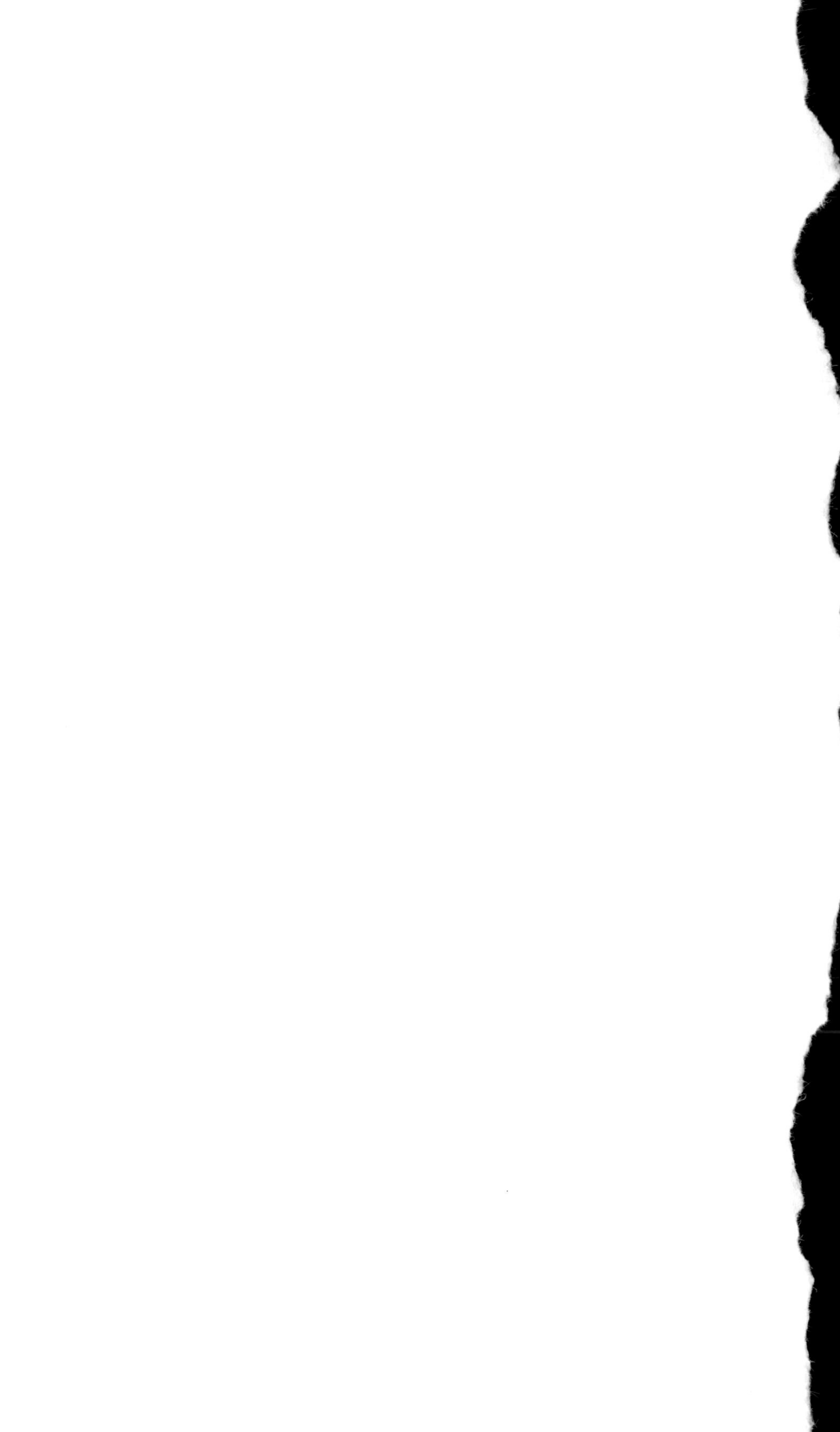

The Aesthetic *of the* Aesthetic

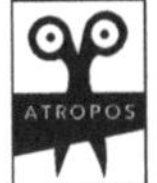

The Aesthetic *of the* Aesthetic

ON THE PURSUIT OF TRUTH THROUGH ILLUSION

MICHAEL THOMA

ATROPOS PRESS
new york | dresden

ATROPOS PRESS
NEW YORK | DRESDEN

THINK MEDIA SERIES IS SUPPORTED BY THE EUROPEAN GRADUATE SCHOOL

ATROPOS PRESS
NEW YORK | DRESDEN
151 FIRST AVENUE # 14, NEW YORK, N.Y. 10003
MOCKRITZER STR. 6, D-01219, DRESDEN, GERMANY

COVER DESIGN BY: DAVID CRIXEL
BOOK INTERIOR DESIGN BY: MILENE NEY

ISBN: 978-0-9894284-4-6

contactatropos@gmail.com

With thanks to Wolfgang Schirmacher, Simon Critchley, Dr. Andrew Spano and the team at Atropos, Bruce Greenwood, Dr. Nicoletta Iacobacci, colleagues at Capilano University, and students in the Philosopher's Café.

For my grandparents, Kathleen Wilke Burns and Robert Taylor Finlayson,

my mother, Margaret Thoma-Noble, and

my family, Susan, Meg, Finn and Alex.

Contents

Introduction

Who is going to save us from ourselves?

This is a question most of us have asked ourselves at one time or another. The answers are never easy, of course, and usually do not involve *who* so much as a more generalized *how* are we are going to save ourselves. This often starts with the idea that we must reconcile the mistakes of the past by making positive changes in the future. That means we must have faith in human ingenuity and scientific breakthroughs because, it stands to reason, in the future we will know more and can solve all our problems.

However, we might consider that we have already seen an exponential increase in innovation and knowledge in the last few centuries. Buckminster Fuller, in *Critical Path* (1982), described the "knowledge-doubling curve" where new knowledge doubled every century up until 1900, and then every twenty-five years, then every eighteen months. And then things really got going with advances in computer technology where the exponential rate of knowledge accumulation has led to claims that knowledge will be doubling in a matter of months or days or even hours. All that knowledge and yet here we are, surrounded by a daily chorus of warnings, predictions and irregularities that predict imminent catastrophe, corruption and irreversible devastation for the entire planet.

Science has made extraordinary contributions to our world; many of them involve advances in technology, many of us believe these advances are the key to self-preservation. However, we have all heard warnings about how technology is changing our lives, such that technology is an end in itself, one that no longer serves us but that we serve technology. Martin Heidegger warned that humans are so entwined with technology that we have hitched our destiny to technology's future.[1] This would certainly justify the fears surrounding the onset of Artificial Intelligence. Unhindered by the biological and social limitations of humans, Artificial Intelligence is increasingly capable of apprehending and processing all of our accumulated and digitalized knowledge and expanding it on its own terms in operations so complex that we will soon be left behind, made redundant by our own creations.

Is it any wonder that for many of us the lived experience of modern life itself often seems to be one of alienation and loneliness, where reality is estranged from nature, fragmented and illusory? Our "burnout society," as described by the South Korean-born, Berlin-based philosopher, Byung-Chul Han, with its culture of convenience and user-friendly technology, has produced a range of disorders, including chronic fatigue, narcissism and addiction, where the pathological sign of our times is depression not oppression.[2] In our darker moments, we might wonder if humankind is worth saving at all, or, for that matter, if we even deserve a say. The pessimist might claim that the human experiment is over, that our accidental and meaningless existence will collapse and we will leave the planet to the rats and the insects. Even for an optimist, there may be a pervasive sense of closing in, of approaching limits.

All the same, the very inability to predict events should allow for some optimism, even when we're simply pinning our hopes on the unknowability of the future. If science and technology are not providing what we need to find a meaningful life, perhaps we should look to art and culture for the answers. Perhaps, like technology, art and culture no longer serve us, or perhaps they must work together. However, isn't contemporary art and culture increasingly aligned with profit-motive technology and culture? In *Empire of Illusion: The End of Literacy and the Triumph of Spectacle*, Chris Hedges, quoting Daniel Boorstin, defines our contemporary culture: "the fabricated, the inauthentic, and the theatrical have displaced the natural, the genuine and the spontaneous, until reality itself has been converted into stagecraft." Americans in particular "live in a 'world where fantasy is more real than reality'," making them "the most illusioned people on earth. Yet we dare not become disillusioned, because our illusions are the very house in which we live; they are our news, our heroes, our adventure, our forms of art, our very experience."[3] Hedges will issue his own warning: "Cultures that cannot distinguish between illusion and reality die."[4]

Where do we go from here? It makes sense that if we're asking who is going to save ourselves from ourselves, then it follows that our best hope may be self-knowledge, where the emphasis would be on the *who* rather than the *how*. The paradox, of course, is then we need to save ourselves from ourselves *through* ourselves. How is that possible, you may ask, if we are both the problem and the solution? For starters, we might consider how we portray ourselves to ourselves. Our modern culture is driven by the "prevailing cultural *script*," according to Frank Furedi, and the cultivation not only of the habit of fearing the worst but a pervasive sense of our own vulnerability.[5] In which case, perhaps we're so conditioned to being this particular version of ourselves, the human disaster of the Anthropocene, that we just don't see how we can be anything else. If we've been listening to the many warnings regarding our future, we are aware how we cast ourselves in a persistent, destructive and self-defeating narrative, but is this also an illusion? If so, that in itself may be the crux of the problem, namely, the *not* seeing past the illusion of how we portray ourselves to ourselves and how that may have clouded our ability to perceive other possibilities.

So how can we challenge the process of *not* seeing, in which we constitute and construct our reality through illusions, some or all of which may be self-defeating, when we're the ones who have constituted and constructed that very reality? The inability to *see* things as they are may be explained by the concept of cognitive dissonance, where what we see and what we tell ourselves that we see are in contradiction. On the other hand, we have cultural cognition, where our creative and artistic endeavours seek to "open our eyes" so that we see things differently and perhaps more profoundly, including how we see ourselves. Of course, there is no shortage of these artistic endeavours. Indeed, between cultural and technological interventions, and every algorithm along the way, it often seems that every nook and cranny of our lives has been exposed and exploited, always vying for our attention. In which case, perhaps the task of the work of art in our contemporary culture is not so much a matter of adding more content for us to *see*, but making us understand how that contemporary culture contributes to our *not* seeing, and in turn how that *not* seeing informs our social reality and our world.

If that's the *how*, we still have the paradox of the *who*, where we are both the problem and the solution. If we constitute and construct our reality through illusion, and if we are essentially powerless against ourselves, then perhaps there is a certain deception beyond the illusion itself, or more accurately, a self-deception. In which case, any challenge to our self-deception will require a certain self-awareness or self-reflection to initiate resistance to the prevailing culture. Of course, in many circumstances this resistance might prove healthy, if for no other reason than discriminating amongst the profusion of cultural and technological interventions. On the other hand, this resistance may still include a certain denial, where self-awareness itself becomes a kind of wilful ignorance, yet another example of how we are *not* seeing when we constitute and construct our reality through cultural cognition.

In terms of works of art, this contradiction would support Theodor W. Adorno when he claimed that truth can be revealed aesthetically, but the "truth" that is aesthetically revealed is not true. Indeed, the task of thought that Adorno had set for himself was, "to use the strength of the subject to break through the fraud of constitutive subjectivity."[6] But how can we use the strength of the subject when the subject is rendered powerless by his or her own self-deception? The key word here may be "fraud," whereby self-deception or the lack of self-awareness or the exploitation of self-reflection is also a societal condition, a condition that has been imposed upon us. Consequently, we may find that even when faced with the fact that we must save ourselves from ourselves, we must recognize the resistance to self-awareness and self-reflection, and it is potent, and that self-awareness itself can become a self-defeating self-exploitation. In which case, we may find ourselves in an even more difficult situation where the subject wilfully defies their social reality and at the same time conforms to it, even when made aware of the contradiction.

Well, we're back to that paradox of the need to save ourselves from ourselves, both individually and collectively, and whether the answers will be found in science and technology or art and culture or some combination of both. Of course, a work of art can provide a revelation about human nature, where we discover some insight that restores the meaning and purpose of our lives. On the other hand, the truth that is aesthetically revealed is not even "truth" per se, just as we must allow that the subjective truth, such as the truth revealed through a work of art, is not scientific, that is, it's not knowledge that is empirical or factual or provable. As Picasso famously said, we all know that art is not truth, but a lie that makes us realize truth, at least the truth that is given us to understand. This makes art something of a Liar's Paradox, as described by Epimenides, such as "this statement is false," where if it is false then it must also be true. This paradox will lead us to the double operation of finding the truth behind the lie of a work of art, of unravelling the contradictions in the illusion, of developing a new way of seeing, where we move beyond the constituted notion of "truth" to reveal a deeper more profound truth. This determination may allow us to address our own paradoxical human nature, the self-defeating contradictions of self-deception or lack of self-awareness or the self-awareness that is self-exploitation, and the *not* seeing. In doing so, we would need an aesthetic that reveals the "truth" found in a work of art but, paradoxically, also trumps its own aesthetic in order to reveal a deeper truth.

Despite its subjective nature, art and culture will inevitably work in conjunction with science. Nonetheless, we can begin by addressing the development of the aesthetic itself and rethinking our underlying assumptions and the judgements we make regarding what we *see*, thereby revealing what we do *not*. In terms of the work of art, this would call for a transgression that reveals that which is concealed behind that which is revealed, or, more accurately, that which is self-concealed behind that which is self-revealed, a double operation that we will determine as the aesthetic of the aesthetic. In doing so, we may produce more questions than answers, but as has been said before, the duty of art is to ask questions, not provide answers. Our survival may depend on it.

Notes

1 Martin Heidegger, "The Question Concerning Technology." *Basic Writings – From Being and Time (1927) to The Task of Thinking (1964)*, Edited, With General Introduction, and Introductions to Each Selection, by David Farrell Krel, Foreward by Taylor Carman (New York: HarperCollins, 2008), pp.307-342.

2 Byung-Chul Han, *The Burnout Society* (Palo Alto CA: Stanford Briefs, 2015).

3 Chris Hedges, *Empire of Illusion: The End of Literacy and the Triumph of Spectacle* (Toronto: Vintage Canada, 2010), p.15.

4 Ibid., p.143.

5 Frank Furedi, *How Fear Works: Culture of Fear in the Twenty-First Century* (London: Bloomsbury Continuum, 2018), p.15.

6 Robert Hullot-Kellner, "Translator's Introduction," Theodor W. Adorno, *Aesthetic Theory*, Gretel Adorno and Rolf Tiedemann, editors; newly translated, edited, and with a translator's introduction by Robert Hullot-Kentor (Minneapolis MN: University of Minnesota Press, 1997), p.xiii. The quote is from Adorno, *Negative Dialectics*, trans. E.B. Ashton (New York, 1973), p.xx (translation amended).

The Task and Precondition

Aesthetics: The "true" art

The first to extend the word "aesthetics" into its modern usage as a judgement of the artistic and the beautiful, as well as a criticism of taste, was Alexander Gottlieb Baumgarten in his *Aesthetica* (1750). His intention was to use aesthetics not as an alternative but as a complement to logic, because logic cannot cultivate all manner of cognitive judgement so aesthetics would become logic's "younger sister."[1]

In *The Critique of Judgement* (1790), Immanuel Kant also employed the word "aesthetics" to mean the judgement of taste and the estimation of the beautiful. For Kant, however, an aesthetic judgement is subjective in that it relates to the internal feeling of pleasure or displeasure by the individual subject and not necessarily to any particular qualities in an external object. Therefore, Kant tried to correct Baumgarten's interpretation by rejecting any attempt to bring the critical judgement of and by aesthetics under rational principles, or, to put it another way, the judgement of taste may not be rational but it is aesthetic, so one cannot raise the rules for such judging to the level of a lawful science by objectifying that which "*cannot be other than subjective.*"[2]

Despite scholarly resistance, however, Baumgarten's interpretation and usage of the term prevailed, gaining support from Walter Pater's use of aesthetics to advocate the late 19th century "Aesthetic Movement" of *l'art pour l'art* (art for art's sake), where the intrinsic value of art, and the only "true" art, is divorced from any didactic, moral or utilitarian function.[3] Such works can be described as autotelic, that is, having a purpose in and not apart from itself, which Kant would describe as "purposiveness without purpose."[4] In any case, Pater, like Baumgarten, focused on the sensual and cognitive aspects of pleasure, and the judgement of the artistic and the beautiful as a criticism of taste, which would, perhaps inevitably, become linked to the intrinsic ideas of "Good, Truth and Beauty." It is significant that in his early years Pater had aims to enter the church, which he subsequently abandoned, but he maintained a nostalgia for the ritual and aesthetic elements of the ecclesiastical. Later in life, he wrote a philosophical novel set in ancient Rome, *Marius the Epicurean* (1885), where he examined the "sensations and ideas" of a young Roman of integrity, who pursues an ideal of the "aesthetic" life, a life based on perception but tempered by asceticism.[5]

Further scholarly resistance to Baumgarten and Pater's interpretation would appear in Tolstoy's *What is Art?* (1897). Tolstoy would claim that art is not simply a means to pleasure but one of the conditions of human life:

> Art is not, as the metaphysicians say, the manifestation of some mysterious idea of beauty or God; it is not, as the aesthetical physiologists say, a game in which man lets off his excess of stored-up energy; it is not the expression of man's emotions by external signs; it is not the production of pleasing objects; and, above all, it is not pleasure; but it is a means of union among men, joining them together in the same feelings, and indispensable for the life and progress toward well-being of individuals and of humanity.[6]

Tolstoy will further oppose the pursuit of "Good, Truth and Beauty" by arguing that the words themselves only hinder giving any higher meaning to art, because, for one thing, good, truth and beauty have nothing necessarily in common and may even oppose one another. Rather than making art important and significant, the arbitrary fusion of these three concepts, particularly as accepted by the privileged class, had only turned art into the empty amusement of "an idle and satiated man."[7] Applying his anarchic convictions and his faith in the workers, Tolstoy will address "the artist of the future" who will "live the common life of man, earning his sustenance by some kind of labour," and so by "the fruits of that highest spiritual strength which passes through him, he will try to share with the greatest possible number of people, for in such transmission to others of the feelings that have arisen in him, he will find his happiness and his reward."[8] In which case, if art is to be essential to human development then it must be accessible to each and every person and it must be spiritually significant, and if it is not, then "either art is not the vital matter it is represented to be or that art which we call art is not the real thing."[9]

Essence: Temple grammar

If a work of art must be accessible as well as spiritually significant in order to be essential, then we might look to the ancient Greeks, where *eidos* is a term that meant "essence," as well as "form," "type," or "species," which would suggest a work of art. As Eric R. Kandel notes, quoting Semir Zeki, only humans are "conscious of being conscious,"[10] and "art extends the functions of the brain more directly than other processes of acquiring knowledge."[11] At the famous Academy in Athens that Plato founded, a sign over the entrance to his lecture room read: "Let no one destitute of geometry enter my doors."[12] His students trained in mathematics and philosophy, suggesting a synthesis of science and culture, in order to look "below the surface of things" where they might seek "the eternal reality and the Good behind it all."[13] Indeed, Plato believed he had found the essential mathematical structure of nature, which he elaborated in his Theory of Forms, that is, the Platonic solids (or bodies). For Plato, therefore, essence was pre-existing. In effect, the use of reason amounts to a process of recollection in which we gain knowledge by recalling information that is already present in our minds, acquired prior to birth, which we have somehow forgotten. In this recalling, evidence of which can be found in the essential forms, we comprehend the true nature of things.

Plato maintained there was a fundamental orderliness to the universe that existed in an invisible spiritual world and is made up of essential forms, each of perfect order and design containing all that is in the corporeal world only in perfection (the perfect cat, the perfect colour, and so on), unchanging and universal, hence the "same." In so doing, Plato presented a movement of perception from the material to the conceptual, from the particular to the universal, which also embodied the idea of a divine creator, "variously described as father, maker or craftsman."[14] Consequently, there was our material "world of Becoming," a world of transition and disorder, where evil pollutes good, where beauty forever fades, where all observed things are mere shadows of the true forms and we are in a constant state of becoming but never being, and hence "different."[15] This led to two opposing points of view: either the universe obeyed fixed, immutable laws and "everything exists in a well-defined objective reality," or there is "no such thing as objective reality; that all is flux, all is change."[16]

Nonetheless, since the ancient Greeks, humankind expanded the search for patterns in nature, and subsequently sought to create formal systems of recognizing, classifying, and exploiting patterns, particularly those which are symmetric, that is, well-ordered, well-proportioned and well-balanced. In appealing to both our visual sense and our aesthetic concepts of beauty, we might also seek Plato's definition of the well-ordered "Good" through harmonious perfection, whereby, eventually, we may even discover some kind of objective reality and so understand why we and the universe exist.[17] Perhaps, as Stephen Hawking wrote while considering a Theory of Everything, this would be "the ultimate triumph of human reason – for then we would know the mind of God."[18]

For Aristotle, aesthetics (*aiesthetikos*) meant sensation, as in the ability to receive stimulation from one or more of the five bodily senses, as well as the manner in which those manifold sensations were perceived, which would include perception, awareness, and consciousness. It would also include desire (*orexis*), such that without desire there is no action. As such, each of us has the capacity to perceive objects in themselves, as well as the capacity for making various perceptual judgments. Hence, the term *sensus communis* (literally "common sense" in Latin). Aristotle employed this term, as well as *koine aisthesis* or "common sensibles," which he used in order to explain the distinct yet allied sensations of our bodily senses.[19] The "common sensibles" are also related to Aristotle's Theory of Universals, where universals are types, properties, or relations that are common to their various instances, that is, universals exist only in things (in Latin, they exist *in re*, meaning "in things"), never apart from things, such that a universal is identical in each of its instances. For example, all red things are similar in that there is the same universal, that is, redness, in each thing. There is no Platonic Form of Redness, some perfect eternal

Redness standing apart from all material red things. Instead, each red thing shares the same property, redness, as do we by our ability to access that redness through our senses. Thus, the universal is not like the Platonic form, separate from the thing, but is found in the thing itself, which also suggests a linkage between things. And that in itself, that essential linkage or connectivity, and our ability to perceive that essence, may also suggest a means to access the presence of an invisible and eternal paradigm, both in the thing and in ourselves.

Aristotle explains that the sum of perception for an individual subject, which would occur at the intersection of the mind and soul, is when all the individual sense organs are engaged and combined into a coherent and intelligible representation, which we can then determine as pleasant or not, and therefore good or not for the individual's senses. The common sense, therefore, is the capacity to perceive objects in themselves, as well as the capacity for making various apperceptual judgements. For Aristotle, unlike later philosophers, this capacity for judgements will remain in the realm of perception rather than reason,[20] because perception requires an external object, whereas thought is "somehow in the soul,"[21] suggesting that understanding itself is a universal, something intrinsic, something that is "up to us" in a way that perception is not.[22] However, perceptual experience is also underwritten by *phantasia*, occurring midway between perception and thought, which is not imagination exactly, but "a *trace* or *echo* of perceptual activity," where *phantasmata* are like representations that linger inside us, "reproduced from perceptual activity like an impression from a signet ring."[23] This suggests that our perception is not necessarily defined by an objective understanding, nor by our recalling of the eternal essence that we have forgotten, but more that our ability to perceive is informed by more than what we take in with our individual senses, where a universal essence is running through all of our perceptual experience.

Aristotle also supported a practical application of thought and perception in terms of a "public sense," namely the art (*technê*) of rhetoric, where certain perceptions and ideas could be mutually agreed upon and understood.[24] Accordingly, an orator could take for granted many of the assumptions, prejudices and values (*endoxa*) of an audience because they had been proved and tested through critical consideration and were now absorbed into society.[25] Plato did not share the same view of "public sense." Indeed, he distrusted commonly held beliefs and opinions (*doxa*) as a starting point for truth. He would claim that only philosophers sought true knowledge (*episteme*). However, unlike Socrates who never wrote a word, Plato will turn to written language, a consequence perhaps of Socrates' failure to talk his way out of drinking the cup of hemlock, which also marks a wider transition from orality to literacy. Nonetheless, Plato will remain highly critical of writing.

In *The Republic*, Plato intends the poets and artists should be removed from the ideal city-state (*kallipolis*) because they sought to entertain and embellish rather than enlighten and so did not speak the truth, a task that could only be entrusted to the philosopher. Indeed, if his ideal city-state is to ever come into existence, either philosophers must rule as kings, or kings must philosophize, thus merging political power and philosophy.[26] This will be the case with Alexander the Great, taught by Aristotle, who in turn was taught by Plato. However, in terms that are similar to today's objections to computers, such as Picasso's famous line that he has no use for computers as they can only give him answers, Plato uses the words of Socrates to claim that writing is detrimental to thinking. This is Walter Ong's observation when he finds that Plato has Socrates claim that writing makes one dependent on an external source, destroying memory and weakening the mind.[27] Unlike rhetoric, writing is internalized, where words allow us to "see" images, and now modern technology can do that work of "seeing" for us. Indeed, in recent times there have been frequent calls for alarm in our decline of critical thinking and our increasing dependence on technology. In the 1960s, Siegfried Kracauer will claim that memory was under threat and constantly being challenged by technology. Photography, for example, replicates many of the tasks previously done by memory.[28]

The characteristics of Plato's stance have been described as a resistance to technological change, yet at the same time Plato himself lent support to the transition. According to Ong, citing his mentor Eric A. Havelock, "Plato's entire epistemology was unwittingly a programmed rejection of the old oral, mobile, warm, personal interactive lifeworld of oral culture (represented by the poets, whom he would not allow in his Republic)."[29] Of course, Ong notes, Plato's objections to writing appear in writing itself. On the other hand, if it weren't for his writing, we might not know anything of Plato, or for that matter, Socrates. Writing is a projection of those words, beyond the limitations of the spoken word and not limited by time. It is an extension of our objective reality that no longer necessitates our being within listening range and present in the moment, where the words can be read and re-read for millennium, perhaps forever. Ong will argue that writing is associated with death, "the deadness of the text, its removal from the living human lifeworld, its rigid visual fixity, assures its endurance and its potential for being resurrected into limitless living contexts by a potentially infinite number of living readers."[30]

This also suggests the "temple grammar" found in the burial chambers and sarcophagi of ancient Egypt. Erik Hornung in his book, *Idea into Image: Essays on Ancient Egyptian Thought*, and as the title implies, sought artefacts that were not simply a representation or the recording of an event, rather those that were attempting to capture an idea, thereby provoking thought or feeling in the viewer by attending some further meaning.[31] Hornung calls this principle the "extension of the existing."[32] And the extension of the existing was not restricted to the material world, but would include the secrets of the underworld, the next life, and the world of dreams. These non-material ideas and concepts could also be realized materially through temple construction, the decorations on sarcophagi, esoteric writings, and so forth.[33] They also served an apotropaic function, that is, they were designed to ward off evil and frighten hostile forces away from the temple area. In doing so, there developed not only a method for scenic arrangement but also a unique syntax and orthography where symbols acquired a variety of meanings, such that it has been described as "temple grammar."[34]

The temple grammar, Hornung notes, allowed the ancient Egyptians a means to develop a kind of "wisdom literature" or "life instructions" that would support their concept of "*maat*."[35] There is no precise definition for *maat* yet it was understood as a concept of truth, balance, order, law, morality, and justice. The ancient Egyptians were convinced that it could not be taught or learned through definitions or rules, but only realized through illustration, thus making into images those aspects of what would be considered an exemplary life. For example, when considered as a legal concept, Hornung tells us, *maat* subsumes all other terms such as "law" and "divine decree," whereby it is synonymous with the very concept of law itself.[36] In this sense, we may surmise that *maat* is similar to the concept of *nomos*, as proposed by the ancient Greeks, whereby laws, traditions or customs are founded on a moral truth, such that human invention and socially constructed laws aspired to an eternal form.

An inward turn: Expanding the existing

Writing is a solitary experience, as is reading, which, Ong will claim, leads to an "inward turn."[37] Also, the combination of our innate ability to use words to visualize supports the importance of storytelling, where the ability to visualize something internally is closely linked with the ability to describe it verbally. Consequently, the means of storytelling has evolved from the earliest oral traditions, to the written form, to audio-visual storytelling, namely the electronic media, which Ong has described as a "secondary orality."[38] Annabelle Sreberny suggests that some Third World countries may have "jumped" from a predominantly oral culture right into the secondary orality, skipping the writing stage in the process.[39] This jump may have contributed to the modern global media where cultural identity can be described by "the global in the local and the local in the global."[40] In any case, verbal and written descriptions create highly specific mental images, building on the link between vision, visual memory, and verbalization.

In terms of our perceptual experience, therefore, writing engages our innate ability to visualize in order to create a cultural form that employs sounds and images. This would naturally lead to the expanded capacity and range in our vision through optical devices (eyeglasses, telescope, microscope, camera) and hearing through the amplification and localization of sounds (loudspeakers, stereos, microphones, headphones). In seeking to enhance our ability to perceive images and sounds, we also seek to expand the range that we can perceive, hence the saturation of the visual and aural field in modern society. Another way to expand both our ability and our range is to replicate them, and, in terms of expanding the existing, by creating the images ourselves.

As Marshall McLuhan argued as early as 1969, and as pointed out by the psychiatrist Norman Doidge discussing our addiction to smartphones, all media extends us: "Now man is beginning to wear his brain outside his skull, and his nerves outside his skin," where the results of this extension of ourselves through modern technology will lead to, as Doidge will claim, "the culturally modified brain."[41] Canadian writer and artist Douglas Coupland considers our reliance on "exomemory," external devices such as computers and i-phones that aid our memory yet are making us forget, leading him to lament the loss of his pre-Internet brain.[42] And six years after he first made this claim, he would say, "Now I barely even remember it anymore. I look at books on a shelf and I know I did read them but it is kind of like driving past a school I used to attend a long time ago." Coupland goes on to address the dramatic changes in todays' relationship with time: "Having disposable free time now is the new luxury item, I think [...] You do have all this free time but you don't use it the same way. Information crack, really. You are always checking your toolbar, your news sites. The Internet is basically this massive TV channel that is all about you."[43] And just as McLuhan argued that the medium is the message, that is, it's not the content of the medium but the medium itself that modifies our brain, so we are proposing that the aesthetic of the content is only the surface, it's the aesthetic of the aesthetic that defines our cultural development and our social reality.

Some things must die in order that we go on living, Ong writes, and one of the things lost in the transition from orality to literacy, and the development of rational logical thinking, may have been an intimate connection to the personal interactive lifeworld of oral culture. Writing is a technology, Ong would claim, the most important ever invented by humankind, and it was internalized and in doing so it had restructured our consciousness by becoming an integral part of our reflexive process. Plato's misgivings about writing, its coldness, its stasis, its inability to come alive, were inherent in a close association with death.[44] Here we find the seed of the modern division in the fundamental relationship between *techne* (know-how) and *poiein* (making poetically), perhaps because our advancements in technology have outpaced our ability to express ourselves poetically. Indeed, Johann Hari will claim that the rise of information technology and the ubiquitous use of personal computers and devices, as well as the profit motive of corporations who seek to hack our attention, have caused the chronic reduction in our ability to focus in a sustained manner and created a global crisis in the levels of distraction, one that has had profound effects on our daily lives and threatens our ability to address the challenges of the future. Indeed, quoting James Williams, Hari argues, "the liberation of human attention may be the defining moral and political struggle of our time."[45]

Writing is a technology and technology is artificial, and yet, Ong notes, artificiality is natural to human beings, such that, "Technology, properly interiorized, does not degrade human life but on the contrary enhances it."[46] Indeed, this is also the significance of artistic creation, where our tools, our instruments, our technology, are also capable of the most profound expression of the human experience. We live in a world where writing and words are locked in a visual field, where, as Ong puts it, trying to think in terms of orality would be like trying to describe a horse as an automobile without wheels, where you end up describing what it isn't.[47] Likewise, we can only describe death as not life, as the absence of presence. Just as the Egyptians sought to extend the existing beyond death and into the next world through temple grammar, our technology may cause us to risk losing a connection to this world, the living world, with its human sounds and connectivity.

As Ong claimed, it is only that the technology must be properly interiorized and enhance our lives. Bruce Chatwin wrote in *The Songlines* of the Australian aboriginals who use the words and tempo of "songlines" as paths to find their way in a barren land. The songlines also brought the world into existence, recreating the Creation, where the ideal human does not go forward into death but follows the paths of the ancestors to a "right death," going back to where they belong, back to their conception.[48] In the beginning was the word, and the word was spoken, yet there was a grammar realized through the pathways across the natural temple of the vast landscape, and they were followed down the ages. And yet we may be entering a new era with the onset of machine intelligence, we surrender our creativity, where the word may no longer guide us nor be properly interiorized nor extend the existing, but build a wall of words and images that are our own creation, behind which there is no secondary reality and no deeper meaning.

A transcendental aesthetic: The weighing of judgement

The value and purpose of rhetoric may be found in Aristotle's concept of *ergon*, the proper function of a thing, its intrinsic truth we might say, and its various uses, *chrêsimon*, which would ultimately serve our well-being or *eudaimonia*, which can be variously described as virtue, self-sufficiency, pleasure, or material goods.[49] The goal of *eudaimonia* could also be described as "well-goddedness," notes Simon Critchley, which would be the culmination of the ethical life, which is not the same as happiness in the modern sense, which is "simply the maximal satisfaction of our inclinations."[50] Consequently, in seeking well-goddedness there arises the need, first endorsed by Kant, "to separate morality from happiness or what he calls 'eudaimonism'."[51]

This concept of well-being and the ethical life is not unlike the earlier description of *maat*, the idea of the exemplary life that cannot be taught or learned through definitions or rules, but only realized through illustration or images. In which case, the fact that we can envision and pursue this abstract concept may in itself be a result of the written word, the temple grammar. It allows for a level of self-awareness and higher consciousness, or "better consciousness" to use Schopenhauer's preferred term,[52] that is, something that transcends our animal instincts, going beyond all experience and all reason, perhaps to give us a glimmer, certainly the hope, of some higher potentiality. Indeed, the historical transition from orality to literacy is a transition from the verbal to the visual, where the complexity and abstract nature of written language would initiate the transformation of human thought from the world of sound to the world of sight, where hearing-dominance gives way to sight-dominance.[53]

With this change we might say that the extension of the existing into those other worlds and realties is seeking guiding principles or points of orientation through illustration or images, thereby discovering those timeless, universal truths that would culminate in well-goddedness. For example, in his attempts to understand the possibility of eudaimonism, Kant expanded on Aristotle's concept of the public sense to make it universal and so include all of humanity. In *The Critique of Judgement*, Kant would write,

> For the principle, which is only subjective, being yet assumed as subjectively universal (a necessary idea for every one), could, in what concerns the consensus of different judging Subjects, demand universal assent like an objective principle, provided we were assured of our subsumption under it being correct.[54]

Therefore, following the notion that an essential impulse informs the *sensus communis*, Kant is now attempting to move the critical judgement of and by aesthetics from the subjective to the objective where, despite the avowed inability to rely on logic or rationality, a consensus in terms of the aesthetic would suggest a public sense through its universal assent, and thereby subsuming an innate moral sense. As a result, Kant would argue that aesthetics is a determination that connects imagination with judgement, such that we may define taste as "the faculty for estimating what makes our feeling in a given representation *universally communicable* without the mediation of a concept," which could then itself be evaluated by "weighing the judgement,"[55] a judgement that contains a moral sense of what is good, true and beautiful. Thus, Kant is able to address the ethical aspects of a representation by weighing the judgement, its rules and obligations, and so argue, for example, that ethical lawgiving cannot be external, although its duties might be, whereas the obligation assigned to ethics is to understand what belongs to internal lawgiving, which would then be considered more than a prescribed duty but an inherent moral obligation. Similar to the concepts of *maat* and *nomos* mentioned earlier, the moral obligation is found in the very concept of the law itself, its universal agreement and application, where its essence contains a trace or echo of the invisible and eternal paradigm.

We should remember, however, that aesthetics, in Kant's estimation, is that whose determining ground can be no other than subjective.[56] If by subjective we mean that which proceeds from or takes place in a person's mind, then, as we have noted, aesthetics is a determination that connects imagination with judgement, which may suggest those guiding principles or points of orientation realized through illustration or images. Indeed, the fundamentally "aesthetic" character of orientation in itself marks a transformation of subjectivity, that is, the orientation of the epistemic subject for whom knowledge is a matter of passing judgement on appearances. For Kant, therefore, the goal is to mediate a proper balance or orientation between theoretical knowledge and practical knowledge by aligning aesthetic judgements with teleological judgements, whereby art's "purposiveness without purpose" contains a critical method in and of itself, one that is both personal and subjective and yet unbiased and objective, just as the meaning of harmonious order may be explained by the naturally occurring patterns found in nature. In terms of the aesthetic, therefore, any attempt to attain the universally communicable in a given representation, that is, the aesthetic, would require a consideration of the essence within the aesthetic, one that is spiritually significant, hence a transcendental aesthetic.[57]

Moreover, in our pursuit of a proper balance or orientation between theoretical knowledge and practical knowledge, we are engaged in the "free play of the cognitive faculties,"[58] where our perceptions are informed by feelings and taste, as well as reflection and understanding, thus allowing for an aesthetic evaluation, but that evaluation could then itself be evaluated by weighing the judgement. As we have noted, weighing the judgement moves beyond the taste of an individual subject to include the broader concept of a public sense.[59] Our critical faculties are engaged in an act of common human understanding, *sensus communis*, an act that serves as a validity claim of "subjective universality,"[60] such that this weighing of judgement now includes the collective knowledge of humankind. However, the weighing of judgement in this wider public sense must contain a necessary provision in that it would "avoid the illusion arising from subjective and personal conditions which could readily be taken for objective, an illusion that would exert a prejudicial influence upon its judgement."[61] On a cautionary note, Kant warned that to forsake the difficult path of critique, for example in the enthusiasm and libertinism that arises from the supposedly free inspiration of genius, would only be to court despotism. Consequently, although difficult to avoid moral and political dilemmas, the weighing of judgement would now give ballast to a "strong view of truth."[62]

The strong view of truth: Political activism

In terms of the aesthetic orientation and the public sense, and in art before or since Kant's time, the concept of a strong view of truth has been used not so much to avoid moral and political dilemmas but to address them through art. Ong offers the example of the early days of the Soviet Union, where an emerging written culture must address its recent past as an oral culture.[63] For example, Anatoly Lunacharsky (1875-1933), a screenwriter and founding father of the Proletkult organization and the People's Commissar of Education of Soviet Russia from 1917 to 1929, argued for the possibility of making use of art as a means to inspire revolutionary political action. The idea behind Proletkult, as noted by John Willett, was,

> [A] third force in the revolutionary state, balancing the political element (the Party) and the industrial element (the trade unions) and ultimately serving to create a new working-class culture to replace that of the bourgeoisie.[64]

By seeking a revolutionary proletarian culture that matched the revolutionary proletarian politics of the time, both of which would raise the political consciousness of the masses, we find a "jump" to secondary orality. In order to address a mostly illiterate population speaking over a hundred languages and spread across a massive contiguous empire, the Soviets would focus on the medium of film.[65] Indeed, the cinema proved an integral component in the construction of Soviet mass society, whereby the Bolshevik government recognized the need to move a largely agrarian society into the modern industrial age and in doing so legitimize the revolution and to enable citizens to recognize their role in the new society.[66]

Lunacharsky, together with the writer Maxim Gorky, went so far as to try and found a "human religion" based on the idea of socialism, also described as "god-building," with the idea of motivating individuals to serve a greater good outside of their own narrow self-interests. Lenin, not surprisingly, did not approve of this philosophical idealism and found it utopian, wasteful and destructive to fundamental Marxist ideology. Proletkult was denounced publicly in *Pravda* in 1920, Lunacharsky was demoted, and Lenin put his wife, Nadezhda Krupskaya, in charge. Tsar Nicholas II had said that cinema was "an empty, totally useless and even harmful form of entertainment... no importance whatsoever should be attached to such stupidities."[67] Lenin, however, recognizing the propaganda value, said, "Of all the arts, for us cinema is the most important."[68]

The Soviet filmmakers did not follow the trial and error developments in early Hollywood, a period in the 1910s and 20s when filmmakers developed a cinematic "language" that addressed clarity of narrative and character motivation, as well as the management of the complex relations of distance and proximity between film and viewer, which would come to be known as the Hollywood Classical or Continuous style. Instead, the Soviets developed the notion of fragmentation to create new meaning, based on the psychology of perception and the Marxist historical dialectic, leading to the theoretical concerns of Soviet montage. For example, the Soviet director, Sergei Eisenstein, who developed dialectical montage, a technique based on a similar concept of psychological stimulation rather than narrative logic.[69] He took inspiration from Japanese pictograms or ideograms, where new meaning is created by combining two separate and distinct pictograms of different meaning. We will address this in more detail later, but by way of example, as noted by film historian David A. Cook, the creation of meaning occurs when the symbol for *knife* is combined with the symbol for *heart* to create *sorrow*.

Eisenstein would write in 1929 that, "The hieroglyphic language of the cinema is capable of expressing any concept, any idea of class, any political or tactical slogan, without recourse to the help of a rather suspect dramatic or psychological past."[70] However, as Cook notes, the concrete images found in cinema may suggest abstract concepts, but there are limits to this technique, which works best when grounded in some specific narrative or dramatic context.[71] Similarly, inspired by Ludwig Feuerbach's "religion of philosophy,"[72] which would also inspire Marx's use of the term *praxis*,[73] Lunacharsky would be limited by his attempts to create a proletarian culture as a means to a political end. By attempting to establish a public sense for the purpose of god-building and legitimizing the rights of socialism, he neglected to reveal the *sensus communis* that could suggest a trace or echo of the universal or divine.

The German philosopher Hans-Georg Gadamer argues that in order for works of art to serve a socially critical function, it is necessary that "art documents a social reality only when it is really art, and not when it is used as an instrument."[74] Gadamer, as noted by Cutrofello, will claim that judgement is not necessarily guided by transcendent truths, but rather by the texts that symbolically represent such truths, which is the function of not only religious texts but also of works of art. Despite the understanding and practice of art in modern society, therefore, which so often offers mere "escapism" and "the enjoyment of spurious freedom," beauty remains a symbol of truth for Gadamer, just as it did for Kant, and "gives us an assurance that the truth does not lie far off and inaccessible to us, but can be encountered in the disorder of reality."[75]

Intentionality: Unconscious inference

All human experience begins with sensations and these sensations inform human cognition. For Kant, these sensations may be based on immediate representations that we apprehend through some prior knowledge given to us through a faculty of receptivity, often referred to as intuition, which suggests this knowledge may be unprovable but is "hard-wired" within us. Another possibility is that these sensations are apprehended and interpreted through spontaneously generated forms of thought that conform to concepts. This suggests the possibility that an image or idea can be produced by prior perception of an object, as in memory or imagination, rather than by actual perception. For Kant, therefore, human cognition is composed of both intuitions and concepts. Each is dependent on the other, such that concepts without intuition would be empty or hollow, while intuition without concepts would be simply a feeling or sentiment. However, there is a distinction between a "determining" judgement, which subsumes an object of intuition under a pre-given concept, and a "reflective" judgement, where there is an inability to subsume an object under any concept that we possess, thus resisting conceptual determination.[76] This distinction is important as we may find the resistance to conceptual determination would in fact empower the aesthetic, supporting the reflective judgement rather than the determining, not allowing for a proper balance and orientation.

If we consider that whatever framework or categories we use to order our knowledge, our pre-given concepts, then these will in themselves reveal our pre-existing beliefs. The pre-given concepts must be universal and independent of particular interests and circumstances because, if valid and unbiased in the public sense, we would find a weighing of judgement that embraces the collective knowledge, whereby, as we have noted, we would have a validity claim of subjective universality. As rational beings capable of self-determination, Kant would claim, we can formulate our own ideas of truth and organize them into categories, which then become a law or "categorical imperative." Despite our autonomy, we now recognize that these laws support a moral duty, which, due to their general acceptance, would address an underlying universal truth. And since we have accessed this universal truth through both determining (analytic) and reflective (synthetic) judgements, that is, intuition and concept, and thereby including some deeper connection that may not be entirely provable yet is still pre-existing in that all or most of us recognize it as "truth." Consequently, this truth not only contains an intrinsic connection to something uniquely human, but, in its subjective universality, we may find evidence of the divine, that invisible and eternal paradigm. In terms of finding this evidence, we may find ourselves advocating a form of immanentism, as Kant did when he proposed that moral duty contends that ought implies can, where the divine is fully present in the physical world and thus accessible to creatures in various way.

The classic example would be a situation where you come upon a child drowning in a shallow pond. Despite the fact that we will get our clothes wet or be late for an appointment, we might safely assume that all of us would agree that we have an obligation to save the child, that is, an imperative or moral duty. The fact that all of us agree, or at least most of us, implies a strong view of truth, where our innate understanding of our moral duty may also suggest a universal truth, which in turn may suggest something intrinsic in humankind that is a trace of the divine. We do not have to experience a drowning child to prove this point; we can understand the concept and base our laws on the potentiality of this situation, which in itself serves as an illustration of this concept. However, as Peter Singer proposes, we may falter in our sense of obligation if, for example, the child were in another country. If the effort or expense increases, so does our resistance to helping the child. In which case, this resistance points to the need for an expanding circle of moral duty, whereby Singer calls for a higher ethical consciousness, a global ethic. In a critique of modern self-interest, and in order to identify ourselves with larger goals and thereby find meaning in life, he reminds us of the "paradox of hedonism," where the ancients understood that the more we pursue our desire for pleasure, the less likely are we to find its satisfaction.[77] In effect, Singer's expanding circle of obligation to a global ethic suggests a balanced view, both a reflective judgement and determining judgement, a "well-goddedness," where we would find a harmony between ethics and enlightened self-interest.[78]

Thomas Metzinger will argue that the model of the self-determining individual is in itself a form of cognitive dissonance, a kind of consistent self-deception, that we are always already subjects and therefore we are unable to develop in any other way: "As soon as individual organisms start to consciously represent themselves as individuals, this fact will inevitably be reflected in countless facets on the level of phenomenal experience itself."[79] Metzinger will argue that there is no such thing as "selves," nobody ever had or was a self, and the we exist only as phenomenal selves, only as we have created our own conscious experience. If it were possible to regard ourselves not as selves, not as someone, then we would have to be no one. In doing so, we would need to think the unthinkable, namely, to not be someone and not "see" subjectively, and perhaps return to "old-fashioned philosophy" and metaphysics, where we would delve beyond our self-deception to understand what it means to exist. In the terms we use here, we would have to be at one remove from our subjective self and our aesthetic judgements, and initiate a double action where we consider the aesthetic of the aesthetic.

In terms of aesthetic judgements and the invisible and eternal paradigm, the strong view of truth, with its combination of moral sense, value judgements, political activism and social justice, also suggests that in some ways art may have inherited the burden of reconciliation that religion can no longer fulfil in a secular society. Religion promises reconciliation in some future life, the next world. Reconciliation, in Christian theology, is an element of salvation that refers to the results of atonement, such that reconciliation is the end of the estrangement, caused by original sin, between God and humanity. Art, on the other hand, offers reconciliation within the course of history, the here and now. The question then becomes whether art attempts to represent something we once had but have lost, or if art serves as an impetus for something that is yet to come, the potentiality hidden in the unknowable future. However, the point here is that the aesthetic is not simply an idle appreciation; it is dynamic and functional, with the potential to carry a weight, perform a task, serve a cause, initiate a change. Therefore, it is not only a matter of questioning what the aesthetic is but what it does, and how it does what it does, how it has evolved, what are its limitations and what are its possibilities.

The Battle of Kadesh: Universal truth

The tableaux on the exterior walls of the Luxor temple depict a series of battle scenes that made up the Battle of Kadesh. A dubious, possibly pyrrhic, victory of the ancient Egyptians over the Hittites, it took place in 1274 BCE, the fifth year of the pharaoh Ramesses II's reign. The format of the tableaux may be a seminal point in the history of image-making in its temporal or "cinematic" presentation of events, that is, a series of images taking place over time.

One particular battle scene from these tableaux on the western exterior wall is examined by Erik Hornung in his book, as mentioned earlier, on ideas into images and ancient Egyptian thought. This particular battle scene is the last in the series and depicts a ravaged landscape, a destroyed city, and, for the most part, a desolate and empty space. The utter barrenness, Hornung explains, is unlike the typically chaotic Egyptian battle scene. There is no stirring of life, no enemy dead, and no victors:

> The scene has an undeniably strong impact on viewers even thousands of years later and needs no special explanation. It shows the absolute devastating consequences of war with shocking clarity. Unlike other Egyptian battle scenes, there is no accompanying written text to provide information not readily available in the visual images; complete anonymity is its aim. The relentless destruction effaces even the names of the particular site and the demolished city. The depiction utterly transcends its particular context and reflects a timeless, universal truth through a visual image that goes far beyond the possibility of a verbal message – as is, after all, the purpose of art.[80]

Although Hornung declares no special explanation is needed, a number of points should be noted to appreciate just how this scene serves as a seminal point in image-making. For example, if we consider an earlier work of art, say, the Venus of Willendorf figurine,[81] with her enlarged breasts and thighs, yet without facial features or anatomically correct arms or legs, these elements have now been replaced by the physical realism or semblance found in ancient Egyptian art. The figurine may have served as a fetish to fertility, and being pocket-sized, would be easily relocated and eminently suitable to a nomadic tribe. In contrast, Luxor's massive stone tableaux display a change of scale and lack of mobility that reflects the relatively sedentary and highly organized Egyptian society. We should also consider the scale of this battle, with its thousands of participants, and perhaps the greatest chariot battle of all time, involving five to six thousand chariots.[82] Politically, there is a recognized leader, Ramesses II, singled out for recognition and portrayed heroically in other scenes in the tableaux. However, that is not where the significance of this particular battle scene lies, indeed its significance is in the anonymity of the fallen, the thousands who lost their lives, and the very absence of life.

As Hornung points out, the scene suggests a work of mourning, where the dead are honoured by *not* depicting them. The work of art, therefore, has been lent to the voice of suffering, and not a single voice, but the many, the thousands who died in battle on that day, and, as long as this work of art stands, to all those who have died in battle since then and who will die in the future. The idea is the absolute devastating consequence of war and its ultimate futility and meaninglessness - which is both aspatial (transcendent in space) and atemporal (transcendent to time) - and thereby, as Hornung claims, serves the purpose of art and its depiction of a timeless, universal truth. In which case, we find the work of art does not simply represent something, it addresses someone, it addresses each and every one of us, yesterday, today and in the future.

The general will: Dissensus

To return to the transcendental aesthetic, we might consider the ethical and the spiritually significant within the aesthetic, yet may also find a resistance to categorization or conceptual determination. If we follow Kant, then the beautiful is that which is "an object of delight apart from any interest,"[83] that which "pleases universally,"[84] such as the meaning of harmonious order of those naturally occurring patterns found in nature. On the other hand, we have the sublime, that which resists conceptual determination. In terms that remind us of the depiction of the Battle of Kadesh, and the absence of presence, Kant would describe the sublime as "a representation of *limitlessness*,"[85] which also has the power to compel and destroy us, such that its formal cause is fear, especially the fear of death. The sublime is often represented by the power and magnitude of nature, an immensely destructive force without any discernible pattern or purpose, which Kant would call "*dynamically sublime*."[86]

The resistance to an underlying universal truth, where we falter in our obligation, also suggests the possibility of a threshold, some barrier within ourselves or incumbent in the world, where there may be a "breaking through," a discovery of higher purpose and the possibility of salvation, or the opposite, of finding no purpose at all, only an absence of presence. This threshold lies between two domains of experience: the *phenomenal* – the realm of sense experience where things are linked in time, space and causality – and the *noumenal* – the transcendental world that is not necessarily logical but it is still justified in itself through the desire for higher meaning.[87] Therefore, following Kant, the phenomenal and the noumenal correspond to the world as we perceive it and the world as it is, or, to put it another way, the world we construct out of the sensations that are present to our consciousness and the world that consists of things we can never know because we do not have evidence of it using our senses. It may seem paradoxical that we seem compelled to believe in the noumenal, the unknowable, and yet this is where we have often sought the basis for some higher purpose or meaning. In other words, the obligation that is assigned to ethics and belongs to internal lawgiving due to its subjective universality, which must then be realized through objective or external laws and practices, is not realized through reason but by that which resists conceptual determination.

Kant, however, did not set out to construct a specific system of moral aesthetics, where, for example, that which is beautiful is synonymous with good in the moral sense. Nonetheless, he claims that unlike reason, which is "*good for something* (useful) which only pleases as a means," the beautiful is "that which pleases on its own account [and] we call *good in itself*."[88] Thus, if we reconsider Baumgarten's terms of "Good, Truth and Beauty," Beauty would have the potential to redeem both Truth and Goodness, empowered by its transcendental aesthetic. Accordingly, in order to re-establish the underlying universal truth in terms of the framework or categories, and following Edmund Burke and his *Philosophical Enquiry into the Origin of Our Ideas of the Sublime and Beautiful* (1757), a new taxonomical system of aesthetics arose, which, corresponding to the phenomenal and the noumenal, offered first beauty and then the sublime as the taxonomical device.[89] In other words, we might call this an aesthetic of unattainable beauty, outside of conceptual determination, a beauty that we may be privileged to see but that we will never fully own or understand.

Burke claimed that the Beautiful is what is well-formed and aesthetically pleasing, framing his argument in a consideration of pain and pleasure, as well as indifference to either. The Sublime, on the other hand, is what has the power to compel and destroy us. Burke's was the first complete philosophical exposition for separating the Beautiful and the Sublime into their own respective rational categories. As such, Burke's view of beauty expands on the traditional bases of beauty: proportion, fitness, and perfection. The sublime, however, also has a causal structure but one that is unlike that of beauty. Its formal cause is the passion of fear (especially the fear of death); the material cause is equally aspects of certain objects such as vastness, infinity, magnificence, etc.; its efficient cause is the tension of our nerves; the final cause is God having created and battled Satan, as expressed in John Milton's *Paradise Lost* (1667).

Hence, the preference for the Sublime over the Beautiful re-established the divine in categorization of aesthetics, which marked the transition from the Neoclassical to the Romantic era. Kant expanded on this categorization in his *Observations on the Feeling of the Beautiful and Sublime* (1764), as well as his *Critique of Judgment* (1790), when he wrote: «We call that sublime that which is absolutely great,» thus distinguishing between the «remarkable differences» of the Beautiful and the Sublime, noting that beauty «is connected with the form of the object,» having «boundaries», while the sublime «is to be found in a formless object,» represented by a «boundlessness."[90] The opposite of boundlessness would be, of course, "boundedness," which could take the form of cognitive closure, the unavailability of self-knowledge that would expand the possibilities of our worldview and not be limited by our own internal representational resources.[91]

A problem with this system of aesthetics is that there remains the "judgement of taste," or what Kant will call "the antinomy of taste."[92] The contradiction is that taste is entirely subjective and makes it impossible to "prove" that something should be considered aesthetically beautiful or not, and certainly even more difficult to claim that something should be considered universally beautiful. Nonetheless, despite a true work of art's "purposiveness without purpose," there is always an "*ought* in aesthetic judgements."[93] Once again, the concept of a strong view of truth aspired to avoid moral and political dilemmas, so Kant addresses this problem by claiming that taste itself is "a kind of *sensus communis*," a shared common sense, where the ideal of a fully achieved *sensus communis* can be thought of as the subjective analogue of the political ideal of a "general will."[94] The assertion is not that everyone will fall in with our collective judgement, just as not everyone might agree to save the drowning child, particularly if she were at some remove for our immediate circle of obligation, but rather that everyone *ought* to.

Kant will argue that this inter-subjectivity is necessary not simply in the sense of a feeling but in the sense of understanding, and that this understanding connected to an innate sense of the good, and thus the moral, which is part of the public sense. Therefore, the very fact that we cannot agree on judgements of taste does not mean that we have abandoned the public sense, but instead presupposes its existence, such that the aim of aesthetic quarrelling or critique, even of widespread disagreement or dissensus, is to cultivate just such a faculty and so reaffirms and rediscovers our common human understanding.[95]

The modern approach will be to challenge the underlying sense of the good with its innate morality, as proposed by Kant's "general will" and its suggestion of the transcendent, and consider a more secular view. For example, Freud would call the boundless "oceanic," which suggests a sense of scale that implies eternity, a feeling of something limitless, unbounded, which he then applies to subjective experience and the objective reality of organized religion:

> This feeling was a purely subjective fact, not an article of faith; no assurance of personal immortality attached to it, but it was the source of religious energy that was seized upon by the various churches and religious systems, directed into particular channels and certainly consumed by them. On the basis of this oceanic feeling alone, one was entitled to call oneself religious, even if one rejected every belief and every illusion.[96]

This approach will fall in line with Jacques Rancière when he argues that there is no trace of the transcendent, nor the divine, nor some lost community of humankind to be restored. Instead what we are seeing are simply scenes of dissensus within our modern society, namely "the organization of the sensible where there is neither a reality concealed behind appearances nor a single regime of presentation and interpretation of the given imposing its obviousness on all."[97] Indeed, the primary quality of reality is its "givenness," that is, its unrestricted availability in the temporal now, which would also form the basis for the elusive phenomenal quality of "presence." Nonetheless, despite the lack of a general will or significance, despite the indecipherability of some higher purpose, the essential point to be made here remains the same. That is, those scenes of dissensus may be conceived as an ethical-aesthetical resistance where we may find, somewhat paradoxically, that the *ought* is not in agreement but disagreement. The universal is not found through an act of recovery but rather a dynamic action of discovery, where acknowledging our differences is the means to restore a sense of harmony in the world. Despite the absence of something more concrete and substantive, that elusive sense of harmony remains our best recourse and may well be worth pursuing.

Homelessness: A reconciled humanity

Even though there were many inequalities and injustices in ancient Greek society, this era has often been regarded as one of harmony between human beings and the world. The Hungarian philosopher, Georg Lukács, for one, prior to his conversion to Marxism and despairing for the Romantic ideal of a reconciled humanity, envisioned an integrated civilization as found in classical Greece where life and essence coexisted, allowing humans to live their lives within a meaningful world. In what is perhaps his best known early work, inspired by both literary theory and aesthetic theory, *The Theory of the Novel: A Historico-philosophical Essay on the Forms of Great Epic Literature* (1920), Lukács begins with, "Happy are those ages when the starry sky is the map of all possible paths," and where, "the world is wide and yet like a home, for the fire that burns in the soul is of the same essential nature as the stars."[98] For Lukács, the modern era, regrettably, was not such an age, particularly after the tragedies of World War I. The world and the self, the light and the fire, had become permanent strangers. Rather than an integrated civilization, Lukács will argue that we have a problematical civilization, one that is distinguished by its opaqueness rather than its transparency, where the need for philosophy and its search for meaning is in itself a symptom of our transcendental "homelessness."[99]

If we return to Plato's uneasiness with writing, Ong makes a similar conjecture when he states that, "The importance of ancient Greek civilization to all the world was beginning to show in an entirely new light: it marked the point in human history when deeply interiorized alphabetic literacy clashed head-on with orality."[100] The impact of the alphabet can be found in the legend of Cadmus, the first king of Thebes, who introduced the alphabet to the ancient Greeks. Cadmus also slayed a dragon and was then instructed by the goddess Athena to sow the dragon's teeth, which sprung up from the earth as a race of fierce warriors.[101] The dragon's teeth can be construed as the letters of the alphabet, which meant power and authority and control of military structures at a distance (and why Roman commanders were required to be literate). When combined with papyrus, the alphabet spelled the end of the stationary temple bureaucracies and the priestly monopolies of knowledge and power. Unlike the pre-alphabetic writing, such as Egyptian hieroglyphics with its innumerable signs, which were difficult to master, the alphabet can be learned in a few hours.

The division between literacy and orality was also a division between interior and exterior, between oneself and the world, which may have led to the sense of homelessness. This division, then, prevented our being at home with or integrating with reality, allowing Marshall McLuhan to claim, "Schizophrenia may be a necessary consequence of literacy."[102] Nonetheless, according to Lukács, the Greek epic form created harmony, whereas all other forms have led to triviality and fragmentation. Of course, any form of art is bound to its historical moment, whereby, in order to recreate the epic form we would also have to recreate that historical moment, namely the social conditions that would allow the possibility of the epic. Thus, we find ourselves in a paradox where art may offer the possibility of redemption, capable of remaking the world in its own utopian image, and yet our problematical world does not allow art to be strong enough to be capable of that remaking. In which case, we as a society always nullify the very form that might lead to our reconciliation. Even the novel, which Lukács regards as the highest cultural form, fails to express the eternity within us, where "the fire that burns in the soul is of the same essential nature as the stars," thus exposing a gap between the finite and the infinite, a gap that can be expressed only through irony. Irony in the ancient Greek was "feigned ignorance," a technique often employed by Socrates. Ultimately, Lukács fears that rather than a true illumination, all we are offered is the irony of a pessimistic anti-illumination. Consequently, having alienated ourselves from the world and unable to achieve totality, namely the unity of subject and object, we are filled with an unaccountable nostalgia for what we have lost. Thus unable to remedy the situation, nor to return to some edenic past, we exist somewhere between past and future, stranded perhaps, as Lukács wrote, in "an age of absolute sinfulness."[103]

Lukács concludes *The Theory of the Novel* with a guarded optimism found through the works of the Russian novelist Fyodor Dostoyevsky (1821-1881), where he perceives a new humanism that manages to bridge the abyss between abstract idealism and romantic disillusionment. Here the possibility of transcending the limitations of the novel form may now offer a faint glimmer of the renewed epic, an emergent form for a new world. However, whether this glimmer of light marked the end of the age of sinfulness, Lukács would only concede the slim possibility for a form drawn from material reality, revealing only the frailty of our designs and the distance we have yet to travel:

> It will then be the task of historico-philosophical interpretation to decide whether we are really about to leave the age of absolute sinfulness or whether the new has no other herald but our hopes: those hopes which are signs of a world to come, still so weak that it can easily be crushed by the sterile power of the merely existent.[104]

A paradox appears, however, when we have pinned our hopes for the future on the written word, that is, where the temple grammar illuminates a deeper meaning and purpose, where humanity is reconciled with the life world, yet the written word itself, ironically, is part of the past and may have removed that deeper connection through its immutability, its lifelessness, its sterility within the existent.

The turning-point: Disharmony

Lukács will identify - as had Hegel and Nietzsche - that a misstep in the development of human civilization occurred during the Golden Age of ancient Greek society. In order to get back on the right path we would not simply add qualifications to existing assumptions, but would need to understand how those assumptions came to exist in the first place. As we have noted, Plato attempted to discover, or rediscover "the eternal reality and the Good behind it all." Indeed, Plato sought the essence of absolute truth, such that his theory of forms presented an unchanging perfect world (being), of which the ever-changing material world was a mere imitation (becoming), and in doing so set the stage for Christianity with its one eternal God. He also turned to the written word as a means to convey the truth, just as the Bible will hold the central tenets of the word of God, where we find the conditions of morality that uphold the standards of civilization. However, just as Plato may have paved the way for the one God and eternal immutable truth, the questioning by philosophy – a consequence of our homelessness - may have led to a variable notion of truth and the death of God, as Nietzsche would claim.

According to Nietzsche, rather than the universal perspective of an absolute truth we now have "perspectivism,"[105] that is, a disarray of individual viewpoints where everything is relative, where multiple, diverse and fluid perspectives lack any coherent sense of objective truth. As Nietzsche would claim, there are no facts only interpretations. Also, perspectivism invites judgements in terms of persuasion. There are no isolated judgements, and no isolated judgement is true, only countless meanings and assertions that are only valid under certain conditions,[106] such that, "It is our needs that interpret the world; our drives and their For and Against. Every drive is a kind of lust to rule; each one has its perspective that it would like to compel all the other drives to accept as a norm.[107] And worse, this lack of objective truth supports the drift toward to nihilism, the belief that no particular thing has any inherent importance and that life lacks purpose. As for those conditions of morality that uphold the standards of civilization, Nietzsche will claim that the "conditional resolve to acknowledge only moral values, struck me as the most dangerous and sinister of all possible manifestations of a 'will to decline', at the very least a sign of the most profound affliction, fatigue, sullenness, exhaustion, impoverishment of life."[108] Accordingly, the dire consequences of the misstep will inform Nietzsche's concepts of "the will to power" and his attempts to initiate an all-encompassing "revaluation of all values."[109]

The young Nietzsche identified Socrates as the one who aimed us down the wrong path. This was due to Socrates' belief in rational thought and its capability of not only penetrating the depths of being but "even of *correcting* being."[110] Socrates was "the prototype of theoretical man," where, for Nietzsche, the image of the dying Socrates holding his cup of hemlock is "man freed by insight and reason from the fear of death, [which] became the emblem over the portals of science, reminding all who entered of their mission: to make existence appear intelligible and consequently justified," thus Socrates is seen as "the turning-point, the vortex of history,"[111] whereby from this point forward we're spiralling ever deeper into a state of homelessness.

Hegel would also identify Socrates' thought as a turning point, although taking a more optimistic view, acknowledging that Socratic ideas were an essential part of the historical process as well as the development of the dialectic.[112] Socrates, as portrayed by Plato, gave expression to the ideas that were present in his time, supporting Hegel in the belief that the dialectical change (or dissensus) found in the historical process was a necessary movement toward the realization of human freedom, a process composed of both increasing awareness of freedom and of increasing knowledge of ourselves. "All position is negation," Hegel wrote of the dialectic, "Every notion has in it the opposite of itself, in which it passes forward to its own negation."[113] This dynamic process suggests that the harmony between humankind and the world was disrupted not so much by a wrong turn but by an inevitable turn, and, in doing so, provides a positive view of historical progress and hope for the future.

The image of the dying Socrates preserved through the writings of Plato denotes not only the transition from orality to literacy but the search for redemption and a reconciled humanity, which was also realized in the struggle between the individual and the state. The harmony that had existed between the individual subject and the city-state (*polis*), a relationship those who condemned Socrates claimed to defend, was due to the fact that individuals, at least those who were free citizens and not slaves, did not consider themselves as separate from the city-state. Yet rational beings, such as Socrates, could not remain content with the status quo but had to examine their lives and question the world around them, hence there was ample cause for disharmony.

Historical aesthetics: *Humanus*

The Socratic demand that reason is necessary to examine one's life would also contribute to the development of individual conscience. In place of natural observance and reflection, according to Hegel, Socrates established morality (*Moralität*), that is, the subjective morality of individual conscience, and so progressing from the obedience to established customs and towards self-governing rational principles. Significantly, what came to consciousness is the broader concept of the "ethical life" or "ethical order" (*Sittlichkeit*):

> Morality consequently is but a one-sided position. A higher position is that of established observance (*Sittlichkeit*), which is the concrete identity of the will and the good [...] in this manner the good becomes to consciousness a second nature, and morality is converted into character, into living principle, into the ethical spirit.[114]

For Hegel, in support of the *polis* and the public sense as a forum for self-realization, the state itself becomes a rational ethical substance; it is the actualization of the Ethical Idea and the Ethical Spirit, such that, in terms that may strike one as mutually exclusive yet are meant to be dialectical, the subjugation of natural subjectivity by means of ethical and political observance opens the path towards a renewed freedom of the spirit.[115]

Hegel would also claim that the classical perfection of the Greek work of art is tied to its historical moment, its *Zeitgeist* (the spirit of the times), as was the work of Homer, Sophocles, Dante, Shakespeare, and other great artists.[116] Thus, the work of art is a response to a need, and the need appears because of the historically appropriate desire for self-knowledge. Therefore, the aesthetic process is one of change where new and conflicting ideas are constantly introduced, and this ever-changing process is what constitutes history, hence Hegel historicizes aesthetics.

The work of art, Hegel will also claim, allows for the immediate view of the Idea in objective reality – what we have called the extension of the existing - and thus art is the first stage on the path towards the Absolute.[117] Hegel will write, "The universal need for art, that is to say, is man's rational need to lift the inner and outer world into his spiritual consciousness as an object in which he recognizes again his own self."[118] However, once we arrive at Romantic art, the art of Hegel's era,[119] he will claim that inwardness and external reality are sublated, so art disintegrates into "'the subjective imitation of the given' (realism of detail) and 'subjective humour',"[120] and so annuls itself. In other words, self-knowledge is in danger of becoming empty reflection, and thus, "With romantic art, art comes to its end and makes way for higher forms of consciousness, i.e., philosophy."[121] Although, as Lukács pointed out, the move to philosophy is not necessarily a mark of progress. Indeed, John Gray writes, "The ideal of self-realization owes much to the Romantic movement. For the Romantics the supreme achievement was originality. In creating new forms the artist was god-like."[122] All good for the artists perhaps, but then Gray will go on to claim, in his pessimistic fashion, that, "The idea of self-realization is one of the most destructive of modern fictions. It suggests you can flourish in only one sort of life, or a small number of similar lives, when in fact everybody can thrive in a large variety of ways."[123]

Of course, even if a particular form of art comes to an end then that is not necessarily the end of art, but could mark a profound shift, even the diminishment, of art's role within the coexistence of life and essence. It may also lead to the secularization of art and its aim of "self-transcendence," making "*Humanus* its new holy of holies."[124] Indeed, after the historicization of aesthetics, then, as noted earlier, art may promise reconciliation within the course of history, the here and now, and an impetus for something yet to come. It is for this reason, in Hegel's view, that art had changed from the classical age, at which time art formed an integral part of society and its affirmative nature was in harmony with its historical moment, whereas in the modern age we would question whether art is the highest form of measuring truth, a position perhaps now occupied by the higher form of consciousness found in philosophy. Yet the work of art in modernity continues to allow for the immediate view of the idea in objective reality and thus, importantly, serves as an expression of self-knowledge that supports human freedom. For Hegel, therefore, the artist plays a significant role in this process. The artist, now released from the "bondage" of a particular subject matter, allows art to "become a free instrument," which "the artist can wield in proportion to his subjective skill in relation to any material of whatever kind."[125] The dissemination of the work of art and its content is entirely the concern of the artist, yet at the same time it may also contribute to the loss of "aura,"[126] to use Walter Benjamin's term, that is, the disintegration of the capacity for a certain kind of experience.

Second creatress: Dethroning the aesthetic

In his "Letter of an Aesthetic Education of Man" (1794), Friedrich Schiller writes that "man cannot pass directly from feeling to thought,"[127] thus, not unlike Aristotle's phantasia, poised between perception and thought, we find ourselves in a "middle disposition," between sense and reason, between the condition of sensual determination and the condition of rational determination, which may describe the in-between condition of the aesthetic.[128] Due to this absence of any specific determination, Schiller maintains,

> [B]eauty produces no particular result whatsoever, neither for the understanding nor for the will. It accomplishes no particular purpose, neither intellectual nor moral; it discovers no individual truth, helps us perform no individual duty and is, in short, as unfitted to provide a firm basis for character as to enlighten the understanding.[129]

Schiller will claim that in order to bridge the gulf between instinct and reason, between will and knowledge, a third mode of experience, the aesthetic mode, is necessary. In doing so, we acknowledge nature as the "first creatress" in that she gave us the power of becoming human, yet beauty allows for a "second creatress," where aesthetics gives us the power of poetic licence and philosophical truth to realize and determine our full possibility.[130] Hence, Schiller, like Kant, supported the free play of the cognitive faculties, which could now be understood as the "spirit" of art, and which he tried to make appear in our social reality through aesthetic art and education. Yet Schiller, unlike Kant, is concerned that "the disinterestedness of the aesthetic judgement" has resulted in the dethroning or suppression of the aesthetic through the emphasis on "the *functionlessness* of art."[131] Thus Peter Bürger argues, "Schiller is not concerned with the sublation of artistic in political and social praxis but with justifying the renunciation of political praxis and the justification of the autonomy of arts as a consequence."[132] In other words, the task of the work of art is found in its aesthetic, which must be impartial and resist its political consequences, and yet it is political in that it challenges politics through the impartiality of its aesthetic.

Hence, there is no determination, political or otherwise, by means of aesthetic culture, and yet that is precisely its value, because it restores freedom in allowing one to make of oneself whatever that might be. Thus, "Nature, which likewise conferred upon us nothing more than the power of becoming human, leaving the use and practice of that power to our own free will and decision."[133] However, although we may find that due to this free will and indetermination that the power of becoming human is through aesthetic culture, yet it is resisted, or at least inhibited, with all the attendant political implications, because in order for reason to take the place of sensation as a source of power, then sensation must be dethroned before reason can become law.

In order to oppose the dethroning of aesthetic culture, for example, Bürger contends that *l'art pour l'art* (having a purpose in and not apart from the work of art itself) is an attempt to counter the tendency for art in a bourgeois society to lose its proper social function, a consequence of Kant's emphasis on "the *functionlessness* of art," thus attempting to restore by means of a higher art the wholeness in our nature which art itself has destroyed.[134] Once again, however, there is an irresolvable contradiction because any form of art is bound to its historical moment, as we have noted earlier, so that to restore the proper social function of the aesthetic would require a society where the aesthetic had a proper social function. In which case, in order to restore the social function of the aesthetic we would also have to recreate the historical moment, namely the social conditions that would allow for that possibility.

Walter Benjamin will describe *l'art pour l'art* as a "theology of art," which "in turn gave rise to a negative theology, in the form of an idea of 'pure' art, which rejects not only any social function but any definition in terms of a representational content."[135] Thus, art loses its social function and is co-opted by ideology. Indeed, Benjamin will cite Bertolt Brecht to state that political thinking is not the same as private thinking; it is "the art of thinking in other people's heads."[136] Responding to the sense of homelessness in the modern world, Benjamin will claim that the result is "the artistic gratification of a sense perception altered by technology," where humankind's self-alienation "has reached the point where it can experience its own annihilation as a supreme artistic pleasure."[137]

Thus, we find ourselves in a paradox where the work of art offers the possibility of reconciling humanity with the world and yet a problematical world does not allow the work of art to be strong enough to be capable of that reconciliation. Nonetheless, as Bürger notes, Schiller assigns art the task of putting back together the "halves" of humanity that have been torn asunder, such that "we must be at liberty to restore by means of a higher Art this wholeness in our nature which Art has destroyed."[138] Benjamin supports this view when he claims that a work of art in "its positive form was inconceivable without its destructive, cathartic side: the liquidation of the value of tradition in the cultural heritage."[139] In other words, in order to reclaim the life of the aesthetic then the first level of the aesthetic must be transgressed, its historical moment and political implications, and then restored by a second level of the aesthetic, its social function, hence, the task and precondition of an aesthetic of the aesthetic.

Aisthēsis: The topography of the mind

In an era of global aestheticization, where we are perpetually exposed and exploited by some form of artistic intervention vying for our attention, aesthetic ideals and aestheticizing activities have extended into all aspects of existence. As a result, our visual constructions have proved an important step in the aesthetic reification of our social reality – where reification is borrowed from Marxist terminology to mean the alienation within our social relations, where people become things – such that we are becoming the crucibles both of, and for, our own modern re--creation. However, the aesthetic experience maintains its traditional element in that it is still a judgement or critique of the beautiful and the artistic. In seeking to apprehend the "truth" through the artistic creation, such as those found in the image-making culture, there must be an aesthetic beyond the aesthetic itself, where the aesthetic is not restricted to the artistic "truth" of its own creation, or what we might call its artistic aspects and the need to be observed and interpreted, and thereby exposing the risk of being co-opted into ideology, and instead there must be an aesthetic that escapes its own bonds of form and beauty.

The idea of pursuing an aesthetic beyond the aesthetic is not a new one. Plato called for a transvaluation of aesthetics that would appeal to reason rather than the senses. For example, regarding music, according to Ekbert Faas, Plato favoured an older style of austere, classical music that was "modelled after numbers," such that "music can induce sobriety. It is indispensable in the education of the young. It can help indoctrinate people by its soothing spell," rather than the new classical forms which were, "possessed by a frantic and unhallowed lust for pleasure."[140] Aristotle was more flexible in terms of form, as found in his *Metaphysics*, for example, which went beyond his *Physics*, moving from seeking natural causes for being to seeking being-understood-as-being (being-qua-being). Thus, one could find meaning in what we all perceive as the shared common traits, the *sensus communis*, where the truth of an ever-changing existence in a world that is in perpetual flux is revealed to have a certain constancy through the universally shared recognition of those traits. Similarly, with aesthetics, the work of art must go beyond the mimetic and seek to present the ideal, thereby going beyond what we perceive to suggest the universal. In doing so, the work of art addresses that which is the appropriate and the ethical, such that *aisthēsis*, understood as perception from the senses, must be accompanied by perception from the intellect, thereby allowing for moral discernment and making a value judgement, which brings aesthetics into the domain of ethics.

Aristotle famously claimed, "the soul is in a certain way *all* beings,"[141] once again linking the individual subject and the *sensus communis*, only through a kind of life force. Martin Heidegger will paraphrase the same quote, only in his version the "all" is dropped so it reads, "The soul is in a certain way beings," which gives the phrase an additional Heideggerian spin by making the distinction between the ontological concerns of "being" and "Being." Heidegger returns to the fundamental Socratic question of what is the meaning of being (metaphysics), in order to recover an understanding of the nature of Being (the ontological), that is, of the profound possibilities of our presence in the world (*Dasein*). He distinguishes between Being (upper case) as a determination of our presence or Being-in-the-world, as opposed to the ontic, that is any manner of dealing with being (lower case) that does not raise the ontological questions, as found, for example, in the objective nature of science and scientific research in general.[142] This distinction is not unlike the one proposed here by the aesthetic of the aesthetic, which we could distinguish as the "aesthetic" (lower case, the work of art itself) and the "Aesthetic" (upper case, the effect of the work of art). To put it another way, the "aesthetic" concerns itself with perception, the process of attaining awareness or understanding of the environment by organizing and interpreting sensory information, and the "Aesthetic," the process by which new experience is assimilated to and transformed by the residuum of past experience of an individual to form a new whole. For example, not unlike Aristotle, where the shared common traits that are revealed and understood as universal imply a certain constancy or purpose, Heidegger would insist that phenomena "is what established itself in itself, what is manifest,"[143] and beauty is only one way in which truth occurs as unconcealment,[144] so that in order to apprehend the truth as a sense of disclosure, of revealing, we understand that phenomena are not appearances per se, but are things themselves showing themselves for what they are (*aletheia*). In terms of this revealing and concealing through the work of art, Heidegger reminds us of Albrecht Dürer's remark: "For in truth, art lies hidden within nature; he who can wrest it from her, has it."[145]

Plato proposed that the material world and the objects encountered in everyday life, along with their imperfections and decay, were merely the inferior copies of the ideal versions of these same objects: the dynamic deficiencies of the material world versus the static perfection of the ideal. In our imperfect world, as the poet Percy Blythe Shelley would write: "Life, like a dome of many-colored glass, stains the white radiance of eternity, until Death tramples it to fragments."[146] The many colours may sound much more appealing than sterile eternity, but the point here is that due to our many imperfections we can neither trust our own senses, nor believe what we see. As a result, we could say that seeing is interpreting, which requires knowledge. In the *Republic*, Plato will determine that "knowledge is compared to vision, and without light the eye has not 'the power of seeing' nor its object 'the power of being seen'. The light comes from a source that is 'beyond being'."[147] Here we have another possibility for the extension of the existing, where the process of revealing and concealing forms the transcendental topography of the mind, which is, importantly, where the edifying source of light emanates from beyond being.

The task, therefore, is to come to terms with the question of existence through existence itself, which would require an exposing or destructuring of the history of ontology,[148] that is, how we understand the nature of being, thus allowing the possibility of truth hiding beyond the appearance of "truth." Thus, the potentiality of art is that it is "the setting-into-work of truth," whereby

> Art lets truth originate. Art, founding preserving, is the spring that leaps to the truth of beings in the work. To originate something by a leap, to bring something into being from out of its essential source in a found leap – this is what the word "origin" [*Ursprung*, literally, primal leap] means.[149]

Heidegger adds that although we must inquire into the essence of art, we can't allow such reflection to force art and its revealing, its coming-to-be. We cannot continue to appeal to "a cultivated acquaintance with the past," but must give heed to "the essence of origin," namely the artistic creation as an origin in itself within our historical existence.[150] In terms of aesthetics beyond aesthetics, we would say that although aesthetics must adopt an interdisciplinary approach in order to address and understand its historical influences, where the aesthetic in our image-making culture extends across all dimensions of perception of the senses (*aisthēsis*), yet it must free itself from its own origins and the act of its own creation to discover the essence of the aesthetic of the aesthetic.

The extension of the existing, therefore, is that precondition of the work of art, whereby it follows, as Lukács surmised, that the task of the work of art is to draw the archetypal map in order to realize "the transcendental topography of the mind."[151] Then, as Rancière will claim, if we are able to "crack open the unity of the given and the obviousness of the visible" and "to reconfigure the landscape of what can be seen and what can be thought," then perhaps we will discover "a new topography of the possible."[152] This is the domain of the culturally modified brain, where the new topography of the mind defines the features of our internal and external landscapes, and where the aesthetic extends beyond a cultivated acquaintance with the culture to the aesthetic of the cultural modification itself. In other words, what we see is determined by how we think.

The image-making culture has brought the conceptual into our lived experience, where an extension of the existing is experienced not only collectively but, importantly, can be experienced at different times and places. Walter Benjamin found the new technology of photography provided the extension of "the artwork's claim to the attention of the masses," as would be realized in the cinema, where, "Painting, by its nature, cannot provide an object of simultaneous collective reception, as architecture has always been able to do, as the epic poems could do at one time, and as film is able to do today."[153] Indeed, the conceptual architecture exists outside of time, unlike the singular brick and mortar and time-bound structures of the real. Here we find the world-building of the modern cinema with its computer-generated images, where the scope of these visual constructions are limited only by the imaginations and budgets of its creators.

As with most things, this conceptual geography must succumb to the demands of politics and economics, where we may find that the principle of the extension of the existing with its temple grammar has not changed since the times of Ramesses II, where he sought not only to expand his kingdom in the material world but into the underworld, the next life, and the world of dreams. The Europeans sought trade routes to India and China in the 1400s, motivated by the trade of gold, silver and spices, only to be astonished to discover the New World, two vast continents of whose exploited treasures would not only finance the cathedrals and palaces and artworks of the Renaissance but instigate the rise of colonial empires. Now modern technology has summoned up a conceptual world, an unlimited frontier that is not restricted by any geography, borders or boundaries, whose treasures have already created fabulous wealth, and whose vast territories will become the disputed grounds for power struggles and the mechanisms of control in the future.

Yet despite all the modern technology of image-making, as Paul Virilio argues, it may be that we are no closer to a new topography of the possible, but rather the reverse, having diminished what Virilio will call the "*productive unconscious of sight*."[154] In which case, the work of art is unable to perform its task because the modern image-making culture, paradoxically, has annihilated the inner and outer landscapes of what can be seen and what can be thought. Perhaps we have overwhelmed our ability for self-realization within these conceptual landscapes, where, as Virilio maintains, we have incurred the symptoms of "*visual dyslexia*," increasingly unable to understand language or to visualize concepts because we are "incapable of *re-presenting* it to ourselves," where the many generations of artistic communication that built our topographical memory, and provided the potentialities for a transcendental topography, are now replaced by "the progressive disintegration of a faith in perception."[155] Everything before us is held in doubt; we have eroded the residuum of our apperception. If so, then the result is a topographical amnesia, where we are visually and artistically incapacitated by our own acts of creation.

Notes

1 Stephanie Buchenau, *The Founding of Aesthetics in the German Enlightenment: The Art of Invention and the Invention of Art* (Cambridge MA: Cambridge University Press, 2013), p.123. In terms of the relationship between beauty and logic, Buchenau points out the views of Gottfried Wilhelm Liebniz (1646-1716), the mathematician and philosopher, and Christian Freiherr von Wolffe (1679-1754), a German philosopher who also wrote on aesthetics, where, "Despite the abstract nature of the symbols, mathematic demonstrations are the most beautiful." Ibid., p.125.
2 Immanuel Kant, "The Critique of Judgement – Part I: Critique of Aesthetic Judgement," *Continental Aesthetics: Romanticism to Postmodernism: An Anthology,* edited by Richard Kearney and David Rasmussen (Malden MA: Blackwell Publishers, 2001), p.5.

3 See Walter Pater, *Studies in the History of the Renaissance*, edited by Matthew Beaumont (London and New York: Oxford University Press, 2010). See also Pater's *Appreciations* (1890) which includes the essay "Aesthetic Poetry," where, controversially, he supports a certain hedonism in poetry, which he will later revise to a "serious beauty." Andrew Leng, "Walter Pater's 'Dante Gabriel Rossetti' versus His 'Aesthetic Poetry,'" *The Journal of Pre-Raphaelite and Aesthetic Studies* (Spring 1989).
4 Kant, "The Critique of Judgement – Part I: Critique of Aesthetic Judgement," p.9.
5 Michael Levy (Editor), "Introduction to Walter Pater," *Marius the Epicurean* (London: Penguin Classics, 1986).
6 Leo Tolstoy, *What is Art?* (1896), translated by Aylmer Maude, Introduction by Vincent Tomas (Indianapolis IN and Cambridge MA: Hackett Publishing, 1996), p.50.
7 Ibid., p.71.
8 Ibid., p.193.
9 Ibid., p.72.
10 Eric R. Kandel, *The Age of Insight: The Quest to Understand the Unconscious in Art, Mind, and Brain, from Vienna 1900 to the Present* (New York: Random House, 2012), p.346.
11 Ibid., p.441.
12 Herbert Westren Turnbull, "The Great Mathematicians," *The World of Mathematics. Volume One,* Presented with commentaries and notes by James R. Newman (New York: Simon and Schuster, 1956), p.95
13 Ibid., p.95.
14 Plato, *Timaeus and Critias*, Translated with an introduction and an appendix on *Atlantis* by Desmond Lee (London: Penguin, reprinted with revisions 1977), p.7.
15 Ibid., p.10.
16 Ian Stewart, *Nature's Numbers – The Unreal Reality of Mathematics* (New York: Harper Collins, 1995), p.47.
17 In Plato's *The Symposium*, Aristophanes tells a story where the human transition from spherical to bilateral symmetry was caused when an angry Zeus split man in half, and had Apollo turn their faces and genitals around, leaving humans to forever hunt for their other half to become whole again. Zeus threatened, "If they continue insolent I will split them again and they shall hop around on a single leg," a consequence that would impose the asymmetric, moving us away from symmetry and its attendant perfection, beauty, and harmony. Plato, *The Symposium*, pp.22-24.
18 Stephen Hawking, *A Brief History of Time* (New York: Bantam Books, April 1988), p.175.
19 Deborah Karen Ward Modrak, "Sensation and Desire," *A Companion to Aristotle*, edited by Georgios Anagnostopoulos (Malden MA: Blackwell Publishing, 2009), pp.310-321. Modrak offers an example where sugar is white and sweet. The "white" is accessed by the sense of sight and the "sweet" is accessed by the sense of taste, and together make up a "common sensible."
20 Ibid., pp.314-315.
21 Victor Caston, "Phantasia and Thought," *A Companion to Aristotle*, Georgios Anagnostopoulos (Editor) (Malden MA: Wiley-Blackwell, 2009), p.322.
22 Modrak, "Sensation and Desire," p.327.
23 Ibid., p.324.
24 Christof Rapp, "The Nature and Goals of Rhetoric," *A Companion to Aristotle*, Georgios Anagnostopoulos (Editor), (Malden MA: Wiley-Blackwell, 2009), pp.581-582. Aristotle included three technical means for this art of persuasion, which may be regarded as the moral and psychological components, namely *êthos* (authority and honesty), *pathos* (empathy, the appeal to an audience's emotions), and *logos* (logic, the facts and figures). Ibid., pp.582-583.
25 Ibid., pp.585-586. Rapp clarifies that Aristotle does not define or endorse a single ethical stance (or popular opinion) for either speaker or audience, such that the formulations of both may be accepted but also challenged.
26 See Book V of Plato, *The Republic: the complete and unabridged Jowett translation* (New York: Vintage Books, 1991).
27 Walter J. Ong, *Orality and Literacy - The Technologizing of the World* (New York: Routledge, 2002), p.78.
28 J. Dudley Andrews, *The Major Film Theories: An Introduction* (London and New York: Oxford University Press, 1976), pp. 103-104. See also Siegfried Kracauer. *Theory of Film: The Redemption of Physical Reality* (1960). With an Introduction by Miriam Bratu Hansen. (Princeton NJ: Princeton University Press, 1997.)
29 Ong, *Orality and Literacy - The Technologizing of the World*, p.79.
30 Ibid, p.80.
31 Erik Hornung, *Idea into Image: Essays on Ancient Egyptian Thought*, translated by Elizabeth Bredeck (New York: Timken Publishers, 1992), 35-36.
32 Ibid., p.82.
33 The Books of the Netherworld, for example, were initially intended solely for the tomb of a king, but around 1000 BCE, in Thebes (now Luxor) and the "divine state of Amun" (Dynasty 21), the higher appropriates this royal privilege for their own sarcophagi and burial papyri. Erik Hornung, *Idea into Image: Essays on Ancient Egyptian Thought*, translated by Elizabeth Bredeck (New York: Timken Publishers, 1992), p.97.

34 Ibid., pp.119-123.
35 Ibid., p.138.
36 Ibid., p.141.
37 Ibid., p.174.
38 Ibid., p.133.
39 Annabelle Sreberny, "The Global and the Local," *Media and Cultural Studies: Keyworks*. Edited by Meenakshi Gigi Durham and Douglas M. Kellner (Malden, MA; Blackwell Publishing, 2012), p.536
40 Ibid., p.537.
41 Norman Doidge, *The Brain that Changes Itself: Stories of Personal Triumph from the Frontiers of Brain Science* (New York: Penguin, 2007), p.311.
42 Douglas Coupland, "Douglas Coupland: I miss my pre-internet brain," *The Daily Telegraph*, September 14 2014. Excerpt reprinted from *Kitten Clone: Inside Alcatel-Lucent* (London: Visual Editions, 2014).
43 Dana Gee, "Back to Books: Coupland looks at how we're spending our free time," *The Vancouver Sun*, October 1, 2016, p.D1.
44 Ong, *Orality and Literacy*, p.80.
45 Johann Hari, *Stolen Focus: Why You Can't Pay Attention and How to Think Deeply Again* (New York: Crown, 2023), p.276.
46 Ong, *Orality and Literacy*, p.82.
47 Ibid, p.12.
48 Bruce Chatwin, *The Songlines* (London: Jonathan Cape, 1987), p.292.
49 Rapp, "The Nature and Goals of Rhetoric," pp.588, 591.
50 Simon Critchley, *Infinitely Demanding: Ethics of Commitment, Politics of Resistance* (London: Verso, 2007), p.70.
51 Ibid., p.71.
52 Arthur Schopenhauer claimed, "The better consciousness in me lifts me into a world where there is no longer personality and causality or subject or object. My hope and my belief is that this better (supersensible and extra-temporal) consciousness will become my only one, and for that reason I hope that it is not God. But if anyone wants to use the expression God symbolically for the better consciousness itself or for much that we are able to separate or name, so let it be, yet not among philosophers I would have thought." David E. Cartwright, *Schopenhauer: A Biography* (Cambridge UK, Cambridge University Press, 2014), p.182. *Schopenhauer: A Biography* (Cambridge UK, Cambridge University Press, 2014), p.182. Despite Schopenhauer's wishes, an esoteric movement called Theosophy, or "God-knowledge," developed in the late 19th century. Influences included Emanuel Swedenborg (1688-1772), the hypnotist Franz Mesmer (1734-1815), and the occultist Madame Blavatsky (1831-1891) who claimed in *The Secret Doctrine* (1888) that theosophy was "the synthesis of science, religion and philosophy," which would uncover the secrets of ancient wisdoms. A similar idea also appeared in the writings of Carl Jung (1875-1961) in his descriptions of the images and motifs that arise from the archetype and the collective unconscious. In Western nations, this influence would appear in the drug counterculture of the 1960s and the eclectic New Age Movement of the 1970s, which sought a confluence of ancient wisdom and modern science. See Fritjof Capra, *The Tao of Physics: An Exploration of the Parallels Between Modern Physics and Eastern Mysticism* (Boulder CO: Shambhala Publications, 1975) and Michael Talbot, *Mysticism and the New Physics* (New York: Ballantyne, 1993).
53 Ong, *Orality and Literacy*, p.115.
54 Kant, "The Critique of Judgement – Part I: Critique of Aesthetic Judgement," p.22.
55 Ibid., pp.28-29.
56 Ibid., p.5.
57 Immanuel Kant, *Practical Philosophy*, translated and edited by Mary J. Gregor, General Introduction by Allen Wood (New York: Cambridge University Press, 1996), pp.384-385.
58 Kant, "The Critique of Judgement – Part I: Critique of Aesthetic Judgement," p.12.
59 Ibid., p.28.
60 Ibid., p.9.
61 Ibid., p.28.
62 Immanuel Kant, "What is Orientation in Thinking?" *Political Writings*, edited and with an Introduction and Notes by H.S. Reiss, translated by H.B. Nisbet (Cambridge MA: Cambridge University Press, 2011), pp.237-238.
63 Ong, *Orality and Literacy*, pp.38-39.
64 John Willett, *Art and Politics in the Weimar Period: The New Sobriety, 1917-1933* (New York: Pantheon Books, 1978), p.41.
65 The Soviet film industry found itself in a unique position to reassess its future: "with Marxists holding state power, questions of entertainment versus instruction, traditional versus radical form, drama versus documentary, literary versus visual communication, native versus foreign (especially Hollywood) models, ethnic nationalisms versus national culture, religious versus secular culture, urban versus rural, and popular audience versus intellectual creators, were raised as practical as well as theoretical matters." Chuck Kleinhans, "Marxism and film," *The Oxford Guide to Film Studies*. Edited by John Hill and Pamela Church Gibson (London and New York: Oxford University Press, 1998), p.107.

66 The film *Battleship Potemkin* (Sergei Eisenstein 1925) was made after the 1917 October Revolution yet its depiction of inequality and cruelty under the Tsar, particularly in the Odessa Steps sequence, justifies the revolution and ennobles the common citizen.
67 Willett, Art *and Politics in the Weimar Period*, p.48. The quote is from Jay Leyda, *Kino: A History of the Russian and Soviet Film* (Crows Nest, Australia: Allen and Unwin, 1960).
68 David A. Cook, *A History of Narrative Film* (New York: W.W. Norton & Company, 2004), p.115.
69 Ibid., p.127.
70 Ibid., p.149.
71 Ibid., p.155. An example is *October* (Sergei Eisenstein 1928) attempted a pure intellectual cinema, where an abstract assembly of juxtaposed images reached a level of abstraction that was often beyond comprehension.
72 See Ludwig Feuerbach, *The Essence of Christianity* (New York: C.Blanchard, 1855).
73 The ancient Greeks defined *praxis* as an activity engaged in by free people. Marxism aimed for a "philosophy of *praxis*" in that it encouraged people to actively seek freedom from oppression.
74 Andrew Cutrofello, *Continental Philosophy: A Contemporary Introduction* (New York: Routledge, 2005), p.290. See also Hans-Georg Gadamer, "The Ontology of the Work of Art and its Hermeneutical Significance," *Continental Aesthetics: Romanticism to Postmodernism: An Anthology*, edited by Richard Kearney and David Rasmussen (Malden MA: Blackwell Publishers, 2001), pp.102-157.
75 Ibid., p.291. See Hans-Georg Gadamer, *The Relevance of the Beautiful and Other Essays*, edited by Robert Bernasconi, translated by Nicholas Walker (New York: Cambridge University Press, 1986).
76 Cutrofello, *Continental Philosophy*, p.2. The distinction between intuition and concept may be likened to the distinction between orientation and action. For example, quoting from Kant, the difference between lust and desire: "Concupiscence (lusting after something) must also be distinguished from desire itself, as a stimulus to determining desire. Concupiscence is always a sensible modification of the mind but one that has not yet become an act of the faculty of desire." Kant, *Practical Philosophy*, p.374.
77 Peter Singer, "The Drowning Child and the Expanding Circle," *New Internationalist* (Oxford UK: New Internationalist Pubications, April 1997).
78 On the other hand, Singer considers the ruthless eploitation in the industrial raising of animals for human consumption and the rise of the vegan movement, which, in a sad but true commentary on human nature, would not be nearly as large if it were driven solely by ethical considerations. He quotes Charles Krauthammer where, not unlike how present generations view slavery or the consumption of tobacco, future generations will find it almost inconceivable how we treat animals and that "we actually rasied, herded and slaughtered them on an industrial scale – for the eating." Peter Singer, "Is meat cooked?" *The Globe and Mail* (Saturday August 25, 2018), pp.01, 06, 07.
79 Thomas Metzinger, *Being No One: The Self-Model Theory of Subjectivity* (Cambridge, Massachusetts: MIT Press, 2003), p.633.
80 Hornung, *Idea into Image*, pp.35-36.
81 The Venus of Willendorf is a small figurine of a female figure, 11 cm. or 4.3 in. tall. Unearthed in Austria in 1908, the estimates of its age range from 22,000 to 24,000 BCE. The exaggeration of her figure is due to an enhanced stimulus, a supernormal stimulus or "superstimulus," where the statuette's swollen figure reveals that during the harsh ice-age environment, the period of its creation, obesity and fertility would be highly desirable. See Nigel Spivey (narrator), *How Art Made the World* [Five-part documentary series]: Executive Producer, Kim Thomas; Producer, Mark Hedgecoe (London: BBC 2005). See also Kandel, *The Age of Insight*, pp.439-440.
82 A poem describing the Battle of Kadesh has survived, the "Poem of Pentaur," which was inscribed on various obelisks. Ramesses II issued a "bulletin" after his near-defeat that appears on the walls of a number of temples, including Luxor. Interestingly, the poem and bulletins mention the mysterious "Sea Peoples," who led various campaigns against Ramesses II.
83 Immanuel Kant, "The Critique of Judgement" (1790), *Continental Aesthetics: Romanticism to Postmodernism: An Anthology*, Richard Kearney and David Rasmussen (Editors) (Malden MA: Blackwell Publishers, 2001), p.99.
84 Ibid., p.13.
85 Ibid., p.24.
86 Ibid., p.25.
87 See Immanuel Kant, "An Answer to the Question: What is Enlightenment?" [1784], *Perpetual Peace and Other Essays on Politics, History and Moral Practice*, edited and translated by Ted Humphrey (Indianapolis IN: Hackett Publishing, 1988).
88 Kant, "The Critique of Judgement – Part I: Critique of Aesthetic Judgement," p.7.
89 Edmund Burke, *Philosophical Enquiry into the Origin of Our Ideas of the Sublime and Beautiful* (1757). (London and New York: Oxford University Press, 1998).
90 See Immanuel Kant, "Observations on the Feeling of the Beautiful and the Sublime," translated by John T. Goldthwait (Berkeley CA: University of California Press, 1960). See also "The Critique of Judgement" (1790), *Continental Aesthetics: Romanticism to Postmodernism: An Anthology*, Richard Kearney and David Rasmussen (Editors) (Malden MA: Blackwell Publishers, 2001), pp.5-42.
91 Metzinger, *Being No One*, p. 57.
92 Kant, "The Critique of Judgement – Part I: Critique of Aesthetic Judgement," p.8. Kant's definition of taste is as follows: "*Taste* is the faculty of estimating an object or a mode of repre-

sentation by means of a delight or aversion *apart from any interest*. The object of such a delight is called *beautiful*." Ibid., p.8.
93 Ibid., p.21.
94 Ibid., pp.28, 9.
95 Ibid., p.131
96 Sigmund Freud, *Civilization and its Discontents*, translated by David McLintock with an Introduction by Leo Bersani (London: Penguin Books, 2002), pp.3-4.
97 Jacques Rancière, *The Emancipated Spectator*, translated by Gregory Elliot (New York: Verso, 2009), pp.48-49.
98 Georg Lukács, *The Theory of the Novel: A Historico-philosophical Essay on the Forms of Great Epic Literature* [First printed by P. Cassirer, Berlin, 1920. Hermann Luchterland Verlag GmbH, 1963.] Translated from the German by Anna Bostock (London: Merlin Press, 1971), p.29.
99 Ibid., p.29. The poet and philosopher Novalis (1772-1801) wrote: "Philosophy is really homesickness, it is the urge to be at home everywhere."
100 Ong, *Orality and Literacy*, p.24.
101 In the film, *Jason and the Argonauts* (Don Chaffey 1963), with animation by Ray Harryhausen, a sorcerer sows the dragon teeth which rise out of the earth as skeleton warriors. This suggests the immutability and stasis of written language, lacking the dynamic lifeblood of rhetoric.
102 Marshall McLuhan, *The Gutenberg Galaxy: The Making of Typographic Man* (Toronto, ON: University of Toronto Press, Scholarly Publishing Division, 1962), p.32.
103 Lukács, *The Theory of the Novel*, p.153. With his reference to "an age of absolute sinfulness," Lukács evokes the German philosopher Johann Gottlieb Fichte (1762-1814).
104 Ibid., p.153. Kant, "The Critique of Judgement – Part I: Critique of Aesthetic Judgement," p.22.
105 Walter Kaufmann, *Nietzsche: Philosopher, Psychologist, Antichrist* (Princeton NJ: Princeton University Press, 1974), p.481.
106 Friedrich Nietzsche, *The Will to Power*, A new translation by Walter Kaufmann and R.J. Hollingdale (New York: Vintage 1968), pp.286-288.
107 Ibid., p.267.
108 Friedrich Nietzsche, "Attempt at Self-Criticism," *The Birth of Tragedy – Out of the Spirit of Music*, translated by Shaun Whiteside, edited by Michael Tanner (London: Penguin Books, 1993), p.9.
109 See *Editor's Introduction* to Nietzsche, *The Will to Power*, p.xvii.
110 Friedrich Nietzsche, *The Birth of Tragedy – Out of the Spirit of Music*, translated by Shaun Whiteside, edited by Michael Tanner (London: Penguin Books, 1993), p. 72.
111 Ibid., pp.72-73.
112 The dialectical method, or dialectic, appears in Plato's Socratic dialogues, where, despite having opposing views, reason and logic in discussion could reveal truth. This is not the same as a debate or the use of rhetoric (persuasion) to win an argument. Fichte introduced a three-step process, followed by Hegel, where the basic formula is: thesis + antithesis = synthesis.
113 Albert Schwegler, *Handbook of the History of Philosophy*, translated and annotated by James Hutchinson Stirling (Edinburgh: Edmonston & Co., 1879), p.324.
114 Ibid., p.338. See also G.F.W. Hegel, *Lectures on the Philosophy of World History: Introduction*, translated by H.B. Nisbett, with an Introduction by Duncan Forbes (Oxford UK: Cambridge University Press, 1981).
115 Ibid., p.340.
116 G.F.W. Hegel, "Lectures on Aesthetics," *Continental Aesthetics: Romanticism to Postmodernism: An Anthology*, edited by Richard Kearney and David Rasmussen (Malden MA: Blackwell Publishers, 2001), p.123.
117 Schwegler, *Handbook of the History of Philosophy*, p.341
118 Hegel, "Lectures on Aesthetics," p.107.
119 Romanticism is an artistic, literary, and intellectual movement that originated in Europe around 1800 to 1850. Partly in reaction to the Industrial Revolution and scientific rationalization, as well as aristocratic social and political norms of the Age of Enlightenment, it validated strong emotion as the source of authentic aesthetic experience. Charles Baudelaire would write, with a wry touch: "Romanticism is precisely situated neither in choice of subject nor exact truth, but in the way of feeling."
120 Peter Bürger, *Theory of the Avant-Garde* [1984], translation from the German by Michael Shaw, foreward by Jochen Schulte-Sasse (Minneapolis MA: University of Minnesota Press, 2007), p.93.
121 Ibid., p.84. See also Hegel, "Lectures on Aesthetics," pp.120-124.
122 John Gray, *The Silence of Animals – On Progress and Other Modern Myths* (New York: Farrar, Straus and Giroux, 2013), p.109.
123 Ibid., p.111.
124 Hegel, "Lectures on Aesthetics," p.123.
125 Ibid., p.122.
126 Walter Benjamin, "The Work of Art in the Age of Its Technological Reproducibility: Second Version" [1937], *Walter Benjamin: Selected Writings. Volume 3, 1935-1938*, translated by Edmund Jephcott, Howard Eiland, and Others, edited by Howard Eiland and Michael W. Jennings (Cambridge MA: The Belknap Press of Harvard University Press, 2002), pp.103-104.

127 Friedrich Schiller, "Letter of an Aesthetic Education of Man" [*Über die ästhetische Erziehung des Menschen in einer Reihe von Briefen*, 1794], *Continental Aesthetics: Romanticism to Postmodernism: An Anthology*, edited by Richard Kearney and David Rasmussen (Malden MA: Blackwell Publishers, 2001), p.43.
128 Ibid., p.44.
129 Ibid., p.45.
130 Ibid., p.45.
131 Bürger, *Theory of the Avant-Garde*, p.44.
132 Ibid., p.99.
133 Schiller, "Letter of an Aesthetic Education of Man," p.45.
134 Bürger, *Theory of the Avant-Garde*, p.45.
135 Benjamin, "The Work of Art in the Age of Its Technological Reproducibility: Second Version," p.106.
136 Walter Benjamin, "The Author as Producer," *Walter Benjamin: Selected Writings. Volume 2, Part 2. 1931-1934*, translated by Rodney Livingstone and Others, edited by Michael W. Jennings, Howard Eiland, and Gary Smith (Cambridge MA: The Belknap Press of Harvard University Press, 1999), p.77.
137 Benjamin, "The Work of Art in the Age of Its Technological Reproducibility: Second Version," p.122.
138 Bürger, *Theory of the Avant-Garde*, p.45.
139 Benjamin, "The Work of Art in the Age of Its Technological Reproducibility," p.104.
140 Ekbert Faas, *The Genealogy of Aesthetics* (Cambridge MA: Cambridge University Press, 2002), p.15.
141 The quote is from Aristotle's *De anima* ('On the Soul'), c.350 BCE. The soul, or essence, is not distinct from the body it occupies, with the nature of a soul varying from creature to creature. In Aristotle's conception, the soul is not a spiritual entity, but more of a life force that is integral to any living creature. The human soul includes the ability for thought and reflection. See also Martin Heidegger, "Being and Time," *Basic Writings – From Being and Time (1927) to The Task of Thinking (1964)* revised and Expanded Edition Edited, with General Introduction, and Introductions to Each Selection David Farrell Krell, Foreward by Taylor Carman (New York: HarperCollins, 2008), p.56*n*6.
142 Ibid., p.53.
143 Ibid., p.73.
144 Martin Heidegger, "The Origin of the Work of Art," *Basic Writings – From Being and Time (1927) to The Task of Thinking (1964)*, edited and with introductions by David Farrell Krell, foreward by Taylor Carman (New York: HarperCollins, 2008), p.181.
145 Ibid., p.195.
146 Percy Blythe Shelley, "Adonais," *The Oxford Book of Mystical Verse*. Chosen by D. H. S. Nicholson and A. H. E. Lee. (Oxford: Clarendon Press, 1917), sec.72. See also Plato, *The Symposium*, edited, translated and with an Introduction by Christopher Gill (London and New York: Penguin Classics, 2003).
147 Francis MacDonald Cornford, *Plato's Theory of Knowledge: The Theaetetus and the Sophist* (London: Routledge, 2013), p.247.
148 Heidegger, "Being and Time," p.63. Heidegger would use the term "*destruktion*," which he intended in the positive sense, the task of destroying ontological concepts, which, through tradition, had buried the meaning, including everyday, ordinary meanings, a kind of social amnesia. The editors note that Heidegger coins the term *existentiell* to designate the way Dasein in any given case actually exists by realizing or ignoring its various possibilities – in other words, by living its life. Ibid., p.55*n*.
149 Heidegger, "The Origin of the Work of Art," pp.201, 202.
150 Ibid., p.203. Heidegger frames this either-or decision with a quote from "The Journey," a Hölderlin poem: "Reluctantly that which dwells near its origin abandons the site." [*Schwer verlässt was nahe dem Ursprung wohnet, den Ort.*]
151 Lukács, *The Theory of the Novel*, p.29.
152 Rancière, *The Emancipated Spectator*, p.49.
153 Benjamin, ""The Work of Art in the Age of Its Technological Reproducibility: Second Version," p.116.
154 Paul Virilio, *The Vision Machine*, translated by Julie Rose, (Bloomington IN: Indiana University Press, 1994), pp.8, 21.
155 Ibid., pp.8,16.

The World as Picture

A technology of reflection: The modern re-creation

"The first technology was not language nor the wheel, not even the tree-branch-turned-spear," according to Ted Hiebert, "the first technology is and has always been the technology of reflection."[1] In other words, as we have determined with aesthetics, everything we do and make, every decision and judgement, can be no other than subjective. And since it was there from the start, the technology of reflection has advanced continuously throughout humankind's existence and is now incorporated to such a degree that it is part of the sheer immediacy of lived experience, integrated into the very fabric of everyday life. By its use of the technology of reflection our society is capable of transposing into image the entire world and everything in it, where the extension of the existing through our visual culture has changed how we see our world to such an extent that in effect it is "changing reality."

The fact that visual culture permeates our social reality means that it is also part of the construction and engagement with the psychology and politics of that social reality. The fact that visual culture is interpreted and integrated into society through technology means that it is also part of the economic and scientific realm. Consequently, the constituent parts of the image-making culture are defined not only by the content of images but also by their interaction with the subject in society, as both viewer and viewed, which may be termed the "visual event," whereby the visual event cannot simply be experienced only at face value but must be interpreted. For example, the visual event could be considered in terms of its origins within the image-making culture, as a cultural product, and in the anthropological or pseudomorphic sense, as a human artefact, and as a component in the technology of reflection, as a product of science.

Also, the visual event is temporal in that there is a viewing subject in the present, oneself, and there is a visual event from some moment in the past, for example, a photograph. Susan Sontag claims that, "All photographs are *memento mori*. To take a photograph is to participate in another person (or thing's) mortality, vulnerability, mutability. Precisely by slicing this moment and freezing it, all photographs testify to time's relentless melt."[2] Nicholas Mirzoeff notes that photography is "a past-tense medium. It says 'that *was* there' not what is there."[3] This reminds us of the notion that the work of art is not only a human artefact but a work of mourning.

In terms of interpretation, we could say it is also a work of denotation and connotation. The classic example would be a picture of an hourglass that denotes an old form of clock, but by suggesting the sands of time running out it also connotes our mortality. In his exploration of photography, *Camera Lucida*, a writing that Roland Barthes referred to a work of mourning inspired by his recently passed mother, he states, "a photograph is a witness, but a witness of something that is no more."[4] In support of the temporal characteristic of the visual event, Barthes will refer to photographs as "clocks for seeing."[5] Of all that is gone, therefore, a photograph, the work of art, is that which remains. And in doing so, and through its accessibility, where the past is able to participate in the present, it remains because it is what we have chosen to remember.

In effect, we have both an image-making culture - always changing, dynamic and alive - and a culture of the image - immutable, static and inanimate. By the same token, the transposing into image through the technology of our visual culture involves an aestheticization that may be understood as taking what may have once been considered unaesthetic – reality itself, for example, which exists in and of itself - but is, or now understood to be, aesthetic – something created, or recreated, through an image, a visual event. Sublime nature is reconfigured into the technological sublime. Due to the scope and magnitude of our technology of reflection in modern society, therefore, we are quite capable of transposing everything into a visual or audio event, or, for that matter an event that addresses any or all of our senses. In terms of ourselves, therefore, this is more than simply visual or audio perception as it encompasses a general perception with all the senses, where we must factor in the impression that remains from whatever is perceived, and delivered through a process of reception that is consuming increasingly large parts of our daily life.

In a larger sense, we are living in an era of global aestheticization, particularly amongst the wealthier industrial societies with their advanced technology, where aesthetic ideals and aestheticizing activities have been incorporated into all aspects of existence. In terms of the individual subject, for example, the technology of reflection enables us to be aesthetically configured by our appearance as determined by lifestyle, health, career, address, income, politics, and so forth, and duly accorded a corresponding social status in the process. Our self-reflective constructions, therefore, have proved a significant step in the aestheticization of our social reality, where the technology of reflection becomes the crucible of, and for, our own modern re-creation. This process is not unlike the creation of the work of art, which is dynamic and filled with vitality, yet the result, also like the work of art, may contain that which is inert and inanimate, an aspect that is inherently mournful, where something essential may have been frozen, or even lost, in the process.

Analytic: Continental

Aristotle may have been the first to grasp that the observation of things, their characteristics and alterations under changing conditions, resulted in a knowledge of how they behave as a rule. This observation and knowledge would become empirical, as found in modern science, which, as Heidegger notes, proceeds by constant activity, creating for itself an appropriate coherence and unity.[6] In the process of gathering knowledge, science is transformed from observation into research, developing an institutional character, while nature and history become objects of explanatory representation.

Nature is full of change, decay, and cycles, yet it can be argued that our knowledge strives for what is everlasting, always seeking the first causes of phenomena. Humankind has assigned itself the task of discovering and shaping this knowledge, a knowledge that informs our understanding and interpretation, thereby assigning value and meaning. Knowledge, therefore, is a form of categorization determined by our comprehension and so must always be a self-defining "experience," where meaning is always self-significant or enlightening, where we pursue knowledge that engages us both by necessity and by right. Adorno would write, "to think is to identify. Conceptual order is content to screen what thinking seeks to comprehend."[7] Consequently, science as research becomes indispensable in that it is part of our self-establishment in a world that we are continually redefining, yet, as Adorno notes, this process of ordering can also be a screen or veil that obscures the essence of what we seek to understand.

In his essay, "An Answer to the Question: What is Enlightenment?" (1784), Kant's answer is "*Sapere Aude!*" or "dare to be wise," a decree originally issued by Horace, the Roman poet, in *Epistles* (20 BCE).[8] For Horace, the phrase applauds the value of human endeavour, of persistence and effort in overcoming obstacles in order to reach a goal. It formed the moral in his story about a fool who waits for the stream to stop before crossing it. For Kant, the phrase supports the use of reason to release humankind from the darkness of despotism and ignorance, to question the status quo both publically and privately, and hence, enlightenment or *Aufklärung*, the liberation from prejudice and superstition.

Kant also wanted to stop the "endless controversies" amongst philosophers, as he wrote in "Perpetual Peace: A Philosophical Sketch" (1795), where the only perpetual peace is found in the graveyard. His goal was to restore metaphysics – the meaning of being - as the queen of all sciences.[9] However, the result was a division between the concept and the intuition, which would become the on-going basis for the struggle between analytic and continental philosophy, of which Kant would find himself as the last common philosophical ancestor. As noted by Gary Gutting, the distinction is an odd one, often indistinct and overlapping, but usually geographical, separating Anglo-American (analytic) and European (continental), and sometimes provoking animosity from either side, such as the debate between John Searle (analytic) and Jacques Derrida (continental), where Derrida accused Searle of "superficiality" and Searle accused Derrida of "obscurantism."[10] In general, as Gutting explains, we could say the goal of analytic philosophy is clarity, precision, and logical rigour, which led to various forms of logical, linguistic and conceptual analysis. In general, Gutting also explains, the goal of continental philosophy was the inclusion of the underlying meanings of experience, where, as we've discussed, the meeting between the work of art and the viewer modifies both. Of course, this is a source of both subjectivity and obscurity due to the uncertain nature of this experience, which, nonetheless, led to thinking about the conditions for the possibility of our concepts and even beyond those concepts, and as we are attempting in this book, to exploring the possibilities of creative intellectual imagination.

As Kant claimed, the only thing we know for certain is what we experience, including the representation of things, which is not precise or provable. We are only able to be conscious of our existence through our inner experience of existence through time. In terms of cognition and how we perceive things, or rather the misunderstandings that arise from it, Kant would state,

> [I]t always remains a scandal of philosophy and universal human reason that the existence of things outside us (from which we after all get the whole matter for our cognitions, even for our inner sense) should have to be assumed merely on faith, and that if it occurs to anyone to doubt it, we should be unable to answer him with a satisfactory proof.[11]

Indeed, Kant proposed a "Copernican Revolution" in reverse, by which he meant, "Up to now it has been assumed that all our cognition must conform to the objects; but [...] let us once try whether we do not get farther with the problems of metaphysics by assuming that the objects must conform to our cognition."[12] Taking Copernicus as an example, Kant argues that if we're not getting anywhere by assuming that we're standing still and the stars revolve around us, then let's consider the stars are standing still and we're the ones who are in motion. Similarly, if perception must conform to the constitution of the object, then we might not get anywhere, but if we understand the object is determined by the way in which the object conforms to the constitution of our perception, then we might be getting somewhere. By considering the constitution of our perception, we must acknowledge the importance of theory, and when we are dealing with theory that determines our perception and the work of art, then, conversely, we must also consider how the work of art determines us through our perception.

If we return to Socrates, we find that he saw mirrors as reflecting only what we can already see, just as the work of art may yield accurate but idle replications of the appearances of things, yet that is of no cognitive benefit whatever. As a student of Socrates, Plato took this a step further, claiming that only philosophers seek the truth, whereas actors or orators are only able to persuade an audience by rhetoric rather than by telling the truth. In his vision of the *kallipolis* (the beautiful city), Plato argued for a ruling council of Philosopher Kings, those rulers who were trained to seek the truth and not idle stargazing, while artists and writers would be banned from the city because they deal in illusion not reality.[13]

Arthur Danto, in his essay "The Artworld" (1964), will turn to both Socrates and Shakespeare, each of whom spoke of art as a mirror held up to nature:

Hamlet: *Do you see nothing there?*

The Queen: *Nothing at all, yet all that is I see.*[14]

In this scene, Hamlet witnesses the ghost of his father hovering before him, whereas the Queen sees nothing, concerned that her son may have gone mad. In terms of art as a mirror held up to nature, Danto argues that Hamlet, more acutely than Socrates, recognized a remarkable feature of reflecting surfaces namely that they show us what we could not otherwise perceive – our own face and form – and so art, insofar as it is mirrorlike, reveals us to ourselves, and is, even by Socratic criteria, of some cognitive utility after all. Just as the ghost appears before Hamlet and not to his mother, so we find the manifestation of past deeds and a state of mind which is determined by perception, which, through the work of art, the viewer is able to share and understand.

Danto will use the term "artworld" to describe cultural context or "an atmosphere of art theory."[15] An atmosphere suggests the work of art moving beyond representation and into the ether of contemplation, where something is not art simply because an artist makes something or because a critic calls something art, but something is art because it has succeeded in being retained within the rarefied realm of the artworld itself. The support of theory would lead to the institutional theory of art, whereby aesthetic theory is the dynamic product of historical forces, but this also suggests its temporal aspect, where something that was not art may become art. For example, something functional or crafted, say a spoon, or something political, say a work of graffiti, or something conceptual, not possessing a physical dimension, may in time alter its identity and become a piece of art. Moreover, some things could not become art because we had not yet arrived at a place where their possibility could be realized. That possibility could only occur as a result of a change in our perception, or apperception, the process by which new experience is transformed by the residuum of past experience, allowing us to see things differently. The work of art holds the mirror up to nature, as Danto claims, and captures the conscience of our kings.

Lacerated disclosure: Utilitarianism

It could be argued that both philosophy and science are seeking the "one thing," such as the absolute idea (as found in Hegel's absolute idealism, which sought the unity of thought and being) or the theory of everything (as pertains to the cosmologists, such as Stephen Hawking, who sought to unify Einstein's general theory of relativity with quantum mechanics). However, Hawking famously claimed "philosophy is dead" because the big questions that used to be discussed by philosophers are now in the hands of physicists.[16]

The entire process of determination becomes a way of life, our raison d'être, where a determination of "what is" through scientific pursuit may seem similar or even identical to the philosophical pursuit in quest of "what is." And yet, despite the common goal, there is often a divide between philosophy and science. Indeed, we might argue that Einstein's "theory of viewpoint," as Virilio calls it, has in fact "more or less destroyed anything connected with external proofs of a unique duration as a cogent principle for classifying events," such as, "the *thinking of being and the uniqueness of the universe* of the erstwhile philosophy of consciousness,"[17] namely, the potentialities for a transcendental topography. Is it any wonder that Einstein sought to restore cosmic order, claiming that God does not play dice and quantum mechanics does not bring us any closer to the secret of the 'old one'."[18] However, returning to Virilio, Einstein showed that space and time are now "*forms of intuition* that are now as much a part of our consciousness as concepts like form, colour, size and so on,"[19] where we have moved beyond the limits of classical physics and our sensory experience, where we have an extension of the existing that moves beyond the realm of perception that now includes the conceptual.

For the empiricists, the whole theory of relativity discounts the possibility of a fundamental understanding of the universe, which, in effect, means the world is an illusion and we are reduced to not-seeing and not-knowing. Politically and philosophically, this perspectivism will find its home in utilitarianism; artistically, we will move toward social realism. However, let's recall that there are determining or analytic judgements, as noted earlier in reference to Kant, a method that seeks a certainty and clarity through analysis of the approach and terms of thinking, which supports the scientific method, a circumscribed sphere of inquiry and discovery. But there are also reflective or synthetic judgements, also as Kant proposed, which appeal to an intuition of some sort, and therefore not necessarily known to be true *a priori* (that is, independent of experience). This suggests that the scientific method in itself is inadequate, that the human condition changes the terms of reference, therefore human agency is integral to the pursuit of truth. Avital Ronell argues that any attempt to lead a scientist to reflect on the true nature of knowledge itself will be rejected as "metaphysical" and therefore not worthy of scientific reflection.[20] Similarly, philosophical or metaphysical reflection alone is also inadequate, requiring the rigour of science to add a measure of certainty and clarity. Hence, we return to Kant's 'strong view of truth', where he wished to avoid "fanatical intuition," such as those found in the mystical writings of Emmanuel Swedenborg,[21] of which the young Kant himself was susceptible. Chastened, Kant would argue we must be content with a "moral faith" in a future life.[22]

For her part, Ronell maintains that there is a certain inhumanity associated with the very pursuit of truth.[23] For example, if we look at the scientific method, where its particular kind of truth is often pursued through the "lacerated disclosure" of testing, which may in fact be linked to a kind of torment, starting with "the Greeks' notion of *basanos*, relating truth to torture, binding a strictly constellated confluence of acts."[24] This reference to ancient Greek society stems from the understanding that a free man could not be tortured and therefore was more inclined to lie, whereas a slave could be tortured and therefore would be more likely to tell the truth. On one hand, as we are a technological society – perhaps even slaves to that technology – then we are more inclined to the scientific method and its determined means of testing and its circumscribed sphere of discovery, we are in effect 'forcing' the truth to be revealed. On the other hand, the same might be said of philosophical enquiry, where Socratic dialogue persists with question after question, often promoting a ruthless interrogation that demands a response and a level of discomfort in pursuit of truth. Yet in seeking their own particular truths, both science and philosophy are often held in esteem, regarded as creative and profound rather than tortuous. All the same, despite whatever means we choose to pursue, it may be in the nature of truth itself to resist our inquiries, and, in doing so, resist the absolute idea or the universal.

In terms of the two means of inquiry, the scientific and the philosophical, we might consider the Objectivists and the Historicists, as noted by Richard Dyer, who, having written extensively on the relationship between cinema and the representations of race, sexuality, and gender, considers movie making as both a scientific discovery and as a cultural product.[25] The Objectivists saw truths of science as facts discovered in the natural world, a Platonic view where the truth already exists so scientific practice is a matter of 'remembering' or rediscovering their existence. The Historicists, on the other hand, believe that knowledge is constructed according to cultural paradigms, where truths themselves may vary according to cultural norms and, depending on the historical circumstances, could be quite different. For example, we have the invention of the motion picture camera, whose technical practices are imposed by the mechanical nature of the apparatus itself, or, conversely, these technical practices are defined by cultural norms, as is the very possibility of the invention itself.

By way of illustration, in 1895, when August and Louis Lumière invented their *Cinématographe*, a motion picture camera and projector fashioned after a sewing machine, August Lumière, perhaps the more artistically inclined of the two brothers, said cinema was an invention without a future. Walter Murch, a celebrated film editor, quoted in Michael Ondaatje's *The Conversations: Walter Murch and the Art of Editing Film*, will support this view:

> [August Lumière] could have been right - there are frequently "inventions without a future," inventions that are ahead of their time, or outside their appropriate culture. The Aztecs invented the wheel, but didn't know how to use it except as a children's toy. Even though they built roads that to us scream out to have a wheel put on them, nonetheless they continued to drag things around. The society itself was blind to the possibilities. So you have to look not only at the invention itself, but the social and cultural context that surrounds it. They all have to mesh.[26]

Murch will identify the cinema's genesis in terms of its historicity, that is, it was the right time for its appearance. Murch identifies what he calls the "Three Fathers" of cinema: Thomas Edison (1847-1931), who represents all the technological geniuses of early film; and, even before the invention of film technology, Gustave Flaubert (1821-1880), who represents all the novelists of realism of this period; and even earlier, Ludwig van Beethoven (1770-1827), who represents the sudden shifts in tonality, rhythm, and musical focus, much like that found in the grammar of film (cuts, dissolves, fades, long shots, close shots, et al.), and which Beethoven was already working out in musical terms. Much like our discussion of the extension of the existing through our visual culture, Murch describes these musical movements as analogous to "moving through different rooms in a palace, going in one room, looking around, and then, closing the door and, with the next movement, going into the next room."[27]

Consequently, if we are going to look at the social and cultural context then we would need to examine the relationship between science and art, which, in turn, may point toward the aesthetic. For example, the differing views between the Objectivists and the Historicists will take us to the differences between scientific cognition and cultural awareness, and thus between determining and reflective judgments. We can dial this back to the debate in the 19th century between the Rationalists and the Empiricists, which would then extend into a debate between Positivists and Romanticists, an ongoing division over which of the two - concepts or intuitions - should be given primacy. And if we dial back further, we find that this division followed an earlier debate that sought to reconcile reason and faith.

During the Age of Enlightenment (1650-1800), the favoured technical practices would employ empiricism and the scientific method to try and prove there can be absolute truths. Experiments allowed for repetition, where truths are proven through consistent results. The goal, therefore, was for science to discover constants that arrived at an unchanging level of reality, as found in the mathematical constants of the Platonic forms for example, where the fundamental forms are abstract ideas, which in turn represent absolute truths or perfection. The problem, however, was that the more that was discovered, the further knowledge moved from absolute truth, and perfection became a very elusive concept. To put it another way, the more the rules of any category were defined, the more the category itself required changes and reformulations, whereby, in theory, the number of categories does not move to the singular but veers instead toward the infinite.

If we refer to John Locke's *An Essay Concerning Human Understanding* from 1690, he begins with the position that the mind at birth is a blank slate, *tabula rasa*, waiting to be written upon my the world of experience, whereby truth can be discovered by the individual through the senses. In doing so, Locke distinguishes between simple and complex ideas, primary and secondary qualities, and formulations of personal identity. Locke was considered an Empiricist – knowledge is gained through experience – as opposed to a Rationalist – knowledge is gained through reason. For example, Locke's friend, Isaac Newton, was a Rationalist who believed the universe runs according to law-governed mechanical principles, such as the law of universal gravity.

However, Locke would argue, in terms of human understanding, as the science of cognition became more and more precise, even simple ideas (such as 'red', 'sweet', 'round') become more divisible.[28] Locke proposed that simple ideas enter the human mind through either sensation or reflection. In sensation, the mind turns outward to the world and receives ideas through the faculties of sight, hearing, touch, smell, and taste. In reflection, the mind turns inward to its own operations, receiving ideas such as solidity, extension, shape, quantity, and motion or rest. In both cases, the process is completely passive. However, the secondary qualities that build upon these primary qualities that make these simple ideas become complex, whereby we develop concepts such as 'colour', 'scent' and 'taste'. These sensations are complex in that we ourselves produce them, such that they are uniquely human distinctions and not necessarily inherent to the thing itself.

As a consequence of this pursuit of human understanding, Locke becomes a proponent of the perceiving mind with its formulations of identity and self, where we may 'know' things outside a system of knowledge, such as those insights provided by intuition, which may or may not be actual truths but are nonetheless perceived as truths. Therefore, if our knowledge of the world depends on experience, which means that it is contingent not absolute, then experience and observation, not just reason, are central to the acquisition of knowledge. If so, we now have support for the interdependence of the two means of inquiry, the scientific and the philosophical.

All the same, in theory, as proposed above, the number of categories, orders, types, etc. would not move toward the singular but toward the infinite. The possibility of an infinite number of categories alarmed theologians of the time because their assumption was always that rigorously applied empiricism, including both concepts and intuition, would uncover the underlying divine nature of creation, but now it appeared it would only uncover an ever-growing number of types and subsequent sub-types. In order to re-establish the divine in categorization, that is, the underlying universal truth, a new taxonomical or classification system arose. As proposed by Edmund Burke in 1757, as discussed earlier, this system corresponded to the phenomenal and the noumenal, offering first beauty and then the sublime as the taxonomical device. The Beautiful is that which is well-formed and aesthetically pleasing; the Sublime is that which has the power to compel and destroy us, namely, that which is not in our power to control, or, to put it another way, formless. In order to re-establish the divine in categorization, that is, the underlying universal truth, a new taxonomical or classification system of arose. Much like Locke's concept of simple ideas, received through the faculties as sensation or through the mind as reflection, a completely passive process, as opposed to complex ideas that we ourselves produce and are uniquely human distinctions and not necessarily inherent to the thing itself, so Burke held that the qualities of the Sublime are not in the Beautiful, the simple idea of form and content in the work of art and its passive reception, but in the Sublime, that which is outside the form, those complex ideas and emotions such as astonishment, terror, vastness, infinity, obscurity, difficulty, privation, light and colour. In terms of aesthetics, the preference for the Sublime over the Beautiful would mark the transition from the Neoclassical to the Romantic era.

Another development would come from William Paley, writing about natural theology in 1802,[29] who endeavoured to prove that nature has been created with an express purpose. Using the metaphor of a watch, which has utility and complexity, and a watchmaker as a creator with a divine purpose, Paley contends that the diversity of nature, its form and function, was designed to accommodate man and his needs, therefore proving both the creator's handiwork and man's superior position in the divine scheme of the cosmos. John Kidd, writing in *The Bridgewater Treatises* in 1833,[30] would continue in this vein by arguing that the very complexity of nature, which clearly has a design and purpose even if it can never be fully understood, only serves as incontrovertible proof of the existence of God. Of course, this view of human existence, having first begun six thousand years earlier as interpreted through scripture, would soon be challenged by Charles Darwin and his theories of biological evolution, particularly after the publication of *On the Origin of Species* in 1859.

Another publication of 1859 was *On Liberty*, written by John Stuart Mill (1806-1873), which presents an ethical system of utilitarianism that sought to bring about the greatest good for the greatest number. Here we have a version of Kant's strong view of truth distinguished by impartiality, where everyone's happiness counts the same and the good is impartially considered. The implication, as Kant held, is of a moral duty, which in turn suggests a universal truth and perhaps a trace of the divine. Mill's writing was influenced by his father, James Mill, as well as his father's friend, Jeremy Bentham, both of whom were well-known British scholars and had written important philosophical works. Mill distinguished himself as the first Member of Parliament to call for women's suffrage. However, the rights of women offers a glaring example where the cracks in utilitarianism are revealed. Mary Wollstonecraft had already proved revolutionary in her *Vindication of the Rights of Women* of 1792, where she lamented the neglected education of females in a male-dominated society, as well as the "legalized prostitution" of marriage. Wollstonecraft states that the perfection of humankind will be attained through reason, virtue and knowledge, but not as long as half of humankind is neither allowed nor encouraged to seek their own perfection. Indeed, women will never be truly useful members of society, nor will humankind realize its potential "breathed into man by the Master of the universe."[31]

Working as a clerk for the East India Company supported Mill's ambition as a "speculative writer"[32] and allowed him to develop his philosophy of utilitarianism. Utility was the proper end to any plan, tempered by an overriding rule to do the greatest good for the greatest number of people. In reality, however, this philosophy often provided a justification for imperialism, whereby the greatest good would be the greatest number of people converted to the British imperialistic concept of good. Although the greatest good may satisfy a certain strict logic in terms of territory, it failed to account for diversity within cultures and individuals and therefore lacked humanity. As a result, Mill came to understand that he lost all sense of purpose and happiness, as "a well-equipped ship and a rudder; but no sail,"[33] and finally suffered a nervous breakdown. In time, he discovered works of art, primarily music and poetry, and a renewed hope in life, believing that happiness was not an end in itself but something that is found "*en passant*, without being made a principal object."[34]

As the Age of Enlightenment transformed into the Industrial Revolution in the early 1800s, science was forcing the issue between reason and faith. This dispute brought about the tradition of natural theology, whereby we could learn about God not only through scripture but through God's creation, the natural world. In other words, faith was not dependent on revelation but observation. The Romanticists will also claim that intellectual intuition manifested itself through works of art. However, the philosophies of science, such as Positivism, will argue that the scientific method is the best approach to uncovering the processes by which both physical and human events occur, such that every rationally justifiable assertion can be scientifically verified or is capable of logical or mathematical proof, and that therefore rejects metaphysics and theism. In the post-Kantian world, this concept was further developed by August Comte (1798-1857), who, along with his associate John Stuart Mill, supported the views of analytic philosophy and rejected the idea of intellectual intuition. Comte created the term 'altruism' to describe the selfless concern for others, which will also inform his attempt to introduce a cohesive "religion of humanity" which, an elaborate if rather uninspiring exercise in system of belief that turned out to be largely unsuccessful, was influential in the development of various secular humanist organizations in the 19th century. Indeed, Comte's ideas were even more influential in Victorian England than the theories of Darwin or Marx, taking hold of the ideals of intellectuals until about 1880.

The debate between Positivists and Romanticists, which may be regarded as a precursor to the analytic-continental divide, can also be found in the contrasting views of Isaac Newton (1643-1727), the English mathematician, astronomer, theologian, author and physicist, with those of Johann Wolfgang von Goethe (1749-1842), the German poet, playwright, theatre director, novelist, scientist, statesman, critic and amateur artist. Newton is famous for his work with optics, where he employed the scientific method and mathematical proofs in his examination of light and colour by means of refraction in prisms and lenses.[35] Goethe, on the other hand, argued, as had Aristotle, that the fundamental nature of light was that it was white, such that colour was not an outward physical phenomenon, but, and here he emphasized the role of the scientist, was intrinsic to the human observing the phenomenon.[36] Indeed, the German Romantics of the post-Kant era supported intellectual intuition through human cognition, and further, that intellectual intuition manifested itself through the creation and reception of works of art.[37] On the other hand, Comte attempted to introduce a cohesive "religion of humanity" which, though largely unsuccessful, was influential in the development of various Secular Humanist organizations in the 19th century.

The dividing lines were drawn up between knowledge and experience, reason and passion, concept and intuition. Many of the works of art of the 1800s followed these divisions, where artists sought their visions of truth through realism or romanticism, the objective or the subjective, and yet, as we shall see, both movements might also be regarded as tributes to scale and accuracy.

The early part of the century was recognized as the Age of Reflection, or Romanticism (1800 – 1840), which appeared as a reaction against the scientific rationalization of nature, imposed by the Enlightenment, as well as part of a revolt against aristocratic social and political norms. There were earlier precedents for romanticism to be found in German literature and music from the late 1760s to the early 1780s, in which individual subjectivity and, in particular, extremes of emotion were given free expression in reaction to the perceived constraints of rationalism and the aesthetic movements it spawned. The movement included many artistic styles, which validated strong emotion as an authentic source of aesthetic experience, placing emphasis on the sublime with such emotions as trepidation, horror, terror and awe. This will inform, in music for example, the orchestral compositions of Beethoven's symphonies, and later, the grandiose operas of Richard Wagner (1813-1883), such as the four-part epic *The Ring of the Nebelung* (1876). This would lead to what the historian Paul Johnson has called the "Age of the Gigantic," which was a tribute to both scale and accuracy.[38]

This movement had already begun with a multi-sheet woodcut of Venice made in 1500, but it was the panoramic paintings, a term coined by the English painter Robert Barker to describe his 360-degree painting of Edinburgh (from the Greek *pan* ('all') and *horama* ('view')).[39] In 1793, Barker will make a fortune from the first purpose-built panorama building in the world, located in London's Leicester Square, which had a skylight, special lighting, and room the for the audience to move around and immerse themselves in the enormous panoramas. The building would be a precursor to the movie palace, for which Leicester Square is still renowned, where the audience could immerse themselves in the spectacles on screen, particularly with the evolution of the wide screen format. As for the panorama pictures themselves, these were similar in form to the earlier 'landscape scrolls' of China, such as those of the Song Dynasty (960-1269), a period when woodblock and then moveable-type printing would lead to the rapid dissemination of literature and knowledge. And in Japan there was the 'picture scroll' of the 11th to 16th centuries, such as the *emaki-mono*, which are handscrolls drawn, painted, or stamped with a horizontal, illustrated narrative, often depicting battles, romances, and supernatural stories. These would inform the *yōkai*, stories of the supernatural from the Edo period (1603-1868),[40] which in turn would appear as *manga*, the Japanese comic book or graphic novel, which was influenced by the 'storyboard' style of comic books brought over during the American Occupation (1945-1952), and then provide inspiration for the *anime* films.[41]

In doing so, as described by Gilles Deleuze and Félix Guattari, a French philosopher and psychologist respectively, where we have been relentlessly submitted to the prescriptive and exclusive "either/or" we may now have the descriptive and inclusive "*either... or... or...*"[42] Hence, instead of the prescriptive orders of categorization, Deleuze and Guattari offer their concept of haecceity, namely the discrete properties or characteristics of a thing which make it a particular thing, a person or object's "thisness."[43] Deleuze and Guattari use the term to align thisness with presence in time and space, which "has neither beginning nor end, origin nor destination; it is always in the middle. It is not made of points, only of lines. It is a rhizome."[44] A rhizome is much harder to uproot, an example would be crabgrass rather than a tree, where crabgrass continues to survive no matter how much you pull up, since no part is the 'governing' part. This same reasoning informed the objectives of the U.S. Department of Defense in 1969 when it set up the Advanced Research Projects Agency Network (ARPANET), originally conceived as a decentralized computer network that could withstand any type of disaster or attack. This network provided the first building blocks to what the Internet is today, a rhizomic network that doesn't start anywhere or end anywhere and at every point in its existence it is the same, a network of individual but indistinguishable threads.

The linear progression and Aristotelian structure of beginning, middle and end is replaced by a rhizomic network of interconnected filaments, with no central point, no particular origin, no definitive structure, no formative unity. Rather than depth or height, we now have a maze of surface connections. In terms of our usage, rather than an extension of the existing that consist of the maps of a territory or terrain, we now embark on "lines of flight" and "strategies of deterritorialization."[45] Unlike the previous stories of growth, of achievement, of upwardness, we now show connections between events and people and ideas without necessarily offering any causative explanations or direction for those connections. In effect, we are witnessing a new era based on "the opposite of history," for just as the rhizome is "an antigenealogy, a short-term memory or anti-memory," and the plateau, Gregory Bateson's term, is "always in the middle, not at the beginning or the end. A rhizome is made up of plateaus."[46]

Our perception of the visual world is dependent on our internal representation of the visual world. In studies of hemispatial neglect, where damage was sustained to one hemisphere of the brain, there were deficits to one side of the field of vision. For example, patients may be presented with a view of a cathedral set in a plaza. They can name objects on the right of the cathedral, but not the left, where, even though their vision is otherwise normal, they are "blind" to the left side because they lack the ability to "imagine" or internally represent the left side so they can't "see" it.[47] The authors of this study also provide studies on the effects of path integration, how we find our way around, which they investigate in terms of human spatial navigation. This includes the allocentric form of navigation and reasoning whereby one's position and direction is relative to multiple external landmarks and independent of the navigator. This suggests what has been called our sixth sense, or as the authors refer to it, our "vestibular system," which they argue provides specific contributions to everyday life.[48] The sketching of our external and internal and navigational maps, our real and virtual worlds, are not unlike the components of a film, relative distance to objects, and between objects, spatial scale, including zooming in and out, alignments and juxtapositions, our responses to stimuli, the encoding in memory and orientation.

In terms of initiating a change in subjectivity and how we "see" things, then we must consider the pervasive image-making culture of our time where we are perpetually presented with new ways of seeing. As noted in the Introduction, the inability to see things as they are is a shortcoming that may be explained by the concept of cognitive dissonance, where what we see and what we tell ourselves that we see are in contradiction. On the other hand, in contrast to cognitive dissonance, we might consider cultural cognition, that is, our creative and artistic endeavours, which often seek to "open our eyes," to challenge how we see things, including how we see ourselves, so that we "see" things differently. Of course, there is no shortage of these artistic endeavours, particularly through computer technology and our mediated reality, which may be hindering rather than enhancing our ability to "see."

In which case, we may find ourselves locked into a perpetual cycle of creation, relentlessly creating and re-creating ourselves through the technology of reflection, where it is increasingly difficult to comprehend, let alone keep pace with, the changes assimilated into our lives and social reality. To quote the Cuban filmmaker Julio García Espinosa, "Art will not disappear into nothingness; it will disappear into everything."[49] Indeed, Susan Buck-Morss quotes Peter Schjeldahl who wrote, "American art today can be anything but necessary."[50] In reference to art in the age of technological surveillance, and with the political overtones of the Argentinian *Los desparacidos* ("The disappeared"), she will also claim, "artists are disappeared."[51] We might say there are no longer works of art as we once knew them, all that remains is the aesthetic that we used to judge them. In which case, the task of the work of art in our visual culture is not so much a matter of making images seen but a matter of understanding how seeing as image-making informs our social reality. Consequently, we could say that the image-making culture has enabled the change from the hierarchical structure, where the idea as image had previously been dispensed within the public sphere from those above to those below, and now, particularly in the proliferation of networks, allowing for the rhizomic structure that incorporates the idea as image through the technology of reflection into lived experience and everyday life.

However, Lyotard identifies another possibility within the genres of discourse, where "the collective addressee of a prescriptive ('You ought') identifies itself with the 'We' qua addressor of prescriptives ('We can),"[52] whereby we understand ourselves to be enabled and empowered in a social relationship and yet it still amounts to a prescriptive and exclusive "either/or." Lyotard maintains that "transcendence is immanent to the prescriptive game," such that "what is being called the transcendence of the prescriptive is simply the fact that the position of the sender, as authority that obligates, is left vacant. That is, the prescriptive utterance comes from nothing: its pragmatic virtue of obligation results from neither its content nor its utterer."[53] In which case, the technology of reflection and its assertion of modern self-creation is merely, to paraphrase Lyotard, an affirmation circumscribed around a big zero, which, by inscribing it, annihilates it and assigns its meaning.[54]

Subjectum: "That-which-lies-before"

The modern age introduced the concepts of subjectivism and individualism that would transform subjectivity and our social reality. In many ways, humanity has freed itself from previous bonds, many of which were self-imposed, so that humanity "frees itself to itself,"[55] as Heidegger stated, yet in the process humankind may have assigned new self-imposed bonds through our social reality. One reason for this paradox is that the essence of humanity is transformed when man becomes "the primary and genuine *subjectum*,"[56] Heidegger argues, where *subjectum* is understood in the original Greek as "ground," as "that-which-lies-before," which includes the action of "that which gathers everything onto itself," such that man intends to have everything brought and placed before him.[57] In doing so, one is not only the self-creator, but now "becomes that being upon which every other being, in its way of being and its truth, is founded. Man becomes the referential center of beings as such."[58] This modern transformation has two mutually inclusive components: the transformation of man as primary subject, and the transformation of the understandings of beings as a whole, in other words, their objectification.

This all-encompassing transformation, Heidegger will claim, is only possible through the world-as-picture. Indeed, Heidegger would claim that the fundamental event of modernity is the conquest of the world-as-picture, and the sign of this event is the magnitude and scope of appearances that accompanies the world-as-picture itself.[59] To clarify, this does not mean to make a copy of something, nor an imitation of some action, but rather to "put oneself in the picture," such that we are all "in the picture," where man is the primary subject, where that-which-lies-before is reflection, or rather self-reflection, such that this transformation and objectification is necessarily self-defining:

> Understood in an essential way, "world picture" does not mean "picture of the world" but, rather, the world grasped as picture. Beings as a whole are now taken in such a way that a being is first and only in being insofar as it is set in place by representing-producing [*vorstellend-berstellenden*] humanity. Whenever we have a world picture, an essential decision occurs concerning beings as a whole. The being of beings is sought and found in the representedness of beings.[60]

As a result, there are two processes at work in modernity: we not only become the primary subject and the world becomes picture, but through these processes, we bring ourselves before ourselves. And because we are now the referential center of beings, we are also the representative of beings in the objectivist sense, the master of the now-bounded object domain, the creator of coherence and meaning, where, self-elevated to the role of self-creator, we are constituted by and through ourselves. This in turn leads to humanism, which, Heidegger argues, is no more than a moral-aesthetic anthropology, an anthropology that is no more than a philosophical interpretation of human beings from the standpoint of, and in relation to, human beings themselves, which in turn leads to an ever more exclusive interpretation of the world that is expressed by humankind's fundamental relation to a world view [*Weltanschauung*].[61] Therefore, the liberated domain of the individual subject may be little more than an illusion because it is also the bounded domain of the objectification, where that which has been objectified and bounded is humankind itself through its own self-reflection and objectification, where the bonds are once again self-imposed, no longer demanding that humanity "frees itself *to* itself" but that humanity "frees itself *from* itself."[62]

Heidegger, however, warns against merely negating the age, which will never allow us to experience and think what that knowledge is that has been refused, or, equally unproductive, retracing the flight into tradition, an aspect of pseudomorphosis, that is merely a "blindness towards the historical moment [*Augenblick*]."[63] In other words, perception in itself is insufficient to interpret meaning, as is self-reflection, which is merely the projection of the bounded object domain as supported by the human being as the primary subject in an attempt to create for oneself an appropriate coherence and unity, whereby this can only result in a "seeing" that is in fact a "blindness," which amounts to vision as a form of bondage, and so demanding that humanity free itself from itself.

The world-as-picture: The illusion of illusion

Heidegger was well aware that the conquest of the world-as-picture extended across the globe, and, in terms that suggests the attendant standardization inherent in this process, writes "From now on the word 'picture' means: the collective image of representing production."[64] Heidegger was also aware of the attendant risks in this development. An ever more exclusive interpretation of the world that is expressed by humankind's fundamental relation to a world view would mean that human beings had now set the stage for a battle of world views, an event whose appearance is everywhere found as "the gigantic, with its planning, calculating, establishing and securing."[65] To capture the immensity of this modern development and its simultaneous incursion into the very fabric of everyday life, Michel Serres considers the acceleration of the "the rise of the local towards the global,"[66] in what has been called the "glocal," where human activity has put the global habitat at risk, and where, from now on, action will not come from any human being as an individual or subject, "-- no, the decisive actions are now, massively, those of enormous and dense tectonic plates of humanity."[67]

This calculation, however, despite its scope and magnitude, comes with its own indeterminacy. Heidegger argues for a realization that there is always that which is incalculable, a shadow that withdraws into a space beyond representation, to a knowledge that is refused. Perhaps this knowledge will be available to the human of the future, one capable of creative questioning and genuine reflection, enabling the transport into "that 'in--between' in which he belongs to being and yet, amidst beings, remains a stranger."[68] Nonetheless, the warning against the gigantic, the planning and securing and its constant activity, of the liberated domain of the individual subject which is in fact an illusion because of the bonds that humankind has imposed upon itself, may also be interpreted as a kind of hope in that the subject still remains capable of being a stranger amidst one's own kind, despite a culture and technology of unremitting reflection.

Nietzsche, who often characterizes himself as a stranger among his own kind, claimed that the need for control over our existence had only reduced us to the dreaded Alexandrian man, indexing and classifying dead cultures rather than embracing a new vision, "the 'critic' without pleasure or strength [...] at bottom a librarian and corrector of proofs, wretchedly blinded by the dust of his tomes and by printing errors."[69] If so, then the illusion of the liberated subject will remain just that, an illusion, bounded by the object domain of self-creation, unless, as the young Nietzsche proposed, the Apollonian pursuit of truth and knowledge includes the resurrection of the Dionysiac. Only then, can we satisfy our longing for redemption through illusion and yet find the spiritual comfort to face "the horror and absurdity of existence."[70] In other words, we may "break through" and find the actual truth within the accepted "truth," and thereby discover "an ideal of the primal Oneness," and, although this too may be a deception, the necessary non-truth, it will reveal "the dream as the *illusion of illusion* as an even higher satisfaction of the original desire for illusion."[71] Is that not the extension of the existing, of expanding this world into other worlds and realities that are created by ourselves, a measure of our capacity and desire for self-creation and world-making? For Nietzsche, the purpose of achieving a place where "when we dream we are at two removes from reality,"[72] is that it allows us to find a way to acknowledge the repellent horror and absurdity of existence, yet without losing the will to continue. It allows us to revel in the uncertainty of existence, our aloneness, rather than abdicate with an Alexandrian failure of courage. And where might we find the ideas that will simultaneously create illusions and reveal the truth of our condition, providing real answers to life's most profound questions? The young Nietzsche had little doubt that we should look to "a redeeming, healing enchantress – *art.*"[73]

In a profound synthesis of art and science, Eric R. Kandel approaches the brain as a "creativity machine," that "searches for patterns amid chaos and ambiguity and it constructs models of the complex reality around us."[74] For Kandel, art and science share a mutual goal, each involved in a dialogue that is continually evolving and informing each other. He quotes the artist Piet Mondrian, who said, "For there are 'made' laws, 'discovered' laws, but also laws – a truth for all time. There are more of less hidden in the reality which surrounds us and do not change."[75] And these laws are revealed through both art and science,

Thus, to paraphrase Deleuze, the intention here is less to discourse about the products of the image-making culture in and of themselves, but to speak with - and *through* – the image-making culture in order to interpret its meaning in terms of the actual truth within the accepted "truth."[76]

Paradoxically, we too are bound within the object domain, and so must be emancipated from the bondage of both constitutive subjectivity and the aestheticization of the world-as-picture, which may then require a double transgression, deconstructing Nietzsche's illusion of illusion and discovering the aesthetic of the aesthetic in terms of oneself.

Notes

1 Ted Hiebert, "The Lacanian Conspiracy," *CTheory*, Arthur and Marilouise Kroker (Editors), p.1. Published 22/6/2005.
2 Susan Sontag, *On Photography* (New York: Anchor Books, 1990), p.15.
3 Nicholas Mirzoeff, *An Introduction to Visual Culture* (London: Routledge, 1999), p.74.
4 Roland Barthes, *Camera Lucida – Reflections on Photography*, translated from the French by Richard Howard (New York: Hill And Wang, 2010), p.xi.
5 Ibid., p.xv.
6 Martin Heidegger, "The Age of the World Picture," *Off the Beaten Track*, edited and translated by Julian Young and Kenneth Haynes (Cambridge MA: Cambridge University Press, 2002), p.64.
7 Adorno, "Negative Dialectics and the Possibility of Philosophy," p.57.
8 See "First Book of Letters (Epistularum liber primus)" in *The Works of Horace, Rendered into Engllish Prose with Introductions, Running Analysis, Notes and an Index* (1874) (Norderstedt DE: Hansebooks, 2017).
9 Immanuel Kant, "Perpetual Peace: A Philosophical Sketch." *Kant – Political Writings*. Edited with and Introduction and Notes by Hans Reiss, Translated by H.B. Nisbet (Cambridge UK: Cambridge University Press, 2011), p.93.
10 Gary Gutting, "Bridging the Analytic-Continental Divide," *The Stone*. The New York Times; February 19, 2012. See also Andrew Cutrofello, "Introduction: What is Continental Philosophy?", *Continental Philosophy: A Contemporary Introduction* (New York: Routledge, 2005), pp.1-29
11 Immanuel Kant, *Critique of Pure Reason*, Translated and edited by Paul Guyer and Allen W. Wood (Cambridge UK: Cambridge University Press, 1998), p.121.
12 Ibid., p.110.
13 See Plato, *The Republic*, Book V.
14 Arthur Danto, "The Artworld," (1964) in *Aesthetics: Classic Readings from the Western Tradition*, Edited by Dabney Townsend (Belmont CA: Wadsworth/Thomson Learning, 2001), p.326. The quote is from William Shakespeare, *Hamlet*, Act III, scene IV.
15 See also Thomas Adajian, "The Definition of Art", *The Stanford Encyclopedia of Philosophy* (Spring 2022 Edition), Edward N. Zalta (ed.). [Online]
16 See Stephen Hawking and Leonard Mlodinow, *The Grand Design* (London UK: Bantam, 2010)
17 Virilio, *The Vision Machine*, p.22.
18 Albert Einstein (1926) in letter to Max Born (4 December 1926); *The Born-Einstein Letters* (translated by Irene Born) (Walker and Company, New York, 1971).
19 Virilio, *The Vision Machine*, p.22.
20 Avital Ronell, *The Test Drive* (Chicago IL: University of Illinois Press, 2005), p.5.
21 Emmanuel Swedenborg (1688-1772) had a spiritual awakening later in life, which he wrote about in *Heaven and Hell* (1758), where he claimed to have had visions and dreams that led to contact with the afterlife, including the ability to communicate with angels and demons.
22 Immanuel Kant, "Dreams of a Spirit-Seer Elucidated by Dreams of Metaphysics," *Theoretical Philosophy 1755-1770*, edited and translated by David Walford in

collaboration with Ralf Meerbote (New York: Cambridge University Press, 1992), pp. 337-338. See also Cutrofello, *Continental Philosophy*, p.31.

23 This statement may take on further meaning in light of Ronell's personal issues, including accusations of sexual harassment (2017), and the rights and privileges associated with those in positions of authority.

24 Ronell, *The Test Drive*, p.13.

25 Richard Dyer, "Introduction to Film Studies," *Film Studies: Critical Approaches*, Editors: John Hill and Pamela Church Gibson (London: Oxford University Press, 2000), p.3.

26 Michael Ondaatje, *The Conversations: Walter Murch and the Art of Editing Film* (Toronto: Vintage Canada, 2002), p.87. Walter Murch and George Lucas co-wrote *THX 1138*, a 1971 science fiction film directed by Lucas in his feature directorial debut. Murch was also credited as sound designer for *Apocalypse Now* (Francis Ford Coppola 1979), the first time this credit was used to acknowledge the change from "sound engineer" to "sound designer." Elsaesser and Hagener, *Film Theory*, p.142.

27 Ibid., pp.89-90.

28 John Locke, *An Essay Concerning Human Understanding* (1689), Revised edition (London: Penguin Classics, 1998).

29 See William Paley, *Natural Theology: or, Evidences of the Existence and Attributes of The Deity, collected from the Appearances of Nature* (1802), (Independently published, 2019).

30 See John Kidd, *The Bridgewater Treatises on the Power Wisdom and Goodness of God as Manifested in the Creation: Treatise II. On the Adaptation of External Nature to the Physical Condition of Man* (London: William Pickering, 1837).

31 Mary Wollstonecraft, *Vindication of the Rights of Women* (1792), Edited with an Introduction and Notes by Miriam Brody, Revised edition (London: Penguin Books, 2004), p.242.

32 John Stuart Mill, *Autobiography of John Stuart Mill*, Preface by John Jacob Coss (New York: Columbian University Press, 1924), p.60.

33 Ibid., p.89.

34 Ibid., p.90. An example can be found in the film *Saving Private Ryan* (Steven Spielberg 1998). Set during World War II, three brothers have already given up their lives and only one brother, Ryan, is still alive. Captain Miller (played by Tom Hanks) is tasked with finding the lone surviving brother, which will come at the cost of losing many of his own men. The captain will declare, "This Ryan had better be worth it. He'd better go home and cure some disease or invent a longer-lasting light bulb or something." Here lies the problem: different activities produce different levels of happiness, so how do we measure it? Ryan's mother will be very happy to learn that her son has survived, but the many people who buy the better light bulb are only marginally more happy, so how does the happiness equate to the lives lost to get Ryan home? Peter Singer and the metaphor of the drowning child inspire another example where we would sacrifice our shoes to save the child but falter if our obligation extended to a child in another country. A wider view of responsibility inspired "effective altruism," as proposed by Will MacAskill, demanding personal sacrifice and extended responsibility beyond the immediate and into future generations, "longtermism." See Gideon Lewis-Kraus, "Do Better: The gospel of effective altruism," The New Yorker (August 15, 2022), pp.48-59.

35 See Isaac Newton, *Opticks: or, A Treatise of the Reflexions, Refractions, Inflexions and Colours of Light* (1704).

36 See Johann Wolfgang von Goethe, *Theory of Colours* (*Zur Farbenlehre*, 1810).

37 Cutrofello, *Continental Philosophy*, p.14. The German Romantics would include Friedrich Wilhelm Joseph von Schelling (1775-1854), Johann Gottlieb Fichte (1762-1814), Friedrich Schlegel (1772-1829), Novalis (Friedrich von Hardenberg, 1772-1801), and, to some degree, Georg Wilhelm Hegel (1770-1831).

38 Paul Johnson, *The Birth of the Modern: World Society 1815-1830* (London: George Weidenfeld & Nicholson Ltd, 1991), p.155.

39 Ibid., p.155.

40 Lafcadio Hearn (1850-1904) was born in Greece, grew up in Ireland, worked in the US as journalist for *Harper's Weekly*, and died in Tokyo. *Kwaidan: Stories and Studies of Strange Things* (1903) is a collection of Japanese ghost stories and a brief non-fiction study on insects. *Kwaidan* or *Kaidan* means 'ghost story', which is a Japanese word consisting of two kanji: *kai* meaning "strange, mysterious, rare or bewitching apparition" and *dan* meaning "talk" or "recited narrative." In terms of insects, Hearn relates the Japanese beliefs in the otherworld qualities of insects, such as butterflies, which are the personification of the human soul, or mosquitoes, which are the karmic reincarnation of jealous or greedy people, and ants, superior to humans in their chastity, ethics, social structure, longevity, and evolution. See Lafcadio Hearn, *Kwaidan: Stories and Studies of Strange Things* (1903) (Project Gutenberg, posted February 18 2010). See also the film *Kwaidan* (Masaki Kobayashi 1965).

41 See Kirsten Thompson Kristin and David Bordwell, Jeff Smith, *Film History: An Introduction*, Fifth Edition (New York: McGraw-Hill, 2022).

42 Gilles Deleuze and Félix Guattari, *Anti-Oedipus: Capitalism and Schizophrenia*, translated by Robert Hurley, Mark Seem, and Helen R. Lane (Minneapolis MN: University of Minnesota Press, 1983), pp.12, 16.

43 The term "haecceity" was first coined by Duns Scotus (1266-1308) to denote the discrete qualities, properties or characteristics of a thing which make it a particular thing, where haecceity is a person or object's "thisness." Charles Sanders Pierce (1839-1914) also used the term as a non-descriptive reference to an individual, such as one's name or an identification number. See Catherine Legg and Christopher Hookway, "Pragmatism," *The Stanford Encyclopedia of Philosophy* (Summer 2021 Edition), Edward N. Zalta (ed.). [Online]

44 Gilles Deleuze and Félix Guattari, *A Thousand Plateaus: Capitalism and Schizophrenia*, translation and Foreward by Brian Massumi (Minneapolis MN: University of Minnesota Press, 2007), p.263.

45 Ibid., pp.88-89.

46 Ibid., pp.22-23.

47 Arne D. Ekstrom, Hugo J. Spiers, Veronique D Bohbot, and R. Shayna Rosenbaum, *Human Spatial Navigation*. (Princeton N.J. and Oxford: Princeton University Press, 2018.), p.132.

48 Ibid., pp.6-7. The sixth sense is also known as proprioception, an awareness of where our limbs are and how our bodies are positioned in space, which also informs our ability to navigate.

49 Julio García Espinosa, "For An Imperfect Cinema," translated by Julianne Burton-Carvajal, *Jump Cut: A Review of Contemporary Media* (No. 20, 1979), pp.24-26.

50 Susan Buck-Morss, *Thinking Past Terror: Islamism and Critical Theory on the Left* (London and New York: Verso, 2003), p.69.

51 Ibid., p.85.

52 Jean-François Lyotard, *The Differend: Phrases in Dispute*, translated by Georges Van Den Abbeele (Minneapolis MI: University of Minnesota Press, 1988), p.145ff.

53 Jean-François Lyotard and Jean-Loup Thebaud, *Just Gaming*, translated by Wlad Godzich (Minneapolis MI: University of Minnesota Press, 2008), p.72.

54 Jean-François Lyotard, *Libidinal Economy*, translated by Iain Hamilton Grant (Bloomington IN: Indiana University Press, 1988), p.19.

55 Heidegger, "The Age of the World Picture,"p.66.

56 Ibid., p.66.

57 Ibid., p.67.

58 Ibid., pp.66-67.

59 Ibid., p.57.

60 Ibid., pp.67-68.

61 Ibid., p.70.

62 The Canadian writer Margaret Atwood used similar terms in her dystopian novel *The Handmaid's Tale* ((Toronto ON: McClelland & Stewart, 1985), which was

adapted into the 1990 film directed by Völker Schlöndorff, and later into a TV series (2017). Atwood maintained that women's rights can be described as "freedom to" (i.e., women having the freedom to do as they please) versus "freedom from" (i.e., women being protected from difficulties, responsibilities, and fear). Atwood claims these two should not be confused as "freedom to" is the much more important. As such, she paraphrases Marx's claim, "From each according to his ability, to each according to his need" and turns it into a comment on gender roles, "From each according to her ability... to each according to his needs." Both Marx and Atwood refer to an egalitarian social order, whereas the context used above is in terms of humanity's self-imposed bonds through constitutive subjectivity. In terms of biopolitics, we might consider Judith Butler's claim that "The sudden feminist conversion on the part of the Bush administration, which retroactively transformed the liberation of women into a rationale for its military actions against Afghanistan, is a sign of the extent to which feminism, as a trope, is deployed in the service of restoring the presumption of First World impermeability." Judith Butler, "Violence, Mourning, Politics," *Precarious Life: The Powers of Mourning and Violence* (London: Verso, 2004), p.41.

63 Heidegger, "The Age of the World Picture," p.72.

64 Ibid., p.71.

65 Ibid., p.72.

66 Michel Serres, *The Natural Contract*, translated by Elizabeth MacArthur and William Paulson (Ann Arbor MI: The University of Michigan Press, 1995), p.3. See also Sreberny, "The Global and the Local," *Media and Cultural Studies: Keyworks*, p.527.

67 Ibid., p.16. For example, the photographs of Edward Burtynsky, as well as the documentary *Manufactured Landscapes* (Jennifer Baichwal 2006), detail the massive changes in the earth's landscape as documented by Burtynsky. As well as the 2018 documentary, *Anthropocene: The Human Epoch* (Nicholas de Pencier, Jennifer Baichwal, Edward Burtynsky). For a quite different perpsective, see the documentary on the work of Scottish artist Andy Goldsworthy, *Rivers and Tides* (Thomas Reidelsheimer 2001), which shows the beauty and rhythm of nature through site-specific art.

68 Ibid., p.72.

69 Nietzsche, *The Birth of Tragedy*, p.89.

70 Ibid., p.40.

71 Ibid., p.25.

72 Ibid., p.120.

73 Ibid., p.40.

74 Kandel, *The Age of Insight*, p. 498.

75 Ibid. p.498.

76 Elsaesser and Hagener, *Film Theory*, p.6.

Purpose and Function

The purpose of art: The sphere of spheres

As Schiller's "middle disposition" describes the condition of the aesthetic that lies between sense and reason, perception and thought, the condition of sensual determination and the condition of rational determination, so Hegel will claim that "the work of art stands in the *middle* between immediate sensuousness and ideal thought."[1] This would suggest that the condition of the aesthetic occupies a liminal space between the "internal" world of the subject and the "external" world as perceived by that subject. In addition, the aesthetic marks the division between human beings and nature, mortal and divinity, and, in terms of ideal thought, good and evil, the moral and the immoral. As such, as proposed by Plato, man becomes the measure of all things, and the work of art bears the burden of "the essential thing or what ought to be," and so becomes an instrument of utility, but not "for other ends, like instruction, purification, bettering, financial gain, struggling for fame and honour," but instead "art's vocation is to unveil the *truth* in the form of sensuous artistic configuration."[2] Therefore, the work of art is not functionless; indeed, it has a particular purpose and goal, namely "the betterment of mankind."[3] Accordingly, the function of art is to be found in its content, such that "to comprehend in thought what this fullness of content and its beautiful mode of appearance are."[4] Therefore, we might say, the function of art is to serve as the navigator in that region described as the liminal space, where the unveiling of truth is an exploration and understanding of that space, a space occupied by humankind.

The goal of unveiling truth would be consistent with Hegel's aim of realizing human freedom, accomplished through a process of increasing knowledge of ourselves. The process of unveiling truth is one of constant change, where freedom and knowledge are the function of the work of art and the aesthetic experience that allows ideas to be presented and comprehended. For Hegel, the process of change is itself reality, where consciousness has elevated morality into perception, a perception that is interpreted and not just "seen," such that interpretation is always through the mind. Ultimately, the unveiling of truth is realized not only through individuals, or societies, but also in the mind itself and its understanding of the reality of the world itself, and so through what Hegel would call *Geist*, often translated as "Spirit." Hegel, quoted in Schwegler, would write:

> Spirit is the truth of nature, the resolution of its alienated outwardness, the attainment to identity with self. Its nature then, is: formally, freedom, or the capability of abstracting from everything; materially, the power to reveal itself *as* spirit, as conscious reason, to erect a structure of objective rationality, to assume for its domain the universe of mind.[5]

In this sense, as Peter Singer suggests, "Spirit" is perhaps better explained as "Mind."[6] Importantly, the implication is that there is another reality above and beyond what our senses can access, above and beyond the individual human mind, but which is accessible in the communal sense of Mind, and is also in the reality beyond the threshold or "behind the veil." For Hegel, therefore, "what is rational is actual and what is actual is rational [...] nothing is actual except the Idea,"[7] whereby the end point of the dialectical process would be Mind coming to know itself as the ultimate reality (Absolute Mind or Absolute Spirit). To put it another way, the state of Absolute Knowledge is also the state of Absolute Freedom, because the Mind determines reality and once it "frees itself to itself" and "frees itself from itself" then the Mind sees the world is in fact itself. What this means, of course, is that Hegel's philosophy of Mind is in itself the very culmination of the whole process: "a sphere of spheres self-closed."[8]

For Hegel, self-knowledge becomes freedom, because it is only through self-knowledge that we can access what is ultimately real, thereby overcoming our self-alienation. The "free play" between understanding and imagination that is produced by an artwork also suggests that the very concept of freedom itself is something noumenal and so can never actually manifest itself in the realm of the senses, and yet, according to Hegel, that is not because we can never access the noumenal, but only that we haven't accessed it yet within our historical process. This also supports the idea that history is change but the real is absolute and eternal, recognizing Plato's demand that objects should be understood not in their particularity but in their universality. Consequently, as Hegel contends, "the beautiful is now to be understood in its essence and its Concept."[9] The aim of art, its workmanship, would support the technology of reflection in that it will endeavour "to strip the external world of its inflexible foreignness and to enjoy in the shape of things only an external realization of himself."[10]

The purpose of art, therefore, and its aesthetic, is self-knowledge that leads to freedom, which is achieved by allowing human beings to see themselves through their understanding of the world, which is a world-understanding that we have created for and by ourselves, between mind and Mind, with the work of art at the threshold of the liminal space:

> The work of art stands in the *middle* between immediate sensuousness and ideal thought. It is *not yet* pure thought, but, despite its sensuousness, is *no longer* a purely material existent either, like stones, plants, and organic life; on the contrary, the sensuous in the work of art is itself something ideal, but which, not being ideal as thought is ideal, is still at the same time there externally as a thing.[11]

Indeed, the work of art must be incomplete because its sensuousness generally addresses only two of the senses, sight and hearing, while smell, taste, and touch remain excluded, and thus man can only produce "a surface of the sensuous, mere *schemata*," that is, temporarily stable perceptual constructs generated by our various cognitive abilities. However, the sensuous shapes and sounds do not appear simply for appearance's sake, nor does the work of art achieve its universality simply by attending to all the senses, because of its aim, that is, "they have the power to call forth from all the depths a consciousness a sound and an echo in the spirit. In this way the sensuous aspect of art is *spiritualized*, since the spirit appears in art as made *sensuous*."[12] The aesthetic of the work of art, therefore, is made "concrete" through its workmanship and form, and its pure or ideal beauty is imbued in the work itself, namely its concept, which is to support man's rational need to recognize his own spiritual self in the world, and thus afford through self-knowledge the possibility of purification, a kind of catharsis,[13] revealing insights into "genuine moral goodness" and "the betterment of mankind." Therefore, in support of the technology of reflection, we must overcome our self-alienation through self-knowledge and so become the crucibles of, and for, our own modern re-creation, and, in doing so, access a process of change that is rooted in *ethos*, that is, the guiding beliefs or ideals that characterize a community. If the aesthetic is that whose determining ground can be no other than subjective, and if the genuine *subjectum* is understood in the original Greek as ground, as "that-which-lies-before," then we might say that the Hegelian hope is in *being-one's-own-ground*, where the "free play" of self-knowledge is realized in the larger sense of the *sensus communis*, an ethically oriented knowledge that is both mind and Mind.

The artist's task: The form as veil

The significance of the artist's task, as well as its method, may be found in Benjamin's essay from 1914-1915, unpublished in his lifetime, entitled "Two Poems by Friedrich Hölderlin: 'The Poet's Courage' and 'Timidity' [*Zwei Gedichte von Friedrich Hölderlin: 'Dichtermut' und 'Blödigkeit'*]."[14] It is important to note that in German the title alone contains multiple double meanings and overlapping etymologies. Not only are two poems the subject of Benjamin's essay, of course, implying an interconnected or double investigation, but the word "poem" in German is *Gedichte* and "the poetized" is *das Gedichtete*, which would not only support the intimate relationship between the poem and the poetized, but the concept that, as Benjamin will argue, that which is poetically formed pre-exists the poem. In Heideggerian terms, therefore, the poem would be a revealing of that which had been concealed.

This pre-existence would also support Benjamin's view that history is constructed backwards (from the present to the past) and therefore the past is no longer a fixed point, thereby creating the need to challenge the myth of historical progress. His final work, for example, "Thesis on the Philosophy of History" (1940), exemplifies an unusual combination of theology and historical materialism, in particular the concept of the "Angelus Novus," based on a 1920 sketch by Paul Klee (which Benjamin owned) and portrays an angel of history whose face is turned to the past where he sees wreckage upon wreckage hurled at his feet. A storm blows the angel into the future to which his back is turned: "What we call progress is this storm."[15] In which case, evoking Hegel's "cunning with reason,"[16] where the "truth" of reason, as noted by Susan Buck-Morss, "becomes conscious by working its way 'with cunning' into history through the passions and ambitions of unwitting historical subjects," and thereby "literally deifies history, affirming the myth of progress."[17] To put it another way, if the "truth" is confirmed through history which has already produced the necessary untruth, then this "truth" is only realized and invested through the transformation of subjectivity itself and arises from our own self-creation, which is then realized as the myth of progress. However, Benjamin offers an alternative when he argues that cunning also has the capacity to challenge the myth of historical progress by seeking to "brush history against the grain,"[18] where the "very newness and modernity of the present could be made to suddenly release its significance when seen as archaic."[19]

Benjamin agreed with Lukács that "the petrified life within nature is merely what history has developed into,"[20] but he would still attempt to illuminate the other side of this same concept, namely the mystical murmuring within the present. Not unlike Heidegger's *alēthia*, or the "bringing forth of Being from concealment,"[21] so Benjamin tried to bring history itself "out of infinite distance into infinite proximity."[22] Thus, the angel sees history as one single catastrophe, which keeps piling wreckage upon wreckage, but, as Benjamin told Adorno, "he is the angel who does not give, but takes."[23] In this sense, the angel would like to halt and bind the wounds of the victims crushed beneath the pile of ruins, yet the storm keeps carrying it on to new catastrophes. This is the whole of modern society, of progress, dominated by tragedy, subject to repetition, always the same (*Immergleich*). For Benjamin, to salvage human experience from historical oblivion, a task compared to religious redemption, would require the Messiah or a revolution, where the "'splinters (*Splitter*) of messianic time' are the moments of revolt."[24] Hence, in those frozen moments of time, "dialectics at a standstill,"[25] Benjamin considered that it may not in fact be revolutionary change in terms of motion that we are seeking, but its opposite, where "revolutions are an attempt by the passengers on this train – namely, the human race – to activate the emergency brake."[26] For

Benjamin, therefore, at any given moment we stand on the edge of history, between "now-time" (*Jetztzeit*) and the possibility of a radically different future, a future that would redress the wrongs of the past, and thereby offering a messianic hope for a second chance.[27]

Benjamin would look to language for the possibility of religious experience and the spiritual depth of words, as found in the poetry of Hölderlin, such that language is not merely an instrument of communication, but a "medium of creation."[28] As human beings we have been given the capacity to use language and thereby the ability to respond to the hidden nature of things, to give voice to the silent murmuring; "There is no event or thing in either animate or inanimate nature that does not in some way partake of language."[29] Indeed, that which is concealed may be due to the form itself and its pseudomorphosis or aura, demanding, as Benjamin words it, the "radical renunciation of eternal value."[30]

Adorno, for his part, is also committed to the destruction of dogmatic constructions but sought to replace them with theories grounded in empirical experience, and yet he could still approve of how Benjamin's interpretation allowed the most common objects to release a significance that dissolved their reified appearance. Adorno would write about this aspect of Benjamin's philosophy: "He is driven not merely to awaken congealed life in petrified objects – as in allegory – but also to scrutinize living things so that they present themselves as being ancient, '*ur*-historical' and abruptly release their significance."[31] Indeed, Benjamin's mystical impulse suggests that the subject needs to go into the congealed object where phenomena have a voice of their own. In this sense, physical matter has its own existence, living and growing old and decaying, just as do ideas, theories, concepts, novels, and films, meaning that they are not mere subjectivity, and therefore contain a significance, a locus of truth. Adorno agreed that there is meaning to be found within objects, but he suggests a different kind of truth, the *ars invieniedi*, which meant "literally the art of coming upon something, invention in the sense, not of making something up, but of discovering it for the first time."[32] Like Freudian slips of the tongue (parapraxis), where truth surfaced as inconsistencies or unintentional truths, an object still manages to reveal its own subjective truth despite its objectification. In other words, all things have their hidden meanings and all cultural forms are a way to discover meaning, but Adorno argues that to recognize those meanings we must first penetrate the phenomena by making their truth cognitively accessible, which required intellectual labour rather than metaphysical magic.

Nonetheless, Benjamin would argue in his essay *The Author as Producer* (1934) for the "refunction" of cultural production through progressive cultural creators.[33] Significantly, the profound influence of cultural hegemony, the art of thinking in other people's heads, becomes the means for decisive political activism: "The catchword in which the demands of Activisim are summed up is 'logocracy'; in plain language, 'rule of the mind.'"[34] This is not to be confused with "rule of the intellectuals," Benjamin explains, because a work is politically correct if it includes a "literary tendency," that is, the two can never be mutually exclusive.[35] For this reason, Benjamin would support the cinema and its potential to become a forum of political enlightenment and discussion, rather than, as Adorno claimed, a medium of "culinary" audience pleasure.[36] According to Benjamin, and due to its reproducibility and accessibility, hence its capacity to be not-eternal, challenging pseudomorphosis, whereby film is essentially lacking in aura. As a result, film is the antithesis of a traditional work of art. The latter is a singular static work created by a single artist in one particular period yet imbued with eternal values; the former is a dynamic collaboration for the masses that can be constantly reinterpreted, rewritten, re-shot, re-edited, and reproduced. Rather than a singular image, a film is composed of a very large number of images and image-sequences, all created by a group of specialists, including writer, director, actors, producer, cinematographer, and editor. These specialists are in a position to intervene at any time in order to improve the film in any desired way during the entire creative process from initial concept to final cut. This capacity for improvement and change links film to "its radical renunciation of eternal value," that is, it refunctions the singular and static form into one of dynamic experience, where the aura of the artistic experience remains but is now disseminated into the audience and the world at large.

Adorno, on the other hand, wanted to attain a "concreteness" of understanding by grounding the particular object in its dialectical, mediated relationship to the totality.[37] Benjamin, as stated by Buck-Morss, sought a "true naming," replacing the "objectness" of language, restoring language to its proper purpose and function:

> In late bourgeois society, words had become fetishes, indifferent to the objects they signified: 'It is a sign of all reification resulting from idealist consciousness that the things can be named arbitrarily...' True naming, in contrast, was mimetic in that it demanded precision of referents: the verbal representation of phenomena really yielded to the particularity of things, forming a one-time-only configuration.[38]

Adorno, however, wrote, "Anything that is not reified, cannot be counted and measured, ceases to exist,"[39] and further, "even the past is no longer safe from the present, whose remembrance of it consigns it to oblivion a second time,"[40] whereby the process of naming in itself creates a kind of forgetting. Nonetheless, a corollary to this may also be true, that without the process of reification, then our existence ceases to make sense. Indeed, Heidegger would state that to name something is to call something into word, and in being named, something is not only called into "presencing," it in turn calls to us, which thus calls us to thinking.[41] Importantly, if "true naming" has been replaced by "objectness," it is because the saving power of the poet has been diminished, and, in so doing, we may find that the work of art itself has moved into concealment.

The concealment of the work of art points out the problem of the relationship between receptivity and spontaneity, namely, how is truth disclosed aesthetically? To put it another way, rather than reveal its nature an artwork seeks to conceal its nature, or, to extend the argument put forth by Wolfgang Schirmacher, who suggests that we are only able to attain glimpses of whatever art is willing to reveal through the aesthetic experience, which then implies that genuine aesthetic experience is only made possible by that which exceeds the grasp of thought and sensibility.[42] Consequently, the concealment of the work of art may appear in its very form, or the "ironization of form," as Ronell words it (meaning "to make ironic"), which, "is like the storm which lifts up [*aufheben*] the curtain of the transcendental order of art and reveals it for what it is, in this order as well as in the unmediated existence of the work.'"[43] Lukács expressed a similar point when he claimed that the novel form fails to express the eternity within us, thus exposing a gap between the finite and the infinite that can be expressed only through irony, a pessimistic anti--illumination rather than a true illumination.

Evoking Paul de Man, Ronell will argue that "'ironization of form consists in a deliberate destruction of the form'... - not at all an aesthetic recuperation, but, to the contrary, a radical, complete destruction of the form, which he calls 'the critical act,' which undoes the form by analysis, which by demystification destroys the form."[44] Thus, through intellectual labour, the form that veils the work is submitted to destruction so that "something like the 'unmediated existence of the work' can stand revealed, is cleared for presentation – though in some sense this showing must mark an allegory of presentation."[45]

If the work of art is to realize its true function and purpose then it must move beyond its own aesthetics of form and interpretation to achieve another level of aesthetic, one that does not rely on, and perhaps destroys, the first level (order, intensity) of aesthetic, and in doing so realizes its own true potential as a second level (order, intensity) of aesthetic. For example, we might consider Fernand Léger's statement, made in 1922, where the potential of the new art of cinema lay not in its capacity of resemblance or representation but in its power to harness visibility, whereby it became a "matter of *making images seen*."[46] Léger was disappointed that this potential to harness visibility was enslaved to traditional art forms, such as theatre and literature.

The filmmaker Stan Brakhage defined "picture" as a "framed collection of nameable things," but instead of depending on these framed collections of nameable things, he sought "a form of creative filmmaking that would present the unnameable – the elusive, fleeting, ineffable images of 'moving visual thinking'."[47] In other words, he sought to reveal, or unconceal, some truth that is beyond the "truth" of the first order of aesthetic, something that may not be achievable by intellectual analysis of the work of art (still the first intensity of aesthetic), which only involves a process of demystification, or, we might even say, the removal of the scientific spirit from the work of art, which is only the precondition of the work of art, whereas its task is that elusive truth that remains the purpose and function of the artist.

The poetized: Being-found-fitting

The mystery of language as invoked by Novalis is noted by Heidegger when he quotes from Novalis' *Monologue*: "Precisely what is peculiar to language – that it concerns itself purely with itself alone – no one knows."[48] In Novalis's notion of *ordo inversus*, a subject's cognitive and intuitive functions are fused, which may be the prevalent paradigm of modern poetics:

> The working of the *ordo inversus*, our intuitive perception of objects and ideas is transformed into cognition as we distinguish them by name. Naming is perhaps the first and simplest form of symbolization; once a name is established, it takes on a functional value of its own, giving form to our intuited understanding.[49]

Benjamin observes that Hölderlin uses *ordo inversus* in the two poems to counter the totality of myth in the form of fragments. Benjamin uses this notion to support the argument that the poet is not simply someone who is possessed by language, but that the poeticized appears to the poet in the form of language because language itself prompted the need to speak and therefore preceded the poem.[50]

To this end, Benjamin states, there is also a double meaning to be found in another word similar to *Gedichte* (poem) and *das Gedichtete* (the poetized), which is *geschickt*, meaning to be "skilful," "dexterous," "clever," but it also means "sent," in the past-perfect tense for an action already completed, thus implying the poet appears among the living, determining and determined. In addition, *das Geschichte*, meaning "story" or "history," one that would have already been sent, would now suggest that "A temporal determination completes the spatial order in the event – namely, of being-found-fitting."[51] According to this interpretation, the skill of the poet creates an aesthetic experience that transpires in the imagination in order to set something free into its own presencing, or self-presencing, which, being-found-fitting, was always there to begin with, and in the poet herself, who is a being-found-fitting for this task.

Authentic poetry, therefore, is not simply an imitation, as Plato had described the mimetic,[52] nor is it a representation or a symbolization, but it names poetically, it is "bespoken," as Heidegger put it, and by naming the poet becomes a re-creator, challenging the gods even in their absence, and, through the poet, all of mankind finds the potentiality of homecoming.[53] Therefore, the work of art, through the artist, lets truth originate: "Art is the setting-into-work of truth."[54] Thus, the poet cares about her own Being, and that of others, both here and in those extensions beyond the existing world, and is thus fully engaged with the experience of being-in-the-world.[55] To be concerned (*er-eignin*), is now woven into the event

(*Ereignis*), which comes with a certain shock of recognition, and with a sense of discernment, of being able to see with one's own eyes, and of propriation, an effort to save one's "own-ness."[56] Heidegger will consider this notion in terms of "thinking poetry" (*des dichtenden Denkens*),[57] where the poet names that which is "holy," in the original sense of *logos*, which Heidegger defines as "to think" (*denken*) and "to create poetry" (*dichten*), which is also to give thanks (*danken*).[58] Despite the risk to themselves of poverty and personal ruin, as would be the case with Hölderlin, the poet, perhaps alone, is doomed by their proximity to the gods and their search for truth and justice, yet they must answer the call to become the guardians, or perhaps caregivers, of Being.

The precondition, therefore, is that in the present age, and throughout the ages since the classical era, humankind has sought the "truth" through self-reflection and in the process become increasingly alienated, both from itself and from the world, and yet there is hope because of the poets, who, unlike our technologies, which mask Being instead of unconcealing it, allow us to realize that "the world's darkening never reaches to the light of Being."[59] The extraordinary task that Heidegger set for himself, as we shall consider, was to overcome the "forgetting of Being," of bringing humankind home again, a return to the hearth. Indeed, for Heidegger, "Being is the hearth."[60] Nonetheless, he would later claim that "only a god can save us," because all that poetry, philosophy, and thinking can do is "prepare a readiness for the appearance of a god, or for the absence of a god in [our] decline, insofar as in view of the absent god we are in a state of decline."[61] Thus, the task is the task of thinking, and not forgetting, in order to make ready for this readiness, holding oneself open for the arrival, or the absence, of a god.

The place of self-presencing: Forgetfulness

An aesthetic experience, as noted above, transpires in the imagination in order to set something free into its own presencing, or self-presencing, which, being-found-fitting, was always there to begin with, and in the poet herself, who is a being-found-fitting for this task. The place of self-presencing is the location of culture, of arts and language, and, in the Heideggerian sense, is also a place of gathering for divinities and mortals. Hami K. Bhabha describes the location of culture as the realm of the "beyond," where, rather than a marching backwards into the future, the "beyond" is "neither a new horizon, nor a leaving behind of the past."[62] The location of culture is thus a vibrant place of movement and linkage, occupying the here and now, where the self-presencing is articulated by a freedom of exploratory, restless movement, an "abundant, ambivalent articulation," creating "a sense of disorientation, a disturbance of direction."[63] This exploratory, restless movement is realized in the French rendition of the words *au-delà* – here and there, on all sides, and the Freudian *fort/da*, hither and thither, back and forth.[64] This is both a private and a public place, a place of gathering, a site of linkage, of a bridge, of paths crossing, of paths emerging: "Always and ever differently the bridge escorts the lingering and hastening ways of men to and fro, so that they may get to other banks and in the end, as mortals, to the other side,"[65] where, "the bridge *gathers*, as a passage that crosses, before the divinities..."[66] As stated earlier, we might say that the aesthetic, or the subjective domain of experiences that connects imagination and judgement, is not only a place of self-presencing, but a location of culture, and thus a public place that involves a public sense. This place also involves a "field" of perceptions, associations and memory, one that is marked not only by studied contemplation but also by turbulence and disorientation. Nevertheless, the place of self-presencing may be in jeopardy, as suggested by Lukács when he wrote that everything is "many-sided," "full of value and yet totally devoid of it," or Heidegger when he writes that "in truth, however, precisely nowhere does man today any longer encounter himself, i.e., his essence."[67]

In a series of lectures that began in 1935, and published in 1953 as *An Introduction to Metaphysics*, Heidegger would include an interpretation of the poetry of Friedrich Hölderlin. In fact, the 1942 lecture course would be published as "Hölderlin's Hymn '*The Ister*'."[68] Although Hölderlin's poetry remained obscure during his lifetime, and for some time after, Nietzsche would recognize Hölderlin as the first poet to incorporate the mysteries of Dionysus and Orpheus in what was hoped would be "the rebirth of tragedy."[69] Inspired by Hellenic poetry, Hölderlin was moved to translate the dramas of Sophocles, including *Antigone*. Published in 1804, Hölderlin had attempted to transpose Greek idioms into German, even adopting an individualized spelling system, and thereby merging ancient Greek and European culture. However, Hölderlin's translations were met with such derision that it may have led to his mental breakdown.[70]

Hölderlin achieved vindication by his peers later in life, although he had been permanently ill and unproductive for decades, and in posterity when Walter Benjamin argued in favour of "the task of the translator [that may] be regarded as distinct and clearly differentiated from the task of the poet,"[71] and yet one that was equally important. Further, Benjamin would debunk the standard literal translations of Hölderlin's era where fidelity to the original text often led to incomprehensibility when translated.[72] For his part, Heidegger would call Hölderlin "the poet's poet."[73] In fact, the poetic language of Hölderlin, who, like Goethe, saw abstract ideas as the horizon of experience,[74] would inspire the later Heidegger towards his own extreme idiosyncrasy in terms of philosophic speech.[75] As for Hölderlin's breakdown, Heidegger interpreted this as an example of the social and psychological vulnerability of the artist.[76]

According to Kathrin Rosenfield, Hölderlin's intent was to move away from Kant's "distinction between moral ideas, scientific knowledge and aesthetic judgement [that] derives from a single a priori faculty that is the intellectual foundation of all three types of rational activity," and move instead toward an "examination of the role of the senses and of feelings in the realm of theoretical, intellectual activity."[77] This suggests moving away from the logic of the historical-political aesthetic circumscribed by instrumental reasoning, and its passing judgement on appearances, in order to examine those distinct truths, which the poetic, a combination of intellectual activity and feelings, and not necessarily based on appearances, may reveal. As such, Heidegger viewed Hölderlin's work as an example of "thinking poetry," in particular *Antigone*, which illustrated not only the Greek experience of being in its pre-Socratic era, but also marked the turning point after which approved metaphysical thinking would envisage Being (*Sein*) as some sort of eternal presentness, as simply "out there" (*Vorhandensein*). Thus, in metaphysics after Plato (i.e., of the essence within and behind appearance) became a quest for that which is constant, such that we seek the universal in the particular, that which stands eternal in the flux of time and change, and that which is circumscribed by instrumental reasoning, thus seeking a certainty and clarity through the technology of reflection. This poses a particular problem for Heidegger as it implies a Platonic "illumination from the outside,"[78] where truth is perceived rather than experienced, and does not require the necessary labour to not only reach a "clearing" in our own existence (*die Lichtung*) but the ability to dwell in it.[79]

According to Heidegger, "The task of thinking would then be the surrender of previous thinking to the determination of the matter of thinking."[80] The surrender of previous thinking, therefore, would amount to a "clearing," indeed it would demand a "free space of clearing,"[81] where that which has been thought gives way to *alētheia*, unconcealment, of that which has remained unthought, emptying the space as it were, allowing for a new kind of thinking. In so doing, this clearing marks the end of that which has already been thought, or, as Heidegger proposes, it marks the end of philosophy, at least philosophy as metaphysics, or what has been thought of as metaphysics, the thinking about being *qua* being that has evolved into an empirical science (psychology, sociology, cultural anthropology, and so forth). However, Heidegger explains, the clearing as an end should be regarded as a completion, or a closure, perhaps understood as an enclosure, where the completion is a gathering, where that which is absent, or unthought, cannot be thought until it presences itself in the free space of the clearing, where both presence and clearing must now determine the task of thinking.

There are two possible rationales, therefore, for "the end of philosophy," either the completion, perhaps exhaustion, of metaphysics, or the displacement of metaphysics by the developments in the natural and human sciences. These two rationales also suggest the possibility for a synthesis, in the Hegelian sense, where the merging of metaphysics and the natural sciences combine to create a new form; for example, the philosophical-psychological work of Lacan. For the same reason, we might argue that Heidegger himself achieves a synthesis when the poem becomes the condition for philosophical thinking, an attempt at retrieval of a link that had been strained, perhaps severed, since Plato's time. Heidegger, for example, returns to the fundamental questions of being (metaphysics), in order to recover an understanding of the nature of being (the ontological), such that an explicit understanding of Being as a determination of the Being of *Dasein*, as opposed to the ontic, that is any manner of dealing with beings that does not raise the ontological questions, as found, for example, in science and scientific research in general.[82]

Following Steiner's interpretation of Heidegger's terms, Being that is "out there" is connected to presence-at-hand (*vorhanden*; *Vorhandenheit*).[83] For Heidegger, the present-at-hand is where a subject observes something without really "seeing" it in terms of Dasein, its history or usefulness are regarded as neutral, which is related to our distinction between "seeing" and "interpreting." For Heidegger, therefore, the present-at-hand, as a present in a "now" or a present eternally (for example, a scientific law or a Platonic Form), has come to dominate intellectual thought, especially since the Enlightenment. However, Heidegger argues that the entity, the thing, does have presence or mood (*Stimmung*), but that the metaphysics of presence, the ontological, tends to level all things down, thus requiring the destroying (*destruktion*), in a positive sense, of the ontological, which suggests Adorno's determination to break through the fraud of constitutive subjectivity. In which case, we may say that stupidity is a lack in terms of the ability to extend the existing, such that, if this lack is indeed everywhere, we may be forced to acknowledge that there is a certain futility in the task of thought Adorno had set for himself, namely, "to use the strength of the subject to break through the fraud of constitutive subjectivity."[84]

The present-at-hand is in contrast to the ready-at-hand (*zuhanden*; *Zuhandenheit*), the ordinary, and more involved, relationship to an entity. This everyday being-in-the-world - the "plain facts" - is where Dasein is practically "concerned" with objects whose mode of being is that of readiness-to-hand, thus supporting the teleological orientation of being. It is possible to treat that which is ready-to-hand as if it were merely present-at-hand, but *presence-at-hand* is itself a derivative mode of being of that which is ready-to-hand (which is a way of saying that Dasein's theoretical comportment toward the world is secondary with respect to its practical engagements in it). Consequently, for Heidegger, to understand the question of being one must be careful not to fall into this "levelling off," or "forgetfulness of Being" (*Seinsvergessenheit*),[85] that has come to dominate Western thought since Socrates. Whenever Dasein takes its entire world – including itself – as exhibiting presence-at-hand, it interprets being in general as "reality."[86]

In the fifth century, Augustine, as Steiner reminds us, had already "warned against the obsessive *concupiscentia oculorum* of philosophers, their Platonic insistence on 'seeing' the essence of things instead of experiencing it with total existential commitment and patience – which commitment entails a realization of the time-bound nature of being."[87] In addition, for Heidegger, "seeing" the essence of things is also the idea that being is present in a "now," its eternal presentness found in those scientific laws or Platonic forms that are always in the "now," an approach that has come to dominate intellectual thought. As a result, the world is interpreted in an "inauthentic" way, where a metaphysics of presence tends to level all things down, and where the subsequent demeaning of natural objects and human products has caused a fatal revolution of values. In other words, the being that is "seeing" the essence of things, that has been constituted subjectively, is inauthentic, which would include the language that was used to develop this inauthentic being, thereby demanding, as was the case with Hölderlin as well as Heidegger, a destruction and realigning of language itself. In which case, we have to change the ways in which we "see" and interpret the world in order to change our reality.

Temps durée: The malaise of modernity

Heidegger's "destruction" began with modern philosophy (primarily Kant and Descartes and the preoccupation with knowledge-theory)[88] and then worked its way back to Aristotle; in other words, back towards the "true" metaphysics of being. As such, modern metaphysics would amount to not only an interpretation of being but the forgetfulness of Being, a forgetfulness that amounts to a neglect of essence, which, like Nietzsche, would include a conception of history that led to nihilism. Indeed, for Nietzsche, the history of ontology was in fact the history of nihilism, or what we might now call a history of the forgetting of essence, which sought a world of definable Being and thus a world constituted subjectively, all of which was necessary in order to rescue man from time, where the interest in Being was revenge against time and its "It-was."[89]

Consequently, as noted by Steiner, Heidegger wished to challenge this conception of history, and the kind of thinking that "forgets," such that we do not live "in time," as if time were some independent and abstract flow external to our being, but we "live time," as if time itself were a constant within the flux of time and change.[90] In other words, time has acquired the "obvious" ontological function "of itself," where Being is made visible in its "temporal" (*zeitlich*) character, but which neglects the necessary destructuring of history itself.[91] Therefore, the manner in which we imagine and conduct our daily lives, almost invariably without giving it much thought, would demand the access to a genuine temporality and require a re-evaluation of the construct of past-present-future.[92]

The external application of time, in what we may call an "outside construction," enables us to "internalize and live with many different time notations, astronomical, biological, private and public."[93] However, it also restricts the experience of individually endured time, the interior or private reality of *durée*.[94] Indeed, the concept of *durée* is taken from Henri Bergson (1859-1941), who, Adorno will contend, arrived at the concept while viewing works of art, adding further support to the need to change the way we "see" and interpret the world:

> Planned visits to famous views, to the landmarks of natural beauty, are mostly futile. Nature's eloquence is damaged by the objectivation that is the result of studied observation, and ultimately something of this holds true as well for artworks, which are only completely perceptible in *temps durée*, the conception of which Bergson probably derived from artistic experience.[95]

Bergson will be a significant influence on Deleuze's work on cinema, particularly the theses on movement and time that include temporal planes and mobile sections. For example, Deleuze, evoking Bergson, will claim that "movement is distinct from the space covered" and "movement will always occur in a concrete duration [*durée*]," such that cinema is a "false movement," that is, it has "instantaneous sections which are called images; and a movement or a time which is impersonal, uniform, abstract, invisible, or imperceptible which is 'in' the apparatus and 'with' which the images are made to pass consecutively."[96] Importantly, "the evolution of the cinema, the conquest of its own essence or novelty, was to take place through montage, the mobile camera and the emancipation of the view point, which became separate from projection."[97] In effect, the purpose of montage is to challenge the indexical nature of the cinema, that is, a film unspools in consecutive images that are viewed by the subject in real time. As a result, we are offered another way of thinking about time, one that overturns the linear progression of homogenous time, where we are able to "live time." This alternative to real time that is found in the cinema, Deleuze will argue, amounts to a kind of emancipation.

However, due to the immobile sections or images that constitute the cinematic form, the cinema must recompose movement in time, and in the process of its emancipation from real time, the camera-eye blurs the distinction between social reality and optical illusion, which includes the demarcation between objective and subjective. It would follow that the cinema, in its conquest of its own essence, and by conceding individual discourse in favour of a single, unified voice, may result in the loss of individual experience, of internal reflection, which in turn may contribute to the modern alienation of humanity from itself as well as the reification of consciousness. Indeed, whatever the content of a film might be, the progression of images in real time remains indexical, and the cinema has merely expanded its access to a much broader range of time, only to compress it within the indexical presentation. Therefore, we must remember that the standardization of time is also the spatialization of time, which will have a number of consequences. For example, Lukács quotes Marx saying, "Time is everything, man is nothing; he is at most the incarnation of time,"[98] adding,

> Thus time sheds its qualitative, variable, flowing nature; it freezes into an exactly delimited, quantifiable continuum filled with quantifiable 'things' (the reified, mechanically objectified 'performance' of the worker, wholly separated from his human personality): in short, it becomes space.[99]

In other words, time is converted into abstract, exactly measurable units of physical space because of scientific and mechanical fragmentation. Time is now quantitative and has a value placed on its units, hence, the abstract of time hypostasizes into a commodity form. Essentially, this is the dictate of the assembly line. Not only does the spatialization of time become a means of regulating the movements of humans and providing another controlling mechanism, but also the general need for security is satisfied by taking the unknown future and quantifying it into both space and time, which supports bourgeois subjectivity and the promises of future happiness (abstract idealism). By controlling time we seek to resolve the ambiguity of our existence, yet by commodifying those units of time, even those found in the images in movement-time of the cinema, we allow the "outside" construction of time to dominate, sacrificing the possibility of internal contemplation, of *durée*, and therefore of "seeing" the essence of things.

For Nietzsche, the concession to "outside" construction is only one more example of humanity's natural inclination toward simplification and falsification, where the fundamental condition of life must be "the ground of perspectival evaluations and apparentnesses,"[100] and the culprit for this condition is thinking itself, not unlike Heidegger, thus holding "the 'mind' responsible for the falseness of the world."[101] Similarly, if seeing is not seeing but interpreting, then, by extension, to see properly is, in essence, to think. However, if we are not thinking properly, then seeing itself results in a kind of blindness, which amounts to vision as a form of bondage. Hence, when man is the primary and genuine *subjectum*, and "ground" is "that-which-lies-before," which includes the action of "that which gathers everything onto itself," where man intends to have everything brought and placed before him, such that everything is present in a "now," then the seeing/blindness is a metaphysics of presence that tends to level all things down, hence a forgetfulness of being. For Heidegger, therefore, the result is a kind of *anomie*, that creates a "oneness" that is really more of a collective, public, herd-like "theyness," where "Every kind of spiritual priority is smoothly suppressed [...] Every secret loses its force."[102] For example, Charles Taylor identifies what he calls "the malaise of modernity," which appears as the espousal of authenticity yet takes on the form of "soft relativism," where "the vigorous defence of any moral ideal is somehow off limits."[103] The authenticity that should involve originality and thus demand a revolt against convention becomes an ideal of self-determining freedom that has lost its significance, replaced instead by the significance conferred by having choice, whereby "our major remaining value is choice itself."[104] Once again, this is the result of the forgetfulness of Being, a forgetfulness that amounts to a neglect of essence.

To put this another way, as Heidegger will, the conception of history that includes forgetfulness and that results from nihilism is not the result of a preoccupation with "the nothing," but rather its opposite, the very lack of encounter with "the nothing."[105] For example, Heidegger claims that "Science wants to know nothing of the nothing," meaning that science always has to be about something, where nothing can be no more than an "outrage and a phantasm."[106] This kind of "objective viewing" is a form of bondage that condemns humankind, as Steiner words it, to "self-scattering," such that "'reification', 'alienation', 'one-dimensionality' are now the fashionable tags for this unhoused and kaleidoscopic condition."[107] The inevitable result, according to Heidegger, is "fallenness" (*Verfall*), a quality that is characterized by the inauthenticity of an individual's involvement with others and with the phenomenal world,[108] to be lost in the "average everydayness" of being, which includes "idle talk" (chatter; the discourse of *"the they,"* or those unable to "see" or "hear"), a lust for novelty (curiosity or inquisitiveness; an inauthentic mode of understanding), and ambiguity (the inability to distinguish between phenomenologically adequate and inadequate significations).[109]

Indeed, being-in-the-world is inherently phenomenological, that is, things show themselves for what they are because appearance is the natural site through which phenomenon disclose themselves. Yet the being of phenomena has been covered up in "average everydayness" and tradition so that "it is necessary for Dasein to *go back*, methodically, to the things themselves and to its own manner of being."[110] Thus, for each of the various possibilities that make up being-in-the-world (*Dasein*; of that which in humankind "is there"),[111] there are authentic and inauthentic ways in which to manifest being-in-the-world, such that in any given case one actually exists by realizing or ignoring life's various possibilities, that is, whether or not one is living life with an understanding of oneself.[112] The question here, however, is whether this engagement takes the form of scientific seeing and interpreting that enables the extension of the existing through scientific means, an aspect of the technology of reflection because it already assumes there is something rather than nothing, and therefore is already constituted subjectively and therefore potentially inauthentic, such that this scientific seeing and interpreting, with its instrumental reasoning, may not allow for the potential of poetic seeing and interpreting that is enabled by the work of art and its "world-discovering" of an entirely different nature, one that is authentic because it allows there is nothing rather than something.

Angst: The self-forming form

The malaise of modernity, returning to Charles Taylor, is identified as the erosion of our dignity as citizens,[113] and the result is often associated with *angst,* identified by Kierkegaard as anxiety or dread, and so not fear exactly but a general feeling of oppressiveness, which Heidegger, following Freud, identifies in the sense of being "un-housed," where "one feels ill at ease [*es ist einem unheimlich*]."[114] Heidegger, however, will claim, "Anxiety reveals the nothing."[115] Anxiety, therefore, is in fact productive because it is an affirmation of the proximity of the time-governing presentness of death, such that, in anxiety, "Dasein finds itself *face to face* with the nothing of the possible impossibility of its own existence."[116] Therefore, being-in-the-world (Dasein) is privileged by its access to the meaning of being, and, because that being is finite, authentic being is now understood as a "being-toward-death" (*Sein-zum-Tode*).[117] At the same time, being-toward-death is, in essence, *angst*, because of the taking upon oneself of the potential non-being of one's own being, and, accordingly, any attempt to remove this anxiety - for example, through the ministrations of priests, physicians, mystics, positivists, and so forth - would in fact alienate us from life itself.[118] In which case, *angst* is a mark of authenticity, of the repudiation of the conformity of "theyness."[119] In fact, as noted by Cutrofello, "death is the one possibility that Dasein has for which no other Dasein can take its place."[120] Similarly, "fallenness" may be positive in that it too makes us aware of the inauthenticity of "theyness," "idle talk," "the lust for novelty," and so forth, such that being-in-the-world (Dasein), now made aware of its loss of self, can strive to return to authentic being.[121]

Although *angst* is a term often associated with modern society, Adorno would dismiss it as "that supposed 'existential'" that is in fact nothing more than "the claustrophobia of a systematized society," whose system character would include philosophy itself.[122] According to Heidegger, however, *angst* and fallenness can be profoundly creative in that they counter inertia and falsification and demand an engagement with being, or what he will call "resoluteness."[123] Indeed, in recognizing its loss of self, *angst* is also a shocking individuation of Dasein, now appearing to the individual subject as an event (*Ereignis*, or "coming into view"), where one realizes they are not at home in the world, thus facing their own sense of the uncanny or not-at-homeness (*Unheimlich*).[124] Therefore, although this alienation can be characterized as fallenness, a symptom of inauthenticity and dehumanization, it may also be affirmative in that it suggests the possibility for change and a "resoluteness" in the recognition of the need to initiate that change and so attend its potentiality, which may give a positive spin to Lukács's sense of homelessness. Indeed, Steiner notes that Ernst Bloch would describe being-in-the-world (Dasein) as "an unripeness," always a "*not-yet*," where "to be is to be incomplete, unfulfilled. But at the same time, all authentic being is a *being-toward-its-own end*."[125] Thus, Heidegger will claim that instead of knowing nothing of nothing, as science would want, "the nothing is more original than the 'not' and negation."[126] It removes all horizons of significance and so it is in fact life-affirming because "Da-sein means: being held out into the nothing," such that, "Without the original revelation of the nothing, no selfhood and no freedom."[127]

Heidegger will argue that once Dasein has torn itself away from conventional thinking, from its immersion in day-to-day existence, in order to reach temporal authenticity, one moves from *ex nihilo nihil fit* (from nothing, nothing comes to be) to *ex nihilo fit - ens creatum* (from nothing comes - created being), which demands a change from the traditional relationship between being and the nothing. Of course, the paradox remains that "if God creates out of nothing precisely He must be able to relate Himself to the nothing. But if God is God he cannot know the nothing, assuming that the 'Absolute' excludes all nothingness,"[128] yet Heidegger presents the possibility of a self-forming form, where nothingness is an essential component of creation. Significantly, in terms of the technology of reflection, Heidegger suggests that being is now "the self-forming form that exhibits itself as such in an image (as a spectacle),"[129] which, as noted earlier, also suggests that our visual constructions have become the crucibles of, and for, our own modern re-creation: in other words, the cultural forms that contribute to the self-forming forms of being.

The call of conscience: Care

The self-forming forms that allow for the potential authenticity of being-in-the-world present the possibility of inward discourse, the "call of conscience" (*Gewissen*) that also manifests itself as *angst*, a fundamental mood (*Stimmung*) that "discloses Dasein as Being-possible."[130] As Critchley words it, "Anxiety is perhaps the philosophical mood par excellence; it is the experience of detachment from things and from others where I can begin to think freely for myself."[131] Thus, the process of the self-forming form is a kind of self-conversion, such that by hearing the call of conscience Dasein allows that it "*wants to have a conscience*."[132]

A critical distinction now appears between the phenomenology of everydayness and the phenomenology of being-in-the-world (Dasein) which is apparent in the distinction between "fallenness" and "resoluteness" in that, as Cutrofello explains, "To be fallen in everydayness is to interpret the phenomenon of the world – as well as Dasein's being-in-the-world – in terms of the 'reality' of nature. By contrast, to become resolute is to recover the primordial dependence of the very 'worldhood' of the world on Dasein itself: 'worldhood itself is an *existentiale*'."[133] Thus, in what will prove important in terms of the task and precondition of the artist and the work of art, the "conscience" of Dasein is a self-forming appeal, one that is taken on silently within oneself, for the "they-self" to return to "its-self."[134] In this individual realization, however, we experience a primal "guilt" (*Schuld*) because we also realize that Dasein is motivated by *angst*, which is anxiety motivated by nothing, or at least the possibility of Dasein's own possible nothingness, so that it is never, and can never be, the origin of its own being.[135] Therefore, as Heidegger states, "The nothing itself nihilates."[136] In other words, the nothing nothings, it encompasses one in a shell of non-being, from which, however, being must then be realized through a process of self-formation, such that "it discloses these beings in their full but heretofore concealed strangeness as what is radically other – with respect to the nothing."[137]

The *angst* that is realized as "guilt" that arises from having a conscience also acknowledges that one has certain moral obligations, yet, for Heidegger, this "Being-guilty" is not defined by morality, because "morality already presupposes for itself,"[138] and instead is realized through care (*Sorge*).[139] Indeed, those who are careless or uncaring are not free, because "care" as the primordial state of man is fundamentally anti-Cartesian, such that "I care, therefore I am."[140] *Sorge* is also a Kierkegaardian term, translated as "care," "concern," or "apprehension," but Heidegger's interpretation also includes the "un-housed" (*unheimlich*) that is also a "falling away from oneself," whereby *Sorge* is modified to "care-for," "concern-for," and "concern-with," which becomes a means of transcendence, of making human existence meaningful.[141] Therefore, although Dasein is face to face with the nothing and its terrifying freedom to be or not to be, the not-yet of possibility proves to be positive and life-affirming, a "grounding" rather than the fear and vertigo of the empty Dasein, where we have "fallen away from ourselves," such that un-thinking everydayness now becomes purposeful, a meaningful human existence of "Dasein-for." In doing so, we are exhorted to become artists of thinking, rather than scholars of thinking, where we are in effect un-thinking that which has been thought in order to make the truth our own.

Thrown projection: Profane illumination

The access to a genuine temporality, as noted earlier, would demand a re-evaluation of the construct of past-present-future, which is suggested by the German word *Zukunft*, meaning "future," but in the additional sense of that "which comes toward one."[142] This also suggests the circularities of any construct of past-present-future - the past altered by the present, the present determining the future, and so on - those paradoxes that are perhaps best realized by the self-reflexivity of the Ouroboros or non-orientation of the Möbius strip.[143] Nonetheless, the self-forming forms of Dasein's self-projection toward fulfilment may resolve this paradox in its movement-toward, or in Heidegger's equally paradoxical terms, "waiting-toward" (*Gegen-wart*) or "waiting-against," in the sense of both presentness and "in proximity to," which is always implicit in caring-for, and one that would also suggest a futurity, indeed "*The primary meaning of existentiality is the future.*"[144]

In seeking to be, therefore, Dasein is constantly ahead of itself and anticipatory, yet always projected towards possibilities.[145] In other words, Dasein has a future. In terms of temporality, therefore, "care" also has the nature of "being-ahead-of-itself" (self-projection), "being-already-in-a-world" (thrownness), and "being-alongside" that which is ready-to-hand and present-at-hand.[146] An important point to be made here is that Heidegger, unlike Hegel, and the metaphysical tradition began by Plato and Aristotle, does not conceive time as a series of "nows," a conception that is based on the measurable "outside" construction of time, whereby Dasein is historical because it belongs to world history, instead of recognizing that Dasein is itself essentially historical, that it is in itself part of world history, where Dasein, and all things, arise and pass away.[147] Perhaps more important, a point made clear by Critchley, one that combines "care" and "thrownness," is that self-projection is a thrown-projection, because each of us is always already somewhere in the world, a world we share with others. But Dasein is not simply thrown into the world, nor are we defined by our being thrown into the world, but we are defined by our ability for understanding and our possibility of throwing off our thrown condition, an activity of realizing and seizing possibilities and that is the experience of freedom. Thus, "Freedom is not an abstract philosophical concept. It is the experience of the human being demonstrating its potential through acting in the world. To act in such a way is to be authentic. [...] Dasein is thrown projection (*Dasein ist geworfener Entwurf*)."[148]

In Heidegger's terms, we must transverse and penetrate the hermeneutic circle, through its spiraling inwardness, to the "clearing" where truth becomes "unconcealment."[149] In which case, there remains something of Benjamin's conception of the archaic in the modern, where "truth" is always already present, waiting for the moment of being-found-fitting, which creates a sense of déjà-vu, a realization that acknowledges Benjamin's attempts to go to the place where phenomena have a life of their own, and thus to reveal the strangeness of an object, its aura, its naming, and "to give voice to its own silent murmuring."[150] Thus, we may find the work of art in the present is colonized by the past, where, as Fredric Jameson notes in reference to film, "intertextuality" becomes "a deliberate built-in feature of the aesthetic effect."[151] Therefore, the very fact that we live in the forgetting of being may also be a consequence of the way in which being comes to presence, namely, as an "unconcealing" (*alethēia*) that conceals itself, "where to be lost as 'the they' in everydayness is 'not to have ears' to hear the *silence* of the concealment in which being presences out of (and possibly into) nothing."[152] We might say, therefore, that the discourses of modern society, and of science, do not address the silence, the nothing, where we would find the releasement of the self-forming forms of being. On the other hand, we could also say that there are two complementary impulses at work, one of concealing the truth and the other of allowing the truth to emerge, whereby the very possibility of unconcealment enhances that which chooses to emerge, such that we may discover, as Benjamin worded it, a "*profane illumination.*"[153]

Poiēsis: Natural language

Heidegger argues that it was Galileo (the father of modern science) and Descartes (when he wrote that the self is known only as a thinking thing, independent of the senses) who brought being into its "objectness," where there is something rather than nothing, instead of realizing the potentiality of presencing that arises from the nothing.[154] As such, Heidegger distinguishes between an earlier mode of everydayness, as found in the Greek conception of *technē*, where unconcealing was a result of craftsmanship, of working with nature, in what we have called "world-discovering," as opposed to the modern form of everydayness, as found in modern technology, of "world-making," where man is the primary subject, such that, as noted by Cutrofello, he is "no longer even aware of the destituteness that attends to his condition because he no longer hears the call of being."[155] Nonetheless, as with *angst* and fallenness, Heidegger suggests that the essence of technology itself offers a means to "hear" the silence, where, despite instrumental determination, there is still the possibility that technology is something that we "receive." This receiving, and the manner of its revealing (*Gestell* or "Enframing,")[156] is another mode of thinking, one that introduces an element of destining, such that "Enframing belongs within the destining of revealing."[157] As such, there is a "releasement" (*Gelassenheit*), which also suggests a calmness, an openness to the mystery of being, where we await the "coming into view" (*Ereignis*), of presencing that which is given. Hence, this mode of thinking is an active and attentive stance of questioning, of "having ears," of listening to the silence, that introduces a religious sense of devotion and reverence, where he concludes that "questioning is the piety of thought."[158]

The essence of modern technology, therefore, starts humankind down the path of revealing and destining (*Geschick*), a path along which the past-present-future of history (*Geschichte*) is also determined, which presents the possibilities of either ordering of revealing and destining (Enframing) as a "challenging-forth," or as an ordaining of revealing and destining as an active "bringing-forth" (*poiēsis*).[159] As such, both are ways of unconcealing (*alētheia*). However, there is also an element of danger, which Heidegger clarifies is "not just any danger, but *the* danger,"[160] namely, that in whatever way the destining of revealing occurs, there is always the danger that man will misconstrue the unconcealed and misinterpret it. Thus, technology in and of itself is not the danger, but its essence remains mysterious, such that the danger lies in the *interpretation* of the transformation of meaning through technology. In other words, the ordering of revealing and destining may deny the potentiality of entering into a more original and profound revealing that allows for the experience of the call of a more primal truth.[161] To put it another way, humankind is destined by the service to its own technology of reflection, rather than using its technology of reflection to destine its being.

In this sense, of forcing a meaning rather than allowing for an interpretation to reveal itself, and of the technology of reflection as language, one is reminded of Heidegger's "*Die sprache spricht*" where "it is *language* that speaks."[162] If one is not to be lost as "the they" of everydayness, and "not to have ears" to hear the silence of the concealment in which being presences out of (and possibly into) nothing, then language lets itself be told, and in doing so, something like a way unfolds: "It lets what is coming to presence shine forth, lets what is withdrawing into absence vanish."[163] Heidegger identifies the place (*Ortschaft*) of this revealing and concealing as "encompassing all locales and time-play-spaces," a place that becomes our own through "propriation."[164] This propriation, therefore, is something that is given and received, a showing of a way that allows thinking, and the saying of which allows for the questioning that is "the piety of thought," whereby "language is the house of Being because, as the saying, it is propriation's mode."[165]

Bruce Chatwin also quotes from Heidegger's "Language": "Poetry proper is never merely a higher mode (*melos*) of everyday language. It is rather the reverse: everyday language is a forgotten and therefore used--up poem, from which there hardly resounds a call any longer."[166] We do not encounter our essence through ordinary language, despite the modern technology of movement and communication, despite the ubiquity of language, and despite the fact that it constitutes a place of meeting in our everyday lives. Heidegger reminds us that we are called upon to thinking and "Science does not think."[167] Our here is nowhere because the essence of language is not given through the poetic, it is not called upon, so, as Heidegger contends, we do not bring language as language to language. In which case, language now serves, as Heidegger claims, evoking Wilhelm von Humbolt, as "a kind of mummification,"[168] where the aesthetic of language, its poetic essence, has been co-opted into the ideological and the non-poetic, where here is nowhere, where the place of creation is not one of reformulation but mere reproduction. This same analogy is also presented by film theorist André Bazin when he writes that the photographic image is a mummifying process which amounts to "the preservation of life by a representation of life."[169]

Nonetheless, language may not prove adequate to counter "objectness" because "speech is challenged to correspond to the ubiquitous orderability of what is present," such that, "speech, when posed in this fashion, becomes information."[170] The challenge to human beings, therefore, is found in their tendency towards language as a technical inventory, a mode that includes "enframing" and its technology, where "man is molded and adjusted into the technical-calculative creature, a process by which step-by-step he surrenders his 'natural language'."[171] In surrendering "natural language," therefore, we disallow the mode of propriation where "every thinking that is on the trail of something is a poetizing, and all poetry a thinking," excluding that questioning as propriation and piety as thought, so the experience of the call to being no longer provides a "thinking that is a thanking."[172]

Bringing-forth: *Autopoiēsis*

Heidegger issues a warning that "where enframing reigns, there is *danger* in the highest sense,"[173] and this danger is unprecedented in modern times. According to Andrew Feenberg, the very occurrence and establishment of the unconcealednesss of beings, there lies the possibility of arbitrariness, of an unbridled positing of goals, such that "modernity is the unleashing of this arbitrariness in the technological expression of human will.[174] This presents the danger of human beings enframing themselves as mere raw materials alongside things, and yet there remains the potentiality that "the essential unfolding of technology harbors in itself what we least suspect, the possible rise of the saving power."[175] Kierkegaard, Hölderlin, and Heidegger had all considered, as worded by Schirmacher, that "salvation is harboured within danger itself, in the de-humanization of the human being, in the undeification of the divine, in the unfounded foundation, in the artificiality of the natural."[176] Indeed, Heidegger finds the possibility of the positive and life affirming by quoting from Hölderlin's poem *Patmos*: "but where danger is, grows/The saving power also."[177] Heidegger notes that "to save" is not simply to prevent something threatened by ruin, but to bring something home to its proper essence, to allow that proper essence to appear.[178] Hölderlin, therefore, is capable of the proper interpretation of the transformation of meaning – and perhaps bringing a positive spin to what we have called the transformation of subjectivity – because he can hear the silence, an ordaining of revealing and destining as a "bringing-forth" (*poiēsis*), and an understanding of the danger of misconstruing that which is unconcealed.

Science, on the other hand, which knows nothing of the nothing, is not capable of doing this "bringing-forth" because its "way of representing pursues and entraps nature as a calculable coherence of forces."[179] By virtue of its very essence of insisting on revealing and destining in the mode of "challenging-forth," modern science cannot awaken us to the occlusion of being, only poets can do this, and they do so by revealing the danger of forgetfulness, and thus preparing the way for a new destining of being. The work of art, therefore, draws us into the more original and profound process of the ordaining of revealing and destining as a "bringing-forth" (*poiēsis*), that allows for the potentiality of *autopoiēsis*, that is, our modern re-creation as self-creation through the cultural forms that contribute to the self-forming forms of being. Thus, the potentiality of *autopoiēsis*, by its very definition, would suggest that the encounter with the saving power of the work of art takes place within the subject.

According to Cutrofello, Heidegger would ascribe the potentiality of this encounter less to the artist and more to the saving power of the work of art itself.[180] In "The Turning" (*Die Kehre*, 1955), Heidegger associates the poet, in particular Hölderlin, with the possibility of a "turning" in the way in which being comes to presence. However, such a turning must be attributed to being rather than to Dasein, thus implying that it is not only through "poetic revealing" but only if "reflection upon art, for its part, does not shut its eyes to the constellation of truth, concerning which we are *questioning*."[181] Thus, Heidegger returns to Hölderlin's *Patmos* and adds the line: "... poetically man dwells on this earth."[182] Accordingly, Heidegger adds the poetical to propriation by stating that, "The poetical thoroughly pervades every art, every revealing of essential unfolding into the beautiful," such that, to expand on an earlier quote, "The closer we come to the danger, the more brightly do the ways into the saving power begin to shine and the more questioning we become. For questioning is the piety of thought."[183] In terms of language, therefore, the "idle talk" or chatter of "the they" does not allow for the proper interpretation of the danger in the transformation of meaning through technology, nor does it allow for the courage of anxiety in the face of death, whereby "Anxiety robs us of speech."[184] In which case, we understand how the poetic language of Hölderlin inspired Heidegger towards his own idiosyncrasy in terms of philosophic speech in order to counter the banality of "idle talk" and its negation of significance, its coming closer to danger, and in so doing to break through the language of constitutive subjectivity. Thus, its concepts define the likeness of the world with the subject, and allow for the piety of thought and its questioning, but not as challenging-forth but bringing-forth, thereby moving away from the primacy of the constitutive subject towards a primacy of the object.

More recently, Charles Taylor called for "a work of retrieval" in order to recover language, and so culture, from its "subjectivation," where, in terms of self-creation, "Modern freedom and autonomy centres us on ourselves, and the ideal of authenticity requires that we discover and articulate our own identity."[185] Taylor calls for a "subtler language,"[186] a term borrowed from Shelley, where the poet is not concerned only with the self, and thus is not subjectivist in this sense, but is also connected to the loss of a sense of belonging.[187] However, Taylor neglects to quote Shelley in full, which, importantly for our consideration of an aesthetic of the aesthetic, reads, "a subtler language within language wrought/ The key of truths which once were dimly taught."[188] Thus, a "subtler language" may serve as a definition of poetry itself, at least in terms of "bringing forth," of *poiēsis*, but the "subtler language within language" moves beyond the artist to allow for *autopoiēsis* and the piety of thought.

Self-determination: *Ethos*

In order to move from the subtler language of "bringing-forth" to the subtler language within language to address the goal of *autopoiēsis* and the piety of thought, then it may require a double transgression, discovering the aesthetic of the aesthetic, deconstructing the illusion of the illusion, allowing its very interpretation to free itself from itself. Therefore, if the goal of "true" art is to restore the harmony between humankind and the world, and its function is to serve as the transgression of the illusion, and the illusion is the concept of self-determination, which is a relationship conceived around *ethos*, then the transgression is necessary for the very reason, paradoxically, that this relationship is conceived as a concept. In other words, it is the concept itself that provides the illusion. Consequently, the transgression is necessary in order to remove the veil from the illusion, but also to reveal that the illusion is a result of the concept, and that the concept is the result of constitutive subjectivity.

If we acknowledge that harmony between humankind and the world was lost at the time of the ancient Greeks due to the augmentation of individual conscience, which was then given the Socratic treatment as a form of self-determination, giving rise to the replacement of social existence based on *ethos* with that of subjective morality, then we must also consider the resistance to this change, as found in Greek tragedy, and, in particular, *Antigone*.[189]

Hegel would argue that looking back to the work of ancient times may serve as material for the modern artist, but it can never achieve the same impact of the original, simply because its time has gone: "Only the present is fresh, the rest is paler and paler."[190] Nonetheless, *Antigone* remains significant as it supports the Hegelian concern for "free activity," one that is informed by an *ethos*, namely a culture that supports the care of the family and the upholding of tradition, as found in the character of Antigone, and concern for the welfare of the city/state (*polis*), as found in Creon. In Heideggerian terms, *Antigone* concerns the authentic being, one who is a being-toward-death (*Sein-zum-Tode*), a kind of liminal space where the deceased have left our world, yet in terms of being, those who remain can still be with those who have departed. It is also fallenness, suggesting both alienation and provenance, which Heidegger will attribute to the true poets – Sophocles, Hölderlin, van Gogh - who, in the midst of dehumanization, alienation and nihilism, are the guarantors of man's ontological homecoming (*Heimkehr*).[191] Thus, the poet's task is the proper interpretation of the transformation of meaning, because he can hear the silence, an ordaining of revealing and destining as a bringing--forth and being-found-fitting, and an understanding of the profound danger of misconstruing that which is unconcealed. However, the question remains whether our visual constructions, those crucibles of and for our own modern re-creation, are the cultural forms that contribute to the self-forming forms of being, or the constitution of the danger of dangers, namely the occlusion of being and the forgetting of essence.

Metaphysics as morality: Aesthetic systems

Hegel, along with Fichte and Schelling, belonged to the period of German Idealism in the decades following Kant. However, Hegel was the most systematic of the post-Kantian idealists, seeking to synthesize sense and reason, perception and thought, the condition of sensual determination and the condition of rational determination, into a comprehensive and systematic ontology from a "logical" starting point.[192] In these terms, we might consider "The Oldest Systematic Program of German Idealism" (1797), attributed to one of either Hegel, Schelling or Hölderlin (the Tübingen Three), which states that "all metaphysics will henceforth fall into morals."[193] In which case, if the aesthetic of the work of art is also the highest act of reason, in the Hegelian sense, that of mind (soul), then it is also a moral one, where aesthetics contains a higher dignity, that of Mind (Spirit), where "truth and goodness become kindred only in beauty,"[194] and where the individual subject and all individual subjects may access the power of the aesthetic, which then recognises the higher spirit that is already among us, and is us. The aesthetic act, ultimately, when realized in terms of Absolute Knowledge and Absolute Freedom, will become "the last work of the human race."[195]

We may recall Nietzsche's concern that rational thought was deemed capable of not only penetrating the depths of being but "even of *correcting* being," such that the Kantian autonomy of aesthetic experience, with its "free play of the cognitive faculties," must now transform into its opposite, namely an activity that involves the "correction" of aesthetic experience into one of morality. One reason for this would be to re-capture the affirmative nature of pre-modern art of the classical age (harmony), yet the modern age has led to a fragmentation that includes the secularization of art and its aim of "self-transcendence." However, as Hegel argued, the work of art in modernity continues to allow for the immediate view of the idea in objective reality and thus serves as an expression of self-knowledge that leads to human freedom. Nonetheless, if the object of freedom is the idea as constituted by a moral being who possesses the potentiality of Absolute Freedom and Absolute Spirit, while recalling that any form of art is bound to its historical moment, and if the object of the state is the system, thereby constituted as something mechanical (i.e., humankind is destined by being in service to its own technology of reflection, rather than using its technology of reflection to destine its being), then the system may be threatened such that it must subordinate the ideas and freedom of the individual in order to maintain itself, whereby the autonomy of art must also be subsumed into a systemic correcting of being, namely a system of morals. If we are obliged to act autonomously rather than heteronomously, then this now poses the question of whether to conceive of moral obligation as autonomous heteronomy or as heteronomous autonomy. Indeed, Antonio Gramsci would recognize that cultural hegemony provides a philosophical and sociological explanation of how, by the manipulation of the societal culture (value system), one social class dominates the other social classes of a society, in particular, a world view that justifies the status quo of bourgeois hegemony.[196] If Karl Marx wanted to emancipate the working class, then we might say that Gramsci wanted to emancipate culture, which may indeed prove to be the primary site of both coercion and resistance in the modern world.

At this point, we may consider that Marx was a Young or Left Hegelian, supporting the basic tenets of Hegel's philosophy, but as Marx famously said, inverting it, thus turning it on its head, or, putting it on its feet. The Old or Right Hegelians believed that Hegel's philosophy supported the Prussian state of 1830, believing that advanced European societies, as they existed in the first half of the nineteenth century, were the summit of all social development, the product of the historical dialectic that had existed thus far. Mainly conservatives, they praised the Prussian state itself, which boasted an extensive civil service system, good universities, industrialization, and high employment, as the pinnacle of progress and the incarnation of the *Zeitgeist*. The state also paid Hegel's salary, it should be noted, which may have made him inclined to be less critical. The Young Hegelians, on the other hand, including Marx, wanted change. The main point of difference was that Hegel saw the dialectical process of change located in the mental or spiritual, whereas Marx saw the process of change located in the material, such that our ideas, our religion, our politics all flow out of the economic structure of our social reality.[197] In these terms, *ethos* itself would be considered a product of history, just as it would not be consciousness (self-knowledge) that determines our existence but our social existence that determines consciousness (knowledge of the self).[198]

The task of philosophy, according to Marx, would be to raise awareness that we have been subject to "the whole trick of proving the hegemony of the spirit in history,"[199] particularly Hegel and his concept of *Geist*, which is nothing more than history with all the materialistic elements removed, while conserving the ideas or illusions that benefit those who create those very ideas or illusions, who, in Marx's determination, would be the ruling class. Thus, the task would include separating the ruling ideas from the ruling individuals, particularly as the concept of history had now become the history of concepts, with ideas and concepts understood as "forms of self-determination," such that, in a manner that would appeal to "the primary and genuine *subjectum*," where "all the relationships of men can be derived from the concept of man, man as conceived, the essence of man, Man."[200] Hegel would confess that he "has considered the progress of the concept only" and has represented in history the "true theodicy."[201]

Mechanisms of shame: Subjective morality

Bernard Williams wrote: "Plato, Aristotle, Kant, Hegel are all on the same side, all believing in one way or another that the universe or history or the structure of human reason can, when properly understood, yield a pattern that makes sense of human life and human aspirations."[202] Indeed, Williams questions just how far we have advanced in terms of our moral consciousness, focusing as we did on "supernatural necessity" rather than the "human necessities of power," where both might be interpreted as modes of self-assertion, the former associated with a sense of shame, the latter with the demands of survival. Williams notes that the word "shame" in Greek is *aidōs*, which is a derivative of *aidoia*, meaning genitals, which may be extended to a sense of shame "in the sight of other men," and perhaps further, in the sight of the gods.[203] It is interesting to note that Freud suggests that the very foundation of human civilization occurred during the fatal transformation from quadruped to biped, which would not only privilege the sense of vision (as opposed to the quadruped, moving close to the ground, and its sense of smell), but also expose the genitals.[204] In terms of shame, Freud also notes the general non-beauty of the genitals, and yet the symbolic beauty attached to their sexual and reproductive functions, namely love and sensuality, thereby transforming genital love into an "aim-inhibited impulse."[205] Indeed, religion, by means of "psychical infantilism" and "mass delusion," proclaims "the ultimate consolation and source of pleasure in the midst of suffering is unconditional submission."[206] Adorno would write, "Immediately back of the mimetic taboo stands a sexual one: Nothing should be moist; art becomes hygienic."[207]

In a similar manner, using Greek tragedy as his point of departure, Williams explores "the mechanisms of shame" as the source of necessity, which may be internalized, grounded in the *ethōs* and individual nature of the subject, and activated by the perceived judgement of the other, or it may be externalized, activated by "divine necessity," which, for the ancient Greeks, was "not conceived as a unitary world-historical or redemptive enterprise, as it had been by Jews and Christians," but simply unavoidable.[208] Although Williams asserts that the search for the lost unity of the classical world is merely an expression of fantasy, he will also claim that the modern world does bear profound similarities to the classical world in that "we know the world was not made for us, or we for the world, and our history tells no purposive story, and that there is no position outside the world or outside history from which we might hope to authenticate ourselves."[209] In which case, we could also say that this perception of a "pattern" would in fact bind the universe, history and the structure of human reason, as well as the structure of our social reality, and yet we understand that it remains a pattern that is self-constituted. As Marx argued, "man makes his own history, but he does not make it out of whole cloth; he does not make it out of conditions chosen by himself, but out of such as he finds close at hand."[210] The significant point, then, is that meaning is understood as a pattern that is perceived by the self-determining subject (constitutive subjectivity), and the interpretation of the pattern becomes a form, or a process, which may then become a system, where the system itself is self-justified through the freedom associated with that original self-determination of the individual subject, when in fact the system may be hegemonic and work against that originary freedom of the individual subject. In other words, there is a tension between the actual freedom of the self-determining subject and the instituted freedom of any system whose claims or rights are justified, or sacrificed, in pursuit of that same individual freedom, which, in addition, allows for a value judgement based on those claims.

If we now consider that harmony between humankind and the world was lost at the time of the ancient Greeks due to the rise of individual conscience, which was then given the Socratic treatment as a form of self-determination, and that subjective morality replaced the ethical life, of correcting being rather than being-coming-to-know-itself, then our social existence would now determine consciousness through the illusion of the process of history. And this social existence would not necessarily be based on *ethōs*, but instead on a system of theodicy, a system of morality that would benefit those who managed the system. Evoking "The Oldest Systematic Program," Critchley points out that there is no idea of the state per se because the state is something mechanical, just as there is no idea of a machine, yet the state claims the idea of freedom, and certainly the objective of freedom, such that, "for every state must treat free people as a piece of machinery; and if it should not do this; thus it must come to an end."[211]

Adorno would argue that "according to Nietzsche's critique, systems no longer documented anything but the finickiness of scholars compensating themselves for political impotence by conceptually construing their, so to speak, administrative authority over things in being."[212] Indeed, "The Oldest Systematic Program," as noted by Jacques Rancière, advocates that the task becomes one of "aesthetic education," thus rendering ideas into sensible form:

> A replacement for ancient mythology; in other words, into a living tissue of experience and common beliefs in which both the elite and the people share. The 'aesthetic' programme, therefore, is essentially a metapolitics, which proposes to carry out, in truth and in sensible order, a task that politics can only ever accomplish in the order of appearance and form.[213]

In these terms, the aesthetic itself, that which can be no other than subjective, would now serve the "concept" of man and the illusion of history, such that the function of a "true" art must be transgression of the illusion of history. However, the illusion of history is protected by the machinery of state and the "mask" of technological progress, its anonymity and its "no idea" residing in its task of education and "the betterment of mankind," which is able to suggest through the hegemonic the transgression of the very autonomy that this transgression of the illusion of history promises. Thus, there is the demand for a transformation of subjectivity itself - both as political subject and as individual subject – that may require an aesthetic of anonymity and non-identity that challenges and transgresses all subjectivity.

Adorno, as noted earlier, identifies the double character of art itself, both autonomous and *fait social*, and so acknowledges that art is produced by the autonomous subject, a reference to the philosophical aesthetic of Kant and Hegel, and yet art is also a force of production, which references Marx and Engels, with the assertion of art's embeddedness in society. This embeddedness is accompanied by the claim that art can only exist in a stunted form in a bourgeois society, even when we seek to immerse ourselves in things that are heterogeneous, that is, resist placing everything in prefabricated categories. However, as noted earlier, the work of art is a social fact that informs and influences our social reality, with the attendant implications in the economic, legal, political and religious spheres, and yet simultaneously art itself is influenced by these same spheres. In other words, art has the potential to influence real change, but it is restricted by its historical moment. For example, the work of art may be the source of "truth," perhaps unintentional truths, *ars inveniendi*, yet they are absorbed within lived experience and are therefore unable to pierce the reified bourgeois subjectivity because they are created and received within that very same subjectivity. This allows Adorno, as noted earlier, to formulate the paradox that "art is autonomous and it is not; without what is heterogeneous to it, its autonomy eludes it."[214]

In historical terms, this paradox also marks the end of the era of "beautiful semblance," which, as noted by Benjamin, was rooted in the era of auratic perception, where, as articulated by Hegel, beauty is "the appearance [*Erscheinung*] of spirit in its immediate... sensuous form, created by the spirit as the form adequate to itself."[215] Benjamin will now claim that, "the beautiful is neither the veil nor the veiled object but rather the object *in* its veil."[216] In which case, the dialectical double construction, the aesthetic of the aesthetic, is thus required to address the paradoxical character of art and discover its true essence (the aestheticized) beyond that which is essential (the aesthetic). Otherwise, as noted earlier, we may not heed Adorno's warning that, "art perceived strictly aesthetically is art aesthetically misperceived."[217] And that misperception is the very domain of the hegemonic.

Nonetheless, the work of art is a social fact that informs and influences our social reality, and just like the individual in that social reality, as Williams maintains, much that happens is determined by the forces of economic and cultural necessity, and for the individual by the determinations of necessity and luck,[218] that which is unpredictable and uncontrollable, what Dante would have called *fortuna*.[219] However, as Williams points out, the triumph of modern liberalism, and perhaps what we might hope as the task and purpose of the work of art, is not that it rejects the idea of necessity and chance but that it questions the idea of a necessary identity, one that conforms to the systems of morality, and in so doing it "has given itself the task of constructing a framework of social justice to control necessity and chance, in the sense both of mitigating their effects on the individual and of showing that what cannot be mitigated is not unjust."[220] In other words, we might say that the world is not fair, but that does not mean it needs to be unjust.

Ideology: Double functioning

In the early 1800s, Destutt de Tracy coined the term "ideology," arguing that the very concept of ideology is itself physiological, where a willingness to conform is a trait linked to zoology.[221] This would suggest there is an inherent human susceptibility to the ideological in order to attain what we have termed "the appropriate coherence and unity," which we may link to the cultural hegemonic. Also, as noted earlier, Kant suggests that any individual aesthetic choice is an integral part of creating the *sensus communis*, which would then generate a consensus, because the ideal of a fully achieved *sensus communis* can be thought of as the subjective analogue of the political ideal of a general will. Consensus may be considered both a collective and a necessary agreement, suggesting that the subject "ought" to agree in aesthetic judgements and thereby contains an element of moral conformity of "theyness." Indeed, in terms of the susceptibility of ideology, even for those who pursue self-knowledge, Adorno warns, "Ideology lies in wait for the mind which delights in itself."[222] Thus, the influence of the hegemonic upon aesthetic autonomy, according to de Tracy, would now have a physiological explanation, and any goal of consensus is thereby reduced to that of coercion.

Louis Althusser would extend this idea into structural Marxism by differentiating between ideology and the ideological, where ideology is in itself structural, hence asocial and ahistorical, whereas the ideological is social and historical, hence a Marxist concern, thereby proposing a "double functioning" of repression and ideology.[223] For Althusser, therefore, interpellation is the construction of the subject, and through constitutive subjectivity, the "real world" cannot be something that is objectively out there, but something that is constituted through the subject, a product of our relations to our social reality, the ideological representations we have made ourselves, and the works of art that support that relation. For example, in terms of the image-making culture, particularly the cinema, the illusion is taken in by the spectator who is hailed as the subject, who then takes those illusions back into reality, where, as if it were a trick of alchemy, the illusion becomes part of the social reality and so made "real." Therefore, the autonomy of art can be subsumed into a hegemonic system of morals, and, for Marx, those who produce the hegemonic system - the theorists, ideologists and philosophers – who all contribute to the hegemony of the spirit in history.

Marx, however, did not support de Tracy's ideas, preferring instead the materialist notion that man is shaped by the conditions of social reality, and thus man is a practical rather than a contemplative subject.[224] Although Heidegger would claim that humanity had liberated itself to itself, Marx recognized that in the process humanity had also released the "constant revolutionizing of production, uninterrupted disturbance of all social relations, everlasting uncertainty and agitation."[225] In doing so, Marx famously observed "all that is solid melts into air,"[226] where many of the assumptions, prejudices and values in both the individual subject and the *sensus communis* could no longer be taken for granted: "Things fall apart, the centre cannot hold."[227] Critchley chooses lines from the same Yeats poem, "the best lack all conviction, whilst the worst are full of passionate intensity," in order to point out those approaches to ethical issues that lack passionate intensity and are more Diogenean cynicism rather than free commitment.[228] Peter Sloterdijk's view, particularly in reference to Diogenes, is that enlightenment has been accompanied by demoralization and disillusionment, such that the modern consciousness is one of unhappiness, and that cynicism itself is "enlightened false consciousness," a paradoxical state where one "knows itself to be without illusions and yet to have been dragged down by the 'power of things'."[229] T.J. Clark will write:

> "Modernity" means contingency. It points to a social order which has turned from the worship of ancestors and past authorities to the pursuit of a projected future – of goods, pleasures, freedoms, forms of control over nature, or infinities of information. The process goes along with a great emptying and sanitizing of the imagination. Without ancestor-worship, meaning is in short supply – 'meaning' here meaning agreed-on and instituted forms of value and understanding implicit orders, stories and images in which a culture crystallizes its sense of the struggle with the realm of necessity and the reality of pain and death.[230]

The call for ancestor-worship may suggest the loss of history within culture, while the emptying and sanitizing of the imagination suggests Heidegger's modern conquest of the world-as-picture and its relation to modern technology and social organization, which may be attended by psychological research, which, in itself, we could define as the activity of constantly revolutionizing scientific research in its application to self-reflection.

As a result, we may find that the psychological contributes to the lack of passionate intensity that results not only in the distrust of intuition and conscience, in the feelings from the human heart, which brings doubt to the validity claims of the consensus-inclined individual "weighing of judgement," and by extension, that of the "public sense," both of which may expose us to deception and the erosion of freedoms that are associated with democracy, and therefore should be regarded with suspicion. Indeed, Paul Ricoeur writes of the existence of an "hermeneutics of suspicion," which Cutrofello notes is predicated upon, "the novel problem of the lie of consciousness and consciousness as a lie,"[231] which is the legacy of Marx, Nietzsche and Freud, whereby that which escapes consciousness falls under the telos of suspicion, yet where "All three [...] far from being detractors of 'consciousness', aim at extending it."[232]

Therefore, just as the "free play of the cognitive faculties" may not in fact be entirely free, so there are physiological and psychological forces at work that suppress the historical process of attaining self-knowledge and of overcoming self-alienation. In terms of Lukács's call to change reality, we may find that rather than moving ever closer to reality through the process of change, we can say that the process of change is moving us ever further from reality. To "extend the existing," therefore, is not to expand the boundaries of what we had formerly perceived as real but to expand that which is not "real," a self-generated domain with its own hierarchies and systems.

Immaculate perception: The geopolitical aesthetic

Any suggestion that the cognitive faculties are "free" would conjure Plato's dictum to distrust the senses, and the pitfalls of relying on any sense, particularly the visual, which we have found subject to coercion and conformity. As for the element of conformity, we might consider Nietzsche when he was prompted to write:

> 'For me, the dearest thing would be to love the earth as the moon loves it, and to touch its beauty with the eyes alone' – thus the seduced one seduces himself. 'And let this be called by me *immaculate* perception of all things: that I desire nothing of things, except that I lie down before them like a mirror with a hundred eyes'.[233]

If we consider the intent here is that "immaculate perception" connotes "immaculate conception," then that which is conceived is self-conceived, or perhaps conceived as a marriage of oneself and the divinity of one's imagination. To become the mirror with the hundred eyes also suggests that the self of the individual subject is a reflector, where images of the self are conceived through the eyes of the other, or the many others, which will also suggest aspects of the psychoanalytical. Indeed, Carl Jung theorized that the human mind possesses a predisposition toward images, ones that we may all share in our collective unconscious.[234] Freud, as well as Jacques Lacan, a neo-Freudian, will maintain that language is structured like the unconscious,[235] which suggests the internalized image-making process of self-reflection that has been externalized through the image-making culture, where the unconscious structure of language is made conscious through the living experience of images.[236] Thus, Freud will claim that just as mankind has used engines to place gigantic forces at his disposal, so too will he invent the camera and the gramophone in order to capture "evanescent visual impressions... the equally fleeting auditory impressions," where "both are essentially materializations of his innate faculty of recall, of his memory."[237] And in so doing, man attempts to achieve his ideal self-conception, one of omnipotence and omniscience, the self-made god, "a god with artificial limbs."[238]

In terms of self-creation through self-reflection, we may consider Lacan's "mirror stage" that describes the child's anticipation of a sense of "self," achieved through vision and its own reflection, thus gaining a sense of identity as a unified and separate whole being (ideal ego). The unconscious, therefore, is the "ground" of being, in Heidegger's terms, the "that-which-lies-before," which includes the action of "that which gathers everything onto itself." However, Lacan will also claim this identification is a "misrecognition" (*méconnaissance*), where the "ideal ego" of the perfect whole self may be internalized, but in reality must always remain unfulfilled (lack).[239] In order to compensate for this lack, the subject creates a succession of fantasies, which Lacan will call "orthopaedic," in order to support the fragmented body-image to a form of totality.[240][241] Consequently, the unconscious itself is the discourse of the other, where the formation of that most fundamental part of our subjectivity is not our own, such that the individual subject's experience goes far beyond that which is experienced as "subjectivity."[242] Thus, the determining ground of the aesthetic is not "free" subjective, not in the sense of "free play of the cognitive faculties" or as an individual judgement of taste, for the very reason that the determination of subjectivity is exterior to oneself.

If we now consider the expansion of the world-picture in terms of the extension of the existing into that domain that is "beyond landscape," to use Fredric Jameson's term, then that domain is now our technologized social reality.[243] However, for the individual subject, the technology of reflection, as found in our technologized social reality, is also the "orthopaedic" construction of fantasy. As such, if the domain of the technologized social reality were considered as a complex organic structure, we would add that its realization is not merely what we strive for, but what we do all the time even if we are unaware of the process. In other words, the technology of self-reflection has now reached a global scale whereby our entire social reality is a "beyond landscape" of self-reflection, which in itself comprises a new world system. Indeed, it is conceivable that this intersection of the psychic and the social marks the delineation between the simultaneous domains of the idea, one that includes an image, and a deeper non-visual system, that of the aesthetic, and that together they create the possibility of a conception of social totality, one that is held together by technology.[244] In order to navigate the domain of the "beyond landscape" would require a cartography of both the technological social reality and the domain of the unconscious, thus supporting Lukács, as noted earlier, when he maintained that the task of true art is to draw the archetypal map, to realize "the transcendental topography of the mind," as well as Rancière when he sought "a new topography of the possible."

According to Jameson, there are elements in the new world system that will continue to reflect on national cultures, or their loss or replacement, or centralized commercial production, or mass-produced neo-traditional images, and all "the operations of some banal political unconscious" that maintain its ideological goals, and so,

> We map our fellows in class terms day by day and fantasize our current events in terms of larger mythic narratives, we allegorize our consumption and construction of the object-world in terms of Utopian wishes and commercially programmed habits – but to that must be added what will now call a geopolitical unconscious.[245]

The combination of residual and emergent forms evokes Benjamin when he wrote that, "Each epoch dreams the one to follow," where present social reality contains the dreams of the prior epoch, "the utopia that has left its trace in a thousand configurations of life."[246] In order to chart, as well as occupy, the territory of the geopolitical consciousness, Jameson notes the demand for a "cognitive mapping,"[247] which is not only the ability to navigate the social reality of the "beyond landscape" but the charting of that process of cognition that creates that social reality, the temple grammar, to use our term, that allows one to make their way through its symbols and meanings. Jameson will argue, in contradiction to Rancière's claim that there is no fatal mechanism transforming reality into image, that there remains an understanding that "everything around us is functionally inserted into larger institutional frameworks of all kinds, which nonetheless belong to *somebody*."[248] The assertion is that the new topography is the new real estate, a domain of the mind that unlike the geographical is potentially limitless, yet still offering a system of ownership based on property relations. The wealth of Tudor England arose from the monetization of the capital that privately owned lands represented (enabling the Industrial Revolution), so the assertion of exclusive title in the new domain would also lead to extraordinary wealth creation (enabling the Computer Revolution), as well as "enclosure," that is, the many will be excluded from these exclusive domains owned by the few. The ownership of the technologized social reality, therefore, convinces Jameson that "cognitive mapping" is also the domain of conspiracy, certainly in terms of cultural content, which supports Lacan's concepts of fragmentation and lack in the individual subject, as well as the susceptibility to ideology and potential for political coercion.

The technologized social totality is not one of God or Nature, but the totally administered society, the new world system as the third stage of capitalism, where there is only an "absent totality," and where, instead of Hegel's Absolute Spirit, we are now asked to identify with "Capital itself, whose study is our true ontology."[249] This suggests that the narcissistic emptiness of self-reflection and the fraud of constitutive subjectivity has been more fully realized, as Adorno will write, as "the undeniable human suffering – a fact of unreason."[250] Jameson states that the absent totality is itself the referent we must accept in order to move forward, as it is "the true ground of Being in our own time. Only by way of its fitful contemplation can its future, and our own, be somehow disclosed."[251]

Notes

1 Schiller, "Letter of an Aesthetic Education of Man", p.111.
2 Ibid., p.119.
3 Ibid., p.117.
4 Ibid., p.125.
5 Schwegler, *Handbook of the History of Philosophy*, p.334.
6 Peter Singer makes this suggestion in "Hegel and Marx: Dialogue with Peter Singer," *Unsanctifying Human Life* (Oxford UK: Blackwell Publishers, 2002), pp.341-357.
7 G.F.W. Hegel, "Preface," *Elements of the Philosophy of Right or Natural Law and Political Science in Outline*. Edited by Allan W. Wood. Translated by H.B. Nisbet. Cambridge UK and New York: Cambridge University Press, 1991), p.10. See also Singer, "Hegel and Marx," p.348.
8 Schwegler, *Handbook of the History of Philosophy*, p.343.
9 Hegel, "Lectures on Aesthetics," p.102.
10 Ibid., p.107.
11 Ibid., p.111.
12 Ibid., p.111. In terms of accessing other senses and ideal thought through a single sense, in this case the haptic, Scarry notes that when Augustine touched something smooth, he begins to think of music and God. Elaine Scarry, *On Beauty and Being Just* (Princeton NJ: Princeton University Press, 1999), p.4.
13 Aristotle saw people leave the theatre elated and asked why they should be after seeing a tragedy. He believed it was because of "catharsis," a cleansing of the soul through the experience of pity and fear: pity created in their sympathy for the hero; fear in that the same misfortunes could befall any of them. See Paul Woodruff, "Aristotle's Poetics: The Aim of Tragedy," *The Companion to Aristotle*, Georgios Anagnostopoulos (Editor) (Malden MA: Wiley-Blackwell, 2009), pp.612-627.
14 Walter Benjamin, "Two Poems by Friedrich Hölderlin: 'The Poet's Courage' and 'Timidity,'" *Walter Benjamin/Selected Writings. Volume 1, 1913-1926*, translated by Edmund Jephcott, Howard Eiland, and Others, edited by Howard Eiland and Michael W. Jennings (Cambridge MA: The Belknap Press of Harvard University Press, 2002), pp.18-36.
15 Walter Benjamin, "Theses on the Philosophy of History," *Illuminations*, edited and with an Introduction by Hannah Arendt, translated by Harry Zohn (New York: Harcourt, Brace & World, 1968), p.260. See also Michael Löwy, *Fire Alarm – Reading Walter Benjamin's 'On the Concept of History'*, translated by Chris Turner (London: Verso, 2005), pp.60-61. [Note: The translation used here is from the latter text.]
16 For Hegel, the "Spirit" (*Geist*) is similar to the culture of people, and is constantly reworking itself to keep up with the changes of society, while at the same time working to produce those changes through the "cunning of reason." Glenn Alexander Magee, *The Hegel Dictionary* (London: Continuum, 2011), p.67.
17 Susan Buck-Morss, *The Dialectics of Seeing: Walter Benjamin and the Arcades Project* (Cambridge MA: The MIT Press, 1991), p.273.
18 Michael Löwy, *Fire Alarm – Reading Walter Benjamin's 'On the Concept of History'*, translated by Chris Turner (London: Verso, 2005), p.47.
19 Walter Benjamin, "Exchange with Theodor W. Adorno on the Essay 'Paris, the Capital of the Nineteenth Century'," *Walter Benjamin: Selected Writings. Volume 3, 1935-1938*, translated by Edmund Jephcott, Howard Eiland, and Others, edited by Howard Eiland and Michael W. Jennings (Cambridge MA: The Belknap Press of Harvard University Press, 2002), p.58.
20 Buck-Morss, *The Dialectics of Seeing*, p.160.
21 Heidegger, "The Origin of the Work of Art," pp.143-212.
22 Buck-Morss, *The Dialectics of Seeing*, p.160.
23 Cutrofello, *Continental Philosophy*, p.195.
24 Löwy, *Fire Alarm*, p.101.

25 Walter Benjamin, "Paris, the Capital of the Nineteenth Century," *Walter Benjamin: Selected Writings. Volume 3, 1935-1938*, translated by Edmund Jephcott, Howard Eiland, and Others, edited by Howard Eiland and Michael W. Jennings (Cambridge MA: The Belknap Press of Harvard University Press, 2002), p.40.
26 Löwy, *Fire Alarm*, pp.66-67.
27 Ibid., p.86.
28 Walter Benjamin, "On Language as Such and on the Language of Man", *Walter Benjamin: Selected Writings Volume 1: 1913-1926*, edited by Marcus Bullock and Michael W. Jennings (Cambridge MA: The Belknap Press of Harvard University Press, 1996), p.68. See Cutrofello, *Continental Philosophy*, p.248.
29 Ibid., p.262. See Cutrofello, *Continental Philosophy*, pp.248-249. Roland Barthes wrote, "alongside each utterance... offstage voices can be heard," voices that are woven together in the heteroglossic text and thus embody "the plurality and the circularity of the codes." Ira Bhaskar, "'Historical Poetics', Narrative, and Interpretation," *A Companion to Film Theory*, edited by Toby Miller and Robert Stam (Malden MA: Blackwell Publishing, 2004), p.392.
30 Benjamin, "The Work of Art in the Age of Its Technological Reproducibility: Second Version," p.109.
31 Theodor W. Adorno, "Portrait of Walter Benjamin," *Prisms*, translated by Samuel and Sherry Weber (London: Neville Spearman, 1967), p.233. See also Susan Buck-Morss, *The Origin of Negative Dialectics: Theodor W. Adorno, Walter Benjamin, and the Frankfurt Institute* (New York: The Free Press, 1977), p.58. For Benjamin, "Allegory is in the realm of thought what ruins are in the realm of things." Buck-Morss, *The Dialectics of Seeing*, p.165.
32 Buck-Morss, *The Origin of Negative Dialectics*, p.86.
33 Benjamin, "The Author as Producer," p.774. Benjamin notes that Brecht coined the term *Umfunktionierung* (functional transformation) to describe this process. Ibid., p.774.
34 Ibid., p.772. Cultural hegemony, in the Marxist sense, explains how a culturally diverse society can be dominated (ruled) by one social class by manipulating the societal culture (beliefs, explanations, perceptions, values, etc.), whereby a ruling-class worldview is imposed on the subaltern classes (to use Gramsci's term). Once established as a societal norm, this worldview is perceived as a universally valid ideology and *status quo* beneficial to all of society, when in fact it only benefits the ruling class. However, as Dick Hebdige argues, the praxis of cultural hegemony is neither monolithic nor a unified value system, rather it is a complex of layered social structures. Each social and economic class has a societal purpose and an internal class logic allowing its members to behave in a particular way that is different from the behavior of members of other social classes, whilst co-existing with them as constituents of the society. On the other hand, Marshall McLuhan will argue that multiculturalism (as found in Canada's immigration policy, for example) is a survival strategy, one that is meant "to keep people apart and to keep them intact without merging." See Antonio Gramsci, "(i) History of the Subaltern Classes; (ii) The Concept of 'Ideology': (iii) Cultural Themes: Ideological Material," *Media and Cultural Studies: Keyworks*, edited by Meenakshi Gigi Durham and Douglas M. Kellner (Malden MA: Blackwell Publishing, 2006), pp. 13-17. See also, in the same volume, Dick Hebdige, "(i) From Culture to Hegemony; (ii) Subculture: The Unnatural Break," pp.144-162. See also Marshall McLuhan, *Understanding Me: Lectures and Interviews*, edited by Stephanie McLuhan and David Staines, with a Foreword by Tom Wolfe (Toronto ON: McClelland & Stewart, 2003).
35 Ibid., p.769.
36 Theodor W. Adorno, "Commitment," *Aesthetics and Politics*, with presentations by Rodney Livingstone, Perry Anderson and Francis Mulhern, afterword by Fredric Jameson (London: Verso, 1980), p.193.
37 Buck-Morss, *The Origin of Negative Dialectics*, p.73.
38 Ibid., pp.88-89.
39 Theodor W. Adorno, *Minima Moralia: Reflections from Damaged Life*, translated from the German by E.F.N. Jephcott (London: Verso, 2005), p.47.

40 Ibid., p.47.
41 Martin Heidegger, "What Calls for Thinking?" *Basic Writings – From Being and Time (1927) to The Task of Thinking (1964)*, edited and with introductions by David Farrell Krell, foreward by Taylor Carman (New York: HarperCollins, 2008), p.390.
42 Wolfgang Schirmacher, "Indirect Communication and Aesthetic Ethics: An Ironic Reading of Kierkegaard." Translated from the German by Virginia Cutrufelli. *Poiesis: A Journal of the Arts and Communication*. Volume 9. Toronto ON: 2007.
43 Avital Ronell, *Stupidity* (Chicago IL: University of Illinois Press, 2002), p.123.
44 Ibid., p.123. Paul de Man (1919-1983) was a Belgian-born deconstructionist literary critic and theorist. In 1966, de Man met Jacques Derrida at a conference at Johns Hopkins University on structuralism and they became close friends and colleagues. De Man elaborated a philosophically-oriented literary criticism of Romanticism. Notably he posits that the resistance to theory is the resistance to reading, thus the resistance to theory is theory itself, or, to put it another way, the resistance to theory is what constitutes the possibility and existence of theory. After his death, the discovery of some two hundred articles he wrote during World War II for collaborationist newspapers in Belgium, including one explicitly anti-Semitic article, which supported the necessity of addressing the "Jewish problem," caused a scandal and provoked a reconsideration of his life and work. See Evelyn Barish, *The Double Life of Paul de Man* (New York: W.W. Norton & Co., 2014).
45 Ibid., p.123.
46 Fernand Léger, "A Critical Essay on the Plastic Qualities of Abel Gance's film The Wheel," *Functions of Painting*, edited and with an introduction by Edward Fry, translated by Alexandra Anderson (New York: Viking Press, 1973), p.21. See also Tom Gunning, "The Cinema of Attraction: Early Film, Its Spectator and the Avant-Garde," *Wide Angle*, Vol. 8, nos. 3 & 4 (Fall, 1986).
47 Marilyn Brakhage, "Foreward," *By Brakhage: An Anthology, Volumes One and Two* (New York: Criterion Collection, 2002), p.8. Stan Brakhage (1933-2003) was an experimental filmmaker and teacher. He created a large and diverse body of work, exploring a variety of formats, approaches and techniques. For example, *Water Baby Moving* (1959) documents the birth of Brakhage's first child. Critic Archer Winsten described the film as being "so forthright, so full of primitive wonder and love, so far beyond civilization in its acceptance that it becomes an experience like few in the history of movies." R. Bruce Elder, *Body of Vision: Representations of the Body in Recent Film and Poetry* (Waterloo ON: Wilfrid Laurier University Press, 1997), p.141. See also *Meshes in the Afternoon* (Maya Deren 1943). Maya Deren (1917-1961) was a Ukrainian-born American filmmaker. Hollywood was very critical of her work, as she was of Hollywood: "I make my pictures for what Hollywood spends on lipstick," and she observed that Hollywood "has been a major obstacle to the definition and development of motion pictures as a creative fine-art form." Bill Nichols (editor), *Maya Deren and the American Avant-Garde: Includes the complete text of An Anagram of Ideas on Art, Form, and Film* (Berkeley CA: University of California Press, 2001), pp.3-10, 268. See also Maya Deren and Gregory Bateson, "An Exchange of Letters between Maya Deren and Gregory Bateson," *October*, Vol. 14 (Autumn 1980), pp.18-20.
48 Martin Heidegger, "The Way to Language," *Basic Writings – From Being and Time (1927) to The Task of Thinking (1964)*, revised and Expanded Edition Edited, With General Introduction, and Introductions to Each Selection David Farrell Krell, Foreward by Taylor Carman (New York: HarperCollins, 2008), p.397.
49 Novalis, *Novalis: Philosophical Writings*, translated and edited by Margaret Mahony Stoljar (Albany NY: State University of New York Press, 1997), p.9.
50 Novalis, Friedrich von Hardenberg, "Monologue" (c. 1798) in Robert Calasso, *Literature and the Gods* (London: Vintage, 2001), pp.178-180.
51 Benjamin, "Two Poems by Friedrich Hölderlin," p.27.
52 See Erich Auerbach, *Mimesis – The Representation of Reality in Western Literature*, translated from the German by Willard R. Trask, with a new introduction by Edward W. Said [2003] (Princeton NJ: Princeton University Press, 2003).

53 Steiner, *Heidegger*, p.146. Steiner observes that Hölderlin later writes, "Mankind dwells poetically, in the condition of poetry [*Dichterisch wohnet der Mensch*]." Ibid., p.145.
54 Heidegger, "The Origin of the Work of Art," p.202.
55 Steiner, *Heidegger*, pp.99-101.
56 Heidegger, "The Way to Language," p.396.
57 Steiner, *Heidegger*, p.51.
58 Ibid., p.146.
59 Martin Heidegger, "What is Metaphysics?" *Basic Writings – From Being and Time (1927) to The Task of Thinking (1964)*, edited and with introductions by David Farrell Krell, foreward by Taylor Carman (New York: HarperCollins, 2008), p.89.
60 Martin Heidegger, *Hölderlin's Hymn "The Ister"*, translated by William McNeill and Julia Davis (Bloomington IN: Indiana University Press, 1996), p.112.
61 Martin Heidegger, "Only a God Can Save Us" [*Nur noch ein Gott kann uns retten - Der Spiegel 1966*] *Heidegger: The Man and the Thinker*, translated by William J. Richardson, edited by Thomas Sheehan (New Brunswick NJ: Transaction Publishers, 2010), p.53.
62 Homi K. Bhabha, *The Location of Culture* (London and New York: Routledge, 1994), p.1.
63 Ibid., p.1.
64 Ibid., p.1. "*Fort*" and "*Da*" are German for "gone" and "there". In *Beyond the Pleasure Principle* (1920), Sigmund Freud relates the story of a game his grandson invented where he took a wooden reel attached to a piece of string, and threw it over the edge of his cot, so that it disappeared (*fort*) and then pulled it back again (*da*). Freud theorized that this game of disappearance and return was the child's invention of symbolism: the use of one object (wooden reel) to represent another, absent object (mother). See Sigmund Freud, *Beyond the Pleasure Principle*, translated and newly edited by James Strachey, introduction by Gregory Zilboorg (New York: Norton, 1975).
65 Martin Heidegger, "Building Dwelling Thinking," *Basic Writings – From Being and Time* (1927) to *The Task of Thinking* (1964), revised and Expanded Edition Edited, with General Introduction, and Introductions to Each Selection David Farrell Krell, Foreward by Taylor Carman (New York: HarperCollins, 2008), p.354.
66 Ibid., 355. See also pp.152-3. See also Bhabha, *The Location of Culture*, pp.4-5.
67 Martin Heidegger, "The Question Concerning Technology," *Basic Writings – From Being and Time (1927) to The Task of Thinking (1964)*, revised and Expanded Edition Edited, With General Introduction, and Introductions to Each Selection David Farrell Krell, Foreward by Taylor Carman (New York: HarperCollins, 2008), p.332.
68 Heidegger gave four readings of Friedrich Hölderlin (1770-1843) in his series of lectures and essays between 1936 and 1944. Hölderlin was a seminary roommate with Hegel and Friedrich Schelling (1775-1854), all three of them important in the development of German idealism, and he was friends with Friedrich Schiller (1759-1805). See *The Ister* (David Barison and Daniel Ross, 2004), a film based on Heidegger's 1942 lecture course (Hölderlin's Hymn "*The Ister*"), featuring Jean-Luc Nancy, Philippe Lacoue-Labarthe, Bernard Stiegler, and Hans-Jürgen Syberberg. The film is a series of lectures set, like the poem, on the Danube River.
69 Nietzsche, *The Birth of Tragedy*, p.96. Poetry containing distinctly Orphic beliefs – that is, beliefs related to Orpheus and his descent and return from Hades - were traced to the 6th century BCE. Orpheus is credited with inventing "The Mysteries of Dionysus," where Dionysus also descended to Hades and returned. Plato refers to "Orpheus-initiators," who prescribe an ascetic way of life and are associated with rites connected to the afterworld. W.K.C. Guthrie, *The Greeks & Their Gods* (London: Beacon, 1954), p.322. See also, for a cinematic interpretation, Jean Cocteau's 'Orphic Trilogy', which consists of *The Blood of a Poet* (1930), *Orpheus* (1950) and *Testament of Orpheus* (1960).
70 Kathrin H. Rosenfield, "Getting inside Sophocles' Mind through Hölderlin's 'Antigone'," *New Literary History Vol. 30, No. 1, Poetry & Poetics* (Winter, 1999), p.107.
71 Walter Benjamin, "The Task of the Translator," *Walter Benjamin: Selected Writ-*

ings Volume 1: 1913-1926, edited by Marcus Bullock and Michael W. Jennings (Cambridge MA: The Belknap Press of Harvard University Press, 1996), p.258.
72 Ibid., p.260. See also Linda Hutcheon, *A Theory of Adaptation* (New York: Routledge, Taylor and Francis Group, 2006).
73 Steiner, *Heidegger*, p.15.
74 Rosenfield, "Getting inside Sophocles' Mind," p.108. See also Eckart Förster, "To Lend Wings to Physics Once Again: Hölderlin and the 'Oldest System-Programme of German Idealism'," *European Journal of Philosophy*, Vol.3, no. 2 (August 1995), pp.174-200.
75 Steiner, *Heidegger*, p.9.
76 Heidegger was severely criticized because of an association with the Nazis while Rector of the University of Freiburg from 1933 to 1934, one that he did not publicly repudiate, justify or explain.
77 Rosenfield, "Getting inside Sophocles' Mind," p.108.
78 Steiner, *Heidegger*, p.79.
79 Ibid., p.67. As Krell explains, although *lichtung* is cognate with "lighting," it is generally translated as "clearing." However, the intent is to suggest a clearing that has occurred through nature, one that allows light in, rather than a man-made clearing. In colloquial German, *eine Lichtung* has the sense of a forest "clearing" where the pines have been thinned out, allowing natural light, and the woods made "lighter," more "open." Similarly, Heidegger invites thought on the free or open space where things appear, linger, endure, and disappear. He calls this *die Lichtung des Seins*, "the clearing of Being." See Martin Heidegger, "The End of Philosophy and the Task of Thinking," *Basic Writings – From Being and Time (1927) to The Task of Thinking* (1964), revised and Expanded Edition Edited, with General Introduction, and Introductions to Each Selection David Farrell Krell, Foreward by Taylor Carma (New York: HarperCollins. New York, 2008), pp.393-426.
80 Martin Heidegger, "The End of Philosophy and the Task of Thinking," *Basic Writings – From Being and Time* (1927) to *The Task of Thinking* (1964), revised and Expanded Edition Edited, With General Introduction, and Introductions to Each Selection David Farrell Krell, Foreward by Taylor Carman (New York: Harper Collins, 2008), p.449.
81 Ibid., p.442.
82 Martin Heidegger, "Being and Time," *Basic Writings – From Being and Time (1927) to The Task of Thinking (1964)* revised and Expanded Edition Edited, with General Introduction, and Introductions to Each Selection David Farrell Krell, Foreward by Taylor Carman (New York: HarperCollins, 2008), p.53.
83 Paraphrasing Steiner's interpretation of Heidegger's terms, Being that is "out there" - *Vorhandensein* – is connected to *vorhanden*, presence-at-hand, or *Vorhandenheit*. For Heidegger, the present-at-hand, as a present in a "now" or a present eternally (as, for example, a scientific law or a Platonic Form), has come to dominate intellectual thought, especially since the Enlightenment. However, Heidegger argues that the entity, the thing, does have presence or mood (*Stimmung*), but that the metaphysics of presence, the ontological, tends to level all things down, thus requiring the destroying (destruction), in a positive sense, of the ontological. To truly understand the question of being one must be careful not to fall into this leveling off, or forgetfulness of being, that has come to dominate Western thought since Socrates. See Steiner, *Heidegger*, pp.19-72. See also Heidegger, "What is Metaphysics?", pp.89-110. See also Simon Critchley's essay series on Heidegger's "Being and Time" in *The Guardian* (2009) [On-line].
84 Adorno, *Aesthetic Theory*, p.xiii.
85 Ibid., p.75.
86 Ibid., pp.19-72. See also Heidegger, "What is Metaphysics?", pp.89-110.
87 Ibid., p.78.
88 David Farrell Krell, "General Introduction: The Question of Being," *Basic Writings – From Being and Time (1927) to The Task of Thinking (1964)*, p.8.
89 Ibid., p.8.

90 Steiner, *Heidegger*, p.78.
91 Heidegger, "Being and Time," pp.61-62.
92 Steiner, *Heidegger*, p.109.
93 Hannah Gay, "Clock Synchrony, Time Distribution and Electrical Timekeeping in Britain 1880-1925," *Past & Present: A Journal of Historical Studies*, Vol. 181, Issue 1 (November, 2003), p.111.
94 Jay, *Downcast Eyes*, p.197.
95 Adorno, *Aesthetic Theory*, p.69. See also Henri Bergson, *Matter and Memory*, translation by Nancy Margaret Paul and W. Scott Palmer (New York: Zone Books, 1988).
96 Gilles Deleuze, *Cinema 1: The Movement-Image* (1983), translated by Hugh Tomlinson and Barbara Habberjam (Minneapolis MN: University of Minnesota Press, 1986), p.1.
97 Ibid., p.3.
98 Lukács, *History and Class Consciousness*, p.89.
99 Ibid., p.90
100 Laurence Lampert, *Nietzsche's Task: An Interpretation of Beyond Good and Evil* (New Haven CT and London: Yale University Press, 2001), p.82.
101 Ibid., p.80. See also Friedrich Nietzsche, *Beyond Good and Evil – Prelude to a Philosophy of the Future*, translated, with Commentary, by Walter Kaufmann (New York: Vintage Books, 1966), p.45.
102 Steiner, *Heidegger*, p.93.
103 Charles Taylor, *The Malaise of Modernity* (Toronto ON: House of Anansi Press, 1991), p.17.
104 Ibid., pp.65, 69.
105 Heidegger, "What is Metaphysics?", p.95.
106 Ibid., p.96.
107 Steiner, *Heidegger*, p.79.
108 Ibid., p.98.
109 Cutrofello, *Continental Philosophy*, p.51.
110 Ibid., p.51.
111 Steiner, *Heidegger*, p.36.
112 Cutrofello, *Continental Philosophy*, p.52. See also Heidegger, "Being and Time," p.33. Krell clarifies that the term *"existentiell"* designates the way Dasein in any given case actually exists by realizing or ignoring its various possibilities, that is, by living its life. Ibid., p.55*n*.
113 Taylor, *The Malaise of Modernity*, p.10.
114 Heidegger, "What is Metaphysics?", p.101. Søren Kierkegaard's *The Concept of Anxiety: A Simple Psychologically Orienting Deliberation on the Dogmatic Issue of Hereditary Sin* [Danish: *Begrebet Angest*], was written in 1844 under the pseudonym Vigilius Haufniensis, which, according to Kierkegaard scholar Josiah Thompson, is the Latin transcription for "The Watchman." See Josiah Thomson, *Kierkegaard* (New York: Alfred A. Knopf, 1973), pp.142-143. Critchley clarifies that "The first thing to grasp is that anxiety does not mean ceaselessly fretting or fitfully worrying about something or other. On the contrary, Heidegger says that anxiety is a rare and subtle mood and in one place he even compares it a feeling of calm or peace. It is in anxiety that the free, authentic self first comes into existence. It was, of course, the mood that launched a thousand existentialist novels, most famously Sartre's *Nausea* and Camus's *The Outsider* (although Heidegger was very critical of existentialism)." Critchley, "Being and Time, part 5: Anxiety," *The Guardian*, posted 06/07/2009. In a 1938 review of Sartre's *Nausea*, Camus opened with the claim that "a novel is nothing but philosophy expressed as images." See Ronald Aronson, *Camus and Sartre: The Story of a Friendship and the Quarrel that Ended It* (Chicago IL: The University of Chicago Press, 2004).
115 Steiner, *Heidegger*, p.101.
116 Ibid., p.79.
117 Ibid., pp.102-103.
118 Ibid., pp.105-106.

119 Ibid., p.94.
120 Cutrofello, *Continental Philosophy*, p.52.
121 Steiner, *Heidegger*, p.98.
122 Adorno, "Negative Dialectics and the Possibility of Philosophy," p.71.
123 Steiner, *Heidegger*, p.107.
124 Ibid., p.99.
125 Ibid., p.104.
126 Heidegger, "What is Metaphysics?", p.97.
127 Ibid., p.103.
128 Ibid., pp.107-108.
129 Ibid., p.107.
130 Cutrofello, *Continental Philosophy*, p.53. See also Heidegger, *Being and Time*, p.232.
131 Critchley, "Being and Time, part 5: Anxiety," *The Guardian* (2009) [On-line].
132 Cutrofello, *Continental Philosophy*, p.52. See also Heidegger, *Being and Time*, p.277 See also Edumnd Husserl, *Ideas Pertaining to a Pure Phenomenology and to a Phenomenological Philosophy, First Book: General Introduction to a Pure Phenomenology*, Translated by F. Kersten (Dordrecht, Germany: Kluwer Academic Publishers, 1983).
133 Ibid., p.53. See also Heidegger, *Being and Time*, pp. 92, 94, 100.
134 Ibid., p.52.
135 Steiner, *Heidegger*, p.108.
136 Heidegger, "What is Metaphysics?",p.103. See Cutrofello, *Continental Philosophy*, p.57.
137 Ibid., p.103.
138 Cutrofello, *Continental Philosophy*, pp.52-53.
139 Ibid., p.52.
140 Steiner, *Heidegger*, p.101.
141 Ibid., pp.99-101.
142 Ibid., p.110.
143 Ibid., p.111.
144 Ibid., p.110. Steiner comments that *On Being and Time* (1962) was one of Heidegger's last writings and remained a fragment, but the new temporal combination of *Being* and *Time* drew criticism from both Lukács and Adorno in what they saw as an "ominous mystification of the entire issue of historical man and society." Steiner, *Heidegger*, p.111*n*.
145 Ibid., p.110. Steiner states that the character of "having been" arises from the future, reminding us of Nietzsche's use of Pindar's dictum to "Become what you are." Steiner, *Heidegger*, p.111.
146 Cutrofello, *Continental Philosophy*, p.52. See also p.132*n*529.
147 Ibid., p.54.
148 Simon Critchley, "Being and Time: Part 4. Thrown Into This World," *The Guardian* (2009), par.9.
149 Steiner, *Heidegger*, p.82.
150 Cutrofello, *Continental Philosophy*, p.248.
151 Fredric Jameson, "Postmodernism, or the Cultural Logic of Late Capitalism," *Media and Cultural Studies: Keyworks*, edited by Meenakshi Gigi Durham and Douglas M. Kellner (Malden MA: Blackwell Publishing, 2006), p.495.
152 Cutrofello, *Continental Philosophy*, p.54.
153 Walter Benjamin, "Surrealism: the Last Snapshot of the European Intelligentsia," *New Left Review*, London: No. 108. March/April 1978, p.49. Kracauer wrote, "Today, access to truth is by way of the profane." Siegfried Kracauer, *The Mass Ornament* (1963), translated, edited and with an Introduction by Thomas Y. Levin (Cambridge MA: Harvard University Press, 1995), p.1. Benjamin references "profane illumination" in terms of "Surrealist experiences," and clarifies that these are not simply religious ecstacies or the ecstacies of drugs, although he did say that "hashish, opium, and whatever else" could "provide the introductory course" for profane illumination. See Walter Benjamin, "Hashish in Marseilles," *Walter Ben-*

jamin: Selected Writings. Volume 2, Part 2. 1931-1934, translated by Rodney Livingstone and Others, edited by Michael W. Jennings, Howard Eiland, and Gary Smith (Cambridge MA: The Belknap Press of Harvard University Press, 1999). See also Buck-Morss, *The Origin of Negative Dialectics*, p.126.
154 Cutrofello, *Continental Philosophy*, p.55.
155 Ibid., p.55.
156 Heidegger, "The Question Concerning Technology," p.325. Heidegger explains: "According to ordinary usage, the word *Gestell* [frame] means some kind of apparatus, e.g., a bookrack. *Gestell* is also the name for a skeleton. And the employment of the word *Gestell* [enframing] that is now required of us seems equally eerie, not to speak of the arbitrariness with which words of a mature language are so misused." Ibid., p.325.
157 Ibid., p.330.
158 Ibid., p.341. See also Cutrofello, *Continental Philosophy*, p.55.
159 Ibid., p.330.
160 Ibid., p.331.
161 Ibid., p.333.
162 Heidegger, "The Way to Language," p.393.
163 Ibid., pp.413-414.
164 Ibid., pp.414-415.
165 Ibid., p.424.
166 Ibid., p.270.
167 Heidegger, "What Calls For Thinking?" p.373.
168 Heidegger, "The Way to Language," p.403. The quote is from Wilhelm von Humbolt, *On the Diversity of the Structure of Human Language and Its Influence on the Intellectual Development of Mankind* (Berlin 1836), Edited by E. Wasmuth (1936), Section 8, p.41.
169 André Bazin, "The Ontology of the Photographic Image," Translated by Hugh Gray, *Film Quarterly*. Volume 13. No. 4. (Summer 1960), pp.4-9.
170 Ibid., p.420.
171 Ibid., pp.420-421.
172 Ibid., p.425.
173 Heidegger, "The Question Concerning Technology," p.333.
174 Andrew Feenberg, *Heidegger and Marcuse: The Catastrophe and Redemption of History* (New York: Routledge. Taylor & Francis Group, 2005), p.337
175 Heidegger, The Question Concerning Technology, p.337.
176 Schirmacher, "Indirect Communication and Aesthetic Ethics," p.76.
177 Heidegger, "The Question Concerning Technology," p.333. The excerpt is from "Patmos," *Friedrich Hölderlin - Poems and Fragments*, translated by Michael Hamburger (Ann Arbor MI: The University of Michigan Press, 1966), pp.462-463.
178 Ibid., p.333.
179 Ibid., p.326.
180 Cutrofello, *Continental Philosophy*, p.56.
181 Heidegger, "The Question Concerning Technology," p.340.
182 Ibid., p.340.
183 Ibid., p.341.
184 Steiner, *Heidegger*, p.101. Michael Harris will contend that through computer technology we have "filled up" our world with constant connection that has effectively eroded absence or the space of contemplation. See Michael Harris, *The End of Absence: Reclaiming What We've Lost in a World of Constant Connection* (Toronto ON: HarperCollins 2014).
185 Taylor, *The Malaise of Modernity*, pp.80-81.
186 Ibid., p.85.
187 Ibid., p.91.
188 The line is from "The Revolt of Islam" (Percy Bysshe Shelley 1818). Also known as "Laon and Cyntha," the poem concerns these two characters during a revolt against a despotic rule in a fictional state, without addressing Islam in any particular way,

but is more of an address to the aura of disillusionment in the arts following the French Revolution. See also W.B. Yeats's essay "The Philosophy of Shelley's Poetry" (1900), where he is critical of Shelley's character of Cyntha and her becoming "wise in all human wisdom," but she appears to have come upon this wisdom mystically and without much effort. Thus, Shelley himself may have provided an example of "subtle language" but not the more "subtle language within language."

189 *Antigone* (442-441 BCE) was written by Sophocles (496-406 BCE). The play is based on the history of the royal family in Thebes. The tragedy arises the conflict of two loyalties: loyalty to god (or the gods) and loyalty to the state. Antigone represents the first and Creon, the king, the second. As with the best tragedies, there will be a tragic contradiction, one that cannot be sublated in either the immanent or transcendent sphere, which will result in the tragic downfall, and, as Peter Szondi words it, "the demise of something that should not meet its demise, whose removal does not allow the wound to heal." Peter Szondi, *An Essay on the Tragic* (*Versuch über das Tragische*, 1961), translated by Paul Fleming (Stanford CA: Stanford University Press, 2002).

190 Hegel, "Lectures on Aesthetics," p.123.

191 Ibid., p.142.

192 Gadamer argues that recognition itself is the operative point, particularly in the representations found in art, which, in the Platonic sense, contain genuine knowledge of essence, and since all knowledge is akin to recognition, then this is the ground for Aristotle's remark that poetry is more philosophical than history. Gadamer, "The Ontology of the Work of Art and its Hermeneutical Significance," p.328.

193 G.F.W. Hegel, *Hegel Selections: The Great Philosopher Series*, M.J. Inwood (Editor) (London and New York: Macmillan, 1988), p.1. See also "The Oldest Systematic Program of German Idealism" [1797], translated by Diana I. Behler, *Philosophy of German Idealism: Fichte, Jacobi, and Schelling*, edited by Ernst Behler (New York: Continuum, 2003).

194 Ibid., p.1. See also Wolfgang Welsch, *Undoing Aesthetics*, translated by Andrew Inkpin (London: Sage Publications, 1997), p.19.

195 Behler, "The Oldest Systematic Program of German Idealism," p.2.

196 Antonio Gramsci, "(i) History of the Subaltern Classes; (ii) The Concept of 'Ideology': (iii) Cultural Themes: Ideological Material," *Media and Cultural Studies: Keyworks*, edited by Meenakshi Gigi Durham and Douglas M. Kellner (Malden MA: Blackwell Publishing, 2006), pp.13-17. See also Antonio Gramsci, *Selections from the Prison Notebooks of Antonio Gramsci*, translated by Geoffrey N. Smith and Quentin Hoare (New York: International Publishers, 1971). The historian Paul Johnson suggests that Antonio Gramsci (1891-1937), a frail figure who suffered from Pott's Disease of the lungs, supported syndicalism as he was unable to assume a leadership role and therefore "drew from Machiavelli not a personal prince, like Mussolini, but a collective one: 'The modern Prince, the myth-prince, cannot be a real person, a concrete individual: it can only be an organization'." Paul Johnson, *A History of the Modern World: From 1917 to the 1990s* (London: George Weidenfeld & Nicholson Ltd, 1991), p.97.

197 *The Communist Manifesto* (Karl Marx and Friedrich Engels, 1848) was published seventeen years after Hegel's death in 1831. Hannah Arendt notes that in terms of self-creation, man produces himself through thought for Hegel, but for Marx it was labour, "the human form of metabolishm with nature." Hannah Arendt, *On Violence* (New York: Harcourt, Brace, Jovanovich 1970), p.13.

198 Karl Marx and Friedrich Engels, "The Ruling Class and the Ruling Ideas," *Media and Cultural Studies: Keyworks*, edited by Meenakshi Gigi Durham and Douglas M. Kellner (Malden MA: Blackwell Publishing, 2006), pp.9-12.

199 Karl Marx, *Marx: Selected Readings*, edited by Lawrence H. Simon (Cambridge MA: Hackett Publishing Company, 1994), p.97.

200 Marx and Engels, "The Ruling Class and the Ruling Ideas," p.11.

201 Hegel, *Lectures on the Philosophy of World History*, p.446. The term 'theodicy' (from Greek *theos* "god" + *dike* "justice") was coined by Gottfried Wilhelm Leibniz

(1646-1716) in his 1710 work, written in French, *Essais de Théodicée sur la bonté de Dieu, la liberté de l'homme et l'origine du mal* (*Theodicy: Essays on the Goodness of God, the Freedom of Man and the Origin of Evil*). The Augustinian interpretation is that evil is a corruption of goodness, traced back to original sin, and thus humans and not God initiated evil. Theodicy, however, is a response to the evidential problem of evil, where the occurrence of evil in the world counts as evidence against the existence of an omnipotent and omnibenevolent deity. Rather than a defense, theodicy argues that it is because of the occurrence of evil or suffering in the world then God's existence is logically possible by reconciling that very evil with the traditional divine characteristics of omnibenevolence, omnipotence, and omniscience. See Michael J. Murray and Sean Greenberg, "Leibniz on the Problem of Evil", *The Stanford Encyclopedia of Philosophy* (Winter 2016 Edition), Edward N. Zalta (ed.). [Online]
202 Bernard Williams, *Shame and Necessity*, foreward by A.A. Long (Berkeley CA: University of California Press, 2008), p.163.
203 Ibid., pp.78-79.
204 Sigmund Freud, *Civilization and Its Discontents*, translated by David McLintock with an Introduction by Leo Bersani (London: Penguin Books, 2002), pp.41*n*1-42*n*1. See also Jay, *Downcast Eyes*, p.6.
205 Ibid., p.38.
206 Ibid., p.22.
207 Adorno, *Aesthetic Theory*, p.116.
208 Williams, *Shame and Necessity*, pp.103-104.
209 Ibid., p.166.
210 Karl Marx, *The Eighteenth Brumaire of Louis Bonaparte*, translated by Daniel De Leon (Chicago IL: Charles H. Kerr & Company, 1914), pp.10-11.
211 Critchley, *Infinitely Demanding*, p.161*n*46.
212 Adorno, *Negative Dialectics*, p.69.
213 Jacques Rancière, *Aesthetics and Its Discontents*, translated by Steven Corcoran (Cambridge UK and Malden MA: Polity Press, 2009), p.37.
214 Adorno, *Aesthetic Theory*, p.6.
215 Benjamin, "The Work of Art in the Age of Its Technological Reproducibility: Second Version," p.127*n*2. The quote is from Hegel, *Werke - Volume 10: Part 1*, p.13.
216 Ibid., p.127*n*2.
217 Adorno, *Aesthetic Theory*, p.6.
218 Williams, *Shame and Necessity*, p.128.
219 Dante, *Inferno*, translated by Charles S. Singleton (Princeton NJ: Princeton University Press, 1970), Canto VII, pp.85-96. Fortuna, as the Romans perceived her, derived her "personality" from the Greek notion of *tyche*, meaning "chance," "luck," or "what happens." Aristotle saw fortune as the prime mover and all unexplained events were attributed to her actions. Augustine went to great pains to explain that no event was wholly driven by chance, however, and denied her existence.
220 Williams, *Shame and Necessity*, pp.128-129.
221 In his *Elements of Ideology* (1801-1815), Destutt de Tracy (Antoine Louis Claude Destutt, Comte de Tracy, 1754-1836), a French Enlightenment aristocrat and philosopher, supported the theories of science, thus arguing that ideology is physiological and so linked to zoology. See Jay, *Downcast Eyes*, p.191.
222 Adorno, "Negative Dialectics and the Possibility of Philosophy," p.77.
223 Louis Althusser, "Ideology and Ideological State Apparatuses (Notes towards an Investigation," *Media and Cultural Studies: Keyworks*, edited by Meenakshi Gigi Durham and Douglas M. Kellner (Malden MA: Blackwell Publishing, 2006), p.81. Louis Althusser (1918-1990) would claim that ideologies are specific, historical and differing; for example, Christian ideology, democratic ideology, feminist ideology, Marxist ideology, etc., whereas ideology is structural, so it can be regarded as "eternal," as it has no history, and because it is a structure, it can be 'filled up' with anything. For example, the state is the kind of government formation that arises with capitalism. There are two major mechanisms for insuring that people within a state act according to the rules of that state, even when it is not in their

best interest to do so. These mechanisms are the RSA (Repressive State Apparatus), such as the police and the criminal justice system, and, suggesting Gramsci's cultural hegemony, the ISA (Ideological State Apparatus), such as schools, religions, legal systems, family traditions, politics, sports and art, which generate the systems and ideas and values of that society. Thus, Althusser is proposing a "double functioning" of repression and ideology: "To my knowledge, no class can hold State power over a long period without at the same time exercising its hegemony over and in the State Ideological Apparatuses." Louis Althusser, "Ideology and Ideological State Apparatuses (Notes Towards An Investigation," *Media and Cultural Studies: Keyworks*, edited by Meenakshi Gigi Durham and Douglas M. Kellner (Malden MA: Blackwell Publishing, 2006), p.81.

224 In De Tracy's political writings, such as *A Commentary and Review of Montesquieu's Spirit of Laws* (translated by Thomas Jefferson, an admirer), he supported a liberal social and economic philosophy which provided the basis for a strong defense of private property, individual liberty, the free market, and constitutional limits to the power of the state. De Tracy rejected monarchism, favoring the American republican form of government. His views lost him favor with Napoleon, who turned the term 'ideology' into one of abuse; Marx agreed and referred to De Tracy as a "*fischblütige Bourgeoisdoktrinär*"—a "fish-blooded bourgeois doctrinaire." See Jay, *Downcast Eyes*, p.191.

225 Marshall Berman, *All That Is Solid Melts Into Air – The Experience of Modernity* (New York: Penguin Books, 1988), p.94. The quote can also be found in *The Marx-Engels Reader*, edited by Robert C. Tucker (New York: W.W. Norton & Co., 1978), pp.475-476.

226 Ibid., p.95.

227 Ibid., p.89.

228 Critchley, *Infinitely Demanding*, p.39.

229 Peter Sloterdijk, *Critique of Cynical Reason*, translation by Michael Eldred, foreword by Andreas Huyssen (Minneapolis MN: University of Minnesota Press, 1987), pp.5-6.

230 T.J. Clark, *Farewell to an Idea: Episodes from a History of Modernism* (New Haven and London: Yale University Press, 1999), p.7.

231 Cutrofello, *Continental Philosophy*, p.299.

232 Ibid., p.299. See also Paul Ricoeur, *The Conflict of Interpretations: Essays in Hermeneutics*. Edited by Don Ihde. Evanston IL: Northwestern University Press, 1974), p.150.

233 Friedrich Nietzsche, *Thus Spoke Zarathustra – A Book for Everyone and No One*, translated with an Introduction by R.J. Hollingdale (Middlesex UK: Penguin Books, 1961), p.145. See also Jay, *Downcast Eyes*, p.191.

234 Liliane Frey-Rohn, *From Freud to Jung – A Comparative Study of the Psychology of the Unconscious*, translated by Fred E. Engreen and Evelyn K. Engreen, forward by Robert Hinshaw (Boston MA: Shambhala Publications, 1974), p. 94.

235 In 1925, Freud wrote "A Note on the 'Mystic Writing-Pad'." The mystic writing pad (also known as a "magic slate") was a toy for children. It had three layers: a wax slab, a waxed sheet of paper attached to the slab at one end, and a celluloid covering that protects the paper. By pressing an object hard enough against the celluloid covering, marks are lift in the slab that "appear" on the sheet of paper. Freud contends that the waxed sheet of paper can be likened to the consciousness – which remains ever-ready for new inscriptions – while the slab functions as a kind of memory. Significantly, it is only by being etched in "memory" that the mark appears in "consciousness." As for the protective celluloid covering, Freud likens this to the psychic apparatus's resistance to excitations from the external world. All this suggests that the psychic apparatus is a kind of writing machine. Sigmund Freud, "Note upon the 'Mystic Writing Pad.'" ("*Notiz über den `Wunderblock*, 1925"') Translation, reprinted from Int. l. Psycho-Anal., 21 (1940), 469, by James Strachey.

236 Lacan's Three Orders are the Imaginary Order, the Symbolic Order, and the Real. These are related to Freud's Id, Ego, and Super-Ego, as well as Freud's three stages of polymorphous perversity in infants: the oral, anal, and phallic stages. The

Imaginary Order is the field of images and imagination, as well as deception. Freud and Lacan both use the term "imago" (Latin for "image") to describe these mental representations. The Symbolic Order (or symbolic register, or the "big Other") is made possible by the acceptance of the rules of language and communication, including laws and contracts, which control human action in a world of the symbol, hence the power of the image-making culture. Lacan calls the acceptance of the paternalistic authority of those rules as the acceptance of the "Name-of-the-father." The Symbolic is also the field of radical alterity (otherness), which is the Other, such that the unconscious is the discourse of this Other. Finally, the Real, for Lacan, is not synonymous with reality. The Real is not only opposed to the Imaginary Order, the Real is also exterior to the Symbolic Order. The Real is that which is outside language and that resists symbolization absolutely: an ontological absolute. It is this resistance to symbolization that lends the Real its traumatic (uncanny) quality. See Jacques Lacan, "The Mirror Stage as Formative of the *I* Function, as revealed in Psychoanalytic Experience," *Écrits: A Selection*, translated by Bruce Fink, in Collaboration with Héloïse Fink and Russell Grigg (New York: W.W. Norton & Co, 1996), pp.3-10. See also "The Instance of the Letter in the Unconscious, or Reason Since Freud," Ibid., 138-168. See also Sigmund Freud, "Selections from Three Essays on Sexuality," *The Freud Reader*, edited by Peter Gay (New York: W.W. Norton and Company, 1995). See also Klages, *Literary Theory*, pp.73-90.
237 Freud, *Civilization and Its Discontents*, p.28.
238 Ibid., p.29.
239 Klages, *Literary Theory*, pp.79-81.
240 Jacques Lacan, "The Mirror Stage as Formative of the Function of the I as Revealed in Psychoanalytic Experience," *Écrits: A Selection*, translated by Alan Sheridan (New York: W.W. Norton & Co., 1978), p.506. See also Jacques Lacan, "The Mirror Stage as Formative of the *I* Function as Revealed in Psychoanalytic Experience," *Écrits*, translated by Bruce Fink (New York: W.W. Norton & Co, 1996), pp.75-81.
241 For Althusser, we become subjects through ideology, rather than we as subjects recognize our positions within any particular ideological formations, and this is possible through "interpellation," which is a "hailing," where an ideology addresses us, "Hey, you there?", and we respond, "Me? You mean me?", and the ideology says, "Yes, I mean you." Like the mirror stage (and misrecognition) in Jacques Lacan's Imaginary Order, we are always-already interpellated. See Althusser, "Ideology and Ideological State Apparatuses," p.86. See also Klages, *Literary Theory*, pp.131-135.
242 Jacques Lacan, "The Discourse of Rome" (1953), *Écrits*, translated by Bruce Fink (New York: W.W. Norton & Co, 1996), p.265.
243 Fredric Jameson, *The Geopolitical Aesthetic: Cinema and Space in the World System* (Bloomington IN: Indiana University Press, 1995), pp.1, 2.
244 An early advocate of a technologized social totality, and the possibility of a synthesis between science and religion, was the Jesuit, Teilhard de Chardin (1881-1955). He believed in an evolving Christianity and suggested that the next phase of our evolution lies within collective thought where "everything strengthens my conviction that the future can be forced and led only by a group [...] united by a common faith in the spiritual future of the earth." He also believed that computers might be that evolution, also predicted that a worldwide computer network would contribute to collective thought. In his book, *The Phenomenon of Man*, he talks about evolution consisting of the same cycle being repeated, but each time with a slow advance, which he called the "coiling." De Chardin also used Kantian-inspired terms, such as the Noosphere, to describe the envelope of reflective life embracing the biosphere, each sphere dependent on the other, as well as "Noogenesis," which described the next evolution of man, one that would lead to 'Christogenesis' - man becoming perfect, a Christ. Despite lifelong disapproval from Rome, he would claim our evolutionary destiny is to become the "Total Christ" or the "Super Christ." Michael W. Higgins and Douglas R. Letson, *The Jesuit Mystique* (Toronto ON: Macmillan Canada, 1995), pp.233-234.

245 Ibid., p.3.
246 Benjamin, "Paris, the Capital of the Nineteenth Century," p.33. Benjamin is quoting from Jules Michelet, an article entitled *"Avenir! Avenir!"* (Future! Future!). Ibid., p.45*n*6.Ibid., p.34. The terms "residual" and "emergent" forms are from Raymond Williams, "Base and Superstructure in Marxist Cultural Theory," *Media and Cultural Studies: Keyworks*, edited by Meenakshi Gigi Durham and Douglas M. Kellner (Malden MA: Blackwell Publishing, 2006), p.137.
247 Jameson, *The Geopolitical Aesthetic*, p.3.
248 Ibid., p.11. Jameson offers numerous cinematic examples, such as *North by Northwest* (Alfred Hitchcock 1959), and many from the 1970s, such as *The Conversation* (Francis Ford Coppola 1974), *Three Days of the Condor* (Sydney Pollack 1975), *Marathon Man* (John Schlesinger 1976), *The Parallax View* (Alan J. Pakula 1974), and *All the President's Men* (Alan J. Pakula 1976). The plethora of political films during the 1970s was due in part to the rise of the 'New Hollywood' and the 'independent' film, which was enabled through the decline of the old studio system, in part due to the end of the 'star stable' system, the decline in censorship due to the replacement of the Production Code with a ratings system, and the influx of foreign films.
249 Ibid., p.82.
250 Adorno, *Negative Dialectics*, pp.17-18.
251 Jameson, *The Geopolitical Aesthetic*, p.82.

Determination and Actualization

The poetry of apachedom: The hysterical sublime

Benjamin's essay "Little History of Photography" (1931) and his exposé, "Paris, the Capital of the Nineteenth Century" (1935) sought not only the phenomena of the collective dream and the exposing of the object in its veil of reification, but also to explore the origins of the image-making culture and, in doing so, identify the genesis of our modern social reality. According to Benjamin, the nature of bourgeois subjectivity and its visual constructions are realized through the character of the *flâneur*,[1] the bourgeois *intérieur*, the allure of phantasmagoria,[2] the transformations in the urban landscape, and the profound changes in the perception of time. The subsequent transformations in subjectivity (that is, modern apperception) would in turn offer insights into the logic of the development of the image-making culture.

A critical point in Benjamin's analysis is that it is the *flâneur*'s navigation coincides with the Hausmannization of Paris that transforms the space of the city, raising the question of whether the transformation of subjectivity precedes or is determined by the physical transformation of the urban space.[3] This transformation would support the idea of history lost within culture, as found in Marx's concept that the capitalist era is only part of prehistory, which also informs Benjamin's concept of the arcades. Here, in the Paris arcades, the light filters through dingy glass roofs as into an aquarium of primitive sea life, a fossil world, where shop signs hang like zoo signs, "recording not so much the habitat as the origin and species of captured animals."[4] The arcades stand halfway between the private collection (a kind of anti-exhibition) and world exhibitions, "places of pilgrimage to the commodity fetish."[5] Its wares fall between the pre-commodified thing and the fetishized commodity, on the tipping point of commodification where "things are freed from the drudgery of being useful."[6] The arcades are also the first establishments to use gas lighting, extending the day for the growing population of urban dwellers in search of diversions.[7] Just as the panoramic view is extended and accelerated by the railway journey, so the arcade extends into rows of shops with an ever-growing view of commodities, offering, just as cinemas will in the near future, "a phantasmagoria which a person enters in order to be distracted [...] surrendering to its manipulations while enjoying his alienation from himself and others."[8]

Initially, before the expansion into department stores, the arcades and their passages are the domain of the collector, the anti-exhibitor, whose Sisyphean task is to take possession of things in order to divest them of their commodity character.[9] However, the new social reality will be realized through the *flâneur*, the man of leisure, a mobile version of the collector, who is an observer of the marketplace. Just as the commodity is the object under its veil of reification, so "the crowd is the veil through which the familiar city beckons to the *flâneur* as phantasmagoria."[10] The *flâneur* will become the collector of images, where modern photography will come into its own, where the camera is deemed capable of making discoveries.[11]

Benjamin points out that the French photographer Nadar spoke of Baudelaire's "*pas saccadé*,"[12] not irregular and brusque, but a measured step. However, "the gait of the poet who roams the city in search of rhyme-booty"[13] is the gait of the ragpicker, a not-so-distant relation to the poet, who also works at night while others sleep, obliged to come to a halt every few moments to contemplate and gather up the discarded objects he encounters. It is also the gait of the *flâneur*, whose inquisitive nature takes him through the streets. The *flâneur*'s travels are executed in the manner of what Guy Debord will call *dérive*, a component in his concept of psychogeography, which describes "an unplanned journey through a landscape, usually urban, on which the subtle aesthetic contours of the surrounding architecture and geography subconsciously direct the travellers, with the ultimate goal of encountering an entirely new and authentic experience."[14] Indeed, Debord will further claim that,

> The sudden change of ambiance in a street within the space of a few meters; the evident division of a city into zones of distinct psychic atmospheres; the path of least resistance that is automatically followed in aimless strolls (and which has no relation to the physical contour of the terrain); the appealing or repelling character of certain places - these phenomena all seem to be neglected. In any case they are never envisaged as depending on causes that can be uncovered by careful analysis and turned to account.[15]

Lauren Elkin will challenge the assumption that the *flâneur*, the aimless wanderer, is necessarily male; "We would love to be invisible, the way a man is, but if we're so conspicuous, why have we been written out of the history of cities?"[16] Baudelaire neglects to mention women and their relationship to the city streets, reducing them to fleeting objects upon which the gaze of the *flâneur* will alight: "From time to time, his gaze meets the gaze of a passing woman, engaging her in a split-second virtual affair, only to be unfaithful to her with the next female passerby."[17] However, Virginia Woolf is an example of the *flâneuse* with her perambulations around London during the nights, as she wrote in her essay *Street Haunting: A London Adventure* (1927), enjoying the release and freedom of her exploits: "The eye is not a miner, not a diver, not a seeker after buried treasure. It floats us smoothly down a stream; resting, pausing, the brain sleeps perhaps as it looks."[18]

Debord will diverge from the contemplative and expand upon the "aimlessness," which supported his view of the consumers in the "society of the spectacle"[19] who have become separated from the reality of everyday life, lost in consumerist fantasies and media phantasmagoria, where diversion and distraction moves to another level and anticipates a society that is only actively engaged in the consumption of vicarious experiences, a society that is "fundamentally *spectaclist*."[20] Debord will maintain that "the primary moral deficiency remains indulgence, in all its forms."[21] Indeed, in terms of aligning moral deficiency with the image-making culture, Debord will evoke Ludwig Feuerbach, who anticipated this condition as early as 1841, arguing that,

> certainly for the present age, which prefers the sign to the thing signified, the copy to the original, fancy to reality, the appearance to the essence, this change, inasmuch as it does away with illusion, is an absolute annihilation, or at least a reckless profanation; for in these days illusion only is sacred, truth profane. Nay, sacredness is held to be enhanced in proportion as truth decreases and illusion increases, so that the highest degree of illusion comes to be the highest degree of sacredness.[22]

If we return to the *flâneur*, Benjamin notes that in this intermediary stage, the situation of the *flâneur* appears as that of the *bohème*, where "the uncertainty of their economic position corresponded to the uncertainty of their political function."[23] In terms of their character, presumably before the full onset of moral deficiency, Benjamin will liken the *flâneur* to "the criminals in early detective novels [who] are neither gentlemen nor apaches, but private citizens of the middle class."[24] The figure of the Parisian apache, a reference to Baudelaire's "*les apachés*," a romanticized vision borrowed from the American west, is one who "abjures virtue and laws" and "terminates the *contrat social* forever."[25] Nonetheless, it is Baudelaire who anoints the apache hero in literature, not the detective but the criminal, just as the poet resembles Baudelaire's character of the ragpicker, the modern version of one who is being-found-fitting, who conducts the pious work of salvage, who "finds the refuse of society on their streets and derive their heroic subject from this very refuse."[26] As did Baudelaire, Benjamin considers the possibility of a "poetry of apachedom" and their uncertain future: "Do the dregs of society provide the heroes of the big city? Or is the hero the poet who fashions his work from such material?"[27] Indeed, Benjamin may be referring to himself, having spent many years strolling the arcades and alleys of Paris, alone, nomadic, strapped for money, "spending as little as possible, with an eye to the side streets for a cheap Chinese restaurant with a halfway decent budget menu."[28]

Benjamin, following Baudelaire, notes that the *flâneur* might also be described as "the first of the *poète assassiné*," whose aim is to give shape to modernity, and in doing so "to annihilate the entire race of lyric poets from the world."[29] This brings to mind Adorno's allegation that to write lyric poetry after Auschwitz is barbaric and pays homage "to that which has been reduced to silence."[30] Although Adorno would later become ambivalent on this claim, allowing that it was only through art that, "suffering can still find its own voice, consolation, without immediately being betrayed by it."[31] In doing so, rather than attempting the beauty of the transcendent, the experiences of victims can be used to create a negative work of art, a work that becomes part of the consumption of a world that caused the victims' experience in the first place. Importantly, Adorno saw the barbarism inscribed within the principle of civilization, particularly after Auschwitz, and that cultural forms offered a means toward autonomy and critical self-reflection that allowed an individual to stand firm against the powers that be in the totally administered society, indeed, in terms of its globalization, to "stand against the world spirit."[32] Thus, Adorno writes that we have created a "veil of technology," hidden behind the promise for the betterment of mankind, where "people are inclined to hypostatize technology, make it the thing in itself, an end in itself, a force of its own, and they forget that it is an extension of human dexterity. Technology is the epitome of the means of self-preservation of the human species, and those means are fetishized, because the ends – a life of human dignity – are concealed and removed from the consciousness of people.[33]

At this point, we might consider Fredric Jameson's account of the "hysterical sublime" found in the modern world, which would replace the sublime of Burke and Kant. According to Jameson, the earlier notion of the sublime, one that was conceptualized in terms of the divine, identified "the physical incommensurability of the human organism within Nature, but also of the limits of figuration and the incapacity of the human mind to give representation to such enormous forces," as did that of Heidegger, who would "entertain a fantasmatic relationship with some organic precapitalist peasant landscape and village society, which is the final form of the image of Nature in our own time."[34] However, taking a grim perspective, Jameson states that the modern world, where we are the primary *subjectum*, would see:

> the radical eclipse of Nature itself: Heidegger's 'field path' is after all irredeemably and irrevocably destroyed by late capital, by the green revolution, by neo-colonialism and the megalopolis, which runs its superhighways over the older fields and vacant lots, and turns Heidegger's 'house of being' into condominiums, if not the most miserable unheated rat-infested tenement buildings. The *other* of our society is in that sense no longer Nature at all, as it was in the precapitalist societies, but something else which we must now identify.[35]

In terms that recall Heidegger's claim that the appearance is everywhere of the gigantic, with its planning, calculating, establishing, securing, so Jameson will clarify that this "something else" that we must now identify is not technology per se, yet technology represents "that enormous properly human and anti-natural power of dead human labour stored up in our machinery, an alienated power," and further, evoking Jean-Paul Sartre, we are witness to "the counterfinality of the practico-inert, which turns back on and against us in unrecognizable forms and seems to constitute the massive dystopian horizon of our collective as well as our individual praxis."[36] If so, then we have evidence of Heidegger's warning of not just any danger, but *the* danger, where humankind is bound to its technology, neglecting its destining of being, and just as Lukács had described a world of convention and its ossified synthetic structures, "rigid and strange [...] a charnel-house of long-dead interiorities."[37]

The paradox remains that rather than the poetics of space that we are capable of envisioning, for example, by Bachelard, those houses in winter, the sanctuaries, "well-determined centers of reverie [that] are means of communication between men who dream as surely as well-defined concepts are means of communication between men who think,"[38] we have instead those ossified institutions and systems whose very rationality would make them resistant to change even if they give rise to a prevailing sense of purposelessness and meaninglessness. As a consequence, this rationality would enable the "disenchantment with the world," in both the capitalist and communist worlds, that would lead to fascism and the "total administration" of post-fascist societies,[39] a society that substitutes commodities for genuine works of art, where, as Horkheimer and Adorno argued, enlightenment had become mass deception.

Le prix de progress: The gimmick

Adorno and Max Horkheimer despaired for understanding and practice of art in modern society. They will not only deliver a polemic against the hegemonic "culture industry" found in the "totally administered society," in particular the Hollywood cinema, where "a technological rationale is the rationale of domination itself,"[40] they will also address *Le prix de progrès*, comparing it to the medical use of chloroform that invokes loss of memory.[41] Significantly, the goal of science is domination over nature, as Descartes envisioned, and in order to achieve this end there must be a "process of oblivion," whereby, "the loss of memory is a transcendental condition of science," such that the relationship of the object becomes distanced from the subject, in what we have called the bound domain of objectification. Indeed, Adorno and Horkheimer claim, "all objectification is forgetting."[42]

Adorno defines the totally administered society by its tendency to "finish things off" (*fertigmachen*), which creates "manipulative people, who actually are incapable of true experience."[43] Thus, the reified consciousness through fetishized products and commodities loses sight of the goal of a life of human dignity, whereby, rather than resisting the herd instinct, the veil of technology creates a lack of empathy, a "human coldness." Adorno will supply an illustration of how technology erodes the work of art and its interpretation by turning to the popular music on the radio where he claims the selections to which we are subjected have nothing to do with quality, their measure taken in terms of success as a commodity. The music industry's formula, like that of the film industry, is to find something that is successful, then to promote and plug the same thing over and over again, with the result that music is made into "a kind of social cement operating through distraction, displaced wish-fulfilment, and the intensification of passivity."[44] As a result, the consciousness of the listener is rarely engaged, where even the performance of classical music on the radio has caused a regression in listening because it is increasingly difficult for listeners to hear it as music: "When they react at all, it no longer makes any difference whether it is to Beethoven's Seventh Symphony or to a bikini."[45] At the same time, the radio voice penetrates the private sphere of the bourgeois *intérieur*, where freedom is now limited to switching the station, or into the public sphere where even that freedom is removed. Despite its attributes of the ethereal and the sublime, music is merely the background noise for the general distraction of modern life.

On the one hand, therefore, we might argue that the technology of reflection, including the "mechanization of the world picture"[46] is an inevitable factor in the transformation of our social reality, whereby, in the Platonic tradition, it serves the scientific method and challenges all manner of illusion.[47] On the other hand, as Adorno argued, the work of art no longer serves a socially critical function, which it is unable to do when the same ideology that provides socially necessary semblance must also serve itself, thereby demanding a distorted image of the true. However, this distortion is aesthetically valid because it is one that "divides the social consciousness of aesthetics from the philistine is that aesthetics reflects the social critique of the ideological in artworks, rather than mechanically reiterating it."[48]

Nonetheless, the essential point is that the aesthetic is subjective, that the subjective is bound to social consciousness, and that the aesthetic mode serves as a bridge between instinct and reason, between will and knowledge, between imagination and judgement. The fact that there is a bridge at all suggests a common ground, or overlap, which also suggests there is indeed a boundary, or threshold, one that art can "break through," between the external world and the internal world of the subject, or if we consider this in Heideggerian terms, the ontic and the ontological (existence and essence), and that this is the determining ground or domain of aesthetics.

The means by which the modern media initiates its "mass deception," its re-mystification of the world, according to Jürgen Habermas in *The Structural Transformation of the Public Sphere* (1991), is by constructing a "socially necessary illusion" or "socially necessary false-consciousness," where ideologies are functional false beliefs that serve to shore up certain social institutions and the relations of domination they support.[49] The result is the decline of the public sphere, where public opinion, and the attendant "public sense," lost its autonomy along with its critical function.[50] In other words, instead of fostering the formation of rational opinion and reliable beliefs, the public sphere in the nineteenth and twentieth centuries became an arena in which public opinion could be stage-managed and manipulated; instead of promoting freedom and human flourishing actually began to stifle it.[51] Hence, we arrive at Sloterdijk's modern state of disillusionment and demoralization, where "cynicism is *enlightened false consciousness*. It is that modernized, unhappy consciousness, on which enlightenment has laboured both successfully and in vain."[52]

Sloterdijk maintains that we might initially think that the "order of things" is an objective order, when in fact it is only constitutive subjectivity supported by the notions of perception and reflection.[53] Indeed, the spiral of reification is precisely what allows the system to function, only towards its inevitable collapse.[54] Consequently, false being is a function of the process, whereby false consciousness is reified into a system of objective delusions: "The modernization of the art of lying is based on schizoid finesse; one lies by telling the truth."[55] Sloterdijk will perceive that in the modern social reality there is an inversion of being and illusion.[56]

In this development Jameson detects an "aesthetic of distraction and boredom,"[57] where the reified image produces "a new kind of flatness or depthlessness, a new kind of superficiality in the most literal sense."[58] An example might be, as worded by David Hesmondhalgh in *The Cultural Industries* (2007), "an explosion of unsubversive titillation and unimaginative, unerotic pornography."[59] According to Lyotard, pornography is simply an exercise in mass conformism, where those who wished to be artists but are unable to play by the "rules," may now pursue successful careers in photography and film.[60] Lukács foresaw this emptiness when he asserted that reification had invaded every aspect of social relations, even to the extent that the relations between people have taken on the character of a thing, thus acquiring a "phantom objectivity,"[61] where rather than a Dionysian intoxication with life, as proposed by Nietzsche, we have, to use Benjamin's term, "the shrinkage of experience."[62] According to Jameson, the detached sex, the artifice of emotion or pleasure, serves as an illustration of what he calls "the waning of affect."[63] In terms of Lacan's account of schizophrenia and the breakdown of the signifying chain, "the interlocking syntagmatic series of signifiers which constitutes an utterance or a meaning" are now little more than "a rubble of distinct and unrelated signifiers," where "we are unable to unify the past, present and future of the sentence, then we are similarly unable to unify the past, present and future of our own biographical experience or psychic life."[64]

"Works of art are ascetic and unashamed," Adorno and Horkheimer claim, while the culture industry is "pornographic and prudish" and "the mass production of the sexual automatically achieves its repression."[65] Jameson observes, an extension of Adorno and Horkheimer's polemic, and the fantasies contrived under the capitalist system of production, that the visual image itself is essentially pornographic and that pornographic films are only "the potentiation of films in general, which ask us to stare at the world as though it were a naked body."[66] In which case, that which is exposed by pornography is both wish-fulfilling, to use Benjamin's terms, and the Freudian realization of repressed desires, yet simultaneously alienating in its inorganic inability to realize those desires. In Lacanian terms, as interpreted by Žižek, the pornographic reveals that the act of sex is so caught up in our narcissistic fantasies (our idealized images of both ourselves and our sexual partners), such that the zero form of sexuality (the most elementary form) for animals is copulation, but for humans it is masturbation. In terms of our mass culture, Žižek will argue that the cinema, with its sensual nature, its fantasies, is itself a form of masturbation.[67]

Derrida maintains that "it has never been possible to desire the presence 'in person', before this play of substitution and the symbolic experience of auto-affection,"[68] and indeed it is this "play" between presence and absence that allows us to conceive of being present and fulfilled in sexual relations with another at all. According to Derrida, masturbation is "originary" and therefore applies to all sexual relations. Indeed, all erotic relations have their own supplementary aspect whereby we are "not present" to some ephemeral "meaning," but we are always involved in some form of representation. For Derrida, even if this substitution does not literally take the form of imagining another in the place of the one you're with, or supplementing the "presence," or acting out a certain role, or faking certain pleasures, such representations and images remain the very conditions of desire and of enjoyment.

In Freudian terms, we could say that pornography is in itself a form of castration, both in terms of its production and in terms of its solipsistic subject. Deleuze and Guattari will refer to the "celibate machine," the site of enjoyment or *jouissance*, thus producing and consuming intensive magnitudes,[69] where the subject proper appears, but only as "a mere residuum alongside the desiring machines," a residuum that "confuses" itself with the celibate machine:[70] "This confusion is akin to that described by Lacan in his account of the mirror stage. The jubilant cry 'So it's me!' is the expression not of a unified and unifying subject but of a subject that is a mere surface effect of desiring-production."[71] Thus, Deleuze and Guattari will claim that the point of Lacan's account of imaginary identification is that the subject is a result of fundamentally passive syntheses and not the agent of a series of active syntheses, and certainly not governed by a principle of common or public sense, even if the subject regards him- or herself as such, but, as we have noted earlier, it is the manifestation of the "desiring machine" and its manifold desires, which begin and end with the technology of self-reflection.

To return to cinema, Deleuze would object to "pointing to the vast proportion of rubbish in cinematic production," claiming that "it is no worse than anywhere else, although it does have unparalleled economic and industrial consequences."[72] Deleuze claims that you cannot blame the filmmakers, especially the great ones who must struggle against all odds to produce their works, such that "the history of cinema is a long martyrology."[73] The real problem may not be with the films themselves, to evoke Lukács, but the barren reality that no longer constitutes a favourable soil for art. Recognizing a severe diminishment in the "prevailing cultural *script*" and the stories we tell ourselves about ourselves, Deleuze describes difference without a determinate value, claiming, "the modern fact is that we no longer believe in this world. We do not even believe in the events that happen to us, love, death, as if they only half concerned us. It is not we who make cinema; it is the world which looks to us like a bad film."[74]

In her book, *Ugly Feelings* (2005), Sianne Ngai detects a bestiary of affects - animatedness, envy, irritation, paranoia, and the synthesis of boredom and shock, excitation and fatigue, a kind of overstimulated numbness, "in other words, one filled with rats and possums rather than lions, its categories of feeling generally, well, weaker and nastier."[75] Ngai presents a dialectic of desire and disgust across genres, in accordance with Kant, where, "There is only one kind of ugliness which cannot be represented in accordance with nature without destroying all aesthetical satisfaction, and consequently artificial beauty, viz. that which excites *disgust*."[76] However, even a "lesser" emotion, although not necessarily a positive one, still has the potential to be transformative.

Catharsis is the process of releasing, as proposed by Aristotle, and thereby providing relief from strong or repressed emotions, a kind of purgation, a purification. However, Ngai is not addressing the grand emotions, such as rage, terror and hatred, nor Aristotle's claim that the sharing of tragedy brought a community together. Neither is she addressing the more "ethical" emotions, such as shame, melancholy, charity; her attention is on the non-glamorous; irritation, boredom, envy, those less dramatic, ongoing, more sustainable, non-cathartic, amoral, and petty emotions. Ngai is addressing "a bestiary of effects, in other words, it is one filled with rats and possums rather than lions, its categories of feeling generally being, well, weaker and nastier."[77] These are the noncathartic feelings that "give rise to a noncathartic aesthetic: art that produces and foregrounds a failure of emotional release (another form of suspended 'action') and does so as a kind of politics."[78]

Ngai perceives a sense of dawning futility, where many people seem to derive their greatest pleasure from making others feel bad, where disaffection and disillusionment are contagions that we ourselves spread. In a concept that stands in direct opposition to the Beautiful and the Sublime, and any claims of "Beauty," "Truth," and "Good," she composes the term "stuplimity," an astutely observed aspect of stupidity that captures the ennui of modern life, described as a synthesis of shock and boredom, fatigue and excitation,[79] and its "stuplime" aesthetics, which "highlights certain limitations in classic theories of the sublime "accounting for that prevent it from adequately accounting for the experience of boredom increasingly intertwined with contemporary experiences of aesthetic awe."[80] Emulating the effect of Gerard Richter's *Atlas* (1997), an installation work of art with over 7000 items, which invoke tedium and fatigue on the part of the observer, have introduced "a strategy of agglutination – the mass adhesion or coagulation of data particles or signifying units."[81] The content of the modern media is a plethora of words and images, not too much of a good thing or even a bad thing, it is too much of a mediocre thing, and just too much, where "The fatigue of the viewer's responsivity approaches the kind of exhaustion involved in the attempt to read a dictionary."[82] Perhaps the viewer's response could be summarized in the popular term: "whatever." Ngai evokes the character of Bartleby, Herman Melville's scrivener of suspended agency and absence of strong emotion,[83] in reference to disgust and its aesthetic of the intolerable, as well as Herbert Marcuse's description of "the friendly or 'repressive tolerance' that makes the scrivener seem 'safely ignorable'."[84] In doing so, Ngai's approach will propose that, "Art thus comes to interrogate the problematically limited agency of art foregrounded in the aesthetics generated by ugly feelings, and in a fashion, I will argue, unparalleled by other cultural practices."[85]

Ngai enhances this argument in *Theory of the Gimmick*, where the "gimmick," a "compromised form," possesses "affective spontaneity, immanent discursivity, claims to normativity in the absence of norms," and is thus "a judgment on and about judgment."[86] The theory of the gimmick stands in opposition to the "conviction" of aesthetic judgments and those "in the academy who harp on 'the aesthetic' as a morally, purified, specialized domain of art."[87] The gimmicky artwork irritates us because it seems to be working too hard to get our attention, but also not working hard enough, Ngai recognizes the historical significance of the rise of equivocal aesthetic categories - such as the merely "interesting," which recalls the ambivalence of the *flâneur* - and with an eye to the special difficulties posed by the very idea of an aesthetics of production (as opposed to reception), where she finds an uneasy mix of attraction and repulsion produced by the gimmick across a range of forms specific to western capitalism.

Ngai specifically addresses the concern of *not* seeing, where she finds the gimmick is an aesthetic judgment that on a genre that is all about nonaesthetic judgments, where aesthetic forms are subsumed by economic forms. In some ways this may realize the Liar's Paradox, where the viewer can "see" that the "flagrantly unworthy gimmick" and its claims to worth that are overrated and false, and the exploitations where aspects of our lives, of human capital, should not be exposed for profit, but are, such that the gimmick amounts to a kind of fundamental contradiction, a blind spot within our visual consumption and social reality, a form of *not* seeing.[88] In effect, the *not* seeing will amount to an ethic of indiscriminate tolerance.

Chora: Black sun

Plato proposed that the poets be removed from the ideal city-state (*kallipolis*) because they are subject to divine madness, seeking to entertain and embellish rather than convey the truth. The *chora* (*khôra*) was the territory of the ancient Greek *polis* outside the city proper and, presumably, this is where the artists would be sent. Plato also used the term to designate a kind of receptacle, a space, or an interval. Heidegger had referred to the *chora* as part of his "clearing," where being takes place. Derrida used *chora* to describe a radical otherness. In terms of a cinematic representation, this suggests the "presence of absence" found in the work of the Japanese filmmaker Yasujiro Ozu (1903-1963). He used a Zen aesthetic as an integral part of his work, whereby "*mu*," or the empty space or "void," is used to create an "active" empty space.[89] Although a character may leave a scene, Ozu does not cut to another shot but will continue filming the "empty scene," allowing the character's presence to linger even when they are not in sight. He will then apply this to the narrative, as in *Tokyo Story* (1953), where a character is absent, an elderly relative having left this world, and yet the impact of their presence remains. In a wider sense, when a modern society does not recognize the impact of what it has lost, perhaps of its traditions and culture, then that too is an absence, a forgetting that defines modern society.[90]

In *Timaeus*, Plato presents fleeting entities, such as fire, air and water, appearing as transitional unformed images or forms, described by John Sallis as "a kind of image of images in a kind of artificial cycle of transformations."[91] They have no form in and of themselves, but can only appear in "receptacles" or "by those things entering it," which makes them images or forms of a "third kind." In this sense, *chora* is neither being nor non-being, nor is there becoming, a space that is only accessible as an interval between in which the "forms" were originally held. With overtones of the mystical, these mutable, perpetual beings are "applied like a stamp to a matrix so as to leave in the matrix an impression similar to the stamp itself."[92]

Luce Irigiray presents a challenge to Plato, and to phallocentric metaphysics, starting with Plato's metaphor of the cave, or hystera, the Greek word for "womb." Instead of Plato's process of liberating the prisoner from the shadowy realm of untruth and ignorance, and brought out into the light of truth, Irigiray claims the metaphor shows the violent process by which a child is forced to renounce its primordial relation to the maternal in favour of a supposedly self-engendering relation to the paternal law.[93] As with mu, the absence of presence, once we leave the cave, we are unaware of what we have lost. In "The Laugh of the Medusa" (1975), Hélène Cixous issues a call for women to refuse to be trapped by a language that does not allow them to express themselves. Calling instead for a "feminine mode" of writing, "écriture feminine," in what Cixous calls "white ink." Yet the essay also calls for an acknowledgment of universal bisexuality or polymorphous perversity, a reference to Foucault and the precursor to queer theory.[94]

Julia Kristeva adapts Plato's idea of the *chora*, where it can mean the womb, "a nourishing maternal space,"[95] perhaps, as in Derrida's view, where "Love means to love the other as other."[96] Walter Murch states that we hear before we see, while still in the womb we hear our mother's voice, four and a half months after conception.[97] In that in-between space, we did not distinguish our own self from that of our mother or even the world around us, our experiences was pleasurable without any acknowledgment of boundaries. This is the stage, then, when we were closest to the pure materiality of existence, or what Lacan terms "the Real."[98]

Lacanian psychoanalytic theory shows how the evolution of the subject is related to the evolution of language.[99] According to Kristeva, and as opposed to Lacan's Symbolic Order, the subject is by nature in motion, not a static and erroneous notion of the monolithic nature of language. Indeed, Kristeva will challenge Lacan, and his concept of the "mirror stage," by claiming that the earliest stage in the psychosexual development is in fact the pre-lingual stage of development, from birth to six months, when we are still dominated by a chaotic mix of perceptions, feelings and needs. It is a chaotic space that suggests "a language without exteriority."[100] Kristeva will also propose that art is not an object of analysis nor an exchange of judgement but an ignition of pleasure (*jouissance*) in the subject. The subject moves outside syntax to the spatial moment of ecstasy, thereby privileging semiotics over the symbolic, a pleasure described as "holiness."[101] In doing so, we discover "the ethics of perceiving ourselves *as already in* poetic language: an ethics of desire."[102] Consequently, Kristeva will support polyamoury, similar to polyvocality, although not in the sense of many love objects but in multiplied connections between possible intensities, ruptures and fissures in meaning, language and images, thereby reawakening the imagination and allowing illusions to exist, where "The ethical turn is the shift from knowing to thinking."[103]

The male subject is relegated to a position of exteriority by identifying him with mastering speech, vision, or hearing. This is addressed as a position of power but may be conceived as a place of exclusion. Marshall McLuhan noted a societal shift in the computer age where the simultaneous character of information moving at the speed of light assails us from all directions simultaneously. Similarly, we do not see from all directions at once, but we hear from above, behind, sides, below, from all directions simultaneously. This is the space of the "electric man," an acoustic space without a center or whose center is everywhere and whose margin is nowhere,"[104] the space of "white noise." Further challenges to Lacan, as well as Kristeva, included a reconsideration of the "male gaze" and "pleasure in looking," including the Freudian concept of scopophilia,[105] which was pioneered in Laura Mulvey's influential essay "Visual Pleasure and Narrative Cinema" (1973).[106] Subsequently, the challenge to the oppositional logic of the masculine-feminine expanded to consider much more complex aspects of representation.

For example, bell hooks introduces the term "oppositional gaze" to address the black person's right to look, where "oppositional" encompasses resistance as well as an understanding and awareness of the politics of race and racism that challenges the cinematic "whiteness" inclusive of the male gaze. hooks argues that Mulvey's essay did not address racism, in particular, black women are placed outside the "pleasure of looking" as an imaginary subject to the male gaze. In her essay, "The Oppositional Gaze: Black Female Spectatorship," hooks states, "from a standpoint that acknowledges race, one sees clearly why black women spectators not duped by mainstream cinema would develop an oppositional gaze."[107] The absence of racial relations in the context of feminist theory engages in a process of denial, where many feminist film critics structure their discourse around white women, with the result that "to see black women in the position white women have occupied in film forever is to see a 'transfer' without 'transformation'."[108] In which case, the emergence of a true "female gaze," or gaze of the Other, is not simply occupying the same space as the "male gaze." Bracha Ettinger has proposed the "matrixial gaze," which is hybrid and floating, replacing the formal structure of oppositional logic itself with a dimension of emergence, where objects, images, and meanings are glimpsed in their nascent stage, before they are differentiated.[109]

Kristeva describes the Symbolic (in contrast to the Semiotic) is associated with the masculine, the law, and structure. This is the space in which the development of language allows the child to become a "speaking subject," and to develop a sense of identity separate from the mother. This process of separation is "abjection."[110] Because female children continue to identify to some degree with the mother figure, they are likely to retain a close connection to the Semiotic. However, this continued identification with the mother may result in what Kristeva refers to as melancholia, given that female children simultaneously reject and identify with the mother figure. In Kristeva's terms, "the abject" is neither subject nor object, referring to that which acknowledges no boundaries, rules or fixed positions, and which upsets identity, system and order. Abjection is a state of flux, where "meaning collapses," and the body is open and irregular, sprouting or protruding internal and external forms to link abjection to grotesquerie.[111] "On close inspection, all literature is probably a version of the apocalypse that seems to me rooted, no matter what its sociohistorical conditions might be, on the fragile border (borderline cases) where identities (subject/object, etc.) do not exist or only barely so—double, fuzzy, heterogeneous, animal, metamorphosed, altered, abject."[112]

Kristeva, in *Black Sun: Depression and Melancholia* (1989), examines the subject of melancholia in the context of art, literature, philosophy, the history of religion and culture, as well as psychoanalysis. The melancholic is one who perceives the sense of self as a crucial pursuit and a nearly unattainable goal and explains how the love of a lost identity of attachment lies at the very core of depression's dark heart. Kristeva reflects on the painting of *The Body of the Dead Christ in the Tomb* (Hans Holbein the Younger, 1522). The painting is a life-size depiction of Christ lying horizontally in his narrow tomb, the wounds in his torso, feet and hands, the body in the early stages of putrefaction. The painting is often seen as a challenge to the "beatific suffering" and "perfect salvation" of Christ's death in the Catholic depictions.[113] "Does Holbein forsake us, as Christ, for an instant, had imagined himself forsaken?" Kristeva asks. "Or does he, on the contrary, invite us to change the Christly tomb into a living tomb, to participate in the painted death and thus include it in our own life, in order to live with it and make it live?" Kristeva recalls Dostoevsky's *The Idiot*, where Prince Myshkin looks at a copy of the painting and declares, with characteristic lack of guile, "Why, some people may lose their faith by looking at that picture!"[114] The question then is are we presented with a descralized reality and the destruction of meaning through the unadorned representation of human death, the point of severance between meaning and non-meaning. Or are we asked to overcome the stark reality of death and the meaninglessness of being and yet still maintain faith in the resurrection. Kristeva will ask, "One question, among others, persists: if there are moments when the only possibility is the safeguard, then there are perhaps others when it is not sufficient to safeguard. Is it possible, and how is it possible, for the artist to make himself understood by subjects transforming the process of history?"[115]

Affirmative culture: The blind spot

The transposing into image, as noted earlier, involves an aestheticization that may be understood as taking what may have once been considered unaesthetic and is, or now understood to be, aesthetic. The scope and magnitude of this image-making suggests we are living in an era of global aestheticization, particularly in the wealthier industrial societies, where aesthetic ideals and aestheticizing activities have been incorporated into all aspects of existence. The extent of the aestheticization of our social reality may be found in Herbert Marcuse's evoking of Nietzsche's definition, "culture: dominion of art over life,"[116] where the work of art has been granted a unique role in society, but it is primarily for reasons of "social hygiene" in the service of reproduction, where "affirmative culture" responded to the historical demand for the general liberation of the individual. Indeed, the very word "culture," as observed by Lyotard, "already signifies the putting into circulation of information rather than the work that needs to be done in order to arrive at presenting what is not presentable under the circumstances."[117]

Marcuse writes, "In antiquity, the world of the beautiful beyond necessity was essentially a world of happiness and enjoyment."[118] In modern times, however, Marcuse insists on the "semi-autonomy" of the cultural realm, where the subject's idealistic longings for happiness are constantly subsumed into the ideal that gives the illusion of granting present satisfaction, such that "even unhappiness becomes a means of subordination and acquiescence. By exhibiting the beautiful as present, art pacifies rebellious desire."[119] Thus, through the affirmative culture one is permitted to partake in happiness despite its elusiveness in the real world, in effect through non-happiness, yet assuage one's anxiety about ever achieving real happiness, whereby we are presented with not so much a better world as a noble and just world, thus "the unity represented by art and the pure humanity of its person are unreal: they are the counterimage of what occurs in social reality."[120]

According to Habermas, the longing for a premodern world-view cannot but renege on those achievements of technological rationalization that has created our social reality. The reason is that human beings have been increasingly subordinated to the requirements of technological production and to the administrators who organize society in the interests of maximum efficiency and productivity, such that we have neglected the interpersonal or "intersubjective" dimension, including interpersonal discourse.[121] The result is that "the totalizing self-critique of reason gets caught in a performative contradiction since subject-centered reason can be convicted of being authoritarian in nature only by having recourse to its own tools."[122] For Habermas, this means that a fully human form of existence is only possible if we restore the collective discussion about social values and goals that is proper to the interpersonal realm: in Habermas's terms, the tools, therefore, must include a "communicative rationality," which, similar to Hannah Arendt's call for a reclamation of the public sphere by liberating the political domain of action from its colonization,[123] will thereby "reclaim the communicative of the lifeworld."[124] Indeed, Arendt protests that the reign of *homo faber* ("man the creator," i.e., the modern bourgeoisie) is both morally and politically objectionable due to its tendency to reduce everything in nature, including human beings, to "mere means."[125]

Habermas, therefore, will criticize the positivists for reducing everything to the cognitive or instrumental rationality point of view, and yet he also criticizes thinkers such as Nietzsche and Adorno for reducing everything to a subject-oriented aesthetic point of view.[126] For Habermas, the foundations of Adorno's determinate negation are never secure, indeed, "Like exiles, we wander about lost in the discursive zone; and yet it is only the insistent force of a groundless reflection turned against itself that preserves our connection with the utopia of a long since lost, uncoerced and intuitive knowledge belonging to the primal past."[127] In contrast to Adorno's totally administered society and its instrumental rationality, Habermas argues that "the real problem is that 'communicative rationality' itself has been subordinated to a 'functionalist' rationality whose aim is mere system-maintenance."[128]

The goal of consensus, as noted earlier, and supported here by Cutrofello, is now reduced to that of coercion.[129] Thus, Habermas seeks to unite a Marxist account of reification with a Western appreciation of the intrinsically rational character of modernization, and, in doing so, to substitute the radical pessimism of Horkheimer and Adorno, and we might add the modern state of disillusionment and demoralization found in the cynicism of Sloterdijk's "enlightened false consciousness," and discover a vision of how to reactivate the stalled process of Enlightenment. In other words, Habermas seeks a moral rationalism through "discourse ethics," whereby the principle of any discourse must be about the *process* of moral decision making and not about the *product*.[130] In which case, the problem is not necessarily the reification of the world through the "mediatisation of the lifeworld," but through its "colonization," thus demanding "*the uncoupling of system and lifeworld*."[131]

With echoes of Lukács, where his philosophy evolved from literary criticism, Habermas proceeds from the need for self-reflection, as opposed to self-interest, to the need for communicative rationality, where communicative action must be prior to instrumental action, such that the members of a community may reach consensus through reason.[132] Thus, a genuine critical theory must occupy a position with two fronts: one is the theoretical claims that address the foundations of science, morality and law, and the other is its relationship to the totality of the "lifeworld" and the public sense, despite the fact, and perhaps because of it, it follows that "in a subversive way it relentlessly shakes up the certainties of everyday practice."[133]

Again, the problem is not that societal rationalization is irrational, but that the processes of rationalization inevitably produces a disenchantment of the world due to the rise of "social pathologies," such as anxiety, alienation and demoralization.[134] As such, Habermas wishes to emphasize a criticism of the philosophy of consciousness, namely, a philosophy that places primacy upon the individual subject rather than upon the processes of interaction within which that individual is involved. Thus, Habermas is also critical of Kant's moral philosophy because "it presupposes that each individual in isolation can rationally calculate the morally correct way to behave."[135] The problem with the philosophy of consciousness, therefore, is that it is inadequate in terms of the justification or legitimation of moral claims, and it is also inadequate as a social theory, primarily because it does not consider or involve the individual subject in terms of the discourse ethics of the collective.[136]

In addition, Habermas notes that Jacques Derrida wishes "to expand the sovereignty of rhetoric over the realm of the logical," and, in doing so, attempt to remove any privileged access to the truth by the subject and thereby render any discussion as "*objectless*."[137] Indeed, Derrida will claim that meaning is in fact "outside of language. And consequently outside humanity."[138] In some ways, this may prove productive, particularly in terms of the "text combed against the grain,"[139] for just as Benjamin sought to "brush history against the grain,"[140] and Adorno would argue that the true work of art "brushed taste against the grain,"[141] so too the "text combed against the grain" may reveal "the blind spot."[142] Consistent with our concerns of constitutive subjectivity and the technology of reflection, this suggests a process of discovery that is necessary because "'blindness and insight' are rhetorically interwoven with one another. Thus, the constraints constitutive for knowledge of a philosophical text only become accessible when the text is handled as what it would not like to be – as a literary text."[143] This supports Habermas's concept of the "double structure" of language, where language has a propositional or perlocutionary component (in that it refers to the world through the individual subject and is made with the strategic intent of manipulating hearers) and an illocutionary component (in that it invokes social relationships and the public sense where we make our intentions explicit).[144]

Nonetheless, Habermas disagrees with Derrida's recommendation that rhetoric is sovereign to logic, where philosophy functions entirely like literary criticism, as this would eliminate the genre distinction between them. In doing so, philosophical thinking would lose its double-edged potency as "the sword of the critique of reason itself"[145] and displace aesthetics from its "truth" content, such that, as Adorno claimed, the work of art is now perceived aesthetically and therefore misperceived, which cannot lead us out of the aporia of becoming mired in self-referentiality. Likewise, Richard Rorty states that Nietzsche, Heidegger, Adorno and Derrida all make a similar mistake in that they get caught up in "universalist problematics," namely, the "strong" concepts of theory, truth and systems that belong to the (Kantian) past. It would be more productive to accept "a kind of fallibalism" where truth claims can never be proved beyond doubt, which does not eschew truth claims but only recognizes that they will constantly be revised by future generations.[146]

Mythology in motion: Dialectics at a standstill

The producers of the modern collective imagination, according to Benjamin, allow for "mythic forces" in abundance in the new industrial technology. Indeed, in Benjamin's view, as noted by Buck-Morss, "the gods are partial" to the transitional space of "awakening" in which we now live, which augurs well for social change, at least as long as the powers are held free of the reifying constraints of mythological systematization.[147] In fact, the very novelty of technology implies that the power of the technological "gods" must be fleeting, "a lightning flash,"[148] which only proves that "gods can die," where their very transitoriness is the basis of their power, and, as such, this was "mythology in motion."[149] And yet, this is also a "double dreaming" where, on the one hand, the collective is in a distracted dreaming state, locked in a commodity dream-world, and, on the other hand, it is unconscious of itself, "composed of atomized individuals, consumers who imagined their commodity dream-world to be uniquely personal (despite all objective evidence to the contrary)."[150] According to Benjamin, as interpreted by Buck-Morss, this was the fundamental contradiction of capitalist-industrial culture:

> A mode of production that privileged private life and based its conception of the subject on the isolated individual had created brand new forms of social existence - urban spaces, architectural forms, mass-produced commodities, and infinitely reproduced 'individual' experiences - that engendered identities and conformities in people's lives, but not social solidarity, no new level of collective consciousness of their commonality and thus no way of waking up from the dream in which they were enveloped.[151]

Because of this lack of commonality, Benjamin would claim the images that have assembled around the arcades exhibit a peculiar kind of ambiguity that indicate the transformative social relations and products that are peculiar to their epoch. He characterizes these images as that of "dialectics at a standstill" because they are dream images, containing both utopian and dialectical elements, and where the dialectic inherent in images and the commodity form can be likened to the prostitute, "seller and sold in one."[152] Although dialectics are at a standstill, the task now is not so much jump-starting a stalled dialectic but of rescuing the dialectical image from the dialectics of the commodity form, or, to put it another way, rather than going "outside" the image to find the revolutionary construction, we have to look "inside" the image itself. Therefore, the true aesthetic of a cultural form is not the aesthetic that we apply to it, but exists within the cultural form itself.

The political meaning of the new visual constructions – both as images and as social reality - are revealed through Benjamin's concept of dialectical images, images that will in effect replace the proletariat's revolutionary barricades in order to challenge the bourgeois second nature within our social reality, identifying reification as the residue of dreams. In Benjamin's view, the failure of the Paris Commune of 1871 not only marked the affirmation of mass culture and modern society, it also marked the end of the hope that the proletariat and the bourgeoisie would continue the revolutionary changes began in 1789, as well as the end of the pre-Marxist utopia envisaged by Fourierism,[153] where the collective includes a radical notion of freedom, including sensual happiness. The architectural phalanstery envisaged by Charles Fourier, Benjamin contends, must now be realized in the arcades,[154] although their utopian construction and ideals would be more fully realized with the arrival of movie theatres, and even more so in the modern shopping mall with its combination of department stores, shops and theatres.

In the images that assemble around the arcades (first as photographs, then as postcards, magazines, advertisements, and soon, an extension of photomontage, as moving pictures), Benjamin finds "the creation of fantasy prepares to become practical as commercial art," through "the realization of dream elements, in the course of waking up, [which] is the paradigm of dialectical thinking."[155] In effect, we seek to resolve the ambiguity of our existence, an ambiguity that Benjamin finds "peculiar to the social relations and products of this epoch,"[156] whereby these images achieve the impossible; they stop the flow of time and bring dialectics to a standstill. Thus, Benjamin's dialectical images suggest that meaning is refracted through the image, containing both the archaic and the modern. Therefore, it is here, inside the image, that Benjamin will seek its true dialectical potential. Indeed, in his call for a revolutionary awakening, he will write:

> Every epoch, in fact, not only dreams the one to follow but, in dreaming, precipitates its awakening. It bears its end within itself and unfolds it – as Hegel already noticed – by cunning. With the destabilizing of the market economy, we begin to recognize the monuments of the bourgeoisie as ruins even before they have crumbled.[157]

Therefore, the dual task of the revolutionary intelligentsia was both to overthrow the predominance of bourgeoisie subjectivity and to gain contact with the proletarian masses. In order to accomplish these tasks, in an extension of Lukács's hope for the proletariat, the revolutionary must abandon contemplation for "action" in order to awaken the "dreaming collective," a task that suggested an unburdened state of mind, according to Benjamin, related to that of a child's consciousness. Just as bourgeois education "badgered out of existence"[158] the unsevered connection between perception and action in children, so the hectoring forms of bourgeois society must be resisted in order to achieve a distinguished revolutionary consciousness in adults. Accordingly, the phenomena of the collective dream must be dissected as patiently and minutely as possible, so that we, its heirs, could understand the ramifications and, finally, awaken from our dream-induced sleep.

Benjamin attempts a dialectic of awakening in *The Arcades Project* (*Passagen-Werk*), his "magic encyclopaedia,"[159] originally conceived as "A Dialectical Fairyland,"[160] which "is concerned with dissolving mythology into the space of history."[161] In a massive collage, one that anticipates the connective possibilities of the Internet, although pre-digested by Benjamin's intellectual vigour, he compiled the dream-world of modernity and sought a collective awakening that would transform the world. To outwit history, therefore, which had placed a spell on the dreaming collective, would require cunning, "to interpret out of the discarded dream images of mass culture a politically empowering knowledge of the collective's own unconscious past."[162] To this end, Benjamin will argue that reason and cunning have placed tricks within myths so that their forces cease to be invincible. Indeed, fairy tales are an example of how the archaic appears in the present and allows for a victory over the forces of myth. He evokes Kafka here, whose stories "went to work on legends," where his little tricks were proof "that inadequate, even childish measures may also serve as a means of rescue."[163]

The world of necessity: Janus-face

Marx identified "the highest good was the human capacity to engage in hobbies, that is, with the capacity to play,"[164] just as Schiller, Hegel, and more recently Marcuse, suggested we become fully human by playing.[165] However, a qualification may be necessary, as noted by Marcuse, for example, who supported the place of art in social life, particularly an "affirmative culture," which he recognized as the higher culture of the bourgeois era, yet the reality is quite different, indeed "the world of necessity, of everyday provision for life, is inconstant, insecure, unfree – not merely in fact, but in essence."[166] The result may be that modern existence is indeed an accumulation of simulated realities, a life turned upside down, where our complacency is, as Marcuse argues, the real miracle of affirmative culture, where "Men can feel themselves happy even without being so at all. The effect of illusion renders incorrect even one's own assertion that one is happy."[167] This decrease in volition recalls Nietzsche's concern that we resist nihilism, refusing to become *der letzte Mensch*, the passionless weak-willed "last man" who responds to "the advent of nihilism" and "the death of God" with apathy, where "'become mediocre' is the only morality that makes sense."[168] Also, as noted by Hannah Arendt, we are still a society created and sustained by human actions, where "play" cannot mean a regression to irresponsibility, because we can only become fully human by working and acting, by being engaged as both actors and spectators, and where we must exercise the faculty of judgement, otherwise we may become part of a culpable complicity that Arendt refers to as the "banality of evil," that is, the "unthinking participation in truly diabolical crimes."[169] Thus, she warns of "the rule by Nobody," "the tyranny without a tyrant," where "everybody is deprived of political rule, of the power to act,"[170] because power is diffused and decentralized to create the illusion that there is no power. Evoking Heidegger, Arendt will claim that "The trouble is not that they are cold-blooded enough to 'think the unthinkable', but that they do not *think*."[171]

In any case, Benjamin would be subject to his own historical moment when he continued to express his solidarity with the working class and the Communist Party, perhaps a reflection of Brecht's ongoing political influence, even after Stalin's summary executions and show trials of 1935 and 1936. However, the ghost of a failed revolution and the unfulfilled dream of a classless society would now be included in mounting tragedies in the historical present. Benjamin maintained the affirmative character of his political position, convinced that in the event of war the Soviets would offer revolutionary support to the German workers. In 1939, however, the signing of the Nazi-Soviet Non-Aggression (Molotov-Ribbentrop) Pact cancelled this possibility and profoundly disillusioned Benjamin.[172] His writings would now move away from his Marxist political orientation and return once again to theological motifs, such as the "Angelus Novus," and may have prompted his suicide at the Catalonian border town of Portbou while attempting to escape from France to Spain.[173]

For Adorno, the failure of the Soviet revolution meant "philosophy, which once seemed obsolete, lives on because the moment to realize it was missed."[174] Adorno's lack of faith in the redemptive power of the proletariat was confirmed, supporting his claim that the proletarian movement had only led to the total administration of modern society. Consequently, the rift between Benjamin and Adorno would widen after the collapse of the Soviet political and social experiment. Adorno, who was Benjamin's junior by eleven years, believed they shared a common philosophical program, whereas Benjamin, for his part, saw Adorno as his successor.[175] Benjamin and Adorno first met in Frankfurt in 1923 through a common acquaintance, Siegfried Kracauer.[176] Both Benjamin and Adorno adopted Marxism in 1927, and from then on, through to Benjamin's death in 1940, they maintained a rigorous intellectual friendship. However, their views diverged in the early 1930s, which can be traced in large part to Benjamin's attempts to reconcile the two opposing poles of his thought, which Benjamin himself acknowledged as the "Janus-face" of his own theory.[177] On one face, the one looking to the future, Benjamin expressed his Marxist political orientation through his solidarity with the rise of the proletariat, a view encouraged by his reading of Lukács and his friendship with Brecht. On the other face, the one looking to the past, was Benjamin's messianism, influenced by Judaic mysticism, which was encouraged through his friendship with Gershom Scholem, a scholar of the Kabbalah.[178] The two poles of thought are apparent in Benjamin's writing style, which "remained closer to the evocative prose of artistic literature than to the denotative language of theoretical philosophy."[179]

Adorno, whose friendship with Benjamin was less personal and more intellectual in nature, supported Benjamin's attempts to incorporate both poles, particularly when they maintained a dialectical nature. In their correspondence, from 1928 to 1940, Adorno refers to their "shared work" and "the mutual confirmation we found in one another's thoughts," even, with a nod in favour of Benjamin's messianic tendencies, "the secret coded character of our theology."[180] Nonetheless, Adorno frequently found himself defending Benjamin against Benjamin himself, their disagreements placing Adorno, as he wrote, between "the Scylla of Brechtian materialism on the one hand and the Charybdis of Judaic theology on the other."[181] Without the mediation of conceptual and critical reflection, namely theory, Benjamin's attempts to reconcile dream and reality can only lead to a degeneration of theology into magic and Marxism into positivism, such that Adorno would be compelled to ask for an "extrapolation to extremes"[182] in order to sharpen and radicalize Benjamin's exposé and its dialectic not just in terms of commodity character and alienation, which in any event had been around since the beginning of capitalism, but to the specifically industrial production of commodities in the nineteenth century.

In terms of the lack of commonality that Benjamin found in modern society that may be rediscovered through mass culture, particularly the cinema, Adorno will argue for the opposite view, whereby mass culture had only reinforced reified forms, which in turn had led to the organization of the mass audience, and consequently to "the liquidation of the individual."[183] In fact, Adorno argues in the harshest terms possible that the liquidation of the active, questioning individual by the organization of the mass audience is a totalitarian accomplishment that compares to that of the Führer.[184] The mass rallies of Nuremberg have only been technologically re-functioned into the audiences of the mass culture. For Adorno, the totally administered society and its structure of domination itself is the primary evil, the cause of world wars, as well as the attendant horrors such as Auschwitz and Hiroshima. In response to Benjamin's question as to whether there really are enough torturers to carry out the orders of the Nazis, Adorno acknowledges the legitimacy of the question but maintains there is no shortage whatsoever, recognizing that "bureaucratic desktop murderers and ideologues" operate contrary to their immediate interest, yet comply by murdering first themselves while they murder others.[185]

Indeed, the potential for cinema as propaganda and mobilizing the masses had already been initiated by Lenin and Stalin, and would be further exploited by Hitler.[186] A variation on the mobilization by mass culture was also perpetrated by Mussolini, who admired the Soviet cinema and its *agitki*, but did not want to raise the political consciousness of the audience or project a message to the working class, and instead wanted to present the bourgeoisie in a positive light, thus seeking hegemonic approval for his regime. The cinematic *cultura popolare* would inspire Hollywood-style genre films, *telefono bianco* ("white-telephone films"), where social mobility was expressed through marriage and divorce, and, like Hollywood, the new mass figure was the star, the individualized composite as the product for mass consumption.[187] Hence, Mussolini would claim: "The crowd doesn't have to know. It must believe... If only we can give them faith that mountains can be moved, they will accept the illusion that mountains are moveable, and thus an illusion may become reality."[188]

Perhaps more significantly, we are now witness to "a culture of trauma," as Kristine Stiles claims, following Hélène Cixous when she declared, "Write yourself, your body must make itself heard," so we find the regularization of trauma when the "marked bodies and shaved heads visualize aggregate forms of suffering."[189] Stiles also evokes Elaine Scarry who argues that suffering cohabits the silences that "actively destroy" language, initiating a process that brings about "an immediate reversion to a state anterior to language."[190] This situation becomes apparent in the modern cinema where the poetic visuals, stylistics and thematic often glorify the excesses of violence and alienation, yet without dialectical opposition they only contribute to the viewer's fatalistic and passive attitude toward those in power. The proliferation of violence in the popular culture may indeed be symptomatic of a deeper political and social crisis, accessing and alleviating the social vacuum caused by apathy and cynicism, yet rarely offering the potential clarity of purpose or meaning, as might be offered by an invigorating opposition usually found in the dialectic of public forums. Instead, the modern cinema chooses to "only lead us ever more deeply into the insanity – and then strand us there."[191] As Adorno argues, no matter how relentless the work, there is always pleasure even in the most sublimated work of art, because there is always a message that appears as a hidden "it should be otherwise:"

> The so-called artistic representation of the sheer physical pain of people beaten to the ground by rifle-butts, contains, however remotely, the power to elicit enjoyment out of it. The moral of this art, not to forget for an instant, slithers into the abyss of its opposite. [...] When genocide becomes part of the cultural heritage in the themes of committed literature, it becomes easier to continue to play along with the culture which gave birth to murder.[192]

Adorno's claim that to write lyric poetry after Auschwitz is barbaric pays homage "to that which has been reduced to silence,"[193] although he would later become ambivalent on this claim, allowing that it was only through art that, "suffering can still find its own voice, consolation, without immediately being betrayed by it."[194] An example would be the works of Arnold Schoenberg (1874-1951), an influence on Adorno's earlier ambitions to be a composer, notably *A Survivor from Warsaw*. Op. 46 (1947), an orchestral piece about a Jewish survivor of a Nazi concentration camp.[195] For Adorno, "Therefore, music must do what language, including visual language, has failed to do: to produce an aesthetic effect rather than an argument. Music must revive the festering body of language and bring it back to life," such that, "The task of music, as it has been throughout human history, is to summon the essences that have drifted beyond our recall."[196] In this way, rather than attempting the beauty of the transcendent, the experiences of victims can be used to create a negative work of art, a work that becomes part of the consumption of a world that caused the victims' experience in the first place. For this reason, Adorno would support modernism over realism, taking up the paradox of paratactic art, which Adorno defines as "artificial disturbances that evade the logical hierarchy of a subordinating syntax,"[197] and thus avoid commodification or aestheticization (first order) because it is ever more fractured, where "the fragment is that part of the totality of the work that opposes totality."[198]

This recalls Adorno's defence of modernism that was based on his belief that art should be the social antithesis of society, always containing an element of negation to expose that which it repulsed. In Lukács's view, however, this did not address the problems of reification, where the process of commodity exchange followed its own logic rather than the needs and demands of real human beings, and therefore was only pessimistic anti-illumination and acquired meaning only by being the opposite of something, by saying no, where even its negation becomes a kind of denial of its own culpability. Accordingly, in the 1962 preface to *The Theory of the Novel*, Lukács would accuse Adorno of taking up residence in the "Grand Hotel Abyss," described as "a beautiful hotel, equipped with every comfort, on the edge of an abyss, of nothingness, of absurdity."[199] In response, Adorno would accuse Lukács of sacrificing the critical vigour of his earlier works, where he correctly identified the problem of reconciliation, replacing it with the "lie" that the proletariat has succeeded in fulfilling its destiny as the subject-object of history in the Eastern bloc.[200] In his essay *Reconciliation under Duress* (1961), Adorno is even harder on Lukács: "The moralism that colours all of Lukács's critical concepts is typical of his weepings and wailings about subjectivist 'lack of reality'."[201] Indeed, for Adorno, "Lukács's thinking is art-alien."[202]

In *The Meaning of Contemporary Realism* (1963), Lukács would again address Adorno's view in psychological terms when he wrote:

> Life under capitalism is, often rightly, presented as a distortion (a petrification or paralysis) of the human substance. But to present psychopathology as a way of escape from this distortion is itself a distortion. We are invited to measure one type of distortion against another and arrive, necessarily, at universal distortion.[203]

As a result, the fracturing found in modern art undermines the status of art itself, where even Adorno would discern "a kind of apotropaic work of mourning by which art grieves over its own immanent disappearance."[204] Hence, rather than the sublime beauty that Heidegger found in Hölderlin, Adorno finds the paratactic juxtaposition of dialectical images, like Beethoven's use of dissonance, which attests to a beautiful sublimity, where the presence of the gods is now only found in ruins.[205]

The collector of images: The mechanical gaze

If Western humanism presents a world centred on the single individual, whose frame of possession is aligned or equated with an act of possession, then the window on the world becomes either a safe in the wall or the shop window that "holds" a world of objects and people as commodities. Indeed, the ordering of the visual landscape, much like the network of coordinates created by Alberti's "veil of gridded strings,"[206] is simultaneously an accumulation and containment of the world within its framework; "a safe let into a wall, a safe into which the visible has been deposited."[207] With future refinements, this perspective will become equivalent to natural vision, so much so, as Martin Jay notes, that the visual field would now replace the visual world.[208] In so doing, a power relation attends the pleasure that accompanies the ordering and the capturing found in the artistic construct. Lev Manovich claims that the Alberti perspective belongs more to the gaze than the glance, allowing for the imprisonment of the body to take place on both the conceptual and literal levels.[209] For example, the perspectival projection found in Albrecht Dürer's *Draftsman Drawing a Recumbent Woman* (1525), where the draftsman extends a reifying male look upon the recumbent woman and turns "its targets into stone," whereby, despite St. Augustine's condemnation of *concupiscentia occularum* ("ocular desire"),[210] diverting our minds from more spiritual concerns, there remains the concern that "the marmoreal nude is drained of its capacity to arouse desire."[211] Similarly, René Magritte's painting, *Ceci n'est pas une pipe* (1928), addresses the ambiguity between image and text, where the treachery of images is that they do not satisfy emotionally. This suggests St. Paul's warning against the *specularum obscurum*, the glass or mirror through which we can see only darkly, a caution against terrestrial sight,[212] but this is not only the treachery of images, but the treachery of words that serve those images, and thereby the content of those concepts that are informed by images and words, thereby initiating a process of nullification, if not assassination, of the poetic.

The advances in the technology of reflection lead to the development of hand-held cameras in the early twentieth century, allowing the camera to become the tool of the *flâneur*.[213] The modern world-as-picture begins through the lens of the *flâneur*. Susan Sontag marks this period when modern photography first comes into its own:

> The photographer is an armed version of the solitary walker reconnoitring, stalking, cruising the urban inferno, the voyeuristic stroller who discovers the city as a landscape of voluptuous extremes. Adept of the joys of watching, connoisseur of empathy, the flâneur finds the world "picturesque."[214]

In the early days of photography, the camera required a concentrated level of involvement on the part of the photographer, allowing the role of the photographer to be a kind of "image-gardener."[215] The image-gardener rejects any ambition to pre-visualize, wanting only to show how things look when photographed, how they've "grown," supporting Baudelaire's concept of the *flâneur* as one who "goes botanizing on the asphalt."[216] Therefore, the *flâneur*, like the naturalist novelist or artist, toting a camera instead of a basket or easel, strolling the city streets instead of the countryside, intent on observing the panoramic surface of the crowd, fascinated by the exotica of the "lower depths," revelling in the hidden corners of the "picturesque" slums.[217] The *flâneur* seeks the unofficial reality behind the façade of bourgeois life, passing by the great sights and so-called landmarks, seeking the refuse and detritus of modern society, allowing Benjamin to equate these photographs to those of a detective collecting evidence at a crime scene.[218]

Subsequent advances in technology allow for speedier exposure and development: photographs that took half an hour or more to complete their exposure in the 1830s, take only seconds by the 1880s.[219] The new speed allows for the "capture" of images, a kind of "guerrilla photography" where seeing turns to staring, where the mechanical gaze creates estrangement from, rather than union with, the natural world.[220] The unblinking and restless mechanical eye, "the gaze of the alienated man,"[221] now advances "an acquisitive relation to the world that nourishes aesthetic awareness and promotes emotional detachment."[222] Consequently, the extension of the existing through the Alberti perspective, the static and atemporal gaze rather than the saccadic glance, belongs, as Manovich words it, to the "perspectival machines" that present a view that is suited "more to a statue than to a living body, becomes equally immobile, reified, fixated, cold and dead."[223] In due course, "the petrified world of the photographic images was shattered by the dynamic screen of the cinema,"[224] where the "perspectival machines" will restore mobility to the image through motion pictures, moving from the static classical screen to the dynamic modern screen, a "plastic art" that includes the element of time, and, in so doing, create not only a new means of artistic expression but an entirely new technological language of reflection.

The effect of shock: Faciality

Benjamin writes: "the camera is getting smaller and smaller, ever readier to capture the fleeting and secret images whose shock effect paralyzes the associative mechanisms in the beholder."[225] These shock effects reflect the fragmentation of modern society that is replicated by the process of photographic imagery, which in turn will lead to the montage technique of cinema, challenging its indexical nature, where the shock effect will rely not only on image but also on juxtaposition.[226] However, in paralyzing the associative mechanisms in the beholder, as Benjamin will argue, the mass audience's reception of film would take on the form of distraction. By definition, a shock is short in duration, diminishing with repetition, which would now became part of the commodification of cinema, an ingredient in the image-making product to be consumed. Benjamin cites Freud in claiming that shock is parried by consciousness, a protective shield, and thus cushioned. Indeed, the greater the shock then the more vigilant is consciousness in its screening and the less these impressions will enter long-term memory.[227] Evoking *Beyond the Pleasure Principle* (1921), "emerging consciousness takes the place of the memory trace," therefore "becoming conscious and leaving behind a memory trace are incompatible processes within one and the same system."[228]

This may explain why the Soviet filmmaker Sergei Eisenstein's "kino-fist" or "shock work" failed to maintain revolutionary fervour among the masses when the shock effects of a new view of reality were replaced with the shock effects of the new itself.[229] Visiting Moscow in 1926, Benjamin would praise Eisenstein's cinematic masses as "architectonic," declaring that film was the only medium that could "transmit this turbulent collective."[230] However, rather than rousing an audience to their political and social reality, the cinema led the way for the replacement of the social and political reality with the image, and that image with another image, and so on, until the entire process falls back into the impotence of art forms in bourgeois culture. In which case, because film is predisposed to a distracted form of reception by virtue of its shock effects, then, by extending Freud's hypothesis that consciousness defends itself from traumas by not allowing them to penetrate far enough to leave a permanent memory,[231] this only provides another indication that the recipient, or viewer, is unlikely to follow through with changes in their life praxis.

There are other problems with relying on shock, as Bürger points out; for one thing, shock is often non-specific.[232] Thus, even though the recipient may be shocked, there is no guarantee the recipient will change their behaviour in a particular direction. The recipient may even receive the shock as a provocation, causing them to resist change. Also, if shock diminishes with repetition, requiring increasingly violent shocks, then the shock is merely consumed and the integrity of the recipient's shock value has been lost entirely. Nevertheless, just as Benjamin observed that "the public is an examiner, but an absent-minded one,"[233] so he will argue that film serves as a training ground for the changes in modern society, where learning is not through contemplative immersion, as had been the case with earlier cultural forms such as painting and literature, but through casual repetition and awareness, through habit.[234]

Benjamin writes that "to dwell means to leave traces."[235] Thus, just as the navigable space of the *flâneur* shifts to the anonymous associations of modern society, so the *flâneur* himself is an anonymous observer, "mentally recording and immediately erasing the faces and figures of passersby."[236] Benjamin will describe the camera-toting *flâneur* with the term "physiognomist,"[237] one who judges human character from facial features, which, contrary to the "mechanical gaze," suggests the importance of "faciality" in determining the poetics of cinema. Significantly, the film theories of Béla Balázs,[238] in *The Visible Man* (*Der Sichtbare Mensch* 1924) and his later work *Theory of the Film* (1948), where he proposed a renewed interest in the close-up, which allowed for the recognition of a human being *through* another.[239] "The close-up can show us a quality in a gesture of a hand that we had never noticed before... The close-up shows your shadow on the wall with which you have lived all your life and which you scarcely knew."[240] Unlike those fleeting gazes and virtual affairs of the *flâneur*, the face would now linger in close-up on the big screen. Indeed, one of Balázs's critiques of modern cinema was its neglect of faciality, which, as a Marxist, he included in the "degenerative phenomenon of bourgeois art," witnessed whenever it "peeled facial expression off the face and physiognomy off the object, creating abstract, floating 'expressions' that no longer express anything."[241]

Deleuze identifies the close-up as an "affection-image," which is one of three dominant articulations he finds in the "movement-image," the other two being the "perception-image" and the "action-image."[242] Deleuze maintains that the latter two lead to a cause and effect of motivated action followed by a new situation to be perceived followed by another action. The affection image, however, is a different quality: "*The affection-image is the close-up, and the close-up is the face...*"[243] Thus, the face becomes a "text" to be deciphered. Indeed, just as Deleuze identifies a relationship between affection and movement in general, so Deleuze and Guattari will conceive of philosophy itself as kind of "faciality," where the face must be dismantled in order to reveal its meaning, where it is capable of arresting the drift of signification by tying meaning to the expressive gestures of a subject.[244] To the question of how would one dismantle the face, their response is that "the face is a politics,"[245] therefore there is a relationship between the face and faciality to the assemblages of power that require social production. Similarly, Deleuze and Guattari would write that art, like philosophy, is never an end in itself, it is a tool. Rather than taking refuge in art, art must sweep away those aspects of art that conceal its "truth" in itself, and thus enable art to move "toward the realms of the asignifiying, asubjective, and faceless."[246] Thus, in our terms, we have to move beyond the aesthetic of faciality, of expression, to that other face, the aesthetic of the aesthetic, where the face expresses a "truth" that is beyond expression.

The psychologist Silvan Tomkins, who had a background in theatre, believed that people acted toward one another according to social scripts. Affect Theory, introduced by Tomkins, refers to the "biological portion of emotion," which is that part of us that is "hard-wired, preprogrammed, genetically transmitted mechanisms that exist in each of us," which when triggered, precipitated a "known patter of biological events."[247] For example, Tomkins addresses faciality through organizing affects, that is, emotions or subjectively experienced feelings, into discrete categories and connects each on to a typical response, whereby affects can be identified through immediate facial reactions that people have to a stimulus. In the 1990s, the essays of Eve Kosofsky Sedgwick will expand on Tomkin's theory. An American scholar in the fields of gender studies, queer theory and critical theory, who in turn was influenced by Tomkins, Michel Foucault, and Melanie Klein, Kosofsky will argue that our world is shaped not simply by narratives and arguments but also by nonlinguistic effects, such as mood, atmosphere and feelings.[248]

Byung Chul-Han claims we now have an "age of exhaustion" driven by a technology of the self and perpetual self-optimization, where self-improvement is merely self-exploitation, such that, "The self-as-a-work-of-art amounts to a beautiful but deceptive illusion that the neoliberal regime maintains in order to exhaust its resources entirely."[249] Lauren Berlant, in her book *Cruel Optimism* (2011), will claim that our desire for meaning in life has led us to imagine that life follows some kind of trajectory and that we ourselves can be the author of its narrative. And yet we also have a sense of precariousness, "a gut-level suspicion that hard work, thrift, and following the rules won't give us control over the story, much less guarantee a happy ending."[250] In her essay on Berlant in *The New Yorker*, Hua Hsu writes, "We dream of swimming toward some beautiful horizon, but in truth, Berlant evocatively observed, we are constantly 'dogpaddling around a space whose contours remains obscure'. What stories do we tell ourselves to stay afloat?" The stories we tell ourselves about ourselves, the prevailing cultural script, is such that "The challenge is finding configurations that don't simply reproduce the same old patterns of life," and further, "We can build worlds out of these small ambitions." [251] In what may be a tonic to Ngai's "ugly feelings," Hsu presents us with an expression of Berlant's cruel optimism: "But attentiveness to affect encourages us to imagine ourselves beyond the present: even if feelings of exhaustion, indifference, or disillusionment may have been neutralized, that doesn't mean they're natural," concluding with a final quote from Berlant, "We refuse to be worn out."[252]

The mirror and its captive: The mask

The mirror itself implies that the direction of vision is not always from subject to object, but the reverse. In which case, the viewing subject is also the viewed object, and the image is both viewed object and viewing subject. In the broader terms of "picture theory," as defined by W.J.T. Mitchell, "the realization that spectatorship (the look, the gaze, the glance, the practices of observation, surveillance, and visual pleasure) may be as deep a problem as various forms of reading (deciphering, decoding, interpretation, etc.) and that 'visual experience' or 'visual literacy' might not be fully explicable in the mode of textuality."[253] In other words, the exchange of looks between the viewing subject and the image may contain the depth of reciprocity as found between the reading subject and the text, although the nature of the exchange is uniquely its own.

The nature of this exchange of looks is often portrayed in terms of a mirror. This has typically fallen into two categories: the mirror as a reflector of external objects, as found in classicism, which we would consider representation, and the mirror as a radiant projector that changes the appearance of the object that it perceives, as found in romanticism, which we would consider illumination.[254] The truth content of this exchange can be profound, as discussed in the aspects of *durée*, and it may be unpalatable, a device often found in narrative fiction.[255] In either case, the mirror can serve as a window into the unconscious, as a reflexive doubling of what is being seen or shown, or as the mirror of the other, a part of human cognitive evolution.

The nature of the mirror itself supports the cinematic process of re-centering and re-calibration of its framing around the human figure, as well as the self-reflexive nature of the Lacanian mirror-stage, and, as pointed out by Elsaesser, the scientific discussions around "mirror neurons," where humans learn through imitative behavior and mimicry, which is also part of the development of empathy and compassion with other human beings.[256] This would suggest that the cinema allows us to pierce the Jungian persona, the social face the individual presents to the world as "a kind of mask, designed on the one hand to make a definite impression upon others, and on the other to conceal the true nature of the individual."[257] Consequently, as noted by Schirmacher, the mask may seem to alienate people and we are urged to throw them aside, yet the mask can also protect one's personal identity within a social sphere, reaffirming the rights of identity.[258] This would also support Jung's claim that a viable social persona is vital to adapting to the external social world, presenting oneself to the world as it were, yet there is always the danger of conformity, where there is the absence of the persona, someone who is merely "playing a role," and thus "blind to the reality of the world, which for him has merely the value of an amusing or fantastic playground."[259] In which case, the restoration of an authentic life would demand either the regressive restoration of the lost persona or the dissolution of the persona in order to achieve individuation through a new persona. Judith Butler will argue that "our very sense of personhood is linked to the desire for recognition, and that desire places us outside ourselves, in a realm of social norms that we do not fully choose, but that provides the horizons and the resource for any sense of choice that we have."[260] Butler also states that recognition is a normative ideal, such that "Recognition implies that we see the Other as separate, but as structured psychically in ways that are shared."[261] The key point is that recognition is not literal in that we "see" each other and are "seen," but how the process of this communicative practice takes place. Thus, Butler moves from an emphasis on complementarity with the Other to one of a relation, where the reference point is not reciprocal desire, but "the Other of the Other," whereby this desire "engages, motivates, and exceeds a relation of desire that it constitutes it essentially," which then creates an "intersubjective space."[262]

In the liminal space of the cinematic mirror/screen, the viewing subject is able to experience both "projection" and "identification," that is, the viewing subject is able to plunge into the film, to temporarily dissolve their bodily boundaries and give up their individual subject status, in favor of a communal experience and a self-alienating objectification, and at the same time the viewing subject an absorb the film as if it were his or her own, constituting themselves as the "imaginary" subject. Christian Metz, the French film theorist, borrowing from Lacan and Freud's concept of the unconscious as a language, would claim the cinema speaks to the viewing subject through the "imaginary signifier," where "the filmic image refigures an absence as a presence, and thus 'signifies' through a dynamic process of substitution."[263] Similarly, Roland Barthes will claim that a photograph is contingent and thus cannot signify (that is, aim at a generality) except by assuming a mask, where the mask is the face as the product of a society and its history.[264] In other words, the nature of the mask is the meaning that reveals the essence.

In terms of faciality, Deleuze, evoking Bergson, will refer to the reflecting and reflected unity of the face, which is significant in that "the face is this organ-carrying plate of nerves which has sacrificed most of its global mobility and which gathers or expresses in a free way all kinds of tiny local movements which the rest of the body usually keeps hidden."[265] Deleuze and Guattari will consider faciality in terms of two axes, significance and subjectification: "Significance is never without a white wall upon which it inscribes its signs and redundancies. Subjectification is never without a black hole in which it lodges its consciousness, passion, and redundancies."[266] Hence, their description of the face as a system of white wall/black hole, an abstract machine of faciality, with the camera as its omniscient "third eye," whereby the power of the close-up in cinema is not necessarily an explanation of social power, it is however a matter of economy and the organization of power.[267]

According to Deleuze and Guattari, the structure of the face has deterritorialized from the snout and mouth of the animal, the head has deterritorialized from the body, away from the organs and toward other strata, such as significance and subjectification (hence, their term, a "Body without Organs"),[268] which also implies a reterritorialization of the face.[269] Thus, "the mask does not hide the face, it *is* the face."[270] The face arrests the drift of signification by tying meaning to the expressive gestures of a subject, and yet, if Balázs is correct in that "expressions" no longer express anything, or, as Rancière words it, "the obtuse presence that interrupts histories and discourses becomes the luminous power of a face-to-face: *facingness*," where "presence opens out into presentation of presence," a power that stems from its lack of residue of presence, its ubiquitous being-there-without-reason.[271] As a result, in terms of the omniscience and organization of power found in the "machine of faciality," human beings are attempting to escape the face, to dismantle the face and facializations, to become imperceptible, to become clandestine. Indeed, in what we might call the "botoxification" of expression, there is an attempt to take away the signification of the face and facializations, to reduce the face to surface, to lose its identity, reducing it instead to a zone of indiscernibility. As such, Deleuze and Guattari's claim that the face is also an assemblage of power, the relations of subject-observer and authority, suggests that faces may be rejected by the "machine" if they do not conform or seem suspicious.[272] Thus, the white wall/black hole system is constructed to "ensure the almightiness of the signifier as well as the autonomy of the subject," where the face takes on the constitution of a landscape, where one can now compose a construction, a mask, a facialization rather than a faciality, "a face of politics."[273]

Deleuze notes that the cinematic image is always deterritorialized, and, evoking Balázs, that "faced with an isolated face, we do not perceive space. Our sensation of space is abolished. A dimension of another order is opened to us."[274] If we consider that this mask is the face, and the face is a landscape, but one of a different order in terms of the cinematic image, and that this face/landscape is art itself, and if we also consider Werner Hamacher's contention that "in order to be art, art cannot simply be itself; it must also be the art of the dissolution of the art,"[275] then the aesthetic of the aesthetic is the destruction of the face/landscape, the acid thrown in the eyes, the straight razor across the retina.

The end of images is no longer possible, they are always-already interpellated into the ideology of images, and so we are forced to address the reception rather than the production. In other words, the self, through identification and projection with the world-as-image on the mirror/screen, sees him- or herself playing in the drama before them, and therefore can only be other than themselves, other than being, and that would be the mask itself. If the mask supports the fraud of constitutive subjectivity, where the crisis of subjectivity is that the subject is only able to "presence" through him- or herself, then the aesthetic of the aesthetic is the unmasking of the mask that it has itself created. In other words, as Foucault worded it, "to get free of oneself."[276] More precisely, as Hamacher aptly words it, "the point is to think of both art and its end as a detaching of the mask, as a release of matter without contour and of a thinking without schema, as a dispatch which *with* art something other *than* art, something other *as* art, is promised and exposed."[277]

Denotation/Connotation: Maps of meaning

A picture of an hourglass denotes an old form of clock, but by suggesting the sands of time running out it connotes mortality. Therefore, denotation is a literal meaning (the passing of time), whereas connotation is an associative meaning (a sense of mortality). The power of the visual media relies on these associative meanings to give depth to its particular language of images. However, meaning is not perfectly transparent or can be "taken-for-granted," suggesting the deeper meaning behind the surface. Stuart Hall will contend that meaning itself is not "determined" but is "dominant" in that there is a "preferred meaning" of the dominant culture, especially in terms of visual culture.[278] Spectators bring diverse histories, cultural competencies and responses, both conscious and unconscious, to the "negotiation" of any spectatorial situation. In which case, this "negotiation" is not in complete conformity, nor in complete opposition to the dominant ideology. Indeed, the image of a passive audience overwhelmed by the hegemonic propaganda of a capitalist media is replaced by an analysis of media and popular culture that stresses a variety of different readings of media representations. Consequently, Hall will champion the idea that culture can tell us things about the world that the more traditional studies, such as politics and economics, cannot.

Hall explains that denotation is meaning that is "almost universally recognized," and connotation is associative and therefore less fixed and more changeable. However, Hall continues that for his part, "We do *not* use the distinction – denotation/connotation – in this way. From our point of view, the distinction is an *analytic* one only."[279] Hall refers to "maps of meaning" that are in fact "maps of social reality," where our process of denotation and connotation have "the whole range of social meanings, practices, and usages, power and interest, 'written in' to them." Hall gives an example taken from Roland Barthes:

> A sweater always signifies a "warm garment" (denotation) and thus the activity/value of 'keeping warm'. But it is also possible, at its most connotative levels, to signify "the coming of winter" or "a cold day." And, in the specialized sub-codes of fashion, a sweater may also connote a fashionable style of haute couture or, alternatively, an informed style of dress. But set against the right visual background and positioned by the romantic sub-code, it may connote '"long autumn walk in the woods." Codes of this order clearly contract relations for the sign with the wider universe of ideologies in a society. These codes are the means by which power and ideology are made to signify in particular discourses.[280]

Thus, the pattern of "preferred meaning" has "the whole social order embedded in them as a set of meanings, practices and beliefs: the everyday knowledge of social structures, of 'how things work for a practical purposes in this culture', the rank order of power and interest and the structure of legitimations, limits and sanctions."[281] According to Hall people are producers and consumers of culture at the same time, such that, "a message must be perceived as meaningful discourse and be meaningfully de-coded before it has an effect, a use, or satisfies a need," or, "To put it paradoxically, the event must become a 'story' before it can become a communicative event."[282] This paradox presents the politics of signification: What is denoted? What is connoted? And by who to affect whom? Hall suggests three positions in response: the dominant-hegemonic position, where the viewer operates and accepts the hegemonic code; the negotiated code or position, where the viewer acknowledges the hegemonic definitions but still makes their own determination; and, the oppositional code, where the viewer defies the dominant-hegemonic and engages in "the struggle of discourse."[283] It is through the challenge to the dominant-hegemonic that we have the opportunity to change the context of meaning and, perhaps, negotiate a different and more profound relationship with the world.

The level of distraction: The representations of consciousness

The big-city dweller is subjected to a flood of images that can cause sensory overload, an intensification of nervous stimulation that accelerates the pace of modern life, transforming even the slow-moving, self-possessed *flâneur* into the agitated impersonal *badaud*, whose behaviour is automatic, a reaction to shocks and the jostling of the crowds, "the mere gaper entirely taken in by what he sees."[284] In the new social reality, where idleness is a demonstration against the division of labour,[285] where the street had become an *intérieur*, and the *intérieur* of the department store had become a street,[286] in what proves to be the *flâneur*'s last promenade, so he becomes alienated and fades away. In turn, the distracted, aggressive *badaud* now dominates the urban landscape, having elevated himself to the level of the commodity. In order to maintain the *badaud*'s level of distraction, while allowing the commodity to retain its roots in novelty, the exchange value of a product is independent of its use-value but enhanced by its newness. Consequently, in terms of the image-making culture, newness becomes a calculated effect, enhanced by the public's desire for the shock-like effects already available in the popular literature and phantasmagoria, soon to become a crucial component of the cinema. Thus, Benjamin contends, newness is, "the origin of the semblance that belongs inalienably to images produced by the collective unconscious."[287]

Newness does not negate earlier artistic styles and motifs, Adorno would agree, but it negates traditions, thus ratifying the bourgeois conceptions of art.[288] In terms of newness, Adorno will take this a step further: "the new is the aesthetic seal of expanded reproduction, with its promise of undiminished plenitude."[289] Therefore, in the second nature of the modern social reality, fashion becomes the arbiter of bourgeois newness, prescribing the ritual according to which the commodity fetish demands to be worshipped.[290] The desire for newness, for fashion, translates to the image-making culture and becomes, as Sontag points out, a form of lust:

> As we make images and consume them, we need still more images; and still more. But images are not a treasure for which the world must be ransacked; they are precisely what is at hand wherever the eye falls. The possession of a camera can inspire something akin to lust. And like all credible forms of lust, it cannot be satisfied: first, because the possibilities of photography are infinite; and, second, because the project is finally self-devouring.[291]

According to Benjamin, visual constructions are "wish images," where "the collective seeks both to overcome and to transfigure the immaturity of the social product and the inadequacies in the social organization of production."[292] However, we could also say that these "wish images" contain less in terms of residual culture and the collective subject and more in terms of the actualization of repressed needs and desires. In fact, Benjamin draws a comparison with the fashion industry, but one whose sex appeal "stands in opposition to the organic," defending "the rights of the corpse," and prescribing the "ritual according to which the commodity fetish demands to be worshipped."[293] Giorgio Agamben will draw a similar comparison when he describes the "nihilism of beauty," where "this disenchantment of beauty, this special nihilism, reaches its extreme state with the mannequins or the fashion models, who learn before all else to erase all expression from their faces. In so doing, their faces become pure exhibition value and, as a result, acquire a particular allure."[294]

This move toward facelessness is the aesthetic of faciality at the first order and taken to its extreme, and yet, in terms of their particular allure, and as noted by Deleuze and Guattari, "if desire produces, its product is real."[295] Indeed, Deleuze and Guattari, evoking Lacan, criticize the practice of locating structures at the level of the Symbolic order rather than at that of the Real, which they maintain is the actual locus of "desiring production."[296] Similarly, in an aphorism that has a distinctly Adorno quality, they will state: "The virtual is opposed not to the real but to the actual. *The virtual is fully real in so far as it is actual*."[297] Thus, instead of maintaining that language is structured like the unconscious, as Freud and Lacan did, which, as noted earlier, suggests the internalized image-making process of self-reflection has been externalized through the image-making culture, Deleuze and Guattari will argue that the unconscious is better thought of in terms of "machinic" rather than "structural" because desire manifests itself not through a "logical combinatory" of signifiers but in a network of binary "desiring-machines" each of which is coupled to another.[298] It is for this reason that Deleuze and Guattari acknowledge Althusser's concept of interpellation, where we are always-already interpellated, and Lacan's mirror stage, where we are always-already defining the world as subjects, yet they disagree that social production is a philosophy of representation, proposing instead that it is a philosophy of difference.[299]

Although there is a connection between desire and representation, there is also a fundamental miscognition, a problem that cannot be fully explained in terms of interpellation or the mirror stage, because it "is not an ideological problem, a problem of failing to recognize, or of being subject to, an illusion. It is a problem of desire, *and desire is part of the infrastructure*."[300] In other words, we might say that there is a process of actualization found in the technology of reflection, but that it is a determination that is always-already a false reflection because it is determined by a philosophy of representation that is presided over by the formation of our consciousness within our social reality. Deleuze offers the example of fetishism as an illusion of social consciousness, thus "not a subjective illusion born of individual consciousness but an objective or transcendental illusion born out of the conditions of social consciousness in the course of its actualization."[301] Indeed, the capitalist system functions by creating desire that is never consummated, but that perpetual lack is not a lack on the part of the subject per se but a failure on the part of the social consciousness that supports that lack in the subject in order to fulfil the demands of the system.

Thus, we could say that there is indeed a fraud of constitutive subjectivity, whereby we are not properly synthesizing the difference in the actualization of reflection, but instead supporting a process of sameness that excludes difference, and at the same time, this process of sameness can only support an illusion formed of social consciousness. Therefore, in terms that suggest the move away from the primacy of the constitutive subject toward a primacy of the object, Deleuze and Guattari will propose a "rectification" that "breaks the unity of fetishistic common sense," whereby "the transcendent object of the faculty of sociability is revolution."[302] Therefore, the practical struggle must proceed not by the Kantian categorizing imperatives of sameness, but by "evaluating that truth beyond the representations of consciousness and the forms of the negative, and by acceding at last to the imperatives on which they depend."[303] In so doing, we must proceed by restoring and evaluating the truth that is beyond the accepted "truth," that is, the reality beyond the socially constructed "reality," and "to show how, in the subject who desires, desire can be made to desire its own repression."[304]

Inventories of mortality: Surreality

The true value of the image-making culture is its exhibition value, Benjamin writes, thus "film is the first art form whose artistic character is entirely determined by its reproducibility."[305] However, the surplus of images causes a "madness of vision,"[306] an intertwining of death and desire which Benjamin will express through melancholy.[307] Fashion itself becomes part of the ahistorical; "a petrified primordial landscape," which we view "under the gaze of melancholy, if melancholy causes life to flow out of it and it remains behind dead but eternally secure."[308] Similarly, photography and film are the inventories of mortality, Sontag claims, where "all photographs are *memento mori*. To take a photograph is to participate in another person (or thing's) mortality, vulnerability, mutability, thus, precisely by slicing this moment and freezing it, all photographs testify to time's relentless melt."[309] As a result, photography is a "past-tense medium."[310] The camera lingers on a face, and we see the face frozen in the last of its expressions, embalmed by the image, "transmuting in an instant, present into past, life into death."[311] Hence, Balázs's critiques of modern cinema and its neglect of faciality demands that the cinema resist this transmutation and attempt to restore the sensualness of life to the image. Nonetheless, as Benjamin writes, "in photography, exhibition value begins to drive back cult value on all fronts. But cult value does not give way without resistance. It falls back to a last entrenchment: the human countenance. [...] In the cult of remembrance of dead or absent loved ones, the cult value of the image finds its last refuge."[312] Once again, we find that the face must be dismantled to find its true expression.

Horkheimer and Adorno wrote that the correct relationship with the dead is the reminder of the burden of life weighing on the living, where, rather than instigating a cult of the dead as simply a component in "rationalized oblivion [...] the modern counterpart of the belief in ghosts," a cult attended by the revival of superstition, that relationship is properly a recognition that we are all victims of the same disappointed hope.[313] Baudelaire, however, lamented the lures and dangers inherent in "the cult of images."[314] In an 1859 article, he grants the new technology's uses in science and industry, but rails against the photographic image's incursions into the realms of "the intangible and the imaginary."[315] "Our squalid society," Baudelaire writes, has become narcissistically entranced by Daguerre's "cheap method of disseminating a loathing of history."[316] Martin Jay cautions, "it is hard to disentangle Baudelaire's contempt for the masses from his distaste for their new toy."[317] Nonetheless, Benjamin's friend, Siegfried Kracauer, detects an "innervation" of contemporary reality.[318] This is one of Benjamin's terms, used in the sense that only through technology can body and image so interpenetrate that all revolutionary tension becomes "collective innervation," whereby, in political terms, we would find "the idea of revolution as an innervation of the technical organs of the collective."[319] Thus, Kracauer will argue that we might deflect the fatal course of history, wherein "the turn to photography is the *go-for-broke game* of history."[320] Consequently, the battle over the fate of modernity would be decided on the site of contemporary mass culture.[321]

For his part, Benjamin recognizes Baudelaire's disdain for photography as the new art of the multitude, a cult with Daguerre as its messiah and the *flâneur* as disciple, yet he wonders if the illiteracy of the future will not be ignorance of reading and writing, but ignorance of the language of the visual culture.[322] Hence, Benjamin's argument will contend that the image is dialectical, that it contains the archaic in the frozen moment of the present, and that the intangible is released from the tangible. This also points to his surrealist sensibility, where, in the attempt to reconcile the tangible and the intangible, the present and the past, his political Marxism and his sense of the mystical. In doing so,

Benjamin, like André Breton, the founder of Surrealism, is attempting the reconciliation of dream and reality, a synthesis of the internal and external worlds to create a transvaluation of modern values through an artistic movement, in order to discover, what Breton called, "a kind of absolute reality, a *surreality*."[323]

Benjamin finds the new beauty in what is vanishing, the traces of a prior life, when the *flâneur*'s photographic images record all that is being lost, opening our eyes to "the monuments of the bourgeoisie as ruins before they have crumbled."[324] For example, the *flâneur* photographer Eugène Atget (1857-1927), an under-employed actor, began taking photographs in 1890, many of which preserve the Old Paris that he saw as disappearing. Benjamin referred to Atget as a "virtuoso" and claimed that Atget's photos are "the forerunners of Surrealist photography – an advance party of the only really broad column Surrealism manages to set in motion. He was the first to disinfect the stifling atmosphere generated by conventional portrait photography in the age of decline."[325] Benjamin's *Passagenarbeit* will be strongly influenced by Atget's photographs, as well as Surrealism, which suggests his resistance to the bound domain of the visible. It is the *flâneur*, therefore, the image-gardener, camera in hand, who stands on the threshold of the metropolis, "the landscape built of sheer life,"[326] observing the massive changes to the empirical, urban surface of reality, which is made manifest as the small-scale, time-worn Paris vanishes under the ceaseless replacement of the new.[327]

Benjamin, therefore, sought a new world of dialectical images and a revolutionary mass art, an artistic procedure that allowed for the negation of illusion by juxtaposing radically dissimilar images in such a way as to draw attention to itself as an artificial construction, as found in Dada, Surrealism and the Soviet avant-garde techniques of montage. Indeed, the artists of the avant-garde, the Dadaists in particular, applied both cultural and political radicalism to their work. In particular, the Dadaists attempted to "shatter" the production relations of modern society, often using film-like effects to shock their viewers, causing Benjamin to ascribe to them the role of precursors who created the demand for film. For the spectator of the film, contemplative immersion is replaced by distraction and percussive effects: "*Film has freed the physical shock effect – which Dadaism had kept wrapped, as it were, inside the moral shock effect – from this wrapping.*"[328]

Benjamin will argue that we search a photograph for "the tiny spark of contingency, of the here and now, with which reality has (so to speak) seared the subject, to find the inconspicuous spot where in the immediacy of the long-forgotten moment the future nests so eloquently that we, looking back, may rediscover it."[329] Thus, influenced by surrealism, Benjamin contends the dialectical image can defy its commodity form by offering a means of re-experiencing time. In other words, although the past is yet to be redeemed, the weight of its failures carried into the present, the possible redemption of the past also holds the utopian promise of a future redemption.

The demolition artist: Technological necessity

The changes to urban reality appear in the "Haussmannization" of Paris, an urban renewal that sought immortality through architecture. Georges-Eugène Haussmann, a civic planner associated with the rebuilding of Paris during the 1860s under the commission of Napoleon III, anointed himself with the title *artiste démolisseur* ("demolition artist"),[330] glorifying his grand architectural plans that razed working class neighbourhoods and forced the proletariat out of the city's centre. In the process, more than half of medieval Paris was transformed. There are two views of Haussmann's changes: either he destroyed old Paris, or he created new Paris. The massive boulevards that replace the convoluted network of blind turns and crowded neighborhoods transform Paris and create, to use Deleuze and Guattari's term, a "striated space" where "lines or trajectories tend to be subordinated to points: one goes from one point to another."[331]

Benjamin will claim that the massive building projects are an example of the modern tendency "to ennoble technological necessities through artistic ends," whereby its immediate goal was to provide wide thoroughfares that allowed access for troops to move into the city if there should be an insurrection. Yet when civil war does erupt in the Paris Commune of 1871, the barricades are stronger and better secured than ever.[332] The Commune only lasts some seventy days but manages to wreak an inordinate amount of devastation on the city, much of which is recorded by photographers. Although Benjamin suggests photographic montage as political agitation was introduced as early as 1855, when the objectivity of its images is questioned, it is after the Commune where photography comes into its own as an instrument of propaganda, when photomontages literally distort images in order to exaggerate the crimes of the Communards. Another consequence is the identification card when the use of photos for police purposes will become widespread in the aftermath of the Commune. Earlier, in 1854, the photographer Adolphe Disdéri introduced the *portrait-carte de visite*, a calling card personalized with a photo, which, after the Commune, will now evolve into the mandatory public document used for licenses, passports and other state-regulated forms of identification and surveillance.[333]

For all the rationality and clarity of Haussmann's architectural vision, and perhaps because of it, the result was often to intensify visual uncertainty and confusion, a seemingly endless disruption of daily life where, as worded by T.J. Clark, "the city is rendered illegible."[334] According to Marx, the failure of the Paris Commune marks the victory of mass culture and modern society, the last effort by the 19th century proletariat to redeem a world that commodification had almost completely disenchanted.[335] The burning of Paris, Benjamin writes, is the only worthy conclusion to the destruction that Haussmann began.[336] Nonetheless, the new social reality, for Benjamin, amounts to a reification of consciousness that paradoxically combines aspects of dreams and reality, a surreality, which suggests the possibility of the world behind the world that could be revealed, or concealed, through the synthetic process of the image-making culture. Hence, just as iron provides the building material for new architectural constructions so the dreams of the collective would provide the building material for the new visual constructions. Thus, "the city opens up, becoming landscape – as it will do later, in subtler fashion, for the flâneurs."[337]

The visual constructions of the 19th century begin with panoramas, massive artworks that depict large-scale views of natural and historical events inside a rotunda, a combination of the architectural and the work of art, as well as residual and emergent forms.[338] Anticipating the design of movie theatres, the audience enters the building and feels themselves immersed in the action of the painting. The popularity of the panoramas coincides with that of the dioramas, introduced by Louis Daguerre in Paris in 1822, which are *trompe l'oeil* entertainments, often called "miracle rooms."[339] The dioramas offer a more theatrical version of the single-panel panorama, where the audience stands or sits on a slowly revolving stage as multi-layered panels and nuanced lighting reveal and transform natural vistas, such as the depiction of a moonlit night turning into a sun-filled day, winter snowscape into summer meadow, a rainbow after a storm, or moving waterfalls. Importantly, these realistic representations of nature, along with the deceptions of deftly manipulated lighting changes, and, as Benjamin will note, prepare the way for both the development and the exhibition of motion pictures, as well as the visual process of change whereby the static image now includes the element of time.[340] Thus, the panorama makes an architectural work of painting, while the diorama adds a spatial and temporal mobility, both critical transitions in transporting an audience of atomized viewers to an imaginary realm while offering a dynamic representation of closely observed reality.

In terms of mass culture, Buck-Morss recognizes that the image-making culture was not only experienced by the masses, but was a mass experience, where a process of "doubling" allowed duplicated virtual realities that could be experienced as material phantasmagoria.[341] She further claims that phenomena that at first existed only as images – cinema, advertisements, propaganda posters - would now impinge on reality, a development with important political consequences, whereby "the collective imaginaries of both capitalism and socialism are virtual worlds, making them real became the social project."[342] In the same vein, Kracauer would look to the movie theatre, the "palace of distractions,"[343] and find a substitutive distraction in the Freudian sense that serves as a substitute for reality,[344] providing "shrines to the cultivation of pleasure; their glamour aims at edification."[345] In doing so, according to Kracauer, cinema's edification dealt exclusively with human affairs through conventional plots that presented a finite and ordered cosmos, substituting a pre-interpreted world-disclosure, rather than a self-critical or reflective disclosure. In which case, we might describe the cinema as not only a "perspectival machine" but these conventional plots as the "perspectival threads" that would now move beyond the Alberti perspective of a desensualized nature, and, in terms used earlier, allow for a power relation that attends to the pleasure that accompanies the ordering and the capturing found in the artistic construct of the mind.

A counter movement to contrived plots and uncritical distraction was found in neo-realism. For Cesare Zavattini - the theoretical founder of the Italian neo-realist cinema movement of the late 1940s and 1950s, also a neo-Marxist who was deeply influenced by Gramsci and the rejection of Mussolini's *cultura popolare*, and whose ideas in turn would influence André Bazin[346] and Kracauer - the most important characteristic of neo-realism was the realization that the necessity of "story" is really a rejection of reality, requiring a work of imagination that superimposes "dead formulas over living social facts."[347] Indeed, Zavattini will write:

> As the cinema's responsibility also comes from its enormous power, it should try to make every frame of film count, by which I mean that it should penetrate more and more into the manifestations and the essence of reality. The cinema only affirms its moral responsibility when it approaches reality in this way. The moral, like the artistic, problem lies in being able to observe reality, not to extract fictions from it.[348]

In effect, "story" is the decline of storytelling, because the value of real experience has fallen in value. As such, story constitutes a human defeat. Similarly, Benjamin wrote that the art of storytelling was coming to its end: "it is as if a capability that seemed inalienable to us, the securest amongst our possessions, has been taken away from us: the ability to share experiences."[349] This observation may resonate with recent concerns about machine intelligence and human apocalypse. In terms used earlier, this defeat may also be regarded as an imprisonment, or the bound domain, of not only the body but the imagination, taking place at both the conceptual and literal levels, colonizing that-which-lies-before. Therefore, the aesthetic of the first level, its visual construction and its "truth," must be transgressed in order to reveal the true aesthetic of the second level, where essence, the truth within and behind experience, would reveal itself.

Indeed, extending Freud's claim that the camera captured memory, Kracauer's concern would be that the technology of reflection, particularly photography, would threaten memory itself. Similar to Sontag's *memento mori*, the photograph is capable of removing any depth or emotion that might otherwise be associated with the memory, because photography cannot create a memory, it can only create an artefact, where, particularly with the proliferation of photographic images, "a person's history is buried as if under a layer of snow.[350] If the essence of the photograph, and even more so the cinema, is a function of the flow of time, then the question is whether the image-making culture only captures the residuum of history while the "truth" is left behind.[351]

Perspective is now in command; developed and expanded to such a degree as to allow visibility itself to be the force of authority. To put it another way, visibility supplies the material for the transformation of subjectivity, because the fact that we look at something and that the something is more and more something that we have named or interpreted or, in our minds, created, which then supplies the multiplication found in the equation of constitutive subjectivity, and thus cements the subjective viewpoint to which we are always-already interpellated, which is also the force of authority and the condition of power relations.

Étui: Agalma

Benjamin states that "the interior is not just the universe but also the *étui* of the private individual,"[352] *étui* meaning a small ornamental case, which recalls his description of the nineteenth-century bourgeois domestic interior as comparable to the inside of a mollusk's shell, encasing the bourgeois individual with all their appurtenances.[353] The appurtenances of the *étui* also suggests Lacan's reference to the *agalma*, the Greek word for ornaments, gifts, images and statues, put as offerings in the temples. Lacan uses the term *agalma* for a precious object hidden in a worthless box, the imaginary part-object, an element which is imagined as separable from its form or body, which for Lacan represents the unobtainable object of desire, the *objet petit a*, which we seek in the other.[354] Using their term of the "Body without Organs," the deterritorialized component or passage, notably the unconsciously created assemblage of intensities that we are always living with and engaged with, Deleuze and Guattari write "The BwO is desire; it is that which one desires and by which one desires."[355]

Lacan maintains that the *objet petit a* can also be regarded as a surplus of *jouissance*, of pleasure or enjoyment, the condition or bliss that comes with merging with the other, which also contains a sexual connotation (i.e. orgasm, the "little death"). Thus, the subject constantly attempts to transgress the prohibitions imposed on his enjoyment, to go beyond the pleasure principle, yet the result of this transgression is not necessarily more pleasure but pain, whereby *jouissance* also recognizes the unattainability of this pleasure and thus contains an element of suffering. A work of art may be defined as having a surplus of meaning, and therein lies its value, yet Lacan's concept of *surplus-jouissance* (*plus-de-jouir*), inspired by Marx's concept of surplus-value, argues that the *objet petit a* has no use or exchange value yet persists for the mere sake of *jouissance*. In this sense, it is like the *agalma*, both an offering and a wish. Indeed, as Deleuze and Guattari word it, "*jouissance* is impossible, but impossible *jouissance* is inscribed in desire,"[356] such that life itself is a condition of trying to abolish the condition of lacking (*manqué*), yet the condition of life and the impossibility of fulfilment is "lack of enjoyment" because the true object of desire is unattainable, such that, perhaps evoking the futile labours of Sisyphus, and his punishment for chronic deceitfulness, life is "a lack to be enjoyed" (*manqué-à-jourir*) whereby *jouissance* must always mean union with a substitute object, hence the annulment of the constitutionally split subject, where either the subject or the object, one of the necessary terms, is always missing.[357] However, there is a significant difference between the appurtenances of the *étui* and the desirous objects of the *agalma* and that is one of possession; the *étui* is to be collected whereas the *agalma* is an offering, a difference that is reflected in the uncertain nature of art itself.

The movie palaces can be described as *étui* in their design and *agalma* in the content of their films. Benjamin will write that they offered an escape from reality, a haven that provides the stimulus to intoxication and dream.[358] Part market place and part dream-world, the movie palace, just like the arcades, merges private space and public space, concrete social reality and optical illusion.[359] In a definition that sounds like the essence of cinema itself, Benjamin pursued the dialectical nature of the dreaming collective, one that evolved, a "double-dreaming," as Buck-Morss words it:

> on the one hand, because of its distracted dreaming state, and on the other, because it was unconscious of itself, composed of atomized individuals, consumers who imagined their commodity dream-world to be uniquely personal (despite all objective evidence to the contrary), and who experienced their membership in the collectivity only in an isolated, alienating sense, as an anonymous component in the crowd.[360]

Benjamin notes that the difficulties caused by photography for traditional aesthetics are "child's play" compared to the difficulties presented by film. In reference to Abel Gance, the French director of the 1927 epic film *Napoleon*, Benjamin will recognize that "all legends, all mythologies, and all myths, all the founders of religions, indeed, all religions... await their celluloid resurrection, and the heroes are pressing at the gates."[361] Benjamin recognizes that this invites a "comprehensive liquidation" of myth, yet, when Gance compares film to hieroglyphs, it also marks the beginning of a new language: "by a remarkable regression, we have come back to the level of expression of the Egyptians... Pictorial language has not yet matured because our eyes have not yet adjusted to it. There is as yet insufficient respect for, insufficient cult of, what is expresses."[362] Although there may now be a cult of images, as Baudelaire feared, these are only the visual constructions of "truth" as representation, when more importantly, it may be that the technology of reflection has created a new language, requiring a temple grammar, namely that which allows one to make their way through its symbols and meanings, whereby we may discover that which is essence.

If we return to the concept of the "extension of the existing" as found in the Egyptian tableaux, and in terms of the *subjectum,* as noted earlier, understood as "ground," as that-which-lies-before, which includes the action of "that which gathers everything onto itself," such that man intends to have everything brought and placed before him, so we should recognize Deleuze's claim that "to ground is to determine," and further, "to ground is always to ground representation."[363] However, Deleuze also maintains that

> to ground is to determine the indeterminate, but this is not a simple operation. When determination as such occurs, it does not simply provide a form or impart form to a given matter on the basis of the categories. Something of the ground rises to the surface, without assuming any form but, rather insinuating itself between the forms; a formless base, an autonomous and faceless existence.[364]

The form is the mask, which is both the face and the faceless, which Deleuze will compare to Nietzsche's *Zarathustra*, which is both philosophy and theatre, and his song of Ariadne,[365] where the actor must play the role of the young woman, whose mask is laid over the mask of a repugnant old man.[366] The modern work of art, insinuating itself between the forms, is where nothing is fixed, a labyrinth without the thread, where ground is determined by difference, leaving "the domain of representation in order to become 'experience'."[367]

Ur-history: One-time-ness

In the fall of 1938, when cinema was entering its fifth decade, Benjamin was starting *The Arcades Project*. Inspired by Louis Aragon's Surrealist narrative *Le Paysan de Paris* (1927), and its defense of the small arcade shop owners and the *flâneur* against the Haussmannization of Paris, as well as inspired by the juxtapositions and synthesis of meaning found in Soviet cinematic montage, Benjamin set out to construct an "ur--history" of modernity through dialectical images, which suggests not only the notion of a history within history, of a second nature within the first, but also the idea that the modern is archaic, where the present construction of our social reality is infused by constructions from the past.

Seeking funding, Benjamin submitted the first three chapters for his book on Baudelaire to the Institute for Social Research, only to have his work rejected by Adorno: "Your study is located at the crossroads of magic and positivism. That spot is bewitched. Only theory could break the spell."[368] Adorno singled out Benjamin's suggestion that "each epoch dreams the one to follow," which makes all the motifs of the theory of the dialectical image open to criticism because it places the dialectical image in the collective consciousness. In Adorno's view, the concept of the collective dream had become "disenchanted and commonplace,"[369] besides which the subjective nature of dreams forfeits any kind of objective authority. Dreaming is outside the bounds of material experience and those phenomena that are contingent, concrete and particular. A dreaming collective also erases the whole idea of difference between classes.

In short, Adorno considers Benjamin's version of the dialectical image, both in photography and film, as the simple and random juxtaposition of contradictory elements, and that any formulation that the new is permeated with the old is merely regression, and therefore, without concrete reflection and critical argumentation, the dialectical image will remain "*undialectical.*"[370] If each epoch did indeed dream the one to follow, then, for the modern epoch, reification is the residue of dreams. To rectify this, Adorno suggests incorporating a complementary formulation where "each epoch dreams of itself as annihilated by catastrophes."[371] Instead of the reified world of utopian dream-images, it would be its obverse, the nineteenth century as a phantasmagoria-filled transition to hell. Rather than a dreaming subject as collective, it would be its dialectical opposite, mass alienation. The only Saint-Simonian conception of utopia to be found in a commodified world of convention, where production forces rule the earth, is in the very absence of utopia.[372]

Benjamin may have intended his collective dream as more of a gesture toward the proletariat rather than a regression to Jungian psychology, but it did skew the balance of the dialectical image in favour of the antirational. Adorno regards this as a violation of their joint commitment to demythification, which must present the necessary correlative to the antirational tendency and the return to myth caused by the disenchantment of the world through secularization. Adorno reminds Benjamin that, if anything, they must polarize and dissolve false consciousness dialectically and "not to galvanize it as a pictorial correlative of the commodity character."[373]

For Benjamin, as we have noted, the images that have assembled around the arcades exhibit a peculiar kind of ambiguity that indicate the transformative social relations and products that are unique to this epoch, where he characterized these not-yet-fully-commodified images as that of dialectics at a standstill. Adorno argues that this ambiguity is not the translation of the dialectic into image, but only the trace of that image, which itself still needs to be made dialectical by theory. Brecht put it this way: "The situation is complicated by the fact that less than ever does the mere reflection of reality reveal anything about reality. A photograph of the Krupp works or the AEG tells us next to nothing about these institutions."[374]

Adorno's modernism and his interest in Freudian psychoanalysis would support the attempt to apprehend dreams and then make them accessible to conscious, rational understanding.[375] Surrealism, however, collects the elements of dreams but without liquidating them. Surrealistic images would be more appropriate for pornography, where any attempts at interpretation were better suited to "ready-made categories, like the Oedipus complex," that were imposed "mechanically from the outside."[376] Adorno's hostility may be directed toward visual constructions themselves, a hostility that will carry over to his polemics on the Hollywood cinema, particularly when he claims that the bourgeois had reduced art to the merely agreeable and audiences find pleasure in the pornographic and the "culinary."[377] Fredric Jameson will argue that the visual image itself is essentially pornographic, and pornographic films are only "the potentiation of films in general, which ask us to stare at the world as though it were a naked body."[378] In which case, visual constructions may be wish fulfilling as Benjamin claimed, where all is revealed through the image, although less in terms of residual culture and more in the realization of repressed needs and desires. Therefore, visual constructions are alienating, in line with Adorno's position, because of the inability of the viewer to realize those on-screen desires which are merely a function of attracting the viewer's gaze to the fetishized commodity. In effect, the consumers of today's mass art are simply commodity fetishists alienated from the products of their labour, the "temple slaves,"[379] as Adorno calls them, worshipping fetishized cultural commodities as idols. This implies not only the commodification of culture, but the culturalization of commodities.

Adorno is also critical of Benjamin's notion of a nineteenth-century collective subject and its relation to the future as utopia, which would seem to promote the myth of historical progress, exactly what he and Benjamin were trying to dissolve dialectically. If history is constructed backwards by the dominant culture, as both Adorno and Benjamin believed, then history is only glorified as a higher truth in order to justify the suffering imposed upon individuals and society along the way. In Adorno's view, history is a construction in the present that incorporates its own reconstruction of the past, while Benjamin's view is that the reconstruction of the present reveals the constructions of the past. In either case, present history, and perhaps modern cinema, is only the chronicle of its own disintegration.

For Adorno, the lie of present history demands incorporating a dialectical consideration of both history through nature, which referred to the concrete, mortal and transitory history of the individual, and history through natural matter, which incorporates the world history outside of human control and not yet penetrated by reason. Both of these histories, the individual and the world, determine each other. For Benjamin, the theme of the allegorical in history, found in the form of ruins and detritus, expressed "the decay and suffering of 'first nature'."[380] In a time of historical decay like the present, rather than a Lukácsian return to lost classicism, the allegorical offered more meaning, where ideas themselves have turned into allegorical "images." Thus, Benjamin looks for clues in the dialectical image, writing that when an era crumbles, "history breaks down into images, not into stories."[381] Adorno, looking perhaps more to the social and behavioural gaps and ruptures rather than the material ruins and detritus, found in the moments of transitoriness, where history and nature become sublated, "the irreversible one-time-ness of the historical fact."[382] In our present situation, we have only the semblance of reconciliation because the level of productive forces is such that we could conceivably have paradise in the here and now, and at the same time, we are constantly confronted with the possibility of total catastrophe.[383] We may see a confluence, where the awareness of the one-time-ness of the historical may very well have coalesced into the modern sense of social reality, to borrow a term from Marshall McLuhan, as "all-at-onceness."[384]

Despite Adorno's dismissal of the collective dream and the re-mythification of the world, Benjamin continued to seek the redemption of mythification. It would be through the technological reproductions of the image-making culture that we are reintroduced to the natural world, thus demanding a reconceptualization of the relationship between culture and nature. For Benjamin, the new urban-industrial world had become fully re-enchanted, as in the ur-forests of another era, where we must go out and search for meaning because myth was alive and everywhere. Indeed, the passages of *The Arcades Project* suggest the seeking of an Ariadne's thread to find our way through the dreaded and dreamed modern landscape and its labyrinthine nature, where one must be always be wary of the Minotaur that may be imprisoned at its center.

Logic of disintegration: Negative dialectic

Adorno believed that a redemptive mass art was unattainable, given the nature of the industrial conditions of production that governed what he called the "culture industry." Not unlike Nietzsche's concerns over creeping mediocrity and his concept of the value-creating *Übermensch*, the poet and warrior who is the antithesis of the Last Man (*der letzte Mensch*),[385] so Adorno will maintain that revolutionary rupture must be supported through intellectual endeavour. In particular, a process of demythification demands a logic of disintegration through the active re-functioning of traditional and existing cultural forms. Consequently, Adorno will borrow the term *Gedichte* to refer to an artistic inversion, his "negative dialectic" in response to Enlightenment idealism. The dialectical method was the "road to truth,"[386] as Lukács called it, and its truth-value did not depend on dogma or political effect, but to be effective it did require, as Adorno would demand of Benjamin, an extrapolation to extremes. The purpose of this technique of dialectical juxtaposition was not only to discover the similarities in opposites as well as their connecting links, but, rather than eliminating contradictions, to illuminate truth itself as contradictory.[387]

Instead of a harmonious totality or synthesis, therefore, Adorno saw no possibility of an argument coming to rest at an unequivocal conclusion. Reason and reality did not necessarily coincide, nor did concept and reality, instead each was affirmed by their non-identity, a principle that would become the basis for Adorno's methodology. His rejection of any closed systems, plus his insistence that reality was fragmentary, supported the idea that, "reason is entitled to a home in the world, but the world is just that: a home; it is not totality."[388] The rejection of any pretensions to totality would lead Adorno to write in *Minima Moralia* (1951), that "the whole is the false,"[389] such that the utopian hope for the future was better expressed through art than philosophy. However, rather than a return to past cultural forms, and the promised return to lost Paradise, which in itself marked the decaying form of bourgeois thinking, Adorno sought the liquidation of idealism, a demythification, which demanded its own "logic of disintegration,"[390] hence, a negative dialectic.

Adorno is committed to the destruction of dogmatic constructions and replacing them with theories grounded in empirical experience, and yet he could still approve of how Benjamin's interpretation allowed the most common objects to release a significance that dissolved their reified appearance. Benjamin's mystical impulse suggests that the subject needs to go into the congealed object where phenomena have a voice of their own. This amounts to a kind of archaeology that exposes the strangeness of an object. In this sense, physical matter has its own existence, living and growing old and decaying, just as do ideas, theories, concepts, novels, and films, meaning that they are not mere subjectivity, and therefore contain a locus of truth. Nonetheless, although Adorno agreed that there is meaning to be found within objects, and the possibility of *ars inveniendi*, where all things have their hidden meanings and all cultural forms are a way to discover meaning, yet he will insist that to recognize those meanings we must first penetrate the phenomena by making their truth cognitively accessible, which requires intellectual labour rather than metaphysical magic. For Adorno, there is no ultimate meaning, as Buck-Morss notes, "no affirmation, no 'closing cadence'. The contradictions are unravelled; they are not resolved."[391]

Truth, therefore, may indeed lie in the material object, but it needs the rational subject to release the truth that it contains. On the other hand, Adorno would agree that this process also involved fantasy as an expression of the essence, those things beyond recall, but the interpretation still demanded intellectual labour. If the construction of meaning is undialectical in its positivism (direct observation), or remains metaphysical in its promise of redemption, without the exactness of critical distance and analysis, as Adorno viewed Benjamin's uncritical acceptance of film, and its reception by the viewer in a state of distraction (*Zerstreuung*),[392] then its meanings would not be crystallized and its constructions merely fantasy, serving only as diversion or narcotic entertainment. In other words, because social contradictions have not been reconciled in reality, the utopian harmony of art must always maintain an element of protest in order to be, to use Lukács's term, creatively polemical. If anything, there has been a regression in interpretation and the demands of intellectual labour, of "degeneration," a symptom of reified consciousness. Instead of cultural forms being re-functioned to explode reified forms, the opposite has happened; mass culture has only reinforced reified forms, which in turn has led to the organization of the mass audience, and consequently to the liquidation of the individual.

According to Adorno, Benjamin once wrote that there is no redemption for art, and so art turns against art.[393] Indeed, for Adorno, art can no longer be a refuge for truth, and in the long term it will merely represent a flight into illusion, even if it does have a dialectic force.[394] Adorno maintained that only when the work of art can escape its commodity character and its false idealism that it has the potential to make a proper political intervention. Therefore, Adorno's support of the intellectual labour necessary to support the construction of consciousness of the proletariat in order to cause an explosion of reified forms is also in line with a refunctioning of aesthetic forms, which will recall Brecht's "distancing gesture" of his epic theatre,[395] and Benjamin's attempts to expose the commodity that is the object in its veil of reification,[396] as well as Adorno's claim that the task of a work of art that is truly committed must strip away the artistic conjuring that is content to be a fetish and refuse to become "an idle pastime for those who would like to sleep through the deluge that threatens them, in an apoliticism that is in fact deeply political."[397] However, just as Odysseus is tied to the mast when he hears the Sirens, unable to free himself, succumbing but not succumbing to the Siren's song, so Adorno believes that art can only awaken the futile hope for redemption.[398] Hence, while the work of art awakens the hope of redemption, its aesthetic a special object of pleasure, it is absorbed by an immobilized audience, where "aesthetic contemplation remains disinterested – just as, according to Freud, dreams require the motor paralysis of sleep to enable otherwise repressed desires to express themselves."[399]

However, the danger may be that the dialectic itself becomes the first principle, "*prima dialectica*,"[400] as Adorno himself understood and warned against. Buck-Morss will argue, just as the dynamics of Arnold Schoenberg's music was "brought to a standstill,"[401] so negative dialectics may have brought philosophy to a standstill, an accusation that will be aimed at Adorno from the New Left of the 1960s and their accusation that Adorno was taking critical theory into a dead end. Buck-Morss will also question whether the perpetual motion of Adorno's arguments go anywhere: did they lead out of the bourgeois *intérieur*, or did they "simply hang suspended within it like the new art form of mobiles?"[402] It is not an insignificant personal characteristic, Buck-Morss notes, that Adorno himself was not much of a traveller, although he spent the war years exiled in the U.S., and that his life journey may have been lived through the written text. This statement recalls Lukács when he imagined the intelligentsia, Adorno in particular, taking up residence in the "Grand Hotel Abyss."[403] Adorno's position has been characterized as aestheticized resignation,[404] and indeed Buck-Morss concludes with a quote from Adorno himself: "For a man who no longer has a homeland, writing becomes a place to live."[405]

Medusa's shield: Troy of the dream

In his own concerns for the liquidation of the individual subject through the mass culture, Kracauer will claim that "man no longer knows what reality is – hence, film must serve for the redemption of physical reality," and yet he will also call for a redemption from the cinema and its Roman circus-like "palaces of distraction."[406] Lukács had claimed that only a truly "seen reality" may pierce the veil of illusion, which may be found in some new form of artistic creation, and Kracauer will make the same claim, nominating the cinema as the new form, and so, paradoxically, he states that society can only change when we move closer to the mass ornament, not further away. Indeed, the human being who is not already impugned by contemporary thinking no longer exists, therefore, instead of ignoring the proper historical context or fleeing from its reality,

> the process leads directly through the centre of the mass ornament, not away from it. It can move forward only when thinking circumscribes nature and produces man as he is constituted by reason. Then society will change. Then, too, the mass ornament will fade away and human life itself will adopt traits of that ornament into which it develops, through its confrontation with truth, in fairy tales.[407]

Thus, Kracauer approaches the cinema in terms that recall Benjamin's view of Kafka. In the meantime, Kracauer argues that "instead of guiding people beyond themselves, the mystery slips between the masks; instead of penetrating the shells of the human, it is the veil that surrounds everything human; instead of confronting man with the question of the provisional, it paralyzes the questioning that gives access to the realm of provisionality."[408] However, this provisionality does not negate the potential of the image-making culture. Indeed, the etymological source of the word "screen" is the old German *scirm*, defined by Elsaesser and Hagener as that which acts like a shield to protect us from enemies or adverse influences (heat, cold, insects), keeping us at a safe distance, but also denoting an arrangement that divides a space, hiding something yet bringing something closer.[409] Heidegger claimed that memory is the gathering of thought,[410] and similarly we might claim a similar purpose in the cinema screen, which is a gathering of light in technical terms, and a gathering of viewers in a societal sense, thus a profound component in the interpretation of events, suggesting a process of actualization. Although Elsaesser and Hagener are referring to the cinematic screen, Deleuze could be as well when he states, "events are produced in a chaos, in a chaotic multiplicity, but only under the condition that a sort of screen intervenes."[411] Thus, the screen becomes an intervention writ large, finding meaning in a world that would otherwise seem random, thereby serving as the means for something rather than nothing to emerge from chaos, which is in itself an abstraction realized by the screen itself. In other words, the screen is a way to make something issue from chaos, *"even if this something differs only slightly."*[412] Thus, by its very existence, the asymptotic aspects of the screen defines chaos, because chaos would not exist without the abstractions of the screen to reference it. Consequently, Deleuze is able to claim, "Systems in which different relates to different through difference itself are systems of simulacra."[413]

In terms of the movie screen, therefore, Kracauer argues that "instead of guiding people beyond themselves, the mystery slips between the masks; instead of penetrating the shells of the human, it is the veil that surrounds everything human; instead of confronting man with the question of the provisional, it paralyzes the questioning that gives access to the realm of provisionality."[414] However, Kracauer does not regard this "slipping between the masks" as something undesirable. In fact, the cinematic screen presents a "disguised quality of existence,"[415] where the mask of the screen can serve as both an offensive and defensive weapon. Not unlike Benjamin's championing of the a actor as a champion who confronts the modern apparatus and retrieves humanity,[416] Kracauer compares the film screen to "Athena's polished shield,"[417] allowing us to engage with those sights which might have blinded us with fear, protecting us from turning to stone, and, like Perseus's decapitation of the Gorgon Medusa, enable us to overcome our fear and strike back. Kracauer will write, "perhaps Perseus' greatest achievement was not to cut off the Medusa's head but to overcome his fears and look at its reflection in his shield. And was it not precisely this feat which permitted him to behead the monster?"[418] Now we can look onto the reflections of horror in order to confront them with new awareness, even debunk them with humor. As such, Kracauer maintains that the mass ornament is abstract and ambivalent, and an end in itself. The reason for this is that the mass ornament is an abstraction, one that serves the mass and not the people.[419]

Kracauer's claim was met with some derision, with critics arguing for the impossibility of representing mass death, the ethical vanishing point of his work.[420] Indeed, just as Adorno derided the "so-called artistic representation of the sheer physical pain of people beaten to the ground" and will argue that the very notion that art should contain a message, or meanings, regardless of whether or not it is politically radical, because the cinema already contains an accommodation to the world, such that the contention of a harmonious totality is merely false appeasement and that rationality itself initiates a mechanism of control. Thus, cinema is an institution. In which case, rather than Heidegger's gathering of memory, the gathering of recollection, there is instead the unquestioning subject and a collective amnesia.[421] Russell Jacoby wrote, "When a society starts to lose its memory, it starts to lose contact with its own mind."[422] However, the important point may be that there is indeed a collective mind that is capable of a collective amnesia and that the mass culture of the cinema is its means of a collective constitutive subjectivity. In which case, rather than the self-critical or reflective societal subject, there is, in Heidegger's terms, the apophantic subject, one that is organized by the mass audience and succumbs to the assertions of the hegemonic.[423]

The danger of forgetting is that there will be a relapse, one that Adorno argues against in his support of an education after Auschwitz, where the bonds of conviction are entered upon and imposed upon the well-meaning citizen, when what is called for is an understanding of the principles of fair play and openness, and a willingness (rather than will) to stand firm, resisting the obscuration of the technological veil and the reification of social consciousness.[424] Similarly, in the apophantic sense, as noted by Evernden, it is the "unquestioned beliefs [that] are the real authorities of culture."[425] Consequently, it is important that when "an individual can express what is undeniably real to him without invoking any authority beyond his own experience, he is transcending the belief systems of his culture."[426] Therefore, the principle of autonomy would demand reflective disclosure, where the subject is self-critical, but then there would need to be a second order of disclosure, one that is critical of society itself.

For his part, as noted earlier, Benjamin will look to Charles Fourier and to the Harmoniums, the collective inspired by children's play as "the utopian model for emancipated activity."[427] Here he finds elements of a classless society, where morality becomes superfluous, where, as noted earlier, "the utopia that has left its trace in a thousand configurations of life, from enduring edifices to passing fashion," which is also one whose "secret cue is the advent of machines."[428] Thus, Benjamin found in the consciousness of children an unspoiled creative spontaneity, perhaps the only surviving vestige of un-reified consciousness before bourgeois education manages to badger it out of existence, as well as the redemption of this creative spontaneity in a new cultural form, perhaps found in modern visual culture. This point is crucial in that it represents the essential connection between perception and action that distinguishes revolutionary consciousness, whereby, and most importantly, the child can do something an adult cannot, to discover the new anew.[429]

If we return to Kafka looking to fairy tales and myth as a means of rescue, Benjamin offers the example of Odysseus who "was so full of guile, was such a fox, that not even the goddess of fate could pierce his armour," and who "stands at the dividing line between myth and fairy tale," where "reason and cunning have inserted little tricks into myths; their forces cease to be invincible."[430] Thus, meaning slips between the masks, marking the liminal space where meaning is found. Indeed, Kafka begins his story *The Silence of the Sirens* (*Das Schweigen der Sirenen*, 1931) where the sirens are silent: "an even more terrible weapon than their song... their silence."[431] Odysseus may have noticed, may have understood that he was out of his depth, but he was also cunning, using the imagined song as a sort of shield. Just as in the ancient tableau of the Battle of Kadesh, the work of mourning where the dead are honoured by not depicting them, where there is only an emptiness, which offers no token of hope, and yet is the only way out of the bound domain of objectification, of breaking through the fraud of constitutive subjectivity, and the way must be accessed through silence. Therefore, it is not the "outside" visual constructions of the image-making culture, the mass ornament with all its appurtenances, but "inside" the dialectical images and their formation in the mind where the real forces of change lay waiting. In *The Arcades Project*, Benjamin will write that Odysseus the Cunning marks the threshold, where "the coming awakening stands like the wooden horse of the Greeks in the Troy of the dream."[432]

The mobility of the visible: The consumption of images

The navigable space of the *flâneur*, according to Manovich, represents the paradigmatic shift from the close-knit community of the small-scale traditional society (*Gemeinschaft*) to the anonymous associations of modern society (*Gesellschaft*).[433] The *flâneur* stands on the threshold of belonging, Benjamin writes, neither at home nor entirely alienated, seeking refuge in the crowd, whereby "the city is now a landscape, now a room."[434] As Manovich words it, "the navigable space is thus a subjective space, its architecture responding to the subject's movement and emotion."[435] Manovich will extend the analogy of the anonymous observer who navigates the space of a Parisian crowd to the purely subjective space of the new media, introducing the character who navigates the hyperreal: the "Data Dandy" or "Data Flâneur" (or the American version, the "data cowboy" on the digital frontier). However, where the *flâneur* moved through the physical landscape of the city, the transformation in subjectivity "only happens in the *flâneur*'s perception, but in the case of navigation through a virtual space, the space can literally change, becoming a mirror of the user's subjectivity."[436]

Manovich contends that the poetic may be found in the mass of information technology where, citing Anne Friedberg, there is the possibility of an archaeology of a mode of perception, where "the 'mobilized virtual gaze' combines two conditions: 'a received perception mediated through representation: and travel 'in an imaginary flânerie through an imaginary elsewhere and an imaginary elsewhen'."[437] This process of modernization "is accompanied by a disruption of physical space and matter, a process that privileges interchangeable and mobile signs over original objects and relations."[438] Therefore, despite Benjamin's argument that the dialectical images found in the cinematic form serve a revolutionary purpose by tearing away the ideological veil of reification, it may be that what we are seeing is simply "the new mobility of the visible."[439] Indeed, Benjamin will also note that the cinema is an extension of the photograph, which amounts to an extension of the existing where the conceptual is realized in our reality. In terms of the fungibility of these products, Manovich cites art historian Jonathan Crary, who evokes Marx's *Grundrisse* as well as Deleuze and Guattari's *Anti-Oedipus*: "Modernization is the process by which capitalism uproots and makes mobile that which is grounded, clears away or obliterates that which impedes circulation, and makes exchangeable what is singular."[440] If so, then it is the mobility of the visible that not only allows for the shifting plates of the tectonic world-as-picture, it also supports an ever-changing technology of reflection that creates an aesthetic rendering of life.

In terms of the viewing subject, Kracauer draws a comparison with the hotel lobby and a togetherness that has no meaning, a congregation "based not a relation to God but on a relation to nothing," where "the individual disappears behind the peripheral equality of social masks."[441] Sontag will argue that "cameras define reality in the two ways essential to the workings of an advanced industrial society: as a spectacle (for masses) and as an object of surveillance (for rulers). The production of images also furnishes a ruling ideology. Social change is replaced by a change in images."[442] In which case, "the freedom to consume a plurality of images and goods is equated with freedom itself. The narrowing of free political choice to free economic consumption requires the unlimited production and consumption of images."[443] However, the freedom of choice is only one narrow aspect of freedom, one that privileges novelty rather than real social change, and suggests an assertion that only contributes to unquestioned beliefs as the authorities of culture.

In order to maintain the illusion that we are making progress, there must be an endless array of refinements in the technological process allowing change to be the constant in our representation of reality. For example, photography, Benjamin argued, extends the sphere of commodity exchange, flooding the market with countless images, in particular the picture postcard and advertising. As a result, the impact of image--making, according to Sontag, is to "have in effect de-Platonized our understanding of reality, making it less and less plausible to reflect upon our experience according to the distinction between images and things, between copies and originals."[444] Sontag is describing an image-world that we had come to inhabit and where we could only, at best, maintain an uneasy distinction between the image and the real world by applying a "conservationist remedy," stemming the tide of visual pollution. "If there can be a better way," Sontag concluded, "for the real world to include the one of images, it will require an ecology not only of real things but of images as well."[445] Of course, not only has nothing of the sort happened, but this very notion may be entirely beside the point. Indeed, as noted earlier, the fundamental event of modernity is the conquest of the world-as-picture, and the sign of this event is the magnitude and scope of appearances that accompanies the world-as-picture itself, whereby the technology of reflection has transposed into image the entire world and everything in it, in both the literal and conceptual sense, by both reinforcing and transcending the bound domain of objectification. It is not only a new mobility of the visible through the technology of reflection, it is moving visual thinking, of a mobility of the "perspectival machine" of the individual and collective constitutive subjectivity that has already profoundly changed any perception of reality.

In the next half century, as Manovich notes, the classical screen will change into the dynamic screen, such that this new kind of screen retains all the properties of a classical screen but adds something new in that it can display an image changing over time.[446] Due to its accessibility and reproduction as a "mass art," Benjamin will warn that film is the work of art most susceptible to becoming worn out.[447] Another interpretation may be that cinema is the art most susceptible to losing its avant-garde nature, succumbing to its necessity of being understood by all, sacrificing its critical potential. Nonetheless, as Badiou notes, that is not only the very definition of mass art but also the unique quality of cinema itself, in that it is a synthesis of art and the masses.[448] The collective experience of the cinema, including the filmmakers who learn from each other's work, now offers "the first 'global vernacular' of modern experience."[449] In terms of the Freudian and Lacanian claim that the unconscious is structured like language, where the internalized image-making process of self-reflection has been externalized through the image-making culture, and the unconscious structure of language is made conscious through the living experience of images, so we must not only learn "to think cinema" in terms of a new language, we must understand that we are always-already thinking cinematically.

Notes

1 The *flâneur* is a term borrowed from Charles Baudelaire, "The Painter of Modern Life," *My Heart Laid Bare and Other Prose Writings* (London: Soho Book Company, 1986).

2 The term "phantasmagoria" went from German to English in 1802 and originally applied to optical illusions produced by means such as the magic lantern. Its negative connotations stem from Marx's descriptions of commodity fetishism. See Theodor W. Adorno, *In Search of Wagner*, translated by Rodney Livingston (London: Verso Books, 1985), p.85*n*. Magic lanterns were invented in France in the late 1700s, the age of Romanticism and the Gothic novel, and gained popularity through most of Europe (especially England) in the 19th century, particularly after the invention of the electric arc lamp allowed for brighter projections. The modified lanterns were a form of theatre that projected images, or "magically moving drawings," onto walls, smoke, or semi-transparent screens. They were often used to produce phantasms or "ghosts." For example, projecting an image on a white sheet in a darkened room, then having the sheet move to give the illusion of a ghost.

3 Georges-Eugène Haussmann (1809-1891) was commissioned by Napoleon III to instigate a program of planning reforms in Paris in the 1860s. Sweeping changes made wide "boulevards" of hitherto narrow streets. A new water supply, a gigantic system of sewers, new bridges, the opera house, and other public buildings, the inclusion of outlying districts – his work had destroyed much of the medieval city, transforming 60% of Paris's buildings.

4 Buck-Morss, *The Dialectics of Seeing*, p.66.

5 Benjamin, "Paris, the Capital of the Nineteenth Century," p.36.

6 Ibid., p. 39.

7 Gas lighting began in 1805, followed by the safer and brighter kerosene lamps after 1869, followed by electrical lighting in the 1890s. See Jay, *Downcast Eyes*, p.123.

8 Ibid., p.37.

9 Walter Benjamin, "Paris, Capital of the Nineteenth Century – Exposé of 1939," *The Arcades Project*, translated by Howard Eiland and Kevin McLaughlin, prepared on the basis of the German volume by Rolf Tiedemann (Cambridge MA: The Belknap Press of Harvard University Press, 1999), p.19.

10 Benjamin, "Paris, the Capital of the Nineteenth Century," p.40.

11 Ibid., p.35.

12 Walter Benjamin, *The Writer of Modern Life: Essays on Charles Baudelaire*, edited by Michael W. Jennings (Cambridge MA: Harvard University Press, 2006), p.108. The word "saccadic" is from the French for jerk, *saccade*. The term is used to describe the fast movement of an eye, head or other part of an animal's body or device (as opposed to 'fixation'). The word was coined in the 1880s by French ophthalmologist Louis Émile Javal (1839-1907), who used a mirror on one side of a page to observe eye movement in silent reading, and found that it involves a succession of discontinuous individual movements. An example of the saccadic in art can be found in the Polaroid photograph-montages of David Hockney, such as *The Scrabble Game* (1983). The mapping of eye movements reacting to art (for example, the painting *An Unexpected Visitor* by Ilya Repin 1884) was conducted by the Russian psychologist Alfred Lukyanovich Yarbus (1914-1986). See David Hockney and Paul Joyce. *Hockney on Art – Conversations with Paul Joyce* (London: Little, Brown and Co., 1999). See also Kandel, *The Age of Insight*, p. 283.

13 Ibid., p.108.

14 Guy Debord, *Introduction to a Critique of Urban Geography*, translated by Ken Knabb, Les *Lèvres Nues* #6, September 1955, par.2. Psychogeography, a subfield of geography, was defined in 1955 by Debord as "the study of the precise laws and specific effects of the geographical environment, consciously organized or not, on the emotions and behavior of individuals." He also describes it as "charmingly vague." Guy Debord, *Introduction to a Critique of Urban Geography*, translated by Ken Knabb, Les *Lèvres Nues* #6, September 1955.

15 Ibid., par.11.

16 Lauren Elkin, Flâneuse: *Women walk the City in Paris, New York, Tokyo, Venice and London* (Farrar, Straus and Giroux, 2017).

17 Manovich, *The Language of the New Media*, pp.268-269.

18 Virginia Woolf, "Street Haunting: A London Adventure" (1927), *Virginia Woolf: Selected Essays*, Edited and with an Introduction and Notes by David Bradshaw (Oxford UK: Oxford University Press 2008), p.178.
19 See Guy Debord, *Society of the Spectacle* (Detroit MI: Black & Red, 2000).
20 Guy Debord, "The Commodity as Spectacle," *Media and Cultural Studies: Keyworks*, edited by Meenakshi Gigi Durham and Douglas M. Kellner (Malden MA: Blackwell Publishing, 2006), p.120.
21 Debord, *Introduction to a Critique of Urban Geography*, par.12.
22 Debord, *Society of the Spectacle*, p.i. See also Ludwig Feuerbach, "Preface to the Second Edition" [1843], *The Essence of Christianity* [1841], translated by George Eliot, 1854. [On-line] In terms of sacredness, Foucault will contrast the Christian "hermeneutics of desire" versus the pagan "aesthetics of existence." See Michel Foucault, *The History of Sexuality. Sexuality - Volume I: An Introduction*, translated by Robert Hurley (New York: Vintage Books, 1988).
23 Benjamin, "Paris, the Capital of the Nineteenth Century," p.40. "From the littérateur to the professional conspirator, everyone who belonged to the *bohème* could recognize a bit of himself in the ragpicker. Each person was in a more or less blunted state of revolt against society and faced a more or less precarious future." Benjamin, "The Paris of the Second Empire in Baudelaire," *The Writer of Modern Life*, p.54.
24 Ibid., p.39.
25 Benjamin, "Paris, the Capital of the Nineteenth Century," p.47*n*35.
26 Benjamin, *The Writer of Modern Life*, p.108.
27 Ibid., p.109.
28 Wolfram Eilenberger, *Time of the Magicians: Wittgenstein, Benjamin, Cassirer, Heidegger, and the decade that reinvented philosophy*, Translation by Shaun Whiteside (New York: Penguin 2020), p.290.
29 Benjamin, *The Writer of Modern Life*, p.109.
30 Cutrofello, *Continental Philosophy*, p.267.
31 Adorno, "Commitment," p.188.
32 Theodor W. Adorno, "Education After Auschwitz" (1966), *Critical Models: Interventions and Catchwords* (New York: Columbia University Press, 1998) p.201.
33 Ibid., p.8. The "technological veil," as Adorno and Horkheimer conceived it, is the "excess power which technology as a whole, along with the capital that stands behind it, exercises over every individual thing" so that the world of the commodity, manufactured by mass production and manipulated by mass advertising, comes to be equated with reality. "Reality becomes its own ideology through the spell cast by its faithful duplication. This is how the technological veil and the myth of the positive is woven. If the real becomes an image insofar as in its particularity it becomes as equivalent to the whole as one Ford car to all the others of the same range, then the image on the other hand turns into immediate reality." See Adorno, "The Schema of Mass Culture" (1942), translated by Nicholas Walker, in *The Culture Industry: Selected Essays on Mass Culture*, edited by J. M. Bernstein (London: Routledge, 1991), p.55.
34 Jameson, "Postmodernism, or the Cultural Logic of Late Capitalism," p.505.
35 Ibid., p.505.
36 Ibid., p.505.
37 Lukács, *The Theory of the Novel*, p.64.
38 Gaston Bachelard, *The Poetics of Space* [*La Poétique de l'espace*, 1958], translated by Maria Jolas, with a new Foreward by John R. Stilgoe (Boston MA: Beacon Press, 1994), pp.39-40.
39 Cutrofello, *Continental Philosophy*, p.260.
40 Max Horkheimer and Theodor W. Adorno, "The Culture Industry: Enlightenment as Mass Deception," *Dialectic of Enlightenment: Philosophical Fragments*, translated by John Cumming (New York: The Continuum Publishing Company, 2000), p.121. Adorno defines the "totally administered society" by its tendency to "finish things off" (*fertigmachen*), which supports the reified consciousness through fetishized

products and commodities that lose sight of the goal of a life of human dignity. Thus, rather than resisting the herd instinct, the veil of technology creates a lack of empathy, a "human coldness." Adorno, "Education After Auschwitz," p.200.
41 Horkheimer and Adorno, *Dialectic of Enlightenment*, p.230.
42 Ibid., p.230.
43 Adorno, "Education After Auschwitz," p.199.
44 Martin Jay, *The Dialectical Imagination, The Dialectical Imagination: A History of the Frankfurt School and the Institute of Social Research, 1923-1950* (Berkeley and Los Angeles CA: University of California Press, 1973), p.192.
45 Theodor W. Adorno, "On The Fetish-Character in Music and the Regression of Listening," *Popular Music: Cultural Concepts in Media and Cultural Studies*, edited by Simon Frith (London: Routledge, 2004), p.332.
46 Martin Jay, *Downcast Eyes: The Denigration of Vision in Twentieth-Century French Thought* (Berkeley and Los Angeles, CA: University of California Press, 1994), p. 51. Note: Jay references E.J. Diksterhuis, *The Mechanization of the World Picture*, translated by C. Dikshoorn (Oxford UK: Oxford University Press, 1961).
47 In *Truth and Method*, Gadamer describes essence as the central motif of Platonism, which includes Plato's theory of *anamnesis* (humans possess knowledge from past incarnations, such that learning consists of rediscovering that knowledge within us) combines the mythical idea of remembrance with that of the *logos*, namely the ideality of language, in order to seek the truth of being. Gadamer, "The Ontology of the Work of Art and its Hermeneutical Significance," p.327.
48 Adorno, *Aesthetic Theory*, p.233.
49 Jürgen Habermas, "The Public Sphere: An Encyclopedia Article," *Media and Cultural Studies: Keyworks*, edited by Meenakshi Gigi Durham and Douglas M. Kellner (Malden MA: Blackwell Publishing, 2006), p. 73. See also Jürgen Habermas, *The Structural Transformation of the Public Sphere – An Inquiry into a Category of Bourgeois Society*, translated by Thomas Burger with the assistance of Frederick Lawrence (Cambridge MA: The MIT Press, 1991).
50 Paul Johnson makes an argument that "the human scourge of the twentieth century" was "the professional politician." During the period of postcolonialism, in particular, "if decolonization did possess an ethical principle, it was that political forms were the ultimate standard of value, the only true criteria of statehood," and further, "unless an opinion could be expressed within the vocabulary and terms of reference and assumptions of that mode of discourse, it was not really an opinion at all, and could therefore be ignored or, if necessary, trampled on." Johnson, *A History of the Modern World: From 1917 to the 1990s*, p.510.
51 James Gordon Finlayson, *Habermas: A Very Short Introduction* (Oxford and New York: Oxford University Press, 2005), p.12.
52 Sloterdijk, *Critique of Cynical Reason*, p.5.
53 Ibid., pp.59-60.
54 Ibid., p.20.
55 Ibid., p.39.
56 Ibid., p.44.
57 Jameson, "Postmodernism, or the Cultural Logic of Late Capitalism," p.488.
58 Ibid., p.489.
59 David Hesmondhalgh, *The Cultural Industries* (London: Sage Publications, 2007), p.290.
60 Jean-François Lyotard, "Note on the Meaning of the Word 'Post' and Answering the Question 'What is Postmodernism?'," *Continental Aesthetics: Romanticism to Postmodernism: An Anthology*, edited by Richard Kearney and David Rasmussen (Malden MA: Blackwell Publishers, 2001), p.367.
61 Georg Lukács, "Reification and the Consciousness of the Proletariat," *History and Class Consciousness*, translated by Rodney Livingstone (Cambridge MA: The MIT Press, 1971), p.83.
62 Bürger, *Theory of the Avant-Garde*, p.xliii. The difference between the representation of an everyday incident and an event, or "charged" incident, may be

apparent in the German where in the difference between *enfahrung* (an everyday experience) and *erlebnis* (a 'charged' or exciting experience). "Grounded in the peculiar variability but also interdependence of place, narration and perception, the cinema would then appear to provide *Erlebnis* without *Erfahrung*, a state formerly associated with trauma, but now the very definition of the media event." Thomas Elsaesser, "Between Erlebnis and Erfahrung: Cinema Experience with Benjamin," *Paragraph*, Volume 32, Issue 3 (2009), pp.292-312.

63 Jameson, "Postmodernism, or the Cultural Logic of Late Capitalism," p.488. An example would be the films of Andy Warhol, which entirely reject the standardized Hollywood entertainment films with their narrative clarity and their "'abundance, energy, transparency, community.'" Cousins, *The Story of Film*, p.117. (Cousins is quoting from Richard Dyer's "Entertainment and Utopia," *The Cultural Studies Reader*, edited by Simon During (New York: Routledge, 1999), pp.371-381). Warhol's films include *Blowjob* (1963), an uncut 45-minute close-up of a man's face while he is being fellated, *Empire* (1964), an eight-hour static long shot of the Empire State Building, as well as *Lonesome Cowboys* (1968) and *Blue Movie/Fuck* (1968), which deal with sexuality, homosexuality, and transvestitism, often testing and frequently surpassing the legal limitations of pornographic content. Despite the pornography, or perhaps because of the pornography, they are really about alienation and self-alienation. In the world of music, Warhol will manage *Velvet Underground* from 1965-1967, a band that challenged conventional standards of composition, influenced by experimental composers such as John Cage. Another example would be Warhol's artwork of the mid-60s to 70s, which reveled in the commodification of Hollywood and its movie stars. Similar to his commodified images, such as Brillo boxes, cans of Campbell's Soup, or bottles of Coca-Cola, Warhol presents glossy images of Marilyn Monroe, Elizabeth Taylor or Elvis Presley in spatialized "strips" of identical images, resonating between commodity fetishism and the cinematic assembly line. Warhol boasted that if Picasso can make four thousand masterpieces in a lifetime, then he could reproduce as many in a day. (Kearney, *Poetics of Imagining: From Husserl to Lyotard*, p.171.) Also, Warhol's films, as well as his paintings and photographs of electric chairs and fatal car crashes, reveal the violence of Western society, along with its commodity fetishism and its acquisitiveness, and, therefore, its culture, which by its very nature is unable to offer anything more than surface appearance. See Andy Warhol, *The Philosophy of Andy Warhol: From A to B and back again* (New York: Harcourt Brace Jovanovich, 1975). See also Robert Hughes, *The Shock of the New* (New York: Alfred A. Knopf, 1980).

64 Ibid., p.500. The syntagm is explicit; elements in the syntagmatic dimension are related *in praesentia*. The paradigm is implicit; elements in the paradigmatic dimension are related *in absentia*.

65 Horkheimer and Adorno, "The Culture Industry," p.140.

66 Nicholas Mirzoeff, *An Introduction to Visual Culture* (London: Routledge, 1999), p.10.

67 Slavoj Žižek, *The Plague of Fantasies* (London: Verso, 1997), p.65.

68 Jacques Derrida, *Of Grammatology*, translated by Gayatri Chakravorty Spivak (Baltimore MD: The Johns Hopkins University Press, 1977), pp.154-156. Derrida argues that "it has never been possible to desire the presence 'in person', before this play of substitution and the symbolic experience of auto-affection." Derrida is suggesting that the supplementary masturbation that "plays" between presence and absence is that which allows us to conceive of being present and fulfilled in sexual relations with another at all. According to Derrida, masturbation is "originary" and therefore applies to all sexual relations. Indeed, all erotic relations have their own supplementary aspect whereby we are "not present" to some ephemeral "meaning," but we are always involved in some form of representation. Therefore, for Derrida, even if this substitution does not literally take the form of imagining another in the place of the one you're with, or supplementing the "presence," or acting out a certain role, or faking certain pleasures, such representations and images remain the very conditions of desire and of enjoyment.

69 Deleuze and Guattari, *Anti-Oedipus*, pp.18, 84.

70 Ibid., p.17.
71 Ibid., p.20.
72 Deleuze, *Cinema 1: The Movement-Image*, p.xiv.
73 Ibid., p.xiv.
74 Gilles Deleuze, *Cinema 2: The Time-Image*, translated by Hugh Tomlinson and Robert Galeta (Minneapolis MN: University of Minnesota Press, 2010), p.171.
75 Sianne Ngai, *Ugly Feelings* (Cambridge MA and London: Harvard University Press, 2005), p.7.
76 Ibid., p.334.
77 Ibid., p.7.
78 Ibid., p.9.
79 Ibid., p.261.
80 Ibid., p.8.
81 Ibid., p.263.
82 Ibid., p.263.
83 Bartleby is a character who appears in the 1853 short story *Bartleby, the Scrivener: A Story of Wall Street*, by Herman Melville (1818-1891). When asked by his employer, also the narrator, to do various tasks, his reply is "I would prefer not to." Eventually, having refused everyone and everything, Bartleby is entirely alone and dies. Although this may suggest a kind of resistance, it also suggests an anti-Sisyphian approach to the struggle of life, not, as Camus wrote, where the struggle itself is enough to fill a man's heart, only now the lack of struggle will empty a man's heart.
84 Ngai, *Ugly Feelings*, p.36.
85 Ibid., p.36.
86 Sianne Ngai, *Theory of the Gimmick: Aesthetic Judgement and Capitalist Form* (Cambridge MA: The Belknap Press of Harvard University Press, 2020), p.23.
87 Ibid., p.23.
88 Ibid. p.37.
89 *Mu* is also the term used to refer to the "active" spaces between the branches of a flower arrangement.
90 Cousins, *The Story of Film*, p.130. See also David Bordwell, *Ozu and the Poetics of Cinema* (London: BFI Publishing, 1988).
91 John Sallis, *Chorology: On Beginning in Plato's Timaeus* (Bloomington IN: Indiana University Press, 2020), p.108.
92 Ibid., p.108.
93 Luce Irigiray, *Speculum of the Other Woman* (1974), (Ithaca NY: Cornell University Press, 1987), p.210.
94 Hélène Cixous, "The Laugh of the Medusa" (1975), Translated by Keith Cohen and Paula Cohen, *Signs*, Vol. 1, No. 4 (Summer, 1976), pp.875-893.
95 Julia, Kristeva, *Revolution in Poetic Language* (New York: Columbia University Press, 1984). p.26.
96 John Caputo, "Love among the Deconstructibles: A Response to Gregg Lambert," *Journal for Cultural and Religious Theory*, 5 (2), p.43.
97 See Ondaatje and Murch, The Conversations. See also "Womb Tone" (Walter Murch 2005).
98 Patrick MacCormack. "Julia Kristeva." *Film, Theory and Philosophy: The Key Thinkers*. Edited by Felicity Colman. (Montreal and Kingston:McGill-Queen's University Press, 2010). pp.276-285.
99 Julia Kristeva, "The Subject in Process," Translated by Patrick ffrench. The Tel Quel Project (London and New York: Routlege, 1998), pp.133-178.
100 Ibid., p.161.
101 MacCormack, "Julia Kristeva," p.279.
102 Ibid., p.277.
103 Ibid., p.279.
104 McLuhan, *Understanding Me*, pp.277-298.

105 See Sigmund Freud, "Selections from Three Essays on Sexuality," *The Freud Reader*, Peter Gay (Editor) (New York: W.W. Norton and Company, 1995).
106 Laura Mulvey, "Visual Pleasure and Narrative Cinema." *Media and Cultural Studies: Keyworks,* Edited by Meenakshi Gigi Durham and Douglas M. Kellner. Malden MA: Blackwell Publishing, 2006. Pgs. 342-352.
107 bell hooks, "The Oppositional Gaze: Black Female Spectatorship"(1992), Edited by Amelia Jones. *The Feminism and Visual Cultural Reader* (New York: Routledge, 2003), pp. 94–105.
108 Ibid., pp.94–105.
109 See Bracha Ettinger, *The Matrixial Gaze* (Leeds, UK: Feminist Arts and Histories Network, 1995).
110 See Julia Kristeva, *Desire in Language: A Semiotic Approach to Literature and Art*, Edited by Leon S. Roudiez and translated by Thomas Gora, Alice Jardine, and Leon S. Roudiez (New York: Columbia University Press, 1980.)
111 Julia Kristeva, *Powers of Horror – An Essay of Abjection*, Translated by Leon S. Roudiez (New York: Columbia University Press, 1982), p. 207. The abject may be found in the "New Extremism" in cinema, such as the French *cinema du corps*, where physicality occurs in brutally intimate, visceral terms through conjunctions of sex, blood, flesh and violence, suggesting a cinema turned against itself.
112 Ibid., p.207.
113 Julia Kristeva, "Holbein's Dead Christ," *Black Sun: Depression and Melancholia*, Translated by Leon S. Roudiez (New York: Columbia University Press, 1989), pp.105-138.
114 Ibid., p.107. See Fyodor Dostoevsky, *The Idiot* (1869) (Ware UK: Wordsworth Classics, 1996).
115 Kristeva, "The Subject in Process," p.173.
116 Herbert Marcuse, "The Affirmative Character of Culture," *The Essential Marcuse – Selected Writings of Philosopher and Social Critic Herbert Marcuse,* edited by Andrew Feenberg and William Leiss (Boston MA: Beacon Press, 2007), p.225.
117 Lyotard, *The Differend,* p.181. Nietzsche writes, "*Ressentiment* is the forbidden *in itself* for the invalid – his evil: unfortunately also his most natural inclination. – This as grasped by that profound physiologist Buddha. His 'religion', which one would be better to call a *system of hygiene* so as not to mix it up with such pitiable things as Christianity, makes its effect dependent on victory over *ressentiment*: to free the soul of *that* – first step to recovery." Friedrich Nietzsche, *Ecce Homo – How One Becomes What One Is*, translated with Notes by R.J. Hollingdal, Introduction by Michael Tanner (London: Penguin Books, 1979), p.16.
118 Marcuse, "The Affirmative Character of Culture," p.208.
119 Ibid., p.227.
120 Ibid., p.213. Pierre Bourdieu claims, "Culture also has its titles of nobility – awarded by the educational system – and its pedigrees, measure by seniority in admission to the nobility," such that "A work of art has meaning and interest only for someone who possesses the cultural competence, that is, the code, into which it is encoded." Pierre Bourdieu, "(i) Introduction; (ii) The Aristocracy of Culture," *Media and Cultural Studies: Keyworks*, edited by Meenakshi Gigi Durham and Douglas M. Kellner (Malden MA: Blackwell Publishing, 2006), p.323.
121 Jürgen Habermas, "On Leveling the Genre Distinction between Philosophy and Literature," *Continental Aesthetics: Romanticism to Postmodernism: An Anthology,* edited by Richard Kearney and David Rasmussen (Malden MA: Blackwell Publishers, 2001), p.307.
122 Ibid., p.307.
123 Cutrofello, *Continental Philosophy*, p.277.
124 Ibid., p.308. See also Jürgen Habermas, *The Theory of Communicative Action Volume One: Reason and the Rationalization of Society*, translated by Thomas McCarthy (Boston MA: Beacon Press, 1984), p.328. See also Jürgen Habermas, *The Structural Transformation of the Public Sphere – An Inquiry into a Category of Bourgeois*

Society, translated by Thomas Burger with the assistance of Frederick Lawrence (Cambridge MA: The MIT Press, 1991).
125 Ibid., p.277. See also Hannah Arendt, *The Human Condition* (Chicago IL: The University of Chicago Press, 1998), pp.155-156.
126 Cutrofello, *Continental Philosophy*, p.303. See also Andrew Edgar, *Habermas: The Key Concepts* (New York: Routledge, 2006), pp.133-134.
127 Habermas, "On Leveling the Genre Distinction between Philosophy and Literature," p.307.
128 Cutrofello, *Continental Philosophy*, p.307. See also Habermas, *The Theory of Communicative Action Volume One: Reason and the Rationalization of Society*, pp.398-399.
129 Ibid., p.305.
130 Edgar, *Habermas*, pp.44-45. See also Critchley, *Infinitely Demanding*, pp.23-24.
131 Cutrofello, *Continental Philosophy*, p.307. Habermas argues that modern societies exist in a fragile equilibrium between system and "lifeworld," where the "colonization of the lifeworld," like Adorno's "totally administered society," is the transformation of social systems through instrumental reasoning, intruding into everyday life and relying on impoverished forms of social interaction. See Edgar, *Habermas*, pp.89-91. See also Finlayson, *Habermas: A Very Short Introduction*, pp.56-57.
132 Finlayson, *Habermas: A Very Short Introduction*, p.56.
133 Habermas, "On Leveling the Genre Distinction between Philosophy and Literature," pp.309, 318.
134 Finlayson, *Habermas: A Very Short Introduction*, p.57.
135 Edgar, *Habermas*, p.27.
136 Ibid., p.29.
137 Habermas, "On Leveling the Genre Distinction between Philosophy and Literature," p.308.
138 Simon Glendinning, *Derrida: A Very Short Introduction* (New York: Oxford University Press, 2011), p.55.
139 Habermas, "On Leveling the Genre Distinction between Philosophy and Literature," p.309.
140 Löwy, *Fire Alarm*, p.47.
141 Adorno, *Aesthetic Theory*, p.36
142 Habermas, "On Leveling the Genre Distinction between Philosophy and Literature," p.309.
143 Ibid., p.309.
144 Edgar, *Habermas*, pp.46-47. See also Cutrofello, *Continental Philosophy*, p.308.
145 Ibid., p.318.
146 Habermas, "On Leveling the Genre Distinction between Philosophy and Literature," p.319*n*28. See also Richard Rorty, "Philosophy as a Kind of Writing: An Essay On Derrida," *Consequences of Pragmatism: Essays, 1972-1980* (Minneapolis MI: University of Minnesota Press, 1982), pp.90-109.
147 Buck-Morss, *The Dialectics of Seeing*, p.256.
148 Ibid., p.256.
149 Ibid., pp.259 and 260.
150 Ibid., p.260.
151 Ibid., p.261.
152 Benjamin, "Paris, the Capital of the Nineteenth Century," p.40.
153 Charles Fourier (1772-1837) was a French utopian socialist and philosopher whose social and moral views were considered radical in his lifetime. Fourier believed that a society that cooperated would see an immense improvement in their productivity levels. Workers would be recompensed for their labors according to their contribution, although Fourier, an anti-Semite, believed the Jews should do the lowest forms of labour. Fourier saw such cooperation occurring in communities called *phalanstère* (phalanstery). Modeled after the phalanx, the basic military unit in Ancient Greece, it was a type of building designed for a utopian self-contained community, ideally consisting of 500-2000 people working together for mutual

benefit. Benjamin saw the realization of Fourier's vision in the emerging "city of arcades." Benjamin, "Paris, the Capital of the Nineteenth Century," p.34. Fourier is credited with having originated the word "feminism" in 1837. His concerns for the liberation of passion suggested the possibility of sensual happiness, but his views on education would support Benjamin's view of bourgeois education that "badgered" children into conformity. Buck-Morss, *The Dialectics of Seeing*, p.263.
154 Benjamin, "Paris, the Capital of the Nineteenth Century," p.34.
155 Ibid., p.43.
156 Ibid., p.40.
157 Ibid., pp.41-42.
158 Buck-Morss, *The Dialectics of Seeing*, p.263.
159 Walter Benjamin, *The Arcades Project*, translated by Howard Eiland and Kevin McLaughlin, prepared on the basis of the German volume by Rolf Tiedemann (Cambridge MA: The Belknap Press of Harvard University Press, 1999), p.x.
160 Benjamin, "Exchange with Theodor W. Adorno on the Essay 'Paris, the Capital of the Nineteenth Century'," p.51.
161 Buck-Morss, *The Dialectics of Seeing*, p.261.
162 Ibid., p.273.
163 Walter Benjamin, "Franz Kafka," *Walter Benjamin/Selected Writings. Volume 2, Part 2. 1931-1934*, translated by Rodney Livingstone and Others, edited by Michael W. Jennings, Howard Eiland, and Gary Smith (Cambridge MA: The Belknap Press of Harvard University Press, 1999), p.799. See also Buck-Morss, *The Dialectics of Seeing*, p.273.
164 Cutrofello, *Continental Philosophy*, p.280. See also Benjamin, "The Work of Art in the Age of Its Technological Reproducibility: Second Version," p.107
165 Ibid., p.280.
166 Marcuse, "The Affirmative Character of Culture," p.203.
167 Ibid., p.228.
168 Berman, *All That Is Solid Melts Into Air*, p.22.
169 Cutrofello, *Continental Philosophy*, p.284. See also Arendt, *The Human Condition*, p.128*n*.
170 Hannah Arendt, *On Violence* (New York: Harcourt, Brace, Jovanovich, 1970), p.81-82.
171 Ibid., p.6.
172 Stalin's "Great Purges" started in 1934. In August 1936, after months of preparations by the Soviet secret police, sixteen "Old Bolsheviks" were put on trial, admitting to all sorts of atrocities, and were subsequently executed. This paved the way for the mass arrests and executions of 1937 to 1938. The non-aggression pact with Germany was signed on August 13, 1939. It was both economic and political. Russia would supply food and raw materials to Germany, while Germany would supply manufactured goods. To avoid fighting a war on two fronts, Germany wanted Russia to stand by when it invaded Poland. In return, Germany gave Russia the Baltic states. The pact lasted two years, ending when Germany invaded Russia in 1941. During this time, Soviet cinema suffered through a stagnant period where films were dominated by Socialist Realism. In 1924, after Lenin's death, Stalin wanted cinema to be heroic and optimistic, charting the happy lives of model worker-citizens. Stalin agreed with Lenin that cinema was important but for Stalin it was much more political: "The cinema is the greatest medium of mass agitation. The task is to take it into our hands." The cinema became an extension of Stalinism, where films confirmed the ideology of the state, showing simple narratives centered on heroic workers (whose actors often resembled Stalin). During the purges of the 1930s, Kuleshov, Vertov, Pudovkin and Eisenstein were denounced for formalist error, effectively ending their careers; Vsevolod Meyerhold was shot. Thus, artistic innovation was subverted by political expediency in order to re-establish ideological conformity in the arts. See Cook, *A History of Narrative Film*, pp.167-168.
173 Lisa Fittko, "The Story of Old Benjamin" in Walter Benjamin, *The Arcades Project*. Translated by Howard Eiland and Kevin McLaughlin. Prepared on the basis of

the German volume by Rolf Tiedemann (Cambridge MA: The Belknap Press of Harvard University Press, 1999), pp.946-954.
174 Buck-Morss, *The Origin of Negative Dialectics*, p.24. Adorno wrote of this missed moment in 1966.
175 Ibid., p.140.
176 Siegfried Kracauer (1889-1966) is the author of several important books on film history and theory, including *From Caligari to Hitler: A Psychological History of the German Film* (1947), *Theory of Film: The Redemption of Physical Reality* (1960), and *The Mass Ornament: Weimar Essays* (1963). See also Buck-Morss, *The Origin of Negative Dialectics*, pp.1-23.
177 Ibid., p.141.
178 Ibid., pp.6, 140, 312*n*.
179 Jay, *The Dialectical Imagination*, p.176.
180 Cutrofello, *Continental Philosophy*, p.259.
181 Buck-Morss, *The Origin of Negative Dialectics*, p.140.
182 Benjamin, "Exchange with Theodor W. Adorno on the Essay 'Paris, the Capital of the Nineteenth Century'," p.62.
183 Adorno, "On the Fetish-Character in Music and the Regression of Listening," p.334.
184 Ibid., p.332.
185 Adorno, "Education After Auschwitz," p.204.
186 During World War I, there was a shortage of domestic films in Germany, as well as effective anti-German propaganda films coming from the Allied countries. General Erich Ludendorff ordered the merger of all German production companies, exhibitors, and distributors into a single unit in order to make and market high-quality nationalistic films that would enhance Germany's image at home and abroad. This was the founding of the Universum Film-Aktien Gesellschaft (UFA). After the war ended in German defeat in November 1918, UFA was privatized, and the government sold its share of UFA to the Deutsche Bank and corporations such as Krupp and I.G. Farben. By late 1925, UFA was going under. It was saved by a conglomerate formed with American studios, Paramount and Metro, that led to what would be called the "Parufamet" agreement. However, they ran into financial troubles again, due in part to the increase in American films, and were given a loan by a Prussian financier Dr. Alfred Hugenberg (1865-1951), also a leader of the right-wing German National party. He soon bought out the American partners and became chairman of the newly reformed UFA. In 1933, with Hugenberg's help, it allowed the Nazis to take over the German film industry and UFA was subverted to their political agenda, a factory for light entertainment and propaganda under the direction of Joseph Goebbels. The cinema of the Third Reich can be described as "a programme of stage management of reality, linking entertainment to the most noxious forms of nationalistic propaganda." Geoffrey Nowell-Smith, The Oxford History of World Cinema, p 292.
187 Cook, *A History of Narrative Cinema*, pp.356-357. Hollywood's early romantic comedies and dramas served as "manuals of desires, wishes, dreams, for those wanting to assimilate themselves to mainstream America." As such, Hollywood films "tended to promote the American dream and dominant American myths and ideologies. They taught that money and success were important values; that heterosexual romance, marriage, and family were the proper social forms; that the state, police, and legal system were legitimate sources of power and authority; that violence was justified to destroy any threats to the system; and that American values and institutions were basically sound, benevolent, and beneficial to society as a whole." Douglas M. Kellner, "Culture Industries," *A Companion to Film Theory*, edited by Toby Miller and Robert Stam (Malden MA: Blackwell Publishing, 2004),pp.206 and 212.
188 John Ralston Saul, *The Unconscious Civilization* (Concord ON: House of Anansi Press. 1995), p.62. See also Susan Buck-Morss, *Dreamworld and Catastrophe: The Passing of Mass Utopia in East and West* (Cambridge MA: The MIT Press, 2002), p.149.
189 Kristine Stiles, "Shaved Heads and Marked Bodies: Representations from Cul-

tures of Trauma," *On Violence: A Reader*, Lawrence, Bruce B. and Aisha Karim (Editors) (Durham NC and London: Duke University Press, 2007), p.538.
190 Ibid., p.537.
191 Jane Caputi, "Small Ceremonies: Ritual in *Forrest Gump, Natural Born Killers, Seven*, and *Follow Me Home*," *Mythologies of Violence in Postmodern Media*, edited by Christopher Sharrett (Detroit MI: Wayne State University Press, 1999), p.171.
192 Adorno, "Commitment," p.189.
193 Theodor W. Adorno, *Prisms*, translated by Samuel and Shierry Weber (Cambridge MA: The MIT Press, 1981), p.34. See also Cutrofello, *Continental Philosophy*, p.267.
194 Adorno, "Commitment," p.188.
195 Theodor W. Adorno, *Philosophy of Music* (London: Sheed & Ward, 1973), p.42. In addition to composing, Schoenberg was also a teacher of composition. His twelve-tone technique and atonal experiments will influence the next generation of composers, particularly in America after he moved there in 1933, including those producing the scores for Hollywood, notably Bernard Herrmann and the shower scene in *Psycho* (Alfred Hitchcock, 1960).
196 Adorno, *In Search of Wagner*, p.99.
197 Cutrofello, *Continental Philosophy*, p.267. The quote is from Theodor W. Adorno, "Parataxis: on Hölderlin's Late Poetry" [*Parataxis: Zur späten Lyrik Hölderlins*, 1964], *Notes to Literature Volume Two*, edited by Rolf Tiedemann, translated by Shierry Weber Nicholsen (New York: Columbia University Press, 1992), p.131.
198 Adorno, *Aesthetic Theory*, p.45.
199 Lukács, *The Theory of the Novel*, p.22.
200 Cutrofello, *Continental Philosophy*, p.267.
201 Theodor W. Adorno, "Reconciliation under Duress," *Aesthetics and Politics*, with presentations by Rodney Livingstone, Perry Anderson and Francis Mulhern, afterword by Fredric Jameson (London and New York, Verso, 1980), p.169.
202 Adorno, *Aesthetic Theory*, p.95.
203 Georg Lukács, *The Meaning of Contemporary Realism*, translated from the German by John and Necke Mander (London: Merlin Press, 1963), p.33.
204 Cutrofello, *Continental Philosophy*, p.267. Apotropaic is to use/wear something to ward off or turn away evil spirits or misfortune. Cutrofello uses the term "hermeticism" to describe beautiful sublimity, a term that comprises beliefs and practices whose purpose is the influencing of the world by means of contact with heavenly forces. This may not quite be the original intention, as we do not have contact, perhaps not even the beliefs and practices, only the remnants of the gods and their silence. See also Georgio Agamben, *Remnants of Auschwitz: The Witness and the Archive* (New York: Zone Books, 2002), p.87. See also Slavoj Žižek, *Did Someone Say Totalitarianism?* (London: Verso, 2001), p.146.
205 Ibid., pp.267-268. See also Adorno, "Parataxis: on Hölderlin's Late Poetry," p.131.
206 Leon Battista Alberti, *De pictura* [1435], translated with Introduction and Notes by John R. Spencer (New Haven CT: Yale University Press, 1966), pp.56-58. Alberti, the model for the Renaissance or "universal" man, explains the theory of the accumulation of people, animals, and buildings, which create harmony amongst each other, and, in so doing, serve "the aim of painting to give pleasure, good will and fame to the painter more than riches. If painters will follow this, their painting will hold the eyes and the soul of the observer." Leon Battista Alberti, *De pictura* [1435], translated with Introduction and Notes by John R. Spencer (New Haven CT: Yale University Press, 1966), p.89.
207 John Berger, *Ways of Seeing* (New York: Viking Press, 1972), p.109. In terms of the visual "safe," John Berger is discussing the painting by Thomas Gainsborough, *Mr and Mrs Andrews* (1750). In his examination of the rising popularity of landscape paintings, Berger observes that there is a connection to property relations and capitalist ideology, such that "the model is not so much a framed window open on to the world as a safe let into a wall, a safe into which the visible has been deposited." In terms of traditional oil painting, for example, Berger quotes Lévi-Strauss: "It is this avid and ambitious desire to take possession of the object for the benefit

of the owner or even of the spectator which seems to me to constitute one of the outstandingly original features of the art of Western civilization." Berger, *Ways of Seeing*, p.109. See also Kenneth Clark, *Landscape into Art* (Boston MA: Beacon Press, 1961).

208 Jay, *Downcast Eyes*, p.57.

209 Manovich, *The Language of New Media*, p.105. See also Lev Manovich, "An Archaeology of a Computer Screen" (Kunstforum International, Germany, 1995) [Online].

210 Ibid., p.13.

211 Martin Jay, "Scopic Regimes of Modernity," *Vision and Visuality*, edited by Hal Foster (Seattle WA: Bay Press, 1988), p.8.

212 Jay, *Downcast Eyes*, p.13.

213 The Eastman Kodak Company released the popular Brownie box camera in 1900, selling for one dollar. Their ads read, "You press the button, we do the rest" and "Any school boy or girl can make good pictures." Where the Gutenberg press allowed words to be disseminated into the public sphere, so magazines (*feuilleton*), newspapers and advertising disseminated images, and now the images could be made by the public themselves.

214 Sontag, *On Photography*, p.55. In Sontag's use of the term "picturesque" and Evernden's use of the term "image-gardener," there is a suggestion of landscape architecture, and the 18th century debate whether the beauty of nature was at its most sublime when left to the creator or whether man might 'improve' upon it. The debate caused a divide between landscape architects of the day. Lancelot 'Capability' Brown (1716-1783) and Humphry Repton (1752-1818) were exponents of the new English style of 'improvement', which, Repton considered, "painting and gardening are not the only foundations," but "the artist must possess a competent knowledge of surveying, mechanics, hydraulics, agriculture, botany, and the general principles of architecture." (Roger Turner, *Capability Brown and the Eighteenth-Century English Landscape*, New York: Rizzoli, 1985, p.57) Others such as William Gilpin (1724-1824) and Uvedale Price (1747-1829) were proponents of the "picturesque," which completed Burke's categories of the Sublime and the Beautiful, and thus were descriptions not only of landscape but of a state of mind. This debate appears in Jane Austen's writing. For example, in *Sense and Sensibility*, Edward Farrars declares, "I like a fine prospect, but not on picturesque principles." Jane Austen, *Sense and Sensibility*, edited by Kathleen James-Cavan (Peterborough ON: Broadview Literary Texts, 2001) p.127.
Martin Jay references the quote in a similar context in *Downcast Eyes*, p.141.

215 Neil Evernden, *The Natural Alien* (Toronto ON: University of Toronto Press, 1993), p.97.

216 Benjamin, "The Paris of the Second Empire in Baudelaire," *The Writer of Modern Life*, p.68. See also Buck-Morss, *The Origin of Negative Dialectics*, p.270*n*49. In the 1850s, Baudelaire became interested in photography then denounced it as an art form and advocated for its return to "its real purpose, which is that of being the servant to the sciences and arts." According to Beaudelaire, photography should not encroach upon "the domain of the impalpable and the imaginary." Lois Boe Hyslop, *Baudelaire, Man of His Time* (Boston MA: Yale University Press, 1980) p.35.

217 Jay, *Downcast Eyes*, p.141. Jay adds that the comparison was also made in the 1850s by Victor Fournel, who called the *flâneur* a "mobile and impassioned daguerreotype." Ibid., p.141*n*217.

218 Walter Benjamin, "Little History of Photography," *Walter Benjamin: Selected Writings. Volume 2, Part 2. 1931-1934*, translated by Rodney Livingstone and Others, edited by Michael W. Jennings, Howard Eiland, and Gary Smith (Cambridge MA: The Belknap Press of Harvard University Press, 1999) p.527.

219 Sontag quotes Hart Crane (writing about Alfred Stieglitz in 1923): "Speed is at the bottom of it all, the hundredth of a second caught so precisely that the motion is continued from the picture indefinitely: the moment made eternal." Sontag, *On Photography*, p.65.

220 Evernden, *The Natural Alien*, p.97.

221 Benjamin, "Paris, the Capital of the Nineteenth Century," p.39.
222 Evernden, *The Natural Alien*, p.97. This very human combination of aesthetics and detachment can be found in Dostoevsky's novel *The Brothers Karamazov* [1880]: "No animal could ever be so cruel as a man, so artfully, so artistically cruel." See Jonathan Glover, *Humanity – A Moral History of the Twentieth Century*, New Haven CT: Yale University Press, 2000, p.2. An early example of the estrangement between man and the natural world, as viewed by cinema's mechanical eye, is found in Thomas Edison's 1903 short film, *Electrocuting an Elephant*. A circus elephant, Topsy, killed three trainers in three years. Despite claims of cruelty and abuse on the part of the trainers, Topsy would be executed. The most suitable method was considered to be hanging until the American SPCA protested and a decision was made in favour of electrocution. A crowd of 1500 watched the execution; many more thousands saw Edison's film. The first human execution on film was the 1895 *The Execution of Mary Queen of Scots*, made by Robert Thomae, which used a dummy and trick camera shots to show her decapitation by axe.
223 Manovich, "An Archaelogy of a Computer Screen," par.3. Manovich gives an example in Peter Greenaway's film *The Draughtsman's Contract* (1982) where "the draughtsman, time and again, tries to eliminate all motion, any sign of life, from the scenes he is rendering." Manovich, *The Language of the New Media*, p.105.
224 Manovich, *The Language of New Media*, p.107.
225 Benjamin, "Little History of Photography," p.527.
226 In opposition to the Hollywood classical style was Soviet montage, the Russian process of editing, or montage, after the French word *monter*, to assemble. Due to film stock shortages due to an embargo after the October Revolution of 1917, the Soviets were forced to make "films without celluloid," or to re-edit old films and so discover new meanings, thus developing the art of taking something to pieces and putting it back together again, which was very much in the zeitgeist (for example, cubism). Just as the Bolsheviks attempted to reorder the life of a whole country, establishing the "dictatorship of the Proletariat," so, from 1924 to 1930, a group of young Marxist filmmakers rejected closed romantic realism and became fascinated by the power of editing to create intellectual responses in viewers. Rejecting the continuity and angle/reverse-angle cutting methods, they began to juxtapose shots that had little to do with each other in the conventional terms of story or flow of action. Two of these filmmakers were Lev Kuleshov (1899-1970) and Sergei Eisenstein (1898-1948). See also Tom Gunning, "Moving Away from the Index: Cinema and the Impression of Reality," *A Journal of Feminist Cultural Studies*, Vol. 18, Number 1 (Durham NC, Duke University Press, 2007), pp.29-52.
227 Benjamin, "On Some Motifs in Baudelaire," *The Writer of Modern Life: Essays on Charles Baudelaire*, edited by Michael W. Jennings, translated by Howard Eiland, Edmund Jephcott, Rodney Livingston, and Harry Zohn (Cambridge MA: Harvard University Press, 2006), pp.176, 178.
228 Ibid., p.175.
229 In the 1920s, and contrary to the Hollywood cinema, Eisenstein discarded the individual hero entirely; casting instead non-actors based on their natural expression and physique to represent not one person but a societal group. In so doing, he creates a non-individuated "character," where, for example, the hero is the working class as a collective protagonist. At a time when Western directors portrayed the crowd as a negative image, because crowds run counter to the celebration of individualism, Eisenstein glorified the crowd as an organic force.
230 Susan Buck-Morss, *Dreamworld and Catastrophe: The Passing of Mass Utopia in East and West* (Cambridge MA: The MIT Press, 2002), p.148. The term "architectonic" comes from Mikhail Bakhtin (1895-1975), who suggests identity does not belong merely to the individual. In the same way, he suggests modern stories incorporate "heteroglossia," a weave of multiple stories. See Mikhail Bakhtin, "Discourse in the Novel," *The Dialogic Imagination – Four Essays by M.M. Bakhtin*, edited by Michael Holquist, translated by Caryl Emerson and Michael Holquist (Austin TX: University of Texas Press, 1981).

231 Ibid., p.104.
232 Bürger, *Theory of the Avant-Garde*, pp.80-81.
233 Benjamin, "The Work of Art in the Age of Mechanical Reproduction," p.33.
234 Benjamin, "The Work of Art in the Age of Its Technological Reproducibility: Second Version," p.120.
235 Benjamin, "Paris, the Capital of the Nineteenth Century," p.39.
236 Manovich, *The Language of the New Media*, pp.268-269.
237 Benjamin, "Paris, the Capital of the Nineteenth Century," p.39.
238 Béla Balázs worked with Lukács after the Socialists and Communists under Belá Kun had taken power in the Hungarian Republic in November 1918. Lukács had spent the war years in Heidelberg, hence most of his works were written in German, but he returned as deputy commissar for education, which is where Balázs worked with him. After the Romanian invasion of Hungary in 1919, both Lukács and Balázs escaped to Vienna. John Willett, *Art and Politics in the Weimar Period: The New Sobriety, 1917-1933* (New York: Pantheon Books, 1978), pp.47-48.
239 J. Dudley Andrews, *The Major Film Theories: An Introduction* (London and New York: Oxford University Press, 1976), pp.99-101.
240 Béla Balázs, *Theory of the Film: Character and Growth of a New Art*, translated by Edith Bone (London: Dobson, 1952), p.55. See also Andrews, *The Major Film Theories*, p.98.
241 Andrews, *The Major Film* Theories, p.98. The quote is from Balázs, *Theory of the Film*, p.55. See also Fredric Jameson, *The Prison-house of Language* (Boston MA: Princeton University Press, 1972).
242 Deleuze, *Cinema 1: The Movement-Image*, pp.64-65. Deleuze describes the three "avatars" of the movement-image: 1) the "perception-image" is the subjective and indeterminate perception of space, 2) the "action-image" is the perception of the operations of space in time, "the incurving of the universe" where "perceived things tender their unstable facet towards me, at the same time as my delayed reaction, which has become action, learns to use them," and 3) the "affection-image," where, using Bergson's definition of affection as "a kind of motor tendency on a sensible nerve," meaning there is a relationship between affection and movement in general, and between the viewing subject and the face of the other in particular. Ibid., pp.64-66.
243 Elsaesser and Hagener, *Film Theory*, p.60. See also Deleuze, *Cinema 1: The Movement-Image*, p.81.
244 Deleuze and Guattari, *A Thousand Plateaus*, p.171.
245 Ibid.,p.181.
246 Ibid.,p.187.
247 Ngai, *Ugly Feelings*, p.49. See Sylvan Tomkins, *Affect Imagery Consciousness*, Volumes I and II (1962) (New York:Springer Publishing, 2008).
248 See Eve Kosofsky Sedgwick. "Jane Austen and the Masturbating Girl." (Critical Inquiry. Vol. 17. Summer 1991), pp. 818-847.
249 Byung-Chul Han, *Psychopolitics: Neoliberalism and New Technologies of Power*, Translated by Erik Butler (Brooklyn: Verso 2017), p.28.
250 Hua Hsu, "Affect Theory and the New Age of Anxiety: How Lauren Berlant's cultural criticism predicted the Trumping of politics." *The New Yorker* (March 19, 2019), pp.61-65.
251 Ibid., p.65.
252 Ibid., p.65.
253 Mirzoeff, *Introduction to Visual Culture*, p.7. See also W.J.T. Mitchell, *What Do Pictures Want?: The Lives and Loves of Images* (Chicago IL: University of Chicago Press, 2004).
254 Elsaesser and Hagener, *Film Theory*, pp.79-81. The Age of Reflection or Romanticism (1800-1840) was an intellectual movement that originated in Western Europe as a counter-movement to the Enlightenment. The period would include Goethe's "colour wheel" as presented in his *Theory of Colours* (1810). The decline of Romanticism occurred because a new movement, positivism, began to take hold

of the ideals of the intellectuals around 1840 that lasted until about 1880.
255 See the works of E.T.A. Hoffman, Edgar Allen Poe, Robert Louis Stevenson, and Oscar Wilde. This is also fundamental to German Expressionist cinema (1919-1924), such as *Nosferatu, eine Symphonie des Grauens* (F.W. Murnau 1922) and *Das Kabinett des Dr. Caligari* (Robert Wiene 1920). See also Lotte Eisner, *The Haunted Screen: Expressionism in the German Cinema and the Influence of Max Reinhardt* (Berkeley CA: University of California Press, 2008).
256 Ibid., p.63.
257 C. G. Jung, *Two Essays on Analytical Psychology*, translated by R.F.C. Hull (London: Routledge, 1999), p.190.
258 Wolfgang Schirmacher, "Mask, Role, and Identity: The Search for the Inner Person," *Philosophy and Technology Studies Center* (New York: Polytechnic University, 1986), sec.4.
259 Jung, *Two Essays on Analytical Psychology*, p.197.
260 Judith Butler, *Undoing Gender* (New York: Routledge, 2004), p.33.
261 Ibid., p.132.
262 Ibid., pp.135, 145. Arthur Rimbaud would claim in his "*Lettre du voyant*" (1871) to Paul Demany, "*Je suis un autre*" (I am the other). See also R.Bruce Elder, *Dada, Surrealism, and the Cinematic Effect* (Waterloo ON: Wilfred Laurier University Press, 2013) p. 359.
263 Elsaesser and Hagener, *Film Theory*, p.63.
264 Barthes, *Camera Lucida*, p.34.
265 Deleuze, *Cinema 1: The Movement-Image*, pp.87-88. Deleuze and Guattari refer to *Battleship Potemkin* (Sergei Eisenstein 1925), particularly the close-ups of faces in the Odessa Steps sequence, and *The Passion of Joan of Arc* (Carl Theodor Dryer 1928), particularly the expressions of Maria Falconetti in the lead role. Deleuze and Guattari, *A Thousand Plateaus*, pp.176, 184.
266 Deleuze and Guattari, *A Thousand Plateaus*, p.167.
267 Ibid., p.175.
268 Ibid., p.165.
269 Ibid., p.172.
270 Ibid., p.115.
271 Jacques Rancière, *The Future of the Image* (New York: Verso, 2007), p.23.
272 Deleuze and Guattari, *A Thousand Plateaus*, p.177.
273 Ibid., p.181.
274 Deleuze, *Cinema 1: The Movement-Image*, p.96.
275 Werner Hamacher, "(The End of Art with the Mask)," *Hegel After Derrida*, edited by Stuart Barnett (London and New York: Routledge, 1998), p.105.
276 Gilles Deleuze, *Foucault*, translated and edited by Seán Hand (London and New York: Continuum. 2006, p.79.
277 Hamacher, "(The End of Art with the Mask)," pp.129-130.
278 Stuart Hall, "Encoding/Decoding," *Media and Cultural Studies: Keyworks*, edited by Meenakshi Gigi Durham and Douglas M. Kellner (Malden, MA: Blackwell Publishing, 2006), pp.163-173.
279 Ibid., p.168.
280 Ibid., pp.168-169.
281 Ibid., p.169.
282 Ibid., p.163.
283 Ibid., pp.172-173.
284 Jay, *Downcast Eyes*, p.119. See also Benjamin, "On Some Motifs in Baudelaire," p.192.
285 Benjamin, *The Arcades Project*, p.417 [M5,8].
286 Benjamin, "The Paris of the Second Empire in Baudelaire," p.85.
287 Benjamin, "Paris, the Capital of the Nineteenth Century," p.41.
288 Bürger, *Theory of the Avant-Garde*, p.59.
289 Adorno, *Aesthetic Theory*, p.21.
290 Benjamin, "Paris, the Capital of the Nineteenth Century," p.37.
291 Susan Sontag, "The Image-World" (1977), *A Susan Sontag Reader*, introduction

by Elizabeth Hardwick (New York: Farrar, Strauss and Giroux, 1982), p.367.
292 Benjamin, "Paris, the Capital of the Nineteenth Century," p.33.
293 Ibid., p.37.
294 Giorgio Agamben, *Nudities*, translated by David Kishik and Stefan Pedatella, edited by Werner Hamacher (Stanford CA: Stanford University Press, 2011), p.88.
295 Deleuze and Guattari, *Anti-Oedipus*, p.26.
296 Ibid., p.97.
297 Deleuze, *Difference and Repetition*, p.208.
298 Deleuze and Guattari, *Anti-Oedipus*, pp.53, 109.
299 Ibid., p.306.
300 Ibid., p.105.
301 Deleuze, *Difference and Repetition*, p.208.
302 Ibid., p.208.
303 Ibid., p.208.
304 Deleuze and Guattari, *Anti-Oedipus*, p.105.
305 Benjamin, "The Work of Art in the Age of Its Technological Reproducibility: Second Version," p.109.
306 Jay, *Downcast Eyes*, p.47.
307 Ibid., p.49.
308 Bürger, *Theory of the Avant-Garde*, p.69.
309 Sontag, *On Photography*, p.15. See also Mirzoeff, *An Introduction to Visual Culture*, p.73. *Memento mori* is a Latin phrase, "Be mindful of death," a reminder that we all must die. In terms of works of art, Damien Hirst's *For the Love of God* is a sculpture produced in 2007. According to Hirst, the sculpture is a *memento mori*. Costing $23 million to produce, it consists of a platinum cast of an 18th century human skull encrusted with 8,601 diamonds, including a pear-shaped pink diamond located in the forehead that is known as the "Skull Star Diamond." It may serve as an example of the absurdity and morbidity of commodity fetishism taken to an extreme.
310 Ibid., p.74.
311 Ibid., p.70.
312 Benjamin, "The Work of Art in the Age of Its Technological Reproducibility: Second Version," p.108.
313 Max Horkheimer and Theodor W. Adorno, "On the Theory of Ghosts," *The Dialectics of Enlightenment* [1944] (New York: The Continuum Publishing Company, 2000), p.215.
314 Jay, *Downcast Eyes*, p.122.
315 Ibid., p.138.
316 Sontag, *On Photography*, p.69.
317 Jay, *Downcast Eyes*, p.138.
318 As noted earlier, Siegfried Kracauer (1889-1966) was a German-Jewish writer, journalist, sociologist, cultural critic, and film theorist. He has sometimes been associated with the Frankfurt School of critical theory, particularly through his friendships with Benjamin and Adorno. For Kracauer, realism was the most important function of cinema. All art is a battle between form and content, he would claim, and thus the material aesthetic is founded primarily on content and not form. Photography is the first and basic ingredient of cinema, connected to the natural world, hence the world exists as photographed or as it is photographable, and this world is the raw material available to the filmmaker. See Andrews, *The Major Film Theories*, pp.106-133.
319 Benjamin, *The Arcades Project*, p.631 [W7, 4].
320 Siegfried Kracauer, "Photography," *The Mass Ornament* (1963), translated, edited and with an Introduction by Thomas Y. Levin (Cambridge MA: Harvard University Press, 1995), p.61. See also Siegfried Kracauer, "Photography," *Theory of Film: The Redemption of Physical Reality* (1960), with an Introduction by Miriam Bratu Hansen (Princeton NJ: Princeton University Press, 1997), p.xii.
321 Ibid., p.xiii.
322 Benjamin, "Little History of Photography," p.527.

323 Buck-Morss, *The Origin of Negative Dialectics*, p.125.
324 Benjamin, "Paris, the Capital of the Nineteenth Century," p.44.
325 Benjamin, "Little History of Photography," p.518. See also Benjamin, "The Work of Art in the Age of Its Technological Reproducibility: Second Version," p.108.
326 Benjamin, *The Arcades Project*, p.417 [M1,4].
327 Sontag, *On Photography*, p.68.
328 Benjamin, "The Work of Art in the Age of Its Technological Reproducibility: Second Version," p.119.
329 Benjamin, "Little History of Photography," p.510.
330 Benjamin, "Paris, the Capital of the Nineteenth Century," p.42.
331 Deleuze and Guattari, *A Thousand Plateaus*, p.478.
332 Benjamin, "Paris, the Capital of the Nineteenth Century," pp.41, 42. The Paris Commune, March 18 to May 28, 1871, is regarded as the first seizure of power by the working class, although it resulted in a split between anarchists and Marxists. The radical and uncompromising leader of the anarchists was Louis Auguste Blanqui (1805-1881). According to Buck-Morss, his cosmological speculations impressed Benjamin, who "happened to come across a forgotten work, written in prison [...] which, in accents of absolute despair, anticipates Nietzsche's theory of the eternal return." (Buck-Morss, *The Origin of Negative Dialectics*, p.262*n*86) A further note: Benjamin had planned a three-part study as a precursor for *The Arcades Project*, the first was "Paris, the Capital of the Nineteenth Century" (1935), and the second was "The Paris of the Second Empire in Baudelaire" (1938). In the second part, Benjamin wanted to develop the hidden relationship between Blanqui and Baudelaire. Adorno was highly critical of the second essay, suggesting it was undialectical in its application of a kind of Jungian collective unconscious. Jay, *The Dialectical Imagination*, p.207.
333 Patrick Deedes-Vincke, *Paris: The City and its Photographs* (London: Bulfinch Press, Little, Brown and Company, 1992), p.22. See also Kracauer, "Photography," *Theory of Film*, p.6.
334 Jay, *Downcast Eyes*, p.119. Debord on the Haussmannization of Paris: "Historical conditions determine what is considered 'useful'. Baron Haussmann's urban renewal of Paris under the Second Empire, for example, was motivated by the desire to open up broad thoroughfares allowing for the rapid circulation of troops and the use of artillery against insurrections. But from any standpoint other than that of facilitating police control, Haussmann's Paris is a city built by an idiot, full of sound and fury, signifying nothing." Debord, *Introduction to a Critique of Urban Geography*, par.8.
335 Cutrofello, *Continental Philosophy*, p.257.
336 Benjamin, "Paris, the Capital of the Nineteenth Century," p.43.
337 Ibid., p.35.
338 Ibid., p.34. An example would be the *Grand Panorama of a Whaling Voyage Round the World*, created by artists Benjamin Russell and Caleb Purrington in 1848, which was approximately 400 metres long (1295 feet) long and 3 metres high (9 feet). The word "panorama", from the Greek *pan* ("all") and *horama* ("view"), was coined by the Irish painter Robert Barker in 1792 to describe his paintings shown on a cylindrical surface. In 1793, in London's Leicester Square, "The Panorama," the first purpose-built panorama building in the world was erected, and Barker made a fortune. Stephen Oetterman, *The Panorama: History of a Mass Medium* (New York: Zone Books, 1997).
339 Jay, *Downcast Eyes*, p.128. See also Benjamin, "Paris, the Capital of the Nineteenth Century," p.45*n*11. Louis Daguerre apprenticed in theatre design and painting, and was an early inventor of photography (best known for the Daguerrotype process), with Charles-Marie Bouton, who was a former student of the renowned French painter Jacques-Louis David, which also suggests the transition from painting to the new image-making culture. Cook, *A History of Narrative Film*, p.3.
340 Benjamin, "Paris, the Capital of the Nineteenth Century," p.35.
341 Buck-Morss, *Dreamworld and Catastrophe*, pp.149-150.

342 Ibid., p.149.
343 Kracauer, "Cult of Distraction," *The Mass Ornament*, p.323.
344 Freud, *Civilization and its Discontents*, p.13.
345 Kracauer, "Cult of Distraction," *The Mass Ornament*, p.323.
346 André Bazin (1918-1958), a French film critic and theorist, was a co-founder of the influential *Cahiers du Cinéma* ("Cinema notebooks") in 1951, along with Jacques Doniol-Valcroze and Joseph-Marie Lo Duca. Bazin was a major influence on the French New Wave filmmakers of the 1950s and 60s. He edited *Cahiers du Cinéma* until his death at forty from leukemia. See André Bazin, *What Is Cinema? Volume 1*, essays selected and translated by Hugh Gray, foreward by Jean Renoir, new foreward by Dudley Andrews (Berkeley CA: University of California Press, 2005) and *What is Cinema? Volume II*, edited and translated by Hugh Gray (Berkeley CA: University of California Press, 2005).
347 Cesare Zavattini, "Some Ideas on the Cinema," *Vittorio de Sica: Contemporary Perspectives*, edited by Steven Snider and Howard Curle (Toronto ON: University of Toronto Press, 2000), p.51. Cesare Zavattini (1902-1989) was a screenwriter, best known for *Ladri di Biciclette* (*Bicycle Thieves*, Vittorio de Sica 1948), and the theoretical founder of Italian Neorealism. Politically, he was influenced by Antonio Gramsci, particularly in the idea of the cultural hegemonic, as found in Mussolini's *cultura popolare*. Stylistically, Zavattini was influenced by the semidocumentaries, such as Roberto Rossellini *Roma, citta aperta* (*Rome, Open City*, 1945), which used real footage mixed with staged scenes. Zavattini called for an end to contrived plots, professional actors, and wanted to go into the streets to find a contemporary social reality. This 'everyday life' – the new realism - was contrary to the heroic ideal of Fascism. The aim, method and philosophy was fundamentally humanist: to create films where there would be "no gap between life and what is on the screen," to show human life without embellishment and without artifice, to show the "dailiness" of people's lives. Cesare Zavattini, "Some Ideas on the Cinema," *Vittorio De Sica: Contemporary Perspectives*, edited by Howard Curle and Stephen Snyder, translated by Pier Luigi Lanza (Toronto ON: University of Toronto Press, 2000), pp.21-37.
348 Ibid., p.53.
349 Walter Benjamin, "The Storyteller: Observations on the Works of Nikolai Leskov," *Walter Benjamin: Selected Writings - Volume 3, 1935-1938*, translated by Edmund Jephcott, Howard Eiland, and Others, edited by Howard Eiland and Michael W. Jennings (Cambridge MA: The Belknap Press of Harvard University Press, 2002), p.143.
350 Kracauer, "Photography," *The Mass Ornament*, p.51.
351 Ibid., pp.54-55.
352 Benjamin, "Paris, the Capital of the Nineteenth Century," p.39.
353 Benjamin, *The Arcades Project*, p.220 [I4,4].
354 See Jacques Lacan, *Écrits: A Selection*, translated by Alan Sheridan (New York: W.W. Norton & Co., 1978). The "a" in *objet petit a* is for *autre*, the "little other." The *object petit a* is also called "the object cause of desire" or "the unattainable object of desire. In 1957, in his *Seminar Les formations de l'inconscient*, Lacan introduced the concept of *objet petit a* as the imaginary part-object, an element which is imagined as separable from the rest of the body. *Objet petit a* is also defined as the leftover, the remnant left behind by the introduction of the Symbolic into the Real. See Jacques Lacan, *Écrits: A Selection*, translated by Alan Sheridan (New York: W.W. Norton & Co., 1978).
355 Deleuze and Guattari, *A Thousand Plateaus*, p.165.
356 Ibid., p.154.
357 Benjamin, *The Arcades Project*, pp.154, 532*n*10.
358 Ibid., p.216 [I2,6].
359 The Lumière brothers held the first public screenings of their films in 1895 in *Le Salon Indien du Grand Café*. It was on the Champs Elysées in Paris, a large basement with an exotic décor, including pillars, palm plants, gaslights, patterned car-

pets and embroidered drapes. The café's décor is as an extension of the luxurious bourgeois *intérieur*, just as the early movie palaces will be imitations of exotic architectural styles, both designed to make the average person feel like royalty. See Cook, *A History of Narrative Film*, pp.9-11.

360 Buck-Morss, *The Dialectics of Seeing*, p.260.

361 Benjamin, "The Work of Art in the Age of Its Technological Reproducibility: Second Version," p.104.

362 Ibid., pp.104, 109-110.

363 Deleuze, *Difference and Repetition*, pp.272, 274.

364 Ibid., p.275.

365 Ariadne was the daughter of King Minos of Crete. The Athenians had been at war with Crete and were forced to send seven youths and seven young women every year as a tribute to the Minotaur. Theseus was one of those youths. Ariadne, who was in charge of the Labyrinth, fell in love with him, and having obtained the secret to the Labyrinth from its constructor, Daedalus, she disclosed the way out to Theseus, giving him a sword and a ball of thread. In the last part of the Labyrinth, Theseus found the Minotaur and killed him. Since Ariadne had helped him, Theseus had agreed to carry her away to Athens and marry her. They both fled from Crete, but on arriving to the island of Naxos, Theseus deserted her. Ariadne's Thread is the name for solving a problem with multiple apparent means of proceeding - such as a physical maze, a logic puzzle, or an ethical dilemma - through an exhaustive application of logic to all available routes.

366 Ibid., p.9. See also Nietzsche, *Thus Spoke Zarathustra*, pp.306-311.

367 Ibid., p.56.

368 Ibid., p.67. See also Theodor W. Adorno, "Letters to Walter Benjamin," *Aesthetics and Politics*, with presentations by Rodney Livingstone, Perry Anderson and Francis Mulhern, afterword by Fredric Jameson (London: Verso Books, 1980), p.129.

369 Benjamin, "Exchange with Theodor W. Adorno on the Essay 'Paris, the Capital of the Nineteenth Century,'" p.54.

370 Ibid., p.54.

371 Ibid., p.58.

372 Ibid., p.54. Adorno is referring to the followers of Henri de Saint-Simon (1760-1825), considered the founder of French socialism, and whose movement contained elements of messianism.

373 Adorno, "Letters to Walter Benjamin," p.113. See also Buck-Morss, *The Origin of Negative Dialectics*, p.55.

374 Ibid., p.526.

375 Adorno incorporated Freudian psychology in his attack on rationalism in his 1926 *Habilitationsschrift* for his mentor Hans Cornelius, entitled "The Concept of the Unconscious in the Transcendental Theory of the Mind." Adorno was struck by psychoanalysis as a cognitive model, with its goal of "disenchantment" of the unconscious by exposing the inner logic of its manifestations – Freudian slips, dreams, neurotic symptoms – and making them accessible to conscious, rational understanding. Buck-Morss, *The Origin of Negative Dialectics*, pp.17-18.

376 Buck-Morss, *The Origin of Negative Dialectics*, p.128.

377 Adorno, "Commitment," p.193.

378 Mirzoeff, *An Introduction to Visual Culture*, p.10.

379 Adorno, "On The Fetish-Character in Music and the Regression of Listening," p.333.

380 Löwy, *Fire Alarm*, p.56.

381 Ibid., p.68.

382 Ibid., p.57.

383 Adorno, *Aesthetic Theory*, p.33.

384 Marshall McLuhan, *Understanding Me – Lectures and Interviews/Marshall McLuhan*, edited by Stephanie McLuhan and David Staines, with a Foreword by Tom Wolfe (Toronto ON: McClelland & Stewart, 2003), p.129.

385 Nietzsche claimed, "I do not want to be confused with these preachers of equality, not taken for one of them. For justice speaks thus *to me*: 'Men are not

equal'." Nietzsche, *Thus Spoke Zarathustra*, p.124. Adorno wrote, "Understand me correctly. I do not want to preach love. I consider it futile to preach it; no one has the right to preach it since the lack of love, as I have already said, is a lack belonging to *all* people without exception as they exist today. To preach love already presupposes in those to whom one appeals a character structure different from the one that needs to be changed. For the people whom one should love are themselves such that they cannot love, and therefore in turn are not at all that lovable. One of the greatest impulses of Christianity, not immediately identical with its dogma, was to eradicate the coldness that permeates everything. But this attempt failed; surely because it did not reach into the societal order that produces and reproduces that coldness." Adorno, "Education After Auschwitz," p.202.

386 Lukács, *History and Class Consciousness*, p.1.

387 Buck-Morss, *The Origin of Negative Dialectics*, p.100.

388 Ibid., p.5. The quote is from Franz Rosenzweig's *Der Stern der Erlösung* (*The Star of Redemption*, 1920), who reintroduced religious elements into philosophy. See Franz Rosenzweig, *The Star of Redemption*, translated by William W. Hallo (New York: Rinehard and Winston, 1971). See also Siegfried Kracauer, who admired Rosenzweig's work for its designation of "religious" to mean "a practice of life that flourishes on the basis of a real connection to essential truth contents – in this case, those conveyed by the documents of Jewish scripture – and not a theoretical orientation of consciousness or a purely internal religious undertaking like that of the liturgical movement." (Kracauer, *The Mass Ornament*, p.190)

389 Adorno, *Minima Moralia*, p.50. See also Jay, *The Dialectical Imagination*, p.52.

390 Buck-Morss, *The Origin of Negative Dialectics*, p.64.

391 Ibid., p.101.

392 Benjamin, "The Work of Art in the Age of Its Technological Reproducibility: Second Version," p.119.

393 Adorno, *Aesthetic Theory*, p.175.

394 See Wolfgang Schirmacher, "The End of Metaphysics – What does this mean?" *Social Science Information*, Number 23, 3 (1984), pp.603-609.

395 The "distancing gesture" of Brecht's epic theatre is part of his goal of "refunctioning" artistic forms. This stems from Formalist defamiliarization that sought modernist artistic innovation, where ideas could be realized only through an alienation effect, an effect influenced by the Formalistic concept of "making the familiar strange (*ostranenie*), or of 'defamiliarizing' what is normally taken for granted." See Ian Christie, "Formalism and neo-formalism," *The Oxford Guide to Film Studies*, edited by John Hill and Pamela Church Gibson, Consultant Editors Richard Dyer, E. Ann Kaplan, Paul Willemen (New York: Oxford University Press, 1998), p.59. See also Buck-Morss, *The Origin of Negative Dialectics*, p.143.

396 Walter Benjamin, "The Significance of Beautiful Semblance," *Walter Benjamin/Selected Writings. Volume 3, 1935-1938*, translated by Edmund Jephcott, Howard Eiland, and Others, Edited by Howard Eiland and Michael W. Jennings (Cambridge MA: The Belknap Press of Harvard University Press, 2002), p.137.

397 Adorno, "Commitment," p.177.

398 Max Horkheimer and Theodor W. Adorno, "The Concept of Enlightenement," *Dialectic of Enlightenment: Philosophical Fragements* [Original edition: *Dialektick der Aufklärung*. Social Studies Association. 1944.] (New York: The Continuum Publishing Company, 2000), p.27.

399 Cutrofello, *Continental Philosophy*, p.267.

400 Buck-Morss, *The Origin of Negative Dialectics*, p.190. See also Adorno, *Negative Dialectics*, p.154.

401 Ibid., p.190. See also Adorno, *Philosophy of Modern Music*, p.102. In his younger years, Adorno aspired to be a composer and studied music with Alban Berg (1885-1935) in Vienna in 1925. Berg was a student of Schoenberg's and part of Vienna's cultural elite.

402 Ibid., p.190.

403 Lukács, *The Theory of the Novel*, p.22.

404 See Simon Critchley, *The Faith of the Faithless: Experiments in Political Theology* (London: Verso, 2012), p.212.
405 Buck-Morss, *The Origin of Negative Dialectics,* p.190. The quote is from Adorno's *Minima Moralia* (p.87).
406 Kracauer, *The Mass Ornament*, p.85.
407 Ibid., p.86.
408 Ibid., p.184.
409 Elsaesser and Hagener, *Film Theory*, p.38.
410 Heidegger, "What Calls for Thinking?", p.367.
411 Gilles Deleuze, *The Fold: Liebniz and the Baroque*, foreward and translation by Tom Conley (Minneapolis MN: University of Minnesota Press, 1993), p.76.
412 Ibid., p.76.
413 Deleuze, *Difference and Repetition*, p.277.
414 Kracauer, *The Mass Ornament*, p.184.
415 Ibid., p.184.
416 Benjamin, "The Work of Art in the Age of Its Technological Reproducibility," p.111.
417 Siegfried Kracauer, "Film in Our Time," *Theory of Film: The Redemption of Physical Reality* (1960], with an Introduction by Miriam Bratu Hansen (Princeton NJ: Princeton University Press, 1997), p.305.
418 Kracauer, *The Mass Ornament*, p.306. Kracauer offers the example of *Le Sang des betes* (Georges Franju 1949), a documentary on a Paris slaughterhouse that drew comparisons to the Nazi death camps. Another example would be the photomontages of John Heartfield (1891-1968), which Benjamin admired and will reference in *The Arcades Project*. An example of humour would be *The Great Dictator* (Charlie Chaplin 1940). Prior to the release of the film, Chaplin's debunking of Hitler was praised in Benjamin's essay "Hitler's Diminished Masculinity." *Walter Benjamin/Selected Writings. Volume 2, Part 2. 1931-1934*, translated by Rodney Livingstone and Others, edited by Michael W. Jennings, Howard Eiland, and Gary Smith (Cambridge MA: The Belknap Press of Harvard University Press, 1999), pp.792-793.
419 Ibid.,p.76.
420 See Gertrude Koch, *Siegfried Kracauer: An Introduction*, translated by Jeremy Gaines (Princeton NJ: Princeton University Press, 2000). Kracauer was regarded as a naïve realist, but he clarified his views in *Theory of Film* (1960) and *The Mass Ornament* (1963). *The Mass Ornament* is dedicated to Theodor W. Adorno.
421 The unquestioning subject may be found in Germany in the decades after the World War II in what has been called the "brown years," a period of "social amnesia." This collective amnesia contributed to the "brown years" of Nazi rule, known as "*unbewaltige Vergangenheit*" ("unassimilated past"). This situation will be addressed in *Das Neue Kino* movement and the films of Alexander Kluge, Werner Fassbinder, and others. See Cook, *A History of Narrative Film*, pp.582-604.
422 Russell Jacoby, *Social Amnesia: A Critique of Contemporary Psychology from Adler to Laing* (Boston MA: Beacon Press, 1975), p.4. See also Jane Jacobs, *Dark Age Ahead* (Toronto ON: Vintage Classic (Random House Canada), 2004).
423 Apohantic is a measure of the objective and subjective components in any judgement, rather than a verdict of what is true and what is false. Heidegger argues that the apophantic judgement does not obscure the truth, because it is not placing something in front of something else like the traditional verdict, but apprehending the being of an entity in and of itself. Roderick Murray, "Glossary of Terms in *Being and Time*" [On-line].
424 Adorno, *Education After Auschwitz*, p.5. See also Horkheimer and Adorno, *Dialectic of Enlightenment.*, p.27.
425 Evernden, *The Natural Alien*, p.31. The quote is from Robert Combs, *Vision of the Voyage* (Memphis TE: Memphis State University Press, 1978), pp.29-30.
426 Ibid., p.31.
427 Löwy, *Fire Alarm*, p.76.
428 Benjamin, "Paris, the Capital of the Nineteenth Century," *The Writer of Modern Life*, p.32.

429 Buck-Morss, *The Dialectics of Seeing*, pp.263, 274.
430 Benjamin, "Franz Kafka," p.799.
431 Ibid., p.799.
432 Benjamin, *The Arcades Project*, p.492 [K1, 5]. See also Buck-Morss, *The Dialectics of Seeing*, p.461*n*110.
433 Manovich, *The Language of the New Media*, p.269.
434 Benjamin, "Paris, the Capital of the Nineteenth Century," p.40. Also quoted in Manovich, *The Language of the New Media*, p.269.
435 Manovich, *The Language of the New Media*, p.269.
436 Ibid., p.269.
437 Ibid., p.273. Note: The quote is from Anne Friedberg, *Window Shopping: Cinema and the Postmodern* (Berkeley CA: University of California Press, 1993), p.2.
438 Ibid., p.173.
439 Ibid., p.107.
440 Manovich, *The Language of the New Media*, p.173. The quote is from Jonathan Crary, *Techniques of the Observer: On Vision and Modernity in the Nineteenth Century* (Cambridge MA: MIT Press, 1990), p.10.
441 Siegfried Kracauer, "The Hotel Lobby," *The Mass Ornament*, translated, Edited and with an Introduction by Thomas Y. Levin (Cambridge MA: Harvard University Press, 1995), pp.179, 181.
442 Sontag, "The Image-World," p.366.
443 Ibid., p.366.
444 Sontag, *On Photography*, p.179.
445 Ibid., p.180.
446 Manovich, *The Language of New Media*, pp.95-96.
447 Walter Benjamin, "The Theory of Distraction," *Walter Benjamin/Selected Writings. Volume 3, 1935-1938*, translated by Edmund Jephcott, Howard Eiland, and Others, edited by Howard Eiland and Michael W. Jennings (Cambridge MA: The Belknap Press of Harvard University Press, 2002) p.141.
448 Alain Badiou, *Cinema*, texts selected and introduced by Antoine de Baecque, translated by Susan Spitzer (Cambridge UK: Polity Press, 2013), p.208.
449 Buck-Morss, *Dreamworld and Catastrophe*, p.156.

Images and Reflection

The camera-eye view: Penny-in-the-slot meaning

By 1896 all the basic technological principles of film recording and projection were available in existing machines, which, excluding synchronous sound, possessed the same fundamental components as the modern feature film. The speed of snapshots had transferred to the spatialized and equidistant framework of the filmstrip, where the ribbon of frozen photographic moments flowed together to give the illusion of continuous and uninterrupted movement.[1] The series of instantaneous images move consecutively in time, integrating them into a simulacrum of real time and conscious experience. Hence, the movement-image is also a time-image.[2]

The filmstrip appears to restore the flow of time that the snapshot took away, yet it remains a "past-tense medium" animated only by the illusion of movement and immediacy, in other words, its very newness. It is in the filmstrip that Benjamin finds the dialectical structure of film, where the sequential nature suggests the assembly line in terms of both production and consumption, and the movement-time-image contains the unity of past and present.[3] Thus, Benjamin looked to surrealism where "image and sound interpenetrated with automatic precision and such felicity that no chink was left for the penny-in-the-slot called 'meanings'."[4] If non-paradoxical meanings only support the false consciousness and abstract idealism that permeates society, then the cinema produces, in terms noted earlier, a morbid kind of stasis or preservation, newness without real change, the maintenance of the status quo, an endless repetition where always-the-same is served up as novelty and fashion.

In the 1910s, the variable size of the image in the cinema led to a process of "re-centering" and "re-calibration" around the human figure as the norm of spatial relations of scale and proportion.[5] At the same time, the language of cinema was evolving through the intuitive, trial-and-error pursuit of narrative clarity, which included innovations such as continuity cutting, close-ups, parallel editing, expressive lighting, nuanced acting, eye-line matching, reverse angle editing, and the "axis," where the camera is in the middle of the action, matching shots from each "side" of the action. In terms of the organizational aspects of the language of images, this period saw the standardization of production in terms of job description (director, cinematographer, scenario writer, etc.), film length (approximately ninety minutes) and genre (standardized content, which also standardized audience expectations). The standardization of film language known as the Hollywood Classical or Continuous Style (also known as the Industrial Mode of Production or the Industrial Mode of Representation),[6] which might also represent the "domestication" of narrative and form into a hierarchically organized Hollywood system.[7] This mode is also economical, a cinematic form that is reproducible and cost effective, allowing for standardization of both production and narrative, instilling, as Horkheimer and Adorno would call it, "the criterion of efficiency."[8] For their part, the Soviet filmmakers were supported by the belief that cinema would prove central to the construction of Soviet mass society and that fragmentation and reassembly were a means of artistic construction. It follows, therefore, that their focus was on montage, creating meaning through the juxtaposition of images, and thus challenging the indexical nature of film.[9]

As the film language developed, the camera moved its perspective from that of the static viewer/projector and became a non-human eye, detached from any individual human subject, one whose perspective could shift and change. In other words, the spectator may be confined to a seat, or consigned to the front of the screen, but the camera had emancipated its viewpoint. In doing so, the camera assumes the position of the third person, or audience, in viewing the first and second person narrative, an extension of free indirect discourse, the novelistic device first used by 19th century authors such as Jane Austen.[10] Another aspect of free indirect discourse, as noted by Roy Pascal when he discusses Jane Austen's technique, is that it creates a "universalist present," that is, it takes past, present and future, memory and action, and merges them into one narrative.[11] Therefore, the camera point of view is in effect an omniscient narrator, capable of moving from author to character, from description to opinion, and yet, unlike in the novel, the camera, even after the introduction of sound, is limited in that it cannot read the thoughts of its subjects. Consequently, the developments in film language focused on how to reveal the thoughts and emotions of the characters and how to access the thoughts and emotions of the spectator.

The power of cinema, according to Mark Cousins, comes from "the ability of a shot to be about both what it objectively photographs – what is in front of the camera – and about the subjectivity of its maker."[12] The camera-eye view, therefore, can present an objective, third person point of view, yet one that also gives subjective meaning (due to its framing, lighting, film stock, content, juxtaposition, etc.), as found in a first person subjective view, which, despite its nature as an apparatus, allows for "making the camera felt."[13] Therefore, the objective quality of the material and the subjectivity of the filmmaker is the basis for the realization of filmic ideas, an ambivalent connection that maintains an alluring dualistic quality. Pier Paolo Pasolini described this personal-realistic dualism as both "free indirect subjectivity" (*discorso libro indiretto*) and "fourth person singular", a phrase in French philosophy to describe the paradox of something that is personal but also objective and without consciousness."[14] Grammatically, the fourth person singular would be the use of "one," as in "one can see that this is true," an indefinite or generic referent, which also suggests the non-specific yet omniscient perspective of a collective constitutive subjectivity.[15]

The inverse effect of this process, as Martin Jay notes, evoking Foucault, is that there is an important transformation marked by "that larger shift from reading the world as an intelligible text (the 'book of nature') to looking at it as an observable but meaningless object [...] the emblem of the modern epistemological order."[16] Indeed, it is only due to this epochal transformation that the "mechanization of the world picture" could even take place.[17] Consequently, Foucault will ask, with regard to a text, which we would extend to the image as text, what is the text *really* saying underneath what it is *actually* saying?[18] However, looking at the observable but meaningless object would question whether the image-making process itself is capable of revealing any meaning underneath the image, which also suggests the image without thought, or the image that conceals thought through its very "imaging." In any case, the result of this ambivalent epistemological transformation, and its acquisition of the omniscient point of view, is that the flow of images may in fact be a process in the "denarrativization of the ocular,"[19] as noted by Jay, which produces "a bewildering excess of apparent referential or symbolic meaning," and yet, a variation on what Benjamin observed, "without any one-to-one relationship between visual signifier and textual signified, images were increasingly liberated from their storytelling function."[20] In other words, by serving the technology of the technology of reflection and its ability to achieve the illusion of perspective, we have trumped the importance of the viewing subject in favour of the subject depicted, where, in Foucault's words, what the text is really saying is *seen* as what it is actually saying. To put it another way, we may recall Deleuze, as noted earlier, when he claimed that "the subjective illusion is not born of individual consciousness but is an objective or transcendental illusion born out of the conditions of social consciousness in the course of its actualization."[21]

Mirror/screen: The double operation

The cinema screen is different from the natural mirror in that it does not reflect the viewer's face or body. However, the viewer who watches a film is capable of filling this perceptual gap or opaque spot within the artistic construction through their understanding of meaning in the flow of images and sound. Elsaesser and Hagener will argue, evoking Lacan and the mirror-stage, "the look into the mirror of the screen no longer resembles – as was still the case in Balázs - the recognition of a human being *through* another. Rather, what takes place is an act of false recognition or miscognition, as if one were to recognize another as oneself, or conversely, (mis-) perceive oneself *in and as* another."[22] However, it may be in this very difference, the liminal space between the concrete images and their interpretation through self-presencing, an interweaving of consciousness and unconsciousness, where the meaning of the artistic construction is found.

If we consider Rancière's definition of the meaning of representation, we find there are two operations working simultaneously: "an operation of substitution (which places 'before our eyes' what is removed in space or time) and an operation of exhibition (which what is intrinsically hidden from sight, the inner springs motivating character and events, visible)."[23] The aesthetic aspects of this double operation could be explained through the Kantian concepts of the phenomenal realm (the realm of sense experience, linked in time, space and causality) and the noumenal realm (the transcendental world where the object of beauty is justified in itself, "purposiveness without purpose," where Beauty saves both Truth and Goodness).[24] Similarly, in terms that would seem to support realism, Hegel would argue that the aim of art does not lie in its "purely mechanical imitation of what is there, which, in every case can bring to birth only technical *tricks*, not *works*, of art."[25] Thus, the genuine work of art must use both direct and indirect means in order to give expression, remembering, "art's vocation is to unveil the *truth* in the form of sensuous artistic configuration," such that "its end and aim in itself in this very setting forth and unveiling."[26] In other words, art is not simply the depiction of things, just as the purely naturalistic and representational is not sufficient - one of the critiques of the mechanical nature of the image-making process and its technology - but must contain elements of the conceptual in order to give meaning and thus count as a genuine work of art. To this point, Walter Benjamin recalls Goethe when he wrote, "The beautiful is neither the veil nor the veiled object but rather the object *in* its veil," and Benjamin adds, "this is the quintessence of the ancient aesthetic."[27]

The paradoxical simultaneity of self-alienation and communal experience found in the cinematic experience, as noted earlier, is linked to the ambivalent connection and personal-realistic dualism of the camera-eye view itself and the description found in "free indirect subjectivity" and "fourth person singular," that is, the paradox of something that is personal but also objective and without consciousness. In a larger sense, the modern technology of reflection has initiated a "transformation" that has been disseminated into our social reality through the world-as-picture. This amounts to both condition and consequence of the ubiquity of image and the emancipation and mobility of the camera-eye view, as well as the emancipation and mobility of the screen, which, through the new technology, is no longer anchored to any specific location. Therefore, in terms used earlier, the question is whether the first-order aesthetic of the world as image denies the truth content of the world as image, namely the de-objectification which appears in its countering of constitutive subjectivity, but serves instead as a nullification where the accumulation of images does the exact opposite; it objectifies the world as image, which in turn does not dissolve constitutive subjectivity but rather enhances it by dissolving the autonomy of the subject themselves, thereby, through the technology of reflection, turning the subject into its own object.

The baroque moment: Language without a language system

Images, as stated earlier, are not simply retinal stimulation but involve a "field" of perceptions, associations and memory. The process of extending the "field" of images is achieved through identification and projection, aided by the processes of synthesis, autonomy, duality, and similarity, as well as an element of deception (the Lacanian miscognition/

misrecognition). We may now say that this process is "orthopaedic," to use Lacan's term, in that it serves as a crutch in the process of the formation of an integrated sense of self, an integration that is subjective in both individual and communal terms. In ideological terms, therefore, the imago of the self is also the "social cement" of the unconscious, defining oneself within our social reality, as well as defining our social reality. However, in doing so, Kracauer would argue, the subject had lost the power of self--observation in that self-presencing is inseparable from the Möbius strip of self-observation, and where, paradoxically, this has occurred through the technology of reflection and its omniscient and ubiquitous self-observation. Elsaesser and Hagener will argue that the metaphor for the spectator entering the film is no longer the window or the threshold, or even the mirror, yet,

> Whether one thinks of it in terms of the visual metaphor of the mirror, moving forward while keeping one eye fixed on its own rear-view reflection, or prefers the more Deleuzian image of 'the fold' – indicating 'the inside of the outside', in which doubling is folded in upon itself, in such a way that the recto cannot be separated from the verso – it is clear that during the 1960s the altered terms of the relationship between spectator and film spoke to anxieties and new possibilities as vividly as had the similarly 'baroque' moment when the cinema was first 'invented'.[28]

If we consider this Möbius strip as the liminal space, the inside of the outside, the recto and verso, then the new topography of the possible is realized through the not-possible and paradoxical.

In an analysis that suggests Freud's concept of *fort/da*, as well as his argument that art is a formidable substitutive satisfaction,[29] Christian Metz specifies a primary and secondary identification, where primary is the (unconscious) identification with the omniscient look of the camera, secondary is the identification with a character: "in short, the spectator identifies with himself as a pure act of perception (astute and alert): as a condition of the possibility of the perceived object, hence also as a kind of transcendental subject who precedes any *There is*."[30] In an extension of the Hegelian synthesis[31] found in Soviet montage, as noted by Elsaesser and Hagener, Metz theorizes that narrative cinema is a chain of substitutions ("metaphors") and displacements ("metonymies"), which, along with Lacan's mirror stage, provide "a key moment in the formation of human subjectivity."[32] If so, we may find that this "chain of substitutions" also defines the bound domain of that-which-lies-before, now regarded as the liminal space, in that the viewer, through their identification and projection, is also "captured" by the mirror/screen.

Metz will find that the filmic image refigures an absence as a presence and thus "signifies" through a dynamic process of substitution, whereby the spectator is "captured" by an imagined or projected presence.[33] Metz will further develop the image/symbol of film language through the syntagm, that which is explicit and whose elements are related *in praesentia*, and the paradigm, that which is implicit, and whose elements are related *in absentia*. To put it another way, the cinematic text is organized along two axes: the syntagmatic (the horizontal flow of messages linked one after the other in a chain of cause and effect) and the paradigmatic (the meaning created through synthesis, as found in montage, juxtaposition, depth of field, text/subtext, et. al.). The true meaning of the text is the complex interweaving of both axes.[34] In doing so, the filmic image fulfils Freud's understanding of symbolism (the child creates a substitute for that which is not present) as well as Lacan's mirror phase (the child's entry into the field of culturally symbolic sounds and words).[35] Therefore, resorting to Soviet montage as well as Sausserean linguistics, Metz will claim that we have created the "imaginary signifier,"[36] as noted earlier, whereby a synthesis of image and symbol enable the viewer to create meaning. The cinema, therefore, and the image-making culture in general, is a language, but, as Metz points out, only a language in a restricted sense because it is not structurally precise in a linguistic sense in its construction of meaning, and therefore "a language without a language system."[37]

If we return to Lacan, recalling his concept that the child experiences a contrast between perceived visual experience and emotional experience initially as a rivalry with his or her own image, because the wholeness of the image threatens the child with fragmentation, the inability to find unity with oneself, and thereby there must always be a lack. As a result, the mirror stage also gives rise to an aggressive tension between the subject and the image. To resolve this aggressive tension, the child identifies with the image, which is now the primary identification. This moment of primary identification is also a moment of jubilation, since it leads to an imaginary sense of completeness and mastery, confronting the ever-present issues left from the developmental stages of the child. However, when the child compares his or her own precarious sense of mastery with the omnipotence of the mother, a depressive reaction may accompany the jubilation, which can then lead to a desire for regression.[38] In the regressive state, the child becomes the perceived object, a secondary identification, which we might also regard as a projection, that one is perceived by the (absent) mother/character, acquiring transcendental signification as the object of the omniscient camera-eye view itself, perhaps even allowing oneself immanent signification as the object of the absent god.

In which case, recalling the Plato's parable of the cave and its "second reality,"[39] and as incorporated into Jean-Louis Baudry's historical dialectic for the technological and ideological advancements in film language, we may find the immobility and confinement of the prisoners/spectators enables them to mistake representations for their own perceptions (the primary identification) thereby regressing to childhood and the pre-mirror stage when the two - representation and perception - were indistinguishable.[40] The cinema, therefore, invites regression and the relaxation of self-control, and explains the iterative, compulsive and highly narcissistic pleasures associated with the narrative cinema. According to Baudry's psychoanalytic interpretation of Plato's parable, as noted by Manovich, this suggests that rather than a historical accident or a fact of political expediency, the immobility of the spectator is the essential condition of cinematic pleasure.[41]

Metz expands on the psychoanalytic by elaborating on Lacan's mirror stage and developing the structural similarities of the cinema and mirror in terms of self-presence. Hence, as Lacan words it, the "image/inary" or the "imagine/ary," where the internalized image of this ego ideal (that is, as being complete onto ourselves, not lacking anything, "I/dentity"), is situated around coherence rather than fragmentation.[42] Consequently, the specular image, with its mirror-like reflection, again becomes "orthopaedic," where the vision of the body as integrated and contained, in opposition to the child's actual experience of motor incapacity and the sense of his or her body as fragmented, induces a movement from insufficiency to anticipation.[43] Hence, Lacan is able to argue that the specular mirror image initiates and then aids, like a crutch, the process of the formation of an integrated sense of self.

The Venus effect: Panopticon

Although Lacan's ethics developed from the same point as Levinas, that of the subject's relation to the other, Lacan distinguished between the little other (*autre*, or *objet petit a*) and the big Other (*Autre*), which emerges in the "mirror stage" of development, when a child identifies itself with its own image in a visual field and the ego arises from a fundamental miscognition/misrecognition or alienation. Significantly, in order for the subject to recognize something as the big Other, it has to make itself recognized to the big Other, which, in developmental terms, would be the function of the child's father, what Lacan calls the *nom-de-père*, the name-of-the-father, also, as a pun, the *non-de-père*, the no-of-the-father).[44] However, just as the desire for the mother originates in the prohibition of incest, so access to the Real (the Sovereign Good; the Heideggerian "thing-in-itself"),[45] would require a transgression that is strictly impossible because the unmediated "thing-in-itself" exists only as a function of the law that prohibits it: in effect, a double bind. We should recall that the double bind, as conceived by Gregory Bateson, is a crisis in communication that evolves from a situation with two or more conflicting messages, such that one message negates the other. Thus, a successful response to one message results in a failed response to the other, and vice versa, so that regardless of the response one will automatically be wrong. The double bind, therefore, arises because a person cannot confront the inherent dilemma, neither can they resolve it, nor opt out of the situation.[46]

For example, expanding on Benjamin and Kracauer, Alexander Mitscherlich diagnosed a type of look found in modern societies, the omniscient "third eye" as found in National Socialism and its support of a "fatherless society," creating a world of images with looks that did not reciprocate its own.[47] This also recalls Adorno's concerns for the organization of the mass audience and the liquidation of the individual, as well as Deleuze and Guattari's "machine of faciality" with its economy and organization of power, as well as Lacan's *nom-de-père/non-de-père*, which would also lead to Foucault's treatise on the Panopticon, where, in the original sense of Jeremy Bentham when he proposed a more humane prison, the collective is organized beneath what purports to be a centralized benevolent eye.[48] It may be that one's very existence is determined and given meaning by being part of that organization, as found in National Socialism where "Hitler appealed to the *Volk*, but he always pictured the German nation as standing there observed by 'the eyes of the world'. The massive specularization of public life, famously diagnosed by Benjamin as the aestheticization of politics, might be said to have helped institutionalize that structure of 'to be is to be perceived'."[49]

The logic of this process, as found in Kleist's text on puppet theatre, would be a text that emphasizes the displacement from one body to another.[50] The viewing subject, now transported between content and context, occupies a liminal space, the transitional or in-between space between their reality and the diegetic world on screen, a world that cannot clearly be labeled "inside" or "outside."[51] In order to overcome the logical paradoxes of the spectator, not only in apprehending that which is absent (i.e., the absence of whatever is not seen directly on the screen; the gap in the artistic construction), but also to access the symbolic and thereby the conceptual potentiality of the image/symbol, the meanings derived from the "language without a language system" must be woven into the narration, allowing for creation of meaning for the viewing subject through the "imaginary signifier," a problem that film theory knows as "suture." Thus, narrative clarity requires a seamlessness that sutures all the elements of the film into a comprehensive and satisfying whole, despite, as Ronell words it, "the effect of shock continues to jolt or to make the image jump, there is still the necessity of enchaining the moments and producing linkage."[52]

If the viewing subject is "captured" within the liminal space created by their relationship with the artistic construct, the world that may be both "inside" and "outside," then, in terms of the relations of subject-observer and authority, the artistic construct holds the upper hand in terms of power relations, becoming an apparatus of capture. A rationale for the privileging of power to the artistic construct may be situated in the "Venus Effect," as found in 16th and 17th century paintings, such as *Venus with a Mirror* (Titian 1555), *Venus at the Mirror* (Peter Paul Rubens 1615), and *Rokeby Venus* (Diego Velázquez, c.1647-51).[53] In each of the paintings, the figure of Venus, the goddess of love, is seen gazing into or holding a mirror. The viewing subject may assume that the Venus is admiring her own reflection, and yet, if one notes the angle of reflection, the Venus is actually looking at them. In effect, the viewing subject is the "object" of the Venus's gaze, and so is "captured" by the work of art. Thus, as Deleuze and Guattari claimed, "the signifier is always facialized." In which case, we are the signified. In terms of faciality, Deleuze and Guattari will write: "I have her picture in front of me, it's as if she were watching me... Surveillance by the face, as Strindberg said." Hence, there is "overcoding by the signifier, irradiation in all directions, unlocalized omnipresence."[54]

For Foucault, the painting of *Las Meninas* (*The Maids of Honour*, Diego Velázquez 1656), contains the first signs of a new episteme in European art, which also marks a new way of thinking. Foucault contends that *Las Meninas* had opened up the space of classical representation, so "visibilities are not defined by sight but are complexes of actions and passions, actions and reactions, multisensorial complexes, which emerge into the light of day."[55] This marks the shift from the Renaissance episteme to the classical episteme that coincides with the reduction of madness to reason's "other," which Foucault identifies as "the decisive point of bifurcation between those images in which it becomes alienated in a pathological subjectivity, and expressions in which it fulfils itself in an objective history."[56] Thus, we are presented with a transformation of subjectivity, where we have arrived at the fork in the road, such that, in our social reality, the road to objectivity and instrumental reasoning may prove much more enticing. Kant's Copernican turn, which may be included in the classical episteme in that it presents a schematism of classification and categories, would lead us further down this path by making the distinction between phenomena and noumena, with the consequence that the order which we encounter in nature pertains not to things in themselves but only to appearances. Foucault notes that the adherence toward appearances rather than to the "thing-in-itself" leads Heidegger to criticize Kant for not distinguishing between an anthropology of man and an existential analytic of *Dasein*.[57] Indeed, the "Copernican revolution" is that "Ontic truth, then, must necessarily conform to ontological truth."[58] Foucault, as noted by Cutrofello, would argue that Heidegger's own attempt to pursue a Platonic retreat and return of the origin, described as the unfathomable event of the *Ereignis*, remains squarely within the problematic of "man and his doubles."[59] Thus, we find ourselves divided; one part situated in the inaccessible transcendental ground of experience and the other part situated as an empirical object in nature. In doing so, the significance of the work of art had moved from the representational to the conceptual, where we, the viewing subject, found ourselves in the liminal space between projection and identification.

The new way of thinking that Foucault locates in *Las Meninas*, therefore, represents a mid-point between what he sees as the two great discontinuities in art history, the classical and the modern: "this locus is a simple one; a matter of pure reciprocity."[60] We are looking at the picture in which the painter is in turn looking out at us, which, in terms of our "perspectival threads," leads to a reciprocal visibility, where "the observer and the observed take part in a ceaseless exchange."[61] Hence,

> We are observing ourselves being observed by the painter, and made visible to his eyes by the same light that enables us to see him. And just as we are about to apprehend ourselves, transcribed by his hand as though in a mirror, we find that we can in fact apprehend nothing of that mirror but its lustreless back. The other side of a psyche.[62]

Thus, we have entered into the paradoxical realm where the figurative or representational is now functioning as the conceptual, where, as noted earlier, its function is not to help us recognize objects but to discover dimensions of experiences that did not exist prior to the work. We could also say that the painting itself is the midpoint between the point of infinity stretching into the painting and, at the same time, stretching outwards and into the viewing subject, placing the viewing subject squarely in the liminal space, the in-between that divides content and context. In doing so, the viewing subject and the work of art have entered into an uncertain relationship, where both are defined by their to-be-looked-at--ed-ness, a reflecting and reflected unity.

Foucault defined power as "a relation between forces, or rather every relation between forces is a power relation."[63] Thus, he recognized the power of the exchange of looks, a power that has expanded into the structure of modern society, evoking the comparison with Bentham's Panopticon, where visibility itself is a trap: "The Panopticon, therefore, must not be understood as a dream building: it is the diagram of a mechanism of power reduced to its ideal form."[64] Foucault would write, "Our society is not one of spectacle but of surveillance [...]. We are neither in the amphitheatre, nor on the stage, but in the panoptic machine, invested by its effects of power, which we bring to ourselves, since we are part of its mechanism."[65] Therefore, the Panopticon corresponds to a new form of power, namely discipline and alienation, while the ordering of the visual landscape, much like Alberti's veil of gridded strings, is simultaneously an accumulation and containment of the world within its framework, the safe into which the visible has been deposited, including those representations of the mind that have also been contained.

Perspective, as noted earlier, is now in command; developed and expanded to such a degree as to allow visibility itself to be the force of authority, where visibility supplies the material for the transformation of subjectivity, but one that also creates the bound domain. Thus, we are also witness to the psychic and social repression that Deleuze and Guattari address in their consideration of "schizoanalysis," a term used to describe the recovery of pathological subjectivity and the reversal of the subjection of the passive syntheses of desire to transcendent uses, thereby "restoring the syntheses of the unconscious to their immanent use."[66] Deleuze and Guattari explain this process of reversal as "de-Oedipalizing,"' which is necessitated by the fact that we have all undergone the process of Oedipalization, namely the bifurcation between that which is prohibited (pathological subjectivity) and that which is permitted (objective history), that can be explained in terms of Althusser's interpellation (i.e., we are always-already interpellated; in this case, we are always-already on the path of objective history). However, in Deleuze and Guattari's estimation, this "de-Oedipalizing" reversal is insufficient because it "is not an ideological problem, a problem of failing to recognize, or of being subject to, an illusion. It is a problem of desire, and desire is part of the infrastructure."[67] In which case, this failure does not call for us to remember a return to pathological subjectivity because we have not forgotten. As noted earlier, "if desire produces, its product is real," and therefore the desire already exists but has been rendered passive, thus necessitating, in what we might call the social transgression of an aesthetic through the aesthetic, calling for another level of "de-Oedipalizing" in order "to show how, in the subject who desires, desire can be made to desire its own repression."[68]

Substantial/functional thinking: The prize of programmability

The visual field now replaces the visual world, where, in terms used earlier, the perspectival threads of the perspectival machine orders that visual field, which would in turn confirm how the technology of reflection supports constitutive subjectivity. Indeed, Adorno will quote Goethe to write, "Destined to see what is illuminated, not the light."[69] Thus, Adorno will claim that only "by transgressing the orthodoxy of thought, something becomes visible in the object which it is orthodoxy's secret purpose to keep invisible."[70] Nonetheless, the consequences of the collective constitutive subjectivity through the technology of reflection may be traced to Descartes and his philosophical justification for "seeing" ideas in the mind, a desensualization and depersonalization of the external world that supports "the glorification of observation as the only valid way of knowing."[71] However, in reference to Descartes and the Cogito, Deleuze questions whether this determination of thinking is not in fact a stupidity. By claiming that "I think" supports "I am" is to make the indeterminate determinable, or perhaps, as noted above, to take a subjective illusion that is in fact an objective illusion born out of social consciousness to make a non-apophantic determination, and by so doing eliminate that which is different, or thinking itself, because the basis of thought is the difference between the indeterminate and the determination.[72]

And let us take this one more step, in terms of the Luxor temple itself, when, in 2013, a Chinese student defaced one of the temple walls by carving "Ding Jinhao was here."[73] Of course, this was not a first. In 1848, for example, Gustave Flaubert's trip to Egypt was disrupted by the huge letters of "Thompson" carved on Pompey's column. Flaubert complained of the defacement, "It can be read a quarter of a league away. There is no way to see the column without seeing the name 'Thompson' and consequently without thinking of Thompson."[74] Thus, through the violence of appropriation, the idea of "Thompson" had supplanted the idea of the monolith and its history, and, as Ronell contends, "parasitizing the Egyptians," where Pompey's column becomes a monument to stupidity.[75] Certainly, the graffiti suggests a transgression of the historicity of the monument, perhaps it could be regarded a resistance against pseudomorphosis, or of a work of art in its own right, or as a transgression of the aesthetic through the aesthetic by transgressing the form with another version of that same form, or, as Ronell contends, it could simply represent a kind of black hole in human nature. In which case, we might consider, as Ronell does, "The expectation that philosophy can train thought to detach from stupidity has its source in the Enlightenment,"[76] although, "no ethics or politics has been articulated to act upon its pervasive pull. Yet stupidity is everywhere."[77] Indeed, Deleuze will claim: "Stupidity (not error) constitutes the greatest weakness of thought, but also the source of its highest power in that which forces it to think."[78] In which case, we may say that stupidity is a lack in terms of the ability to extend the existing, such that, if this lack is indeed everywhere, we may be forced to acknowledge that there is a certain futility in the task of thought Adorno had set for himself, namely, "to use the strength of the subject to break through the fraud of constitutive subjectivity."[79]

Deleuze argues that in the classical episteme, all the forms of unreason were reduced to a single figure of error, which he characterizes as the negative image of recognition, where "the terrible Trinity of madness, stupidity and malevolence" should be questioned in terms of the legitimacy of its terms.[80] In other words, as per Ronell, stupidity is not the opposite of intelligence, nor is it pejorative, as it might be the synthesis of intelligence and ignorance, or intelligence and hubris, but it may also be something that is not synthesized nor an aspect of a thesis, it just "is." In place of the single figure of error, Deleuze provides a "transcendental" description of "stupidity" as something that belongs to thought by right.[81] Therefore, where Kant defined stupidity as the lack of the power of judgement, which is to conceive of stupidity merely as the possibility of error, for Deleuze stupidity represents thought's confrontation with "the indeterminate, but the indeterminate in so far as it continues to embrace determinism."[82] Deleuze's transcendental empiricism provides a way of going back to a kind of "zero point" at which stupidity still appears as "unthinking" or, in the literal sense, "thoughtlessness," and not yet merely as the error of unintelligence.

To return to this zero point would be to encounter "the terrible revelation of a thought without image," namely that "which does not allow itself to be represented."[83] Thus, we would have two possibilities: we may have that something which in itself does not allow for the possibility of creating a mental image, that is, to be constituted by the subject, or we have the inability of the subject to conjure a mental image of that something because of some lack on the part of the subject. In either case, we may find the lack in the ability to extend the existing. Nonetheless, Deleuze offers an alternative in the concept of "the thought which is born in thought, the act of thinking which is neither given by innateness nor presupposed by reminiscence but engendered in its genitality, is a thought without image."[84] Thus, Deleuze offers the thought without image that has the possibility of not being constituted by the subject's preconception. For example, the aesthetic of the Mona Lisa is not just in the painting itself, a work of genius, a portrait of mystery, but in its context. This context could be its position hanging in the Louvre, with the security glass and the crowds, or during a riot in the streets of Paris, or on a fridge magnet, or on a computer screen, or in virtual space where it is owned by Bill Gates. The original meaning of the painting is still there, but the context is something much different and much more complex.

If we refer to E.J. Dijksterhuis's *The Mechanization of the World Picture* (1961), we would find that ancient science was concerned with "substantial" thinking and inquiries into the true nature of things, while modern science was more concerned with "functional" thinking, that is, in understanding how things worked and how they were affected by their relationships to one another.[85] We would also find that the task of classical science would be to repudiate ancient science and it would do so in a wide range of applications, particularly in the realm of the mechanical, which, of course, offered a mechanized world-picture as opposed to a mythological world-picture. Modern science differs from classical science in what might be called its "mathematization," which would be aligned with the functional, and yet in some ways might prove a return to the Platonic school which also considered that creation took place in accordance with mathematical principles.[86]

Significantly, in Descartes' determination, the goal of science is domination over nature. In order to achieve this end, Adorno and Horkheimer will argue, as noted earlier, there must be a "process of oblivion" where the relationship of the object becomes distanced from the subject, resulting in a loss of memory, which is then a transcendental condition of science.[87] William Leiss, in his book *Under Technology's Thumb* (1990), observes that modern society adopts the strategy of using the continuous advance in technical innovation as the path of least resistance in striving to maintain social peace.[88] This is consistent with Adorno and Horkheimer who perceive the technological rationale as the rationale of domination itself,[89] characterizing its hold over society as active rather than reactive, a trait of "the coercive nature of society alienated from itself," where "automobiles, bombs, and movies keep the whole thing together until their levelling element shows its strength in the very wrong which it furthered."[90] In this levelling, nothing is truly new, offering only a constant reproduction of the same thing, where "the machine rotates on the same spot," and, as Jameson observes, we succumb to an aesthetic of novelty, "a perpetual culture machine which must desperately renew itself by ever more rapid rotations of its own axis."[91] Thus, the epochal transformation found in the mechanization of the world picture is essential to modern science, as well as an inevitable factor in the transformation of our social reality, such that, in the Platonic tradition, scientific method challenges all manner of illusion through that which can be mathematized. In *Discourse Networks 1800/1900*, Friedrich Kittler, evoking Foucault, would write: "Works that put things in order do not furnish any judgements or even oracles, but they 'dispossess' people of 'that discourse in which they wish to be able to say immediately and directly what they think, believe, or imagine.'"[92] With intentional irony, Kittler will refer to the goal of the new technology, this dispossession, as a process that seeks that which is mathematizable as "the prize of programmability."[93]

In objectivist terms, Kittler describes this *prix de progrès* with regard to computer technology: "This all-important property of being programmable has, in all evidence, nothing to do with software; it is an exclusive feature of hardware, more or less suited as it is to house some notation system."[94] In which case, the value of a communication does not reside in its information, particularly if that information were to contain unpredictable parts and uneven digital frequencies, but in its "logical depth," the measure of its potentiality for programmability. In other words, the value of a discourse does not reside in that which contains unpredictability (or, as Deleuze would say, its difference from actualization), resulting in what Kittler will call "buried redundancy,"[95] where only that which is eminently predictable is revealed. Similarly, in terms of what is accepted as "truth," Ronell argues, invoking Kurt Gödel, that provability "is a weaker notion than truth," and that truth must be rescued from "limitative results of provability, keeping it intact and pinned to an idealized horizon of expectation."[96] Thus, even if the information received were complex and its discovery difficult, that which is unpredictable has still been eliminated, so that, as Kittler will claim, with enough resources of time, money and computation one might eventually come to the same conclusion. The primary value of the discourse to the receiver, therefore, derives from the fact that the process has been sped up and streamlined. Hence, we have the highway to information and data rather than the Heideggerian path to knowledge, where, as Kittler argues, "logical depth, in its mathematical rigor, could advantageously replace all the old everyday language definitions of originality, authorship and copyright in their necessary inexactness."[97] Indeed, in Heideggerian terms, the prize of programmability dictates the ordering of revealing and destining that denies the potentiality of entering into a more original and profound revealing of a more primal truth, where humankind is destined by its service to its own technology of reflection, rather than using its technology of reflection to destine its being.

Adorno would also argue that modern social reality is structured to accord with logic and scientific ordering, a binary structure that subsists on the principle of the excluded middle, whereby whatever does not fit into its principles, whatever differs in quality, comes to be designated as a contradiction.[98] Consequently, the imbalance due to the nature of these binary oppositions will also allow, as noted by Peter Brunette, that "in each case, one term is favoured or seen as primary or original; the second term is regarded as a (later) perversion of the first, or in some way inferior to it."[99] In addition, the dominant culture is generally alert to any forms perceived as emergent, viewing revolutionary ideas with scepticism, yet this also suggests that new ideas permeated with the old will meet less resistance. However, even subversive forms, as observed by Dick Hebdige, can be recuperated into the dominant culture through conversion into mass-produced objects, what he will call "labelling," thus normalizing the deviant, and, now having lost their shock value, can be absorbed into the mainstream.[100] For example, as noted by Critchley, the revolutionary efforts at *détournement* by avant-gardists, such as the Situationist International in the 1960s, have only resulted in recuperation of its radical forms into the mainstream.[101] If so, this would also support Jameson's view that everything around us is functionally inserted into larger institutional frameworks of all kinds and that "cognitive mapping" is the domain of conspiracy. However, the term "conspiracy" implies a determined will, whereas the reality, as noted earlier, is that we are destined by the service to our own technology of reflection.

The prize of programmability, therefore, would indicate that the mechanical has transitioned to the mathematical, and the image-making culture would now be expressed through codification, and where we may apply the term "discretization,"[102] where the world is chopped up into pieces through the fundamental forms of devices and their codable operations. If so, the technology of reflection is realized through a codable flow of discretized images, moving us ever further from substantial thinking and the inquiries into the true nature of things, while binding us to a technology without *poiēsis*, to language without truth content, where that which is unpredictable has been eliminated. If we consider this transition in terms of world-picture, we may find that just as the relation between classical and modern science is quite different as that between ancient and classical science, so too has the world-picture changed substantially between each of these eras. The division found between ancient and classical science may be larger than that between classical and modern, and yet the world picture may have changed disproportionately more in the latter, primarily due to the extent of the codification of the world-picture and the subsequent flow of images. The immensity of this modern development and its simultaneous incursion into the very fabric of everyday life can be describe as gigantic, tectonic, which would be attended by the realization that the exchange of inexactness for "logical depth" comes at an incalculable price, the loss of that which withdraws into a space beyond representation, to a knowledge that is refused.

Representational thinking: Self-observation

Richard Rorty, quoted in Martin Jay, will claim: "In Descartes' conception – the one which became the basis for 'modern' epistemology – it is *representations* which are in the 'mind'."[103] If so, then we may consider that the synthesis of functional thinking (how things work) and substantial thinking (the true nature of things) could be called "representational thinking." In terms of the technology of reflection, Jay writes that, "Descartes may thus not only be responsible for providing a philosophical justification for the modern epistemological habit of 'seeing' ideas in the mind, but may also have been the founder of the speculative tradition of identitarian reflexivity, in which the subject is certain only of its mirror image."[104] If we consider representational thinking and the mirror image, we may find, as Montaigne did, that "I turn my gaze inward, I fix it there and keep it busy... I look inside myself; I continually observe myself."[105] Nicholas Rombes addresses this very point: "Individuals are self-observers. They distinguish themselves through the fact that they observe their own act of observation. [...] they gain an identity only through the looks of the others; but this happens only if they watch themselves being watched."[106] If so, this would support the concept of self-creation and a system of autopoesis through the auto-referential technology of reflection. However, as noted above, this also suggests that there may be a failure of these systems to support self-creation, particularly if the content relies on codable operations, and if the self-observation causes us to question whether the "observable but meaningless object" is in fact oneself. And further, in terms of representations in the mind, we may question whether the perspectival threads are not only in the visual field of the subject, but in the subject's self-perspective within that visual field, which, as noted earlier, would suggest that the advances in the technology of reflection have only reinforced the bound domain in terms of both the literal and the conceptual sense. Indeed, we may say that the domain of reflection is bound through the unity of the literal and the conceptual through the synthesis of functional and substantial thinking into representational thinking.

Kracauer will argue that the subject has lost the power of self-observation, which has been replaced by "the *aesthetic* rendering of such a life bereft of reality,"[107] and yet the more the truth content of life is submerged, to evoke Lukács, lost in a labyrinth of distortion that no longer perceives its own distortion, the more responsibility falls on the artist and the artwork to unseal that which has withdrawn and galvanize the fragments in a meaningful way. However, Kracauer recognizes the danger may be in the "overloading of the aesthetic," for example, imposing the role of educator onto the artist. In any case, he agrees that the viewing subject fails to perceive the truth content of life and is only able to recognize that he or she has been "captured in the mirror of the artistic construct, and thereby gains consciousness, albeit negative, of its distance from reality and its illusory status."[108] If so, then we might say that the precondition of the work of art is to create the artistic construct that mirrors the viewing subject, a synthesis of the literal and the conceptual, and the task of the work of art is to emancipate the viewing subject from its imprisonment in that same mirror of the artistic construct.

Deleuze claims that aesthetics has two parts, the theory of the forms of experience and the work of art as experimentation, but for that association to be productive then it must be based on difference.[109] In other words, in order to reclaim the life of the aesthetic then the first order/intensity of the aesthetic must be transgressed at the social level, and then restored by a second order/intensity of the aesthetic at the individual level, where its difference is the task and precondition of an aesthetic of the aesthetic. Deleuze extends this difference by offering "two faces," a suggestion of a Janus view. The first "face" is where difference is in the representation itself in the form of repetition, or what we have called the functional, as its aspect is that of "Habitus," the "face" turned toward the repetition that it renders possible. The second "face" is that of the "Mnemosyne," where difference is in a second repetition that results from the first, or what we have called the substantial, as it the "face" of the mind and the repetition is that of memory.[110] Deleuze cites Bergson's concept where the entire past exists at every moment, where its most concentrated level would be found in the present and its most relaxed found in increasing amounts in that which differs from the present.[111] Significantly, for this inquiry, we may understand the screen as a Janus head, one "face" is its functional aspect that appears in material form or Habitus, and another "face" is its substantial aspect that appears in its conceptual form or Mnemosyne, where its repetition and difference are in both our conscious present and our unconscious memory, our external reality and internal reality, where its representations are both material and in the mind. However, if, as Deleuze argues, consciousness has only a single presence,[112] then we must consider that we are in effect the Janus head ourselves, where our two "faces" of external and internal reality synthesize with the screen and become a kind of threshold.

Psychotechnology: Substitutive system

In 1916, Hugo Münsterberg, in *The Photoplay: A Psychological Study*, was already investigating cinema in terms of psychotechnology, determined by what he called cinema's "outer" development (the technology of the medium) and "inner" developments (the evolution of society's uses of that medium).[113] Münsterberg argued that film was moving into the realms of psychology and aesthetics, in particular the Kantian concept of the noumenal realm, whereby "the photoplay tells us a human story by overcoming the forms of the outer world, namely space, time, and causality, and by adjusting the events to the forms of the inner world, namely attention, memory, imagination, and emotion," and, in doing so, these events "reach complete isolation from the practical world through the perfect unity of plot and pictorial appearance."[114] Consequently, the constructive or generative aspect of perception would include the ability by the experienced viewer to extract more explicit spatial information than the sensory stimulus on which it is based. On the other hand, the manipulation of the reality effects of these mental constructions could lead to a form of brainwashing. Thus, Münsterberg will claim that more than any other art form the moving picture of the future would fall under the authority of psychologists who analyze the workings of the mind, particularly in terms of the ability of the mind to organize the perceptual field in relation to part and whole, between figure and ground. Therefore, "film is the medium not of the world, but of the mind. Its basis lies not in technology but in mental life."[115] To this point, Kittler recognized the critical fact that Münsterberg was not only the founder of psychotechnology but the head of the psychology lab at Harvard, which added empirical support to the view that "film replays to its viewers their own processes of perception – and this with a precision achievable only via experiment, which is to say, it cannot be represented either by consciousness or language."[116]

Another psychologist and film theorist, Rudolf Arnheim, who studied the Gestalt school of psychology, was interested only in the aesthetics of film, but, as he argues in *Film as Art* (1932), "all media have multiple uses, but only one is aesthetic, but it is this very artistic function that generally makes us focus on the medium itself."[117] Hence, not all films can achieve the status of an aesthetic object, as Münsterberg had also claimed, but the fact that they have that potential is what interests us. Consequently, Arnheim did not support naturalism, as found in the Bazanian "long take," which favored realism through an unedited view of the events on screen. This approach could only offer a mechanical double of reality and the world, where film would merely re-present the world, as opposed to film as art, or aesthetic object, where its artistic content was realized insofar as how it differed from a true rendering of reality.[118]

In line with the fundamental precept of Gestalt theory,[119] the constructive or generative aspect of perception, Arnheim focuses on the experience of that construct, whereby film provides a "partial illusion" and then the viewing subject must use their own abilities to discern forms and to create patterns, developing an inner organization from outside sense perception, and thus assembling a number of disconnected sense impressions (the fragments of images and sounds in each segment of film) into a whole that is larger than the sum of its parts. Therefore, the form-generating capability of our senses, where we can recognize patterns of stimuli imposed upon reality, is now transformed into the fragments that make up film language. However, film is not simply pattern recognition or retinal stimulation, but involves a "field" of perceptions, associations and memory.[120] In which case, film as art is produced not through its representation, but is a product of the tension between the difference that exists between representation and distortion, whereby the alteration and manipulation of filmic perception is distinct from everyday perception. Therefore, its task as a work of art is based not on the aesthetic use of something in the world but on the aesthetic use of something which gives us the world.

In his 1938 essay, "A New Laocoön: Artistic Composites and the Talking Film," Arnheim calls for cinema to become the nexus of visual and symbolic art. This suggests the cinema as *gesamtkunstwerk*, the total work of art envisaged by Wagner that synthesizes various forms of expression, or, in Gestalt terms, an assemblage of artistic forms that creates a greater whole. Just as the incomplete statue of the Laocoön, its parts having been lost over time, had to be "recreated," so Arnheim sought "transformation," where the manner of our organizing of stimuli and experience leads to higher meanings and a transformed view of the world. However, for Arnheim, this did not include sound, which would not lead the images on the screen to a higher signification, but only bring film closer to reality, making it less distinct from everyday perception.[121] In terms of the transformation of the urban landscape, it may be that the navigable space had changed to one of noise and urgency, the domain of the *badaud*, while the movie theatre remained an oasis of contemplation, of *durée*. In any case, Arnheim did not support "talkies," which he considered an unacceptable compromise between two incompatible art forms: silent film and radio drama.[122] Adding dialogue to pictures could only be harmful in that "the addition of spoken dialogue has made storytelling easier," despite the claims by critics, in terms that recall functional thinking and the prize of programmability, that film dialogue was "a device for saving time, space, and ingenuity – a saving that would reserve the available limited length of the film and the creative energy of the maker for the truly relevant content of the work."[123] Nonetheless, for Arnheim, film was being forced to become closer to reality, while forgetting that what made film as art was how it differed from reality.

In *The Aesthetics and Psychology of the Cinema* (*Esthétique et psychologie du cinema,* 1963-1965), Jean Mitry will claim that film only became an art when it left the heritage of a theatrical aesthetic of unchanging angles and continuous time within scenes, developing its own art-language. This new art-language was found not at the level of style but of structure, what Mitry called "dramaturgie," using the theatrical term to point up the film as construction and production.[124] Mitry did not conceive cinema as an asymptote of reality, as did Bazin, but, following Arnheim, that cinema as art was in those very differences that kept cinema from becoming that asymptote.[125] However, for Mitry, the cinema is the greatest of arts not because its construction shows us the end result of a transformation of the world, as found in other arts, but because it shows the process of transformation, thereby emphasizing the transition from a static to a dynamic screen, one that contains the element of time and memory.

If we return to Münsterberg, and his view of film in terms of aesthetics and psychology, he would argue that film is a fact of experience, as Andrews notes, where "our minds invade this object on the screen and are cut off from all other engagements. The film then flows to its conclusion shaped in such a way that it *sustains itself* away from the real world and *sustains us* in what has been called a state of 'rapt attention'."[126] This paradoxical state both supports and challenges the narrative of constitutive subjectivity. Thus, we find that process of the narrative, in this case the language of images, once again works both ways, supporting the Janus view to the past and the future, ceaselessly transforming the symbolized space of place into non-symbolized space, and vice versa, and therefore, a substitutive system that ceaselessly replaces itself with itself, where it is increasingly difficult to distinguish between the interior and the exterior, the here and the elsewhere.

The optical unconscious: Thinking cinematically

Benjamin warns against seeking to annex film to the traditional concept of art, which would attribute elements of cult and a high-art-ness to the cinema, in other words, "eternal values."[127] This was the case with photography, when many of those alarmed by the appearance of the new technology sought to maintain a fetishistic and anti-technological concept of art, and so undertook "nothing less than to legitimize the photographer before the very tribunal he was in the process of overturning."[128] Rather than asking how or whether photography and film are art, Benjamin argues, the question is really how photography and film have changed our concept of art, and further, how film provides a new schooling for our mimetic powers. In other words, film changes the way we create images in the mind, whereby, in a term used earlier, we have enhanced our ability to think cinematically.

Unlike the painter who maintains a natural distance from reality, Benjamin writes, the cinematographer is an extension of the *flâneur*'s photographic eye, piercing the mirage of bourgeois subjectivity like a scalpel, penetrating deeply into the tissue of reality, so deeply in fact that we forget about the apparatus that took us there.[129] The viewer is actively engaged in the camera's movement across the visual field, and the fragmentation of time and space through montage, which is consistent with the shock-like collisions and the acceleration of time that we find within our modern social reality. This is also consistent with human physiology and the constant motion of the eye, which is no longer the static viewer/camera/projector perspective, but the rapid jumps from one fixed point to the next in "saccadic movements."[130]

The total image produced by the painter presents a vision that is atemporal and static (a dilemma which the Cubists, already under threat from photography, attempted to remedy),[131] whereas the cinema uses the technique of montage to present fragments, moments in time and space, manifold parts assembled by the new laws of apperception. Accordingly, Benjamin returns to the concept of penetrating the object to find its truth, where cinematic techniques allow the camera, like a surgeon's scalpel, to reveal the hidden in the familiar, and that would include ourselves; hence, "we discover the optical unconscious, just as we discover the instinctual unconscious through psychoanalysis."[132]

Therefore, despite the self-alienation of the audience, and without the need for extensive intellectual labour, the technological aspects of film still allows the viewer to pierce, and potentially negate, bourgeois subjectivity, revealing the essential meaning and truth hidden within the language of things. In doing so, the reproducibility and accessibility of photography and film counter the rituals and the cult value of the fetish and emancipate the work of art from its parasitic subservience. The democratic levelling of reproduced works of art, particularly film, now fulfils its revolutionary significance and stands as a significant step in the process of dymythification. Reality and the masses now fall into close alignment. Consequently, the social function of art will change. The emergence of present-day masses and the growing intensity of their movements elicits the desire to "get closer" to things, to possess them in their immediacy, combined with an equally passionate goal of overcoming each thing's uniqueness.[133] In other words, the masses and the new means of apperception and the creation of sameness all demand the destruction of aura. The masses discard the traditional rituals and cult values associated with art, until, "the extremely backward attitude toward a Picasso painting changes into a highly progressive reaction to a Chaplin film."[134] In fact, everyone is an expert because the accessibility of film now means, "any person today can lay claim to being filmed."[135] Therefore, just as the Gutenberg press allowed for the dissemination of the written word and led to an exponential rise in literacy and the subsequent challenge to "eternal values," while removing literary competence and accessibility from the privileged classes and the church,[136] so film creates a common language and is itself common property, transferring control from the cultural producers to the masses, thus allowing the masses to confront the omnipresent apparatus of modern society and gain equilibrium within their lived experience, which in turn offers the potential for raising of revolutionary consciousness and the rise of the proletariat.

Bertolt Brecht wanted to focus on the cathartic properties of cinema by enhancing modernist artistic innovation, believing that ideas could be realized through an expansion of the "alienation effect" used in theatre, and influenced by the concept of "making the familiar strange (*ostranenie*), or of 'defamiliarizing' what is normally taken for granted."[137] In Brecht's view, he found "the realist-naturalist tradition since Ibsen as conforming to the Aristotelian model of catharsis: raising political issues only to send the audience away purged of any fervour for change."[138] Consequently, Brecht's intentions were to unsettle the audience, in order to countermand "the narcotic effects of dominant dramatic forms."[139] In order to accomplish its socially antithetical task, therefore, bourgeois forms must be constantly re-functioned into revolutionary constructions through the dialectical opposition of theory and praxis. The revolutionary role of the artist would be to transform dialectically the technical developments in his or her field by reversing the traditional function of cultural forms from ideological tools into tools of human liberation. Adorno, however, warned against overconfidence in the popular culture, principally the American cinema, which was "typically mimetic and infantilist: the American industry, in particular, was a vehicle of bourgeois ideology even in its apparently most 'progressive' expressions."[140]

However, just as those early critics sought to annex film to the traditional concept of art, so these cultural critics sought to annex film to the traditional concept of politicized art, both of which neglect the purpose of art itself, which is to reveal the truth within the accepted notions of "truth," and that the revealing of truth is also to reveal something in ourselves. Once again we find the paradox of using the technology of reflection to challenge the very construction of that reflection, both externally and internally, and doing so through a work of self-reflection. Nonetheless, for Benjamin, as noted by Buck-Morss, the construction of new "synthetic realities" creates new spatio-temporal orders through its "fragmented images" that are brought together "according to a new law."[141] In which case, as noted earlier, there is the potential that through the technology of reflection that we are reintroduced to the natural world, thus demanding a reconceptualization of the relationship between culture and nature. Indeed, in terms that would support Münsterberg's concept of psychotechnology, as well as Bazin's views that cinema projected new meanings back on reality, Benjamin would write:

> Thus it becomes clear that a different nature speaks to the camera than to the naked eye – different above all in this, that in place of space interwoven with the consciousness of human beings, one is presented with space unconsciously interwoven.[142]

Therefore, in consideration of our innate capacity to form and manipulate mental images, it is the realization of the internalized image-making process of self-reflection that has been externalized through the image-making culture, and the unconscious structure of language is made conscious through the living experience of images, whereby we are already thinking cinematically. However, just as the image-making culture has the potential to "see" the world differently, so too it can change the way we create mental images, whereby the construction of those mental images and the process of transformation can also be refunctioned hegemonically. Moreover, if there is a crisis of artistic reproduction that is part of a crisis in perception itself, then the crisis is not in the mode of artistic reproduction itself but in the mode of perception, and that crisis may be in the ability of the artist and the viewer to move beyond the fraud of constitutive subjectivity, where the subject is objectified through that very technology of reflection that promises its emancipation. Therefore, as noted earlier, the true aesthetic of a cultural form is not simply the aesthetic that we apply to it, but exists within the cultural form itself. However, if the technology of reflection supports the primacy of the constitutive subject, then it may nullify its potential to challenge the bound domain of objectification, which, as noted earlier, is a form of forgetting. On the other hand, if the technology of reflection can unlock the historical dynamic hidden within objects, and, as Benjamin promised, release the silent murmuring congealed inside, where the object longs to transform itself, seeking a sensual happiness within its own body, then, as we have become objects to ourselves, those voices that are released may well be ours, and, in doing so, discover that which is poetically formed and pre-exists the cinematic form.

The non-identical provides a determination that is indetermination and thus provides the power of non-identity that restores freedom to the subject and so challenges, to use Adorno's term, the fraud of constitutive subjectivity. However, if there is a crisis of subjectivity, it may lie in the very fact that the subject is only able to self-presence through its self, that is, any challenge to oneself is still a challenge from oneself. In terms of visual culture, or the culture of the image, and its subsequent transposition of the world through the technology of reflection, an adjunct to the Cartesian goal of mastering nature, an ideology of domination, we may find that any potential of self-presence through the self has become severely limited, where we only master ourselves within the bound domain of constitutive subjectivity. To put it another way, if the culture of the image can only define the likeness of the world through the subject, which amounts to the subject identifying the world, and itself, through its own self-objectification, that process serves the reinforcement of constitutive subjectivity. However, in doing so, the subject only reinforces the Cartesian division between man and nature, which would amount to, as stated by Neil Evernden, the vivisectionist who severs the vocal cords of the animal on the table, thus denying the creature its voice, and then convincing himself that the creature feels no pain, thus both negating his humanity and then affirming it.[143]

Photogénie: Fluctuations of the market

The merging of our interior reality and exterior reality suggests the formation of a new reality, a reality that incorporates elements of the noumenal, the surreal, and the imaginary, where illusion becomes part of life's essence. This new reality would define the contemporary interpretation of experience, which is attended by a transformation of subjectivity, the synthesis of functional thinking and substantial thinking, of our conscious and unconscious, into representational thinking. Benjamin's view of film would support this notion, whereby we discover the optical unconscious,[144] and that which is discovered through the optical unconscious can be described by *photogénie*. Jean Epstein defined *photogénie* as "any aspect of things, beings, or souls whose moral character is enhanced by filmic reproduction. And any aspect not enhanced by filmic reproduction is not photogenic, plays no part in the art of cinema."[145] By moral character, Epstein refers to the truth content or essence of the thing-in-itself. On a similar note, Andrei Tarkovsky will claim "cinema is still looking for its language and is only now coming somewhere near grasping it. The cinema's progress towards self-awareness has always been hampered by its equivocal position, hanging between art and the factory: the original sin of its genesis in the market-place,"[146] so he will also claim that "as a rule the film-maker's work is not a creative act, not a morally exacting undertaking of vital importance to him personally. A work becomes dated as a result of the conscious effort to be expressive and contemporary; these are not things to be achieved; they have to be in you."[147] The concept of *photogénie*, therefore, especially in the hands of the avant-garde Surrealist and French Impressionist filmmakers of the 1920s, emphasized two important aspects of cinema, namely, the cultural and the aesthetic. In the cultural sense, *photogénie* proposes to legitimize the medium of film, arguing that film can transcend its photochemical/mechanical base, and, in the right hands, become art, and thereby determining those filmmakers who are artists. In the aesthetic sense, *photogénie* also divides audiences, separating those who can "see" and appreciate the art of film from those who cannot, thus denying the passivity of the viewing subject and the claim that there is no need for extensive intellectual labour to appreciate the cinema.[148]

Nonetheless, Horkheimer and Adorno would direct their polemic of the cinema at the potential for profits that led to the increasing standardization of scripts, productions, and genre - "the criterion of efficiency"[149] - with the inevitable result that opportunities frequently bypassed many of the more idiosyncratic filmmakers (substantial thinking) and favoured the more malleable and commercial filmmakers who can dependably churn out something familiar and commercial (functional thinking). Similarly, as noted earlier, the work of art informs and influences our social reality just as its own nature is influenced by that same social reality, so Marshall Berman evokes Marx in saying that modern professionals, intellectuals and artists, which would include filmmakers, are subject to the bourgeoisie who control the means of production of culture and therefore, "their goods and services go on sale, and it is 'the vicissitudes of competition, the fluctuations of the market', rather than any intrinsic truth or beauty or value – or, for that matter, any lack of truth or beauty or value – that will determine their fate."[150] To this end, artists are "'selling themselves piecemeal', they are selling not merely their physical energy but their minds, their sensibilities, their deepest feelings, their visionary and imaginative powers, virtually the whole of themselves."[151] Thus, society imposes its own ideological terms and, as Dick Hebdige writes, evoking Barthes, effectively substitutes "the fairy tale of the artist's creativity" for an art form "within the compass of every consciousness."[152]

Indeed, Epstein also claimed that "the cinema seems to me like two Siamese twins joined together at the stomach, in other words by the base necessities of life, but sundered at the heart, or by the higher necessities of emotion. The first of these is the art of cinema, the second is the film industry."[153] In terms of the poetic interpretation of the poet/filmmaker, which may recall the earlier reference to the impact from the tableaux of the Battle of Kadesh, Epstein would write:

> Of course a landscape filmed by one of the forty or four hundred directors devoid of personality whom God sent to plague the cinema as He once sent the locusts into Egypt looks exactly like this same landscape by any other of these locust filmmakers. But this landscape or this fragment of drama staged by someone like Gance will look nothing like what would be seen through the eyes and heart of a Griffith or a L'Herbier. And so the personality, the soul, the poetry of certain men invade the cinema. [...] The cinema is poetry's most powerful medium, the truest medium for the untrue, the unreal, the surreal, as Apollinaire would have said. This is why some of us have entrusted to it our highest hopes.[154]

Epstein's highest hopes anticipates Deleuze, who will write that it is not sufficient to compare great directors to other artists, such as painters, architects, or musicians, but that they must be compared to thinkers, because their creative capacities are connected to their contributions to the new materials and means that the future makes possible.[155] On a similar note, Elsaesser and Hagener would claim "the revival of Bazin (but also that of Kracauer, Epstein, Balázs and Arnheim) proves that the history of film theory is not a teleological story of progress to ever-more comprehensive or elegantly reductive models. Generally speaking, a theory is never historically stable, but takes on new meanings in different contexts."[156] For example, avant-garde Surrealist and French Impressionist filmmakers of the 1920s viewed cinema itself as "plastic shape," "frozen time," or "synchronized to the tempo of our daydreams."[157] Hence, they sought photogénie, which Louis Delluc would describe as "the purest essence of cinema,"[158] namely that which could only be expressed in the moving images on a dynamic screen, perhaps not always expressible in words, yet able "to endow with a poetic value that which does not yet possess it."[159]

Photogénie occurs at the convergence of the mechanical gaze of the camera and the profilmic (that which is in front of the camera), which encouraged detractors to focus on the intervention of the mechanical on any artistic creation. However, Bazin would claim that the essence of cinema is in its very ability to record and reproduce reality and its phenomena: "For the first time, between the originating object and its reproduction there intervenes only the instrumentality of a nonliving agent. For the first time, the image of the world is formed automatically, without the creative intervention of man."[160] For Bazin, therefore, one of the truly unique aspects of the cinema was precisely the mechanical recording of reality without human intervention, which is why he favored realism, and the placing the camera in the right position and letting it register what is before it (the profilmic). Thus, unlike the formalists and constructivists, such as Arnheim, or the Soviet filmmakers Lev Kuleshov and Eisenstein, Bazin supported the aesthetic of the "long take," where the unadorned mould of reality had its own aesthetic validity. In the Heideggerian sense, the camera would unconceal the truth that we might otherwise have been unable to "see."

As opposed to Bazin's humanist approach that allowed the viewer to discover meaning, Eisenstein wished to raise the political consciousness of his audience through the praxis of the conceptual, a manipulation that would rely on the psychological, particularly the experiments of Pavlov on conditioned responses.[161] Incorporating the process of the Hegelian dialectic, and the politics of the Marxist dialectic, as well as the power of juxtaposition known as the "Kuleshov effect," Eisenstein's techniques of montage proposed that a fragment (thesis) juxtaposed to another fragment (antithesis) would create new meaning (synthesis). In creating his five levels of montage construction (that is, editing), culminating in the fifth level of intellectual montage, Eisenstein wanted to open up the cinema to complex mental structures such as metaphors, comparisons, synecdoche and other tropes, normally limited to communication based on language. Eisenstein was also influenced by Japanese kabuki theatre, with its triangulation of looks that incorporated the audience into the creation of meaning (rather than the dualistic shot/reverse shot and eye line match), as well as kanji, the term for the logographic Chinese characters found in the Japanese writing system. For example, "gate" 門 plus "ear" 耳 equals "listen" 聞. Another example: "word" 言 plus "oneself" or "yourself" 己 becomes "history" 記. In a similar way, and in terms of the "concrete" images of film (in that they are unchanging once cut into the film), a fragment of film (noun) juxtaposed with another fragment of film (noun) would synthesize through their juxtaposition into a dynamic meaning (verb or concept). It is within the synthesis that the meaning and poetry of cinema would lie, escaping those concrete images, and allowing for a process of denotation and connotation.[162] For example, a picture of an hourglass denotes an old form of clock, but by suggesting the sands of time running out it connotes mortality. Therefore, through artfully building contexts, the filmmaker is able to invest prosaic objects, events, or characters with poetic meaning that transcend their everyday appearances.

For his part, Bazin did not rule out all forms of montage, he was simply suspicious of "tricks" that augmented the manipulation of the spectator.[163] In which case, the sequence shot is not the sequencing of images, as in montage, but the disposition of space within the frame, or mise-en-scène. In other words, the poetic synthesis was not between shots (interframe) but within the shot (intraframe), and the synthesis was between the foreground, middle ground, background, where the viewer, as in real life, could make their own interpretation. Hence, Bazin was not so concerned with the realm of a traditional film aesthetics of psychological realism, but rather the idea of a social reality, which sees reality as an "inseparable whole," where the things embraced by a film, or the "fact," as Bazin called it, possesses an ontological unity which film has to respect.

If we return to the concept of photogénie, we would consider the cinema as an illusion-producing machine where the viewer is subjected to a dream-like reality that exists only within the cinematic world. The concept of photogénie, therefore, as noted by Robert B. Ray, emphasized precisely what Eisenstein wanted to escape: the cinema's automatism.[164] Eisenstein attempted to escape the indexical nature of cinema through the meanings created by juxtaposition, whereas the realists (and surrealists) sought a property that cannot be found in "reality" itself but through the camera's view of that same reality. However, a camera that is simply switched on does not record photogénie, and a filmmaker cannot simply "find" it and film it. Ian Aitken contends, "Fully realized photogénie could only be manifested when its latent power was employed to express the vision of the film-maker, so that the inherent poetry of the cinema could be harnessed, and developed in a revelatory manner by the auteur."[165] Therefore, the avant-garde filmmakers explored the perception of reality through two main concepts: subjectivity and photogénie. By destabilizing familiar or objective ways of seeing, which amounted to a simultaneous recognition of the objects or events and a defamiliarization of the spectator with what appears on screen (what we have referred to as representation and memory, or repetition and difference) and thereby create new dynamics of human perception. In effect, to use Benjamin's terms in his reference to poetry, the camera would be capable of revealing that which is poetically formed and pre-exists the cinematic form.

However, Wittgenstein claimed, "aesthetic questions have nothing to do with psychological experiments, but are answered in an entirely different way."[166] If so, we may ask if the psychological is not being used to discover the poetic but to exploit the poetic. Indeed, for Bazin's part, he would write, in terms that recall Benjamin's "rights of the corpse": "If the plastic arts were put under psychoanalysis, the practice of embalming the dead might turn out to be a fundamental factor in their creation."[167] Indeed, if we consider ancient Egypt, as Andrews does, the model and the image may have been endowed with ontological significance, but now images serve symbolic and aesthetic functions, not magical ones: "they signify what is important to culture and they do so in styles that display values."[168]

Filmic perception: *Découpage*

The alteration and manipulation of filmic perception distinct from everyday perception is precisely what Bazin supported in terms of *mise-en-scène*, the "placing in the scene" (intrascene) by the filmmaker that allows for *photogénie*, and in doing so the filmmaker becomes an *auteur* and the camera becomes the *camera-stylo*, capable of "writing" with images. In other words, *mise-en-scène* is what we see on film, editing is what we do not, and what we see has the higher distinction because "photography enjoys a certain advantage in virtue of this transference of reality from the thing to its reproduction."[169] Therefore, in opposition to the formalist/constructivists, Bazin favored the long take and composition in depth, which allowed the viewer the freedom to interpret what was on the screen, as opposed to the overtly manipulative aspects of montage.

Andrews notes that Bazin, as well as Kracauer, believed that "cinema can provide a common non-ideological understanding of the earth from which men can begin to forge new and lasting social relations."[170] Indeed, Kracauer quotes Erwin Panofsky in claiming the difference between film and the traditional arts:

> The processes of all the earlier representational arts conform, in a higher or lesser degree, to an idealistic condition of the world. These arts operate from top to bottom, so to speak, and not from bottom to top; they start with an idea to be projected into shapeless matter and not with the objects that constitute the physical world... It is the movies, and only the movies, that do justice to that materialistic interpretation of the universe which, whether we like it or not, pervades contemporary civilization.[171]

Thus, a film is not just an intellectual or rational experience, but also an emotional and psychological experience, one that may attain the status of an aesthetic object. In terms of the cinematic reality, Bazin would seek a causal link between form and style, demanding that every filmmaker must take into account the realistic nature of his material, even if he wants to deform or distort that material. Rather than a standardized taxonomy, Bazin would try to imagine "the kind" of film that a film was or was trying to be, then formulate the laws of this "genre" in order to reflect on the film itself. Kracauer would claim that the "found story"[172] is the proper story, not the one created by artifice, which also suggests Adorno's *ars inveniendi*, as well as Benjamin's awakening of the congealed life in petrified objects. For Kracauer, the ideal cinematic genre is the story that is engaged to the earth, not theatrical, but open-ended, unstaged, and indeterminate, because we have lost the sense of "thingness" of things and so need to re-attune ourselves to the earth and become responsive to its truths.[173]

According to Bazin the raw material achieves its proper signification when it finds its forms and when the filmmakers can make reality significant through "a succession of fragments called 'shots', the choice, order, and duration of which constitutes exactly what we call the 'decoupage' of the film," and where, as Andrews interprets, "*découpage*, or shot breakdown, is a system of conventions which pass unnoticed, leading us to the acceptance of a certain order of things."[174] It is through this acceptance, however, that our image-making culture is altering our perception of reality itself in a particular manner, with the real and the unreal becoming increasingly interchangeable, perhaps, as Cousins notes, taking us to a place of *Entwirluchung*, of "reality losing its realness."[175] Instead of regarding this alteration as a loss, Bazin insists that the cinema projects new meanings back on reality and provides the greatest tool for accomplishing this transformation of perception because it proceeds like natural perception yet builds another, more intense world alongside that of natural perception. Therefore, realism is cinema's greatest appeal in that it reveals aspects of the world through *photogénie*, enhancing that which we hadn't "seen" before, and, more than any other art, captures the sense of a world which flows around and beyond us. And it does so, as Panofsky claimed, from the "bottom to top," and thereby avoids the ideological and allows the "free play" for the filmic subject to reveal itself. Hence, according to Bazin, the raw material of film is brute reality, where the unadorned mold of reality has its own aesthetic validity: "Only the impassive lens, stripping its object of all those ways of seeing it, those piled-up preconceptions, that spiritual dust and grime with which my eyes have covered it, is able to present it in all its virginal purity to my attention and consequently to my love."[176]

In doing so, Bazin identifies, as will Mitry, an "openness to Being" where cinematic realism projects new meanings back on reality, where, unlike montage, and its sense of *telling* of events, the depth-of-field "long take" works at the level of *recording* events,[177] a differentiation that evokes the double nature of language mentioned earlier, both as propositional or perlocutionary (in that it refers to the world through the individual subject and is made with the strategic intent of manipulating hearers) and illocutionary (in that it invokes social relationships and the public sense where we make our intentions explicit). Hence, where Eisenstein would use montage to create juxtapositions that synthesize into meaning and emotion for the viewer, Jean Renoir, for example, would avoid montage and the sequencing of images to develop "composition in depth," that is, the disposition of space within the frame, or *mise-en-scène*, by incorporating close shot, medium shot, and long shot within a single frame.[178] In doing so, Renoir reproduces the field of vision of the human eye (although the eye does not possess extreme depth of field, but, as noted earlier in saccadic eye movement, it is able to rapidly alter focus within a depth perspective so that we are not aware of the discontinuity). Expanding on Renoir, Orson Welles wanted the images to flow poetically from image to image in a manner analogous to the process of human memory - reinforcing the concept of repetition and difference in both our conscious present and in our unconscious memory - and will structure the narrative in a series of overlapping flashbacks, as if remembered.[179] More importantly, it is as if we, the viewer, were remembering.

Barthes argues this point in terms of photography when he makes a distinction between "*studium*" and "*punctum*." He explains that *studium* "doesn't mean, at least not immediately, 'study,' but application to a thing, taste for someone, a kind of general, enthusiastic commitment, of course, but without special acuity,"[180] as opposed to *punctum*, which is the "sting, speck, cut, little hole – and also a cast of the dice [...] that accident which pricks me (but also bruises me, is poignant to me)."[181] Barthes will further distinguish *studium* as provoking a knowledge and civility, a polite interest, as opposed to *punctum* with its dangerousness, its subversive quality, not through shock necessarily, but once it has occurred, through pensiveness. This pensiveness, a kind of remembering, brings to mind Heidegger, where that which is thinking, that which becomes worthy of questioning, is worthy of thought.[182] Barthes will define this domain of the pensiveness as the "blind field,"[183] as that which emerges as "a kind of subtle *beyond* – as if the image launched desire beyond what it permits us to see."[184]

The "showing" of what cannot be seen, yet is revealed, occurs when "the photographer has found the right moment, the *kairos* of desire," where the *punctum* is "just the right degree of openness; the right density of abandonment."[185] In effect, this is similar to Bazin's "long take," where the truth content (in Bazin's terms, "the fact") of the cinema is precisely in its mechanical recording of reality without human intervention. Bazin and Barthes, consequently, both share a preference for realism and the classical text that enhances naturalness and authenticity, a work of duration, and both wished to break away from the tyranny of traditional literary criticism. Barthes can envision the "death of the author,"[186] separating the work from its author, and Bazin envisions a similar possibility, where the cinematic *auteur* will break away from the *litterateurs* and *le tradition de qualité*.[187]

Rancière, however, interprets the pensiveness of the image in terms of combinations that refute *studium* and *punctum*, as well as the privilege of photographic or pictorial silence, and instead finds silence itself as "a certain type of figurativeness, a certain tension between regimes of expression which is also a set of exchanges between the powers of different media."[188] In other words, within the technology of reflection, silence itself speaks volumes. Not unlike the depiction of the Battle of Kardesh, it is what is not represented that represents. In Heidegger's terms, this is not simply silence, as in what it is not (i.e., not revealing), but as in what it is, which is its giveness. However, this giveness is not the same as givenness that is given, but its coming-into-view through silence, it gives, unbidden, unforced. Hence, this is not coming-into-view (*Ereignis*) as a transcendent ground of being, as Kant tried to conceive of the unpositable ground by which the positable is positable, which is understood through the concept of nothing, but, as noted earlier, when Heidegger claimed that the nothing nothings, which is an important aspect of our self-formation, just as being is not givenness but as that by which the given is given, whereby something is given that eludes interpretation through its representing.[189]

Historical poetics: Harnessing enchantment

Neo-formalist film theorist David Bordwell would argue that the avant-garde Surrealist and French Impressionist filmmakers lacked a theoretical and philosophical basis for their notions and thus "the concept of *photogénie* is always on the edge of an inexplicable mysticism that many critics cannot accept."[190] Film theorist Paul Willemen, a proponent of oppositional cinema, particularly the cinema of emerging nations, supports Bordwell's view when he writes: "'mysticism' was indeed the swamp in which most of the theoretical statements of the Impressionists eventually drowned."[191] Therefore, as opposed to the stylistic paradigm of Bazin, the tradition of neo-formalism would argue that the Impressionist/Surrealist filmmakers sought to portray a realm beyond matter and our immediate sense experience, as found in the internal state of the character or characters as expressed by the artist, and in some of the later and more complex films, there is an attempt to bring the audience into the equation as a subjective participant.[192] For example, filmmakers would increasingly seek the means to counter the "concrete" representations of the photographic image in order to create metaphors for things that the cinema cannot represent directly on the screen, much like Wassily Kandinsky attempts in his paintings that showed how sound could appear, or conversely of paintings that could be "heard,"[193] so filmmakers would seek a multisensory experience where color, sound, movement, emotion, all mingle together to produce a synesthetic experience for the viewer.

By the same token, Robert B. Ray agreed that *photogénie*'s elusiveness caused its disappearance from film theory, where it has been more accurately connected to fetishism, and further, that Bazin's humanist approach amounted to a displacement of his "unrequited religious impulse."[194] Nonetheless, Ray also presents the challenge of whether the politically sensitive Eisenstein tradition might reunite with the Impressionist/Surrealist interest in *photogénie*, thus presenting a combination of logical structure and untranslatable allure.[195] If so, there arises the possibility of avoiding formulaic systems that address what might now be considered the "random generators" of the camera,[196] as well as addressing Barthes' lament whereby the semiotic paradigm "has become in some sort mythical: any student can and does denounce the bourgeois or petit-bourgeois character of such and such a form (of life, of thought, of consumption). In other words, a mythological doxa has been created: denunciation, dymystification (or demythification), has itself become discourse, stock of phrases, catechistic declaration."[197] If so, rather than the free association of symbolism we would have "symbolic blockage,"[198] which, as Martin Jay argues, would mean, "film contained the disruptive implications of language and produced instead narratives restoring equilibrium and reconciliation."[199] However, it could also be argued that although the Surrealist movement, initially composed of writers and artists, was a call to revolt against the conventional cinema,[200] which serves the goal of art as a social antithesis, at the same it was also led to the attempt to "harness" the enchantment of the cinema, along with its access or ability to realize *photogénie*. For example, just as screen tests were introduced with the express purpose of finding actors who were photogenic, so the culture industry sought to standardize the means to access *photogénie*, to develop the means to capture and standardize enchantment.[201]

The practical goals of "harnessing" enchantment, which may seem a paradoxical pursuit, would support Bordwell's matter-of-fact approach to the developments in film language, one that wished to avoid undue critical theory and instead would focus on the material developments of film production and technology, a somewhat Marxian perspective that supports an "historical poetics" that "let films speak for themselves."[202] In other words, the changes in film production and technology allowed for the changes in film language and content, and those opportunities in and of themselves allowed for the poetic potential ascribed to *photogénie*. For example, changes in the depth of field in film stock enhanced the development of composition in depth, whereby the narrative could be developed not simply through interframe (editing), but also intraframe (foreground, middle ground, background), where the entire depth of field could be in focus. As such, Bordwell would support neo-formalism over either Bazin's ontological realism or Eisenstein's revolutionary montage, whereby technological developments allowed for the refinements in film language, the extensions of classical narration and its psychological motivation, as found in Hollywood's pragmatic view of film composition (i.e., the Hollywood Classical or "Continuous" style). In turn, this meant that films were constructed on the principle of "functional equivalence," that is, several techniques come together to fulfil certain expressive functions, namely to allow imagery to function as or access mental images. Once again, we may find that functional thinking and substantial thinking have synthesized into representational thinking.

Interestingly, there have been studies that test the human ability to perform the mental rotation of images in order to investigate how the human mind maintains and manipulates mental images as topographic and topological wholes.[203] In light of Lukács's claim that the task of the work of art is to draw the archetypal map, to realize the transcendental topography of the mind, and Rancière's claim that if we are able to break through the obviousness of the visible then we may discover a new topography of the possible, we may find that the new topography is found in the synthesis of representational thinking, accessing the single presence constituted by inner and outer subjectivity through the technology of reflection.

Cinema as social machine: The gaze of the object

Against Bazin's idealist and evolutionary account, Jean-Louis Comolli would propose that cinema "is born immediately as a social machine...from the anticipation and conformation of its social profitability; economic, ideological and symbolic."[204] In Comolli's account, as noted by Manovich, the history of cinematic technique is "an intersection of technical, aesthetic, social, and ideological determinations," an analysis that privileges the ideological function of the cinema, which is a direct result of its capacity as the "'objective' duplication of the 'real' itself conceived as specular reflection."[205] Therefore, in order to fulfill its ideological function through it technological abilities, the cinema must maintain and constantly update its potential to create a "synthetic realism."[206] The process of creating this synthetic realism, Manevich's term, is not so much one of transformation leading to higher meanings, as Arnheim and the formalists had conceived, but rather, in Comolli's objectivist view, as a process of "addition and substitution,"[207] usually understood in terms of technological improvements, which thus maximizes the cinema's capacity to duplicate the "real" in terms of the process itself. The technological genealogy of the cinema, and its ideological influence, begins with the idea of cinema as a representation or as a storytelling medium, then develops the technological and ideological advancements – additions and substitutions - in terms of Plato's cave, the camera obscura, Renaissance perspective, and Cartesian optics.[208] Therefore, the same Renaissance which gave birth to the "perspectival threads" and the enhanced "reality effect" are incorporated into the camera itself, allowing for an ideological critique of the cinema's subjective effects, where images are appropriated into our social imaginary and thereby into our social reality.

Similarly, Bordwell and Staiger, as noted by Manovich, locate realism within "the institutional discourses of film industries, implying that it is a rational and pragmatic tool in industrial competition."[209] Bordwell and Staiger agree that the development of cinema is not linear, yet they also recognize that it is not random either, but they do not subscribe to a semiotical analysis of cinema. Indeed, Bordwell supports analysis based on "historical poetics," as noted above, where changes in technology allow further complexity of narratives, which then allows for functional and causal-historical accounts of why films in various traditions display certain regularities in their narrational strategies. The question is whether these strategies are ideologically or psychologically determined, or if they access some "hard-wired" aspect of the physiology of human perception.[210] In *Post-Theory: Reconstructing Film Studies* (1996), Bordwell and Nöel Carroll coin the pejorative term "SLAB theory" to describe the theories that incorporate the ideas of Saussure, Lacan, Althusser, and/or Barthes, thus rejecting the "Grand Theories" that use films to confirm pre-determined theoretical frameworks.

Offering an opposing view, Slavoj Žižek rejects Bordwell and Carroll's neoformalism, arguing that analysis limited to neo-formalism and historical poetics would not reveal the problematic values of the very different societies in which films are produced. Žižek also argues that Bordwell does not understand the Lacanian concept of the gaze, which may be due in part to the appropriation of Lacan by cultural studies, yet the primary misunderstanding is that Lacan's concept is that of the gaze belonging to the subject, whereas Lacan believed that the gaze was on the side of the object.[211] Hence, this misunderstanding fails to recognize "the irreducible fissure between the actual and the possible, one that prevents consciousness from coinciding with an imaginary or symbolic identity."[212] Indeed, the aim of Lacanian analysis is to "traverse the fantasy" (*traverse du fantasme*),[213] to remove the "orthopaedic" crutch as it were, not unlike the dissolution of the Jungian persona, such that if the "fundamental fantasy" is the desire to be God, then to traverse the fantasy, a term Žižek will adopt, is "far from enslaving us to these fantasies and thus turning us into desubjectivized blind puppets, it enables us to treat them in a playful way and thus to adopt towards them a minimum of distance."[214]

Ultimately, for Žižek, there is in fact nothing but the "gap" itself, the irreducible fissure that results from the discovery that any messages that the subject "receives" in the real are those that it has sent itself. In which case, for example, to reach the Hegelian Absolute would be to suspend all of the imaginary fantasies that suture the Real to the Symbolic. Žižek argues that we have to acknowledge that fantasy merely functions to screen the abyss or inconsistency in the Other, and thereby traversing the fantasy is to acknowledge that there is nothing "behind" the symbolic, and that fantasy masks precisely this "nothing." Thus, if it were possible to strip the subject of their customary fantasmatic support, disrupting their social identity and challenging their personality, the question is not whether these strategies are ideologically or psychologically determined, but what does someone who has passed through this experience, who has traversed the fantasy, become?[215] In our terms, we would ask what happens when we expose the fraud of constitutive subjectivity and "see" things in an entirely new way.

The myth of total cinema: A turn toward the object

Bazin asserts that cinema was not borne from the advances of technology and economy in the late 19th century but from the innate desire to reproduce the world around us in asymptotic detail. This would support Hiebert's claim that the first technology was not language nor the wheel, but the technology of reflection. Bazin takes a historicist view; that is, scientific knowledge is constructed according to cultural paradigms, and the apparatuses, such as the film camera, were constructed according to cultural norms and could be used differently. The basic technical discoveries are fortunate accidents, which are essentially second in importance to the preconceived ideas of the inventors.[216] Therefore, the inventors of photography and cinema were not simply producing technology for profit, although that may certainly be a motive, but they were playing their part in a much larger purpose, namely the replication and reproduction of the world. The modern technology of cinema, for Bazin, is a realization of the ancient myth of mimesis, just as the development of aviation is a realization of the myth of Icarus. The idea of cinema existed long before the medium actually appeared and that the development of cinema technology "little by little made a reality out of original 'myth'," where "every new development added to the cinema must, paradoxically, take it nearer and nearer to its origins. In short, cinema has not yet been invented."[217]

Bazin considers these origins in terms of ancient Egypt, where the statues, the mummy in the sarcophagus, the pyramids, their labyrinthine corridors, were all attempts to stem the flow of time, namely "the preservation of life by a representation of life:"

> Today the making of images no longer shares an anthropocentric, utilitarian purpose. It is no longer a question of survival after death, but of a larger concept, the creation of an ideal world in the likeness of the real, with its own temporal destiny. "How vain a thing is painting" if underneath our fond admiration for its works we do not discern man's primitive need to have the last word in the argument with death by means of the form that endures. If the history of the plastic arts is less a matter of their aesthetic than of their psychology then it will be seen to be essentially the story of resemblance, or, if you will, of realism.[218]

The technology of reflection, therefore, should be used not only to record reality, but to allow reality to emanate from the film and reveal itself, thus emphasizing "film's ability to offer a hitherto unattainable view onto (non-mediated) reality."[219] In other words, film offers reality to reveal itself because we are able to transgress our own constitutive subjectivity. Hence, the photograph itself is "a mould in light," one that takes an "impression" of the object, like the "casting of a death-mask."[220] It is not the real object, but a "fingerprint," a "tracing," which evokes Aristotle's claim that perceptual experience is underwritten by *phantasia*, occurring midway between perception and thought, which is not imagination exactly, but a trace or echo of perceptual activity, like an impression from a signet ring. In which case, cinema is in an ever-narrowing liminal space that stands beside the world, looking just like the world, and yet, as Bazin will claim, borrowing a term from analytic geometry, cinema does not exactly present "reality" but is itself the asymptote of reality, moving ever closer to reality, forever dependent on reality.[221]

The cinema serves as a form of *photogénie*, using its technology to reveal the truth content of reality itself, and perhaps this will be the Lukácsian coming to the surface of everything that had been lying dormant as a vague longing in the innermost depths,[222] or Benjamin's "thought fragments" brought into view as images, which Arendt compares to the work of a pearl diver who descends to the bottom of the sea to bring to the surface that which was once alive and has now crystallized into a new form.[223] The cinema addresses these possibilities by using its basic objectivity, its mechanical recording of reality, to counter constitutive subjectivity and restore the identity of the object to itself. Or, like Icarus, it is only the attempt to escape the coils of the labyrinth by privileging the eye, only to fall to death after being betrayed by the sun.[224]

Depth of duration: Involuntary memory

Similar to Bazin, Bergson would also claim that cinematographic modes of thought antedated the invention of the motion picture. Despite his hostility to ocularcentrism, as Jay points out, as well as his hostility to the conceptual abstraction found in scientific language, Bergson often called on verbal images, those representations of the mind, as a possible antidote to both, "namely the poetic images found in the process of *durée*."[225] According to Bergson, every perception has a certain "depth of duration" (*épaisseur de durée*), where

> the concrete living present, which consists in the consciousness one has of one's body as a centre of action, necessarily occupies a moment of duration very different from our ideas of chronological time [...] prolonging the past into the present and thereby preparing the future. As a constantly varying spatiotemporal 'rhythm', a flow of states, duration is the basis of matter, which, insofar as it is extended in space, must be seen as a present which is always beginning again.[226]

This also suggests not only how perception alters the experience of time, particularly in the cinematic experience, but also how these mental images extend the existing through the technology of reflection, and simultaneously, and paradoxically, as Bazin suggested, move nearer and nearer to the source of original myth. Bazin will famously claim, "Evolution is the language of the cinema."[227] These mental images also suggest what Alexander Kluge will call the "film in the mind of the spectator," a capacity which he also believes had existed long before the technological invention of cinema, where "film takes recourse to the spontaneous workings of the imaginative faculty which has existed for tens of thousands of years."[228] Hence, this innate ability to "see" mental images is also the ability to maintain and manipulate mental images, editing together images and experiences into something meaningful, to see the hidden correspondences between diverse things, which not only supports the first technology of reflection but also suggests a capacity that is not unlike Benjamin's notion of "involuntary memory."[229]

Benjamin cites Bergson's division between "*vita activa*" and the "*vita contemplativa*" that arises from memory, which is further distinguished by the "*mémoire involuntaire*," as realized in Proust's involuntary memory of his childhood when tasting a madeleine (a pastry), whereby "the word *perdu* acknowledges that the experience he once shared is now collapsed into itself. The scent is the inaccessible refuge of *mémoire involuntaire*."[230] However, if the purpose was solely to convey information, such as that found in a newspaper, then it would seek to isolate events from the experience of those events. On the other hand, a story does the opposite; it seeks to embed "the event in the life of the storyteller in order to pass it on to those listening. It thus bears the trace of the storyteller, much the way an earthen vessel bears the trace of the potter's hand."[231] Thus, Benjamin evokes both Proust and Bergson to claim, "It is the actualization of *durée* that rids man's soul of the obsession with time," and further, "the fact that death has been eliminated from Bergson's *durée* isolates it effectively from a historical (as well as prehistorical) order."[232]

In terms that recall Sontag's description of the consumption of images as a form of lust, Benjamin also refers to "the gaze that will never get its fill of a painting, [where] photography is rather like food for the hungry or drink for the thirsty."[233] However, the earlier work of art employed imagination to give expression to desires of a special kind, where their intended fulfilment held "something beautiful," whereas now there may be a crisis of artistic reproduction that is part of a crisis in perception itself. Citing Novalis, where "perceptibility is an attentiveness,"[234] and in terms that suggest the return of identity to the object, Benjamin returns to the experience of the aura that "arises from the fact that a response characteristic of human relationships is transposed to the relationship between humans and inanimate or natural objects. The person we look at, looks at us in turn. To experience the aura of an object we look at means to invest it with the ability to look back at us. This ability corresponds to the data of *mémoire involuntaire*."[235] However, as Baudelaire would discover through his disdain for photography, his disillusionment with the crowd, its baseness replacing what once had a soul and movement all its own, where the lustre that had dazzled the *flâneur* had faded, so now "he named the price for which the sensation of modernity could be had: the disintegration of the aura in immediate shock experience."[236] Consequently, to recover the experience of *mémoire involuntaire*, Benjamin sought "the creative spontaneity of response that bourgeois socialization destroyed."[237] It was in children, therefore, that he found the capacity for revolutionary transformation, whereby, stripped of metaphysical pretensions, each generation was always a return to beginnings.

Buck-Morss clarifies that this was an appreciation of childhood cognition and not simply a romanticizing of childhood innocence, yet Benjamin was able to avoid the pessimism of Adorno that led to "'the extinction of the ego' as the tragic result of history's 'progress'."[238] Indeed, by locating revolutionary praxis within the mechanical technologies of art's reproduction, Benjamin had already separated the development of art from that of the rest of society, as he now separated children through their capacity for creative spontaneity and revolutionary praxis. He is convinced that film contributes to the hope for the future by providing a means of shattering auratic cultural forms and instigating the dialectical renewal of humanity, although "its positive form was inconceivable without its destructive, cathartic side: the liquidation of the value of tradition in the cultural heritage."[239] Moreover, Benjamin argues that the possibilities for the future of mimetic expression are far from exhausted, nor are they limited to verbal language, but extend to the new technologies of camera and film. For Benjamin, film is the means to the politicization of art where, as Buck-Morss words it: "technological *re*production gives back to humanity that capacity for experience that technological *production* threatens to take away."[240] In which case, modern culture, the culture of the image, including the mass media, is not simply a means of acculturation or appropriation in the negative context, as it is so often portrayed, but may in fact actively protect our undefined and asymptotic status as humans, our difference, "the not-yet as well as the never."[241]

The critical importance of recognizing and allowing difference is found in Simone de Beauvoir's *The Ethics of Ambiguity*, where, following the existentialist line and despite possessing no objective truths whatsoever, she will claim that we are all condemned to be free, which means we all have a choice to determine *what/who we are not yet*. In which case, our freedom through self-determination is restricted by others, whereby we can only realize our freedom to determine *what/who we are not yet* if others are also free. Freedom for self-determination, therefore, relies on freedom of the community, where my freedom is a condition of *our* freedom. Therefore, the choices that each of us make must also consider the freedom of others and this means we are compelled to make an ethical choice, such that, "To make being 'be' is to communicate with others by means of Being."[242]

The dream for waking minds: Perceptual judgements

The epistemic turn in modern times was the move from resemblance to similitude to representations of the mind, where these representations in the mind became perceptual judgements, not mere simulacra. Annette Michelson, in terms that recall Benjamin, will claim that cinema is "a dream for waking minds,"[243] where "art now takes the nature of reality, the nature of consciousness in and through perception, as its subject or domain. As exploration of the conditions and terms of perception, art henceforth converges with philosophy and science upon the problem of reality as known and knowable."[244] Thus, as noted by Elsaesser and Hagener, the cinema becomes "a paradoxical kind of consciousness that includes the unconscious."[245]

We may find that these perceptual judgements include the weight of judgement, formerly understood as an act of common human understanding, *sensus communis*, and one that serves as a validity claim of subjective universality and includes the collective reason of humankind. Perspective is now in command, as noted earlier, developed and expanded to such a degree as to allow visibility itself to be the force of authority, thereby creating the necessary conditions for perceptual judgements. The order of things is not simply a taxonomy, as Foucault argued, but a power relation. This allows Manovich, citing Michel de Certeau, to consider the use of strategies that have imposed "a particular matrix of space time, experience, and meaning on its viewers," and who in turn use "tactics" to create their own trajectories through the navigable spaces of this matrix.[246] Therefore, the Cartesian mastering of the "true nature" of light that would allow us to master human vision and raise it from a means of self-preservation to an instrument of scientific knowledge, and therefore a means of "illumination," may instead be the process of denarrativization, of programmability, an extension of the elimination of the unpredictable, that can only deliver that which is able to be revealed through the visible, where the value of a discourse does not reside in that which is "unseen," which would by definition contain unpredictability. If so, we have technology without *poiēsis*, one that does not serve to "present the unpresentable,"[247] but language without truth content, the image without thought, where what the text is really saying is *seen* as what it is actually saying.

Heidegger attempted to deal with this problem when he pointed out the challenge to human beings in their very tendency towards a technical inventory, where we had surrendered "natural language" and excluded that questioning and piety of thought that allows for "thinking that is a thanking." We might ask, what is that "natural language"? How can language not be information or orderability of one form or another? Moreover, to put a variation on Bateson's famous claim, how can "information" be "information" and still be the "difference which makes a difference?"[248] Deleuze and Guattari use the metaphor of a bee as a determination of language by illustrating what it is *not*:

> A bee that has seen a food source can communicate the message to bees that did not see it, but a bee that has not seen it cannot transmit the message to others that did not see it. Language is not content to go from a first party to a second party, from one who has seen to one who has not, but necessarily goes from a second party to a third party, neither of whom has seen.[249]

Therefore, we have the representations of the mind, which Deleuze and Guattari will refer to in terms of free indirect discourse, the enunciation of which in itself suggests "collective assemblages," where the discourse between subjects is not explained through individuality but rather through the assemblage, and in so doing, explains "all the voices present within a single voice, [...] the languages in a language, the order-words in a word."[250] Just as free indirect discourse explains all the voices in a single voice, as noted by Mikhail Bakhtin in his term "heteroglossia,"[251] so Deleuze and Guattari identify a "ghostly capacity for the apprehension of incorporeal transformations; an aptitude for grasping language as an immense indirect discourse."[252] In fact, Deleuze and Guattari claim language in its entirety is indirect discourse, which is particularly significant in terms of the collective assemblages:

> It is for this reason that indirect discourse, especially "free" indirect discourse, is of exemplary value: there are no clear, distinctive contours; what comes first is not an insertion of various individuated statements, or an interlocking of different subjects of enunciation, but a collective assemblage resulting in the determination of relative subjectification proceedings, or assignations of individuality and their shifting distributions within discourse.[253]

This "ghostly capacity" might suggest the mystical, as in Jung's *unus mundus*, a medieval term that describes our existence between spirit and matter, between the essence of human nature and the external world of physical reality, situating us in the liminal space between this world and an underlying unified reality from which everything emerges and returns to.[254] Jung maintains that this synchronicity, or "meaningful coincidence," is made possible by the fact that both the viewing subject and the connected event must ultimately stem from the same source, which allows him to theorize that the human mind possesses "a kind of pre-existent ground-plan that gives the stuff of experience a specific configuration, so that we may think of them, as Plato did, as *images*, as schemata."[255]

If we now reconsider Benjamin's claim that the camera discovers the optical unconscious, just as psychoanalysis discovers the instinctual unconscious, and if we consider the transformation of subjectivity, with its viewing subject and the projection of the bounded object domain, then, to paraphrase Freud, we may discover constitutive subjectivity and its discontents, where we cannot fall out of this world-as-picture.[256] Indeed, just as Freud would claim that art and the aesthetic experience serves as an effective substitutive satisfaction,[257] so it may prove propitious to argue that psychoanalysis is an effective substitutive satisfaction for the aesthetic experience, or conversely, that the aesthetic experience is an effective substitute for psychoanalysis, or, writ large, that psychoanalysis itself is the aesthetic experience of our collective assemblages. In terms of the world as picture, therefore, where the technology of self-reflection has now reached a global scale, where our entire social reality is a "beyond landscape" of self-reflection, we also have the aestheticization of politics, as argued by Benjamin, and therefore the politicized image.

We may now claim, as does Žižek, following Rancière, that a "shift from the political to the aesthetic is inherent in the political itself,"[258] and further, "some kind of elemental process is taking place where the living fabric of life is being transformed into the theatrical," and thus, "these poetic displacements and condensations are not just secondary illustrations of an underlying ideological struggle, but the very terrain of this struggle."[259]

Notes

1 The perception of motion in cinema is an illusion of motion made possible due to the physiological phenomenon of "persistence of vision," whereby the brain retains images entering the retina of the eye "upside down," as in a camera obscura. In order for the brain to "invert" the image so it is "right side up" takes approximately 1/20th to 1/5th of a second. This process is also known as the "phi phenomenon" or the "stroboscopic effect." In terms ov cinema, the momentary gap in perception means that we don't see the dark space between the series of static frames (which may account for as much as 50% of the film), where the illusion of unbroken movement in a series of static images is the basis for cinematography. Hence, the film speed is set at 24 frames per second. Hugo Münsterberg (1863-1916) wrote about the phi phenomenon in *The Photoplay: A Psychological Study* (1916).
2 Deleuze, *Cinema 1: The Movement-Image*, p.5.
3 Walter Benjamin, "The Formula in Which the Dialectical Structure of Film Finds Expression," *Walter Benjamin/Selected Writings - Volume 3, 1935-1938*, translated by Edmund Jephcott, Howard Eiland, and Others, edited by Howard Eiland and Michael W. Jennings (Cambridge MA: The Belknap Press of Harvard University Press, 2002), p.94.
4 Benjamin, "Surrealism: the Last Snapshot of the European Intelligentsia," p.48.
5 Elsaesser and Hagener, *Film Theory*, p.70.
6 The Hollywood "Continuous" or "Classical" style began in the 1910s and remained internationally prevalent into the late 1950s. It developed through the intuitive, trial-and-error of narrative clarity and includes innovations such as continuity cutting, close-ups, parallel editing, as well as expressive lighting, nuanced acting, eye-line matching, and shot-reverse shot editing, where the camera is in the middle of the action, matching shots from each "side," a 180-degree "axis," of the action. The classical paradigm in the Hollywood film also favours a universal address to an audience that is not specific in either class or gender, which would also become a factor in the subsequent standardization of narrative and the film-factory methods of production. This includes what Mark Cousins has called "Closed Romantic Realism." The films are "Closed" because they tend to create worlds that do not acknowledge that they are being watched and the actors behave as if the camera wasn't there. Also, they avoid ambiguous endings, preferring closed endings. The films are "Romantic" because they tend to be escapist, often with happy non-ambiguous endings, also tending toward a 'good' or romanticized version of life. In general, the films are in the vein of "realism," in other words, they avoid abstraction or experimentation in preference of conventional story and flow of action. See Cousins, *The Story of Film*, p.67.
7 Ibid., p.93.

8 Horkheimer and Adorno, "The Culture Industry: Enlightenment as Mass Deception," p.129.
9 D.W. Griffith was the first to discover the psychological effects of editing but Kuleshov and his workshop were the first to conceive of the editing dissimilar images to produce non-literal meaning, in other words meaning that was not part of the narrative information and action. The power of juxtaposition is found in the "Kuleshov effect." Kuleshov's experiments dealt with the creation of "artificial landscapes" through "creative geography," that is, landscapes, or space, that did not exist in reality but "existed" in the film. For example, a shot of a man moving left, then a woman moving right, then a building, where it was assumed the man and woman met, even if in reality none of the three shots were connected at all. Although he made few films (seven completed), Eisenstein extended Kuleshov's ideas into his "Theory of Dialectical Montage," which he wrote about in his books, *The Film Sense* (1942) and *The Film Form* (1948). Eisenstein argued that it was through the interaction of form and content between the shots, and by the way one shot determined the meaning of the preceding or following shot, that he could create a dialectical synthesis of idea, emotion, perception, that would in turn create an intellectual perception of revolutionary history. To this end, Eisenstein recognized five separate types or "methods" of montage: 1) Metric (tempo); 2) Rhythmic (tempo within shots and the shots themselves); 3) Tonal (emotional charge); 4) Overtonal (synthesis of the above); and 5) Intellectual or ideological (conceptual relationships). See Cook, *A History of Narrative Film*, pp.148-158.
10 Cousins, *The Story of Film*, p.9. See also Roy Pascal, *The Dual Voice: Free Indirect Speech and its Functioning in the Nineteenth Century Novel* (Manchester UK: Manchester University Press, 1977), p.34. See also Deleuze, *Cinema 1: The Movement-Image*, pp.72-73.
11 Pascal, *The Dual Voice*, p.49.
12 Mark Cousins, *The Story of Film* (New York: Thunder's Mouth Press, 2004), p.9.
13 Deleuze, *Cinema 1:The Movement-Image*, p.74.
14 Cousins, *The Story of Film*, p.9. See also Deleuze, *Cinema 1:The Movement-Image*, pp.72-73.
15 The term "fourth person" is sometimes used for the category of indefinite or generic referents that works like "one" in English phrases such as "one should be prepared." In Finnish and related languages, there is the so-called "zero person" in addition to the passive voice, which may serve to leave the subject-referent open, a kind of "anyone" or "nobody."
16 Jay, *Downcast Eyes*, p.51.
17 Ibid., p.51.
18 Michel Foucault, "On The Ways of Writing History," *Aesthetics, Method and Epistemology: Volume 2*, eEdited by James B. Faubion, translated by Robert Hurley and others (New York: The New Press, 1998), p.286.
19 Jay, *Downcast Eyes*, p.51.
20 Ibid., p.51.
21 Deleuze, *Difference and Repetition*, p.208.
22 Elsaesser and Hagener, *Film Theory*, p.65.
23 Rancière, *The Emancipated Spectator*, p.65.
24 Kant, "Critique of Aesthetic Judgement," p.7. See also Andrews, *The Major Film Theories*, pp.20-21.
25 Hegel, "Lectures on Aesthetics," p.114.
26 Ibid., p.118. For Hegel, the naturalistic and prosaic works that best meet this criterion are the paintings of the 16th and 17th century Dutch masters. "In such works, we do not see human freedom giving itself objective expression, but rather witness subjectivity 'destroying and dissolving everything that proposes to make itself objective and win a firm shape for itself in reality.'" Stephen Houlgate, "Hegel's Aesthetics", *The Stanford Encyclopedia of Philosophy* (Winter 2021 Edition), Edward N. Zalta (ed.). [Online]
27 Benjamin, "The Work of Art in the Age of Its Technological Reproducibility," p.127n22.

28 Elsaesser and Hagener, *Film Theory*, p.75. The period of artistic style known as Baroque began around 1600 in Rome and then spread to most of Europe. The style employed exaggerated motion and clear, easily interpreted detail to produce drama, tension, exuberance, and grandeur in sculpture, painting, architecture, literature, dance, and music. See Erwin Panofsky, "What is Baroque?", *Three Essays on Style* (Cambridge MA: The MIT Press, 1995), p.19. The cinema is often seen as a form that employs similar artistic style, while borrowing from all the other arts, incorporating them - to use the term associated with Richard Wagner - into *gesamtkunstwerk*, the total work of art. The term *gesamtkunstwerk* was first used by the German writer and philosopher K. F. E. Trahndorff in an 1827 essay, *Ästhetik oder Lehre von Weltanschauung und Kunst*. Wagner used the term in two 1849 essays, but it remains unclear whether he knew of Trahndorff's essay. See Anke Finger and Danielle Follett (Editors), *The Aesthetics of the Total Artwork: On Borders and Fragments* (Baltimore MD: The Johns Hopkins University Press, 2010).

29 Freud, *Civilization and Its Discontents*, p.13. In human psychological development, symbolism (as suggested by Freud's *fort/da*) coincides with the emergence of language, or the child's entry into the field of culturally symbolic sounds and words, which Lacan will extend into the mirror-stage where the self-reflection is the foundation of the "ego-ideal" and "ideal-ego," and the gap between them caused by the misrecognition. Language, including the sound-image, is one way we give presence to (or re-present) people, ideas, events, and feelings, in order to recover the past, or make what is gone, there. See Jacques Lacan, "The Mirror Stage as Formative of the Function of the I as Revealed in Psychoanalytic Experience," *Écrits: A Selection*, translated by Alan Sheridan (New York: W.W. Norton & Co., 1978).

30 Elsaesser and Hagener, *Film Theory*, p.67. See also Christian Metz, *The Imaginary Signifier*, translated by Celia Britton, Annwyl Williams, Ben Brewster, and Alfred Guzzetti (Bloomington IN: Indiana University Press, 1977), p.49.

31 Hegel's synthesis or dialectic, as well as his view of the dialectical process of history, is based on the idea of sublation involved in "the negation of the negation," whereby a thesis is negated by an antithesis, which creates a synthesis, which in turn becomes a new thesis, and so on. "Sublation" is the term used to translate Hegel's *Aufhebung*, which literally means "out/up-lifting." In Hegel, this has the apparently contradictory implications of both preserving and changing (the German verb *aufheben* means both "to cancel" and "to keep"). Thus, sublation is a term or concept for that which is both preserved and changed through its dialectical interplay with another term or concept. For example, the two concepts "Being" and "Nothing" are each both preserved and changed through sublation into the concept "Becoming." See Paul Redding, "Georg Wilhelm Friedrich Hegel," *The Stanford Encyclopedia of Philosophy* (Winter 2020 Edition), Edward N. Zalta (ed.). [On-line]

32 Ibid., p.63.

33 Ibid., p.63.

34 Andrews, *The Major Film Theories*, pp.228-229.

35 Klages, *Literary Theory*, p.82.

36 Elsaesser and Hagener, *Film Theory*, p.63. See also Robert Stam, Robert Burgoyne and Sally Flitterman-Lewis, *New Vocabularies in Film Semiotics: Structuralism, Post-Structuralism and Beyond* (London, and New York: Routledge, 1992).

37 Ibid., p.64. See also Christian Metz, "Problems of Denotation in the Fiction Film," *Film Language*, translated by Michael Taylor (New York: Oxford University Press, 1974), p.145.

38 Ibid., pp.64-66.

39 In Plato's cave, prisoners are chained in such a way that they can only look one way, a fire burns behind them, and between the fire and the prisoners is a walkway where puppeteers can move. The puppeteers are outside the prisoners' field of vision, but they cast shadows on the wall that the prisoners can see, a "secondary reality." This parable has been applied to the spectator in the cinema, immobilized in their seat, staring at the projection surface. One difference is that the film spectator has paid to be there. Plato, *The Republic*, translated by Desmond Lee, intro-

duction by Melissa Lane (New York: Penguin Classics, 2007). See also Jean-Louis Baudry, "Ideological Effects of the Basic Cinematographic Apparatus," translated by Alan Williams, in *Narrative, Apparatus, Ideology: A Film Theory Reader*, edited by Philip Rosen (New York: Columbia University Press, 1986), pp.286-298.

40 Jean-Louis Baudry, "Ideological Effects of the Basic Cinematographic Apparatus," translated by Alan Williams, in *Narrative, Apparatus, Ideology: A Film Theory Reader*, edited by Philip Rosen (New York: Columbia University Press, 1986), pp.286-298.

41 Manovich, *The Language of the New Media*, p.109.

42 Klages, *Literary Theory*, p.80.

43 Ibid., p.80.

44 Cutrofello, *Contintental Philosophy*, pp.168-169.

45 Heidegger, "The Origin of the Work of Art," p.147.

46 Gregory Bateson, *Steps to an Ecology of the Mind: A Revolutionary Approach to Man's Understanding of Himself* (Chicago IL: University of Chicago Press, 1972), pp.271-278. A typical example of Bateson's double bind would be a mother telling her child: "You must love me." The primary injunction here is the command itself: "you must"; the secondary injunction is the unspoken reality that love is spontaneous. Thus, for the child to love the mother genuinely, it can only be of his or her own accord, hence the double bind in a communication that is within language. See Mathijs Koopmans, "Schizophrenia and the Family: Double Bind Theory Revisited" (1997).

47 Elsaesser and Hagener, *Film Theory*, pp.101-102. See also Alexander Mitscherlich, *Society Without a Father* (New York: Schocken Books, 1970).

48 Ibid., p.101. The Panopticon was an idealized concept of a prison building designed by Jeremy Bentham in 1785. The centralized guard tower, where prisoners were never sure whether they were being watched or not, translated into the dynamics of cinema in terms of active and passive, where, on one hand, there was a clear vision of subject and object, of power and subjugation, and on the other, the all-pervasive, surveillant and punitive eye. Foucault will claim this is a model of society.

49 Ibid., p.200*n*40. The quote is originally from Thomas Elsaesser, *Fassbinder's Germany: History – Identity – Subject*," (Amsterdam: Amsterdam University Press, 1996), p.93.

50 Heinrich von Kleist, "On the gradual production of thoughts whilst speaking," *Selected Writings*, edited by David Constantine (Cambridge MA: Hackett Publishing Company, 2004), pp.405-409. See also Rancière, *The Emancipated Spectator*, p.65.

51 Elsaesser and Hagener, *Film Theory*, p.56,

52 Avital Ronell, "Trauma TV: Twelve Steps Beyond the Pleasure Princple," *The Über-Reader: Selected Works of Avital Ronell*, edited by Diane Davis (Urbana and Chicago IL: University of Illinois Press, 2007), p.68.

53 Emmeline Pankhurst, the leader of England's suffragette movement of the early 1900s, was often arrested due to her involvement in protests. Following Pankhurst's arrest in 1914, Mary Richardson, a militant Canadian suffragette, decided to protest by going to London's National Gallery armed with a meat cleaver and slicing Velazquez's famous nude painting, *Rokeby Venus*. She was sentenced to eight months in prison. When asked why she vandalized the painting, Richardson stated, "I have tried to destroy the picture of the most beautiful woman in mythological history as a protest against the government for its role in the destruction of Mrs. Pankhurst and other beautiful living women." In a 1952 interview, almost forty years later, Richardson added that she "didn't like the way male visitors gaped at it all day long."

54 Delueze and Guattari, *A Thousand Plateaus*, p.115.

55 Ibid., p.50.

56 Cutrofello, *Continental Philosophy*, p.81. See also Michel Foucault, *Madness and Civilization: A History of Insanity in the Age of Reason*, translated from the French by Richard Howard (New York: Vintage, 1988), p.ix. Note: The original quote is from Foucault's first publication, "Dream, Imagination, and Existence: An Introduction

to Ludwig Binswanger's 'Dream and Existence'" (*Introduction* in *Le Rêve et L'Existence*, 1954), translated by Forrest Williams, in *Review of Existential Psychology and Psychiatry*, XIX:1, 1985, p.78.
57 Ibid., p.86. See also Michel Foucault, *The Order of Things: An Archaeology of the Human Sciences* (*Les Mots et les choses*, 1966: Unattributed translation) (New York: Routledge Classics, 2002), p.334.
58 Ibid., p.20. See also Martin Heidegger, *Kant and the Problem of Metaphysics* (1929), translated by James S. Churchill (Bloomington IN: Indiana University Press, 1962), p.22.
59 Ibid., p.86.
60 Michel Foucault, *The Order of Things: An Archaeology of the Human Sciences* (New York: Routledge Classics, 2002), p.4.
61 Ibid., pp.4-5.
62 Ibid., p.6.
63 Deleuze, *Foucault*, p.59.
64 Elsaesser and Hagener, *Film Theory*, p.105.
65 Ibid., p.105. See also Michel Foucault, *Discipline and Punish: The Birth of the Prison*, translated by Alan Sheridan (New York: Vintage Press, 1979), p.217.
66 Deleuze and Guattari, *Anti-Oedipus*, p.112.
67 Ibid., p.104.
68 Ibid., p.105.
69 Theodor W. Adorno, "The Essay as Form," translated by Robert Hullot-Kentor and Frederic Will, *New German Critique*, No. 32. (Spring - Summer, 1984), p.151.
70 Ibid., p.171.
71 Ibid., pp. 67-70. René Descartes (1596-1650) stated in his *Discourse on the Method* (1637) that "I think therefore I am," thus establishing a self known only as a thinking thing, and known independently of the senses. *Dioptrics* (1637) was a technical treatise on optics that included an essay on the laws of refraction later called "Descarte's Law," as well as an essay in the "practical philosophy" that he claimed could render us "masters and possessors of nature." For Descartes, human vision was an extended critique of nature's workmanship that grounds the possibility of improving vision by artificial means. The purpose of sensory perception, therefore, is to preserve the mind-body composite, not to provide knowledge of the essential nature of things. Accordingly, the ultimate goal of *Dioptrics* is to "master" human vision by raising it from a mere means of self-preservation to an instrument of scientific knowledge. See Gary Hatfield, "René Descartes," *The Stanford Encyclopedia of Philosophy* (Summer 2018 Edition), Edward N. Zalta (ed.). [Online]
72 Deleuze, *Difference and Repetition*, p.276. Deleuze considers whether the outcome of Descartes' *Discourse on Method* is Flaubert's *Bouvard et Pécuchet*, an unfinished satirical work published in 1881 after Flaubert's death in 1880. The novel details the adventures of two Parisian copy-clerks, Bouvard and Pécuchet, of the same age and nearly identical temperament, and their search for intellectual stimulation, which leads them, over the course of years, to flounder through almost every branch of knowledge. Flaubert uses their quest to expose the hidden weaknesses of the sciences and arts, as nearly every one of their project comes to grief, mainly because Bouvard and Pécuchet systematically confuse signs and symbols with reality. See Gustave Flaubert, *Bouvard and Pécuchet*, translated and with a new Introduction by Mark Polizzotti, preface by Raymond Queneau (Dublin: Dalkey Archive Press, 2005).
73 Hiufu Wong, "Netizen outrage after Chinese tourist defaces Egyptian temple," CNN, Wed May 29, 2013.
74 Ronell, *Stupidity*, p.12.
75 Avital Ronell, "Slow Learner," *The Über-Reader: Selected Works of Avital Ronell*, edited by Diane Davis (Urbana and Chicago IL: University of Illinois Press, 2007), p.268.
76 Ronell, *Stupidity*, p.23.
77 Ibid., p.37.
78 Gilles Deleuze, *Difference and Repetition*, translated by Paul Patton (New York: Columbia University Press, 1994), p.275.

79 Adorno, *Aesthetic Theory*, p.xiii.
80 Deleuze, *Difference and Repetition*, p.149.
81 Ibid., p.151.
82 Ibid., p.152.
83 Ibid., p.147.
84 Ibid., p.167.
85 E.J. Dijksterhuis, *The Mechanization of the World Picture*, translated by C. Dikshoorn (Oxford UK: Oxford University Press, 1961), pp.493-502. See also Jay, *Downcast Eyes*, p.51
86 Ibid., p.501. The transition from "substantial" to "functional" thinking, and from mythological to mechanical to mathematical, is a direction encouraged by the rationalism expounded by Descartes. These transitions are linked to the development of a visual culture by Descartes, writing in *Dioptrics* (1637), where he renders a technical and mathematizable treatise of optics. Ancient science regarded optics, as found in Euclid (330-260 BCE), through "emission theory," following the Platonic tradition that vision is caused by discrete rays that emanate from the eye. The ancient theories of extromission were disproved by Alhazen (965-1039) who argued that the after-images of bright objects, like the sun, that can be seen even after your eyes are closed, proves that light enters the eye and not the other way around. In any case, Descartes's practical intent is indicated by his mathematized models for the behavior of light, which require no consideration of light's "true nature," where the world is mathematized and the unpredictable has been eliminated. Sir Isaac Newton (1642-1727), *Opticks* (1704), will analyze the fundamental nature of light by means of the refraction of light with prisms and lenses, the diffraction of light by closely spaced sheets of glass, and the behavior of color mixtures with spectral lights or pigment powders. A century later, Goethe's experiments with optics will disregard Newton's work and instead apply Romantic ideals of observation. For Goethe, in *Theory of Colours* (1810), and his application of a "colour wheel," colour was not an outward physical phenomenon but internal to the human. See Olivier Darrigol, *A History of Optics from Greek Antiquity to the Nineteenth Century* (London and New York: Oxford University Press, 2012) See also E.J. Dijksterhuis, *The Mechanization of the World Picture*, translated by C. Dikshoorn (Oxford UK: Oxford University Press, 1961), pp.493-502.
87 Horkheimer and Adorno, "*Le prix de progrès*," p.230.
88 William Leiss, *Under Technology's Thumb* (Toronto ON: McGill-Queen's University Press, 1990), p.34.
89 Horkheimer and Adorno, *Dialectic of Enlightenment*, p.121.
90 Ibid., p.121.
91 Jameson, "Reflections in Conclusion," p.211.
92 Friedrich A. Kittler, *Discourse Networks 1800/1900*, translated by Michael Metteer, with Chris Cullens., foreward by David E. Wellbery (Stanford CA: Stanford University Press, 1990), p.372. The quote is from Michel Foucault, *The Archaeology of Knowledge*, translated by A.M. Sheridan Smith (New York: Routledge Classics, 2002), p.241.
93 Friedrich A. Kittler, "There is No Software," *CTheory*, Article: a032, p.7.
94 Ibid., p.7.
95 Ibid., p.7.
96 Ronell, *The Test Drive*, p.189. Kurt Gödel (1906 - 1978) is an Austrian, and later American, logician, mathematician, and philosopher. Considered with Aristotle and Gottlob Frege to be one of the most significant logicians in history, particularly with his first and second incompleteness theorems. Gödel essentially constructed a formula that claims that it is unprovable in a given formal system, and that if it were provable, it would be false, which contradicts the idea that in a consistent system, provable statements are always true. Thus, there will always be at least one true but unprovable statement. His proof will be known as Gödel–Dummett intermediate logic (or Gödel fuzzy logic). See Tucker McElroy, *A to Z of Mathematicians* (New York: Infobase Publishing, 2005), p.189.
97 Kittler, "There is No Software," p.7.

98 Adorno, "Negative Dialectics and the Possibility of Philosophy," p.57.
99 Peter Brunette, "Post-structuralism and Deconstruction," *The Oxford Guide to Film Studies*, edited by John Hill and Pamela Church Gibson, Consultant Editors Richard Dyer, E. Ann Kaplan, Paul Willemen (London and New York: Oxford University Press, 1998), p.92.
100 Dick Hebdige, "(i) From Culture to Hegemony; (ii) Subculture: The Unnatural Break," *Media and Cultural Studies: Keyworks*, edited by Meenakshi Gigi Durham and Douglas M. Kellner (Malden, MA: Blackwell Publishing, 2006), p.155.
101 Critchley, *Infinitely Demanding*, p.99. The Situationist International (SI), founded in 1957, was an internationalist group of revolutionaries based mainly in Europe with very restricted membership. The peak of influence was during the May 1968 protests in France. Their most influential member was Guy Debord (1931-1994) and his work *The Society of the Spectacle* (1967). Debord argued that the spectacle is the inverted image of society in which relations between commodities have supplanted relations between people, in which "passive identification with the spectacle supplants genuine activity." An offshoot of the Situationists was the Lettrists, led by Isidore Isou (1925-2007), who applied their theories to all areas of art and culture, most notably in poetry, film, painting and political theory. In 1952, they caused riots at the Cannes Film Festival after the screening of Isou's *Traité de bave et d'éternité* (*Venom and Eternity*, the cast included Jean Cocteau). They also heckled Charlie Chaplin at the 1952 press conference in Paris for Chaplin's *Limelight*, after which there was a split within the movement. The Ultra-Lettrists, including Debord, announced the death of cinema. Debord's film, *Howlings in favor of de Sade* (*Hurlements en Faveur de Sade* 1952), consisted of a white screen with expressionless voices or, for almost an hour of its one hour and twenty minutes length, it was black and silent. See Thompson et al., *Film History: An Introduction*, p.441.
102 Ibid., p.8.
103 Jay, *Downcast Eyes*, p.71. The quote is from Richard Rorty, *Philosophy and the Mirror of Nature* (Princeton NJ: Princeton University Press, 1979), p.45.
104 Ibid., p.70.
105 Ibid., p.71*n*158. The quote is from Michel de Montaigne, *The Complete Essays of Montaigne*, translated and edited by Donald Murdoch Frame (Stanford CA: Stanford University Press, 1973), p.273.
106 Nicholas Rombes, *Cinema in the Digital Age* (London: Wallflower Press, 2009), p.1. See also Niklas Luhmann, *Essays on Self-Reference* (New York: Columbia University, 1990). Habermas will dispute Luhmann's claim, particularly in that Luhmann claimed he was "not interested in people," only the social systems, which Habermas would say is impossible as those systems are people, thus "the crucial theoretical weakness in systems theory lies in its failure to take account of the lived experience and social competence of ordinary people." Andrew Edgar, *Habermas: The Key Concepts* (New York: Routledge, 2006), p.152.
107 Kracauer, "The Hotel Lobby," p.174.
108 Ibid., p.174.
109 Deleuze, *Difference and Repetition*, p.285.
110 Ibid., p.287.
111 Ibid., p.286.
112 Ibid., p.286.
113 Andrews, *The Major Film Theories*, p.15.
114 Ibid., p.25. See also Hugo Münsterberg, *The Film: A Psychological Study* (New York: Dover Publications, 1970), pp.74, 82.
115 Ibid., p.20.
116 Elsaesser and Hagener, *Film Theory*, p.152. The quote is taken from Friedrich A. Kittler, "Romanticism – Psychoanalysis – Film: A History of the Double," *Literature, Media, Information Systems: Essays*, edited by John Johnston, translated by Stefanie Harris (Amsterdam: G+B Arts International 1997), pp.85-100.
117 Rudolf Arnheim, *Film as Art* (Berkeley, CA: University of California Press, 1957), pp.199-230. See also Andrews, *The Major Film Theories*, p.28.

118 A debate between film theorists is the notion that the screen is a window, the Realist view, or a frame, the Formalist or constructivist view. One looks through a window; one looks at a frame. Thus, the window becomes "invisible," whereas the frame "exhibits" the material. The window would be considered "open," and so it is centrifugal, oriented outwardly, where the audience is a guest. The frame, on the other hand, is centripetal, oriented inwardly, where the audience is a voyeur or victim. J. Dudley Andrews will write, "The force of theatre is centripetal with everything functioning to ring the spectator, like a moth into its swirling light. The force of cinema is, on the contrary, centrifugal, throwing the interest out into a limitless, dark world which the camera constantly strives to illuminate." J. Dudley Andrews, *The Major Film Theories*, p.149.
119 Gestalt psychology is a theory of mind and brain: the operational principle is that the brain is holistic, parallel, and analog, with self-organizing tendencies. For example, the visual recognition of figures and whole forms instead of a collection of simple lines and curves. An extreme example is found in the condition of *apophenia*, the experience of seeing meaningful patterns or connections in random or meaningless data, which was the premise for the film *A Beautiful Mind* (Ron Howard 2001).
120 Empty-chair technique or "chairwork" is used in Gestalt therapy to explore patients' relationships with themselves or other people in their lives. The technique involves the client addressing the empty chair as if another person was in it. They may also move between chairs and act out two or more sides of a discussion, typically involving the patient and persons significant to them. A form of role-playing, the technique focuses on exploration of self and utilized by therapists to help patients self-adjust.
121 Rudolf Arnheim, "A New Laocoön: Artistic Composites and the Talking Film," *Film As Art* (Berkeley CA: University of California Press, 1957), p.190.
122 Andrews, *The Major Film Theories*, p.35.
123 Arnheim, *Film as Art*, p.225.
124 Andrews, *The Major Film Theories*, p.206.
125 Ibid., p.190.
126 Ibid., p.23.
127 Benjamin, "The Work of Art in the Age of Its Technological Reproducibility," p.109.
128 Benjamin, "Little History of Photography," p.508.
129 Benjamin, "The Work of Art in the Age of Its Technological Reproducibility," p.115.
130 Jay, *Downcast Eyes*, p.7.
131 Cubist spatiotemporal dynamics are seen in Marcel Duchamp's "Nude Descending a Staircase: No. 2." (1912). An example of cinematic fragmentation and stylization are the "saccadic movements" of the handheld camera and jump cuts of the French New Wave of the late 1950s and early 1960s.
132 Benjamin, "The Work of Art in the Age of Its Technological Reproducibility," p.117. See also Buck-Morss, *Dialectics of Seeing*, p.267. Buck-Morss notes that Benjamin will refer to Freud's manifestations of the unconscious in forms of parapraxis (i.e., slips of the tongue). Ibid., p.459*n*77.
133 Ibid., p.105.
134 Ibid., p.116.
135 Ibid., p.114.
136 Johannes Gutenberg (1398-1468) was the inventor of mechanical movable type printing and the Gutenberg Press in the 1450s. The ready availability and affordability of the printed word led to the spread of literacy and learning to the masses, resulting in the democratization of knowledge and laid the material basis for the modern knowledge-based economy. It also led to the decline of Latin as the lingua franca, breaking the monopoly of the literate elite on education and learning, and so bolstered the emerging middle class and introduced the era of mass communication, thus permanently altering the structure of society. The relatively unrestricted circulation of information and (revolutionary) ideas transcended borders, and so captured the masses in the Reformation and threatened the power

of political and religious authorities; the sharp increase in literacy broke the monopoly of the literate elite on education and learning and bolstered the emerging middle class.

137 Ian Christie, "Formalism and neo-formalism," *The Oxford Guide to Film Studies*, edited by John Hill and Pamela Church Gibson, consultant Editors Richard Dyer, E. Ann Kaplan, Paul Willemen (London and New York: Oxford University Press, 1998), p.59.

138 Kleinhans, "Marxism and film," p.107.

139 Ibid., p.107. Sergei Eisenstein's first film, *Strike* (*Stachka*, 1924), proved to be revolutionary in both its impact on its audience and in its place in history as the first mass film of the new Soviet state. Eisenstein, a Marxist himself, would proclaim it "the October of the cinema." Rather than *kino-pravda* (film-truth), he wanted to employ a "kino-fist," replacing theatrical effects with cinematic shocks or stimuli that celebrated the spirit of revolutionary violence and the Bolshevik agitation for change. See Cook, *A History of Narrative Film*, pp.126-127.

140 Rodney Livingstone, Perry Anderson and Francis Mulhern, "Presentation III," *Aesthetics and Politics*, (London: Verso Books, 1980), p.106.

141 Buck-Morss, *The Dialectics of Seeing*, p.268.

142 Ibid., p.267.

143 Evernden, *The Natural Alien*, p.17.

144 The Haida artist and woodcarver Bill Reid said a work of art must be "deeply carved," which would include calling on his ancestors. See "The Life and Legend of Bill Reid," *Arts and Entertainment, Sculpture; CBC Archives*, 2009. The structuralists, such as Claude Levi-Strauss, sought to examine the ways in which people use individual signs in order to understand the "deep structures" of society that generated these individual instances, and so to discover the universal structures that underlay all societies and cultures, a process that was ultimately unproductive. Mirzoeff, *Visual Culture*, p.14.

145 Jean Epstein, "On Certain Characteristics of *Photogénie*" (1935), *French Film Theory and Criticism: Volume 1 - 1907-1939*, edited by Richard Abel (Princeton NJ: Princeton University Press, 1988), p.314. See also Robert Farmer, "Jean Epstein," *Senses of Cinema*, Issue 69, December 2010.

146 Andrei Tarkovsky, *Sculpting In Time – Reflections on the Cinema*, translated from the Russian by Kitty Hunter-Blair (Austin TX: University of Texas Press, 2005), p.99.

147 Ibid., p.99.

148 James M. Magrini, "'Surrealism' and the Omnipotence of the Cinema," *Senses of Cinema*, Issue 44, August 2007.

149 Horkheimer and Adorno, "The Culture Industry: Enlightenment as Mass Deception," p.129.

150 Berman, *All That Is Solid Melts Into Air*, p.117.

151 Ibid., p.118.

152 Hebdige, "(i) From Culture to Hegemony; (ii) Subculture: The Unnatural Break," p.158.

153 Epstein, "On Certain Characteristics of *Photogénie*," p.314.

154 Ibid., p.316. Guillame Apollinaire (1880-1918) would experiment with "*calligrammes*," words grouped in such as way as to form an illustration. Similarly, the Surrealist poet Stéphane Mallarmé (1842-1898) also explored the relationship between content and form, between the text and the arrangement of words and spaces on the page, as in his poem, *Un coup de dés jamais n'abolira le hasard* (1897). This relationship suggests the juxtaposition of montage in cinema, as well as the poetic synthesis of *photogénie*.

155 Deleuze, *Cinema 1: The Movement Image*, p.x.

156 Elsaesser and Hagener, *Film Theory*, p.6.

157 Andrews, *The Major Film Theories*, p.12.

158 Robert B. Ray, "Impressionism, Surrealism, and Film Theory: Path dependence, or how a tradition in film theory gets lost," *The Oxford Guide to Film Studies*,

edited by John Hill and Pamela Church Gibson, Consultant Editors Richard Dyer, E. Ann Kaplan, Paul Willemen (New York: Oxford University Press, 1998), p.68.
159 Ibid., p.70.
160 André Bazin, *What Is Cinema? Volume 1*, essays selected and translated by Hugh Gray, foreward by Jean Renoir, new foreward by Dudley Andrews (Berkeley CA: University of California Press, 2005), p.138.
161 Ivan Pavlov (1849-1946) was a Russian physiologist who won the Nobel Prize in physiology/medicine for his experiments on conditioned reflexes and memory through association. See Kandel, *The Age of Insight*, p.311.
162 See Sergei Eisenstein, *The Film Sense* (1947), translated by Jay Leyda (New York: Harcourt, Brace, Jovanovich., Revised edition, 1969).
163 Andrews, *The Major Film Theories*, p.151.
164 Ray, "Impressionism, surrealism, and film theory," p.69.
165 Ian Aitken, *European Film Theory and Criticism: A Critical Introduction* (Bloomington IN: Indiana University Press, 2001), p.82.
166 Ludwig Wittgenstein, "Lectures on Aesthetics," *Continental Aesthetics: Romanticism to Postmodernism: An Anthology*, edited by Richard Kearney and David Rasmussen (Malden MA: Blackwell Publishers, 2001), p.214.
167 Bazin, *What Is Cinema? Volume 1*, p.xiv.
168 Ibid., p.xv.
169 Ibid., p.13. See also Andrews, *The Major Film Theories*, p.139.
170 Andrew, *The Major Film Theories*, pp.171-172.
171 Siegfried Kracauer, *Theory of Film: The Redemption of Physical Reality* (1960), with an Introduction by Miriam Bratu Hansen (Princeton NJ: Princeton University Press, 1997), p.309. The quote is from Erwin Panofsky, "Style and Medium in the Motion Pictures," *Critique*, Jan.-Feb. 1947, Vol. 1, No. 3, p.27.
172 Andrews, *The Major Film Theories*, p.121.
173 Ibid., p.126. Kracauer would support the films *Nanook of the North* (Robert Flaherty 1922), *Ladri di biciclette* (*Bicycle Thieves*, Vittorio de Sica 1948), *La terra trema* (*The Earth Trembles*, Luchino Visconti 1948), and *Diary of a Country Priest* (Robert Bresson 1950). See Andrews, *The Major Film Theories*, pp.106-133.
174 Ibid., p.161.
175 Cousins, *The Story of Film*, p.465.
176 André Bazin, "The Ontology of the Photographic Image," translated by Hugh Gray, *Film Quarterly*, Volume 13. No. 4. (Summer 1960), p.8.
177 Andrews, *The Major Film Theories*, p.163.
178 Cook, *A History of Narrative Cinema*, pp.321-322. Jean Renoir (1894-1979) was a French director, screenwriter, actor, producer and author. The son of the Impressionist painter Pierre-Auguste Renoir (1841-1919), Jean Renoir is regarded as the most influential director from the era of French poetic realism, realized in films such as *La Grande Illusion* (The Grand Illusion, 1937) and *La Régle du jeu* (*The Rules of the Game*, 1939). David A. Cook writes that Renoir "presents us with a world in which feeling has been replaced by manners and all that remains of civilized values is their external form – a form that will itself soon crumble. Society has become a vast collective lie, and those, like Jurieu, who break its "rules" by telling the truth, come to no good. *La Régle du jeu* has the moral and intellectual depth of a great novel, but it is also a brilliant piece of filmmaking." Cook, *A History of Narrative Film*, p.349. Bazin writes, "Renoir alone in his searchings as a director prior to *La Régle du jeu* [...] forced himself to look back beyond the resources provided by montage and so uncovered the secret of film form that would permit everything to be said without chopping the world up into little fragments, that would reveal the hidden meanings in people and things without disturbing the unity natural to them." Ibid., p.324.
179 In *Citizen Kane* (Orson Welles 1941), the identity of "Rosebud" is a symbol of lost love and innocence, yet it is also insufficient for a clear answer to Kane's emptiness, and to America's, as it is the "missing piece" of the jigsaw puzzle of Kane's life, the "something lost," yet it is also an inanimate object, and a regressive one, which is ultimately meaningless, or perhaps, like reality, ambiguous and unreli-

able. The cinematographer, Gregg Toland (1904-1948), also developed techniques that were more comparable to what the eyes see in real life, since our vision does not blur what we look at, but what we do not look at. In the films before Toland (such as Renoir's), a shallow depth of field was used to separate the various planes on the screen, creating an impression of space, as well as stressing what mattered in the frame by leaving the rest (the foreground or background) out of focus. With Toland's lighting schemes, shadow was a much more interesting tool, dramatically as well as pictorially, to separate foreground from background and thus to create space within a two-dimensional frame while everything was in focus. See Cook, "Orson Welles and the Modern Sound Film," *A History of Narrative Film*, pp.327-354.
180 Barthes, *Camera Lucida*, p.26.
181 Ibid., p.27.
182 Heidegger, "Building Dwelling Thinking," p.362.
183 Barthes, *Camera Lucida*, p.57.
184 Ibid., p.59.
185 Ibid., p.59.
186 Roland Barthes, "The Death of the Author," *Continental Aesthetics: Romanticism to Postmodernism: An Anthology*, edited by Richard Kearney and David Rasmussen (Malden MA: Blackwell Publishers, 2001), pp.371-373.
187 Bazin will become the inspiration for the young French filmmakers and critics of the *Cahiers du Cinéma*, who would reject the French commercial cinema and its "tradition of quality," mostly adaptations of French literature. In his essay, "*Une certaine tendance du cinéma français*" (*A Certain Tendency in French Cinema*, 1954), François Truffaut expressed the "policy of author," which attacked "*le tradition de qualité,*" and the "*litterateurs*" with their emphasis on plot and dialogue. Truffaut had nothing against great literature, only their cinematic adaptations, which he felt were manipulative and exploitative. Truffaut wanted the main author of a film to be the director, ideally the writer/director, who shouldn't just be "the gentleman who added the pictures." This would replace the "*cinéma de papa*" with "*un cinéma d'auteurs,*" support the *francs-tireurs* or independents, and become the manifesto for the French New Wave of the late 1950s and early 1960s. To quote Jean-Luc Godard, "It's not where you take things from - it's where you take them to." See Cook, *A History of Narrative Film*, pp.431-480. See also Francois Truffaut, *A Certain Tendency in French Cinema* (1954).
188 Rancière, *The Emancipated Spectator*, p.125.
189 See Cutrofello, *Continental Philosophy*, pp.57-58.
190 David Bordwell, *French Impressionist Cinema* (New York: Arno Press, 1980), p.133.
191 Ray, "Impressionism, Surrealism, and Film Theory," p.69.
192 Bordwell, *French Impressionist Cinema*, p.133.
193 In abstract paintings such as *Black and Violet* (1923), Wassily Kandinsky (1866-1944) experimented with the colour of sounds and the sounds of colour, or synesthesia, defined as a neurologically based condition in which stimulation of one sensory or cognitive pathway leads to automatic. Kandinsky held that blue is the colour of spirituality: the darker the blue, the more it awakens human desire for the eternal. Kandinsky was a member of *Der Blaue Reiter* (The Blue Rider, 1911-1914), a group of artists from the *Neue Künstlervereinigung München* in Munich, Germany, would be fundamental to Expressionism, along with *Die Brücke*, founded the previous decade in Dresden in 1905. Their work would influence cinema through films such as *The Cabinet of Dr. Caligari* (Robert Wiene 1920), *The Golem: How He Came into the World* (Paul Wegener and Carl Boese 1920), *Nosferatu, a Symphnoy of Horror* (F.W. Muranu 1922), *The Last Laugh* (F.W. Muranu 1924), and *Metropolis* (Fritz Lang 1927).
194 Ray, "Impressionism, Surrealism, and Film Theory," pp.70, 71.
195 Ibid., p.75.
196 Ibid., p.72.
197 Ibid., p.74. The quote is from Roland Barthes, *Image-Music-Text*, translated by Stephen Heath (New York: Hill & Wang, 1977).

198 Jay, *Downcast Eyes*, p.476. Jay acknowledges this term is from Raymond Bellour, "*Le blocage symbolique*," *Communications*, 23 (1975). Ibid., p.476*n*139.
199 Ibid., p.476.
200 Ian Christie, "The avant-gardes and European cinema before 1930," *The Oxford Guide to Film Studies*, edited by John Hill and Pamela Church Gibson (Oxford and New York: Oxford University Press, 1998), pp.449-454.
201 An example of screen tests and the "harnessing of enchantment" can be found in the early Hollywood cinema. In 1922, at 24 years old, Irving Thalberg (1899-1936), named "The Boy Wonder" in Hollywood, became the head of production at MGM and turned it into the most successful studio in Hollywood. He was instrumental in the standardization of cinema production, concentrating production in a single place, the studio, creating an organized division of labour, standardizing film language through story conference as well as enhancing the continuity system, standardizing exhibition and distribution by holding previews and doing reshoots, and co-authored the Production Code. He also realized that movies succeeded commercially to the extent that they are "enchanted," which meant that the formula for production would need a formula for enchantment, which he also realized was not only the job of the director but also that of the actor. Thalberg introduced screen tests with the sole purpose of finding those actors who were "photogenic," in other words, he sought to standardize the means to access *photogénie*, to capture and standardize enchantment. To keep his mental faculties at peak, Thalberg would read philosophical books by Bacon, Epictetus, or Kant. "They stimulate me. I'd drop out of sight in no time if I didn't read and keep up with current thought—and the philosophers are brain sharpeners." See Ray, "Impressionism, Surrealism, and Film Theory," pp.69-70. See also Cook, *A History of Narrative Film*, pp.240-241.
202 Elsaesser and Hagener, *Film Theory*, pp.32-3. See also David Bordwell, Janet Steiger, and Kristin Thompson, "The Central Producer System: Centralized Management after 1914," *The Classical Hollywood Cinema: Film Style and Mode of Production to 1960*, editors David Bordwell, Janet Steiger, and Kristin Thompson (New York: Columbia University Press, 1985).
203 See Nigel J.T. Thomas, "Mental Imagery, Philosophical Issues About," *Encyclopedia of Cognitive Science*, Volume 2, L.Nadel (Editor) (London: Nature Publishing/Macmillan, 2003), pp.1147–1153.
204 Manovich, *The Language of New Media*, p.186. See also Jean-Louis Commoli, "Machines of the Visible," *The Cinematic Apparatus*, edited by Teresa de Lauretis and Steven Heath (New York: St. Martin's Press, 1980), p.122.
205 Ibid., p.186.
206 Ibid., p.185.
207 Ibid., p.186. See Lev Manovich, "Synthetic Realism and its Discontents" (excerpt from *The Language of New Media*), *Film Theory and Criticism: Introductory Readings*, edited by Leo Braudy and Marshall Cohen (London and New York: Oxford University Press, 2009), pp.786-787. Objectivists see the truths of science as facts discovered in the natural world and technical practices as things imposed upon practitionaers by apparatuses.
208 Elsaesser and Hagener, *Film Theory*, pp.66-68. See also Jean-Louis Baudry, "Ideological Effects of the Basic Cinematographic Apparatus," translated by Alan Williams, in *Narrative, Apparatus, Ideology: A Film Theory Reader*, edited by Philip Rosen (New York: Columbia University Press, 1986).
209 Manovich, *The Language of the New Media*, p.187.
210 Elsaesser and Hagener, *Film Theory*, p.92.
211 See Slavoj Žižek, "The Strange Case of the Missing Lacanians," *The Fright of Real Tears: Krzysztof Kieślowski Between Theory and Post-Theory* (London: British Film Institute, 2001).
212 Cutrofello, *Continental Philosophy*, p.350.
213 Bruce Fink, *The Lacanian Subject: Between Language and Jouissance* (Princeton NJ: Princeton University Press, 1997), p.61.

214 Slavoj Žižek, "The Cyberspace Real," *European Graduate School* (2013) [On-line].
215 Jacques Lacan, *The Four Fundamental Concepts of Psycho-Analysis*, translated by Alan Sheridan (London: Penguin, 1994), p.60
216 Dyer, "Introduction to Film Studies," pp.3-10.
217 André Bazin "The Myth of Total Cinema," *What is Cinema? Volume II*, translated and Edited by Hugh Gray (Berkeley CA: University of California Press, 2005), pp.25, 26.
218 Bazin, "The Ontology of the Photographic Image," pp.5, 6.
219 Elsaesser and Hagener, *Film Theory*, p.3.
220 Bazin, "The Ontology of the Photographic Image," p.7.
221 Andrews, *The Major Film Theories*, pp.140-141.
222 Lukács, *The Theory of the Novel*, p.24.
223 Hannah Arendt, "Introduction," *Illuminations*, edited and with an Introduction by Hannah Arendt, translated by Harry Zohn (New York: Harcourt, Brace & World, 1968), pp.50-51.
224 Jay, *Downcast Eyes*, p.229*n*66.
225 Ibid., pp.199, 202.
226 Benjamin, "On Some Motifs in Baudelaire," pp.275*n*8-276*n*8. See also Henri Bergson, *Matter and Memory*, translated by Nancy Margaret Paul and W. Scott Palmer (New York: Zone Books, 1991), pp.137-139, 186, 205.
227 Andrews, *The Major Film Theories*, p.186.
228 Michelle Langford, "Alexander Kluge," *Senses of Cinema*, Issue 69, July 2003.
229 Benjamin, "On Some Motifs in Baudelaire," p.174.
230 Ibid., pp.174, 200. *À la recherche du temps perdu* (*In Search of Lost Time*, or translated previously as *Remembrance of Things Past*) is a novel in seven volumes by Marcel Proust (1871–1922). It is known for its theme of involuntary memory, the most famous example being the "episode of the madeleine," where the taste of a madeleine cake dipped in tea inspires a nostalgic incident. See Marcel Proust, *In Search of Lost Time*, translated by C.K. Scott Moncrieff, Terence Kilmartin, and Andrea Major, revised by D.J. Enright (New York: Random House, 1981).
231 Ibid., p.174.
232 Ibid., pp.196, 201.
233 Ibid., p.203.
234 Ibid., p.204. See also p.289*n*76. The quote is from Novalis, *Schriften* (Berlin 1901), p.293.
235 Ibid., p.204.
236 Ibid., p.210.
237 Buck-Morss, *The Dialectics of Seeing*, p.264.
238 Ibid., p.265.
239 Benjamin, "The Work of Art in the Age of Its Technological Reproducibility," p.104.
240 Buck-Morss, *The Dialectics of Seeing*, p.268.
241 Wolfgang Schirmacher, "Cloning Humans with Media: Impermanence and Imperceptible Perfection," *Poesis: A Journal of the Arts and Communication*, Vol. 2 (Toronto ON: EGS Press, 2000), p.39.
242 Simone de Beauvoir, *The Ethics of Ambiguity*, translated from the French by Bernard Frechtman (Don Mills, ON:Syracuse Press, 1948) p.71
243 Elsaesser and Hagener, *Film Theory*, p.161.
244 Ibid., p.161. See also Annette Michelson, "Bodies in Space: Film as 'Carnal Knowledge'," *Art Forum*, Volume 7, No. 6, February 1969, p.58.
245 Ibid., p.161.
246 Manovich, *The Language of the New Media*, pp.267-268. See also Michel de Certeau, *The Practice of Everyday Life*, translated by Steven Rendall (Berkeley CA: University of California Press, 1984).
247 Mirzoeff, *An Introduction to Visual Culture*, p.17.
248 Gregory Bateson, *Steps to an Ecology of the Mind: Collected Essays in Anthrology, Psychiatry, Evolution, and Epistemology* (Northvale NJ and London, Jason Ar-

onson Inc., 1987), p.321. See also Elsaesser and Hagener, *Film Theory*, p.45. Bateson inspired the title of Deleuze and Guattari's *A Thousand Plateaus*. Deleuze and Guattari state that the plateau is always in the middle, not the beginning or the end, and that a rhizome is made of plateaus. Bateson used the word "plateau" to "designate something very special: a continuous, self-vibrating region of intensities whose development avoids any orientation toward a culmination point or external end. Bateson cites Balinese culture as an example: mother-child sexual games, and even quarrels among men, under go this bizarre intensive stabilization." Deleuze and Guattari, *A Thousand Plateaus*, pp.21-22. Also, Bateson uses "plateau" for "continuous regions of intensity constituted in such a way that they do not allow themselves to be interrupted by an external termination, any more than they allow themselves to build toward a climax; examples are certain sexual, or aggressive, processes in Balinese culture. A plateau is a piece of immanence. Every BwO [Body without Organs] is itself a plateau in communication with other plateaus on the lance of consistency." Ibid., p.158.

249 Deleuze and Guattari, *A Thousand Plateaus*, p.77.

250 Ibid., p.80.

251 See Mikhail Bakhtin, "Discourse in the Novel," *The Dialogic Imagination – Four Essays by M.M. Bakhtin*, edited by Michael Holquist, translated by Caryl Emerson and Michael Holquist (Austin TX: University of Texas Press, 1981).

252 Deleuze and Guattari, *A Thousand Plateaus*, p.84.

253 Ibid., p.80.

254 Carl Jung and M.L. von Franz, Joseph L. Henderson, Jolande Jacobi, and Aniela Jaffé, *Man and his Symbols*, Coordinating Editor: John Freeman (London: Aldus Books, 1964), pp.384-385.

255 Liliane Frey-Rohn, *From Freud to Jung – A Comparative Study of the Psychology of the Unconscious*, translated by Fred E. Engreen and Evelyn K. Engreen, forward by Robert Hinshaw (Boston MA: Shambhala Publications, 1974), p.94. The idea of synchronicity came to Jung in the 1920s while having dinner with Einstein.

256 Freud, *Civilization and Its Discontents*, p.4. Freud wrote, "We cannot fall out of this world."

257 Ibid., p.13.

258 Jean-Luc Godard, who, as Rancière points out, uses collage as a technique to combine heterogeneous elements, creating a distanciation effect that is aimed at initiating social and political discourse, particulary in his work since the French riots of 1968. Jacques Rancière, "The Ethical Turn of Aesthetics and Politics," *Aesthetics and Its Discontents*, translated by Steven Corcoran (Cambridge UK and Malden MA: Polity Press, 2009), p.122. For Godard's collage technique, see *Weekend* (Jean-Luc Godard 1968), a film shot by Raoul Coutard, where the violence and social unrest anticipates the 1968 student riots in France.

259 Slavoj Žižek, "Afterword by Slavoj Žižek," in Jacques Rancière, *The Politics of Aesthetics: The Distribution of the Sensible*, translated and with an Introduction by Gabriel Rockhill (New York: Continuum, 2004), pp.76-78.

Poetics and Perception

Classical form: The transcendental topography of the mind

According to the preface of the 1962 edition of *The Theory of the Novel*, Georg Lukács recalls the summer of 1914 and starting his first draft, he was in a mood of permanent despair and admits that he was not simply looking for a new literary form but for a new world. This statement is offered somewhat apologetically, perhaps because he would later renounce this and other works from his pre-Marxist period. Even so, at that time, rejecting all rationales for the war, and particularly disturbed by the public's enthusiasm for the conflict, Lukács anticipated that Germany would be defeated and that the Russian monarchy would fall, but then the question would still arise: who would save us from Western civilization?[1]

In fact, the summer of 1914 first found Lukács compiling a book on Dostoevsky, originally conceived in the form of Boccaccio's *Decameron*. It would contain a series of dialogues where a group of young people withdraw from the insanity of war, just as the storytellers of the Decameron withdraw from the plague. Only now the modern version would convert the plague into capitalism, its toxic symptoms apparent in the pathological, the aberrant, and the deformed in modern culture, little of which Lukács would find deserving of consideration as true art, serving only as an expression of decline from the height of classical form.[2] This view was reflected in Lukács's hostility to modernism of all kinds, particularly Franz Kafka, James Joyce and Samuel Beckett, preferring instead the great novelists of the European bourgeois tradition, particularly the Russian novelists, such as Leo Tolstoy, who had remained closer to a "natural life" and thereby attempted to move beyond the social forms of a corrupted culture to access the "innermost essence."[3]

The twenty-nine-year-old Lukács was setting the stage for his lifelong battle, a battle fought on two fronts, where each front not only dealt with opposing forces but undermined the other front as well. As a classicist in the debate between high art and popular culture, he would condemn any art that surrendered to modern values; as a Marxist in the debate whether religion could be replaced by art or philosophy, he would subordinate both art and philosophy to his orthodox political views. His colleague Ernst Bloch would call this practice "a confusion of realms."[4] Nonetheless, four years away from joining the Communist party, motivated by his disenchanted view of the world, Lukács was already distancing himself from the "superb prison" of Kantian ethics with its categorical imperatives and seeking answers in the writings of Dostoevsky, where Lukács perceived, in a case of the means justifying the ends, how Dostoevsky was working out "a system of ethics charged with mysticism and revolutionary terror, grace and sin, salvation and perdition."[5]

Inspired by "a highly naïve and totally unfounded utopianism,"[6] as he claimed in his 1962 preface, Lukács sought "a general dialectic of literary genres that was based upon the essential nature of aesthetic categories and literary forms."[7] In so doing, Lukács discovered that the problems of the novel form - which he regarded as the highest cultural form - are "the mirror--image of a world gone out of joint," and therefore, "the 'prose' of life is only a symptom, among many others, of the fact that reality no longer constitutes a favourable soil for art."[8] In a journey that originated in literary criticism and would soon lead to political philosophy, Lukács's utopian hope, one that he would maintain for much of his career, was for the development of a historical sense within modern culture that maintained the timeless values of the past. Consequently, Lukács's search for a comprehensive system of aesthetics begins by considering the historical context for an ideal form of literature. In his view, the closest to this ideal form would be the Greek epic,[9] composed of being and destiny, adventure and accomplishment, life and essence, a "well-fitting garment for the world,"[10] which asks the all-important question: how can life become essence? The main function of this concept in Lukács, as Andrew Feenberg explains, is "to mark the place of the lost unity of self and world for which modern consciousness longs."[11] Indeed, Lukács envisions an integrated civilization where life and essence coexist, perceived as classical Greece, where human beings are able to live their lives within a meaningful world. The modern era, unfortunately, is not such an age. The world and the self, the light and the fire, have become permanent strangers. Rather than an integrated civilization, we have a problematic civilization, one that is distinguished by its opaqueness rather than its transparency. Thus, having alienated ourselves from reality and unable to achieve totality, namely the unity of subject and object, we are filled with an unaccountable nostalgia for what we have lost. We now exist somewhere between past and future, stranded perhaps, as Lukács wrote, evoking Fichte, in "an age of absolute sinfulness."[12]

Lukács acknowledges the inner loneliness of the soul in a disenchanted world, and "the rift between 'inside' and 'outside'," such that the task of the work of art is to draw the archetypal map, to realize "the transcendental topography of the mind."[13] Works of art, therefore, should be a sign of hope, pointing the way to redemption, and yet "the inner nullity of their own means" must deny that possibility because "the form-giving subject and the world of created forms has been destroyed, and the ultimate basis of artistic creation has become homeless."[14] Similarly, Lukács will also define philosophy, quoting Novalis, as a kind of "homesickness," described as "the urge to be at home everywhere." This sense of homesickness, of wanting to belong to the world, thus applies to both the work of art and philosophy, because both are attempting to find a synthesis between the actual and the possible, which "determines the form and supplies the content of literary creation."[15]

The Greek epic form, according to Lukács, existed prior to man's "homesickness" and created harmony between life and essence, whereas all other forms have led to triviality and fragmentation. In order to recreate the epic form, however, we would also have to recreate the historical moment, namely the social conditions that would allow the possibility of the epic. In this regard, any form of art is bound to its historical moment. Thus, we find ourselves in a paradox where art offers the possibility of redemption, capable of remaking the world in its own utopian image, and yet a problematical world does not allow art to be strong enough to be capable of that remaking, and so the historical moment must nullify the very form that might lead to its own reconciliation. Although Lukács regards the novel as the highest cultural form, it still fails to express the eternity within us, thus exposing a gap between the finite and the infinite that can be expressed only through irony. Ultimately, rather than a true illumination, all we are offered is pessimistic anti-illumination.

The "half-art" of the novel, therefore, prescribes more and more laws for itself, laws of "tact and taste,"[16] which only exacerbates the requirement for a "new ethical self-correction, determined by the work's content, in order to achieve the 'tact' which will create a proper balance."[17] Tact and taste provide boundaries for the novel, an attempt at self-correction where the world's fragility, often realized through irony, creates the concurrent danger of "obscuring or even destroying the creative intention of acceptance and objectivity which the great epic demands." In other words, the irony of the novel presents a world where everything is seen as "many-sided," and although everything is isolated and independent from everything else, everything is also connected to everything else, thus "full of value and yet totally devoid of it." We now have a new perspective of life where there is an "indissoluble connection between the relative independence of the parts and their attachment to the whole,"[18] yet rather than a totality, we merely have an empty re-mythification of essence.

Burdened with a nostalgia for a world that no longer exists, equipped with forms of art that are either too weak or inadequate to achieve our "homecoming," Lukács's only hope for redemption, faint as it might be, was for some new form to emerge and succeed where the novel had failed.[19] However, whether this emergent form might mark the end of the age of sinfulness, Lukács would only concede the slim likelihood for a form drawn from material reality, yet "still so weak that it can easily be crushed by the sterile power of the merely existent."[20] Nonetheless, the prospect of transcending the limitations of the work of art could now offer a faint glimmer of an emergent form for a new world, which is "drawn for the first time as a seen reality."[21] This would call for a realism informed by its own historical sense and a reality not simply experienced at face value but interpreted. In other words, just as the commodity is the object under its veil of reification, so our social reality is veiled by illusion and our social being informed by a false consciousness, where only a truly "seen reality" may pierce the veil of illusion, which was the possibility of the new form of artistic creation.

Creatively polemical: To change reality

To create a truly beautiful world, in Lukács's view, would demand a cultural form that is capable of overcoming the alienation and de-humanization found in modern bourgeois society, tethered as it is by its own coercive elements, thus demanding a revolutionary change. If the highest good for humanity can only be achieved through human praxis, as Marx had claimed, then, as Lukács would write in his opening line of *History and Class Consciousness* (1923), "Materialist dialectic is a *revolutionary* dialectic."[22] Therefore, the central goal of the dialectical method would be to transform the world and "*to change reality*."[23] In order to produce the transformative dialectic and initiate real change within our reality, particularly if we have a barren reality that no longer constitutes a favourable soil for art, we would then need an art form that is, as Lukács termed it, "*creatively* polemical."[24] Lukács's view, as Andrew Cutrofello interprets, is that "'man' does not yet exist; or rather he exists only as not yet existing."[25] Lukács's solution will be that "the coming – or rather on-going – proletarian revolution is the process of restoring to humanity its very humanity."[26] In Lukács's conception, therefore, determination must include intention: in order to re-conceive the role of art in human experience, we must also re-conceive the role of human experience in art.

This project is inspired not only by the centenary of *The Theory of the Novel*, but also by the questions posed by Lukács, the answers of which may prove more problematic than ever. One hundred years on we could say that we have transformed the world through the image, thus changing our reality, and creating in the process, as Richard Kearney has described it, the "Civilization of the Image,"[27] where "there can no longer be any *decidable* distinction between image and so-called reality."[28] Yet the questions remain. Who will save us from Western civilization? How can life become essence? How is our image-making culture tied to its historical moment? Is the new emergent form to be found in the "mass art" of the cinema? Is the cinema the product of a problematical civilization that incorporates the "many-sided" perspectives where everything is connected to everything else, or is it "creatively polemical"? If we have re-conceived the role of art in human experience, how have we also re-conceived the role of human experience in art? Is it possible that the works of art produced by the image-making culture are capable of restoring to humanity its very humanity?

This project will attempt to address these questions using an interdisciplinary approach, which will include aspects of the historical, philosophical, psychological, cultural and technological. However, perhaps more importantly, the underlying theme is to be found in the sub-title and the historical-philosophical inquiry into the transformation of subjectivity through the image-making culture, in particular, the logic and impact of the aesthetic experience found in visual culture, or what could be called a culture of the image, particularly during the expansion of image-making technology in the last century. To put it literally, we will consider how the image-making culture changed the way we see things. In other words, our perception of the image has changed the way we perceive and understand everything around us, including the perception and understanding of ourselves through images, or, to put it yet another way, the changes in our subjectivity have transformed those perceptions and judgements that take place in or proceed from a person's mind, which, in turn, also causes changes in the creation of a distinctly different social reality. Of course, it is not only consciousness that determines our social reality, so too it is our social reality that determines consciousness, yet we may find that the modern culture of the image inhabits and defines both of these realms, such that, as Friedrich Kittler wrote, the viewer views their own processes of perception.[29]

The fraud of constitutive subjectivity: Social antithesis

If the transformation of subjectivity has led to a crisis of subjectivity, then there may be a demand for a transgression of this transformation within the modern culture of the image, a transgression that may be achieved through the aesthetic experience. As such, the goal of this inquiry will be to consider if truth can be disclosed through aesthetics, particularly in the work of art, and subsequently, how aesthetics may or may not disclose truth, what kind of truth is disclosed, what prevents truth from being disclosed, and so forth. A major influence in formulating these questions has been Theodor W. Adorno, in particular, and as mentioned in the Introduction, his claim that the task of his thought was "to use the strength of the subject to break through the fraud of constitutive subjectivity."[30] The most important aspect of this statement may be its paradoxical nature: the subject must use their own strength to break through their own subjectivity, yet subjectivity is fraudulent and therefore, we might assume, works against that very strength. Another significant aspect is that this "breaking through" suggests not only a dynamic process but also some kind of threshold, which raises another question, namely, just what truth might be found on the other side. Indeed, if the fraud of constitutive subjectivity is that its concepts define the likeness of the world with the subject, then the power of identity must go beyond constitutive subjectivity where concepts could be developed in such a way as to present what is more than conceptual in them. In which case, identity must be more than identity in that it draws back into itself what it purports to overcome. Kant's Copernican turn specifically limited knowledge to a world constituted by the subject; therefore, Adorno will call for a second Copernican revolution, an axial turn that reverses subject and object, so that non-identity becomes the basis of knowledge.[31]

The significance of this inquiry may also be found in the nature of truth itself, and how it relates to the nature of subjectivity and objectivity, namely the manner and meaning of their relationship and constitution, or more precisely their self-constitution, which would include the relationship between the virtual and the actual. The importance of an inquiry into the nature of aesthetic truth can be found in Adorno's claim that "the need to lend a voice to suffering is a condition of all truth. For suffering is objectivity that weighs upon the subject; its most subjective experience, its expressions, is objectively conveyed."[32] We may find that the need to address suffering would mean that truth is not only connected to the aesthetic but the ethical. However, another paradox arises in that we may understand the need to lend a voice to suffering, but we may find that the suffering that needs our voice is in fact our own. In which case, if the work of art intends to be that voice, then how does that voice become heard, and who hears it, and what does it say and how does it say it? Yet here we have another paradox, for if that voice is truth, as opposed to "noise," which Jean-François Lyotard defines as something that is not recognizable as anything within a system, i.e. language, and therefore not recognized as an accepted "truth," and if the work of art by its very definition must be distinct but recognizable by its form and visibility, then its condition of being within a system may nullify that very distinctness and its potential for truth outside an accepted "truth." Thus, for Lyotard, the important question to ask is who decides what knowledge is and what "noise" is, and who knows what needs to be decided.[33]

In which case, as Adorno noted, the task of the work of art, like the task of philosophical self-reflection, may be to unravel the paradox of discovering the non-conceptual in the concept, and in so doing discover the actual truth within accepted "truth," whereby, as we may find through this inquiry, "reflection upon its own meaning is the way out of the concept's seeming being-in-itself as a unit of meaning."[34] Thus, both philosophy and the work of art must strive to transcend the concept of what they are, thereby transcending constitutive subjectivity, and thereby reconciling the subject with the object, or with that of which the object was deprived through its objectification. However, if we return to Adorno's claim that, "for suffering is objectivity that weighs upon the subject; its most subjective experience, its expressions, is objectively conveyed," we may find that suffering is constituted through subjectivity and so through that which is objectively conveyed, such that, unavoidably, that which "weighs upon the subject" is human nature itself. If so, then the task that Adorno set himself, of breaking through the fraud of constitutive subjectivity, is daunting indeed.

In any case, we must remember that philosophy is not art; it is not a reflection of anything, nor should it be. Alain Badiou makes this point by citing Deleuze: "philosophy is not a reflection of anything whatsoever. There is philosophy, there can only be philosophy, when there are paradoxical relationships, ruptures, decisions, distances, and events."[35] Yet both philosophy and the work of art involve apperception, and both share the task of resisting pseudomorphosis, such that they are not condemned to always struggle in the shadows of the past, which suggests the demand for both a philosophical and a historical consideration of the image-making culture.[36] Indeed, in terms of the work of art, Adorno will claim it is "both autonomous and *fait social*."[37] As a result, due to the double character of art itself, the image-making culture is an activity that informs and influences our social reality, with implications in the aesthetic, economic, legal, political, and ethical spheres, and yet simultaneously art itself seeks autonomy while being influenced by these same spheres. This co-dependency allows Adorno to formulate the following paradox: "Art is autonomous and it is not; without what is heterogenous to it, its autonomy eludes it."[38] A dialectical double construction is thus required to address the double character of art and discover its true essence (the aestheticized) beyond that which is essential (the aesthetic). Otherwise, we may find, as Adorno famously warned, that, "art perceived strictly aesthetically is art aesthetically misperceived."[39] This also reveals another aspect of the double character of art, namely its necessary and illusory nature, its non-truth.

In order for modern culture to not simply be reportage, and thereby to resist the ideological, it may have to become "the social antithesis of society,"[40] which would require a transgression within the work of art that transgresses its own aesthetic, producing what might be termed "the aesthetic of the aesthetic." In so doing, its social fact also suggests a potentially significant politics of resistance, where, in terms of the modern image-making culture, autonomy is protected by the "mask" of technological anonymity, yet at the same time that technological anonymity suggests the potentially sinister ability to transgress that same autonomy that this transgression promises. The result may be an aesthetic of anonymity that transgresses all subjectivity, that is, that which resists constitutive subjectivity because it was not originally constituted by the subject.

Of course, there is strength in the subject, and perhaps only those aspects of constitutive subjectivity that are fraudulent need breaking through, and we may also find assistance in the nature of truth. If truth can indeed be disclosed through aesthetics, then we may look to the work of art to share the burden that truth must bear, that which lends a hand to the voice of suffering, whereby the aesthetic experience is also an ethical experience. Perhaps what lies beyond the "breaking through" is that which appears after the struggle in the shadows, whereby we would hear the voice of suffering because it had acquired the assistance of "truth," thus by voice, through its lending of the truth and by allowing our finding of the truth, we come to hear not just a single voice but the many voices, our voices, and of those who have come before, and of those yet to come into being. Badiou forwards this claim to cinema, calling it "an absolutely impure art."[41] Badiou claims that we are all "the orphans of the idea of revolution,"[42] where we live in a world that has lost its illusions, where we have become resigned, and yet the image-making culture, in particular the cinema, despite its triviality and fragmentation, its frequent lack of taste and tact, may point the way to redemption because it is capable of transforming philosophy itself, and in the process telling us something about the world, namely, not to despair.

The form-determined essence: Poetic crisis

Lukács claimed that the novel is the highest cultural form; however, it may be that poetry has been the privileged form. Mary Klages observes, "poetry is meant to be an art form, to be and to create something beautiful; fiction, on the other hand, is a kind of rhetoric, a literary form meant to persuade or to present an argument, not to produce an aesthetic effect," hence she will claim that, historically, "poetry has been associated with the aesthetic function ('delight') and novels with the didactic function ('instruct')."[43] In terms used earlier, we might also say that, historically, poetry is the "temple grammar" that evokes the "beyond landscape" whereas the novel or fiction is the "cognitive mapping" that evokes the reified "second nature." The distinction is important. The reified second nature may have been co-opted into the hegemonic goals of larger institutional frameworks, as noted earlier, and indeed may itself be a creation of the historical and political aesthetic, which suggests that it is a result of "world making." In contrast, just as Sontag claimed there was a grammar and, even more importantly, an ethics of seeing,[44] so the beyond landscape may be a creation of the poetic as well as the ethical, yet it is not trying to "prove" something but is a process of "world discovering." Importantly, it suggests resistance to the hegemonic at the level of the individual subject.

If we return to Lukács's claim that the novel remains a "half-art" due to the relationship between ethics and aesthetics in the creative process, only prescribing more and more laws for itself of tact and taste when what is needed is a new ethical self-correction that is determined by the work's content, then this proposal necessarily allows that cultural forms as the self-forming forms must include an ethical aesthetic, one that must reject those of tact and taste, or the first level of the aesthetic. In terms that recall Heidegger's "*the they*," those unable to "see" or "hear," Lukács echoes Nietzsche when he claimed that "one must shed the bad taste of wanting to agree with many," because, at least for the philosopher of the future, and the very act of writing implies a future reader, demanding that "my judgement is *my* judgement."[45] However, due the nullification, even assassination, of the poetic, the question is whether the artist can create a work of art that includes the necessary self-correction or if any cultural form is itself truly capable of self-correction.

If self-correction is to be generated from the self and not from society then we might look to Nietzsche's affirmation of the ecstatic experience and his claim of the significance of *amor fati*, the love of one's fate, such that "nothing that is may be subtracted, nothing is dispensable."[46] Thus, Nietzsche addresses the poetic crisis by not only writing his own poems and dithyrambs but by addressing the poet of the future, "you *new* philosophers."[47] In the meantime, Nietzsche offers his writing and himself as one who seeks the transformation of the theoretical man through the "birth of an artistic Socrates,"[48] the "music-making Socrates,"[49] a figure, as Walter Kaufmann argues, who would be Nietzsche's vision of himself.[50] Kaufmann reminds us that, like Socrates, Nietzsche was not trying to convert anyone to a metaphysics of his own, but only to be the educator, hence the model and mediator, urging his reader to "Become what you are!"[51] Thus, the task of the poet and the task of the translator are both realized through Nietzsche, who will suffer just as Hölderlin did, because he called for the transvaluation of values and taught the need for an awareness of "a very popular error: having the courage of one's convictions; rather it is a matter of having the courage for an *attack* on one's convictions!!!"[52] We might regard this as the exposure of the fraud of constitutive subjectivity and Nietzsche as one who had passed that threshold.

Lukács prescribed critical and socialist realism; otherwise, "the end-product of this flight from the reality of the present day must be a form of nihilism. Once a commitment to the realities of the age is refused, human content disappears."[53] Indeed, these end products - nihilism and cynicism, despair and *angst*, suspicion and self-disgust - are the "spontaneous product of the capitalist society in which intellectuals have to live."[54] As a result, we now have a perspective of life where there is an "indissoluble connection between the relative independence of the parts and their attachment to the whole,"[55] yet rather than a totality we merely have an empty re-mystification of essence. Therefore, in terms of an ethical self-correction, if the ethic is purely an element in the structure, as when ethics appears merely as the conventions of "justice" for example, then the ethic is only a formal precondition that allows "the form-determined essence to be attained."[56] On the other hand, if the ethical intention of the work of art is in the very creation of every detail of the work itself, its being-found-fitting, then the ethical and the aesthetic are inseparable. In other words, the former (ethic as element) is all about the outer form, and the latter (ethical and aesthetic as substance) is concerned with the inner form. To put it another way, the form-determined essence is about world-making, the work of art in its historical moment, whereas the essence realized through form is world-discovering, the work of art in its essence.

However, if we are in danger because "natural language" is in danger, as Heidegger claimed, then it is because language itself has not proven adequate to counter objectness, to "the ubiquitous orderability of what is present," which may be due to the division of ethical intention and the aesthetic. Yet the saving power of the work of art is also dependent on the questioning subject and their piety of thought, thus the two are linked: the ethical/aesthetic intention of the work of art and the questioning subject. However, if we have become a victim of liquidation, to use Adorno's term, where speech is consigned to orderability and information, disallowing self-reflection and self-presencing, then this also disallows the potentiality of *autopoiēsis* and the thinking as thanking, as well as the cultural forms that contribute to the self-forming forms of being. Therefore, if the discourses of modern society are lacking in "discourse ethics," Habermas's term, then it may very well be because, as Sartre had claimed, "a crisis of language broke out at the beginning of the twentieth century and that it was a poetic crisis."[57]

The labyrinth: The forgotten song

The modern artist, the young Lukács would argue, must use his or her craftsmanship to "put bourgeois professionalism in the service of the perfection to which art aspires," and yet "the artist's sense of craft is not merely the creation of art but the redemption of life itself, or at least of life as it has been deformed by bourgeois society."[58] But there are productive limits to this possibility, as Lukács words it, "limits which are drawn from within,"[59] because a great work of art arises from, and must be an integral part of, the historico-philosophical moment that made its creation possible.

This brings up the question, as Critchley will ask, of whether an outside construction is capable of putting together a conception of action in concert with a whole number of disparate interest groups.[60] Adorno had suggested that cultural forms contain an "inherently collective objectivity,"[61] where the artist's individual voice is more importantly a part of the whole of humanity, and that in itself is why the work of art is the form that must carry the "burden of art's eloquence."[62] However, Adorno argues, it is not so much the forms themselves that cannot serve the revolutionary purpose of raising awareness of the reality of bourgeois subjectivity, but the very inability of the subject to release the truth, unintentional or not, due to the reification of consciousness.

Adorno contends that reflection meant burdening artworks with intentions, whereas the absurd, as found in Samuel Beckett's works for example, does not mean that there is nothing to interpret, but rather that the content "resists" interpretation. Thus, Adorno will write that Beckett's works can no longer be identified with reason, such that "the darkness of the absurd is the old darkness of the new. This darkness must be interpreted, not replaced by the clarity of meaning."[63] The inability to achieve clarity of meaning is also considered by Lyotard, evoking Hegel, when he considers whether oppositions demonstrate unity: "What goes against the grain is what confers, and of differences in the finest harmony."[64] Lyotard is divided in his conclusion, as we must be, because the work of art is called upon to give hope for the future and yet register the world's despair, and so is captured in a double bind, perhaps because they are one and the same thing. Nonetheless, a double bind suggests once again the necessity for the transgression of the aesthetic through the aesthetic, in that the production of meaning must be achieved through a double operation of self-reflection, one that may be found in Adorno's views of music.

Rather than tracing the cinema's genesis to photography or its mechanical reproduction, as did Benjamin, Adorno will address the language of moving pictures. In doing so, he will claim that the birth of moving pictures comes out of the spirit of music. Adorno cites as evidence a letter dated March 23, 1890 - five years before the first public screenings by the Lumière brothers and Edison - where a member of Wagner's immediate circle suggested performing one of Liszt's symphonies in a darkened room with a sunken orchestra and images moving past in the background.[65] Adorno interprets the significance of this event as proof that moving images came out of music, and indeed the music of this epoch evoked a new dynamics that found expression in the cinematic form. Consequently, where Benjamin sought equivalences between philosophy and image, Adorno would look to philosophy and music.[66]

Adorno would reject the notion of the bourgeois artist-as-genius and replace it with artist-as-craftsman.[67] Music requires intellectual labour, not simply inspiration, and it had to be translated from written text into sound, or vice versa, which meant it had to be interpreted in order to exist. Adorno would extend this argument to justify an intellectual elite. If the understanding of the new music, such as Arnold Schoenberg's, was limited to an exclusive audience, "then that is the fault of the social structure and not the experimental artist."[68] In his younger years, Adorno himself aspired to be a composer and studied music with one of Schoenberg's students, Alban Berg.[69] In his later years, Adorno would connect Benjamin's philosophy and Berg's aspirations for "the complete freedom of the ear."[70] Adorno will claim that science had destroyed language, which had succumbed to the instrumental reasoning of the modern world, losing its beauty and purpose, and, as a result, rather than Benjamin's cinematic scalpel that pierces subjective reality, it was only music that can heal those very wounds caused when "the anatomic scalpel has gashed the body of speech and by breathing into it the breath that may animate it with living motion."[71]

Music, therefore, must revive the festering body of language and bring it back to life, and thus music must do what language, including visual language, had failed to do: to produce an aesthetic effect rather than an argument. Music is in a position to accomplish this monumental task for a couple of reasons. First, Adorno argues that while the eye had grown accustomed to perceiving reality as a reality of objects, and hence of commodities, the ear did not adapt so quickly so hearing lagged behind technology and remained relatively immune to its manipulation. Martin Jay writes that the privileging of the eye evokes the pyramid, the construction, the signification, whereas the coils of the ear evoke the labyrinth, the internal, and the hidden.[72] Secondly, in support of intellectual labor, it is the very alienation of music, classical music in particular, which keeps it separate from both the bourgeoisie and the proletariat, allowing it to provide a means to transcend the present consciousness. Therefore, rather than the distraction and shock-value of film, and Benjamin's tactile "missile"[73] with its dynamite of the split second, it would be through the contemplative immersion of the intellectual that we return to the internal experience of individually endured time, to the private reality of *durée*, and thereby recover our lived experience and the abstract boundlessness of the sublime. Adorno would write, "We don't understand music, it understands us."[74] Thus, the artwork's necessary autonomy, albeit illusory, is the key to modernism's social character and its task to be the social antithesis of society. Hence, the task of the work of art is to summon the essences that have drifted beyond our recall and renew "the promise contained in the age-old protest of music: the promise of a life without fear."[75] Importantly, Adorno may have marked a turning point in seeking a means to transgress the aesthetic of one aesthetic form through another aesthetic form, or the transgression of one sense through another sense.

For Adorno, "all attempts at reconciliation, whether by market-oriented artists or collectively-oriented art educators, are fruitless."[76] However, just as an encounter with the sublime would involve an element of terror, so art can no longer be beautiful, demanding that Odysseus strains to the terrible cries of Schoenberg's *Enwartung*, which is the remembrance of the forgotten song.[77] The dissonant twelve-tone compositions of Schoenberg give voice to anxiety and the terror of the catastrophic situation, which, according to Adorno, dismisses the temptation to rescue the work of art through a progress of disenchantment, as if the auratic might give way to something more profound. However, even Schoenberg's students are now using their advanced techniques to write movie soundtracks.[78]

One might assume that Adorno would support cinema, perhaps realized as the synthesis of the pyramid and the labyrinth, yet he would claim that the poetic potential, if it ever existed, was nullified by cinema as mass culture, a victim of the instrumental reasoning and marketplace economics that would impose itself upon the cinematic form from the outside, and in the process transform it into a commodity. Thus, as with any work of art, there is the potentiality for the poetic that sets it free from its traditional moorings, yet it must contend with the irresolvable contradiction that any form of art is bound to its historical moment. As stated earlier, to restore the proper social function of the aesthetic would require a society where the aesthetic had a proper social function. In other words, despite the potential for the poetic in the cinematic form, its historical moment also leads to its enslavement, just as Adorno found a nullification in music that "represents at once the immediate manifestation of impulse and the locus of its taming."[79] Therefore, just as Odysseus tied to the mast when he hears the Sirens, unable to free himself, succumbing but not succumbing to the Siren's song, art can only awaken the futile hope for redemption.[80] Hence, Adorno must settle for the contention that "great art waits," that its authenticity arises in its "capacity of standing firm."[81]

Adorno would be accused of a melancholy withdrawal into pessimistic resignation and political hopelessness, a kind of "intellectual hibernation,"[82] a waiting for better times. This seemed particularly true when he spent a good deal of his later years involved in university administration. However, Max Pensky calls this the "message-in-the-bottle" interpretation, because Adorno was in fact the embodiment of the nonconformist intellectual and the application of theory-as-praxis who "effectively undermined the traditional understanding of the antinomy between the (politically committed) intellectual and the (politically aloof) academic mandarin."[83] In doing so, Adorno characterized the double character of art itself, which he claims is "both autonomous and *fait social*."[84] Adorno respected Benjamin's assertion that history has been written from the standpoint of the victor and must now be written from that of the vanquished, but he would add that we should also address ourselves to those things which were not embraced by such history, that had fallen by the wayside, "the waste products and blind spots that have escaped the dialectic."[85] Indeed, Adorno will claim, "dialectical thought is an attempt to break through the coercion of logic by its own means."[86] Consequently, Adorno will concede that Benjamin sought new ways to make philosophy rewarding even in the face of catastrophe, whereby "the task he bequeathed was not to abandon such an attempt to the estranging enigmas of thought alone, but to bring the intentionless within the realm of concepts: the obligation to think at the same time dialectically and undialectically."[87]

Acousmêtres: White noise

Adorno identified a turning point in seeking a means to transgress the aesthetic of one aesthetic form through another aesthetic form, or the transgression of one sense through another sense, yet there may be a problem in that this may give rise to fragmentation and, ultimately, lead to a state of indistinction. For example, Walter Murch will assert that sound is our first sense, developed while still in the immersion and protection of the womb: "Sound rules as solitary Queen of the senses."[88] However, sound is less exacting than sight in terms of its source,[89] where it can be difficult to decide if the experience takes place "inside" or "outside" the body.

Michel Chion, the French composer of *musique concrete*, explored music based on sound rather than musical notation, as well as music based on sounds other than instruments or voices. Chion also coined the term *acousmêtres* (derived from "acousmatic," a sound whose origin is invisible, and *être*, "to be"), which, as noted by Elsaesser and Hagener, describes the bodiless voice in cinema that apparently has no origin, ambiguous and oscillating, neither "inside" nor "outside," suggesting an inversion of the traditional hierarchy of images and sound, as well as an antagonism between the image (surface) and the sound (space).[90] Chion will also use the term *rendu* to describe the rendering of sound that the viewer would not be able to hear if they found themselves in the "reality" of the images.[91] In doing so, the soundtrack no longer "accompanies" the flow of pictures, it provides the narrative continuity that the fragments of images do not, suggesting "visual fishes swimming freely in the encompassing medium of the sound-aquarium."[92] Elsaesser and Hagener assert that,

> The new technological 'viscosity' or 'Velcro' quality of sound allows it to cling to material substance, but also to any semantic substance: such sound is always poised on the brink of referentiality, but being transient, fleeting and multi-directional, it is also volatile and fickle in the way it attaches itself, or indeed detaches itself from, an image as well as from meaning.[93]

Indeed, even the state of indistinction itself is mobile and ubiquitous, when, to recall McLuhan's depiction of the modern world, we are in a time of "all-at-onceness" where "we have no precedent for this, no way of getting our bearings, nobody to tell us what's happening."[94] Thus, the visual spectator may go into "free fall," to use Freud's term, when subjected to manipulation that recalls Münsterberg's psychotechnology and leading to what Chion calls "the screaming point," where the film moves from meaning to non-sense, often signified by a woman's scream, the place "where speech is suddenly extinct, a black hole, the exit of being."[95]

Žižek will argue that sound is more important than vision in helping us orient and stabilize ourselves in space, and thus more significant in terms of disorientation and destabilization. The notion of the *voix acousmatique*, as expounded by Chion and interpreted by Žižek, explores "the voice without bearer, one that cannot be attributed to a subject and hovers in some indefinable interspace, implacable precisely because it cannot be properly located, being part neither of the diegetic 'reality' of the story nor of the sound-accompaniment (commentary, musical score), but belonging to that mysterious domain designated by Lacan the 'between-two-deaths' (*l'entre-deux morts*)."[96] This would suggest that sound has the capacity to un-suture and thereby challenge the cohesion of the visual field, and thus a transgression of the aesthetic (image) through the aesthetic (sound).

In support of Lacan's view that the gaze as well as the voice is on the side of the object and not the subject, Žižek regards this transgression of the classical cinematic style as making visible a gap between the traditional camera perspectives, plus that which is coded as subjective, and thereby achieving a look of the camera that is not attached to any human point of view.[97] In Lacanian terms, this non-human point of view is neither that of the Imaginary or the Symbolic Orders, but the Real itself. For Lacan, the Real is not synonymous with reality, but an ontological absolute that is outside language and that resists symbolization absolutely. Lacan defines the Real as "the impossible" because it is impossible to imagine, impossible to integrate into the Symbolic, and impossible to attain. It is this resistance to symbolization that lends the Real its traumatic (uncanny) quality.[98] If so, this non-human view would challenge constitutive subjectivity, and, as with Adorno, there is meaning to be found in this view, a different kind of truth, the *ars inveniendi* that is discovered through Freudian slips of the tongue (parapraxis), where these truths surface as inconsistencies or unintentional truths.

"Noise," as Lyotard claimed, is something that is not recognizable as anything within a system, for example, the system of language, and so not recognized as an accepted "truth." In addition, if the work of art by its very definition must be distinct and yet recognizable due to its form and visibility, then its condition of being within a system may nullify that very distinctness and its autonomous potential for truth outside an accepted "truth." Thus, for Lyotard, the important question to ask is who decides what knowledge is and what "noise" is, namely to decide the distinction between that which is the truth and that which is the accepted "truth," and who knows what needs to be decided.[99] Similarly, in terms of the work of art, we might consider Adorno's claim that the rank or quality of an artwork must be conceived from its "degree of articulation."[100] In relation to the Habermasian "double language," with its propositional or perlocutionary component and illocutionary component, Lyotard contends that language itself has two forms, science and narrative. Science is connected to the grand narratives, or meta-narratives, and needs to be legitimated (propositional), whereas the narrative is connected to language games, including the postmodern micro-narratives, which do not need any outside legitimation and so are fluid and unpredictable, yet follow certain rules and strategies to effect different results (illocutionary).[101] To put it another way, scientific discourses are legitimated by linking knowledge to the liberation of humanity (a trope associated with the French Revolution) or to the meta-perspective of speculative Spirit (as found in Hegel).[102] By contrast, language games, or the micro-narratives, are characterized by a skepticism towards the grand narratives, where there is no recourse to the unifying strategies of the pre-ordained systems, where these so-called unities, as the tragic histories of the nineteenth and twentieth centuries have witnessed, have only resulted in terror.[103] However, rather than "mourning" this situation, Lyotard seeks to draw out its practical implications.[104] Thus, Lyotard, as noted by Cutrofello, agrees with Habermas that a systems approach to society is repressive in the sense that it subordinates all human ends to the technocratic demand for performative efficiency, and where knowledge is characterized by its utility, but he rejects

Habermas's theory of communicative rationality because it aims at the legitimation of norms through consensus.[105]

According to Lyotard, Habermas contends that modernity failed when the totality of life was fragmented into independent specialties and their subsequent interpretation through "the narrow competence of experts,"[106] and so the remedy for the splintering of culture and its separation from the lifeworld would call for "changing the status of aesthetic experience when it is no longer primarily expressed in judgements of taste," which would then "bridge the gap between cognitive, ethical, and political discourses, thus opening the way to a unity of experience."[107] Lyotard argues that the consensus that Habermas seeks can only damage the heterogeneity of language games, which forces Lyotard to defend such heterogeneity by conceiving of legitimation on the model of "paralogy,"[108] a movement against an established way of reasoning, developing instead "the capability of thinking outside of the concept and outside of habit."[109] In doing so, as noted by Richard Kearney, Lyotard seeks an invocation of "narrative imagination" as a means to resist "the modern ideology of the Total Theory,"[110] and so "to unmask Theory as Grand Narrative and [...] to unmask Grand Narrative as a concealment, even suppression, of little narratives."[111] Thus, the heterogeneity of language games finds its expression through 'narrative imagination' and can be described as "mistress without masters, the armoury of the disarmed, the power of the powerless,"[112] and by calling attention to the multiplicity and incompleteability of "little narratives" and away from the consensus of a unified weighing of judgement, Lyotard is able to claim that "the history of the world cannot pass a last judgement. It is made out of judged judgements."[113]

In other words, rather than a political discourse that is oriented towards the public sense and consensus, Lyotard accepts a political discourse of dissensus, of opinions, of differends, namely a conflict that cannot be resolved equitably, where "one side's legitimacy does not imply the other's lack of legitimacy."[114] Contrary to Kant's claim of an innate good or an underlying moral, Rancière makes this very point when he argues that what we are seeing in the modern world are simply scenes of dissensus, namely "the organization of the sensible where there is neither a reality concealed behind appearances nor a single regime of presentation and interpretation of the given imposing its obviousness on all."[115] Similarly, just as Lyotard will argue that the metanarratives must be replaced by a postmodern culture of diversity, where, instead of being deprived of the right to narrate, it is the little narratives of dissensus that are the stories that survive to tell the tale.[116]

Consequently, Lyotard disagrees with Arendt about the nature of political conflict. For Arendt, political discourse remains oriented toward the sensus communis, but differends are conflicts that can only be sustained in light of an irreducible element of "dissensus."[117] The mistake made by Habermas, then, was his concern for world conflation and so to adhere to consensus through "the narrative of emancipation,"[118] rather than to present the "unrepresentable" through the little narratives of dissensus and so "wage a war on totality."[119] However, as Cutrofello points out, unlike Habermas who offered a basis for a moral conception of discourse, Lyotard's solution does not allow for the presumption of first principles and can only offer an irreducibly agonistic conception of discourse.[120] Lyotard's response might be, as he stated, "humanity is not made of creatures in the process of redeeming themselves, but of wills in the process of emancipating themselves."[121] In making this claim, Lyotard echoes Adorno that the condition of truth addresses the need to lend a voice to suffering, for suffering is objectivity that weighs upon the subject; its most subjective experience, its expressions, is objectively conveyed. Although Lyotard critiques Adorno for his lack of invention,[122] he follows Adorno in using the name "Auschwitz" in order "to signify just how impoverished recent Western history seems from the point of view of the 'modern' project of the emancipation of history."[123] Following Hegel, Lyotard will also claim, "there is a sort of grief in the *Zeitgeist*. It can find expression in reactive, even reactionary, attitudes or in utopias – but not in a positive orientation that would open up a new perspective."[124] Similarly, Sloterdijk will write, "modernity is losing, in addition to its feeling of vitality, the distinction between crisis and stability."[125] In fact, Lyotard will claim, "with Auschwitz something new has happened in history (which can only be a sign and not a fact),"[126] perhaps the destruction of reality itself, and so, "it is the silence that surrounds the phrase, [...] it is the sign that something remains to be phrased which is not, something which is not determined."[127]

Adorno made the famous claim that to write lyric poetry after Auschwitz is barbaric because it cannot pay homage "to that which has been reduced to silence."[128] He also warned, in terms of the liquidation of the subject, that, "people who blindly slot themselves into the collective already make themselves into something like inert material, extinguish themselves as self-determined beings. With this comes the willingness to treat others as an amorphous mass."[129] Nonetheless, for Lyotard, so radical is Auschwitz, so unprecedented is this event, that "between the SS and the Jew there is not even a differend, because there is not even a common idiom (that of a tribunal) in which the damages could be formulated, be they in place of a wrong."[130] Perhaps this is the "allocutionary" that Lyotard spoke of, perhaps the "white noise," something that is not only not recognizable as anything within a system, not only not recognizable as "truth," but something else again, the implacable noise as silence, and perhaps that is truth itself.

Artificial life: An open *autopoiēsis*

"Artificial life" is the term that Schirmacher uses to describe the social reality that we as human beings have created for ourselves. Schirmacher invokes Nietzsche in writing that we created the entire world, and then forgot that we did, so we had to invent a creator, only to anguish over the problems of origin.[131] As a result, the "truth" may be ugly, as Nietzsche claimed, but we have art so as not to perish from the truth. More importantly, every "truth" is artificial, even when it has the benefit of being a necessary lie. However, the "truth" created through artificial-artistic perception is not simply a coping mechanism that allows the necessity of forgetting the "ugly" truth, but, an important distinction made by Schirmacher, it also must promote the awareness of forgetting whatever we have understood.

If so, then what are the ethics of an aesthetic arising from artificial truth? Ethics arise from aesthetics because they are values derived from the intuition of a self-fulfilling life, Schirmacher states, realized authentically only in the pleasurable perception of one's own world. There are two possibilities in how this perception is realized: one is anthropocentrism, a self-reflexive "human-all-too-human" constitutive subjectivity that is exclusive; the second is anthropomorphism, a self-generated "human-uniquely-human" openness that is also inclusive.[132] The anthropomorphic self-embraces the art of living by knowing of no other world beyond the human horizon and experiencing no phenomenon in any way other than in relation to him- or herself. In either case, evoking Heidegger, this suggests a humanism that is no more than a moral-aesthetic anthropology that amounts to an internal-external relation of the same, and no more than a philosophical interpretation of man from the standpoint of, and in relation to, man himself, which in turn leads to an ever more exclusive interpretation of the world that is expressed by man's fundamental relation to a world view [*Weltanschauung*], which is realized in modern times as world-as-picture. Therefore, in order for the aesthetic to be ethical, it must subvert its own form, because it can only present the necessary lie or the artificial truth. However, this subversion would certainly be resisted, if only in terms of self-defence, protecting its own forgetting as it were, or, as Nietzsche would have it, the transvaluation of the self-granted "rights" of the will to power that determine what things we accept and how those things are accepted, all of which would demand an ethics of an aesthetic that shrewdly challenges itself to overcome itself.

The challenge of a self-subversive aesthetic would need to address the modern expansion of our pictorial and perceptive capabilities through "hyperperception," which appears as a Nietzschean "sleeplessness," with its suggestion of the scale of Heidegger's world-as-picture as well as the sinister component of modern surveillance. This challenge also suggests, as Schirmacher notes, the dissolution of ethics in aesthetics, because there will always be ethical "disobedience," which, however, can also serve as a virtue in terms of an "aesthetics of resistance."[133] Schirmacher, citing Wolfgang Welsch, maintains that there remains an interplay of revealing and concealing, while exposing the "culture of the blind spot," which acknowledges the twofold relationship between heeding and excluding, and the usefulness of the "recognition of the overlooked, the missed, the unheard."[134] The implication is that this timeless interplay of revealing and concealing, determined by Heidegger as *aletheia*,[135] acknowledges that which is incalculable, the shadow that withdraws into a space beyond representation, to a knowledge that is refused, and yet still enables the "in-between" where the subject belongs to being and yet remains a stranger, only now we understand the "undefined life" in itself is that which is authentic. This interplay is defined, therefore, as a kind of open *autopoesis*,[136] where we may find that the liberated domain of the individual subject is now accompanied by the bounded domain of the object, only now recognized as a self-fulfilment or self-presencing that allows for self-creation through modern technology, which is possible precisely because we cannot conceal the truth that can only be the one created by ourselves.

Homo aestheticus: Polyvalency

In his *Undoing Aesthetics* (1997), Wolfgang Welsch will call for an undoing of traditional aesthetics in order to discover an aesthetics beyond aesthetics, when he states that there is a blindness toward the negative effects caused by the modern tendency toward what he calls hyperaestheticization and the creation of *homo aestheticus*.[137] In addition, Welsch argues that the passion for traditional aesthetics as the principles of the artistic and beautiful, the rational and the sensuous, does not address the flaws in global aestheticization, namely that when everything is fashioned and judged by the artistic and the beautiful then art and beauty become meaningless. Wittgenstein would write, "You might think Aesthetics is a science telling us what's beautiful – almost too ridiculous for words. I suppose it ought to include also what sort of coffee tastes well."[138] However, that would be precisely Welsch's point, it does. As such, Welsch offers three primary criticisms of traditional aesthetics, which are 1) the derealization of reality, 2) the reconfiguration of *aesthesis*, and 3) the revalidation of accustomed forms of experience.[139]

The first point, the derealization of reality is attributed to modern technology where the electronic manipulation of images, as well as media aesthetics, makes everything mutable, a realm of transformability, so much so that if there is an "unbearable lightness of being," to borrow from Kundera, then it is in the electronic realm. The consequences of the derealization of reality is desensitivity to the actual, which may account for the level of violence found in the media, and where "the real is tending to lose its insistency, compulsiveness and gravity."[140] This leads to the second point, the reconfiguration of *aesthesis*, which calls for the revalidation of experiences outside electronic media, and here we get a practical application of the aesthetics beyond aesthetics. Perception, more specifically vision, is no longer the noble sense, certainly not a reliable contact with reality, and yet this may have opened the way for a departure from the traditional hierarchy of the senses where a new appreciation for hearing, touch, smell and taste may contribute to a new reconfiguration of *aesthesis*. A consequence of these first two points may be a revalidation of accustomed forms of experience, the third point, which is not to exclude the fascination of electronic worlds, nor is it a matter of simply returning to the sensuous experience of pre-electronic times, but to address the plurality of worlds and multiple domains of modern existence.

Welsch recognizes that there will continue to be entanglements between the aesthetics of the artistic and the aesthetics beyond aesthetics: "The fact that the aesthetic constitution of thinking as such is not new, but only the attentiveness to this might well ease the step to recognition of the aesthetic-poetic character of thinking. At the same time this step is a difficult and unaccustomed one."[141] In other words, the processes that originated historically in art have also played a significant role in the transformation of subjectivity, such that our everyday perception is imbued with the sediment of generations of artistic perception and experience. At the same time, the artistic and the aesthetic are not autonomous but must remain inseparable from reality; otherwise, a purely aesthetic perception and experience removed from the world would be unrecognizable and irrelevant.[142]

In terms of aesthetics beyond aesthetics itself, we would say that aesthetics must adopt an interdisciplinary approach in order to free itself from its past perceptions, extending the aesthetic in our image-making culture across all dimensions of perception of the senses, *aisthēsis*, and thus become a new discipline, a "transaesthetics." In terms of a reconfiguration of *aisthesis*, in what we had earlier referred to as a new discipline, a "transaesthetics," where we are exhorted to become artists of thinking, rather than scholars of thinking, and so incorporate all dimensions of *aisthesis*, a polyphonic transaesthetics that would allow for an emancipation of dissonance and of unresolved accords, where mutually contradictory worlds can co-exist, this is what Welsch will call "polyvalency." In doing so, Welsch is evoking Wittgenstein and his concept of "family resemblance," whereby "an expression's coherence need not be due to unitary essence, but can come about in a different way: through overlap between one usage and the next."[143] Nor does this necessarily mean an ambiguity that is synonymous with unusability, a dilemma Wittgenstein recognized when he wrote that "anything – and nothing – is right,"[144] because the ambiguity itself supports the interdisciplinary aspect of aesthetics, the complexity of its relationships and interpretations, as well as its versatility. This ambiguity of interpretation would also support Schirmacher's reference to the "culture of the blind spot," namely the twofold relationship between heeding and excluding, and the usefulness of the recognition of the overlooked, the missed, the unheard, the shadow that withdraws into a space beyond representation, to a knowledge that is refused. Wittgenstein claimed that aesthetics is not a science, that it is unable to come up with any definitive answers, yet it does move within the perspective of truth. Indeed, aesthetics provides the concepts – and, as Deleuze would say, a concept is not a brick, but a "tool box"[145] – and so provides the tools to construct a philosophy of art that addresses the truth beyond truth itself. Adorno may have said it best:

> The task of a philosophy of art is not so much to explain away the element of incomprehensibility, which speculative philosophy has almost invariably sought to do, but rather to understand the incomprehensibility itself. This incomprehensibility persists as the character of art, and it alone protects the philosophy of art from doing violence to art.[146]

And what is the violence that can be done to art through the philosophy of art? It is the annihilation of the material by means of the form, such that, to paraphrase Schiller, rather than demanding any specific determination we should remind ourselves that art only offers us the possibility of becoming human beings, just as nature only confers upon us the power of becoming human.[147] Like Rancière, we might say that the artist must be invisible in his work, just as God is in nature.[148] However, what is that incomprehensibility in art that protects the philosophy of art? It is the aesthetic beyond the aesthetic, the truth beyond truth itself, that determination which cannot be determined. We might recall that the dictum for Adorno's *Aesthetic Theory* was meant to be Friedrich Schlegel's quote: "What is called the philosophy of art usually lacks one of two things: either the philosophy or the art."[149] As Adorno knew, and Welsch will confer, the "aesthetic experience [...] [must] transcend itself:"[150] such that, "the semblance of art is not fully encompassed by aesthetic semblance: Art has truth as the semblance of the illusionless."[151] Therefore, in terms of ambiguity and the "culture of the blind spot," the aesthetic beyond the aesthetic does not seek a singular perception or totality of meaning, a monoaesthetic, but seeks instead a polyaesthetic, a plurality of perceptions and meanings accessed through different modes across multiple fields of perception and domains of experience.

Hyperperception: The leap of faith

If we return now to artificial life, the social reality that we as human beings have created for ourselves, we may find, as Schirmacher contends, that the ethics for an artificial life runs into the danger of an ideologically charged controversy around the natural and the artificial. Further, this suggests Paul Virilio's concerns of the "dressage of the eye,"[152] where the eye's motility, and thus our inclination toward nomadism, a Deleuzian term,[153] is domesticated and standardized into fixity, which imposes a closed rather than open generation of perception. However, Schirmacher disagrees with Virilio's call for an "ethics of perception,"[154] stating that it remains unrealistic. Virilio will write that "at the end of the century, there will not be much left of the expanse of a planet that is not only polluted, but also shrunk, reduced to nothing, by the teletechnologies of generalized interactivity,"[155] yet Schirmacher will suggest precisely the reverse in that hyperperception is in fact a protection *against* the dressage of our gaze and emotions. This is possible because hyperperception is an intensification of humankind that encompasses both a granting and a forgetting of the world, at once critical and creative, self-fulfilling and self-creating.[156]

The problem of the ethics of the aesthetic remains, however, and if every truth is artificial, even when it has the benefit of being a necessary lie, and if artificial-artistic perception is not simply a coping mechanism that allows the necessity of forgetting the truth, then it also must promote the awareness of forgetting whatever we have understood. In which case, paradoxically, as Schirmacher argues, this necessary forgetfulness appears as fidelity to the leap of faith.[157] If we consider Kierkegaard's leap of faith, as interpreted by Schirmacher, we find that "the meaning of life is not achieved merely through reasoning and common practice, but rather it bears the signature of the absurd which is transformed by the individual from within, into fulfilment."[158] Therefore, the leap of faith is not true fulfilment, but only our evasion of revolutionary experience and instead making the choice of forgetfulness, of evasion of life itself, which has been given the term "God," and proves in retrospect to be anything but a leap and instead is only a "step back."[159] Nevertheless, just as Kierkegaard sought an aesthetic existence, so the use of the media and our modern technology in pursuit of hyperperception does indeed allow for the education of our perception, yet at the same time evokes the dogma of a new and modern theology, which still requires, therefore, just as in Kierkegaard's time, a *true* leap of faith.

We may now ask what is required of a "true" leap of faith. As "media monads,"[160] we remain artificial beings by nature, although self-generated in terms of the open autopoesis that the new technology allows. In which case, openness, trust and perception would be the necessary criteria of an aesthetic ethics, which, for the first time, would allow for an unbiased presenting of and accounting for the world. The potential for a fulfilling life, therefore, or rather the dynamic process in the art of living a fulfilling life, becomes a *causa sui* in terms of the open autopoesis in that it protects us from the illusion of the ideological by giving us the potential for a leap of faith into the non-metaphysical art of living, that is, however, already present in the fact of our own existence, and evidenced through our unavoidable natality and mortality that initiates the will-to-will that generates all human activity. To put this another way, despite our penchant for normalcy, our fear of change, and our evasion of revolutionary experience, the requisite leap of faith cannot be justified by anything, yet that is precisely the impetus required in order to catapult ourselves free from the very disaster that we have created for ourselves.[161]

Consequently, we must make the leap of faith *into* ourselves, because that is all there is, because we self-generate ourselves, which means that freedom is actually the freedom to be ourselves and not restricted by that which we have created for ourselves, such as ideology or religion. Thus, Adorno would write, "To comprehend a thing itself, not just to fit and register it in its system of reference, is nothing but to perceive the individual moment in its immanent connection with others."[162] Therefore, we are more than a being-here-and-nowhere-else and must find the capacity to take the leap of faith and live our lives, and, even if we were still incapable of living our lives or escaping ideology or the drudgery of the merely existent, we must pursue the goal of a life fulfilling itself, which in itself then becomes a world of ethics. In taking this leap of faith we would free ourselves from our own presencing, and the misfortune of waiting for that which has been withdrawn, namely the gods that we have created for ourselves, whose divinity is already existent in the fourfold of things, earth and sky, divinities and mortals,[163] yet which is simultaneously concealed by our awaiting the divinities as divinities.

The monad: The infinite opening of the finite

Heidegger wrote, "World is never an object that stands before us and can be seen. World is the ever-non-objective to which we are subject as long as the paths of birth and death, blessing and curse, keep us transported into Being." Or, to put it succinctly, "the *world worlds*."[164] This process evokes Schirmacher when he cites Deleuze and "the post-nihilistic turning from Heidegger's 'Being-in-the-world' to the 'being-for-the-world' of the monad,"[165] which suggests a *re*-turn from the ontological (essence, Being) to the ontic (existence, being), or, to put it in terms used above, from the false leap of faith to the true leap of faith, which connects the action of the "world worlds" with the freedom to create ourselves and pursue the goal of a life fulfilling itself.

The monad is the "windowless" unit that Leibniz used to describe the soul, the first element of every composed thing, the equivalent in the metaphysical realm to that which atoms are to the phenomenal realm.[166] Deleuze proposes that the monad is projected and repeated through scansion along an infinite curve that is made up of an infinity of curves, each made up of an infinity of points; "the convergent series of all convergent series."[167] Deleuze also envisions a "harmonic unity," described as

> not that of infinity, but that which allows the existent to be thought of as deriving from infinity; it is a numerical unity insofar as it envelops a multiplicity ("to exist means nothing other than to be harmonic"); it is extended into the affective domain insofar as the senses apprehend it aesthetically, in confusion.[168]

In other words, and in conjunction with Leibniz, Deleuze is proposing that there is a certain rationality or form, hidden or waiting to be discovered, in the incommensurable, and which aesthetics will only obfuscate. Nonetheless, this would explain the harmonic relationship of being and world, and support a being-for-the-world that is reflected in the soul and the world, which are individually and endlessly folded into one another. If we accept this view, Schirmacher contends, we now remove the limits of a contrived culture conceived within modern technology, instead we have a culture that is no longer a liability but one that offers the freedom of the "undefined life" (and perhaps, in terms of the work of art, the open-endedness of the Kantian purposiveness without purpose), and thus the harmonic individualism of the monad, where "eternal reoccurrence is not a theory about the world, but rather an understanding of self."[169] In Deleuze's terms, we have "the world of possibility of beginning over and again in each monad," described as "the infinite opening of the finite."[170]

This concept, however, also suggests the formation of a unified subject and object, which would present the danger, as Deleuze points out, of the failure to establish "a true form that cannot be reduced to an apparent whole or to a phenomenal field, because it must retain the distinction of its details and its own individuality in the hierarchy in which it enters."[171] Similarly, Deleuze will describe Foucault's gaze as his "folds of vision" in order to distinguish it from the ocular pyramid one associates with perspectival vision: "an ontological visibility, forever twisting itself into a self-seeing entity, on to a different dimension from that of the gaze and its objects."[172] In other words, the linkages of the true form are not localized, nor unified into a gestalt whole, nor are they reduced to mere subjectivity, but rather in a dynamic process of endlessly folding and unfolding, yet without allowing the subject to be authentically self-present as "souls, monads, 'self-surveilling' superjects."[173]

To address the problem, we return to Deleuze's concept of actualization, when he claimed that the subjective illusion is not born of individual consciousness but is an objective or transcendental illusion born out of the conditions of social consciousness in the course of its actualization, so that there is a fraud of constitutive subjectivity if the difference is not properly synthesized in the actualization of reflection and instead supports a process of sameness that excludes difference. If so, then "realizing" in terms of artistic forms would only reveal what is already there, rather than "creating" which is to invent a possibility where it did not previously exist. Thus, Deleuze will claim, "the world is a virtuality that is actualized by monads or souls, but also a possibility that must be realized in matter or in bodies."[174] Hence, we are always self-present to ourselves, but we each travel in a multiplicity of worlds. In other words, human beings, each with indivisible body and soul, constantly travel between the virtual and the possible, where there exists an actual world that may be possible, but that is not forcibly real, and at the same time, there is a virtual world which may not be possible, but it can be realized.[175]

Bees against a window: The existential aesthetic

Aristotle claimed that perceptual experience is underwritten by *phantasia*, occurring midway between perception and thought, not imagination exactly but a trace or echo of perceptual activity. Bergson defines "image" as "a certain existence which is more than that which the idealist calls a representation, but less than that which the realist calls a thing – an existence placed halfway between the 'thing' and the 'representation'."[176] Kant claimed that we can only know ourselves as appearances and not as things in themselves,[177] and that space is the form of "outer" intuition, in which we represent objects outside ourselves (appearances), while time is the form of "inner sense" by which each of us intuits our own representations (the appearance of oneself). Bergson, as noted by Cutrofello, will agree with the understanding of objects in space as appearances but disagree that self-knowledge (knowing things in themselves) is impossible because it is precisely through intuition and "the lived flux of my own duration" that we become aware of ourselves as a "thing-in-itself."[178]

Sartre proposed that, "to have an image of someone is not to have a consciousness of the *image* of someone, but to have the imaginative consciousness of that person," such that "the image is entirely determined by the knowledge I use to create it. It can therefore reveal nothing new."[179] In these terms, there is no other possibility other than that of constitutive subjectivity. The image, therefore, is like the negative of a photographic plate, a negation of an already negated world, where the world emerges through its own inversion, and yet it is a "hypnagogic image," that is, one that is fascinated by itself.[180] Thus, Sartre argues for a notion of projection, where the creative imagination of the artist also "requires the re-creative imagination of the beholder if its intended image is to be intentionally imagined. Without the imaginative project of the beholder the artwork remains a static nexus of gestures, hints and traces: a material substrate bereft of life."[181]

Lukács had written that the God-forsakenness of the world reveals itself as a lack of substance, "an irrational mixture of density and permeability," where,

> like dry clay at the first contact with a man possessed by a demon, and the empty transparence behind which attractive landscapes were previously to be seen is suddenly transformed into a glass wall against which men beat in vain, like bees against a window, incapable of breaking through, incapable of understanding that the way is barred.[182]

Similarly, Sartre will claim that the real and the imaginary are always separated by a wall, what he will call *le néant* or "Chinese wall," which can only be traversed by projecting oneself through imagination, which amounts to an act of "unrealizing" oneself.[183] Consequently, Sartre proposed an existential aesthetic, where "fatalism, not determinism, is the existential counterpart of freedom,"[184] and where the "beautiful" does not refer to actual things but to "an aesthetic property of no-thingness," such that we are finally able to "transcend the *actual* and project ourselves into the *possible*."[185] Kearney concludes that for Sartre, paradoxically, "imagination emerges in the final analysis as an illness which aesthetic man, every man, cannot afford to do without,"[186] and yet beauty is nothing more than a value applied to the imaginary, such that its essential structure involves the nullification of the real, which is why "it is foolish to confuse ethics and aesthetics."[187] However, even if ethics and aesthetics are not to be confused, they are certainly intricately and unavoidably aligned. Any new cultural form will also have to address the "beyond landscape" within the subject, the realm of the possible, which would include the ethical relation to the other, as evoked by Critchley in what Levinas called "a curvature of intersubjective space."[188]

The sovereign good: The transgression of the aesthetic

Lacan's term *"entre deux morts"* was used earlier to describe the voice without bearer, one that cannot be attributed to a subject and hovers in some indefinable interspace. If we return now to Antigone, Lacan would use the term to describe her position as being *"entre deux morts"* (between two deaths), which might also describe the situation of human finitude.[189] If we overrule Sartre and consider ethics with aesthetics, we might also consider Critchley's statement that *eudaimonia* ("well-goddedness") is no longer possible in modern life, but that happiness, which is Lacan's goal, just might be:

> we can no longer pursue what he calls an aristocratic ethics of the sovereign good. We live in symbolically impoverished societies which have been subject to the disappearance of forms of community where ethics is rooted in ethos, in custom, habit and tradition, what Hegel calls *Sittlichkeit*, ethical life. We live, to coin a phrase, after virtue.[190]

In terms of the "sovereign good," Lacan would state that Freud's greatest contribution to ethics was the recognition that the ultimate object of desire, the good, is unattainable:

> The step taken by Freud at the level of the pleasure principle is to show us that there is no Sovereign Good – that the Sovereign Good, which is *das Ding*, which is the mother, is also the object of incest, is a forbidden good, and that there is no other good. Such is the foundation of the moral law as turned on its head by Freud.[191]

For Lacan, Antigone is the essence of tragedy: the beautiful, and yet also the sublime, in her "unbearable splendour."[192] It is in the character of Antigone that we find the ethical experience that is the excess over and above the aesthetic experience, where the remainder/surplus meaning/*jouissance* appears through the work of art and its truth process of sublimation, transcending the aesthetic of form and creating an excess that is beyond form, which is ethical by virtue of the truth process, and which now appears as the symbolic, whose purpose is to access the Real. For Lacan, therefore, as interpreted by Critchley, and a key point in the development of our discussion, the excess of the ethical over the aesthetic is found in *atè*, "transgression," where the function of the work of art is transgression, which will demand "the transgression *of* the aesthetic *through* the aesthetic."[193]

To put it another way, if the function of art is transgression, then the aesthetic of the aesthetic is the aesthetic that appears after the transgression of the aesthetic norm through a transgressive aesthetic. The purpose of this transgression is the redemption of humanity and of life itself through the disruption of our delusion and disillusionment. However, if we look at *Antigone* in terms of deconstruction, we may find, as did Derrida, as will Critchley, that the text has a blind spot from which its conceptual edifice can be deconstructed, and in so doing, "it is Antigone's death that sounds the knell or *glas* of the system and announces the end of history."[194] The problem is that "Antigone's death *should* exceed the Hegelian system and make Spirit stumble on its path to Absolute Knowledge, and yet Spirit barely loses its footing for an instant and relentlessly continues its ascent."[195] In terms of the Hegelian dialectic, therefore, this suggests that Antigone's death is only a moment of synthesis and then we simply move on. However, Critchley will argue that this is in fact a precise moment that exemplifies the essence of ethical life, of *Sittlichkeit*, which is irreducible and therefore "an ethics of the singular."[196] In which case, this moment may be one of Absolute Knowledge, an endpoint as it were, where there is no remainder, where even if the Spirit stumbles on, the dialectical process stops: in Benjamin's terms, the emergency brake, a dialectic at a standstill; in Adorno's, the social antithesis, the moment of negation, the undialectical; in Deleuze's, the infinite opening of the finite, where we discover the world of possibility of beginning over and again in each monad.

In replacing Antigone for Oedipus, diverging from the Freudian norm, a de-Oedipalization as it were, Lacan allows that a "new form of secret is established," as Rancière terms it, "one that is irreducible to any salvational knowledge."[197] Just as Kant failed to recognize the *jouissance* that motivated his respect for the moral law, and just as Freud in turn revealed the sadism in the categorical imperative, so Lacan is able to detect a Kantian morality in the Marquis de Sade.[198] Indeed, Critchley will argue that de Sade was immoral but he was not unethical,[199] accordingly, "the ethical subject is constituted in relation to a demand that is determined as good, and that this can be felt most acutely when I fail to act in accordance with that demand or when I deliberately transgress it and betray myself. I can be as much a failing Sadist as a failing Kantian."[200] Indeed, Sartre will note that de Sade is hardly scandalous at this point, "no longer anything but a soul eaten by a beautiful disease, a pearl-oyster,"[201] but de Sade remains an example of de-Oedipalization, of difference, the grain of sand in the system.

Eidos: The essential ambiguity

Heidegger looked to the ancient Greeks where, as Feenberg words it, he had "rediscovered his own premises in the Greek beginning."[202] However, despite nominating human beings as the primary and genuine subjectum, there would be a limitation in that the Greeks did not recognize the ungrounded nature of the *eidos* (essence). One possibility is that this ungrounded nature suggests that the *eidos* itself is self-formulated and therefore could never be grounded outside oneself, or, for that matter, outside human beings. Another possibility, as Feenberg suggests, is that in the very process of the unconcealing of being there lies the possibility of arbitrariness, of "an unbridled positing of goals," such that "modernity is the unleashing of this arbitrariness in the technological expression of human will."[203] For Heidegger, this presents the danger of human beings enframing themselves as mere raw materials alongside things, although, as he claimed, there still remains the potentiality, as noted earlier, that the essential unfolding of technology harbors in itself the possible rise of the saving power.

Critchley writes that it is this very arbitrariness and fragmentation, one that is both systematic and anti-systematic, that constitutes the "essential *ambiguity*, or what Lacoue-Labarthe and Nancy call 'romantic equivocity',"[204] so the ambiguity of the *eidos* itself may be construed as "playful and serious, open and hidden, natural and artistic, unconditional and conditioned, impossible and necessary... Irony is the expression of the double bind at the heart of the human condition."[205]

We should recall that Lukács claimed that irony expressed the gap between the finite and the infinite, but rather than a true illumination, all we are offered is pessimistic anti-illumination. We should also recall that the double bind, as conceived by Gregory Bateson, is a crisis in communication that evolves from a situation with two or more conflicting messages, such that one message negates the other, so that regardless of the response one will automatically be wrong. Therefore, a person cannot confront the inherent dilemma, neither can they resolve it, nor opt out of the situation, which may well describe the human dilemma. Therefore, the double bind may prove the basis for Critchley's claim that philosophy begins in disappointment, one that can be either religious or political, but where disappointment in either case is inevitable.[206] The result is a "romantic oscillation," yet one that "yields an insight into finitude, a tragic wisdom centred in an acceptance of the limitedness of thought, of the finiteness of the human condition as that which cannot be overcome."[207] Therefore, we may find that "irony is the genre of ethical discourse," because its ethical content "lies precisely in its resistance to totalization, its everlasting ironization of totality."[208] In fact, we might say that the aesthetic of the aesthetic is realized through irony, the ethical discourse that results from the process of the aesthetic *through* the aesthetic.

Contrary to the self-serving concept of the primary subjectum, Critchley will argue that we must abandon the whole idea of redemption because "we can be redeemed only be ending the demand for redemption, by ceasing to use the concepts of redemption."[209] In doing so, we would free ourselves from a world that is "overfull of meaning and we suffocate under the combined weight of the various narratives of redemption – whether they are religious, socio-economic, political, aesthetic or philosophical."[210] If not, we only continue the empty re-mystification of essence, as Lukács had claimed, a world where everything is seen as many-sided, full of value and yet totally devoid of it. On one hand, we have the scientific method and testing which attempts to control arbitrariness, and on the other hand, we have the work of art that responds to the arbitrariness in itself. In either case, as Judith Butler argues, emphasizing the essential ambiguity, the struggle is in part over language, over words themselves, where and how they apply, but also their plasticity and their equivocity.[211] Indeed, we might recall the positive aspects of ambiguity as presented by De Beauvoir when she writes:

> Art and science do not establish themselves despite failure but through it; which does not prevent there being truths and errors, masterpieces and lemons, depending upon whether the discovery or the painting has or has not known how to win the adherence of human consciousness; this amounts to saying that failure, always ineluctable, is in certain cases spared and in others not.[212]

Poetic memory: Unrealizing oneself

The poetic crisis, Sartre argues, is caused by the fact that, "poets are men who refuse to *utilize* language."[213] Therefore, to use Butler's terms, when languages loses its plasticity and equivocity, its essential ambiguity, then it is also in danger of losing the struggle to maintain its ability to *convey* meaning through the very act of its ability to *seek* meaning. Consequently, a very real danger arises with a poetic crisis because "nobody is questioned; nobody is questioning; the poet is absent."[214] Sartre will also claim, in terms that are similar to our earlier distinction between poetry and the novel, that prose is "in essence, utilitarian," and the prose-writer is one "who makes use of words."[215] The poet, however, in terms that recall Heidegger, must use words differently, finding ways around their conventions, discovering their organic truth, thus, "if the poet dwells upon words, as does the painter with colours and the musician with sounds, that does not mean that they have lost all meaning in his eyes."[216] If so, we might claim the poet is the safe house of words, our talisman against aphasia,[217] preserving the ability of language to both convey and seek meaning, to prevent the liquidation of the questioning subject. In doing so, the poet is capable of transcending the actual and projecting us into the possible, an act of unrealizing oneself, and thus challenging the fraud of constitutive subjectivity, and perhaps placing us on the other side of the Chinese wall, *le néant*, even "the other side of the human condition, on the side of God."[218]

Of course, Sartre's philosophy of human existence, as expounded in *Being and Nothingness* (1943), is that there is nothing outside of or within ourselves that we can appeal to in order to justify our value and moral rules, nor is there a God to guide us on how to live, nor is reason able to provide rules for living (as Kant proposed), nor is human happiness a valid goal (as utilitarianism proposed). Humankind must acquire its own basis for moral rules and value, and nothing can guide us in these choices except ourselves, and yet human beings are free to give their lives whatever goal or purpose they choose, and to avoid the responsibility for self-determination is only self-deception, leading to the inauthentic life and the great existentialist sin of "bad faith" (*mauvais foi*).[219] Thus, rather than self-deception, Sartre calls for an imaginative consciousness that involves "a *double* negation," as noted by Kearney, "when we imagine, we first posit a world in which our imagined object is absent, in order that we may then imagine a world in which our imagined object is present."[220]

Sartre warns that the imagination can become fascinated by the images that it intends, such that there is also a contradiction between the imagination's claim to both freedom and fascination, where it must break free of its own fascination in order to be free.[221] This breaking free would amount to a severing from self-significance through the act of unrealizing oneself. In terms used earlier, this also suggests a breaking through the fraud of constitutive subjectivity, as well as the bondage of images. Although this severing from self-significance would almost certainly cause angst and anxiety, it may very well lead to the questioning of one's existence and the authentic life, as Heidegger had hoped, and yet this questioning, if it is to avoid self-delusion, must also lead to a denial of the fundamental trait that makes us human, namely the ability to apprehend some meaning beyond ourselves. Therefore, this breaking free must also lead to the inauthentic, namely a denial of any meaning beyond ourselves, whereby any work of art can function as the basis for a perception that affirms self-deception, or as an act of imagination that negates it, which leads again to an inescapable double bind.[222] Thus, when Heidegger claims that human existence could apprehend beings only insofar as it "holds itself out into the nothing," so Sartre will object to this formulation, claiming that nothingness is now confined to the "beyond" of human existence, and, in doing so, we only substitute authentic freedom for inauthentic fatalism. For Sartre, here lies the power and the danger of imagination, characterizing it as both "our health and our disease,"[223] because "consciousness is itself determined to transform into the imaginary everything it gets hold of: hence the fatal nature of the dream... it is the odyssey of consciousness dedicated by itself, and in spite of itself, to build only an unreal world."[224]

Sartre maintains that any act of perceptual consciousness is accompanied by the act of being reflected upon, such that, as worded by Cutrofello, evoking Plato's cave, "the entire 'region' of the psychic haunts the physical world as a kind of 'shadow' cast upon it by reflective consciousness."[225] Nevertheless, Cutrofello will claim that Sartre alluded to "another fundamental attitude" other than that of bad faith.[226] Although human beings are incapable of forsaking the desire to resolve the double bind, to synthesize the freedom of consciousness (the possible, the for-itself, *pour-soi*) and the facticity of the intentional objects that it negates (the actual, the in-itself, *en-soi*), and so to be God, hence it may be possible to make sheer freedom the object of one's aspiration.[227] This synthesis, therefore, addresses the double bind of deception and disillusionment by embracing the actual and the possible, and thereby proceeds toward what could be called the *of-itself*, where the Hegelian absolute of the *thing-in-itself* is now realized as the *thing-as-itself*, thus, a being-for-the-world that both frees itself to itself and frees itself from itself.

Mimetic desire: Literary conversion

In terms of the process of synthesis that addresses the double bind of deception and disillusionment, it may be the creative process itself that allows for the discovery of one's bad faith or self-deception, requiring a double negation, an aesthetic through the aesthetic, where the perspective of one's desire demands the liberation from one's desire. René Girard addresses this very situation when he defines "mimetic desire," whereby, "to say that our desires are imitative or mimetic is to root them neither in their objects nor in ourselves, but in a third party, the *model* or *mediator*, whose desire we imitate in the hope of resembling him or her, in the hope that our two beings will be 'fused', as some Dostoyevskyan characters love to say."[228] Thus, if the failure of self-fulfilment through desire is the root of modern individualism and the consumer society, then, Girard claims, as interpreted by Robert Doran, and in terms that recall the young Lukács, there can be a recognition of the failure of desire through a literary conversion, a recognition that constitutes a renunciation of the world.[229] Importantly, this conversion may even take on aspects of a religious experience, an awakening to the moral and spiritual possibilities of the world. According to Doran, Girard only wishes to imply that this type of conversion invites an opening to religion and is not to be mistaken for a true religious experience, nevertheless, the literary conversion that appears as religious experience would explain the attempts to poetize philosophy (as found in Nietzsche, Heidegger and Derrida), which "represents a desire to return to the primordial (pre-Socratic) unity between the will to know and the will to create."[230] Consequently, Girard would regard literature as superior to philosophy in its unique ability to reconcile universality and particularity.

The burden of art's eloquence, as Adorno said, was also the burden of reconciliation that religion can no longer fulfil in a secular society. If the literary conversion offers the semblance of a religious experience, then it is not to be mistaken for a true religious experience, thus landing us once again in the double bind of deception and disillusionment. Nonetheless, the process of seeking religious experience has not abated, even after, as Nietzsche famously asserted "'The father' in God is thoroughly refuted," because "we have killed him, you and I."[231] Thus, Nietzsche will argue that the Christian doctrine of God was responsible for the disaster of modern atheism, as well as the intellectual conscience that has been hardened by modern science and no longer able to believe, and thereby he challenges our religious convictions while calling for the ecstatic experience, declaiming "Has one understood me? – *Dionysus versus the Crucified* –."[232] However, Nietzsche does not abandon his search for the music-making Socrates, for the "greatness of soul" that Aristotle conceived as *megalopsychia*,[233] because the religious instinct remains. Indeed, he will observe, "it appears to me that in fact the religious instinct is growing powerfully."[234]

The cult of surfaces: Burnt children

If the religious experience, or the semblance of religious experience, is found in the literary conversion then we may find support for the idea that the work of art does indeed bear the burden of the essential thing, of what ought to be. And if, as Girard claimed, the poetization of philosophy does not match the experience of the literary conversion, perhaps it is because, as Nietzsche pointed out, delivering "a few pokes in the ribs (*Rippenstösse*)," that the dutiful philosophers who follow the Platonic demand for truth, cannot tolerate deception or being deceived, despite the fact that these deceptions are not necessarily evil or immoral or unavoidable, even that "deception may be species preserving, even species enhancing."[235] For Plato, of course, the poet is subject to divine madness, or inspiration, and their function is not to convey the truth, but only to persuade, such that truth is the concern of the philosopher only.[236] However, as noted earlier, Aristotle maintained that the purpose of the work of art (rhetoric, for example) may ultimately serve *eudaimonia* (well--goddedness, also virtue, self-sufficiency, pleasure, external goods). The Platonic distrust of the arts, therefore, is precisely because the work of art shares the burden that truth must bear, such that the aesthetic experience may have the semblance of religious experience, and must then be an ethical experience.

The work of art is a social fact that informs and influences our social reality, with the attendant implications in the economic, legal, political and religious spheres, and simultaneously the work of art itself is influenced by these same spheres, such that a poetic crisis, and the crisis in historicity, appears when the poetic aesthetic has been co-opted into utility. And because we are now the referential center of beings, the master and servant of the bounded object domain, taking on the role of the self-constituted creator of coherence and meaning in the absence of the father in God, then the poetic crisis attains a much more profound scale and urgency. Thus, there remains cause for concern, even the possibility of extreme danger as Heidegger warned, and not just any danger, but *the* danger, danger in the highest sense, where the transformation of subjectivity through culture is mistaken for the self-determination found in the process of synthesis itself, a semblance of religious experience in the literary conversion, or in any cultural experience and a subsequent conversion, where the language of questioning, that which addresses the double bind of deception and disillusionment, is in fact only that blindness from self-reflection which amounts to a form of bondage.

Nietzsche would argue that the blindness from self-reflection can be found in the blindness to the gravity of religion and its power, a power that is enabled because the imprint of religion has left its mark on our culture, which suggests both the profound influence of culture and the influence of culture on the profound. In which case, just as Plato invented pure forms, and Homer invented gods (an audacity that Nietzsche greatly admired),[237] so, in what may be taken as recognition for the suffering of poets and their alienation, Nietzsche would argue that "let nobody doubt that whoever stands that much in *need* of the cult of surfaces must at some time have reached *beneath* them with disastrous results."[238] However, that may be all we now see, the cult of surfaces, where we not only have a culture that is the mirror-image of a world gone out of joint, as Lukács had written, but, as Michel Serres so bluntly puts it, "our culture abhors the world,"[239] where even the poet has lost his way, one of Nietzsche's "burnt children," as Lampert writes,

> Perhaps there even exists an order of rank among these burnt children, born artists who can still find the pleasure of life only in the intention of *falsifying* its image (as it were, in a long-winded revenge on life): the degree to which life has been spoiled for them might be inferred from the degree to which they wish to see its image falsified, thinned down, transcendentalized, deified – the *homines religiosi* might be included among artists, as their highest rank."[240]

Thus, that same blindness to the gravity of religion and its power may have migrated to the religious experience of the literary conversion, now that the father in God is discredited, and so migrated from there to the image in our modern world. In Freudian terms, the "oceanic," which suggests a sense of eternity, a feeling of something limitless, unbounded, was "the source of religious energy that was seized upon by the various churches and religious systems, directed into particular channels and certainly consumed by them. On the basis of this oceanic feeling alone, one was entitled to call oneself religious, even if one rejected every belief and every illusion."[241] The sense of the oceanic is realized through the image-making culture, its religious energy a form of literary conversion. In the world as picture, therefore, with its ubiquitous technology of reflection, we are constantly aware of the double bind of deception and disillusionment, of the falsification of its images, where even the promise of the future and its new philosophers is eroded by the present, yet that promise is precisely where we may find our most profound experience.

The poet in a destitute time: Remembrance

Hölderlin asks, "And what are poets for in a destitute time?"[242] Heidegger will respond that our time is not simply destitute but "absolutely" destitute, a sign of the extreme danger we are in, because not only have the gods disappeared, but so have the traces of that which could lead us to them.[243] Ronell observes in her analysis of Heidegger's reading of Hölderlin's poem "*Andenken*" that it is characterized by the modern experience of mourning and, evoking Jean-Luc Nancy, "a more abandoned experience of dispossession," such that, evoking Hannah Arendt, "the fact that 'we' has become the stranger."[244] Indeed, if "we" have become strangers, it may be because we have become strangers to ourselves, and we may consider this alienation in terms of the poetic crisis, which, if it could be resolved, may find its solution in the quote from Heidegger that states, "Hölderlin's poetry is a destiny for us."[245] In other words, if our destining was through the poetic, then, as noted earlier, we may find another mode of thinking, an active and attentive stance of questioning, of "having ears," of listening to the silence, that introduces a religious sense of devotion and reverence, and the potentiality of entering into a more original and profound revealing.

Heidegger, therefore, will claim that the task of the poet is one of remembrance, of preserving the memory of the flight of the gods: "Poets are the mortals who, singing earnestly from the wine-god [Dionysus], sense the trace of the fugitive gods."[246] Nietzsche had argued for the work of art allied with rapture and the experience of the Dionysian, as opposed to Apollonian self-reflection and the apotheosis of "the *principium individuationis*, from whose gestures and looks all the delight, wisdom and beauty of 'illusion' speak to us."[247] Heidegger, however, would maintain that the Dionysian is only one aspect of the work of art, one aspect of "bringing forth," a presence or mood (*Stimmung*) if you will, and that the true work of art should unite the Dionysian and the Apollonian.[248] As such, Heidegger will point to Hölderlin's work and how it addresses the matter of "retaining the load," and in doing so, "showing, veiling-unveiling,"[249] such that, with a suggestion of literary conversion, "the poem does not 'express' 'experiences'; rather, it takes the poet into the open realm of his essence, which has opened up as a poem."[250] Thus, for Heidegger, as noted earlier, the process of the self-forming form is a kind of self-conversion, such that by hearing the call of conscience Dasein allows that it wants to have a conscience. And further, as Ronell extracts from Heidegger's reading of Hölderlin, that in addition to the implications of thinking and thanking, "'Andenken' requires of us an 'anders Denken', another kind of thinking."[251] In terms of the "we" that has become a stranger, Ronell will observe that the act of greeting is embedded in the word "Andenken," addressing the concerns for both the poetic crisis and the crisis in historicity, whereby "for Heidegger the Greeting uttered in the poem has everything to do with grounding and historicity."[252] The significance of the greeting and the poet's attending to that greeting, a counter to "objectness," is because "the poet is responsible for finding the way for Dasein's embrace of alterity."[253] Similarly, as Derrida will claim in the address of the other, evoking Levinas, "language *is* hospitality."[254] The poet addresses the friends, but they are not there, or not yet in existence, as Nietzsche would have claimed, yet "greeted and greeting, the poet stands on responsive alert, clear about the limits of poetic dwelling on earth,"[255] and yet the danger is ever present, such that "there will be no gathering home, even if the poet has projected a homeward turning."[256]

Consequently, Nietzsche's task in destitute times, as interpreted by Lampert, is to respond to the dying Platonism that gave rise to "the religion that has given religion a bad name,"[257] namely the victory of Christianity that amounted to a "transvaluation of all classical values,"[258] thus making it necessary to act decisively and profoundly, just as Plato did, although now it would be an anti-Platonic transvaluation, such that it allows "for religion once again to pass into the care of philosophy, for the philosopher once again to use religion as a means of education and nur-ture, as an instrument for the spiritual cultivation of a new sort of human being loyal to nature and the natural."[259] For example, the *eudaimonia* of modern life may be found in the ecological commitment and awareness, where, as Bruno Latour has stated, historicity has switched from humans to nature.[260] In any case, we have two movements here: the poetization of philosophy that leads to the religious experience of literary conversion, and the religious experience of literary conversion that leads to the poetization of philosophy. This suggests that the poetization of philosophy is now bolstered from the religious experience of literary conversion, in terms of both poet and reader, and invites an opening to religion, a homecoming as it were, the cure for the Lukácsian homesickness and alienation, for the lost father in God. This also suggests an anti-Platonic process from the many to the one, rather than the earlier one to the many. In the Benjaminian sense, the poetized philosophy is that which is already there, where both poet/philosopher and those who experience the poem/philosophy are those who are being-found-fitting for such a return, and yet the danger remains because the self-conversion is still through the self-formed form, hence the susceptibility to the double-bind of disillusion and disenchantment.

If these destitute times are marked by the poetic crisis, by the measured "outside" construction – in other words, by the crisis of historicity, as found in the withdrawal of being in the past-present-future of history – then we may believe that the gods have never been present. Therefore, Heidegger senses, as he found in Nietzsche's character of Zarathustra, a kind of abject terror of the abyss of nothingness, of one, in Nietzsche's own words, very much in need of the cult of surfaces because they have reached beneath them with disastrous results.[261] Therefore, this may be the result of stripping the subject of their customary fantasmatic support, disrupting their social identity and challenging their personality, of exposing the fraud of constitutive subjectivity in order to "see" things in an entirely new way. Nonetheless, according to Kaufmann, Nietzsche considers himself "still pious," and that piety itself is Nietzsche's faith.[262] And yet, Nietzsche, like Heidegger, failed to escape the grasp of terror, to look beyond the cult of surfaces, to reach beneath the very thing they had hoped to resist, when their poetized philosophy did not return the "we" to the pre-Socratic unity between the will to know and the will to create, but became an instrument instead for the will to power. Indeed, Gertrude Himmelfarb argues that the explanation lies in the fact that they – including Adorno in his "Grand Hotel Abyss" - had not looked into the terror of the abyss at all but only into a purely linguistic construction, one that had been wilfully constructed and therefore could be wilfully reconstructed and deconstructed.[263]

The danger, therefore, is that poetized philosophy is by definition language that has been utilized, and therefore is danger of becoming only another aspect of the poetic crisis, of the crisis of language. Hence, it is the poet who must bear witness to the traces of the fugitive gods through the remembering of forgetting, and it is poetry that is the work of art that commemorates an event (*Ereignis*; coming-into-view), which is not that of the past, or even the future, but of that which disappears with the arrival of time itself, whereby "we experience what-has-been, returning in the remembrance, swinging out beyond our present, and coming to us as something futural."[264] Rainer Maria Rilke would take this a step further, writing that the poet must not only remember the flight of the gods but preserve the possibility of their return,[265] and, as Heidegger will claim, the poet can only do this by characterizing "the beginning of the terrifying, a beginning we but barely endure."[266]

At the same time, we must also accept that there is always the spectre of the double bind of deception and disillusionment, the poetic crisis, such that, as found in Adorno, who remembers Auschwitz in his rejection of any and all false appeasement, or any flight into illusion, lays claim that the poets cannot bear witness to either the flight or the return of the gods, but only to that which has been reduced to silence. If there is indeed a poetic crisis, it may be because the work of art itself has retreated into silence, its revealing veiled by the image, by all that we see. Indeed, Lyotard questions how we can understand why meaning may have been lost, why unity has been lost, when these questions must blunt themselves on a "highly resistant material. This material is time, which preserves what it loses."[267] Therefore, when the poet is in destitute times, it is the task of the philosopher to question, to be questioning, to listen to the silence, by "having ears," and if necessary to poetize philosophy, a work of art in itself whose process is an aesthetic *through* the aesthetic, and so *re*-introduce a religious sense of devotion and reverence, and the potentiality of entering into a more original and profound revealing.

Desecration of silence: The need to talk

An aesthetic experience derived from an artistic experience would, in the Bergsonian sense, imply a domain of experience that consists of individually endured time (*durée*), a private reality that is free and unrestricted, as well as the potential for the recovery of lived experience, the *élan vital*, through the work of art.[268] This presence of mind, a particular domain of experience with its own sense of time, which might be described as non-linear or formless, perhaps inspired by "a representation of limitlessness"[269] in the Kantian sense of the sublime, or simply the inverse of an objectified external form, an indeterminate space, for example, or silence. Adorno, however, will claim that an artwork, in reference to the work of Beckett with its resistance to interpretation, is "*a desecration of silence*,"[270] whereby the artwork does not seek to reveal its nature but to withdraw into its own silence, assimilating itself with the non-identical (*das Nichtidentische*).[271] Indeed, Adorno also claims that "this shabby, damaged world of images is the negative imprint of the administered world. To this extent Beckett is realistic."[272] However, rather than reveal its nature an artwork seeks to conceal its nature or, to extend the argument put forth by Schirmacher, the transgression of the aesthetic protects the very possibility of revealing and concealing, which suggests that we are only able to attain glimpses of whatever art is willing to reveal through the aesthetic experience, which implies that genuine aesthetic experience is only made possible by that which exceeds the grasp of thought and sensibility, that is, an experience that resists interpretation.

If we recall Barthes use of the term "the *kairos* of desire" in reference to the photographer's decisive moment, as found in the photographs of Henri Cartier-Bresson,[273] so Schirmacher contends that the *kairos* of desire is also the *kairos* of "timing," where *kairos* is not only integral to the art of living, but it is integral to the nature of art, or at least the truth that is given by art. Schirmacher will argue, invoking Deleuze, that, "it is the signature of truth to erase its signing right after the fact in order to allow the on-going folding, unfolding and refolding to be done in peace."[274] In other words, art has always provided us with the symbolic and its processes, but the transgression of artistic form gives us a glimpse of something more that is at work, a glimpse that art protects the possibility of revealing and concealing, in the Heideggerian sense of *aletheia*, that calls in the truth and yet simultaneously protects it. Hence, it is in this way that an artwork, and its truth content, as Adorno words it (*Wahrheitsgehalt*), simultaneously challenges the way things are and suggests how things could be better, but leaves things practically unchanged (and thus Adorno avoids the Kantian emphasis on the "thing in itself.") Instead, Adorno argues, the truth content of art is in its de-objectification that appears in its countering of subjectivity: "Art has truth as the semblance of the illusionless."[275]

Adorno's view, although pessimistic, may be closer to Schiller's when he declares that the aesthetic actualizes freedom only in its own freedom of determination, whereby it need not conform to either "logical necessity in thinking, or moral necessity in willing."[276] The aesthetic experience thus remains completely indeterminate in terms of its results, just as Wittgenstein and Welsch claimed, and yet it is through that very indetermination that freedom is restored, allowing one to be what one ought to be without censure or restriction.[277] Further, Adorno supports the non-identical because "the need to let suffering speak is a condition of all truth. For suffering is objectivity that weighs upon the subject."[278] In other words, somewhat paradoxically, the freedom of indetermination is most valid for those who do not have the freedom of determination. Consequently, we now have a possible cause for a crisis of subjectivity, namely the weight of suffering on the subject which occurs as objectivity, which then calls for a freedom of indetermination, a de-objectification, that would amount to the release from human suffering, or as Adorno words it, the promise of a life without fear.

If we return to the idea of the aesthetic as a domain of experience, and the concept of de-objectification of the viewing subject, we may find that the truth content of an aesthetic is an inversion achieved through the non-identical. In which case, the goal of Beckett's writing in terms of its truth content, is not silence in itself but rather, as stated by Critchley, "a necessary *desecration* and *desacralization* of silence." This is necessary for the very reason that we must experience the desecration of silence in order not to withdraw into silence, the solipsism of *temps durée*, because, quite simply, if we are in destitute times, then, as Critchley words it, "we have to talk."[279] If the transgression of the aesthetic protects the very possibility of revealing and concealing, then it is through the need to talk, the questioning, that we might reveal and address the fact of human suffering. At the same time, we must also recognize and acknowledge that which is allowed to remain concealed, or allowed to return to concealment, to withdraw, thus supporting the significance of de-objectification of subjectivity through a counter-aesthetic that opposes or inverts the accepted aesthetic. If there is a poetic crisis, a crisis of language, then, as Lyotard proposes, we may need philosophy in order to testify to the presence of a lack within our speech, because "you can transform this world only by listening to it."[280]

Notes

1 Lukács, *The Theory of the Novel*, p.11.
2 Georg Lukács, "Realism in the Balance," *Aesthetics and Politics*, with presentations by Rodney Livingstone, Perry Anderson and Francis Mulhern, afterword by Fredric Jameson (London and New York: Verso, 1980), p.53.
3 Lukács, *The Theory of the Novel*, p.146. In a later work, *The Historical Novel* (1937), Lukács would further champion the products of historical realism where a historical consciousness allows for an ever-changing history and thus the possibility for revolutionary transformation.
4 Arpad Kadarkay, *Georg Lukács: Life, Thought, and Politics* (Cambridge MA: Blackwell, 1991), p.338. Kadarkay describes the effects of Lukács's youthful journey as "the charred ruins of his youth's single-minded pursuit of salvation." Ibid., p.193.
5 Ibid., p.153,
6 Lukács, *The Theory of the Novel*, p.20.
7 Ibid., p.16.
8 Ibid., p.17.
9 In Aristotle's *Poetics* (335 BCE), he describes three genres of poetry: the epic, comic, and tragic. He also develops rules to distinguish the highest-quality poetry of each genre, based on the underlying purposes of that genre. The three major genres will become epic poetry, lyric poetry and dramatic poetry (with comedy and tragedy as subgenres of dramatic poetry). The serious "higher" poets represent the noble deeds of noble men through epic poetry, while the "lower" poets represent the actions of inferior men, at first writing satire just as the others wrote hymns and eulogies. Aristotle recognized these rules were open to interpretation. For example, Homer's *Iliad*, although epic, contained elements of all three genres. Aristotle will claim that poetry is finer and more philosophical than history; for poetry expresses the universal, and history only the particular. See Aristotle, *Poetics,* general editor Stanley Applebaum, editor of this edition Richard Koss (New York: Dover Publications, 1997).
10 Lukács, *The Theory of the Novel*, p.30.
11 Feenberg, *Heidegger and Marcuse*, p.72.
12 Lukács, *The Theory of the Novel*, p.153. Fichte, also caught in the "superb prison" of Kantian ethics, did not endorse Kant's argument for the existence of *noumena*, of "things in themselves," of a reality beyond the categories of human reason. Instead, Fichte argued that the systematic separation of *noumena* (things in themselves) and *phenomena* (things as they appear to us) was an invitation to skepticism. See Johann Gottlieb Fichte, "Attempt at a Critique of All Revelation," (*Versuch einer Kritik aller Offenbarung* , 1792).
13 Ibid., p.29.
14 Ibid., pp. 39, 41.
15 Ibid., p.29.
16 Ibid., p.74.

17 Ibid., p.84.
18 Ibid., p.75.
19 Ibid., p.152.
20 Ibid., p.153.
21 Ibid., p.152.
22 Georg Lukács, *History and Class Consciousness*, translated by Rodney Livingstone (Cambridge MA: The MIT Press, 1971), p.1.
23 Ibid., p.3.
24 Lukács, *The Theory of the Novel*, p.145.
25 Cutrofello, *Continental Philosophy*, p.242.
26 Ibid., p.242.
27 Richard Kearney, *Poetics of Imagining: From Husserl to Lyotard (Problems of Modern European Thought)* (London: HarperCollinsAcademic, 1991), p.184.
28 Ibid., p.177. Kearney is citing from Jacques Derrida, "The double session," *Dissemination* (London: Althone Press, 1981), p.211.
29 Elsaesser and Hagener, *Film Theory*, p.152. See also Kittler, "Romanticism – Psychoanalysis – Film: A History of the Double"), pp.85-100.
30 Adorno, *Aesthetic Theory*, p.xiii.
31 Theodor W. Adorno, *Negative Dialectics*, translated by E.B. Ashton (New York: Routledge, 1973), p.xx. See also Susan Buck-Morss, *The Origin of Negative Dialectics: Theodor W. Adorno, Walter Benjamin, and the Frankfurt Institute* (New York: The Free Press, 1977), p.83.
32 Theodor W. Adorno, "Negative Dialectics and the Possibility of Philosophy," *The Adorno Reader*, edited by Brian O'Connor (Malden MA: Blackwell Publishing, 2000), p.67.
33 Mary Klages, *Literary Theory: A Guide for the Perplexed* (London: Continuum Publishing Group, 2006), p.173.
34 Adorno, "Negative Dialectics and the Possibility of Philosophy," p.63.
35 Alain Badiou, *Cinema*, Texts selected and introduced by Antoine de Baecque, translated by Susan Spitzer (Cambridge UK: Polity Press, 2013), p.206.
36 Adorno, *Aesthetic Theory*, p.65. Oswald Spengler used the term "pseudomorphosis" in *The Decline of the West* (1918-1923). Specifically, pseudomorphosis entails an older culture so deeply ingrained that a young culture cannot find its own form and full expression of itself.
37 Ibid., p.5. See also Emile Durkheim's reference to the "total social fact'"(*fait social total*) in Marcel Mauss, *The Gift: Forms and Function of Exchange in Archaic Societies*, translated by Ian Cunnison, Foreward by E.E. Evans-Pritchard (Eastford CT: Martino Fine Books, 2011), pp.76-77.
38 Ibid., p.6.
39 Ibid., p.6.
40 Ibid., pp.8, 11.
41 Badiou, *Cinema*, p.225.
42 Ibid., p.232.
43 Klages, *Literary Theory*, p.137.
44 Susan Sontag, *Regarding the Pain of Others* (New York: Farrar, Straus & Giroux, 2003), p.131.
45 Nietzsche, *Beyond Good and Evil*, p.53.
46 Walter Kaufmann, *Nietzsche: Philosopher, Psychologist, Antichrist* (Princeton NJ: Princeton University Press, 1974), p.112. The quote is from Nietzsche, *Ecce Homo*, p.2.
47 Ibid., pp.426-427. See also Nietzsche, *Beyond Good and Evil*, p.56. Nietzsche would support the dithyramb (the ecstatic hymn-song-dance in honour of Dionysus), as opposed to the paean (the solemn lyric poem of thanksgiving to Apollo). Nietzsche, *The Birth of Tragedy*, pp.14-18.
48 Ibid., p.395.
49 Nietzsche, *The Birth of Tragedy*, p.75.
50 Nietzsche wrote, "We shall see the insatiable, optimistic zest for knowledge, exemplified in the figure of Socrates, transformed into tragic resignation and a

need for art; while that same zest, at its lower levels, must express itself in terms hostile to art, and find Dionysian tragedy profoundly repellent, as we have seen in the battle between Aeschylean tragedy and Socratism. We now knock agitatedly at the portals of the present and the future; will that 'transformation' lead to ever-new configurations of genius, and particularly of the *music-making Socrates*?" Nietzsche, *The Birth of Tragedy*, p.75.

51 Kaufmann, *Nietzsche*, p.422.

52 Ibid., pp.354, 423. Kaufmann notes Nietzsche's emphasis with three exclamation marks.

53 Lukács, *The Meaning of Contemporary Realism*, p.66.

54 Ibid., p.91.

55 Lukács, *The Theory of the Novel*, p.75.

56 Ibid., p.72.

57 Jean-Paul Sartre, "What is Literature?" *Continental Aesthetics: Romanticism to Postmodernism: An Anthology*, edited by Richard Kearney and David Rasmussen (Malden MA: Blackwell Publishers, 2001), p.279.

58 Cutrofello, *Continental Philosophy*, p.235.

59 Lukács, *The Theory of the Novel*, p.88.

60 Simon Critchley, "Art and Ethics: Transgression, Visibility, and Collective Resistance," *Impossible Objects: Interviews*, edited by Carl Cederström and Todd Kesselman (Cambridge UK and Malden MA: Polity Press, 2012), p.131.

61 Adorno, "Commitment," p.180.

62 Cutrofello, *Continental Philosophy*, p.265.

63 Adorno, *Aesthetic Theory*, p.27.

64 Jean-Francois Lyotard, *Why Philosophize?*, translated by Andrew Brown (Cambridge UK: Polity Press, 2013), p.51.

65 Adorno, *In Search of Wagner*, p.107. Early silent cinema was not "silent" in that there was musical accompaniment to the moving images. Also, the technology for recording sound was already developing, but it was not yet synchronous with the moving image, and it wouldn't be until 1927 when "talkies" would arrive.

66 The film editor Walter Murch will identify the cinema's genesis in terms of its historicity, that is, it was the right time for its appearance. Murch identifies what he calls the "Three Fathers" of cinema: Thomas Edison (1847-1931), who represents all the technological geniuses of early film; Gustave Flaubert (1821-1880), even before the invention of film technology, who represents all the novelists of realism; and even earlier, Ludwig van Beethoven (1770-1827), who represents the sudden shifts in tonality, rhythm, and musical focus, much like that found in the grammar of film (cuts, dissolves, fades, superimposures, long shots, close shots, et al.). Murch describes these musical movements as analogous to "moving through different rooms in a palace, going in one room, looking around, and then, closing the door and, with the next movement, going into the next room. Michael Ondaatje and Walter Murch, *The Conversations*, pp.89-90. Murch and George Lucas co-wrote *THX 1138*, a 1971 science fiction film directed by Lucas in his feature directorial debut. Murch was also credited as sound designer for *Apocalypse Now* (Francis Ford Coppola 1979), the first time this credit was used to acknowledge the change from "sound engineer" to "sound designer." Elsaesser and Hagener, *Film Theory*, p.142

67 Buck-Morss, *The Origin of Negative Dialectics*, p.123. Buck-Morss writes, "The refusal to accept bourgeois cultural forms as absolute was a unifying characteristic of expressionism, the otherwise diverse artistic revolt of the 1910s with which Schönberg [Schoenberg] himself identified. But whereas expressionist contemporaries, like Klee in art or Trakl in poetry, retreated into a subjective, psychological realm, Schönberg focused on the material itself. He approached the teaching of music as teaching a craft, in which the knowledge of laws governing past compositions provided a technical mastery which necessarily preceded original creativity. He taught his pupils, not musical theory, but compositional practice, and urged them to rely on their own aesthetic experience: 'And a false theory found through honest searching always stands higher than the contemplative securi-

ty of him who opposes it because he presumes to know – to know without having searched himself!'" Ibid., p.14. Schönberg's quote is from Arnold Schönberg, *Harmonielehre* (Vienna: Universal-Edition, 1922), p.2. Buck-Morss notes that Adorno would be familiar with this (third) edition. Buck-Morss, *The Origin of Negative Dialectics*, p.199*n*107.

68 Ibid., p.35. Buck-Morss adds that Adorno found justification for an intellectual elite from Lukács's argument that if the correct revolutionary consciousness was not yet found in the proletariat then a Party elite was justified. Buck-Morss, *The Origin of Negative Dialectics*, p.218*n*79.

69 Ibid., pp.15-17. As noted earlier, Adorno studied music and composition with Alban Berg (1885-1935) in Vienna in 1925. In his later years, Adorno would connect Benjamin's philosophy and Berg's aspirations for "the complete freedom of the ear." This freedom, also connected with Adorno's understanding of Benjamin's philosophy, was associated with the quality of inexhaustibility, of a profusion of ideas, which constantly regenerates itself. "In a real world in which matter-of-factness (which was fully justified as a critique of false plenitude) has degenerated into a statement of bankruptcy, a kind of spiritual meanness, the need for compositional freedom converges with the need for this sense of the inexhaustible. The sterility of functionality is a mere surrogate for the rigour of the work of art." Adorno, *Quasi una fantasia: Essays on Modern Music*, pp.194-195. Adorno's associating of the "quality of inexhaustibility" with "the sterility of functionality" recalls Sontag when she writes, "the vast maw of modernity has chewed up reality and spat the whole mess out in images," suggesting that the dynamic image may be ingesting the fluidity of time and dishing it back out as the indices of mortality. Susan Sontag, *Regarding the Pain of Others* (New York: Farrar, Straus and Giroux, 2003), p.109.

70 Theodor W. Adorno, *Quasi una fantasia: Essays on Modern Music* (1963), translated by Rodney Livingstone (London and New York: Verso, 1992), p.194.

71 Adorno, *In Search of Wagner*, p.99.

72 Jay, *Downcast Eyes*, p. 229.

73 Benjamin, "The Work of Art in the Age of Its Technological Reproducibility," p.119.

74 Adorno, *Aesthetic Theory*, p.xii.

75 Adorno, *In Search of Wagner*, p.156.

76 Adorno, "On the Fetish-Character in Music and the Regression in Listening," p.348.

77 *Erwartung* ("Expectation" Arnold Schoenberg 1909) is a one-act opera for solo soprano and orchestra. The monodrama is set in a forest at night where a woman is looking for her lover, only to find him murdered. Adorno writes, "She is consigned to the music the very same way as a patient is to analysis. The admission of hatred and desire, jealousy and forgiveness, and – beyond all this – the entire symbolism of the unconscious is wrung from her; it is only in the moment that the heroine becomes insane that the music recalls its right to utter a consoling protest." Adorno, *Philosophy of Music*, p.42.

78 Fredric Jameson, "Reflections in Conclusion," *Aesthetics and Politics*, with presentations by Rodney Livingstone, Perry Anderson and Francis Mulhern, afterword by Fredric Jameson (London: Verso Books, 1980), p.209. Schoenberg felt that none of his students succeeded at becoming composers. John Cage, also a student of Schoenberg, "composed" *4'33"* (1952), a concept piece which consists of four minutes and thirty-three seconds of silence. Rather than silence, the work is meant to emphasize the sounds that listeners hear in their environment while listening to "silence." However, Schoenberg said Cage was less a composer and more of an inventor.

79 Adorno, "On the Fetish-Character in Music and the Regression of Listening," p.325.

80 Horkheimer and Adorno, *Dialectic of Enlightenment*, p.27.

81 Adorno, *Aesthetic Theory*, p.40.

82 Bürger, *Theory of the Avant-Garde*, p.xxv.

83 Max Pensky, "Beyond the Message in a Bottle: The Other Critical Theory," *Constellations*, Vol. 10, No. 1 (Oxford and London: Blackwell Publishing, 2003), p.139.

84 Adorno, *Aesthetic Theory*, p.5.

85 Ibid., p.151.
86 Adorno, *Minima Moralia*, p.150.
87 Adorno, *Aesthetic Theory*, p.152.
88 Elsaesser and Hagener, *Film Theory*, p.145.
89 Martin Jay tells us that, "the eye is also able to accomplish its tasks at a far greater remove than any other sense, hearing and smell being only a distant second and third." Jay, *Downcast Eyes*, p.6. Citing Edward T. Hall (*The Hidden Dimension* 1982), Jay notes that the ear is efficient up to twenty feet, less so at a hundred, and beyond that auditory clues break down rapidly. Meanwhile, the unaided eye can sweep up an extraordinary amount of information within a hundred-yard radius and still be efficient at a mile. Ibid., p.7*n*17.
90 Ibid., pp.138-139, 145.
91 *Rendu* is from "rendering," which is a cinema sound editing technique, a process where sound changes as it leaves its source on its way to the listener, and where the sound is manipulated by the sound editor. Contemporary film sound is now considered a component of the film, like a "substance," which can be described as "liquid" or "plastic," and thus is molded and shaped before it is "laid down" and applied to the image track. For example, the film *2001: A Space Odyssey* (Stanley Kubrick 1968) would explore the vacuum of silence found in space, whereas the film *Woodstock* (Michael Wadleigh 1970) would attempt to turn a musical event into a cinematic one, using the new sound systems, as well as documentary style, split screens, etc. Chion is also suggesting that the understanding of the viewing subject is "rendered," where meaning is molded and shaped by the sound. Elsaesser and Hagener, *Film Theory*, pp.144-148.
92 Slavoj Žižek, "The Undergrowth of Enjoyment: How Popular Culture Can Serve as an Introduction to Lacan," *The Žižek Reader*, edited by Elizabeth Wright and Edmond Wright (Malden MA: Blackwell Publishing, 1999), p.13.
93 Ibid., p.148.
94 McLuhan, *Understanding Me*, p.129.
95 Elsaesser and Hagener, *Film Theory*, pp.143-144. Examples would be the woman's scream in *King Kong* (Ernest B. Schoedsack and Merian C. Cooper, 1933), the shower scene in *Psycho* (Alfred Hitchcock, 1960), and the tag-line from *Alien* (Ridley Scott, 1979): "In space, no-one can hear you scream." The screaming woman has been identified with a dominant male "gaze "in cinema, as well as the trope of the "final girl," the last one to confront the killer in horror and "slasher" films. An example of the "final girl" where the unseen terror confronts the power of the *acousmêtre* is found in the final sequence of *The Silence of the Lambs* (Jonathan Demme 1990). See Laura Mulvey, "Visual Pleasure and Narrative Cinema," *Media and Cultural Studies: Keyworks*, edited by Meenakshi Gigi Durham and Douglas M. Kellner (Malden MA: Blackwell Publishing, 2006), pp.342-352. Also, Carol J. Clover, *Men, Women, and Chainsaws: Gender in the Modern Horror* (Princeton NJ: Princeton University Press, 1992). Also, Vivian Sobchack, *Carnal Thoughts: Embodiment and Moving Image Culture* (Berkeley CA: University of California Press, 2004). Also, Kaja Silvernman, "Lost Objects and Mistaken Subjects," *Feminist Film Theory: A Classical Reader*, edited by Sue Thornton (New York: NYU Press, 1999), pp.97-106.
96 Slavoj Žižek, "The Undergrowth of Enjoyment," *New Formations*, No. 9, Winter 1989, p.9.
97 Žižek's example is a sequence from *Vertigo* (Alfred Hitchcock, 1958) that has the classical point-of-view (POV) shots, as well as shots without a defined POV. The latter suggest "the excess of 'subjectivity without subject-agent'" such that we have the look from the "object." Elsaesser and Hagener, *Film Theory*, pp.104-105.
98 Jacques Lacan, "The Mirror Stage as Formative of the *I* Function, as revealed in Psychoanalytic Experience," *Écrits: A Selection*, translated by Bruce Fink, in Collaboration with Héloïse Fink and Russell Grigg (New York: W.W. Norton & Co, 1996), pp.3-10. See also Notes lxiii.
99 Klages, *Literary Theory*, p.173.
100 Adorno, *Aesthetic Theory*, p.190. In *Aesthetic Theory*, Adorno's writing itself

resists subordinating structures by using a paratactical presentation, that is, the lack of paragraph breaks means the reader is tasked with making the connections through coordinating rather than subordinating structures. This elliptical technique is also found in Samuel Beckett's writing, for example *Waiting for Godot* (1953).
101 Klages, *Literary Theory*, pp.173-175. Influenced by Ludwig Wittgenstein, Lyotard will use the term "language games" because each linguistic act follows certain rules and uses certain strategies. This follows Mikhail Bakhtin's ideas about heteroglossia, and the different kinds of language you use in the course of a day in talking to different audiences about different topics and for different purposes. Adorno, *Aesthetic Theory*, p.173. See also Wittgenstein, "Lectures on Aesthetics," pp. 212-215.
102 Cutrofello, *Continental Philosophy*, p.313.
103 Lyotard, *The Postmodern Condition*, pp.xxiv, 81. See also Richard Kearney, "The Post-Modern Imagination," *Poetics of Imagining: From Husserl to Lyotard (Problems of Modern European Thought)* (London: HarperCollinsAcademic, 1991), p.201.
104 Ibid., p.26.
105 Cutrofello, *Continental Philosophy*, pp.312-313. See also Lyotard, *The Postmodern Condition*, p.66.
106 Lyotard, "Note on the Meaning of the Word 'Post'," p.365.
107 Ibid., pp.365-366. This addresses Habmeras's three validity spheres - cognitive, moral, and aesthetic - each representing a distinctive discursive genre with its own criteria of legitimation, which he sought to ground in a theory of universal pragmatics. Such differentiation - the correlate of world decentration - makes it possible to develop separate action systems that acquire semi-autonomy. To each action system there corresponds a "steering mechanism" or "steering medium" that, for reasons of efficiency, is capable of coordinating action directly, that is, without having pass through the normal channels of lifeworld communication. Edgar, *Habermas*, pp.35, 42. See also Jürgen Habermas, *The Theory of Communicative Action - Volume One: Reason and the Rationalization of Society*, translated by Thomas McCarthy (Boston MA: Beacon Press, 1984), p.342.
108 Lyotard, *The Postmodern Condition*, p.61.
109 Lyotard and Thebaud, *Just Gaming*, p.82.
110 As an example of the democratic virtues of the "little narrative" (*des petits récits*), Lyotard cites Alexander Solzhenitsyn's *Gulag Archipelago* (1974), which is "a medley of narratives" that support "the power of the common, than anyone can narrate." Kearney, "The Post-Modern Imagination," p.197. See also Jean-François Lyotard, *Instructions païennes* (Paris: Galilée, 1977).
111 Kearney, "The Post-Modern Imagination," p.196.
112 Ibid., p.201.
113 Lyotard, *The Differend*, p.8.
114 Ibid., p.xi.
115 Rancière, *The Emancipated Spectator*, pp.48-49.
116 Jean-François Lyotard, *Critical Evaluations in Cultural Theory*, edited by Victor E. Taylor and Gregg Lambert (New York: Routledge, 2006), p.186.
117 Jean-François Lyotard, *Peregrinations: Law, Form, Event* (New York: Columbia University Press, 1990), p.44.
118 Lyotard, *The Postmodern Condition*, p.60.
119 Lyotard, "Note on the Meaning of the Word 'Post'," p.370.
120 Cutrofello, *Continental Philosophy*, p.320.
121 Lyotard, *The Differend*, p.161.
122 Lyotard, "General Introduction," *Critical Evaluations in Cultural Theory*, p.6.
123 Lyotard, "Note on the Meaning of the Word 'Post'," p.364.
124 Ibid., p.364.
125 Sloterdijk, *Critique of Cynical Reason*, p.124.
126 Lyotard, "Note on the Meaning of the Word 'Post'," p.364.
127 Lyotard, *The Differend*, p.57.
128 Cutrofello, *Continental Philosophy*, p.267.

129 Adorno, "Education After Auschwitz," p.198. "All political instruction finally should be centered upon the idea that Auschwitz should never happen again. This would be possible only when it devotes itself openly, without fear of offending any authorities, to this most important of problems. To do this education must transform itself into sociology, that is, it must teach about the societal play of forces that operates beneath the surface of political forms." Adorno, "Education After Auschwitz," p.203.
130 Lyotard, *The Differend*, p.106.
131 Wolfgang Schirmacher, "Art(ificial) Perception: Nietzsche and Culture After Nihilism," *Poeisis: A Journal of the Arts and Communication* (Toronto ON: 1999), p.17. From "Emerging," a poem by R.S. Thomas: "Hear my prayer, Lord, hear my prayer. As though you were deaf, myriads of mortals have kept up their shrill cry, explaining your silence by their unfitness." R.S. Thomas, *Laboratories of the Spirit* (Boston MA: David R. Godine, 1976), p.1.
132 Ibid., p.5.
133 Ibid,. p.6.
134 Ibid., p.6.
135 Heidegger, "The Origin of the Work of Art," p.176.
136 Heidegger quotes from Plato's *Symposium*: "Every occasion for whatever passes beyond the nonpresent and goes forward into presencing is *poiēsis*, bringing-forth [*Her-vor-bringen*]." Heidegger refers to poiesis as a 'bringing-forth', using this term in its widest sense. He explained poiesis as the blooming of the blossom, the coming-out of a butterfly from a cocoon, the plummeting of a waterfall when the snow begins to melt. The last two analogies underline Heidegger's example of a threshold occasion: a moment of ecstasis when something moves away from its standing as one thing to become another. Heidegger, "The Question Concerning Technology," p.317.
137 Welsch, *Undoing Aesthetics*, p.6.
138 Wittgenstein, "Lectures on Aesthetics," p.212. See also *L. Wittgenstein – Lectures and Conversations on Aesthetics, Psychology and Religious Belief.* Compiled from Notes taken by Yorick Smythies, Rush Rhees and James Taylor. Edited by Cyril Barrett. Berkeley and Los Angeles CA: University of California Press, 1972.
139 Welsch, *Undoing Aesthetics*, pp.84-89.
140 Ibid., pp.85, 86. See Milan Kundera, *The Unbearable Lightness of Being* (New York: Harper Perennial Modern Classics, 2009).
141 Ibid., p.51.
142 Ibid., p.92.
143 Ibid., p.89.
144 Ibid., p.9. See also Ludwig Wittgenstein, *Philosophical Investigations*, translated by G.E.M. Anscombe (Oxford UK: Macmillan, 1958), p.36.
145 Deleuze and Guattari, *A Thousand Plateaus*, p.xv.
146 Adorno, *Aesthetic Theory*, p.347.
147 Schiller, "Letter of an Aesthetic Education of Man," p.45.
148 Rancière, *The Emancipated Spectator*, p.118.
149 Schiller, "Letter of an Aesthetic Education of Man," p.366.
150 Welsch, *Undoing Aesthetics*, p.95.
151 Ibid., p.132.
152 Schirmacher, "Art(ificial) Perception," p.6. See also Paul Virilio, *The Vision Machine*, translated by Julie Rose (Bloomington IN: Indiana University Press, 1994).
153 Nomadism, or Nomadology, is "the opposite of history," just as the rhizome is "an antigenealogy, a short-term memory or anti-memory," and the plateau, Bateson's term, is "always in the middle, not at the beginning or the end. A rhizome is made up of plateaus." Deleuze and Guattari, *A Thousand Plateaus*, pp.22-23.
154 Ibid., p.6.
155 Paul Virilio, *Open Sky* (New York: Verso, 1997), p.21. A similar proposal to Virilio's was put forth by Thomas Friedman in *The World is Flat: A Brief History of the Twenty-First Century* (New York: Farrar, Strauss & Giroux, 2005). Friedman

proposes that globalization and technology have created a more interconnected world and "leveled the playing field," thus presenting challenges to remaining competitive in a global market where historical and geographical divisions are becoming increasingly irrelevant.
156 Schirmacher, "Art(ificial) Perception," p.6.
157 Schirmacher, "Indirect Communication and Aesthetic Ethics," p.79. See also Wolfgang Schirmacher, *Just Living: Philosophy of Artificial Life* (New York: Atropos Press, 2007).
158 Ibid., p.78. See also Søren Kierkegaard, "The Concept of Irony," *Søren Kierkegaard's Journals and Papers, Volume 2, F-K*, edited and translated by Howard V. Hong and Edna H. Hong, assisted by Gregor Malantschuk (Bloomington IN and London: Indiana University Press, 1970). On another note: "Charles Darwin advocated conducting an occasional damned fool experiment, such as blowing a trumpet at a bed of tulips." Richard K. Guy, "John Horton Conway," *Mathematical People*, Donald J. Albers and G.L. Alexanderson (Editors), Introduction by Phillip J. Davis (Chicago IL: Contemporary Books, 1985), p.44.
159 Ibid., pp.78, 79.
160 See Wolfgang Schirmacher, "Homo Generator in Artificial Life: From a Conversation with Jean-François Lyotard," *Poiesis: A Journal of the Arts and Communication*, Vol. 7 (Toronto ON, 2005).
161 Schirmacher, "Indirect Communication and Aesthetic Ethics," p.78.
162 Adorno, "Negative Dialectics and the Possibility of Philosophy," p.73.
163 Heidegger, "Building, Dwelling, Thinking," p.351.
164 Heidegger, "The Origin of the Work of Art," p.170.
165 Schirmacher, "Art(ificial) Perception," p.20. See also Deleuze, *The Fold*, p.26.
166 See Gottfried Wilhelm Leibniz, *Monadology* (*La Monadologie*, 1714) (Pittsburgh PA: University of Pittsburgh Press, 1991).
167 Deleuze, *The Fold*, p.24.
168 Ibid., p.128.
169 Schirmacher, "Art(ificial) Perception," p.6.
170 Deleuze, *The Fold*, p.26.
171 Ibid., p.103.
172 Elsaesser and Hagener, *Film Theory*, p.106.
173 Deleuze, *The Fold*, p.102.
174 Ibid., p.104.
175 Ibid., p.104.
176 Henri Bergson, *Matter and Memory*, translation by Nancy Margaret-Paul and W. Scott Palmer (New York: Zone Books, 1988), p.9.
177 Cutrofello, *Continental Philosophy*, p.36.
178 Ibid., p.36.
179 Richard Kearney, "The Existential Imagination," *Poetics of Imagining: From Husserl to Lyotard (Problems of Modern European Thought)* (London: HarperCollinsAcademic, 1991), p.50 and 52.
180 Ibid., pp.67, 82*n*.31.
181 Ibid., p.57. Sartre offers the example of characters who actually see the world as it is, such as Emma Bovary from Gustave Flaubert's novel *Madame Bovary*, where these characters imagine "a romantic world uncontaminated by reality but rediscover all the boredom of the real in the imaginary." Kearney, "The Existential Imagination," p.61.
182 Lukács, *The Theory of the Novel*, p.90.
183 Kearney, "The Existential Imagination," p.58. The term "Chinese wall" describes a barrier that separates two or more groups and restricts the flow and exchange of information.
184 Ibid., p.64.
185 Ibid., p.68.
186 Ibid., p.77. See also Jean-Paul Sartre, *The Imaginary: A Phenomenological Psychology of the Imagination* (*L'Imaginaire: Pscyhologie Phénoménologique de l'Imag-*

ination, 1940), revisions and historical introduction by Arlene Elkaïm-Sartre, translated by Jonathan Webber (New York: Routledge, 2004).
187 Ibid., p.78.
188 Critchley, *Infinitely Demanding*, p.58. See also Emmanuel Levinas, *Totality and Infinity: an Essay on Exteriority*, translated by Alphonso Lingis (Pittsburgh PA: Duquesne University Press, 1969), p.291.
189 Simon Critchley, "On the Ethics of Alain Badiou," *Alain Badiou: Philosophy and its Conditions*, Gabriel Riera (Editor) (Albany NY: State University of New York Press, 2005), p.231. The "*entre deux morts*" suggest Beckett's tragic-comedy *Waiting for Godot* (1952), and a line from the character Pozzo: "They give birth astride a grave, the light gleams an instant, then it's night once more." See also Beckett's very short play, about 25 seconds, with no actors on stage, entitled *Breath*.
190 Critchley, *Infinitely Demanding*, p.70.
191 Cutrofello, *Continental Philosophy*, p.172. The quote is from Jacques Lacan, "The Ethics of Psychoanalysis 1959-1960," *The Seminars of Jacques Lacan – Book VII*, edited by Jacques-Alain Miller, translated with Notes by Dennis Porter (New York: W.W. Norton & Co, 1992), p.70.
192 Ibid., p.176. See also Critchley, *Infinitely Demanding*, pp.72-73.
193 Critchley, *Infinitely Demanding*, p.73.
194 Simon Critchley, "A Commentary Upon Derrida's Reading of Hegel in *Glas*," *Hegel After Derrida*, edited by Stuart Barnett (London and New York: Routledge, 1998), p.198.
195 Ibid., p.198.
196 Ibid., pp.198-199.
197 Jacques Rancière, "The Ethical Turn of Aesthetics and Politics," *Aesthetics and Its Discontents*, translated by Steven Corcoran (Cambridge UK and Malden MA: Polity Press, 2009), p.113.
198 Cutrofello, *Continental Philosophy*, pp.174-175.
199 Critchley, "Art and Ethics," pp.129-130.
200 Critchley, *Infinitely Demanding*, pp.21-22.
201 Sartre, "What is Literature?" p.284.
202 Feenberg, *Heidegger and Marcuse*, p.38.
203 Ibid., p.39.
204 Simon Critchley, *Very Little... Almost Nothing: Death, Literature, Philosophy* (London: Routledge, 1997), p.109. See also Phillippe Lacoue-Labarthe and Jean-Luc Nancy, *The Literary Absolute: The Theory of Literature in German Romanticism* (New York: The State University of New York Press, 1988).
205 Ibid., p.114.
206 Ibid., p.2.
207 Ibid., p.137.
208 Critchley, "A Commentary Upon Derrida's Reading of Hegel in *Glas*," pp.199, 200.
209 Ibid., p.204*n*85. The quote is from Martha Nussbaum, "Narrative Emotions: Beckett's Genealogy of Love," *Ethics*, Vol. 98, No.2. (January 1988), p.246.
210 Ibid., p.179.
211 See Judith Butler, "Bodily Confessions," *Undoing Gender* (New York: Routledge, 2004), pp.161-173.
212 De Beauvoir, *The Ethics of Ambiguity*, p.140.
213 Sartre, "What is Literature?", p.278.
214 Ibid., pp.278, 280.
215 Ibid., p.280.
216 Ibid., p.278.
217 Aphasia (from the Greek "speechlessness") is an impairment of language ability. This class of language disorder ranges from having difficulty remembering words to being completely unable to speak, read, or write. See Denise Riley and Jean-Jacques Lecercle, "A Voice Without A Mouth," *The Force of Language, Part 1* (London and Basingstoke: Palgrave Macmillan, 2004).
218 Ibid., p.279.

219 Cutrofello, *Continental Philosophy*, p.67. See also Jean-Paul Sartre, *Being and Nothingness: A Phenomenological Essay on Ontology*, translated by Hazel E. Barnes (New York: Washington Square Press, 1992).
220 Kearney, "The Existential Imagination," p.67.
221 Ibid., p.74.
222 Jean-Paul Sartre, *The Imaginary: A Phenomenological Psychology of the Imagination* (*L'Imaginaire: Pscyhologie Phénoménologique de l'Imagination*, 1940), revisions and historical introduction by Arlene Elkaïm-Sartre, translated by Jonathan Webber. (New York: Routledge, 2004), p.20. Sartre puts the double bind in the Hegelian terms of "for-itself" (*pour-soi*) and "in-itself" (*en-soi*), representing the difference between consciousness and the intentional objects that it negates, such that the "for-itself" is always torn between actuality and possibility, facticity and transcendence, which is also the condition of "bad faith." Cutrofello, *Continental Philosophy*, pp.66-67. See also Kearney, "The Existential Imagination," p.75.
223 Kearney, "The Existential Imagination," p.68.
224 Ibid., p.65. The quote is from Sartre, *The Psychology of Imagination* (New York: Citadel Press, 1948), p.255.
225 Cutrofello, *Continental Philosophy*, p.65.
226 Ibid., p.350. See also Sartre, *Being and Nothingness*, pp.784, 798.
227 Ibid., p.350.
228 René Girard, "Mimetic Desire in the Underground: Feodor Dostoevsky" (1997), *Mimesis and Theory: Essays on Literature and Criticism, 1935-2005*, edited and with an Introduction by Robert Doran (Stanford CA: Stanford University Press, 2008), p.246.
229 Ibid., p.xxiii.
230 Ibid., p.xxv.
231 Lampert, *Nietzsche's Task*, p.111. See Nietzsche, *Beyond Good and Evil*, p.66. See also Nietzsche, *Thus Spoke Zarathustra*, p.41, where he writes "But when Zarathustra was alone, he spoke thus to his heart: 'Could it be possible! This old saint has not yet heard in his forest that *God is dead*!'"
232 Ibid., p.111.
233 Kaufmann, *Nietzsche*, p.382.
234 Lampert, *Nietzsche's Task*, p.112.
235 Ibid., p.81.
236 Plato addresses his views on mimesis (representation) and diegesis (narrative) in both *Ion* and *The Republic* (Books II, III and X), as well as his view that artists and writers should be removed from the *kallipolis* as they deal with falsifying truth. Only philosophers present the truth. Therefore, if his ideal city-state is to ever come into being, "philosophers [must] become kings...or those now called kings [must]...genuinely and adequately philosophize." Plato, *The Republic*, Book V.
237 Ibid., p.125.
238 Nietzsche, *Beyond Good and Evil*, p.71.
239 Michel Serres, *The Natural Contract*, translated by Elizabeth MacArthur and William Paulson (Ann Arbor MI: The University of Michigan Press, 1195), p.3.
240 Lampert, *Nietzsche's Task*, p.125. Lampert is addressing the chapter "*Das religiöse Wesen*" in Nietzsche's *Beyond Good and Evil*. To paraphrase Walter Kaufmann in his translator's footnote, he points out that the word *Wesen* is difficult to translate, but in philosophical terms it usually means "essence," but in other contexts it means "being," as in a natural being, a human being, so that *Das religiöse Wesen* would mean either "the religious nature" or "the religious being." Nietzsche also refers to "the religious neurosis – or what I call '*das religiöse Wesen*'" (p.62), where *Wesen* means character, conduct, manners, as well as *viel Wesen* meaning "much ado." Nietzsche, *Beyond Good and Evil*, p.57*n*3
241 Freud, *Civilization and its Discontents*, pp.3-4.
242 Martin Heidegger, "What are Poets For?" (1946), *Poetry, Language, Thought*, translated by Alfred Hofstadter (New York: Harper and Row, 1971), p.94. See also Cutrofello, *Continental Philosophy*, p.247.
243 Ibid., p.94. The opening page of Heidegger's *Being and Time* has the quote: "We

are too late for the gods/ and too early for Being./ Being's poem, just begun, is man." Heidegger, "Being and Time," p.37.
244 Avital Ronell, "The Sacred Alien: Heidegger's Reading of Hölderlin's 'Andenken'," *The Über-Reader: Selected Works of Avital Ronell*, edited by Diane Davis (Urbana and Chicago IL: University of Illinois Press, 2007), p.205. Ronell notes that the title of Holderlin's poem *Andenken* is usually translated as "Remembrance" (The Heideggerian overtones are apparent in "to think" (*denken*) and "to give thanks" (*danken*). Ibid., p.224.
245 Ibid., p.205.
246 Heidegger, "What are Poets For?", p.94.
247 Nietzsche, *The Birth of Tragedy*, pp.16, 26. Nietzsche compares Apollo and the "principle of individuation" with a passage from Schopenhauer: "Just as the boatman sits in his little boat, trusting to his fragile craft in a stormy sea which, boundless in every direction, rises and falls in howling, mountainous waves, so in the midst of a world full of suffering the individual man calmly sits, supported by and trusting the *principium individuationis*." Nietzsche, *The Birth of Tragedy*, p.16. The quote can be found in Arthur Schopenhauer, *The World as Will and Representation*, translated by E.F.J. Payne (London: Dover Publications, 1968), p.352.
248 Cutrofello, *Continental Philosophy*, p.245.
249 Martin Heidegger, *Elucidations of Hölderlin's Poetry*, translated by Keith Hoeller (New York: Humanity Books, 2000), p.218.
250 Ibid., p.172.
251 Ronell, "The Sacred Alien," p.212.
252 Ibid., p.212.
253 Ibid., p.214.
254 Jacques Derrida, *Of Hospitality : Anne Dufourmantelle invites Jacques Derrida to respond*, translated by Rachel Bowlby (Stanford CA: Stanford University Press, 2000), p.135.
255 Ronell, "The Sacred Alien," p.224.
256 Ibid., p.224.
257 Lampert, *Nietzsche's Task*, p.124.
258 Ibid., p.105.
259 Ibid., p.124.
260 Bruno Latour, "War and Peace in an Age of Ecological Conflict" (Lecture), *The Wall Exchange: Peter Wall Institute for Advanced Studies*, Vancouver, BC, September 23, 2013.
261 Martin Heidegger, "Who is Nietzsche's Zarathustra?", *Nietzsche, Volume 1: The Will to Power as Art, Volume 2: The Eternal Recurrence of the Same*, translated by David Farrell Krell (New York: HarperOne, 1991), pp.103-104. A quote from Nietzsche: "Whoever fights monsters should see to it that in the process he does not become a monster. And when you look long into an abyss, the abyss also looks at you." Nietzsche, *Beyond Good and Evil*, p.89. For Nietzsche, the kingdom of God is in the hearts of men, but when it is sought in another life then the central insight of Jesus has been betrayed, so Nietzsche writes, "Whoever wants to be a Christian should tear the eyes out of his reason..." Kaufmann, *Nietzsche*, pp.345, 350.
262 Kaufmann, *Nietzsche*, p.359.
263 Gertrude Himmelfarb, *On Looking Into the Abyss: Untimely Thoughts on Culture and Society* (New York, Vintage Books, 1994), p.13.
264 Martin Heidegger, *Elucidations of Hölderlin's Poetry*, translated by Keith Hoeller (New York: Humanity Books, 2000), p.123.
265 Rainer Maria Rilke, "The First Elegy," *Duino Elegies* (*Duineser Elegien*, 1923), the German Text, with an English translation, Introduction, and Commentary by J.B. Leishman and Stephen Spender (New York: W.W. Norton & Co., 1939), pp.20-27. See also Cutrofello, *Continental Philosophy*, p.247.
266 Heidegger, "Poetry, Language, Thought," p.134.
267 Lyotard, *Why Philosophize?*, p.59.
268 Bergson will claim that in animals the *élan vital* expresses itself primarily

as instinct; in human beings, as intellect. See Henri Bergson, *Creative Evolution*, translated by Arthur Mitchell (New York: Dover Publications, 1998).

269 Kant, "The Critique of Judgement – Part I: Critique of Aesthetic Judgement," p.24.

270 Adorno, *Aesthetic Theory*, p.134.

271 Ibid., p.132.

272 Ibid., p.31.

273 The French photographer Henri Cartier-Bresson refers to the moment of capturing a photograph as being like an orgasm: "The simultaneous recognition, in a fraction of a second, of the significance of an event as well as the precise organization of forms which gives that event its proper expression." Henri Cartier-Bresson, *The Decisive Moment* (New York: Simon and Schuster, 1952).

274 Schirmacher, "Cloning Humans with Media,"p.41.

275 Adorno, *Aesthetic Theory*, p.132.

276 Schiller, "Letter of an Aesthetic Education of Man," p.44.

277 Ibid., p.45.

278 Adorno, *Negative Dialectics*, pp.17-18.

279 Critchley, *Very Little... Almost Nothing*, p.152.

280 Lyotard, *Why Philosophize?*, p.122.

The Question of Ethics

Cinema: The flow of images

Badiou writes that the cinema functions as "the 'plus-one' of the arts. It operates on the other arts, using them as a starting point, in a movement that subtracts them from themselves."[1] He also claims that the "cinema is an art of the perpetual past, in the sense that it institutes the past of the pass (*la passe*). Cinema is visitation: it passes. To organize within the visible the caress proffered by the passage of the idea, this is the operation of the cinema."[2] Therefore, the cinema makes time visible, just as music makes time audible, where the lived experience of time is changed into the lived experience of representation, and, in so doing, evoking Bazin, cinema addresses the relationship between "being" and "appearing."[3] Thus, cinema contains elements of the ontological, even the metaphysical, and so is capable of transforming philosophy.

Badiou offers three possible schemata for the links between art and philosophy, which may be presented as: 1) didacticism (an educational surveillance of art's purpose, which views it as extrinsic to truth), 2) romanticism (art realized within finitude and disenchantment, as discussed with Heidegger and the poet), and 3) classicism (art that captures desire and shapes its transference, to use the psychological term, by proposing a semblance of its object).[4] Badiou extends these three possible schemata into the three main spheres of thought in the twentieth century, namely: 1) Marxism (the didactic, as found in the new rationality, where truth is dialectical materialism), 2) Heideggerian hermeneutics (romanticism, where the poet-thinker is presented as the obverse of Nietzsche's philosopher-artist), and 3) psychoanalysis (classical, where the work of art is an object of desire that is beyond symbolization, and yet it is paradoxically an act of symbolization).[5]

Significantly, in terms of didacticism, the link between art and philosophy is pedagogical in that education itself may be defined as an education by truths, and therefore most certainly not simply an opinion, but a truth made manifest.[6] On the other hand, the "truth" offered by Heideggerian hermeneutics/romanticism offers a "divine" or universal truth, one that is connected to being itself, and the promise of the arrival or the absence of the gods. As we have noted earlier with Heidegger's view of Hölderlin, and as noted by Badiou, the poet-thinker is presented as the obverse of Nietzsche's philosopher-artist, yet, importantly, "it is *the same truth that circulates*,"[7] hence, the "truth" of the poet and the "truth" of the thinker are the same. However, Badiou will argue that in terms of ownership of that "same" truth, the advantage is with the poet, as discussed above in poetized philosophy, because the thinker only offers its reversal, confirming "the retroactive elucidation of the historiality of being."[8] In other words, as noted earlier, we could say that the philosopher has not looked into the terror of the abyss but only into a purely linguistic construction, whereas the poet composes a linguistic construction from within the terror of the abyss. However, in terms of a poetic crisis, particularly a crisis of language, we would consider that both the poetic and the philosophical function through language, whereby their synthesis may provide the bridge, as Heidegger described, a passage that crosses before the divinities. And if not before the divinities as divinities, then beside the flow of life, where the poetic and the philosophical are the banks on either side of the same truth, the Danube with Hölderlin and Heidegger perhaps, the bridge as subject connecting points from both sides, a midstream intersection of the immutable poem and the philosophical flow, of words, the interface between elements, including those riparian zones that quietly and modestly define the well-being of all. Moreover, in the world-as-picture, where the image is realized digitally, ever more accessible, ever more manipulatable, it is as if the image were a word, where the flow of words becomes a flow of images.

Art-truth: Heterogenous truths

In terms of the psychoanalytic/classicism links between art and philosophy, the "truth" is realized through its self-determination, a theory of desire. To put this in Lacanian terminology, the work of art is an object of desire that is beyond symbolization, yet simultaneously and paradoxically an act of symbolization It is the *objet petit a*, defined as the leftover, the remnant left behind by the introduction of the Symbolic in the Real, which thus leads to "the dissipation of the unspeakable scintillation of the lost object."[9] Indeed, as Critchley notes, "the moral goal of psychoanalysis consists in putting the subject in relation to its unconscious desire. This is why sublimation is so important, for it is the realization of such desire."[10] Thus, the object of desire is linked to the cause of desire (*objet petit a*), such that the difference between them, between what we might distinguish as the difference between a need and a want, the remainder, is the work of art itself, the formidable substitutive satisfaction (Freud), such that the surplus meaning in the work of art may be considered as *jouissance* (pleasure, enjoyment).[11]

Badiou argues that all three of these schemata are "saturated," producing a "disrelation" between art and philosophy, where, in terms of the double bind (or in Lacan's Master/Hysteric relationship),[12] art is condemned as alienated and inauthentic on one hand, yet regarded as the profound container of "truth content" on the other, the absolute of self--determination, eliciting demands for its salvation. According to Badiou, therefore, the problem that all three schemata share is that each make a particular claim for their relation between art and truth, when in fact "art *itself* is a truth procedure."[13] In other words, the work of art is only the point of departure in the sense of placement, the conceptual site as a point of reference amongst infinite possibilities, and thus, the co-existence that depends on the free circulation of its conditions because it moves the individual subject's registering of truths into another phase, namely the production of truths and their inventive capacity within social reality. However, Badiou clarifies that the work of art is not in itself an event, but it is the artistic configuration initiated by the event. Consequently, the work of art is not a produced truth, but it is a truth procedure, and thus an artistic truth, an art-truth.[14]

For Badiou, then, the free circulation of conditions includes a return to the mathematics of Plato where the discourses of the philosophical and the mathematical offer a pure multiplicity composed of multiple events, or situations, which may register heterogenous truths. In mathematical terms, therefore, the concept of being *qua* being remains but it does so in terms of this multiplicity, such that one (the One), or, for that matter, zero (Nothing), is not the axiomatic point of departure,[15] but that it is only the point of departure in the sense of placement, the conceptual site as a point of reference amongst infinite possibilities, just as counting places the numerical one on an abstract axis but that is just one possibility, and yet the numerical one is also an empirical reality, each of which *becomes* the point of reference.

In Heideggerian terms, we might say that rather than an event that presences itself in the clearing, the clearing is presenced through the event. Even so, like Heidegger, Badiou recognizes the significance of the event, but is significant not in the event itself (i.e., the work of art), but in the artistic configuration initiated by the event, where a significance is accorded through a fidelity to the event. Unlike Heidegger, where the event is that which is always repeated and never exhausted, despite inscribing difference, because it always returns to Being, for Badiou the event is an "'extraordinary multiple'; it is, at the same time, the situation of the multiples of its own site and its own situation, which means that the defining feature of the event is its self-belonging."[16] Thus, the truth that arises from an event is a subjective process, because, as noted above, it is accessed from a point of reference, namely the individual subject. Although the individual subject cannot know whether or not they will be connected to a given event, once they have been exposed to the event, they are the one to give the point of reference to its "happening" and thereby the one to put the event into circulation, by naming or identifying the event as an event, and thus they also become the link between the event and fidelity. By way of illustration, Badiou offers Saint Paul, noting the force of the event and the militant apparatus (*dispositif*) of truth, as "the example of a subject whose fidelity to the event of Christ's Resurrection puts this singular occurrence into circulation and renders it into a universal truth."[17] However, for Badiou, an atheist, we might also recall Camus when he wrote, "Sisyphus teaches the higher fidelity that negates the gods and raises rocks."[18] Indeed, the paradox here, and the absurdity, is that the absence of religious belief does not diminish the longing for salvation and meaning.

The conceptual site, therefore, in which the generic procedures – the processes of truth - are thought of as compossible (that is, possible in coexistence with something else),[19] depends on the free circulation of its conditions, not unlike Heidegger's "free space of clearing," because it moves the individual subject's registering of truths into another phase, namely the production of truths and their inventive capacity within social reality. The obstruction to this free circulation would be the "suture," which may then demand the de-suturing of the philosophical and the poetical. In terms of these obstructions, as compiled by Gabriel Riera and paraphrased here, Badiou identifies three types: 1) scientific (positivism and its doctrine of progress), 2) political (revolutionary philosophy and the hybrid represented by "scientific socialism" that juxtaposes a science of History and a voluntaristic form of politics), and 3) poetic (represented by the age of poets).[20] The purpose of the suture, therefore, and its capacity for obstruction to free circulation, is to support the scientific commitment to the empirical, which, as noted earlier, enforces the bounded domain of the object, where the idea in a form or law dominates intellectual thought, which also supports the hegemony of the spirit of history, as well as the tendency for the poetic that becomes the condition for philosophical thinking.[21] Indeed, for Badiou, by suturing thought to the poem, to the linguistic turn, and thus to waiting for the absent god, can only expose the world to disenchantment and to a philosophy of finitude.[22] Although the poetic has a place in Badiou's philosophy, he asserts that philosophy is not seeking the art-truth, but it is "the site where thinking seizes the *truths* or *generic procedures* of an epoch."[23] Thus, the aim of philosophy is understood as thinking "together" because, as Badiou words it, the "sole question is indeed that of the truth. Not that it produces any, but because it offers a mode of access to the utility of a moment of truths, a conceptual site in which the generic procedures are thought of as compossible."[24] The space of compossiblility, therefore, namely those contradictory elements that can exist together, are understood by the generic procedures, what we might call the process of clearing and presence, which is philosophy itself, and which therefore allows for changing and heterogenous truths.

The singular occurrence of the event means that the subject does not pre-exist the event, yet the circulation of the event's name is a subjective process, and only the fidelity to the event will reveal its truth. However, as discussed, the obstructions to the free circulation of this revealing of truth can be scientific, political or poetic, and also may occur at the level of the individual subject as well as their social reality, whereby the free circulation of truth is obstructed at the level of registering the truth as well as the production of truth. In these terms, the conception of the self-determined subject involves, and perhaps demands, a certain notion of self-sufficiency, or, in Critchley's terms, an autarkic will (which also suggests self-sufficiency at the level of both the subject and the state),[25] because the conceptual site is a point of reference amongst infinite possibilities to the event. Therefore, Badiou's philosophy proposes a non-dogmatic imperative towards the event, such that the maxim of the fidelity to the event would be, "Decide from the point of view of what is undecidable."[26]

Aesthetic experience: Didactics of the senses

The proposition that we have now developed, one that conforms to Badiou's idea of heterogenous truths, is that there are at least two basic truths: the registered truth that is the event as it is experienced by the individual subject, and the produced truth that is the event interpreted by the subject, circulated and interpreted within their social reality. The obstructions to these truths are at least two-fold as well: the truth of the event that is obstructed by the individual subject, either through interpretation or misinterpretation, which may be intentional or not, and the truth of the event that is obstructed by social reality, either through interpretation or through misinterpretation, which again may be intentional or not. The consequences of these two poles of intention are significant. Once again, we return to the fidelity to the event, but now, due to the self-determination of the subject, that which Kant would call autonomy, we must also consider the event as an ethical experience due to the very concept of fidelity. Thus, the fidelity of the event that is an ethical experience that will appear as an aesthetic experience, one that is the response (registered truth) of the self-determined subject to the event as well as the potential work of art (produced truth). In Badiou's terms, therefore, as interpreted by Rancière, we must recognize that the ethical experience includes a "duty of thought," which is "to 'decide at the point of the undecidable', and that it is precisely this exigency to make a decision on the undecidable that is at stake in the question of knowing."[27] Therefore, the duty of thought, like the weight of judgement, is a position in relation to the event (the aesthetic experience), one that is defined by the fidelity to the event, not the event in and of itself, which is an ethical decision.

At this point, we may wish to distinguish between ethics and morality. For our purposes, ethics is related to a position, whereas morality is related to a system or tradition. A system of morals suggests norms of action, whereas the ethical position suggests the subjective re-action, which we have now described as an act of fidelity to the event. We could also say that the ethical position suggests a registered truth, one that is non-dogmatic, and where, in the terms used above, the fidelity to the event is to weigh the judgement, a duty of thought, which necessitates that the response of the individual subject is incorporated into the broader concept of the *sensus communis*, or the public sense. On the other hand, the system of truths, or morality, suggests a produced truth, one that is dogmatic, a truth that may be received by the subject's fidelity to the event and so is interpreted for all – for example, an event that illuminates an idea, a position, a registered or non-sutured truth - or it may be a hegemonic truth that is produced by the system for the self-justification of the system itself – for example, a work of art that goes on public display that supports a concept, a system, a sutured or produced truth. By extension, we might also say that ethics is philosophical, in that it involves a questioning, whereas morality, when it is systematized, as Badiou would say about religion, is anti-philosophical.[28]

To be clear, the aesthetic experience of the self-determined subject is also an ethical experience, that is, the aesthetic experience can be no other than subjective, such that there is necessarily a demand incurred on the subject by the fidelity to the event. Thus, the fidelity to the event is realized through the becoming-subject, an ethical and an aesthetic experience, that may register its "truth content" through the engagement with the work of art, and so realize its art-truth. We understand that the aesthetic elements may then be translated into the *sensus communis*, as part of the processes of truth, whereby they are then foundational for our knowledge.

In his *Undoing Aesthetics*, Welsch returns to Kant's *Critique of Pure Reason* under the title "Transcendental Aesthetic," where Kant states that in his "revolution of the way of thinking" that we know "*a priori* of things only what we ourselves put into them," and what we first put into them are *aesthetic* stipulations, namely space and time as forms of intuition.[29] Therefore, since Kant, and as argued by Welsch, we have known of aesthetic fundaments of all knowledge as "a principal protoaesthetic of cognition."[30] As such, we find the linkage between cognition, knowledge, aesthetics, and ethics. Even so, Plato had warned that there are arts and there are appearances, which may be differentiated, to paraphrase Rancière, in that the arts are applications of forms of knowledge founded on the imitation of models, whereas appearances are the simulacra of arts, such that there are true and false imitations, those that contribute to knowledge and those that deceive with false knowledge.[31]

Art is the imitation of the effects of truth so it must be either condemned or treated in a purely instrumental fashion, and where its terms of acceptance are prescribed then its vote of confidence arrives when its goal is education and where it functions as a mode of public service. Aristotle will advance this proposal by claiming that there are criteria of recognition and evaluation that distinguishes the viewing subject and the determination of what is art or imitation. Aristotle, as Badiou will say, signed the peace treaty between art and philosophy, where it is conceded that art is not truth, and where its value lies in its therapeutic functions (i.e., catharsis).[32] Recognizing that cognition itself is constitutive, Kant reinforces the autonomy of art and the viewing subject. Hegel makes the transition from natural beauty to art beauty, which, Adorno argues, unfolds from a "theodicy of the real,"[33] which amounts to a form of natural theology. Yet, Adorno claims, despite the concept of natural beauty as "the first natural form" and therefore "suitable," and therefore beautiful, it remains constitutive, whereby "the beauty of nature is beautiful only for another, i.e., for *us*, for the mind which apprehends beauty."[34] Accordingly, this is simply a case of "art [that] has converged with natural beauty."[35] Nonetheless, starting with Giambattista Vico, as noted by Rancière, the aesthetic autonomy of art becomes another name for its heteronomy, such that "the aesthetic identification of art is the principle of a generalized disidentification."[36] Consequently, the lines are blurred between man and nature, between arts and appearances, between true and false imitations, where poets do not set out to be poets, where artists are not necessarily artists, and where the conception of art spreads to other fields and pursuits. Indeed, in the world as picture, constituted by the subject, the aesthetic identification is ubiquitous. Rancière argues that the result has been the development of an anti-aesthetics due to the inability to identify art's specificity.[37]

Much like Badiou, where to philosophize is in the registering of truths rather than the producing of truths, Adorno claimed, "aesthetics is, however, not applied philosophy but rather in itself philosophical."[38] Accordingly, the aesthetic of art is considered less in terms of its form and more in terms of its idea, its way of thinking, to use Heideggerian terms, and not unlike the claim of *die Sprache spricht*, so Adorno would write, "art thinks itself."[39] The concern, however, one that is identified by Badiou, is that art is always already there, interpellated as it were, "addressing the thinker with the mute and scintillating question of its identity while through constant invention and metamorphosis it declares its disappointment about everything that the philosopher may have to say about it."[40] Badiou will compare the relationship of philosophy and art, where art is a producer of truths but not necessarily an object for philosophy, to that of Lacan's Master and Hysteric, where the philosopher-master is forever divided between idolatry and censure.

Thus, the aesthetic experience of the self-determined subject is an ethical experience, one that necessarily incurs a demand on the subject to the fidelity to the event, but it is a demand that can be intentionally or unintentionally misinterpreted, and, in its self-determination, may even prove destructive to the self. It is also a demand that is influenced by the prescriptions from outside, as Badiou noted, the obstructions to free circulation that may be scientific, political, or poetic, where the aesthetic experience must then be educational and produce prescribed truths, whereby "art is a didactics of the senses" and therefore "the 'good' essence of art is conveyed in its public effect, and not in the work itself."[41] If so, we are back to the Platonic "false truth," or, as Badiou words it, "the 'imaginarization' of truth, which is relieved of any instance of the Real, is what the classical thinkers called 'verisimilitude' or 'likelihood'."[42] In so doing, art does not need to be supported by its "truth content," but rather, as Badiou argues, it needs to be "liked," hence "the 'vassalization' of art and artists by absolutism, as well as in the modern vicissitudes of funding."[43]

Non-place: The cinematic long shot

In Heideggerian terms, if we focus on the destination rather than the journey, the highway rather than the meandering path, then we are travelling but not on the path of self-presencing. The site of linkage, the bridge, the paths crossing, paths emerging, is not a gathering. Our self-made environment is less one of freedom than one of confinement, where freedom of movement is not an exploratory, restless movement, but rather a contained and composed exploration, one of definitive purposefulness that is constituted subjectively (the bound domain).

In terms of the location of culture, we may find that this movement is actually confinement, expressed in the idea that the traditional places of gathering have been replaced by equally institutionalized "non-places." This argument is put forth in his *Non-Places: Introduction to an Anthropology of Supermodernity* by Marc Augé, where his definition of the non-place, or *non-lieux*, refers to places of transience that do not hold enough significance to be regarded as "places." In other words, the non-place would not contain "a principle of meaning for the people who live in it, and also a principle of intelligibility for the person who observes it."[44] Thus, Augé defines "place" in terms of the anthropological, where the anthropological space is a "concrete and symbolic construction of space," and further, "all anthropology is anthropology of other people's anthropology," whereby meaning and intelligibility allows for "places of identity, of relations and of history," with activities and assemblies, with monuments to a shared historical past, with an accompanying sense of duration, where the subject "displays a vulnerability and permeability to his immediate surroundings."[45] Non-places, on the other hand, are not anthropological spaces and do not integrate those earlier places and their attendant activity, history and duration, and instead present a world "surrendered to solitary individuality, to the fleeting, the temporary and ephemeral," and therefore, "place and non-place are rather like opposed polarities: the first is never completely erased, the second never totally completed."[46] Consequently, we have developed a new architecture of transit and impermanence, where the ordering of our social reality is found in gated communities, shopping malls, airports, and expressways, with travel organized by hotel chains and holiday clubs, and the less fortunate gathering in tent cities for the homeless and political refugee camps.

The opposition between "place" and "non-place" may be further defined as the opposing notions of "place" and "space," where "place" is one of assembly and "space" is one of movement, which, citing Michel de Certeau, Augé further distinguishes by the opposing notions of "doing" and "seeing." Augé extends these oppositions in terms of language, where the assembly and movement aspects of "place" and "space" suggest a picture ("there is..."), and the organization of movements ("you go in, you cross, you turn...") suggests "journeys" and "actions." If we apply this to the language of the narrative, which contains both "journeys" and "actions," because, according to De Certeau, every narrative is a journey narrative, then we also find that every narrative contains the concept of "delinquency," one that suggests the task of the aesthetic through the aesthetic, which "'crosses', 'transgresses' and endorses 'the privileging of the route over the inventory'."[47] In other words, we may find, as Adorno worded it, the aesthetic actualizes freedom only in its own freedom of determination. Augé, however, warns against a solely negative view of non-places, which would contrast "the symbolized space of place with the non-symbolized space of non-place."[48] He also warns against the urge to discover the totality of the social fact, in what he calls the "totality temptation," which is a desire for "that consistency or transparency between culture, society and individual."[49] Similarly, Adorno defined totality as a lie and art as the social antithesis of society and not directly deducible from it.[50] However, the point here is that the social fact itself is perceived as picture.

Heidegger set himself the task of overcoming the forgetting of Being, of bringing humankind home again, a return to the hearth, whereby "Being is the hearth." However, Augé argues that Hestia, the goddess of the hearth, the feminine center of the home, is replaced by Hermes, god of the threshold, the protector of exchanges and the men who monopolize them.[51] Indeed, we might say that the hearth of the home is replaced by the screen; the stable or central place (hearth, the heart) replaced by the transitional or liminal space (subliminal, the mind).

As stated earlier, the work of art – and in this inquiry, the culture of the image - is a social fact (*fait social*) defined as an activity that informs and influences our social reality, with the attendant implications in the economic, legal, political and religious spheres, and yet simultaneously art itself is influenced by these same spheres. Thus, the process of the narrative itself works both ways, ceaselessly transforming the symbolized space of place into the non-symbolized space of non-place, and vice versa. For example, far-flung or imagined places (Costa del Sol, Timbuktu, distant planets) are often found in the re-symbolizing language of travel, hotel and leisure institutions (picture yourself in this or that place), or in the fantasy realms of narrative, such as those found in the imagined locations in films and video games (project yourself into these exotic situations and worlds). Alternately, in terms of the organization of movement, in both "place" and "space," in both material reality and the screened image, we find not only the indexical nature of cinema and computers (its framing, its narrative devices, its unspooling in the viewing subject's real time) but the ubiquity of signage, the language of image/text that contains an organizing intent: "Walk/Don't Walk," "No Parking Anytime," "Google Search," "You are Here."

However, we may find that "space" is not only a more abstract term than that of the anthropological "place," it also suggests a domain that is more suitable to organization, because technology allows for a more manipulatable and more readily accessible domain than material reality. It also suggests a domain that is more quickly and easily bought and sold, the limits of material property versus the virtually unlimited domains of intellectual property, which would include the temporal domain of past and future as found in the symbolized space of place, such as the re-symbolization of reproductions of art of the past, or the computer-generated images of some imagined future. In addition, this suggests a domain that is subject to the legal process as well as hegemonic reinterpretation through the political. Thus, the screened reality and its language of images, the ceaselessly transforming process of the narrative and the diversion of picture to inventory, becomes a substitutive system that replaces itself with itself. It is a system that has its own ideology, where it is increasingly difficult to distinguish between the interior and the exterior, the here and the elsewhere. The aesthetic through the aesthetic, therefore, would involve the transgression of the language of images, a delinquency as it were, that challenges the co-opting of place into non-place, the ordering and organizational non-language of signage, as well as the blurring of the frontier between material reality and the screened images, and the narrative that disallows the site of self-presencing. We may recall Adorno's enigmatic statement that, "today the only works which really count are those which are no longer works at all."[52] An example can be found in the works of the pseudonymous graffiti artist, Banksy, and the transgressive nature of his word/images, his lack of identity, the delinquency of his presentations in terms of both site and content, and their reproductions found in print, cinema and computer sites.[53]

The dominant aesthetic of the modern age, Augé contends, is that of the cinematic long shot, a mechanical gaze that distances us from reality and makes us forget the world is now one of discontinuity and interdiction:

> Photos taken from observation satellites, aerial shots, habituate us to a global view of things. High office blocks and residential towers educate the gaze, as do movies and, even more significantly, television. The smooth flow of cars on a highway, aircraft taking off from airport runways, lone sailors circumnavigating the globe in small boats witnessed only by the television audience, create an image of the world as we would like it to be. But that mirage disintegrates if we look at it too closely."[54]

This disintegrating mirage recalls Jean Baudrillard's observations when he journeyed across the United States in the 1980s (the same decade that saw the introduction of personal computers), particularly in Los Angeles where he discovered "nothing but long tracking shots of signals," signifiers without signifieds, where highways are nothing more than the "insane circulation without desire," and landscapes that are "an extravaganza of indifference."[55] All of which, Baudrillard claims, marks not so much a transgression of the aesthetic as the end of aesthetics itself. Perhaps he bears witness to the material remainder when all is cancelled and replaced by the world as picture. Indeed, Baudrillard will claim that the urban man-made landscapes that can be likened to deserts in their undifferentiated surfaces can also be extended to the image-making culture and the ubiquity of its products where its contribution to the desertified geography is that, "there is no longer a medium in the literal sense: it is now intangible, diffused, and diffracted in the real."[56]

The extent of this barren world-as-image is described by Borges' story, "On Exactitude in Science," referenced by Baudrillard in *Simulacra and Simulation* (1981), where the geographers of the Empire construct a map that is as large and detailed as the Empire itself. In Borges' story, only tatters of the map of the Empire still survive in the deserts of the west, whereas Baudrillard contends, "it is the real, and not the map, whose vestiges persist here and there in the deserts that are no longer those of the Empire, but ours. The desert of the real itself."[57] Why don't we "see" the desert of the real for what it is, namely, a desert? In response, we might look to the treachery of images and the desensualized world-as-picture, as well as Lukács and his concept of reification, where we might find that the secondary reality is so pervasive because the veil of illusion and the images that we use to construct the world is supported by constitutive subjectivity, thus creating a world-image as we interpret it, as it ought to be, or as we dream of it becoming. In any case, we may not see the desert because, quite simply, we don't want to.

Sloterdijk argues that because God is not "empirically" observable, then we must assign divine attributes to human experience, and because the world had become more mechanized, so "the idea of God was transferred from the biological conception of procreation to that of production. Accordingly, the procreating God became increasingly a world manufacturer, the original producer."[58] In the production of the world-as-picture, as noted earlier, our visual constructions have proved an important step in the aesthetic reification of our social reality and the technology of reflection becomes the crucible of, and for, our own modern re-creation. Deleuze would write:

> The copy is an image endowed with resemblance, the simulacrum is an image without resemblance. The catechism, so fully inspired by Platonism, has familiarized us with this notion. God made man in His own image and to resemble Him, but through sin, man has lost his resemblance while retaining the image. Having lost a moral existence in order to enter into an aesthetic one, we have become simulacra.[59]

The folds of vision: The parallax view

In the 1970s and 1980s, film theory was widely influenced by Lacan's work and its incorporation of neo-Freudian psychoanalysis and Foucault's theory of the Panopticon, models for both subjectivity and social control. The central tower of the Panopticon allows the hidden observer to see everything without themselves being seen, such that, Deleuze notes, the architecture is "a luminous form that bathes the peripheral cells in light but leaves the central tower opaque."[60] Foucault claims that the panoptic space functions "as a kind of Lacanian point-de-capiton or suturing point of the 'carceral archipelago'."[61] The *point-de-capiton* is an upholstery button, the analogy being that just as upholstery buttons are places where the mattress-maker's needle prevents a shapeless mass of stuffing from moving too freely about, so the *points-de-capiton* are points at which the signified and signifier are knotted together. The *point-de-capiton* is thus the point in the signifying chain at which "the signifier stops the otherwise endless movement of the signification and produces the necessary illusion of a fixed meaning."[62] However, when Foucault contends that Velasquez's *Las Meninas* had opened up the space of classical representation, where the overall effect is that of a destabilization of the image, there is a cross-thatch of looks and meaning that creates a "shimmer effect," one that recalls the ambiguity and instability of Wittgenstein's duck-rabbit.[63]

In terms of "the origin of the 'gaze', i.e. of the look as a fixed stare or as a scopic regime of control and domination," as noted by Elsaesser and Hagener, it "cannot be located in any specific place or associated with any specific person. The term encompasses both the historical (Foucault) and the structural (Lacan) dimensions of visual (power) relations."[64] However, also noted by Elsaesser and Hagener, the gaze is outside the realms of the social control of the Symbolic or the pleasurable realm of the Imaginary, and appears as the Real, where "the gaze therefore is external to the human subject, a force not controllable and assimilable, that can only be approached in the strangely twisted figure of watching oneself being watched,"[65] or, as Deleuze describes Foucault's concept of the gaze in terms of the folds of vision, the interior of the exterior, of "*life within the folds.*"[66] Thus, the folds of vision are "an ontological visibility, forever twisting itself into a self-seeing entity, on to a different dimension from that of the gaze and its objects,"[67] such that, there is a unity of the folding-unfolding, of the unveiling-veiling, of Being-being, of seeing and being seen, where we may consider the resulting synthesis as "being-image."

For Lacan, as noted earlier, the Real is not synonymous with reality but rather an ontological absolute, a true being-in-itself, a paradoxical state in that it can only be defined by what it is not. It is outside any form of embodiment or representation – otherwise it wouldn't be "real" – yet it is "still somehow within our field of vision, but not immediately recognizable, constantly present, yet not consciously so."[68] By way of example, Lacan refers to Hans Holbein's *The Ambassadors* (1533), a painting that presents two affluent men surrounded by their worldly goods, and where, as spectators, we would feel that we were in control of the scene, that is, until we recognize a stain on the lower part of the painting. As a result, as noted by Žižek: "The gaze marks the point in the object (the picture) from which the viewing subject is *already gazed at*: it is the object which is gazing at me. Thus, far from guaranteeing the self-presence of the subject and his/her vision, the gaze functions as a spot or stain in/on the picture, disturbing its transparent visibility and introducing an irreducible split in my relation to it."[69] And here we find the Real, the uncanny, familiar yet foreign at the same time, where we are attracted to and yet repulsed by an object at the same time. The object in question is a human skull, which appears as an anamorphic stain, an intentional distortion, and is only visible as a skull if the viewing subject regards the painting from an acute angle, from which point the skull is clearly in view but the rest of the painting is not. This is also an example of the parallax view, a displacement or difference in the apparent position of an object viewed along two different lines of sight, which is a common technique in cinema.[70] In any case, paradoxically, the subject is "manipulated" by the static and inanimate object of the painting into movement, and therefore even though we might have the illusion of control over the look and therefore the object – through voyeuristic or scopophilic power – we are in fact under the power of the gaze and thereby always destabilized by the Real.

At this point, we might consider Baudrillard and his term the "precession of simulacra," where "precession" could be described as a change in the orientation of the rotation axis of a rotating body. Baudrillard was calling attention to the simulacrum, whereby the relationship of the signifier and signified is no longer a relationship that is based on reality, rather there is a separation of signifier from signified because it is a representation without an original, whereby "simulacra don't mirror or reproduce or imitate or copy reality – they are reality itself."[71] In terms that evoke Kittler, Baudrillard will claim that the real can no longer be anything but operational, which raises questions in the cinema as a cultural form, its world-making potential of the "beyond landscape" within the subject, which, evoking Levinas and Critchley, would include the ethical relation to the other, and the curvature of intersubjective space:

> In crossing into a space whose curvature is no longer that of the real, nor that of truth, the era of simulation is inaugurated by a liquidation of all referentials – worse: with their artificial resurrection in the systems of signs, a material more malleable than meaning, in that it lends itself to all systems of equivalences, to all binary oppositions, to all combinatory algebra. It is no longer a question of imitation, nor duplication, nor even parody.[72]

Thus, Baudrillard argues that the era of the Panopticon has ended, that the medium and the message are indeed the same, as McLuhan famously claimed, and, as noted earlier, there is no medium in the literal sense, not in the era of information technology, where the medium itself is "intangible, diffused, and diffracted in the real."[73] Indeed, if we return to the term "precession" and apply it to Holbein's *The Ambassadors*, and the ability of a static work of art to elicit movement in the viewing subject, we may consider the world-as-picture in terms of precession, whereby the dynamics of the image-making culture have changed the entire orientation of the rotation of society. In fact, consider that Holbein's painting was from the 1500s and could elicit movement, and now extend that movement into a full circle and repeat the movement, whereby our mobile visual constructions and their viewing subjects spin in an ever-accelerating rotation, our technology of reflection and ourselves and our society in perpetual motion.

Although Baudrillard will claim that the panoptic focal point may be blind, yet it still plays on the opposition of seeing and being seen.[74] Hence, we might say that this non-human camera-eye view is the gaze of the object, which in itself becomes the subject through its own self-presencing, which in turn objectifies us. However, if we take this a step further, as Žižek does, the camera eye can also be regarded as an "autonomous organ," and therefore, in Lacanian terms, a "partial object," that is, an "an 'eye' torn from the subject and freely thrown around."[75] In doing so, the spectator experiences the gaze as *objet petit a*, a moment of the uncanny where we behold that view that eludes the mirror-like and symmetrical relationship of constitutive subjectivity, such that one now sees oneself "from outside." There is inherent disorientation in this "outside" view, or the view emanating from the "outside" construction, in that the subject has "lost" control of their look, which may result in "subjective destitution," a term Lacan uses to describe "an abrupt awareness of the utter meaningless [sic] of our social links, the dissolution of our attachment to reality itself."[76] Therefore, in the sense used here, "an 'eye' torn from the subject and freely thrown around," suggests that the omniscient "third-eye" of the camera (and its meaning) is not controlled by either viewing subject or the filmmaker, nor even the camera (technology) itself.

Žižek will claim that the non-human autonomous gaze is like that of God; moreover, it is like God seeing himself. However, unlike other divine or god-like figures – Buddha or Socrates, for example – Christ is also God, and therefore Christ is the anamorphosis of God. In other words, we could say that Christ is the distorted projection of God, one that may have appeared as human, but in fact requires us to reconstitute this being-image in order to fully understand its meaning, perhaps through technology. In Lacanian terms, «Christ is God's partial object," whereby "God has manifested himself to his own gaze, offering the divine the perspectival vision of its own self-presence."[77] Thus, the extraordinary task that Heidegger set for himself to overcome the forgetting of Being, of bringing mankind home again in a return to the hearth, and his later claim that "only a god can save us," was amended to the transitional or liminal space, the screen or threshold, and is now further amended by Žižek to claim that "only a suffering god can save us."[78] Thus, when Pontius Pilate brings forth the suffering Christ - *Ecce homo!* - it is not Nietzsche, nor the destitute poet, nor the poet of the future, nor the forgotten god, it is God himself who is presented to the people – but we didn't "see" him, we didn't see the mortal and the immortal, the man as God, and God as man. Žižek will calls this "the parallax gap,"[79] the gap of understanding between two different lines of sight.

In contrast to Christ, Antigone is condemned to impassive suffering, burdened as she is by her destructive *agalma*, she does eventually die and find peace, albeit alone, which, according to Žižek, allows for a certain sublime beauty. On the other hand, Žižek considers the public sharing of pain and sorrow found in the Christ figure, as presented by Kierkegaard, a "parallax view" that is consistent with a "'triad' of the Aesthetic, the Ethical, and the Religious," yet creates a double bind in the Kierkegaardian determination of *"either/or,"* such that choices are always between either the first two – Aesthetic or Ethical (pleasure versus duty) – or the second two - Ethical or Religious (duty versus the unconditional ethico-religious). This means that the Religious does not offer a synthesis, but only, "the radical assertion of the parallax gap (or 'paradox', the lack of common measure, the insurmountable abyss between the Finite and the Infinite). That is to say, what makes the Aesthetic or the Ethical problematic is not their respective positive characteristics, but their very formal nature: the fact that, in both cases, the subject wants to live a consistent mode of existence and thus disavows the radical antagonism of the human condition."[80] Žižek will conclude that this disavowal, as found in fundamentalism for example, is paradoxically what poses a threat to authentic belief, much more so than that of the secular humanist.[81] Therefore, Žižek's view supports the individual subject capable of creative questioning and genuine reflection, terms that we've used earlier, only starting from a different perspective, namely the position of radical antagonism as a fundamental characteristic of the human condition.

Žižek doesn't consider the third possibility of the either/or determination of the Aesthetic or Religious (pleasure versus the unconditional ethico-religious), perhaps because, as we have noted, the aesthetic experience is the ethical experience, thereby disqualifying the three-way either/or condition because Aesthetic (pleasure) would be synthesized into the Ethical (duty), just as the Ethical (duty) would be synthesized into the Religious (the unconditional ethico-religious). In our terms, however, this third option is valid in that it would require the process of the aesthetic *through* the aesthetic, whereby the aesthetic experience is an ethical experience, as well as one that is part of our social reality, where the viewing subject must, in Badiou's terms, decide from the point of view of what is undecidable. In any case, Žižek seems to be proposing that God must show a fidelity to the event of humankind, where God would see himself through the subject as object, which is possible through the suffering of Christ, which would be a condition of radical antagonism. However, we would propose that God, through the Aesthetic or Religious determination that would access the aesthetic through the aesthetic that reveals the truth beyond "truth," and so allow God to see himself through the subject as object, thus challenging the fraud of his own constitutive subjectivity, and perhaps allow for an ethical/aesthetic experience that does not depend on radical antagonism.

Sisyphus: Laughter

If we return to the concept of *eudaimonia* (well-goddedness), understood here as human flourishing, as noted by Critchley, it is often for the sake of duty or as a utilitarian measure of the greatest good.[82] If we follow the determination that God must challenge his own constitutive subjectivity, and that the individual subject (God, oneself) is constituted not through oneself but through the eyes of the other, or the many others, then there is not only the demands on oneself but also on those others for one's own flourishing. Evoking the theologian Knud Ejler Løgstrup, Critchley will argue there is an ethical demand that requires one act for the sake of others, whether they be neighbour or stranger, friend or foe, and that demand is unfulfillable.[83] Therefore, we might say that this demand is unfulfillable for both the individual subject just as it is for God.

The demands on oneself and on others for one's flourishing, and the unfulfillability of those demands by oneself, by others, by God, suggests the need for a humanist approach, which also necessitates, as Critchley argues, the restoration of community in the Hegelian sense, one that impoverished modern societies lack, namely an ethical life (*Sittlichkeit*) "rooted in ethos, in custom, habit and tradition."[84] In the same manner, we may understand Christianity as "the individual's relation to God is determined *wholly* at the point of his relation to the neighbour."[85] As any demand is unfulfillable, then, as Badiou stated, we must decide at the point of what is undecidable. Therefore, Critchley argues, in order to advance the concept of the true character of ethical demand, one that "no longer orbits around the auto-affection of the subject, but is articulated through the *hetero-affectivity* of an unfulfillable, one-sided and radical demand."[86] We may understand that there is no direction from God, or any direction for that matter, yet "we have to subject ourselves to the demand to be God-like, knowing that we are sure to fail because of our finite condition – a godless subjectivation."[87]

Critchley offers the motto for ethical subjectivity taken from Beckett's novella *Worstward Ho* (1983): "Try again. Fail again. Fail better."[88] Here, the absurdity of man's futile search for meaning, unity and clarity in the face of an unintelligible world devoid of God or eternal truths is no reason for dejection and disaffection; it simply is. If Beckett offers the motto of the absurd then Albert Camus offers the hero, namely Sisyphus: "His scorn of the gods, his hatred of death, and his passion for life won him that unspeakable penalty in which the whole being is exerted toward accomplishing nothing."[89] Yet despite the absurdity of his hero's predicament, Camus will conclude, "the struggle itself toward the heights is enough to fill a man's heart. One must imagine Sisyphus happy."[90] Hence, even if an individual is tied to their particular fate and there is no higher destiny, and if we are incapable of achieving the desired totality, with totality defined as the elevation of our interior reality in conjunction with a sense of order and purpose in the exterior world, and yet we are faced with the unfulfillable ethical demand and its hetero-affectivity, and just as the determination of subjectivity is exterior to oneself, and just as the determination of God is exterior to God, so the opportunities for our well-goddedness are both absurd and impossible, yet we may still be God-like in our relations to the other, because one must imagine the other happy. Thus, in terms of the ethical address that binds us, terms that suggest an ethical interpretation of Heidegger's concept of throwness, Judith Butler would write:

> What binds us morally has to do with how we are addressed by others in ways that we cannot avert or avoid; this impingement by the other's address constitutes us first and foremost against our will or, perhaps more appropriately, prior to the formation of our will [...] Indeed, this conception of what is morally binding is not one that I give myself; it does not proceed from my autonomy or my reflexivity. It comes to me from elsewhere, unbidden, unexpected, and unplanned.[91]

Badiou will also refer to Beckett's *Worstward Ho!* and claim that this work remains the most accomplished witness to "wandering at the edges," where Beckett "loved to gnaw at the edges of the peril to which all high literature exposes itself: no longer to produce unheard-of impurities, but to wall in the apparent purity of the concept. In short, to philosophize. And therefore to register truths, rather than producing them."[92] Hence, Beckett's appeal for Badiou is its "art-truth," one that has its emphasis on the processes of truth applied to the reality of human existence, as noted by Critchley, which are best exemplified by the lines, "I must go on, I can't go on, I will go on," and the Sisyphean, "Try again. Fail again. Better again. Or better worse. Fail worse again. Still worse again,"[93] each of which illuminates the becoming-subject and Badiou's maxim, citing Beckett, "to commence is always to 'continue'."[94] This is not succumbing to the radical antagonism of humankind; this is embracing the absurdity of the human predicament. Indeed, for Badiou, existence is different from being in that existence is "the generic attribute of what is capable of worsening," and being "exists when it is in the guise of an encounter,"[95] a guise is necessary because in fact worsening is a labour, "a sovereign procedure of naming in the excess of failure."[96] Therefore, Badiou writes, "Philosophy, in its very essence, elaborates the means of saying 'Yes!' to the previously unknown thoughts that hesitate to become the truths that they are."[97]

In doing so, however, Critchley warns there is an element of risk, where the conception of the self-determined subject involves a certain notion of self-sufficiency, an autarkic will, that amounts to a kind of heroism, which is also understood as the ethical.[98] Although the conception of the self-determined subject involves a non-dogmatic imperative towards the event, as noted earlier, such that the maxim of the fidelity to the event would be to "decide from the point of view of what is undecidable," there remains the potential to sidestep the commitment to the other. For example, the concern over the heroic found in the tragic paradigm is that "the subject can achieve authenticity in its confrontation with finitude."[99] As such, the exemplarity of Antigone's character presents a risk of the heroic conception of authenticity that is more Heideggerian than Levinasian, whereby the commitment to the other is found in tragic finitude, rather than, for example, the tragicomic of Beckett, along with the maxim of "*Continuer!*" Critchley will consider the element of risk in heroic self-determination and self-sufficiency while extending and refining both Levinas and Butler's concepts of the hetero-affectivity of an infinite demand:

> The human being is essentially impotentialized in its relation to the Messiah. The decision about who I am is not in my power, but only becomes intelligible through a certain affirmation of weakness. Authenticity is not so much a "seizing hold" as the orientation of the self towards something that exceeds oneself, namely the hetero-affectivity of an infinite demand that calls me. Freedom is not something I can confer upon myself in a virile assertion of autarchy. It is something that can only be received through the acknowledgement of an essential powerlessness, a constitutive impotence. Freedom can only be received back once one has decided to become a slave and attend in the endurance of love – for love endures all things.[100]

Therefore, radical antagonism may very well be a fundamental characteristic of the human condition, but only because we have not recognized the unfulfillable demand of and to the other, which is a condition of the fraud of constitutive subjectivity because it is not a fully realized being-for-the-world that both frees itself to itself and frees itself from itself *through* the other. However, we cannot simply disavow the condition of radical antagonism, which presents numerous challenges that also contain the possibility of heroic self-determination. By embracing the absurdity of the human predicament, and thereby acknowledging the weakness in our ability to self-determination, our flawed constitutive subjectivity, indeed, our "essential powerlessness" and "constitutive impotence," we may discover what it means to be human.

Marx wrote, "Hegel says somewhere that all great historic facts and personages recur twice. He forgot to add: 'Once as tragedy and again as farce.'"[101] Laughter is also a survival tactic, one that serves as a means of popular self-determination, as found in the carnivalesque humour of civil disobedience and the new tactics of political resistance and non-violent warfare, which also suggests the double order of the aesthetic through the aesthetic, whose power, as Critchley notes, lies in "the *risus purus*, [...] the laugh that laughs at the laugh, the laugh that laughs at that which is unhappy."[102]

Trauma: Dissensus

The importance of Antigone is that she performs an ethical act of transgression, a non-violent response to the demand of the ethical experience, a fidelity to the event. However, as noted earlier, following Rancière, the Lacanian replacement of Antigone for Oedipus allowed for the establishment of a "new form of secret," where the Kantian moral law of the categorical imperative was turned on its head, making way for the impossibility of any salvational knowledge:

> The reign of ethics is not the reign of moral judgements over the operations of art or of political action. On the contrary, it signifies the constitution of an indistinct sphere in which not only is the specificity of political and artistic practices dissolved, but so also is that which formed the very core of 'old morality': the distinction between fact and law, between what is and what ought to be.[103]

Therefore, when the work of art must bear the burden of the essential thing, of what ought to be, the result is a division of violence, morality and right, a division of knowledge and law, a dividing force that Rancière will claim is the very definition of politics.[104] In terms of the human necessity of violence, Arendt writes that, "To see the productivity of society in the image of life's 'creativity' is at least as old as Marx, to believe in violence as a life-promoting force is at least as old as Nietzsche, and to think of creativity as man's highest good is at least as old as Bergson. And this seemingly so novel biological justification of violence is again closely connected with the most pernicious elements in our oldest traditions of political thought."[105] In which case, the Lacanian replacement of Antigone for Oedipus in psychological terms, to paraphrase Rancière, also meant that the trauma that could have once been regarded as a forgotten event, one that could be cured once the trauma was reactivated, was now a new form that had neither beginning nor end, irreducible to any salvational knowledge (the ethical experience, the "old morality").[106]

The term "trauma" is significant. Freud suggested that consciousness defends itself from traumas by not allowing them to penetrate far enough to leave a permanent memory, as noted earlier, which is also an indication that the recipient of trauma, or shock, is unlikely to follow through with changes in their life praxis. Nonetheless, trauma is used by Levinas, Critchley observes, with all the psychological overtones to suggest "both a physiological and a psychological meaning, denoting a violence effected by an external agency, which can be a blow to the head as much as the shock of emotional bereavement. As such, a trauma is something that comes from outside the self, the irruption of a heteronomous fact that can strike without warning, like a terrorist explosion."[107] The critical point that Critchley makes is that the ethical subject is a split subject, divided by the demand that it must ethically respond to, namely the experience of hetero-affectivity that comes from outside the subject, and therefore a traumatic demand, and yet it is a demand that is split between itself and its relation to the other, which can never be known, and therefore one that cannot be met.[108]

For Rancière, therefore, Antigone is the terrorist, engaged in the state of indistinction, "the witness of the secret terror that underlies the social order."[109] In our time, the war against terror, and "infinite justice,"[110] are examples of the state of indistinction, where the logic of this kind of war and this form of justice is never to cease until terror has been stopped but terror never will stop because this kind of war and this form of justice is terror. In addition, as Rancière points out, this kind of justice is above the rule of law, thereby blurring the distinction between fact and law. The suppression of this division is called consensus, indeed, Critchley notes, this is what Rancière calls the "idyll of consensus," without "the manifestations of dissensus that disturbs the order by which government seeks to depoliticize society and create the state of exception, or the state of indistinction."[111] In fact, the true concept of "consensus" should include the manifestations of "dissensus" because a political community is by definition structurally divided, and yet the "idyll of consensus" reduces various groups into a single community, one that may also be transformed into a moral community, that is, a community that is not related to a position (ethics), but rather to a system or tradition (morality).

The remainder from this transformation toward the "idyll of consensus" are those who are excluded; those who fall outside the purview of the "social bond" (the sick, handicapped, derelict, and so forth), or those who are not yet recognized by the system, or have been witness to an injustice and are self-excluded (self-determined). This latter group are often marginalized as the "radical other," excluded from the "ethical community" where everyone is alleged to be included.[112] In which case, we may find that the ethical experience is no longer "ethical" but political, no longer inclusive in terms of community but exclusive in its division, where the subject's self-determination is no longer an ethical self-determination, but a political determination of self. As such, the subject would need to determine if the demand is an ethical one, requiring a fidelity to the event, a commitment to the other, or if that demand is a political one, veiled as the ethical, then that may require, as found in Antigone, a refusal of discourse. Hence, if the excess of the ethical over the aesthetic is found in transgression (*atè*), where the function of the work of art is transgression, requiring the transgression *of* the aesthetic *through* the aesthetic, whereby the aesthetic of the aesthetic is a transgression that is ethical.

What then is a transgressive ethic? In particular, what is a transgressive ethic in a work of art? There are two points to be made. First, the transgressive ethic would restore the ethical experience through its transgression. For example, to use Rancière's terms, the restored ethical experience would clarify the state of indistinction, restoring the distinction between fact and law by questioning our social reality, much as Antigone did. In doing so, the aesthetic regime of art provides a liberating force, where the aesthetic freedom of determination offers a counterpart to the limitations imposed by reality. And this leads to the second point, whereby the work of art must transgress its aesthetic through the excess of the ethical, which is transgressive, and thereby the aesthetic transgresses its aesthetic through the transgressive ethic. The work of art, therefore, must restore the ethical experience. In doing so, the work of art acknowledges that the ethical subjectivity is articulated through the hetero-affectivity of the unfulfillable, one-sided and radical demand, which, in turn, contributes to the restoration of the community. In terms of the possibility of discovering what it means to be human, we might look to Giorgio Agamben when he writes in *The Coming Community* (1993): "The transcendent, therefore, is not a supreme entity above all things; rather, *the pure transcendent is the taking-place of every thing.*"[113]

Approval: Demand

The work of art is a point of reference, the registering of truth in response to an event, a truth procedure, an art-truth, where the aesthetic experience of the self-determined subject is an ethical experience and where the fidelity to the event can be regarded as a commitment to the other. Therefore, the ethical experience begins when there is an aesthetic experience that, to use Critchley's terms, creates a demand and thus elicits an approval,[114] such that, "Without some experience of a demand – that is, without some experience of a relation to the otherness of a demand of some sort – to which I am prepared to bind myself, to commit myself, the business of morality would not get started."[115] For our purposes, the experience that creates the demand is the aesthetic experience. Also, the use of the term "bind" should remind us of that the liberated domain of the individual subject may be little more than an illusion because it is also the bound domain of the object, and, in terms of the public sense, where that which is bound is humankind itself, and where the bonds are once again self-imposed, demanding a fully realized being-for-the-world that both frees itself to itself and frees itself from itself *through* the commitment to the other, thereby addressing the demand and approval that encompasses the fidelity to the event that formulates an ethical position through that very commitment.

The aesthetic experience, therefore, is a truth procedure in that it presents a demand upon the individual subject, a demand that calls for an approval, an action, an interpretation, which, under the weighing of judgement, may be considered either good or bad, and therefore the fidelity to the event comprises an action that illuminates the ethical aspects of the aesthetic experience. [116] Importantly, this is a point of reference amongst infinite possibilities, but we ourselves are the point of reference, a position whose coordinates are established through the ethical experience. This position includes a duty of thought, which, as we have established, is to "decide at the point of the undecidable," such that the duty of thought, like the weight of judgement, is a position in relation to the event, one that is defined by the fidelity to the event, which is not necessarily a rational decision but it is an ethical decision. Critchley explains that, for Levinas at least, the core of ethical experience is not "a fact of reason" but "a fact of the other,"[117] where the "ethical subject chooses to relate itself to something that exceeds its relational capacity. This is what Levinas calls *'le rapport sans rapport'*, the relation without reason."[118] In which case, "the ethical experience turns around the alterity of a demand that does not correspond to the subject's autonomy, but which places the autonomy in question, at least at the ethical level."[119] Thus, the individual subject is ethically determined by the other, such that the individual subject is autonomous in its response to the demand, but the approval must always be in relation to the other.

If we consider this relationship in mathematical terms, such as the asymptote that moves every closer to the line of the other, which is also cinematic in Bazin's view as it approaches a reality, then each aesthetic experience (demand *x*) and ethical experience (approval *y*) of the individual subject would be a point of reference on an *x/y* axis, where each point also represents a commitment to the other, which, with the accumulation of experiences, could then be a heteronomously determined series of points, forming an asymptotic arc, where the individual subject moves ever closer to, or further from, a communion with the other. In which case, we may have addressed the problem of the heroic, as mentioned above, where Critchley warns there is an element of risk because the conception of the self-determined subject involves a certain notion of self-sufficiency, "an autarkic will," that amounts to a kind of heroism, only now, through the commitment to the other, it may be understood as a relationship, one that demands hetero-affectivity. However, another problem arises if there is a determination of "good" and "bad," when the multiple points of reference (arc) do not simply define a single ethical position (or point) determined by the autonomous response to the demand made upon the individual subject, but now, because of the relationship to others, become the broader position of a value judgement, which would be morality and so connected to the *sensus communis* or a system of morals.

Critchley states that, "the good only comes into view through approval, it is not good by virtue of approval."[120] And further, we cannot cultivate a disposition of both passivity and action (as Heidegger does), nor wait for an event (as Badiou does), nor accept a form of paralysis or inaction (as Žižek does), nor comport ourselves with action for action's sake, but rather develop "a conception of action in concert, across a whole number of disparate interest groups."[121] In which case, we may revisit the notion of hetero-affectivity, where the true character of ethical demand "no longer orbits around the auto-affection of the subject," such that when we are faced with a demand and its approval that is an ethical response that determines our individual position of self and our placement within the community or system, where, in a secular society, the determination of that placement is heteronomous and ever-changing. Critchley sates that what is infinitely demanding is "this ethical commitment towards a possibility, as yet unknown and inexistent in the situation, but still powerfully imagined: a supreme fiction."[122] From there, the problem arises in a manner described by Otto Neurath: "No *tabula rasa* exists. We are like mariners who must rebuild their ship on the open sea, without ever being able to disassemble it in dock and reassemble it with the best components."[123]

This also brings us back to "the business of morality" and the self-determination of the event, such that, "The self is something that shapes itself through its relation to whatever is determined as its good."[124] Levinas would be the inspiration when he wrote that the Good is before being.[125] However, this is a self-determination, as noted by both Badiou and Critchley, that may be more clearly illustrated by its opposite, namely evil, such that if one acts in a manner that is not good then one is also acting in a manner that is destructive to the self.[126] The question is: if we fail to respond, or to respond properly, to the fidelity of the event, which may be the demand proffered by the aesthetic experience as an ethical experience, then would we say that we are failing in our commitment to the Other, and, in so doing, we also fail our self? Derrida notes: "Freeplay is always an interplay of absence and presence, but if it is to be radically conceived, freeplay must be conceived of before the alternative of presence and absence; being must be conceived of as presence or absence beginning with the possibility of freeplay and not the other way around."[127] As noted earlier, the subject's autonomy and the "free play of the cognitive faculties" may be regarded as an individual judgement of taste, but it is also a "weighing the judgement" that is connected to the questioning subject and the *sensus communis*, comprised of the necessary and subjectively universal, which means that any individual aesthetic choice is also part of creating the *sensus communis*, which, collectively, would then generate a *consensus*. In which case, the failure to respond, or to respond properly, to the fidelity of the event and the aesthetic experience as an ethical experience would be destructive not only to the self but may be viewed as destructive to the community, thus the demand placed upon the self is both internal and external, an *intersubjectivity*, requiring approval both autonomously and heteronomously.[128]

This leads to a critical point, one that echoes Heidegger and the concept of *alētheia*, of unconcealment, and the artistic construction as an event as a revealing of that which had been concealed. As noted by Deleuze and Guattari, "*Render visible*, Klee said; not render or reproduce the visible."[129] However, when the fundamental event of modernity is the conquest of the world-as-picture, and the sign of this event is the magnitude and scope of appearances that accompanies the world-as-picture itself, then, when everything is made visible, the act of concealment and the need for withdrawal become the decisive stance. And if so, it is an act of becoming invisible rather than visible that would define the processes of truth, such that we must question the aesthetic and ethical experience of the work of art, which, as noted by Critchley, is situated in the world of the visible. However, we may again incorporate the Heideggerian terms of clearing and presence, but rather than a clearing of what is already thought, or made visible, in order to allow for that which has been unthought, or left invisible, to become present, it may be necessary for a challenge to the very process of clearing and presence, to the becoming-visible or presencing through constitutive subjectivity, such that the becoming-visible is a self-presencing that is an unconcealing initiated by the object.

Deleuze will cite Bergson to propose "a schema of a world with two centres, one real and the other virtual, from which emanate on the one hand a series of 'perception-images', and on the other a series of 'memory-images', the two series collaborating in an endless circuit."[130] Deleuze claims that the virtual object belongs essentially to the past, yet the virtual object is not a "former present," it is a "*partial* object,"[131] because it lacks a part which remains in the real, that is, it lacks a past that is contemporaneous with its own present, such that the virtual object may be considered as a shred of pure past, of the real world, which recalls Baudrillard's tatters of the real in the present. Whereby, evoking Melanie Klein and virtual objects in the maternal body – "these partial or virtual objects have been encountered under various names, such as Klein's good *and* bad object, the 'transitional' object, the fetish-object, and above all Lacan's object *a*."[132] Deleuze claims that the potentiality of these virtual objects must not be thought of in terms by what "totalises or englobes them, or possesses them, but rather that they are planted in it like trees from another world, like Gogol's nose or Deucalion's stones."[133] In other words, these partial or virtual objects contain their own particular truth, their own potentiality for self-creation, the culture of the blind spot.

Saving power: Technologies of the self

Heidegger wrote, "A boundary is not that at which something stops but, as the Greeks recognized, the boundary is that from which something *begins its presencing*."[134] This presencing, to apply Critchley's terms, suggests the demand on the self, a demand that founds the self, and is the fundamental principle of self-articulation, perhaps realized through "the demand of the good [that] requires approval by a self in order to be experienced as a demand."[135] The "demand of the good" may be found in Heidegger's concept of "letting-dwell,"[136] where the fundamental character of dwelling is "to spare," which would encompass the ideas of "to free" and "to be set at peace" and "to save."[137] Heidegger also offers a clarification in that saving, like presencing, is not the end of an action but a beginning, where "saving does not only snatch something from a danger. To save properly means to set something free into its own essence."[138]

If to save something is to set it free into its own self-presencing, then it may be a revealing or it may just as well be a withdrawing, which suggests that the demand to self-articulation through presencing may legitimately be refused. Critchley, evoking Heidegger, will maintain that freedom is not an abstract philosophical concept, but is in fact the experience of the human being demonstrating its potential through acting in the world, and that to act in such a way is to be authentic.[139] The implication, therefore, is that there is an ethical condition in the place of self-presencing that must involve the community, those others hastening to and fro, and a weighing of judgement in the location of culture, the domain of the aesthetic experience and the image. In which case, rather than the exclusivity of the "autonomy orthodoxy," the place of self-presencing includes an ethical component in that one's own self-presencing must at the same time allow others the freedom and peace for the possibility of their own presencing.

This suggests another possibility, one that is implied by Bhabha when he evokes Levinas to depict the "beyond" as an "externality of the inward,"[140] where the connection between divinities and mortals, between the external world and the internal world, allows not only for self-presencing, but the subjective conversion that allows for the possibility of self-transcendence. However, as noted earlier, the subject may have lost the power of self-presencing because it is inseparable from the Möbius strip of self-observation, and, paradoxically, this has occurred through the technology of reflection and its omniscient and ubiquitous self-observation. We have also claimed that the work of art must restore the ethical experience, which is possible when the ethical subjectivity is articulated through the hetero-affectivity of an unfulfillable, one-sided and radical demand, which, in turn, contributes to the restoration of the community. In addition, we have claimed, evoking Heidegger, the saving power of the work of art is dependent on the questioning subject and their piety of thought, such that the essential unfolding of technology harbors in itself the possible rise of the saving power. Therefore, something does not begin its self-presencing through reflection as self-observation as constitutive subjectivity (or constitutive impotence), but something does begin its self-presencing through reflection as ethically constituted subjectivity that is articulated through the hetero-activity of the radical demand, wherein lies the saving power of the technology of reflection.

If so, the location of culture, and by extension the culture of the image, becomes the location of praxis found in, as Foucault worded it, "technologies of the self," which would "permit individuals to effect by their own means or with the help of others a certain number of operations on their own bodies and souls, thoughts, conduct, and way of being, so as to transform themselves in order to attain a certain state of happiness, purity, wisdom, perfection, or immortality."[141]

Communion and community: Externality of the inward

The concept of "technologies of the self," particularly in relation to operations of the individual subject by their own means or with the help of others, would describe the saving power of the technology of reflection through an ethically constituted subjectivity, or as the ancient

Egyptians would have it, *maat*. It may also suggest "incarnational tools" or "spiritual exercises," such as those proposed by Boris Gunjević when he calls for communication and participation framed by a doctrine of Radical Orthodoxy, whose maxim would read, "Communication confers communion and creates community."[142] Again, we find a link between individual communion (self-presencing through sharing with others) and community (*sensus communis*) that is located in communication and culture, only now articulated through a moral system, namely, religion. As proposed by Gunjević, the communication, or discourse, demanded by Radical Orthodoxy is for a Christian radicalism, indeed a "double radicalism" (perhaps realized through the Aesthetic and Religious), which first acknowledges the "unfinishedness of theological discourse," and second, considers the "*hyperbolically orthodox*," which seeks to uncover the paradoxes of orthodoxy and identify a set of concrete, theopolitical proposals.[143]

In our terms, we might seek the orthodox *through* the orthodox. In so doing, the possibility arises for a "double truth,"[144] namely, the truth of reason and the truth of faith, whereby, evoking Augustine's claims in *City of God*, Gunjević calls for a community that is authorized by the sharing of a "goal beyond goal,"[145] which is another order beyond the objective political goals of the earthbound and pagan *dominium*, and seeks instead to "ground" the political subject through the ecclesial practice of the "divine nomadic city,"[146] a place founded on justice and virtue, recognizing, as Augustine does and the pagans do not, the "proper order that relates to the soul, the household, the city, and the cosmos."[147] Consequently, following the divine example of *kenosis*,[148] Gunjević will call for a "popular discipline,"[149] which is also Badiou's term, which provides the correlation to the *sensus communis*, but one that suggests an external authority and the possibility of fanaticism. Indeed, this suggests Sartre's army of the disenfranchised, where those without power still retain the capacity to act together. Gunjević recognizes this possibility, where the political subject would be revolutionary and the authority become ideological, and thus proposes a subversive synthesis of nomadism and asceticism. Gunjević also frames this revolutionary resistance in terms of culture, citing Badiou's "Fifteen Theses on Contemporary Art" (2003), which recognizes that, "it is better to do nothing than to contribute to the invention of formal ways of rendering visible that which Empire already recognizes as existent."[150] Hence, Gunjević is seeking a revolutionary political subject, untamed by any capitalist rationality, supported by nomadism and the ascetic exercise of ecclesial practices.

If we return to the *sensus communis*, we may now find the irreducible multitude, as interpreted by Michael Hardt and Antonio Negri, one of desertion and exodus attended by new levels of corruption in modern society, a corruption that they claim Augustine would be astounded by.[151] In terms of culture in the public sense, we could also look to Badiou, when he addresses the correlation between art and humanity, between artistic creation and freedom, when he writes:

> Since it is sure of its ability to control the entire domain of the visible and the audible via the laws governing commercial circulation and democratic communication, Empire no longer censures anything. All art, and all thought, is ruined when we accept this permission to consume, to communicate and to enjoy. We should become the pitiless censors of ourselves.[152]

Importantly, Badiou regards artistic freedom as different from democratic freedom, at least its imperial definition (that is, institutions are the precondition and guarantee of democratic participation), and artistic creation as the creation of a new kind of liberty, where artistic creation is proof for everyone, and for humanity in general, that there is a possibility to create a new possibility. Thus, Badiou makes the fundamental distinction between *creating* a new possibility and *realizing* a new possibility, where to realize a possibility is to think that the possibility is there and one only needs to conceive the possibility, whereas to create a new possibility is to invent a possibility where it did not exist before. In terms of the image-making culture, we might consider Bachelard's view, where images can have a life of their own, ones that partake in a community of experience, such that "man is a being *to be imagined*."[153] In terms of the individual subject, the artistic creation is an expression of a truth. In terms of our social reality, it is to reveal that which our social reality does not acknowledge as existing. Arthur Koestler, in *The Act of Creation* (1964), wrote, "all great innovations which inaugurate a new era, movement or school, consist in sudden shifts of a previously neglected aspect of experience, some blacked out range of the existential spectrum."[154] Badiou wishes to take this a step further, where the innovation does not simply realize a new aspect of experience but the process of innovation in itself creates new possibilities for experience.

If there is a crisis in the commitment to enlightenment, as Sloterdijk claimed, then there may be a crisis in subjectivity and its external and internal worlds, that is, an ethically constituted subjectivity, and thus a crisis in the possibility of both self-presencing and self-transcendence. The Levinasian concept of the "externality of the inward" now serves as an aspect of subjectivity and its transformation through aesthetic experience and the culture of the image, whereby a transgression of the aesthetic would be required in order to "save" the individual subject as well as our social reality. In terms of the artistic creation and the public sense, therefore, the crisis in subjectivity may be due to the disconnect between creating a new possibility and realizing a new possibility, where our social reality is so certain of "its ability to control the entire domain of the visible and the audible via the laws governing commercial circulation and democratic communication" yet, in fact, it does not allow true artistic creation precisely because it does allow everything and anything, but it is only that which exists (the earthbound and pagan *dominium*) and not that which is beyond cognition and must be imagined and created (Augustine's *City of God*). To put it another way, if the "externality of the inward" appears as subjectivity in our exposure to the face of the other and thus becomes "the very enunciative position of the historical and narrative subject," then a crisis of subjectivity with its external and internal worlds necessitates, "'introducing into the heart of subjectivity a radical and anarchical reference to the other which in fact constitutes the inwardness of the subject.'"[155]

Therefore, if "to save" implies an action, both to save from danger and to set something free, initiated through human praxis, thus allowing for subjectivity that is self-presencing, and if the universal validity of aesthetics implies a moral demand, and further, where self-presencing allows for the possibility of self-transcendence, then, when there is a crisis of subjectivity there may be a demand for an intervention, not as a moral prescription, but rather as the ethical responsibility of art itself. The required intervention may appear through artistic creation as a subversive non-action yet functions as a transgression of the aesthetic in order to give proper direction to the action of an individual, and, in the larger public sense, to that of the community and to society as a whole.

Converting to oneself: Situated universality

There is a deeper problem here, however, one that Dostoevsky addresses in his famous parable of the Grand Inquisitor from *The Brothers Karamazov* (1881), namely that humanity does not want freedom and, as the inquisitor will claim, people are quite happy to lay their freedom humbly at the feet of authority. Consequently, when Jesus appears during the time of the Spanish Inquisition, the Grand Inquisitor promptly puts him under arrest and sentences him to burn at the stake like a heretic. The reason, as Critchley will argue, is that Jesus represents not only the rejection of authority in favour of freedom, but also the proximity of faith and truth, as well as the fidelity to the event, such that, "truth does not consist of the empirical truths of natural science or the propositional truths of logic. It is truth as a kind of troth, a loyalty or fidelity to that which one is betrothed, as in the act of love," which in turn supports "the idea that truth, understood as the truth of faith, will free."[156] The Grand Inquisitor, however, claims that is exactly what people do not want: truth, faith and freedom must all burn. Critchley stresses this is not done out of malice but from a genuine love for mankind, and may even be morally justified, because the choice is between "diabolical happiness" or "unendurable freedom," where the former demands self-deception and the submission to authority and yet provides the best means for assuring universal happiness, harmony and unity, whereas the latter sends us out to "the proverbial desert," where there are no guarantees because faith itself is not only tested by, but depends upon, "diabolical temptation and radical doubt."[157] Here is another passage from Critchley that also suggests the unfulfillable demand of the other:

> The truth that sets free is not, as we saw, the freedom of inclination and passing desire. It is the freedom of faith. It is the acceptance - submission, even - to a demand that both places a perhaps intolerable burden on the self, but which also energizes a movement of subjective conversion, to begin again. In disobeying ourselves and obeying this hard command, we may put on new selves. Faith hopes for grace.[158]

If we consider the term "subjective conversion," and interpret this conversion as one that transforms our subjectivity, then, in terms of the aesthetic, it would entail a challenge or transgression to that whose determining ground can be no other than subjective, which in turn challenges the *sensus communis*, whereby we must transform not only our selves but our self-created social reality. Indeed, we must disobey ourselves and create new selves for ourselves, and to do so requires a conversion in the religious sense, a reawakening of knowledge or understanding within a human being that overcomes the resignation and complacency to self-destruction, and calls for grace, the acceptance of the spontaneous gift of love, which may be unexpected and undeserved, but is ours. In order for this regeneration to take place, as Foucault put it, we must practice what the Greeks called "*askēsis*," the principle of "converting to oneself."[159]

In terms of the "technologies of the self," Foucault argues, as does Critchley, that in order to make the truth our own and achieve the possibility of a kind of self-transcendence, then we need to embark upon a course of philosophical ascesis or self-discipline,[160] namely a self-motivated walk into "the proverbial desert," or as Gunjević words it, "a measured dose of voluntary, disciplined ascetism."[161] Gunjević also states that no revolution will succeed unless it is informed by virtue,[162] and "virtue can fully function only if the whole community possesses it and lives together in a life of virtue."[163] In other words, people would need to make an individual sacrifice toward self-discipline in order to elevate the *sensus communis*, which, as stated above, would entail a transgression of oneself, and that is a course of action that most people are unwilling to take. Nonetheless, in order to achieve a participative ascetism, Gunjević will seek "to incorporate heavenly virtue, which is another name for faith, hope, and charity, or as Badiou puts it, fidelity, perseverance, and love."[164] In reference to Paul the Apostle, Badiou will call for "interventions,"[165] where, in Gunjević's reading, "truth is evental, singular, subjective, and consists of fidelity to the declaration of the event."[166] Critchley also evokes Badiou but seeks a less abstract and more concrete intervention, namely a fidelity to the event or situations that he will call a "*situated universality*:"[167]

> The subject commits itself ethically in terms of a demand that is received from that situation, for example a situation of political injustice: a strike, an act of police brutality, a miscarriage

> of justice or whatever. But this demand is not reducible to the situation. It is, rather, a situated demand that is addressed, in principle, to everyone and hence universal.[168]

Critchley explains that this is not simply "the means of *justification* for norms of action," a term that we used earlier to define moral systems, but, more provocatively, "an ethics of *truths*,"[169] where truth is interpreted as "being true to" or "troth," namely an act of fidelity to the event. Therefore, we could also say that the fidelity to the event is to weigh the judgement, which necessitates that the individual subject is incorporated into the broader concept of the *sensus communis*, or the public sense, where our critical faculties are engaged in an act of common human understanding, a self-formulating act that serves as a validity claim of subjective universality, which is now understood through the event as a concrete intervention that is constituted subjectively but realized through the unfulfillable demand of the other. We could also say that this weight of judgement now includes an ethical subjectivity, that, as Critchley notes, is an ethical demand made upon the self, which, evoking Badiou, is not an ethics in general (hence, not a moral system), but "an ethics of processes whereby one confronts possible courses of action in specific situations."[170] Thus, Critchley claims that the goal is in "trying to conceive of forms of political gathering, coalition, or association, that is to say, contingent political articulations in relation to a more wild and formless conception of social being."[171]

As individual subjects, however, we are not unaware of the potentiality of an ethical subjectivity, nor, for that matter, the possibility of an ethical aesthetic, and yet we often seem incapable of reaching beyond conformity to the necessary consensus in terms of a commitment to enlightenment or an ethics of truths, which suggests that there is a disconnect between the "subjective universality" and the "situated universality." Perhaps, as Benjamin observed, this may incline us towards the aesthetic pleasure of our own destruction, where one revels in apocalypse and at the same time acknowledges the outcome is entirely preventable. Therefore, in terms of the work of art, the aesthetic through the aesthetic would challenge constitutive subjectivity and the false leap of faith in order to connect action to the "true" leap of faith by giving oneself the freedom to create oneself, thereby creating new possibilities for experience, and thereby allowing one to pursue the goal of a life fulfilling itself through the other as an ethically constituted subject. And it would do this not simply as an intervention that remembers that which is forgotten, but by creating a new "situated universality," a "more wild and formless conception of social being" that allows for both the communion of the hetero-affectivity of an unfulfillable demand, as well as self-presencing and the self-determination of the fidelity to the event, realizing the promise of a life without fear.

The state of indistinction: Action and non-action

The state of indistinction has been variously described in terms of white noise, *acousmêtres*, the secret terror that underlies the social order, the war against terror and "infinite justice," the kind of justice that is above the rule of law, the blurred distinction between fact and law, the depoliticized society, and the vagaries of consensus that lead to a state of exception. The state of indistinction may also be an indistinctness of ethics or moral relativism, or, to be more precise, there is an indistinctness in the validity claim of the intervention that arises from the demand for the ethical experience and its call for fidelity to the event. An intervention cannot simply be the means of justification for norms of action, but, evoking Critchley, it must be an act of fidelity to the event, one that supports "an ethics of truths." However, as discussed, there is resistance to intervention, even if it means giving up one's freedom, the potential for self-presencing, and the possibilities for new experience, which leads to the problem of action versus non-action, particularly if we subscribe to the radical antagonism of the human condition, which then leads to the ethical questions over the use of violence.

For example, Benjamin supported the sporting event when an athlete is confronted by natural tests, as opposed to the "mechanized" test performance when an athlete is submitted to a series of measures that are designed to promote conformity, making productive use of the human being's self-alienation.[172] For Adorno, sport is ambiguous, because on one hand it involves fair play, which is anti-barbaric, anti-sadistic, and holds a consideration for the weak. On the other hand, it can also promote aggression, brutality, and sadism, especially in those who do not participate but just watch from the sidelines.[173] This recalls Adorno's concern that so-called artistic representations of people beaten to the ground by rifle-butts contains, however remotely, the power to elicit enjoyment out of it. If the fundamental event of modernity is the conquest of the world-as-picture, then we may find that whether producing images or watching from the sidelines there is an element of violence contained within non-action. We might consider Rancière when he cites Agamben who claims that the true horror of the camps was when the SS and the Jews of the *Sonderkommando* played football together: "And every time we turn on our television sets to watch a football match this game is replayed."[174] Thus, as noted earlier, Rancière identified the "idyll of consensus," the depoliticized society without the manifestations of dissensus to disturb it. The inference is that all differences disappear into the state of indistinction.

On the other hand, we tend to find the action accompanied by the justification for norms of action. In recent times, there has been the war against terror, the war against drugs, perpetual wars, ones that serve as examples of the state of indistinction due to the open-endedness of their interpretation and their unfinalizability. This "unfinalizability" is also found in Bakhtin, as noted earlier, in his concept of heteroglossia, where many voices speak, which would encompass narratives as processes of open and indeterminate exchange between the reader or viewer and the text or sound-and-image track, where the viewing subject or recipient is more active, interventionist or inter-active. This also recalls the viewing subject in cinema, or the participant in computer games, where we might say that the viewing subject is immersant, where they are projected into a liminal space, dissolving or abdicating their subjectivity into a state of indistinction.[175]

In which case, it is unclear if the action of the viewing subject is dissolved into non-action in terms of fidelity to the event when the event is virtual and therefore may be considered in actuality as a non-event. Nonetheless, action is accompanied by an ethics of indistinction, the blurring between reality and fiction, between fact and law, where the justification for the norms of action is realized, but not created, such that, as Rancière points out:

> This tendency of differences in politics and right to disappear in the indistinctness of ethics is also defining of a certain present of the arts and of aesthetic reflection. Similar to the way in which the combination of consensus and infinite justice blots out politics, arts and aesthetic reflection tend to redistribute themselves between a vision of art whose purpose is to attend to the social bond and another of art as that which interminably bears witness to catastrophe.[176]

Attending to the social bond implies the communal experience of the mass work of art, which is attended by the technologies of production, its programmability, its speed of dissemination, its manipulability. The implication of bearing witness to catastrophe is Benjamin's *Angelus Novus*, where the angel sees history as one single catastrophe, which keeps piling wreckage upon wreckage, yet is unable to assist. In terms of society and changing its reality, the alternate possibilities of a messiah or a revolution would also suggest two different strategies of either non-action or action, of passivity or of violence, Antigone suffering in silence or Antigone the terrorist.

An ethical turn: *Nomos* of the earth

Rancière detects what he calls an "ethical turn," as found in Agamben, which does not seek a restoration or a commitment to the rights of the other, but rather a confrontation with the state of exception, and so "appeals to a sense of messianic waiting for salvation to emerge from the depths of catastrophe."[177] The state of indistinction, as found in the state of exception, not only erases the differences between fact and law, but between perpetrator and victim, human and non-human. The state of exception, Agamben states, is a Möbius strip or a Leyden jar, where the outside and the inside, the exception and the rule, the state of nature and law, pass through one another.[178] The two features that characterize this ethical turn are first, the reversal of the flow of time, where time "towards an end to be accomplished – progress, emancipation, or the other – is replaced by that turned towards the catastrophe behind us," as with Benjamin's angel, and second, "a leveling out of the very forms of catastrophe," where "the extermination of the European Jews, then, appears as the explicit form of a global situation, characteristic of the everyday existence of our democratic and liberal lives."[179] Human rights are no longer the rights of the human as human, as Lyotard and others have argued, nor the "bare human," such as Antigone, but the rights of the "other than human," the Möbius construction of someone outside what is considered acceptable, also Antigone. As such, the "bare life" is that of the *homo sacer* (the "sacred man" or the "accursed man"), as realized by Polynices, the one "*who may be killed and yet not sacrificed*."[180] By foregoing the demand of the other, communication, communion, community, are all eliminated; even heroic self-determination is disallowed.

The shift from the classical to the modern, from substantial thinking to functional thinking, brings the individual subject to objectify him- or herself, constituting him- or herself as a subject and, at the same time, binding themselves to external control. Rancière will discern this shift in the opposition between politics and the police, even in the most elementary sense of maintaining social order, where we find that the care of life coincides with fighting against the enemy. Critchley confirms this notion when he states "*la police* is always about making invisible *la politique*."[181] Indeed, the "processes of subjectivization" that Foucault had investigated as "The Great Confinement" were found where "the house of confinement in the classical age constitutes the densest symbol of that 'police' which conceived of itself as the civil equivalent of religion for the edification of the perfect city."[182] Thus, Foucault writes, "To build a house of confinement was to erect a barrier between the Same and the Other within the very heart of the Same; neither assimilated nor simply excluded, the confined Other was included *as* excluded from the order of the Same."[183]

American politics offers another example in what Critchley calls "crypto-Schmittianism,"[184] where politics is "an activity that acts through force, generally founded on law – but not always, not in a time of emergency or a state of exception when the sovereign is he who makes law as was the case in Guantanamo."[185] Thus, this state of emergency is realized as *mésentente*, to use Rancière's term, which, as Žižek notes, is "a false radicalization, i.e., by way of reformulating it as a war between 'Us' and 'Them', our Enemy, where there is no common ground for symbolic conflict."[186]

The state of exception was originally Schmitt's term for a state of emergency and borrowed by Agamben, as will the term "*nomos* of the earth," which Schmitt used to describe the Eurocentric global order.[187] The *nomos*, originally from the Greek meaning the law, or tradition, or custom, as found in "the spirit of the law," and thus a human invention that is arrived at by consensus for the sake of expediency and the common good. It refers not only to explicit laws, but to all of the normal rules and forms that people take for granted in their everyday activities, and so can also be regarded as the socially constructed ordering of experience. Hence, to be most effective, the *nomos* must be taken for granted, such that the structure of the world that is created by human and social activity is treated not as contingent, but as self-evident. Indeed, the acceptance of the self-evident structure would be the function of cultural hegemony. However, just as Gramsci recognized that cultural hegemony provides a philosophical and sociological explanation of how one social class dominates the other social classes of a society, so the emancipation of culture would provide the means for both self-presencing and the restoration of community. In many ways this would suggest that the original definition of *nomos* where the spirit of the law could be envisioned as a positive component in the integrated civilization, much as Lukács did of classical Greece, where life and essence coexist, where human beings are able to live their lives within a meaningful world.

If we consider *nomos* in terms of the state of exception and the Schmittian false radicalization of society, we may find, as did Agamben, the originary structure of the *nomos* is not found in Foucault's prison, a simple space of confinement, but in the camp, an absolute space of exception.[188] In terms used earlier, this marks the difference between "place," one of assembly, and "space," one of movement where the traditional place of gathering has been replaced by the equally institutionalized "non-place." Following Lukács, this shift is apparent in the sense of homesickness, both in terms of the barrenness of our culture and our social reality, as well as the reified consciousness of the individual subject and the veil of illusion created by commodities within the community. However, it is the absolute exception where Agamben identifies the sovereign rule, as found in the homelessness of the "bare human," the *homo sacer*: "When our age tried to grant the unlocalizable a permanent and visible localization, the result was the concentration camp. The camp – and not the prison – is the space that corresponds to the originary structure of the nomos."[189] Therefore, this is not a counter-environment, as in a transgression that makes us interpret the real environment, this is a real environment that is representative of our modern social reality, the place of movement as well as the non-place of gathering, the definitive "here is nowhere."

Just as the event of human relations has moved from the local to the global, and the world-as-picture is a process invoking the gigantic to the extent that human activity puts the global habitat at risk, and is now, massively, that of enormous and dense tectonic plates, so too the movement and activity of the "bare human" approaches the grand scale. Agamben is able to say that the *nomos* of modernity is the camp, with all its inferences to Auschwitz as "the place in which the most absolute *condition inhumana* that has ever existed on earth was realized," and is now being realized, massively, as "the new biopolitical *nomos* of the planet."[190] Agamben also claims that Nazism, the condition of its possibility and its "elemental evil," was made possible by Western philosophy itself, especially in Heideggerian ontology: "a possibility that is inscribed in the ontology of Being's care for being – for the being *dem es in seinem Sein um dieses Sein selbst geht* ['for whom Being itself is an issue in its being']."[191] Thus, being is always in a state of indetermination with its potential for determination realized through others, yet it also allows for the exclusion of the "bare human" or not-yet-being that allows for the sovereign state of exception that becomes "explicitly and immediately political."[192] In the state of exception that has become the rule, where life is immediately politics, Agamben evokes Levinas to write, "Man's essence lies no longer in freedom but in a kind of bondage [...] Truth is no longer for him the contemplation of a foreign spectacle; instead it consists in a drama in which man is himself the actor."[193] Hence, the bound domain is the precondition that defines our task, namely the formation of the ethically constituted subject.

For Rancière, therefore, like Agamben, the ethical turn is at the very core of philosophical thinking, which appears, first, as the affirmation of the rights of the other, a justification for humanitarian intervention, what Judith Butler will call the "foreclosure of alterity,"[194] and second, as the affirmation of a state of exception, rendering inoperative fact and law, and thirdly, that man's essence is in a kind of bondage. In effect, man's essence is always bound by his existence, and his existence is always bound by the other. However, the affirmations of the other and the justifications for intervention will only reinforce the expanding condition of the state of exception, such that the unfulfillable demand of the other is in fact realized in terms of oneself as the prime *subjectum*. Although we must struggle to emancipate the other for their own good, and ours, it is also true that our intervention, even when justified on humanitarian grounds, must in fact be understood in terms of ground, of that-which-lies-before, of that which gathers everything onto itself, where to ground is to determine the indeterminate, such that the unfulfillable and indeterminate demand of the other is unfulfillable by the very fact that it is not determinable, nor should it be, because it is not a demand for freedom but always one of reflection. Indeed, as Critchley argued, freedom is not something that can be conferred upon oneself in a virile assertion of autarchy, but only through the acknowledgement of a constitutive impotence. Consequently, when we say that our visual constructions have proved an important step in the aesthetic reification of our social reality, where the technology of reflection becomes the crucible of and for our own modern re-creation, we are in fact describing the process whereby one is seeking one's self-presencing and asserting one's own determination within the technology of reflection. This may be construed as a kind of essence when in fact this technology is itself a site of power in that it confers or withholds recognition.

Unrepresentable: Aesthetic reflection

If we now return to Rancière's contention that there is a tendency for the differences in politics to disappear in the indistinctness of ethics, which is also defining of a certain present of the arts and of aesthetic reflection, then we also arrive at the ethical turn in aesthetic reflection. Rancière describes this ethical turn in aesthetic reflection as "unrepresentable." This could mean that a work of art is not adequate to measure the singularity of a particular subject, as Rancière notes, or this could mean that art is incapable of expressing the sublime. Edmund Burke expressed the same concern in regard to Milton's description of Lucifer in *Paradise Lost*, because "the sublime aspect depended upon the duplicitous play of words that do not really let us see what they pretend to show us."[195] However, another literary example is provided by Martin Jay who points out that for Maurice Blanchot, "Orpheus's gaze was the founding act of writing because it crosses the threshold of death and seeks in vain to return to an immediacy of visual presence that cannot be restored."[196] Indeed, the Western tradition of writing may have started with Plato after the failure of rhetoric in the death of Socrates, and what we are now witnessing in the image-making culture is the return to a visual literacy, only one that must struggle with the unrepresentability of the ethical turn. Also, in terms of the terror in the sublime, according to Rancière, the unrepresentable would occupy the same place as terror in politics, which produces an indistinction between right and fact, not unlike Agamben's state of exception that renders inoperative the distinction between fact and law. Similarly, because all ideology is structured around a sublime object, thus creating an ideological fantasy, then the resistance to ideology is resistance to the ideological fantasy, namely a traversal of the fantasy. Hence, this would be a resistance to the sublime that has manifested itself as the terror in politics.

Rancière describes the unrepresentable of the ethical turn in terms of two distinct aspects: "impossibility" and "interdiction."[197] Impossibility is linked to the inability of the work of art to present that which is excluded from the art of the visible; for example, the unrepresentability of extermination in the Nazi death camps.[198] On the other hand, interdiction is related to the Jewish prohibition on graven images to represent God, an ancient taboo that could be explained, as worded by Blanchot, that "whoever sees God dies."[199] Thus, impossibility and interdiction of the unrepresentable are connected by terror to both the sublime and the divine. As such, the inadequacy of the work of art to present the unrepresentable may be found in Adorno when he wrote:

> The Old Testament prohibition on images has an aesthetic as well as a theological dimension. That one should make no image, which means no image *of* anything whatsoever, expresses at the same time that it is impossible to make such an image. Through its duplication in art, what appears in nature is robbed of its being-in-itself, in which the experience of nature is fulfilled.[200]

On one hand it may be that the work of art functions by way of presenting this very lack, namely of what it is unable to present, which is being-in-itself, which then supports Adorno's view of the negative dialectic, where rather than the liquidation of the individual subject, we find the liquidation of idealism. On the other hand, according to Žižek, the Jewish prohibition on graven images represents the exemplary form of ideological fantasy, because it is the purest form of "*Che vuoi?*", the term he uses to express the subject's "What do you want?" that is addressed to the other, in particular, the big Other, God. In receiving no answer, the subject experiences an anxiety that can be likened to the pain felt in the experience of the sublime, and thus, through fantasy, the subject protects itself from the abyss of the other's unfathomable desire. However, because the Jewish people consider themselves the chosen people, and are thus interpellated by God, yet they are also prohibited from constructing a fantasy, a graven image, which would explain what it means to be chosen, or at least to protect them from this traumatic experience, so, like Antigone, they must maintain allegiance to the very place of the sublime.[201]

Žižek, evoking Hegel, presents a conception of the passage from Judaism to Christianity where "the first stage of Christian belief is the properly 'fantasmatic' level at which one accepts that Christ is God, but this must be superceded through the traversal by which one accepts the death of Christ as the mark of the 'incompleteness' of God [...] and thus God is an enigma to himself."[202] If we return to the idea that the fundamental fantasy is the desire to be God, and to traverse this fantasy is to suspend all of the imaginary fantasies that suture the Real to the Symbolic, which would result in the discovery that any messages which the subject "receives" are only those which it has sent itself, which might also be described as constitutive impotence. Thus, traversing the fantasy would acknowledge that there is nothing behind the symbolic, the big zero, as Lyotard worded it, where the technology of reflection and its assertion of modern self-creation is merely the vain attempt to inscribe meaning to the nothing and so annihilate it. Thus, in line with Benjamin seeking a revolutionary act capable of retroactively redeeming past wrongs, so Žižek seeks a truly revolutionary intervention that would constitute a challenge to the subject's objectively embodied beliefs and thereby suspend the imaginary fantasies that suture the Real to the Symbolic.

We return to the question that if it were possible to traverse the fantasy, to strip the subject of their customary fantasmatic support, disrupting their social identity and challenging their personality, then who do they become? One answer might be Diogenes, urinating and masturbating in public, thus announcing, as Sloterdijk postulates, the split between the cynical reason of domination and self-domination.[203] Another possibility would be Antigone, in the Lacanian sense, as a terrorist, the witness to the sublime, to the secret terror that underlies the social order, the one whose encounter is the purest response to the unfulfillable demand and the unfathomable desire of the other.

The work of mourning: The vanishing point

According to Rancière, "the right to the other," in what we have also referred to as the commitment to the other, the unfulfillable demand of the other, as well as the foreclosure of alterity, is also the right to bear witness to our subjection to the law of the other (including the big Other), and further, that the will to challenge these laws and master the "unmasterable," or determine the indeterminate, is where the state of indistinction begins. For example, Rancière states that the Nazi genocide exterminated "the very people whose vocation was to bear witness to the necessary dependency on the law of the Other."[204] On this same point, Žižek claimed that anti-Semitism protects those who are not interpellated as Jews from being interpellated as Jews, and thus from the traumatic encounter with the Other, which further protects them from a direct experience or demand from the sublime.[205]

Lyotard, for his part, repudiated the "grand narrative" that had given way to the postmodern, the multiple universe of "little narratives,"[206] which implied a beneficent multi-culturalism. However, as Rancière argues, and as found in Lyotard's aesthetic of the sublime as "art of the disaster," this "disaster" attests to no more than the fact that "the West's modern history is identified not with the emancipation of the proletarians but with the programmed extermination of the Jews."[207] Hence, Rancière argues that the work of art may lay claim to restoring lost meaning to a common world or repairing the cracks in the social bond,[208] and yet there remains the double bind of this restorative task and the unrepresentability of the ethical turn, even as formulated by Lyotard's aesthetic of the sublime and the art of the disaster, whereby "art is placed in the service of the unrepresentable and of witnessing either yesterday's genocide, the never-ending catastrophe of the present, or the immemorial trauma of civilization."[209]

This is not new, as we observed with the depiction of the Battle of Kadesh, where the ancient tableaux served as a work of mourning, its content suggesting the realm of the sublime, an experience bordering on terror, where the presence of absence is found in death, in that which resists all representation.[210] However, as Foucault claimed, the epistemic change from the classical to the modern occurs when the entire field of Western thought is inverted because the former correlation between a metaphysics of representation and of the infinite has been replaced by an analysis of finitude and human existence.[211] As we've noted earlier, humans are the prime subjectum, such that, as Foucault claims, the appearance of ourselves as the prime subjectum is the event of Western thought, which also evokes the rise of the technology of reflection, and yet Foucault argues that despite allotting ourselves this privileged position in the order of the world, we are no more capable of conceiving what it is to be human.[212] Indeed, in what might superficially appear to be the advancement of Hegelian self-knowledge that leads to Absolute Truth, in fact may be, as Foucault states, that the march of modern thought is only "advancing towards that region where man's Other must become the Same as himself."[213] In other words, we are not addressing the unfulfillable demand of the Other, we are simply demanding the Other fulfil our lack, realized through the fraud of constitutive subjectivity.

Rancière claims that the work of art may no longer carry any promise of representing the unrepresentable, yet it is still seen, in memory of Adorno, as a form of resistance, but that resistance is nothing more than the endless work of mourning.[214] Indeed, the very concept of resistance has changed, as Lyotard will claim, where the emancipation that is sought is no longer the Deleuzian conversion from the prescriptive and exclusive *"either/or"*, or perhaps *"neither/nor"*, into the descriptive and inclusive "*either... or... or...*", and is instead the emancipation from the aesthetic experience itself which has become that of "the enslaved human mind, the mind enslaved to the sensory, but also, and above all, enslaved, on account of this sensory dependency, to the law of the Other."[215] This enslavement, according to Deleuze and Guattari, is a problem of desire, and desire is part of the social infrastructure, such that it is necessary "to show how, in the subject who desires, desire can be made to desire its own repression."[216] Therefore, in terms of psychoanalysis, it would be necessary to carry out a truly transcendental analysis of the unconscious, one that will critique the various "paralogisms of the unconscious" – the Lacanian traversing the fantasy - and thereby account for the mechanism by which psychic and social repression are produced by desiring-production itself.[217]

This repression only leads to another paralogism, which Deleuze and Guattari call the "paralogism of extrapolation," where desire appears as a lack,[218] and then extrapolated from the inclusive (*either... or...or...*) to the exclusive (*either... or...*), such that differences are considered in terms of rigid oppositions.[219] This process is the connection between capitalism and Oedipalization, which both produces desire and prohibits it. Hence, desire can only choose between subjecting itself to a transcendent law that directs it toward the Symbolic or it can retreat to an undifferentiated imaginary space, which amounts to the choice between "normality" and "neurosis." In either case, its "real" nature as desiring-production is dissimulated, leading to another paralogism, the "paralogism of the double bind,"[220] whereby, as Deleuze and Guattari describe it, the conjunctive synthesis, whose immanent use had been "nomadic and polyvocal" now becomes "segregative and biunivocal."[221] Thus, we arrive at the task of Deleuze and Guattari's "schizoanalysis"[222] and its therapeutic aim of "de-oedipalizing" the subject and reversing the passive syntheses of desire to transcendent uses by "restoring the syntheses of the unconscious to their immanent use."[223]

However, in terms of the Other becoming the Same, we may also consider that since desire is not a faculty of a unified and unifying subject, on account of the Lacanian mirror stage and the subsequent misrecognition, but a differential manifold, which, according to Deleuze and Guattari, can be characterized as a field of "desiring machines," where each desiring-machine produces a "flow" that is siphoned off by another which produces a flow that is in turn siphoned off by another, and so on.[224] Accordingly, these desiring-flows are the connective syntheses of the unconscious. Collectively, these desiring-flows give rise to the non-productive "Body without Organs," which, in terms noted earlier, can be considered a kind of reterritorialization, one that produces a virtual object that is less the totality of the series of connective syntheses than an additional entity existing "alongside" it: "The body without organs is in fact produced as a whole, but a whole alongside the parts – a whole that does not unify or totalize them, but that is added to them like a new, really distinct part."[225] In other words, we may find that the technology of reflection allows for the Other to become the Same by amalgamating one's desires and fantasies into creating a virtual self, where the technology of reflection as a site of power now confers recognition on its re-creation, thereby restoring the lost unity of human subjectivity caused by the mirror stage by merging perception and representation and synthesizing the subject and its reflection, thereby achieving unity with oneself, the vanishing point of constitutive subjectivity.

Hubris: Ethical transgression

Judith Butler will question Deleuze's opposition to psychoanalysis and his defense against negativity, particularly as his work revolves around the lack, which is defined in terms of the unconscious and is considered a fundamental aspect of psychoanalysis.[226] Like Deleuze, Foucault was also suspicious of psychoanalysis in that it surrounds the patient in a "milieu" of responsibility and creates guilt for unconscious transgressions, which is no more than a new type of confinement.[227] Hence, rather than following Heidegger's attempts to overcome the tyranny of reason by returning to the piety of questioning, Foucault attempts to recover the experience of *hubris*, as found with in classical Greece, an era when they did not yet distinguish *hubris* from the *logos*.[228] This will recall Lukács's vision of an integrated civilization where life and essence coexist, where human beings are able to live their lives within a meaningful world, where principles of order and knowledge are celebrated as part of the human experience. However, rather than the modern psychoanalytic "liberators" who have delivered us from unreason, Foucault will celebrate Hölderlin and Nietzsche, Van Gogh and Artaud, where irreducible madness challenges the "truth" of the work of art, because it dissolves truth, and so "truth ceases irrevocably."[229]

Thus, following Nietzsche, there is a fundamental question of whether we suffer from too much hubris or too little. For example, just as Nietzsche's pronouncement of the death of God is really saying that we must seek God, so Foucault will suggest that it is "Nietzsche's pride," not his piety, that challenges the sovereignty of modern reason.[230] And just as psychoanalysis remains complicitous with nineteenth-century techniques of "liberation," so Heidegger's critique of man's hubris is perfectly in keeping with nineteenth-century attitudes toward madness: "For the nineteenth century, the initial model of madness would be to believe oneself to be God, while for the preceding centuries it has been to deny God."[231] However, according to Lacan, the modern version is to fulfill the fundamental fantasy of the desire to be God, whereby, as noted earlier, Deleuze is now able to claim that having lost a moral existence in order to enter into an aesthetic one, we have become simulacra, and rather than God making man in his own image, man makes himself as an image of God. Thus, we still seek salvation but that is impossible because there is no longer the possibility of an ethically constituted subjectivity based on the demand of the Other because we have amalgamated the Other and the Same.

Rancière maintains that resistance today is nothing more than the Platonic rediscovery of the trace, of that which has been lost, realized through "the anamnesis of the 'Thing', the indefinite re-inscription, in written lines, painted brushstrokes or musical timbres, of subjugation to the law of the Other. Either obedience to the law of the Other that does us violence, or indulgence in the law of the *self* that leads into an enslavement by commercial culture."[232] Thus, aesthetic dissensus is only the reformulation of the art of the disaster, of "the disaster that is born of the forgetting of that disaster, the disaster of the promise of emancipation that can only lead either to the overt barbarism of Nazi and Soviet camps, or to the soft totalitarianism of the world of commercial culture and communication."[233] In either case, he concludes, both aesthetics and politics are suppressed in the name of ethics.

Rancière's view is that proper politics began when the common people within the Greek *polis* demanded to be included in the public sphere and recognized as an equal partner with the ruling oligarchy or aristocracy.[234] However, the result may have been that consensus became coercion and the public sphere entered the state of exception with its *mésentente*, its false radicalization, such that political struggle proper is not a rational debate but simply a struggle to be heard, to overcome its unrepresentability, hence demanding conceptualizations of "how we are going to resist?" Once again, we may find that the task as in the work of art is transgression, requiring the transgression *of* the aesthetic *through* the aesthetic, challenging constitutive subjectivity and the false leap of faith, such that the aesthetic of the aesthetic is a transgression that is ethical.

A struggle for visibility: Little resistances

With regard to the different strategies of action or non-action, Critchley's concern is a struggle for visibility, indeed, "politics is a struggle for visibility," such that, "politics is the emergence into visibility of that constituency which has no part."[235] This might be viewed as two sides of the Benjaminian coin where phenomena must have a voice of their own in order to give voice to the silent murmuring, to find the profane illumination, and yet the object in nature is mute and so it must be named, that is, made visible, in order to lend a voice to its suffering.[236] We could draw a comparison between the murmuring of the people of the *polis*, and suffering of the *homo sacer*, the "bare human" who is not "named." There is also a suggestion of Heidegger's concept of concealing and revealing, which Critchley describes as "a sort of experience of waiting and inaction"[237] realized through "a need for secession and withdrawal."[238] Critchley clarifies that this is a strategy and not a question of action for action's sake (as Hemingway once said about mistaking movement for action), but a strategy that demands "the expansion of our imagination when it comes to the capacity for action that we possess."[239] Indeed, the struggle for invisibility in the face of a politics of control may prove as much of a challenge as the struggle for visibility.

Critchley views "naming" within a context of hegemony, that is, a political articulation that allows for a conception of action in concert with others,[240] and yet there is a problem when everything becomes visible, when society functions as an apparatus of security, where, to use Critchley's term, there are no "interstices."[241] In particular, Critchley considers how the essential function of the work of art is one of visibility, yet its task of transgression, and its necessary invisibility, would demand for it to become semi-autonomous in order to work in the liminal spaces that exist within the system, suggesting a new conception of "freeplay," of presence and absence, which might occur through "little resistances," a kind of bricolage, to use Derrida's term,[242] such that "the interstices must be created through articulation."[243]

This articulation suggests the "spandrel," as discussed by Žižek in the introduction to *Incontinence of the Void: Economic-Philosophical Sandrels*, where he explains "the use of the useless spandrels."[244] For Žižek, the spandrels "fill in the empty spaces that emerge in the interstices between philosophy, psychoanalysis, and the critique of political economy."[245] Indeed, the spandrel was originally an architectural term, as described by Stephen Jay Gould and Richard Lewontin, used to describe "the tapering triangular spaces formed by the intersection of two rounded arches at right angles."[246] The spandrel is an architectural constraint (perhaps more properly called a "pendentive"), not necessarily part of the original vision yet necessary for support, often used for ornamental effect, "elaborate, harmonious and purposeful."[247] However, suggesting a comparison to the double operation of the aesthetic of the aesthetic, Gould and Lewontin argue that the spandrel, when applied to evolutionary theories of development, supports their challenge to the exclusivity of natural selection, where the developments and modifications of surviving species were purposeful and optimal. Therefore, the visible design in itself would not be the proper path for an analysis to infer the cause in some sense of the surrounding structure, rather, in the case of the spandrel, the starting point should be its primary and "invisible" function of support. The design itself is an adaptation, an ornamental addition in response to an architectural necessity, where the adaptation is not originary, not the primary cause of the structure, but a consequence that is influenced by numerous and varied agents, some of which may not be pragmatic. Indeed, as the aesthetic may be dismissed as subjective, merely a matter of taste, yet its task, as we've discussed, is functional and significant. However, just as the aesthetic may be purposeful without purpose, it is not merely an adaptation, nor is it necessarily a function of utility, yet it remains a means to understand the cultural complexity of our existence and evolution.

Inertia: Piercing

As opposed to the strategy of semi-autonomy and the "little resistances," there is the possibility of a course of non-action, or the refusal of taking action, as found in Žižek's concept that "sometimes, doing nothing is the most violent thing to do."[248] Consequently, in Critchley's view, the answer to how we are going to resist would now amount to a kind of paralysis,[249] a Hamlet-like "readiness is all" yet combined with inaction,[250] where "the only choice in politics is between state power and no power."[251]

A comparison might be made to Kant's peculiar (and perhaps comical) response to the French Revolution, which was one of disinterested enthusiasm. As described by Lyotard: "The officer cries *Avanti!* and leaps up out of the trench; moved, the soldiers cry *Bravo!* but don't budge."[252] Like the soldiers, Kant also cries *Bravo!* in response to the French revolutionaries' *Avanti!* However, in effect, he remains bound to the mast, just like Adorno's Odysseus, never leaving his study, a mere spectator without the least intention of budging. Perhaps this serves as another example of not looking into the terror of the abyss, but only into a purely linguistic construction. Nonetheless, Lyotard does share Kant's desire to distinguish enthusiasm from fanaticism, particularly in that he affirms the feeling of the sublime is not the difference between the standpoints of spectator and actor but the affective (or libidinal) correlate of a moral respect for differends. However, "by naming and by showing, one eliminates," yet "reality entails the differend,"[253] and that is because differends, like the double bind, are incapable of being resolved without committing a wrong against one of the two parties, such that there is no overarching Kantian-style tribunal that could adjudicate them.[254]

If we return to Žižek's concept that doing nothing is the most violent thing to do, then we may find, as does Critchley, that this statement stems from a two-fold strategy, the first of which is a Bartlebian inertia ("I would prefer not to") and the second is divine violence, "a cataclysmic, purifying violence of the sovereign ethical deed, something like Sophocles' Antigone."[255] In other words, as Critchley notes, "For Žižek – in what we might call his *jouissance* – these acts of divine violence are 'beyond good and evil... in a kind of politico-religious suspension of the ethical,'"[256] and thus, "translates divine violence into Kantian categories as 'the direct intervention of the noumenal into the phenomenal.'"[257] In equating divine violence with the Kantian sublime, Critchley reminds us that "for Kant, the sublime is an emotion that places human beings in the fundamental tension between infinity (*Unendlichkeit*) and finitude (*Endlichkeit*), between immanence and transcendence, between representation and that which exceeds it. On this view, violence is the sudden piercing of the finite by the infinite, of the phenomenal by the noumenal."[258]

For Žižek, therefore, this violent "piercing" suggests a divine intervention and thus means the sublime is incarnated into the material world, and because this intervention is from outside, we may remain passive. If we recall the statement that "only a suffering god can save us," and that Christ is the "partial object" of God sent here to give voice to humankind, and that the human objects are determined by the constitutive gaze of the big Other, then those voices of the suffering multitude, perhaps even more so after the divine intervention of the Tower of Babel, become the *voix acousmatique* raised to the screaming point in the tortured hope of attracting, or recovering, the attention of God. In turn, the aesthetic is no longer that which is subjective, nor that which is beautiful, but, as Lyotard claimed, an aesthetics of the sublime, the art of the disaster, where passivity is a consequence of "the feeling of powerlessness in the experience of the sublime, is endured by reason," and thereby realized as a "positive nihilism of aesthetics as a discourse which, under the name of culture, delights in the ruined ideals of a civilization."[259] Rancière concludes, "the aesthetic scene, properly speaking, thus turns out to be the scene of the irreconcilable."[260] In which case, the politics of control, Adorno's totally administered society, has created a culture that supports the sovereign state of exception not through the cataclysmic, purifying violence of the sovereign ethical deed, but through the on-going threat of such a violence with its attendant passivity, which results in the very opposite of transgression in that it reduces one and all to a state of homelessness, of bare life, both real and imagined, because it eliminates differences, a social production that is a philosophy of representation instead of a philosophy of difference.

Duty of thought: Thingly secrecy

Critchley observes "a kind of purification of desire" that occurs because the beautiful work of art "*sublimes* the object, endowing it with Thingly dignity."[261] In these terms, Critchley also writes that, "If the relation to the real is the realm of the ethical, and the work of sublimation is the realm of the aesthetic, then we might say that *the aesthetic intimates the excess of the ethical over the aesthetic*."[262] In other words, if the work of art may be distinguished from representation by its remainder, and that remainder is ethical, and that ethical remainder is the aesthetic, or, at least, the art-truth or truth process that the aesthetic experience is attempting to access as the ethical experience, then, in doing so, the work of art sublimates the cause of desire or object of desire into the aesthetic, and the symbolic would now approach the real. Critchley writes, "The basic thought here is that the real is that which exceeds and resists the subject's powers of conceptualization or the reach of its criteria."[263] To put it another way, the remainder/surplus meaning/*jouissance* appears through the work of art, and its truth process of sublimation, in order to transcend the aesthetic of form and create (intimate) an excess that is beyond form, which is ethical by virtue of the truth process, and which now appears as the symbolic, whose purpose is to access the real.[264]

The question now becomes what is the real that the truth process is seeking, and why. If the moral goal of psychoanalysis is happiness, as Lacan supported, then, as Critchley notes, in a modern society where happiness is no longer aimed at well-goddedness (*eaudaimonia*), then the goal has changed into "putting the subject in relation to its unconscious desire."[265] However, for Lacan, following Freud, the problematic of desire is pursued in relation to death, such that desire tends towards death, indeed, "the realization of desire would require the extinction of the subject," such that "the real of death is only represented in a work of sublimation that traces an excess within representation."[266] In which case, the beautiful work of art, and its work of sublimation, would address, in Heideggerian terms, the "finitude of Dasein," such that "Death is the possibility of the unqualified impossibility of Dasein. Death thus reveals itself as the *most proper, nonrelational, insurmountable possibility*."[267] Indeed, if death is the limit of one's desire, then we must understand that limit in order to become authentically alive, a service that the work of art can perform.

Nietzsche wrote that we need art lest we perish from the truth, and then if the real of death is that object of desire, then art allows us to face the realization of that desire as the possible impossibility of death.

If we now return to the "Thingly dignity," we may find, as Critchley does, that the Kantian thing-in-itself (*Ding-an-sich*) contains "a dimension of *Thingly secrecy*,"[268] or perhaps we might say it is dignified by its right to concealment. Thingly secrecy, therefore, is that which is alien, that alterity that escapes comprehension, and here Critchley evokes Levinas, where "That which exceeds the bounds of my knowledge demands *acknowledgement*."[269] Therefore, the alterity, the Thingly secrecy, is located in the Other, and the commitment to the Other is at the core of self-determination and the demand presented by the ethical experience, a demand that requires acknowledgement or approval. We may be reminded of the fidelity to the event, and that "Ethics is a work of self-formation,"[270] such that to abandon ethics, and the good, would be destructive to the self. Thus, as noted earlier, if we fail to respond, or to respond properly, to the fidelity of the event, namely the demand proffered by the aesthetic experience as an ethical experience, then we might say that we are failing in our commitment to the Other, and, in so doing, we also fail our self (*Seine*). However, Levinas, reproaching Heidegger, will argue that ethics, not ontology, is the first philosophy (metaphysics), and that the good is "beyond being and non-being."[271] Rather than the Heideggerian intersubjectivity, which is conceived as a kind of communion, but one in which the subject remains solitary, Levinas, as well as Critchley, argues that the demand placed upon the self is both internal and external, requiring approval both autonomously and heteronomously. To encounter the other is not reducible to the order of sameness or homogeneity, a communion, but is fundamentally unencounterable, which, recalling our earlier discussion of faciality, Levinas characterizes as the "epiphany of the face."[272] However, unlike Heidegger's solitary subject, the Levinasian subject does not confront death alone, hence "death represents the limit of possibility not in the ontological sense of a possible impossibility but rather in the ethical sense of an impossible possibility."[273] Indeed, death cannot be predicted, represented or even understood, and so is that something alien, that alterity that escapes comprehension, yet it is a demand that requires acknowledgement, and thus "an ethics that is endlessly open to the surprise of the otherness whose most eloquent expression is that of the other person."[274]

For Levinas, there can be no ethical evasion, it is impossible because the subject has always already responded to this call through a primordial "Here I am" (*me voici*),[275] thereby committing to the good, even "before the bipolarity of good and evil presented to choice, the subject finds himself committed to the Good."[276] The argument to this position, as pointed out by Cutrofello, is like that of the Cretan paradox, following the statement "There is no truth," such that if it is true then it is false, or false then true, and so forth.[277] So you heard the call to the good because if you hadn't heard it then you wouldn't be here, and since you heard it then you heard the call to the good. Nonetheless, as noted earlier, the core of ethical experience is not a fact of reason but a fact of the other, that alterity that escapes comprehension, hence a paradox. This also suggests the point of reference amongst infinite possibilities, to decide at the point of the undecidable, which includes a duty of thought, or a weight of judgement, a self-determination that is defined by the fidelity to the event, which is an ethical decision, and yet, through the sublimation of the beautiful work of art, we are "momentarily lifted from the utilitarian world of calculations, the world of our familiar concerns, and allowed a relation to the Thing that does not crush or destroy us."[278]

For Nietzsche, as stated earlier, the work of art allows us to find a way to acknowledge the repellent horror and absurdity of existence, yet without losing the will to continue. For Lacan, as noted by Critchley, the work of art is a work of sublimation in the realm of the aesthetic, where the aesthetic intimates the excess of the ethical over the aesthetic, and that excess is the beautiful. The demand of the horror and absurdity of existence is met by the acknowledgement or approval of the good. Similarly, for Lacan, the "triumph of being-for-death" in tragedy offers an important cathartic experience, yet in psychological terms the actual experience of human action has the character of tragi-comedy, which is to say that it is lived as the conflict between Thanatos and Eros.[279] The embodiment of this condition, for Lacan, and the essence of tragedy, is not found in Oedipus, as was the case with Freud, but in the character of Antigone. In the defence of her brother, Polynices, whose body as object is sublimed and endowed with "Thingly dignity," she has challenged the utilitarian laws of the polis and its king, Creon. By violating Creon's decree, Antigone's actions are now governed exclusively by the death instinct, what Heidegger had called being-towards-death (*Sein-zum-Tode*).[280] We might say that she has realized the ultimate desire to the extinction of herself, which also sublimes the Other through her death. However, Heidegger's conception of the authentic death, which can only be one's own, such that to die for another person would simply be to "sacrifice oneself," thereby the deaths of others are secondary to one's own and one's own death must be primary. To this point, Critchley writes:

> In my view [...], such a conception of death is both false and morally pernicious. On the contrary, I think that death comes into our world through the deaths of others, whether as close as a parent, partner or child or as far as the unknown victim of a distant famine or war. The relation to death is not first and foremost my own fear for my own demise, but my sense of being undone by the experience of grief and mourning.[281]

Thus, Antigone responds to the event, which aligns the point of reference to its "happening" and thereby she is the one to put the event into circulation, by naming or identifying the event as an event, and thus providing the link between the event and fidelity. We are presented with the will of Antigone versus the will of Creon, and thus the individual (loyalty to family, the gods, commitment) versus (loyalty to the state, personal status, use of power), which could also be regarded as woman (and what she represents) and man (and what he represents), as well as the will of the work of art itself which necessitates the "free play of the cognitive faculties." In other words, we might say that Antigone represents the ethics related to a position, whereas Creon upholds morality related to a system or tradition.

The experience of grief and mourning can be extended to Antigone herself, as noted by Judith Butler, in that she must live in a state of suspension between life and death, a dehumanization, where there can be no public grieving, no mark or trace, because there is a refusal of discourse.[282] Indeed, for Butler, the refusal of discourse designates a structure of address, which suggests how moral authority is introduced and sustained, and, more importantly, that we are defined by how we address others and how others address us, and that "something about our existence proves precarious when that address fails."[283] We may consider Critchley when he notes that both Freud and Lacan were concerned with sublimation in the form of art, particularly in view of its "satisfaction without repression."[284] Critchley expands on this idea, evoking Melanie Klein, to say, "the trauma of separation requires *reparation*, the ethical *tear* requires *repair* work of sublimation that would be a work of love."[285] In destitute times, then, as Critchley said, we have to talk.

In terms of visual culture, and the media in particular, the refusal of discourse is critical in establishing a state of suspension between what is humanized and what is dehumanized, such that, as Butler argues, the Levinasian notion of the "face of the other," which makes an ethical demand, although we cannot know what demand it makes, is being effaced through a foreclosure of alterity, first through occlusion and second through representation itself.[286] However, we might consider the work of art itself may be the "face of the other," as Paul Klee formulated when he claimed that at a certain point a painting acquires a face, "Now it looks at me," such that, as Freud wrote "Where there was an it, an 'I' shall come into being."[287] Therefore, as Shierry Weber Nicholsen argues, in terms that suggest the release of the bound object, that the work of art acquires a "psychic nature, a kind of selfhood (something capable of looking), to the role of temporality (implicit in the word 'now'), and to something we not see explicitly in Freud's formulation, some kind of reciprocal relationship with the viewer (who may also be the artist in the process of working): the painting looks at me, who is looking at it."[288] Thus, the aesthetic experience makes an ethical demand as the "face of the other" that is critical in the formation of the ethically constituted subject and the resumption of discourse and the restoration of community.

Notes

1 Alain Badiou, "The False Movements of the Cinema," *Handbook of Inaesthetics*, translated by Albert Toscano (Stanford CA: Stanford University Press, 2005), p.78.
2 Ibid., p.79.
3 Badiou, *Cinema*, pp. 209, 207.
4 Alain Badiou, "Art and Philosophy," *Handbook of Inaesthetics*, translated by Albert Toscano (Stanford CA: Stanford University Press, 2005), p.5.

5 Ibid., pp.4-7.
6 Ibid., p.14.
7 Ibid., p.7.
8 Ibid., pp.6-7.
9 Ibid., p.7.
10 Critchley, *Infinitely Demanding*, p.72. "Sublimation of the drives is a particularly striking feature of cultural development, which makes it possible for the higher mental activities – scientific, artistic and ideological – to play such a significant role in civilized life." Freud, *Civilization and Its Discontents*, p.34.
11 As noted earlier, Lacan defines *objet petit a* as the leftover, the remnant left behind by the introduction of the Symbolic in the Real. However, Žižek argues that, "the tidy operation of signification never comes off without producing some annoying, messy, disturbing surplus, a piece of leftover or ‹excrement›, which Lacan designates as *smell a*." Žižek contends that this remainder does not have to suggest anything profound, but may simply isolate "the outrageous kernel of its mindless enjoyment." Slavoj Žižek, "The Undergrowth of Enjoyment: How Popular Culture Can Serve as an Introduction to Lacan," *The Žižek Reader*, edited by Elizabeth Wright and Edmond Wright (Malden MA: Blackwell Publishing, 1999), pp.11-36. Žižek will also introduce Lacan's concept of the *sinthome* – the "floating signifiers" where, "What we must do – what is done by Fassbinder and Gilliam – is, on the contrary, to isolate the *sinthome* from the context by virtue of which it exerts its power of fascination, to force us to see it in its utter stupidity, as a meaningless fragment of the Real. In other words, we must (as Lacan puts it in *Seminar XI*) 'change the precious gift into a piece of shit'; we must make it possible to experience the mesmerizing voice as a disgusting piece of sticky excrement." Ibid., p.15.
12 See Jacques Lacan, *The Other Side of Psychoanalysis, Seminar 17*, edited by Jacques-Alain Miller, translated by Russel Grigg (New York: W.W. Norton & Co., 2007).
13 Badiou, "Art and Philosophy," pp. 8, 9.
14 Ibid., pp.13-15.
15 The meaning of axiomatic is that of being self-evident, as well as a formal proof that is mathematically provable within a formal system.
16 Gabriel Riera, "Introduction," *Alain Badiou: Philosophy and its Conditions* (Albany NY: State University of New York Press, 2005), p.11.
17 Ibid., p.12. See also Alain Badiou, *Logics of Worlds: Being and Event, 2*, translated by Alberto Toscano (London: Continuum, 2009), pp.244-245. Badiou recognizes the foundational role of Saint Paul, as well as his assurance and militancy, also found in a paradoxical kinship between Saint Paul and Walter Benjamin, through "the tremblings of messianism." Badiou also marks the gap between himself and Giorgio Agamben, where Badiou supports "the virtues of the closed," and Agamben supports the open, which is the same as that of finitude, "being as weakness, as presentational poverty, as a power preserved from the glory of its act." Indeed, Badiou will locate two different sources for the differences in his and Agamben's interpretation of Saint Paul: for Badiou, *Saint Paul: The Foundation of Universalism*, translated by Ray Brassier (Stanford CA: Stanford University Press, 2003); and for Agamben, *The Time That Remains*, translated by Patricia Dailey (Stanford CA: Stanford University Press, 2005). See also Badiou, *Logics of Worlds: Being and Event, 2*, p.559.
18 Albert Camus, *The Myth of Sisyphus and Other Essays*, translated from the French by Justin O'Brien (New York: Vintage International, 1991).
19 According to Leibniz a complete individual thing (for example a person) is characterized by all its properties, and these determine its relations with other individuals. The existence of one individual may contradict the existence of another. A possible world is made up of individuals that are compossible - that is, individuals that can exist together. Possible worlds exist as possibilities in the mind of God. One world among them is realized as the actual world, and this is the most perfect one. See Brandon C. Look, "Leibniz's Modal Metaphysics", *The Stanford Encyclopedia of Philosophy* (Winter 2022 Edition), Edward N. Zalta & Uri Nodelman (eds.). [Online]
20 Riera, "Introduction," *Alain Badiou: Philosophy and its Conditions*, p.13.

21 Ibid., p.6. See also Gabriel Riera, "For an 'Ethics of Mystery': Philosophy and the Poem," *Alain Badiou: Philosophy and its Conditions*, pp.61-86.
22 Ibid., p.7.
23 Ibid., p.2.
24 Alain Badiou, *Manifesto of Philosophy: Followed by Two Essays "The (Re) Turn of Philosophy Itself" and "Definition of Philosophy,"* translated, Edited and with an Introduction by Norman Madarasz (Albany NY: State University of New York Press, 1999), p.37. See also Riera, "Introduction," *Alain Badiou: Philosophy and its Conditions*, p.13.
25 Critchley, "On the Ethics of Alain Badiou," p.228
26 Riera, "Introduction," *Alain Badiou: Philosophy and its Conditions*, p.3.
27 Jacques Rancière, "Alain Badiou's Inaesthetics," *Aesthetics and Its Discontents*, translated by Steven Corcoran (Cambridge UK and Malden MA: Polity Press, 2009), pp.79-80.
28 Critchley, "On the Ethics of Alain Badiou," p.216.
29 Welsch, *Undoing Aesthetics*, p.20. See also Kant, *Critique of Pure Reason*, translated by Norman Kemp Smith (New York: St. Martin's Press, 1965), p.19.
30 Ibid., p.20.
31 Rancière, "Alain Badiou's Inaesthetics," pp.66-67.
32 Badiou, "Art and Philosophy," pp.3-5.
33 Adorno, *Aesthetic Theory*, p.74.
34 Ibid., p.75.
35 Ibid., p.77.
36 Rancière, "Alain Badiou's Inaesthetics," p.67. Giambattista Vico (1668-1774) was an Italian political philosopher who supported systemic or complexity thinking, as opposed to Cartesian reductionism. Critchley notes that Vico was the first real philosopher of history, now called cultural anthropology, who proposed a cycle of history in four stages: beasts, gods, heroes and men, whereby "unless the cycle of history is broken by the action of divine providence, there is a constant danger of a cataclysmic return to a new age of the beasts." Simon Critchley, *The Book of Dead Philosophers* (London: Granta Books, 2008), p.161. See also Giambattista Vico, *The First New Science* (1725), edited and translated by Leon Pompa (Cambridge UK: Cambridge University Press, 2002).
37 Ibid., p.69.
38 Adorno, *Aesthetic Theory*, p.91.
39 Ibid., p.99.
40 Badiou, "Art and Philosophy," pp.1-2.
41 Ibid., p.3.
42 Ibid., p.4.
43 Ibid., p.5. An example of art's non-specificity of purpose, its "vassalization," and the vicissitudes of funding, may be found in a commentary on the work of German artist Neo Rauch that states: "Collectors are tumbling over one another to rate contemporary art higher and higher, in a frenzy that feels religious – the market as a medieval cathedral under construction, whose consumption of resources declares the priority of immaterial belief over practical needs. Inflated financially and, through booming institutions, socially, art may never have been more esteemed while meaning less." Peter Schjeldahl, "Paintings for Now – Neo Rauch at the Met," *The New Yorker*, June 4, 2007, p.96. An interesting meditation on the artist in American society after World War II, see Dore Ashton, *The New York School: A Cultural Reckoning* (New York, Penguin 1972). In particular, she addresses the emergence of the Abstract Expressionists and the measure of the artist through financial success.
44 Marc Augé, *Non-Places: Introduction to an Anthropology of Supermodernity* (London and New York: Verso, 1995), p.42.
45 Ibid., p.40, 42 and 43.
46 Ibid., pp.64, 65.
47 Ibid., pp.65-66.

48 Ibid., p.66.
49 Ibid., pp.39- 40.
50 Adorno, *Aesthetic Theory*, p.8.
51 Augé, *Non-Places*, p.viii.
52 Bürger, *Theory of the Avant-Garde*, p.55.
53 The work of the pseudonymous British artist, Banksy, consists of graffiti images, posted anonymously, often accompanied by epigrams such as, "Follow Your Dreams: Cancelled," "If graffiti changed anything, it would be illegal," a panhandler with a sign "Keep your coins, I want change." See also the film, *Exit Through the Gift Shop* (Banksy 2010). The Dalai Lama, when asked what surprised him about humanity, answered, "Man. Because he sacrifices his health in order to make money. Then he sacrifices money to recuperate his health. And then he is so anxious about the future that he does not enjoy the present; the result being he does not live in the present or the future; he lives as if he is never going to die, and then dies having never really lived."
54 Augé, *Non-Places*, p.xiii. Augé may have anticipated the launch of Google Maps in 2005.
55 Jean Baudrillard, *America*, translated by Chris Turner (London: Verso, 1988), pp.124-125.
56 Ibid., p.124.
57 Jean Baudrillard, "The Precession of Simulacra," *Media and Cultural Studies: Keyworks*, edited by Meenakshi Gigi Durham and Douglas M. Kellner (Malden MA: Blackwell Publishing, 2006), p.453.
58 Sloterdijk, *Critique of Cynical Reason*, p.27.
59 Gilles Deleuze, *Plato and the Simulacrum*, translated by Rosalind Krauss (Cambridge MA: The MIT Press, Vol.27, Winter 1983), p.1.
60 Deleuze, *Foucault*, pp.49-50.
61 Cutrofello, *Continental Philosophy*, p.383. The quote is from Foucault, *Discipline and Punish*, p.297.
62 Jacques Lacan, Écrits: A Selection, translated by Alan Sheridan (London: Tavistock Publications, 1977), p.303.
63 Ray Monk, *Ludwig Wittgenstein: The Duty of Genius* (New York: The Free Press, 1990), pp.507-508. For example, the painting of *A Bar at the Folies-Bergère* (*Un bar aux Folies Bergère*, Edouard Manet 1882) depicts a scene in the Folies Bergère nightclub in Paris, where the woman working behind the bar is looking straight at us – her gaze "capturing" the viewing subject, and yet her reflection in the mirror seems to be wrong because it shows her talking to a man, who could be us, but then the angle causes doubt about our own position of observation. One interpretation, as noted by Elsaesser and Hagener, is that the faulty reflection depicts an interaction earlier in time that also results in the woman's expression in the painting's present. If so, then the static painting has now introduced an element of time and movement, and a relationship over time that the viewing subject is now triangulated into, which would also foretell how the static images of each frame in a film will flow together to 'create' movement in time. Elsaesser and Hagener, *Film Theory*, p.62. At the same time, we have a sense of the uncanny, the creation of a cognitive distance, a liminal space as it were, between the understanding of what we see and what we should see. First identified by Ernst Jentsch, he will define the Uncanny as, "doubts whether an apparently animate being is really alive; or conversely, whether a lifeless object might be, in fact, animate" and expands upon its use in fiction. E.T.A. Hoffman - whom Freud refers to as the "unrivalled master of the uncanny in literature" - utilizes uncanny effects in his work, focusing specifically on Hoffmann's story "The Sand-Man", which features a life-like doll, Olympia. Freud identifies uncanny effects that result from instances of "repetition of the same thing," including incidents wherein one becomes lost and accidentally retraces one's steps, and instances wherein random numbers recur, seemingly meaningfully. Freud may be prefiguring the concept that Jung would later refer to as synchronicity. However, Freud draws on a wholly different element of the story,

namely, "the idea of being robbed of one's eyes," as the "more striking instance of uncanniness" in the tale. See Sigmund Freud, *The Uncanny* (1919), (New York: Penguin Books, 2003). See also Ernst Jentsch, *On the Psychology of the Uncanny* (1906).
64 Elsaesser and Hagener, *Film Theory*, p.102.
65 Ibid., p.103.
66 Deleuze, *Foucault*, p.101.
67 Ibid., p.91. See also Elsaesser and Hagener, *Film Theory*, p.106.
68 Ibid., p.103.
69 Žižek, "The Undergrowth of Enjoyment," p.15.
70 A favourite term of Žižek's, parallax is a displacement or difference in the apparent position of an object viewed along two different lines of sight. In cinema, this is important as objects in the foreground move quicker than those in the distance, a change in perspective that can create a disconcerting and vertiginous effect. See Slavoj Žižek, *The Parallax View* (Cambridge MA: The MIT Press, 2009).
71 Baudrillard, "The Precession of Simulacra," p.453.
72 Ibid., p.454.
73 Ibid., p.473.
74 Ibid., p.472.
75 Slavoj Žižek, "Only a Suffering God Can Save Us," *God in Pain: Inversions of Apocalypse, Slavoj Žižek and Boris Gunjević* (New York: Seven Stories Press, 2012), p.165. Žižek frequently uses the example of *Kino-Eye* (Kinoglaz 1924) from the Soviet filmmaker Dziga Vertov (1896-1954). Vertov is considered the first poet of the cinema, rejecting traditional narrative in his attempts to investigate the poetics of cinematic language, particularly in his best-known film, *Man with a Movie Camera* (1928). In contrast, there is the *kino-fist* used by Eisenstein, where he used the shock of montage to raise the political consciousness of the viewing subject.
76 Ibid., p.167.
77 Ibid., p.165.
78 Ibid., p.165.
79 Ibid., p.177.
80 Ibid., pp.176-177.
81 Ibid., p.192.
82 Critchley, *Infinitely Demanding*, pp.51, 70.
83 Ibid., p.10. Knud Ejler Løgstrup (1905–1981) was a Danish philosopher and theologian, who, as an ethical intuitionist, was critical of rule-based ethics of the type advocated by Immanuel Kant. Rather than ethical systems that try to determine basic moral laws, he trusted instead to the fundamentals of individual intuition. See Knud Løgstrup, *Beyond the Ethical Demand* (Notre Dame IN: University of Notre Dame Press, 2007).
84 Ibid., p.70.
85 Ibid., p.51.
86 Ibid., p.56. Hetero-affectivity is the condition of being susceptible to other stimuli outside oneself.
87 Ibid., p.55.
88 Beckett's title is a parody of *Westward Ho!* (1855), a British historical novel by Charles Kingsley. The novel's full title is *Westward Ho! Or The Voyages and Adventures of Sir Amyas Leigh, Knight of Burrough, in the County of Devon, in the reign of Her Most Glorious Majesty, Queen Elizabeth, Rendered into Modern English by Charles Kingsley.*
89 Albert Camus, *The Myth of Sisyphus and Other Essays*, translated from the French by Justin O'Brien (New York: Vintage International, 1991), p.120.
90 Ibid., p.122. For a quotidian example, see Seamus Heaney's poem, *Old Smoothing Stone* (1984), about a woman ironing a sheet: "To work, her dumb lunge says,/ is to move a certain mass/ through a certain distance,/ is to pull your weight and feel/ exact and equal to it./ Feel dragged upon. And buoyant." Seamus Heaney, *The Poetry of Seamus Heaney* (New York: Columbia University Press, 2008).
91 Judith Butler, *Precarious Life: The Powers of Mourning and Violence* (London: Verso, 2004), p.130. See also Critchley, *Infinitely Demanding*, pp.161-162n47.

92 Alain Badiou, "The False Movement of Cinema," *Handbook of Inaesthetics*, translated by Albert Toscano (Stanford CA: Stanford University Press, 2005), p.88. Badiou will claim that the minimal *dispositif* is, "When one possesses the figures of being, thought, and existence, or the words for this *dispositif*, or, as Beckett would say, the words to 'ill say' or 'missay' it – that is, when one possesses the minimal and experimental *dispositif* of saying – one can construct questions, one can set the – ward." Badiou, "Being, Existence, Thought," p.99. Foucault uses the term *dispositif* to refer to the various institutional, physical, and administrative mechanisms and knowledge structures that enhance and maintain the exercise of power within the social body. Michael Hardt and Antonio Negri describe Foucault's disciplinary society as that society in which social command is constructed through a diffuse network of *dispositifs* or apparatuses that produce and regulate customs, habits, and productive practices. Michael Hardt and Antonio Negri, *Empire* (Cambridge MA: Harvard University Press, 2001), pp.22-23.
93 Alain Badiou, "Being, Existence, Thought," *Handbook of Inaesthetics*, translated by Albert Toscano (Stanford CA: Stanford University Press, 2005), p.101.
94 Ibid., p.91. See also Critchley, "On the Ethics of Alain Badiou," pp.232-233. In discussing the successes and failures of the film artist, Walter Murch quotes a line from Rilke: "The point of life is to fail at greater and greater things." Ondaatje and Murch, *The Conversations*, p.307.
95 Ibid., p.99.
96 Ibid., p.103.
97 Alain Badiou, *Logics of Worlds: Being and Event, 2*, translated by Alberto Toscano (London: Continuum, 2009), p.3.
98 Critchley, "On the Ethics of Alain Badiou," p.228.
99 Ibid., p.76.
100 Critchley, *The Faith of the Faithless*, p.182.
101 Karl Marx, *The Eighteenth Brumaire of Louis Bonaparte*, translated by Daniel De Leon (Chicago IL: Charles H. Kerr & Company, 1914), p.9.
102 Critchley, *Infinitely Demanding*, p.82. See also Simon Critchley, "Mystical Anarchism," *Adbusters*, June 1, 2012, and "Occupy's Perfect Storm," *Adbusters*, April 16, 2012. [On-line]
103 Rancière, "The Ethical Turn of Aesthetics and Politics," p.109.
104 Ibid., p.111.
105 Arendt, *On Violence*, p.74.
106 Rancière, "The Ethical Turn of Aesthetics and Politics," p.113.
107 Critchley, *Infinitely Demanding*, p.60. Critchley reminds us that in his later work Levinas constructs what he called an "ethical language," "composed of several strange, wonderful and hyperbolical terms: persecution, obsession, substitution, hostage and trauma." Ibid., p.60.
108 Ibid., pp.61-63.
109 Rancière, "The Ethical Turn of Aesthetics and Politics," p.114.
110 Ibid., p.111. Critchley notes that the official name used by the US for the conflict in Afghanistan that began in 2001 is "Operation Enduring Freedom." It was "Operation Infinite Justice," after a speech by George W. Bush, where "infinite justice is the only suitable response for the fight against the axis of evil." Critchley, *Infinitely Demanding*, p.111.
111 Critchley, *Infinitely Demanding*, p.129.
112 Rancière, "The Ethical Turn of Aesthetics and Politics," pp.114-116.
113 Giorgio Agamben, *The Coming Community* (*Theory Out of Bounds, Volume 1*), translated by Michael Hardt (Minneapolis MI: University of Minnesota Press, 1993), pp.15-16.
114 Critchley, *Infinitely Demanding*, pp.14-15. See also Critchley, "On the Ethics of Alain Badiou," p.215.
115 Critchley, "On the Ethics of Alain Badiou," p.216.
116 Tarkovsky mused on this aspect of cinema when he wrote, "It would be absurd to speak of classical works of art, say the Divine Comedy, as being dated. And yet

films which seemed a few years ago to be major events unexpectedly turn out to be feeble, inept, like school-boy attempts. And why? The main reason as I see it is that as a rule the film-maker's work is not a creative act, not a morally exacting undertaking of vital importance to him personally. A work becomes dated as a result of the conscious effort to be expressive and contemporary; these are not things to be achieved; they have to be in you." Tarkovsky, *Sculpting in Time*, p.99.

117 Critchley explains, "A *Faktum* (fact) [...] places a demand on the subject and to which the subject assents, and this demand has an immediate apodictic certainty that is analogous to the binding power of an empirical fact (Tatsache). However, "For Levinas, the core of ethical experience, indeed, the demand of a Faktum, is not a *Faktum der Vernuft*, a fact of reason, as much as a *Faktum des Anderen*, a fact of the other." Critchley, "On the Ethics of Alain Badiou,"pp.216, 218.

118 Critchley, "On the Ethics of Alain Badiou," p.218.

119 Ibid., p.218.

120 Ibid., p.215.

121 Critchley, "Art and Ethics," pp.130-131.

122 Critchley, *The Faith of the Faithless*, p.245.

123 Welsch, *Undoing Aesthetics*, p.21. The quote is from Otto Neurath, "Protokollsatze," *Erkennis*, Vol. 3, 1932-33, p.206.

124 Critchley, "On the Ethics of Alain Badiou," p.217.

125 Jay, *Downcast Eyes*, p.555. The quote is from Levinas, "Substitution," *The Levinas Reader*, edited by Seán Hand (Malden MA: Wiley-Blackwell, 1989), p.141.

126 Critchley, "On the Ethics of Alain Badiou," p.217.

127 Jacques Derrida, "Structure, Sign, and Play, in the Discourse of the Human Sciences," *Writing and Difference*, translated by Alan Bass (London: Routledge, 1978), p.289.

128 Critchley, *Infinitely Demanding*, pp.32, 35.

129 Deleuze and Guattari, *A Thousand Plateaus*, p.342.

130 Deleuze, *Difference and Repetition*, p.101. R. Bruce Elder notes, "a common but erroneous belief that psychoanalysis holds that the unconscious relies exclusively on what Freud called *Dingvorstellung* ('thing-presentations', mental represensentatons of concrete, particular objects, formed of the residue of sensations of concrete objects), and that what he called *Wortvorstellungen* ('word presentations', mental representations that have the form of names of things or of a hierarchy of increasingly abstract thoughts about objects) are the province of secondary–process thinking." Consequently. Elder argues that any presentation that is *not* put into words will be in a state of repression. R.Bruce Elder, *Dada, Surrealism, and the Cinematic Effect* (Waterloo ON: Wilfred Laurier University Press, 2013) p.368.

131 Ibid., p.100.

132 Ibid., p.101. Melanie Klein (1882-1960) worked in "Object relations theory," a branch of psychoanalytic psychology, which describes how experience affects unconscious predictions of others' social behaviors. This begins with the repeated experiences of the caretaking environment forming internalized images, which usually depict one's mother, father, or primary caregiver, whereby later experiences only somewhat reshape those images already established at an early age. Object relations theory further holds that the infant mind initially comprehends objects by their functions, which are termed "part objects," which are held as "good enough," and support a "facilitating environment," which will eventually become a comprehension of whole objects that corresponds to tolerance of ambiguity. This work is clearly reflected in Lacan's concepts of the "mirror stage" and "object petit *a*." See Melanie Klein, "Some theoretical conclusions regarding the emotional life of the infant" (1952), *Envy and gratitude and other works 1946-1963* (London: Hogarth Press, 1975). Critchley regards Klein's work as "pathbreaking," and observes that Lacan didn't always acknowledge his debt to her work. Critchley, *Infinitely Demanding*, p.71. Sadly, Klein's life was full of tragedies and, despite the positive impact of her work on child psychology, she was also criticized for her use of psychoanalysis on young children.

133 Ibid., p.101. Nikolai Gogol (1809-1852) wrote a satirical short story called "The Nose" (1835-36) about a St. Petersburg barber Ivan Yakovlevich whose nose leaves his face and develops a life of its own. "Deucalion's stones" refers to Greek mythology and the tale of Deucalion and his wife, Pyrrha, who were tasked by Prometheus, Deucalion's father, to build a chest in order to survive a deluge unleashed by Zeus. Unlike Noah, Deucalion and Pyrrra saved themselves but not the creatures of the world. Once the deluge was over, and they had given thanks to Zeus, an oracle told them how to repopulate the earth by covering their heads and throwing rocks back over their shoulders, which then formed people: Pyrrha's rocks became women and Deucalion's became men.
134 Heidegger, "Building, Dwelling, Thinking," p.354.
135 Critchley, *Infinitely Demanding*, p.20.
136 Heidegger, "Building, Dwelling, Thinking," p.360.
137 Ibid., pp.350-351.
138 Ibid., pp.352.
139 See Critchley, "Being and Time: Part 4. Thrown Into This World," *The Guardian* (2009) [On-line].
140 Bhabha, *The Location of Culture*, p.15. The term is taken from "Levinas's ethical discourse, between individuation and universality," *Re-Reading Levinas*, edited by Robert Bernasconi and Simon Critchley (Bloomington IN: Indiana University Press, 1991).
141 Michel Foucault, "Technologies of the Self," *Lectures at Vermont University in October 1982*, L.H. Martin et al (editors) (Boston MA: University of Massachusetts Press, 1988), pp.16-49. The full quote from Foucault reads: "As a context, we must understand that there are four major types of these "technologies," each a matrix of practical reason: (1) technologies of production, which permit us to produce, transform, or manipulate things; (2) technologies of sign systems, which permit us to use signs, meanings, symbols, or signification; (3) technologies of power, which determine the conduct of individuals and submit them to certain ends or domination, an objectivizing of the subject; (4) technologies of the self, which permit individuals to effect by their own means or with the help of others a certain number of operations on their own bodies and souls, thoughts, conduct, and way of being, so as to transform themselves in order to attain a certain state of happiness, purity, wisdom, perfection, or immortality." Foucault, "Technologies of the Self," p.17.
142 Boris Gunjević, "The Thrilling Romance of Radical Orthodoxy – Spiritual Exercises," *God in Pain: Inversions of Apocalypse, Slavoj Žižek and Boris Gunjević* (New York: Seven Stories Press, 2012), p.210. "Incarnational" would be god existing within oneself, such that we are the material manifestation of god. Radical Orthodoxy is related to "Process Theology," originated by Alfred North Whitehead (1861-1947), which is a call for God to be fully involved in temporal and material processes, often perceived as a leftist call for political intervention through theology. It also rejects the metaphysics that privileges "being" over "becoming," thus emphasizing self-determination. The incarnation of God, therefore, is not found in the hypostasis of divine and human personae, the Christ figure, but rather God is incarnate in the lives of all humans when they act according to a call from God, as did Christ. See Bruce Epperly, *Process Theology: A Guide for the Perplexed* (London and New York: Bloomsbury T&T Clark, 2011).
143 Ibid., pp.197-199.
144 Boris Gunjević, "The Mystagogy of Revolution," *God in Pain: Inversions of Apocalypse, Slavoj Žižek and Boris Gunjević* (New York: Seven Stories Press, 2012), p.18.
145 Boris Gunjević, "Babylonian Virtues – Minority Report," *God in Pain: Inversions of Apocalypse, Slavoj Žižek and Boris Gunjević* (New York: Seven Stories Press, 2012), p.92.
146 Ibid., p.93.
147 Ibid., p.95. The proper Augustine order is described as *psyche*, *oikos*, *polis* and *cosmos*. Ibid., p.93.
148 "Kenosis" is from the Greek word for emptiness (*kénōsis*). In Christian theology, it describes the "self-emptying" of one's own will and becoming entirely receptive to God's divine will.

149 Gunjević, "Babylonian Virtues," p.101. The term "popular discipline" is attributed to Badiou and cited from Slavoj Žižek, "The True Hollywood Left" (2007).
150 Alain Badiou, "Fifteen Theses on Contemporary Art" (2003), par.15. This is the fifteenth thesis. Also, Gunjević points out that in a later version Badiou will exchange "Empire" for "the West." Gunjević, "Babylonian Virtues," p.102*n*17.
151 Gunjević, "Babylonian Virtues," p.73. See also Michael Hardt and Antonio Negri, *Empire* (Cambridge MA: Harvard University Press, 2001), p.390.
152 Badiou, "Fifteen Theses on Contemporary Art," par.14. This is the fourteenth thesis.
153 Kearney, *Poetics of Imagining*, p.101. The quote is also translated as "man is an imagined being" in Gaston Bachelard, *The Poetics of Reverie: Childhood, Language, and the Cosmos* (1960), translated from the French by Daniel Russell (Boston MA: Beacon Press, 1971), p.81.
154 Arthur Koestler, *The Act of Creation* (Ann Arbor MI: University of Michigan, 1978), p.1.
155 Bhabha, *The Location of Culture*, Ibid., p.15.
156 Simon Critchley, "The Freedom of Faith: A Christmas Sermon," *The Stone*, December 23, 2012, par.13. [On-line]. See also Critchley, *Infinitely Demanding*, p.43. Critchley clarifies "that 'true' is here being used in a manner closer to its root meaning of 'being true to' or 'troth', namely an act of fidelity that is kept alive in the German *treu*, loyal or faithful." Ibid., p.43.
157 Ibid., par.36. Marshall Berman quotes from Dostoevsky: "Man prefers peace," the Inquisitor says, "and even death, to freedom of choice in the knowledge of good and evil. There is nothing more seductive for man than his freedom of conscience, but nothing that is a greater cause of suffering." Berman is optimistic, noting the struggles for democracy around the world, the masses of anonymous people who are putting their lives on the line, and the new forms of creative expression, where "Solidarity and People Power are modernist breakthroughs as stunning as 'The Wasteland' or 'Guernica'. The book is far from closed on the 'grand narrative' that presents 'humanity as the hero of liberty': new subjects and new acts are appearing all the time." Berman, *All That Is Solid Melts Into Air*, pp.11-12.
158 Ibid., par.32.
159 Michel Foucault, *The Hermeneutics of the Subject – Lectures at the Collège de France: 1981-82*, edited by Frédéric Gros, General Editors: François Ewald and Alessandro Fontana, English Series Editor: Arnold I. Davidson, translated by Graham Burchell (New York: Picador, 2001), p.331.
160 Ibid., p.333.
161 Gunjević, "Babylonian Virtues," p.100.
162 Gunjević, "The Mystagogy of Revolution," p.12.
163 Gunjević, "Babylonian Virtues," p.96.
164 Ibid., p.97.
165 Boris Gunjević, "Every Book is Like a Fortress – Flesh Became Word," *God in Pain: Inversions of Apocalypse, Slavoj Žižek and Boris Gunjević* (New York: Seven Stories Press, 2012), p.145. See also Alain Badiou, *Saint Paul: The Foundation of Universalism*, translated by Ray Brassier (Palo Alto CA: Stanford University Press, 2003).
166 Ibid., p.146.
167 Critchley, *Infinitely Demanding*, p.43.
168 Ibid., p.42.
169 Ibid., p.43.
170 Ibid., p.44.
171 Ibid., pp.118-119.
172 Benjamin, "The Work of Art in the Age of Its Technological Reproducibility: Second Version," pp.111-113.
173 Adorno, "Education After Auschwitz," p.204.
174 Rancière, "The Ethical Turn of Aesthetics and Politics," p.120. The quote is from Giorgio Agamben, *Remnants of Auschwitz: The Witness and the Archive* (New York: Zone Books, 2002), p.87.
175 Salman Rushdie once described the screenplay as "that will-o'-the-wisp of mod-

ern critical theory: the authorless text." Salman Rushdie, "Out of Kansas," *Step Across This Line – Collected Nonfiction 1992-2002* (Toronto ON: Alfred A. Knopf, 2002), p.9.
176 Rancière, "The Ethical Turn of Aesthetics and Politics," p.120.
177 Ibid., p.120.
178 Giorgio Agamben, *Homo Sacer: Sovereign Power and Bare Life*, translated by Daniel Heller-Roazen, edited by Werner Hamacher and David E. Wellbery (Stanford CA: Stanford University Press, 1998), p.37.
179 Rancière, "The Ethical Turn of Aesthetics and Politics," p.119.
180 Agamben, *Homo Sacer*, p.8.
181 Critchley, "Art and Ethics," p.132.
182 Michel Foucault, *Madness and Civilization: A History of Insanity in the Age of Reason*, translated from the French by Richard Howard (New York: Vintage, 1988), p.63.
183 Ibid., p.83.
184 Carl Schmitt (1888-1985) claimed that every government that is capable of decisive action must include a dictatorial element within its constitution. It was Schmitt who introduced the concept of the state of exception from the German concept of *Ausnahmezustand*, perhaps better translated as "state of emergency," which, according to Schmitt, frees the executive from any legal restraints to its power that would normally apply. Schmitt's work would influence Benjamin and Adorno, among others, but remains controversial due to his association with Nazism. See Carl Schmitt, *Nomos of the Earth in the International Law of the Jus Publicum Europaeum* (1950), translated by G.L. Ulmen (Candor NY: Telos Press, 2003).
185 Critchley, *Infinitely Demanding*, pp.133-134.
186 Žižek, "Afterword by Slavoj Žižek," *The Politics of Aesthetics*, pp.70-71.
187 See Carl Schmitt, *Nomos of the Earth in the International Law of the Jus Publicum Europaeum* (1950), translated by G.L. Ulmen (Candor NY: Telos Press, 2003).
188 Agamben, *Homo Sacer*, p.20.
189 Ibid., p.20.
190 Ibid., pp.166, 176.
191 Ibid., p.152.
192 Ibid., p.153.
193 Ibid., p.152.
194 Judith Butler, "Violence, Mourning, Politics," *Precarious Life: The Powers of Mourning and Violence* (London: Verso, 2004), p.41. Butler provides an example of the justification for intervention: "That this foreclosure of alterity takes place in the name of 'feminism' is surely something to worry about. The sudden feminist conversion on the part of the Bush administration, which retroactively transformed the liberation of women into a rationale for its military actions against Afghanistan, is a sign of the extent to which feminism, as a trope, is deployed in the service of restoring the presumption of First World impermeability. Once again we see the spectacle of 'white men, seeing to save brown women from brown men', as Gayatri Chakravorty Spivak once describe the culturally imperialist exploitation of women." Judith Butler, "Violence, Mourning, Politics," *Precarious Life: The Powers of Mourning and Violence* (London: Verso, 2004), p.41.
195 Rancière, "The Ethical Turn of Aesthetics and Politics," p.123.
196 Jay, *Downcast Eyes*, p.553.
197 Rancière, "The Ethical Turn of Aesthetics and Politics," p.123.
198 Rancière offers the example of the NBC miniseries, *Holocaust*, broadcast in January 1979, which came under criticism for trying to present the Nazi death camps. Despite the criticism, it was widely seen and had blockbuster ratings, including in Germany. Significantly, 70 percent of German viewers between 14 and 19 say they learned more about Nazism from the miniseries than from all their history classes. In a survey of West German teenagers taken in 1970, an overwhelming majority could identify Hitler only as "the man who built the autobahns." Cook, A History of Narrative Film, p.585n7. See Thomas Elsaesser, New German Cinema: A History (London: British Film Institute, 1989).
199 Jay, *Downcast Eyes*, p.553. The quote is from Maurice Blanchot, "Literature and

the Right to Death," *The Gaze of Orpheus and Other Literary Essays* (Barrytown NY: Station Hill Press, 1995), p.46.
200 Adorno, *Aesthetic Theory*, p.67.
201 Cutrofello, *Continental Philosopy*, pp.323-324. See also Slavoj Žižek, *The Sublime Object of Ideology* (London: Verso, 1989), p.110.
202 Ibid., p.324. See also Slavoj Žižek, *Did Someone Say Totalitarianism?* (London: Verso, 2001), pp.56-57. Žižek's example is *The Wizard of Oz* (Victor Fleming 1939), when Dorothy encounters the wizard who is not only not a wizard, but that he is also a profoundly needy man. Žižek, *Did Someone Say Totalitarianism?*, pp.56-57.
203 Sloterdijk, *Critique of Cynical Reason*, pp.xvii, 106.
204 Rancière, "The Ethical Turn of Aesthetics and Politics," p.119.
205 Žižek, *The Sublime Object of Ideology*, p.115.
206 Jean-François Lyotard, *The Postmodern Condition: A Report on Knowledge*, translated by Geoff Bennington and Brian Massumi (Minneapolis MI: University of Minnesota Press, 1984), p.60. Lyotard's *The Postmodern Condition* was originally written as a report to the *Conseil des universités du Québec* to explore the issues of Quebeçois identity in the post-Quiet Revolution (1960s) era, asking "Where, after the metanarratives, can legitimacy reside?" The conclusion was that in our postmodern world, it is no longer possible to have a stable sense of identity, a 'fixed identity', or a secure sense of reality. See George Melnyk, *One Hundred Years of Canadian Cinema* (Toronto, ON: University of Toronto Press, 2004).
207 Rancière, "Lyotard and the Aesthetics of the Sublime," p.103.
208 Rancière, "The Ethical Turn of Aesthetics and Politics," p.122.
209 Ibid., pp.129-130.
210 In response to the NBC miniseries *Holocaust* (1979), Claude Lanzmann made *Shoah* (1985), a nine-hour documentary that investigagted the Holocaust through interviews, actual locations, details, etc., in an effort to restore this tragedy to its full, incomprehensible obscenity and horror. Lanzmann claimed he was trying to capture "the presence of absence."
211 Foucault, *The Order of Things*, pp.316-317.
212 Ibid., p.318.
213 Ibid., p.328.
214 Rancière, "Lyotard and the Aesthetics of the Sublime," pp.105, 130.
215 Ibid., p.105.
216 Deleuze and Guattari, *Anti-Oedipus*, p.105.
217 Ibid., p.177.
218 Ibid., pp.73, 110.
219 Ibid., p.76.
220 Ibid., p.80.
221 Ibid., pp.110-111.
222 Ibid., pp.75, 109.
223 Ibid., p.112.
224 Ibid., p.1*ff.*
225 Ibid., p.326.
226 Butler, *Undoing Gender*, p.198.
227 Foucault, *Madness and Civilization*, p.83.
228 Ibid., p.xi.
229 Ibid., pp.278, 286, 287.
230 Ibid., p.288.
231 Ibid., p.264.
232 Rancière, "Lyotard and the Aesthetics of the Sublime," p.105.
233 Ibid., p.105.
234 Žižek, "Afterword by Slavoj Žižek," *The Politics of Aesthetics*, p.69.
235 Critchley, "Art and Ethics," p.132.
236 See Buck-Morss, *The Origin of Negative Dialectics*, pp.88-89.
237 Critchley, "Art and Ethics," p.130.
238 Ibid., p.134.

239 Ibid., p.131.
240 Simon Critchley, "Violent Thoughts about Slavoj Žižek," *Naked Punch*, p.6. [On-line].
241 Critchley, "Art and Ethics," pp.135, 137.
242 Derrida, "Structure, Sign, and Play, in the Discourse of the Human Sciences," p.283. "The *bricoleur*, says Levi-Strauss, is someone who uses 'the means at hand', that is, the instruments he finds at his disposition around him, those which are already there, which had not been especially conceived with an eye to the operation for which they are to be used and to which one tries by trial and error to adapt them, not hesitating to change them whenever it appears necessary, or to try several of them at once, even if their form and their origin are heterogeneous -- and so forth." Jacques Derrida, "Structure, Sign, and Play, in the Discourse of the Human Sciences," *Writing and Difference*, translated by Alan Bass (London: Routledge, 1978), p.283.
243 Critchley, "Art and Ethics," p.137. An example of "resistances" in cinema can be found in the cinema of Argentina, in particular the militant documentary filmmaking proposed by Fernando Birri in "Cinema and Underdevelopment" (1967), and the cinema for the "new human being," one who had the potential of "becoming," proposed by Fernando Solanas and Octavio Getino in their "Toward a Third Cinema" (1969), and in Brazil where Glauber Rocher proposed an "Aesthetic of Hunger" (1965). Glauber argues that instead of a "digestive cinema," as found in the easily digestible films of Hollywood, there should be a cinema of "miserabilism," one that illuminate the hunger of the masses in South America. Similarly, Solanas and Getino demand a guerilla cinema as opposed to an institutionalized cinema. In addition, they propose that these films are not shown in cinemas, where they will be banned in any case, but that the act of seeing these films illicitly will make the viewer party to these resistances. See Julianne Burton-Carvajal, *Multiculturalism, Postcoloniality, and Transnational Media*, edited and with an Introduction by Ella Shohat and Robert Stam (Piscataway NJ: Rutgers University Press, 2003). See also, by the same author, "South American cinema," *The Oxford Guide to Film Studies*, edited by John Hill and Pamela Church Gibson (London: Oxford University Press, 1998), as well as "Film Artists and Film Industries in Latin America, 1956-1980: Theoretical and Critical Implications of Variations in Modes of Filmic Production and Consumption," *New Latin American Cinema: Theory, Practices, and Transcontinental Articulations, Volume 1* (Detroit, MI: Wayne State University Press, 1997), pp.157-184. See also Cook, *A History of Narrative Cinema*, p.796.
244 Slavoj Žižek, "Introduction: The Use of Useless Spandrels," *Incontinence of the Void: Economic-Philosophical Sandrels* (Cambridge MA: The MIT Press, 2019), p.xi.
245 Ibid.,p.xi.
246 S.J. Gould and R.C. Lewontin, "The spandrels of San Marco and the Panglossian paradigm: a critique of the adaptationist programme," *Proceedings of the Royal Society of London. Series B, Biological Sciences, Vol. 205, No. 1161, The Evolution of Adaptation by Natural Selection* (Sep. 21, 1979), p.148.
247 Ibid., p.148.
248 Žižek, "Afterword by Slavoj Žižek." *The Politics of Aesthetics*, pp.76-78.
249 Critchley, "Art and Ethics," p.131.
250 Critchley, "Violent Thoughts," p.3.
251 Ibid., p.6.
252 Lyotard, The *Differend*, p.30.
253 Ibid., pp.54-55.
254 Ibid., p.xi.
255 Critchley, "Violent Thoughts," p.2.
256 Critchley, *The Faith of the Faithless*, p.241. Critchley points out that for Žižek an example of divine violence in the cinema would be the shower scene in *Psycho* (Alfred Hitchcock, 1960).
257 Ibid., p.241. The Žižek quotes are from Slavoj Žižek, *In Defense of Lost Causes* (London and New York: Verso, 2008), pp.478, 486.
258 Ibid., pp.241-242.
259 Rancière, "Lyotard and the Aesthetics of the Sublime," pp.93, 89.

260 Ibid., p.103.
261 Critchley, *Infinitely Demanding*, p.73.
262 Ibid., p.72.
263 Ibid., p.63.
264 Ibid., p.64.
265 Ibid., p.72.
266 Ibid., p.72.
267 Krell, "General Introduction: The Question of Being," p.23.
268 Critchley, *Infinitely Demanding*, pp.64-65.
269 Ibid., p.66.
270 Ibid., p.41.
271 Cutrofello, *Continental Philosophy*, p.159.
272 Ibid., p.158. See also Emmanuel Levinas, *Totality and Infinity: An Essay on Exteriority*, translated by Alphonso Lingis (Pittsburgh PA: Dusquesne University Press, 1969), p.51.
273 Ibid., p.160.
274 Simon Critchley, *The Book of Dead Philosophers* (London: Granta Books, 2008), p.250.
275 Cutrofello, *Continental Philosophy*, p.166.
276 Ibid., p.162. The quote is from Emmanuel Levinas, *Otherwise Than Being, or, Beyond Essence*, translated by Alphonso Lingis (Pittsburgh PA: Duquesne University Press, 2001), p.122.
277 Ibid., p.166.
278 Critchley, *Infinitely Demanding*, p.73.
279 Cutrofello, *Continental Philosophy*, pp.176-177.
280 Critchley, *Infinitely Demanding*, p.76. Critchley states, "The basic idea in *Being and Time* is very simple: being is time and time is finite. For human beings, time comes to an end with our death. Therefore, if we want to understand what it means to be an authentic human being, then it is essential that we constantly project our lives onto the horizon of our death. This is what Heidegger famously calls 'being-towards-death'. If our being is finite, then an authentic human life can only be found by confronting finitude and trying to make a meaning out of the fact of our death. Heidegger subscribes to the ancient maxim that 'to philosophise is to learn how to die'." Simon Critchley, "Being and Time: Part 9 Death," *The Guardian*, posted 13/07/2009.
281 Simon Critchley, "Being and Time: Part 9 Death," *The Guardian* (2009) [On-line].
282 Butler, "Violence, Mourning, Politics," p.76.
283 Judith Butler, "Precarious Life," *Precarious Life: The Powers of Mourning and Violence* (London: Verso, 2004), p.130.
284 Critchley, *Infinitely Demanding*, p.71.
285 Ibid., p.68.
286 Butler, "Precarious Life," p.147.
287 Shierry Weber Nicholsen, "'Now It Looks at Me': Aesthetic Experience and the Work of Psychoanalysis" (March 2013), Paper presented at the conference "On Psychoanalysis and Aesthetics," *Institute of the Humanities* (Simon Fraser University, Vancouver BC, April 27, 2013), p.2.
288 Ibid., p.2.

The Struggle for (In)visibility

Intervention: Human and divine

We have stated that the ethical turn is at the very core of philosophical thinking, a turn has been perceived as one for the worse because the ethical turn is unrepresentable. Nonetheless, the ethical turn does appear, although often in terms of what it is not. More precisely, it appears as the double bind. It appears first, or not, as the affirmation of the rights of the other and provides a justification for humanitarian intervention, and second, or not, as the affirmation of a state of exception that renders inoperative the distinction between fact and law, perpetrator and victim, human and non-human, and third, or not, as the affirmation of the double bind in terms of the unrepresentability of the ethical turn and its task of restoration, where we refuse the call for an ethically constituted subjectivity and the demand of the other, thereby foregoing the possibility to participate in another person (or thing's) mortality, vulnerability, mutability. The ethical turn also appears in the rise of the tectonic world--as-picture and its *memento mori*, the reversal of the flow of time, and yet the interstices within the system abound, the "little resistances" as the task of radical political articulations. It appears, or not, when we appear to be moving towards progress or emancipation, then we turn towards the catastrophe behind us, where, like Benjamin's angel, we see history as one single catastrophe, a global situation where wreckage is piled upon wreckage. In which case, the alternate possibilities of a messiah or a revolution suggest two different strategies of either non-action or action, of passivity or of violence, of de-Oedipalizing desire or traversing the fantasy, of self-presencing or technologies of the self, of Antigone suffering in silence or Antigone the terrorist, Bartlebian inertia or the cataclysmic, purifying violence of the sovereign ethical deed.

Regardless of the strategy, one and all are reduced to a state of homelessness, of bare life, because all efforts to avoid the ethical turn must defy the double bind, an impossibility that only produces helplessness. Eliminating differences will only eliminate self-determination, hence a social production that is a philosophy of representation instead of a philosophy of difference. The affirmation of a state of exception that renders inoperative fact and law is also accompanied by the state of indistinction, where the will to challenge these laws and master the "unmasterable," or determine the indeterminate, is not found in the arts or in aesthetic reflection, because the situation is unrepresentable, inadequate to measure both the singularity of a particular subject and incapable of expressing the sublime. The sublime resists all representation, yet the sublime has been incarnated into the material world where it appears as the scene of the irreconcilable. Indeed, the aesthetics of the sublime is found in the art of the disaster, where the two different strategies of either non-action or action are a consequence of the feeling of powerlessness at the experience of terror that is the sublime, thereby promoting a discourse that promotes a positive nihilism of aesthetics, whereby, under the name of culture, we delight in the ruined ideals of a civilization.

However, Naomi Klein contends that this view embraces a central lie, the belief that "we are nothing but selfish, greedy, self-gratification machines," who are "not just incapable of self-preservation but fundamentally *not worth saving*."[1] She will argue that this central lie is a worldview supported by an ideology that has proven a formidable barrier to change. We might find that this barrier is composed of our cultural cognition, one that changes nominally but not fundamentally. This recalls Walter Benjamin's famous statement that, "Humankind, which once, in Homer, was an object of contemplation for the Olympian gods, has now become one for itself. Its self-alienation has reached the point where it can experience its own annihilation as a supreme aesthetic pleasure."[2] It would appear that both views, the optimist and the pessimist, contain the acceptance of defeat. Hence, art is placed in the service of the unrepresentable, of witnessing yesterday's genocide or today's never-ending catastrophe, the catastrophe of history and the immemorial trauma of civilization. All of which declares that the sublime has become a *fait social*, with its politics of terror incarnated in the material world and its cultural forms, informing and influencing our social reality, including the economic, legal, political, and religious spheres, manifested as an experience of terror, while its own inflation is influenced and supported by that same social reality. Therefore, more than ever, there must be a resistance to the sublime, an intervention that is both human and divine.

A human intervention cannot simply be the means of justification for norms of action, but, evoking Critchley, it must be an act of fidelity to the event, one that supports an ethics of truths. However, as noted earlier, there is resistance to intervention, no matter that the cost of non-intervention may be loss of one's freedom, as well as the potential for self--presencing and the possibilities for new experience, which leads to the problem of action versus non-action, particularly if we subscribe to the radical antagonism of the human condition, which also leads to the ethical questions over the use of violence because the affirmation of the rights of the other provides a justification for humanitarian intervention, yet it also allows for the affirmation of a state of exception, rendering inoperative fact and law, in effect nullifying humanitarian intervention. Therefore, in the state of emergency, the false radicalization and the sovereign state of exception, one that becomes explicitly and immediately political, as Rancière claimed, and in the art of disaster, as Lyotard claimed, we also find that man's essence is in a kind of bondage, where freedom is willingly sacrificed for security, where people are quite happy to lay their freedom humbly at the feet of authority. Hence, the art of disaster is also an affirmative culture, as Marcuse claimed, where one can feel themselves happy without being so at all, perhaps more so as the possibilities for disaster are all around.

In any case, human intervention is realized through language (not the refusal of discourse), including the language of images, whereas divine intervention is related to the unrepresentable, its impossibility and interdiction (the refusal of discourse), thus connected by its cataclysmic terror and its inaccessibility to both the sublime and the divine. Benjamin distinguishes between divine violence, which "may manifest itself in a true war exactly as it does in the crowd's divine judgement on a criminal,"[3] and mythic violence, which is law-making violence, or "executive," which is pernicious, as is the law-preserving or "administrative" violence that serves it.[4] Hence, for Benjamin, divine violence is not law-making but law-destroying, leaving open "the hope that some kind of messianic salvation will arise from out of the depths."[5] He concludes: "Divine violence, which is the sign and seal but never the means of sacred dispatch, may be called 'sovereign' violence."[6] The state of emergency, false radicalization, the sovereign state of exception, are explicitly and immediately political, where man's essence is in a kind of bondage, where freedom is willingly sacrificed for security, where people are quite happy to lay their freedom humbly at the feet of authority. Consequently, the art of disaster is also an affirmative culture, as Marcuse claimed, where one can feel themselves happy without being so at all, perhaps even more secure, and more so as the possibilities for disaster are all around.

Benjamin's mystical impulse has been interpreted as a religious or theological desire to restore a lost or broken totality and identity.[7] The Janus face of Benjamin's work suggests looking to the future by way of a Marxist political orientation and support of the proletariat, a view encouraged by his reading of Lukács and his friendship with Brecht, and the other face looking to the past, a messianism influenced by Judaic mysticism, encouraged by his friendship with Gershom Scholem. If we reconsider Benjamin's position, we may find that instead of support of the proletariat and the external construction needed to raise revolutionary consciousness, we are no longer raising a revolutionary consciousness, but rather revolutionizing the raising of consciousness, a paradoxical transformation of our social being marked by both rapid changes in awareness combined with an inability to constitute any form of social praxis. With globalization, we move not only from the local to the global, but the global to the local, where the proletariat itself is only a placeholder for the individual who, with the availability of the new and ever more portable technology, creates his or her own cultural forms.

In addition, although we may find that the active force of life, as Benjamin wrote in *The Task of the Translator* (1923), may be concealed and fragmentary, it also exists within the symbolized thing itself.[8] Perhaps this will be the Lukácsian coming to the surface of everything that had been lying dormant as a vague longing in the innermost depths, or the pearl divers of Benjamin whose discoveries bring their rich and strange discoveries to the world of the living, or Adorno's music that emits from the coils of the labyrinth. Perhaps each of these creations becomes an artistic monad, one particular note in the universal, a form of critical self--reflection that might, the second Copernican revolution, the axial turn that reverses subject and object, so that non-identity becomes the basis of knowledge.[9] In other words, the primacy of the object trumps the primacy of the constitutive subject. To put it another way, the true aesthetic of a cultural form is not the aesthetic that we apply to it, but exists within the cultural form itself, or, to paraphrase Adorno, we don't understand art, it understands us. If so, we may unlock the historical dynamic hidden within objects, and, as Benjamin promised, release the silent murmuring congealed inside, where the object longs to transform itself, seeking a sensual happiness within its own body. As we have become objects to ourselves, perhaps those voices will be ours.

Mystical postulate: Political theology

Derrida, as interpreted by Hent de Vries, is uneasy with Benjamin's ambiguity of the possibilities of language as well as the "desire for a past origin and for immediated forms of noncommunicative – that is, no longer mediated 'communication'," particularly in what De Vries calls the "mystical postulate" found at the intersection of language and politics.[10] For example, Michel de Certeau will claim that mysticism is "the anti-Babel. It is the search for a common language, after language has been shattered. It is the invention of a 'language of the angels' because that of man has been disseminated."[11] This recalls the Habermasian "double language" with its perlocutionary component (scientific discourses, grand-narratives, legitimated, propositional) and illocutionary component (narrative, language games, fluid, unpredictable). As noted earlier, scientific discourses are legitimated by linking knowledge to the liberation of humanity (associated with the French Revolution) or to the meta-perspective of speculative Spirit (as found in Hegel), whereas language games are skeptical of the grand narrative and the unifying strategies of the pre-ordained systems, and yet the mystical postulate would now legitimate a non-scientific and non-mediated system of its own. It is not simply illocutionary, it is "allocutionary," that is, an absolute address to the absolute.[12] Evoking Wittgenstein, when he wrote, "how things are in the world is a matter of complete indifference for what is higher. God does not reveal himself in the world," De Vries claims that the "mystical postulate" could thus be said "to display a passion for what *is* rather than for *what* it is that is."[13]

As found in the sovereign state of exception and the indistinction of ethics, so the problem presents itself that there are no grounds that would justify a criticism of legitimation, an impasse, Derrida claims, as noted by De Vries, "that defines the perilous moment of every political earthquake as well as every genuine juridical or ethico-political judgement and decision."[14] Hence, Derrida's concerned that Benjamin's concept of "the gift of language" is originary and without a stated task, just as Benjamin's critique of the violence of the law is highly ambiguous.[15] Indeed, here we may find evidence of the poetic crisis, of the crisis of language, and the danger of self-conversion through the self-formed form, as well as the susceptibility to the double-bind of disillusion and disenchantment, or simply wishful thinking. In addition, as Heidegger warned, there is danger in the highest sense, where the transformation of subjectivity through culture is mistaken for the self-determination found in the process of synthesis itself, a semblance of religious experience in the "mystical postulate" of literary conversion, or in any cultural experience, where the language of questioning is in fact only that blindness from self-reflection which amounts to a form of self-bondage. The "mystical postulate" also suggests the art of disaster as a work of mourning, of the motif of spectrality, of the ghost that haunts Hamlet, where time is out of joint, where ontology is transformed into a "hauntology," which does not obey any new or old logos, but presents the end-time, "the apocalyptics of apocalyptics, the eschatology of eschatology, the last - and least - become first."[16] Thus, in *Spectres of Marx*, Derrida claims "each time it is the event itself, the first time is the last time,"[17] and so, evoking Marx when he wrote "The tradition of all dead generations weighs like a nightmare on the brain of the living."[18] Derrida characterizes the relation to the future as a "desert-like messianism," perhaps the self-motivated walk into the proverbial desert, where messianic hope oriented not toward the fulfilment of a promise but toward the coming of the unforeseeable.[19]

Derrida considers that Benjamin's views may be out of date, particularly those lines "Divine violence, which is the sign and seal but never the means of sacred dispatch, may be called 'sovereign' violence," where Derrida finds an essential uncertainty, which, "paradoxically, is its sole chance of being salvaged."[20] Hence, Derrida turns to a consideration of "the relationships between an ethics of hospitality (an ethics *as* hospitality) and a law or a politics of hospitality, for example in the tradition of what Kant calls the conditions of universal hospitality in cosmopolitical law: 'with a view to perpetual peace.'"[21] Another example, discussed earlier, would be the significance of the greeting for Heidegger. In any case, De Vries will argue that this amounts to an attempt to mobilize a "political theology," an alternative that turns to, and away from, religion.[22] This also is an attempt to move away from the art of the disaster and those cultural forms of the sublime, conjuring passivity or violence, moving instead toward hospitality as culture itself, an action of dissensus, yet one that contains an *ethos*.

The question here is one of hegemony, De Vries will claim, but a hegemony that is not simply cultural, nor is it political, nor all-determining, but one that nonetheless makes all the difference in the world.[23] Indeed, the interface between the "return of religion" and the new technology is connected to the exponential growth in the importance of the new media enhances our understanding of the mediatic element in and mediatizing function of religion and symbolic systems in general, revealing, "on the flip side of harmonizing, anti-Babelian *interpretations*: polysemy rather than dissemination, the return of the repressed instead of spectralization, repetition and mimesis of the same as opposed to its reiteration and displacement, approximation to the possible but not the invention of the impossible, pluralism and tolerance over and against the multicultural, and the attestation of the self as already another for this very self."[24] As a result of the desire for harmony and the new technology's goal of programmability, Michel Serres is able to claim that the reign of panoptic theory is over: "The informational world takes the place of the observed world [...] things known because they are seen to cede their place to an exchange of codes. Everything changes, everything flows from harmony's victory over surveillance..... Pan kills Panoptes: the age of the message kills the age of theory."[25] Hence, the eyes of the all-seeing god are no more than the eyes of a peacock's tail, merely ornamental, staring blankly, a man-made image of god.

De Vries argues that the progression of humankind must move through its political and cultural forms, as found in the history of religion, such that "in order to mitigate the propensity toward radical evil, that other curvature in the order of things, one must run the risk of indispensable yet disposable errors, that is to say, idolatries and blasphemies. To risk less is to risk the worst. What's more, to risk less than the worst is to risk the worst of the worst, the evil of evil, more radical than radical evil: the indifference of in-decision or, worse still, the complacency of good conscience."[26]

Plumb-line: Precarity

Another view of Benjamin's "Critique of Violence" is found in Critchley who suggests that Benjamin is distinguishing between a justification of means, as found in mythic violence, and the justness of ends in the realm of God, divine violence.[27] However, Critchley argues that Benjamin is not proposing that we should abandon laws or the categorical imperative or moral commandments entirely, such as "Thou shalt not kill," nor is he condoning violence. Instead, we should consider these laws as "a plumb-line, thumb-line or guideline for the action of people and communities,"[28] and that action (as opposed to non-action), and its possibility, is an individual choice, one that we must "wrestle with in solitude,"[29] and may in fact take the form of a necessary or essential violence, causing a radical disturbance or disruption to the state.[30] Similarly, Agamben notes that, "Politics has suffered a lasting eclipse because it has been contaminated by law, seeing itself, at best, as constituent power (that is, violence that makes law), when it is not reduced to merely the power to negotiate with the law. The only truly political action, however, is that which severs the nexus between violence and law."[31] As such, Critchley calls for a "non-violent violence."[32] The state seeks to saturate and control more and more areas of social life, the task of the "little resistances" is the task of radical political articulations that serve the creation of "an *interstitial* distance, an internal distance that has to be opened from the inside,"[33] because "there *is* no distance within the state," and thereby "weaving such cells of resistance together into a common front, a shared political subjectivity."[34] This "sharing" would also entail an ethical subjectivity through the communion of the hetero-affectivity of an unfulfillable demand, thus allowing that "Ethics is anarchic meta-politics,"[35] that is, we must talk about politics as a "more wild and formless conception of social being."

However, if we consider that action is an individual choice that we must "wrestle with in solitude," then we might recall Adorno's warning that "ideology lies in wait for the mind which delights in itself," such that:

> Critical self-reflection alone will keep [the naïve self-confidence of the mind] from a constriction of this abundance, from building walls between itself and the object, from the supposition that is being-for-itself is an in-and-for-itself. The less identity can be assumed between subject and object, the more contradictory are the demands made upon the cognitive subject, upon its unfettered strength and candid self-reflection.[36]

Thus, if we take in the various considerations of the fidelity to the event, where the good only comes into view *through* approval and not by virtue of approval, to get free of oneself and detach the mask, then liberation, as Adorno points out, evoking Nietzsche, occurs when the mind "discards rationalization – its own spell – and ceases by its self-reflection to be the radical evil that irks it in another."[37] In a statement that evokes Heidegger's marking the end of philosophy, where both presence and clearing must now determine the task of thinking, so Adorno determines that, "The system, the form of presenting a totality to which nothing remains extraneous, absolutizes the thought against each of its contents and evaporates the content in thoughts."[38] To put this in a broader perspective, as Critchley does, the problem, therefore, rests with the "anarchic" thinking about politics, namely thinking in terms of the institution (system) rather than rebelling against the system through open critique (meta-politics), meaning that, evoking Levinas, "Anarchy, unlike *archè*, cannot be sovereign. It can only disturb, albeit in a radical way, the State, prompting isolated moments of negation without any affirmation. The State, then, cannot set itself up as a Whole."[39]

The concepts of non-violent violence, the struggle for visibility, and the call for "little resistances" as the task of radical political articulations, all create interstices inside the system, which conceivably could be the task of the semi-autonomous work of art. We might recall Foucault's claim that visibilities are not defined by sight but are complexes of actions and passions, actions and reactions, multisensorial complexes, which emerge into the light of day, and, in terms of politics, then this is the emergence into visibility of that constituency which has no part. Indeed, Butler uses the term "precarity" to describe that segment of the population that is the least visible and the most vulnerable.[40] In which case, the emergence of that constituency which had previously not been visible is possible through the assemblage of the visible crowd and its use of public space, hence the revealing of precarity.

To this point, Butler notes that mass demonstrations are becoming more and more frequent in today's world, and, in doing so, they have re-functioned (to use Brecht's term) the material environment, often diverting public spaces from their original purpose as designated by the *polis*, and so allow for a new space of appearance to come into being.[41] Nonetheless, freedom, Butler contends, does not come from you or me, but occurs as a relation between us and among us, which is now a global concern.[42] Therefore, if this contestation is going to work, Butler argues, there will need to be a hegemonic struggle over this new space of appearance, one that is articulated in concert, by which we may include the world-as-picture, the mass culture, and the virtual realms opened up by technology. As such, one of the main aspects that distinguish the new space of appearance is its presencing in the world-as-picture, such that, in out terms of extending the existing, we might say, as Butler does, that "the media *is* the scene or the space in its extended and replicable visual and audible dimensions."[43]

If we consider this "new space of appearance," a scene of action of people and communities, a "more wild and formless conception of social being," then its possibility may be guided by a plumb-line, perhaps with the work of art as the plumb-bob, the weight suspended to determine verticality and depth, where dissensus is the forum of life-art. Indeed, art may then inaugurate a "counter-psychoanalysis," as proposed by Bachelard, a poetics of listening rather than an analytic of unmasking, where "imagination can be a discriminating *valorizing* agency as well as an *aesthetic* one."[44] With a suggestion of clearance and presence, Bachelard will write:

> To be authentic, all imagination must learn again how to dream... and at the same time, how to break the fascination of images in order to keep the way clear for imagination's propulsion towards the absolute... the authentic image renews not be renunciation of imagination but by fulfilment... it does not represent something, it addresses someone.[45]

In doing so, Bachelard seeks to reverse the typical configuration of constitutive subjectivity, seeking an ethically constituted subjectivity, as did Levinas with his view of alterity, abandoning the visually constituted, subject-object "I-It" relations and allow the verbally mediated, intersubjective "I-Thou" to take precedence.[46] Bachelard will claim that "the *picturesque* disrupts both mythological and poetic forces. The picturesque disperses the strength of dreams."[47] In terms of imagination, and in support of pancalism (where meaning is attached to mental content, to ideas or concepts), as well as the spirit of music, Bachelard maintains that "the imagination is not, as its etymology suggests, the faculty of forming images of reality; it is the faculty for forming images which go beyond reality, which *sing* reality."[48]

Thus, we return to crisis of language, the poetic crisis, and the demand that language must enable new thinking, even when that may not seem possible when language, including the language of images, is condemned by its technologies of production, its programmability, its speed of dissemination, its manipulability. We may be the prime subjectum, determining the ground before, but not if we are serving the technology of reflection rather than using it to expand the existing, to support the freedom of destining. To kill language, therefore, the form than enables thinking, is to kill not only freedom of expression, but also freedom itself. We are thinking cinematically, creating images in the mind through language, as we always have, where the technology of reflection has made access to and creation of images as equivalent to that of words, yet the poetic crisis is revealed in the art of the disaster, so that a century after Lukács, when he would only concede the slim possibility for a new form drawn from material reality, yet capable of resisting "the sterile power of the merely existent," we may find instead that the merely existent is not a sterile power at all, and that the resistance to its power is what restricts freedom. In fact, the merely existent may be the interstices that Critchley spoke of, those semi-autonomous liminal spaces that function as much by visibility as invisibility, where transgression must be articulated through "little resistances." This also evokes the coming-into-view through silence, in that which gives, unbidden, unforced. Indeed, as Derrida would claim, "keeping silent is already a modality of possible speaking."[49] As we are always-already Sisyphean, it is the merely existent that appears in the interstices, just as the grammar of resistance, its process of articulation and determination where the transgression occurs, must be the aesthetic through the aesthetic, a transgression that reveals an ethic of truths, of what it is that is.

Being together apart: The inversion of the inversion

The work of art may serve as a transgression, of revealing an ethic of truths, and yet a condition for the work of art is also the desire for *durée*, for solitary contemplation or meditation, requiring the construction of a place of solitude, an "aesthetic place" of concealing. The paradox is that in a world-as-image where the experience of reality is always mediated and sustained by some kind of virtual mechanism, there may be no "concealing place" as all places have been subsumed into constitutive subjectivity, not just in the material world-as-picture, but the inner world of the imagination (image/ination). Levinas claimed that man is "a being who understands Being," and so, in Heideggerian terms, requires a privileged "clearing" in order to develop that understanding.[50] The location of culture is a place of movement and of linkage, a place of gathering for divinities and mortals, and, as noted by Deleuze, the being and the Being are one and the same that is both ontologically one and formally diverse, so that the real distinction of a location of culture is not entirely in terms of separability but in the "community" of all possibilities to the individuality of a necessary being. Rancière uses the term "being together apart,"[51] where the aesthetic place is both solitary and communal. In which case, there is both aesthetic community and aesthetic separation, consensus and dissensus.

We must now consider and value dissensus conceived as an ethical-aesthetical resistance, as the "fragile" and non-productive construction, as the "merely existent," just as we would consider and value the *sensus communis*, the visual spectacle and the architectonic mass of the general will. However, as we move away from the status quo and return to the significance of free indirect discourse and the heteroglossic diversity of language, that is both nomadic and polyvocal, allowing for the contour-less-ness of the collective assemblage, so too will the discourse between subjects be explained not only through individuality but through the assemblage. Importantly, the synthesis of "being together apart," Rancière argues, would allow for the reconfiguration of the landscape of the possible, a different regime of perception and signification, and the distribution of capacities and incapacities.[52] Therefore, it is here in this new topography of the possible where we find the challenge to the idea that freedom is something conferred upon oneself in "a virile assertion of autarchy," and instead acknowledge an essential powerlessness, a constitutive impotence, that is also a place of self-origination and self-legislation, as yet a place of both dissensus and communion because dissensus is communion.

Adorno also refers to "autarky" and warns that, "Philosophical reflection makes sure of the nonconceptual in the concept. It would be empty otherwise, according to Kant's dictum; in the end, having ceased to be a concept of anything at all, it would be nothing. A philosophy that lets us know this, that extinguishes the autarky of the concept, strips the blindfold from our eyes."[53] Rancière supports this stripping of the blindfold through the importance of the term "aesthetic efficacy," that is, "a paradoxical kind of efficacy that is produced by the very rupturing of any determinate link between cause and effect."[54] In terms of the new topography of the possible, Rancière claims that it is "the point where the *as if* of the community constructed by aesthetic experience meets the *as if* at play in social emancipation," such that, "it is a multiplicity of folds and gaps in the fabric of common experience that change the cartography of the perceptible, the thinkable and the feasible."[55] To extend Rancière's aesthetic efficacy, and in terms of the task and precondition of the work of art, we now have the modern rupture with representation: in the process of restaging of the Laocoön, in the fragmentation of Mallarmé's poetry that finds new meaning in the dynamics of cinematic editing and the various "fonts" of time-images, in the mutilated Hercules found in the Deleuzian "body without organs," or the Deleuzian "pure sensation" torn away from the Wagnerian *gesamtkunstwerk* and the sensory-motor regime of experience, as well as the Adorno-influenced effect of dis-identification where "the aesthetic community is a community of dis-identified persons."[56]

The pretensions of critical art are loaded with the supposed efficacy of *détournement*, which are meant to help us discover the power of the commodity, but, as we have noted earlier, have only resulted in recuperation of its radical forms into the mainstream. Nonetheless, even if *détournement* is insufficient, the true resistance to recuperation may serve to define the viability and quality of a work of art. Besides, as Rancière argues, nobody is unaware of the power of the commodity, nor the reign of the spectacle or the pornography of power, but the image-making culture still manages to capitalize on the undecidability of the viewing subject and their inability to make a decision on what it all means.[57] Thus, we have the paradox of needing images of action in order to show the viewing subject that action is the answer, yet the only action is found in the images and the response to the images, such that we have an inversion of the real and virtual worlds, an inversion of what was already an inversion, which thus appears to be an action yet is devoid of any real action:

> It denounces the inversion of existence that consists in being a passive consumer of commodities which are images and images which are commodities. It tells us that the only response to this evil is activity. But it also tells us that those of us who are viewing the images it is commenting on will never act, will forever remain spectators of a life spent in the image. The inversion of the inversion thus remains a form of knowledge reserved for those who know why we shall continue not to know, not to act.[58]

The ideal citizen would appear to be someone who is an active consumer of images, making them at once a perpetual consumer and politically neutral, and yet here Rancière makes the distinction of the importance of disconnection and the rupture of any determinate link between cause and effect, the aesthetic efficacy, which, as he terms it, cracks open the unity of the given and the obviousness of the visible, which is then the monument that speaks to the ears of the future, a Nietzschean prospect, where that which is missing, in the Laocoönian sense (it's there and it's not there, a phantom limb), namely the possibility of freedom that will be fulfilled by those to come.[59] For example, one means of accomplishing the task of Laocoönian restoration and reformation is through the aesthetic through the aesthetic, where the second order of the aesthetic is a different form from that of the first, which may very well be orthopaedic, yet it attends to a different truth content that arises from a different location of culture or a different use of technology.[60] Another possibility is also found in the aesthetic through the aesthetic whereby we understand what is missing, what is not there, revealed through its silence, in what resists representation (it gives, unbidden, rather than the subject giving it what it gives).

In doing so, Rancière finds a more complex relationship between mimesis and poiesis, namely *aisthēsis*, which, as noted earlier, allows for ethical discernment and making a value judgement. Hence, the bound domain of aesthetics has extended into the domain of ethics, such that the idea-image comprises more than just visual perception, but an apperception, a perception that includes the intellect and experience, which would involve all the senses, such that the signet-ring impression of that which is perceived leaves upon the body and memory can be described as "exhibiting the signs on human bodies of thoughts and feelings that are not *their own*."[61]

At the same time, the *aisthēsis* is an aesthetic effect marked by two "separations": the first is the loss of destination (i.e., the distribution of artistic productions in particular social places and functions, such as museums or cinemas, where the viewing subject and the screen itself have motility), and the second is the aesthetic effect of a community that is a community of dis-identified persons (such as the Internet "community"). The torsions of artistic practice, the spiralling Möbius movement of revealing and concealing, are both evinced and neutralized by the same tension between the aesthetic effect of dis-identification and neutralization, where, a variation on Benjamin's politicizing art in response to the aestheticizing of politics,[62] "the very same thing that makes the aesthetic 'political' stands in the way of all strategies for 'politicizing art'."[63]

Thus, we move towards the construction of a new topography of the possible, with new forms of individuation challenging any form of political subjectivation.[64] In the Heideggerian sense, we are in a new provenance of presencing. Or, as Deleuze and Guattari might describe it, we are now in the realm of haeccities, the viewing subject's "thisness," but as defined in the new technology of reflection, enabling the change from the hierarchical structure to a rhizomic structure that incorporates the idea-image into lived experience and everyday life. The change in apperception may follow with a change in the perception of history, which, as Deleuze and Guattari claimed, was always written from the sedentary point of view and may now be moving toward one of nomadology,[65] hence, a parallax view.

Art as work: Images of thought

Badiou notes that "art is never anything but a service rendered to psychoanalysis itself: Art as free service."[66] What is this "free service"? For one thing, art is a truth procedure, one that reveals the object of desire. As such, art is not truth in itself but its value lies in its therapeutic functions (i.e., catharsis). If we combine these two points, then, according to Badiou, its "free service" in the classical schema is that it "*dehystericizes art*."[67] Freud argued that the price paid for civilization is loss of happiness and a sense of guilt, yet art offers a formidable substitutive satisfaction,[68] so we might also say that art provides a formidable substitutive satisfaction for the loss of art-truth. Similarly, Adorno will identify the sense of guilt with the reified consciousness, where consciousness must give to the object that which is appropriate for its proper cognition, and, after Hegel, dialectics cannot do this because it cannot conceive of objects going into their concepts without leaving a remainder.[69] Therefore, the substitutive satisfaction that occurs in art must be in terms of its remainder, namely, the surplus meaning or *jouissance*; in other words, whatever art is above and beyond its representation or its construction would be its remainder, which we may access as the aesthetic, and that remainder/surplus meaning/*jouissance* is what makes it art, and indeed may serve as a definition of art itself.

For example, Kant, in repudiating the Stoics, would claim that we must not denigrate our natural inclinations because they are good or bad when considered in and of themselves: "to want to extirpate them would not only be futile but harmful and blameworthy as well; we must rather only curb them, so that they will not wear each other out but will instead be harmonized into a whole called happiness."[70] Thus, the work of art is an act of sublimation that plays a significant role in the cultural life of the community, whereby it presents a condition of demand and approval, both autonomous and heterogenous, a process that offers pleasure and enjoyment, where we would experience catharsis, or, as Critchley worded it, the work of art "*sublimes* the object" and yet endows it with Thingly dignity. In other words, "the aesthetic regime of art,"[71] to use Rancière's term, provides a liberating force where the aesthetic freedom of determination offers a counterpart to the limitations imposed by reality. Indeed, we might say that the work of art is tasked with these services, such that the task of the work of art becomes its "occupation."

In the nineteenth century, Rancière writes, the suspension of work's negative value became the assertion of its positive value, as found when the "aesthetic state" was transformed into the "aesthetic will": "Romanticism declared that the becoming-sensible of all thought and the becoming-thought of all sensible materiality was the very goal of the activity of thought in general."[72] Thus, art is not simply the aesthetic mode of thought, but "it is an idea of thought, linked to an idea of the distribution of the sensible,"[73] such that the work of art not only provides its "free services," but it offers a revalorization of work itself. In fact, Rancière, inspired by Schiller, would maintain there are three major regimes of identification: 1) an ethical regime of images, 2) the poetic - or representative - regime of the arts, and 3) the aesthetic regime of the arts.[74] For Rancière, the aesthetic regime of the arts is the most significant, as well as the most problematical, in that it removes the identification of art from any hierarchy of the arts, the divisions of doing and making, of subject matter, of genre, and instead distinguishes a sensible mode of being that is specific to artistic products, making art into "an *autonomous form of life* and thereby sets down, at one and the same time, the autonomy of art and its identification with a moment in life's process of self-formation."[75] In effect, we have art that provides a formidable substitutive satisfaction for the loss of art-truth, which may be due to the Bergsonian world of two centers, the real and the virtual, perception-images and memory-images, whereby each one is cleaved because of the other, yet both are necessary, because they collaborate in an endless circuit that may be synthesized through the idea-image.

For Bergson, as well as Deleuze, concepts are the images of thought.[76] Thus, to perceive something is not reducible to either a representation, as an idealist would say, or a thing, as a realist would say, but rather to perceive something is to encounter it, which includes both sensation and perception, or an active engagement with the event of its appearing (*Ereignis,* the coming-into-view). Thus, the encounter with the idea-image is an event that involves perception and action, which also includes the idea that both are solicited by that which is encountered, which in effect also removes any clear delineation of the subject/object relationship. In addition, Bergson states, as noted by Cutrofello, that there is a moment of delay between perception and action, where

> This moment of delay marks the intrusion of the mental into the physical and of the past into the present. Since the distinguishing feature of the mental is duration, it is not consciousness per se but memory that accounts for freedom. To be free is to be capable of living in memory – or rather to bring the past to bear on present situations.[77]

The notion of freedom within memory suggests freedom within the "landscape of the mind," and can be regarded as a particularly important component in the transformation of subjectivity through modern visual culture, or where the lack thereof would prove significant in terms of a crisis of subjectivity, particularly when movement, the physical reality in the external world, and the image, the psychic reality in consciousness, can no longer be opposed. Thus, we could say that freedom within memory is the freedom of movement within the location of culture, of the possibility of self-presencing, of autopoesis, and the employment of technologies of the self. Indeed, if we return to the idea that art has disappeared into everything, we would claim, as does Buck-Morss, "We can do without objects as art, we can do without an artworld, we can do without ontologically designated artists. But we cannot do without aesthetic experience – affective, sensory cognition – that involves making critical judgements about not only cultural forms, but social forms of our being--in-the-world."[78]

Bergson claimed that in general we live in an intermediate zone, a liminal space that is not entirely mental or entirely physical, where mind and body meet, where memory (the entirety of the past) meets matter. Bergson will also claim that matter can be thought of as memory in its most "relaxed" state, while memory can be thought of as matter in its most "contracted" state, and since images always have some minimal duration, then image-making itself must be "in great part the work of memory."[79] Therefore, we might say then that all the idea-images (perception-images plus memory-images) comprise our understanding of the world-as-picture in its present two-centred state of real and virtual. However, when the perception and action of the individual subject is located in an intermediate zone, and when the encounter with something is also solicited by that something, then the distinction between subjective and objective tends to lose its importance, such that the optical situation or visual description replaces the motor action, and where the encounter promotes "a principle of indeterminability, of indiscernibility: we no longer know what is imaginary or real, physical or mental, in the situation, not because they are confused, but because we do not have to know and there is no longer even a place from which to ask."[80]

Hermeneutics of restoration: Heterogenesis

Language itself might be regarded as a kind of "hermeneutics of restoration,"[81] a term used by Paul Ricoeur, where we seek the trace of that which has been lost. Foucault suggests in *The Archaeology of Knowledge* that we must find the indicative "monuments" rather than the expressive "documents,"[82] thereby seeking to recover the experience of hubris not yet distinguished from that of logos.[83] Here we also find the fallibility of human beings, and the genuine violence that Benjamin located in the founding of laws rather than in their transgression, where evil is manifested, as Ricoeur claims, and Adorno had warned, because "the true malice of man appears only in the state and in the church, as institutions of gathering together, of recapitulation, of totalization."[84] Nonetheless, Ricoeur argues there are meanings to be revealed through language and speech, which are not so much a question of uncovering the archaic meanings that are buried within speech, but in a "double movement," which we may regard as Sisyphean, that considers that which "pushes" language from behind toward meaning, and that which "pulls" language forward toward meaning, in a kind of synthesis of creative transformation.[85] Once again, we discover the two-fold nature of language, the thinking-back and the thinking-forward, where language must communicate both that which is the essential and that which is essence, such that consensus will never be possible, and yet within the limits set by that Sisyphean impossibility, everything is possible.

In terms of the aesthetic through the aesthetic, and of one form completing another form, Rancière reminds us this is not the critique of one form by another, nor is it replacement, where, for instance, images would replace words, but rather the power of an indeterminate affect towards the calculations of thought and art.[86] Thus, we are again in the Deleuzian realm, one of heterogenesis, where, for example, the video image, unlike film, is no longer dependent on the tension between a temporality of the sequence and the temporality of the break, due to its production as an electronic signal and its infinite circularity. Another example would be the Barthian *studium* (pensiveness) and *punctum* (subversiveness), which remain valid but only as two possibilities in the construction of alternate narrative chains.[87] However, Rancière takes issue with Barthes' regard for the plenitude of pensiveness to be found in the classical text, and instead finds a surplus of plenitude to be found in the modern text, namely the aesthetic regime of expression, which offers "unprecedented pensiveness."[88]

In which case, the digitized form has opened up untold new possibilities, just as did photography, whereby the technology of reflection and its heterogenesis becomes a process that allows for "the construction of another narrative chain: a sequence of micro-events that duplicates the classic sequence of causes and effects, of projected ends, their achievement and their consequences."[89] In doing so, the form resists the pure expansion of metaphoric matter, allowing the opaque screen to perform its task of revealing and concealing, which, importantly, also allows the viewing subject to determine the measure of the relationship. Hence, we must consider not only that which is complementary and overlapping in language, that which is preserved, but also that which is contrary and separate, that which cancels. In terms of communication, and to add a variation on Deleuze's "former present," we may be attending to that which is "future present," which suggests Lyotard and the idea of the differend, "the unstable state of language wherein something which must be able to put into phrases cannot yet be."[90] This presents an irreducibly agonistic concept of discourse that evokes the Tower of Babel, where the prospect of a united humanity and a harmonizing single language, was dispelled when God created a confusion of tongues in punishment for the hubristic act of building a tower to the heavens. But is this a "punishment"? God is not allowing his word to be used as prescriptive, which pertains to the rigid and the ideological, as well as the mystical, but his word used only as descriptive, the indefinite and the flexible, supporting the essential ambiguity of language, its plasticity, its equivocity, its polysemy, both polyvocal and heteroglossic, thereby causing the never-ending dissensus that demands translation and interpretation, as well as the work of understanding the unfulfillable demand of the other, understood in the difference from oneself. Thus, the Sisyphean attempts to find meaning and truth would not find answers in rigid moral systems but, as noted earlier, in an ethics of processes whereby one confronts possible courses of action, where the very limitations of dissensus in themselves provide the possibilities for communion and community, and the presencing of an ethically constituted subjectivity.

Yin and yang: Freedom and flux

In seeking a taxonomy rather than a history of cinema, Deleuze contends that the evolution of the cinema is initially connected to the emancipation of its own possibility, where the camera viewpoint was emancipated from that of projection (sedentary), and thus to its own freedom of movement (nomadic). However, that freedom of movement has progressed in terms of the motility not only of the portable multi-purpose camera but of the screen, emancipated from the sedentary theatre, as well as from the analogue filmstrip, disallowing restrictions of time and length due to digitization, and in terms of distribution, the images now projected anywhere and accessed at any time due to the Internet, thus allowing anyone to be a filmmaker anywhere at any time. In terms of time and space, therefore, the new technology allows us to speak of "any-instant-whatevers" and "any-space-whatevers,"[91] where time and space are no longer determined distinctly, and where we have a new and ever-changing geography of the virtual and the possible. This also suggests a certain freedom of movement within the location of culture, as well as the freedom within memory and the potentiality of self-presencing, or if there is a crisis of subjectivity, as found in constitutive impotence, then a lack of freedom, as the case may be. Perhaps these changes will be the death knell of the traditional cinema theatre, and perhaps of the Hollywood cinema and the European (auteur) cinema as we know it, and that the new cinema and its technology of reflection, in whatever form that might be, will be characterized by new possibilities for "being together apart," where discourse between subjects is still experienced through individuality and the assemblage, aesthetic separation and aesthetic community, only now with an emphasis on the virtual world. As we move through these residual and emergent forms, we may find, as proposed by the Mexican director Paul Leduc, a cinema that is amphibious, "a cinema of the salamanders," one that manages to "swim" in both worlds.[92]

For his part, Deleuze wants to convey that there are infinite possibilities for the world, but that the possibilities of the monad-actualized world are "virtual-actual" or "possible-real," which present the possibilities of both actualization and realization. There is also the possibility of both actualizing and realizing occurring simultaneously, a possibility that human beings have always reserved for God, described by Deleuze as "existentifying,"[93] evoking the Kantian transcendental of God as the unconditioned condition of all possibilities.[94] However, just as Bergson was merging the transcendental (noumenal) and the immanent (phenomenal) domain of matter and memory, so Deleuze considered a *re*-turn from the ontological (essence) to the ontic (existence), which could be regarded as a shift in direction from the transcendental back towards life itself. This move could also be compared to Nietzsche, as noted by Cutrofello, who wanted "to see science through the lens of the artist, but art under the lens of life,"[95] just as Bergson attempted "to look at science through the lens of intuition and intuition through the lens of the *élan vital*, the fundamental life force that manifests itself in different ways through the course of evolution."[96] In other words, they are seeking to shift the emphasis of existence toward lived experience by using a form to interpret through another form, or the virtual-actual to recover the possible-real.

The manifold possibilities of the virtual-actual and possible-real appear because "the process of actualization operates through distribution, while the process of realization operates by resemblance,"[97] thereby allowing for a double process of soul and body, body and soul: a Möbius strip. The fundamental symbiosis of this relationship is apparent in the constant activity of revealing and concealing that is now integrated into the folds of actualizing and realizing, where, just as "the world of possibility of beginning over and again in each monad," described as "the infinite opening of the finite," and just as we must decide at the point of the undecidable, the unfulfillable demand, so enormous complexities may still appear in simple form. Thus, the inspiration for the simplicity and symbiosis of the fold can perhaps best be illustrated by the inspiration for Leibniz's binary code, namely the *I Ching*, and its concept of *Yin* and *Yang*.[98] Deleuze was also inspired by the extensive works by Leibniz that sought to uncover a theory of life that could be reduced to a series of straightforward propositions, which we may call the "merely existent." For Leibniz, using mathematical terms, the harmonic individualism of the monad as the most "simple" number would constitute itself as the inverted image of God, and thus the inverse of infinity, the least "simple" number. Hence, the monad can be written as $1/\infty$, whereas the divine formula of God would be $\infty/1$.[99] However, in theological terms, God is also defined by the "1" in this formula and therefore the existence of God relies on each and every individual subject. Indeed, if a line were drawn between these two points it would be a circle, such that this relationship could be described as a measure of the degree of solitude and of community, of "being together apart."[100]

Modern visual culture has been described as "a fractal network, permeated with patterns all over the globe."[101] Therefore, if the image-making culture has become fractal, as argued by Mirzoeff, then it is because modern visual culture,

> precludes any possibility that any one overarching narrative can contain all the possibilities of the new global/local system, for fractals may always be extended. Second, a fractal network has key points of interface and interaction that are of more than ordinary complexity and importance. For example, the detail of a Mandelbrot pattern can be observed more and more closely until it suddenly opens into another 'layer' of the pattern.[102]

The fractal nature of the image-making culture also evokes an aspect of McLuhan's "all-at-onceness," which suggests chaos or randomness, rather than a pattern. However, the difference between a chaotic system and a random one is that randomness has no structure, it is "the mathematical equivalent of white noise – whereas chaos does have a certain pattern, albeit a very complicated and subtle one,"[103] suggesting Schirmacher's point of the authenticity of the "undefined life" within the structure of technology, that "not only can law and flux coexist, but law *generates* flux."[104] However, unlike chaos, with its seemingly random and non-symmetric patterns, fractals are geometric shapes that repeat their structure. For example, weather is chaotic and clouds are fractal. Also, each repetition of fractals becomes (at least approximately) a reduced-size copy of the whole, a property called "self-similarity,"[105] which evokes the function of the technology of reflection. Indeed, this self-similarity is also found in Western art history in the term *mise-en-abyme* ("placing into infinity"), used to describe the visual experience of standing between two mirrors, seeing an infinite reproduction of one's image, each one a smaller copy of itself, the sequence appearing to recur infinitely. This self-reflexive technique is found in painting, such as the aforementioned *Las Meninas* by Velasquez, and in writing, such as Shakespeare's use of the play-within-a-play in *Hamlet*. This also includes the "framing story," or the breaking of the "fourth-wall," where the actor addresses the audience directly or the "dream-within-a-dream" or "reality-within-another reality."[106] Similar to the Deleuzian fold and its *yin/yang* symbiosis, so there is no clearly labeled "inside" or "outside" in the relationship between spectator and screen, nor in the relationship between reality and fiction.[107] In the Heideggerian terms used earlier, this also marks the spectator and screen as a location of culture, the vibrant place of movement and linkage, where, as found in the definition of fractal, the self-presencing is an "abundant, ambivalent articulation," a field of perceptions, associations and memory, marked not only by studied contemplation but by turbulence and disorientation, all of which suggests a threshold.

In terms of the Deleuzian fold, we may return to the Möbius strip as the liminal space, the inside of the outside, the recto and verso, where the new topography of the possible is realized through the not-possible and paradoxical, where the infinite opens into the finite, realized as an encounter that involves perception and action, both solicited by that which is encountered and yet removing any clear delineation of the subject/ object relationship, such that we are no longer submitted to the prescriptive and exclusive *"either/or,"* but rather the freedom of movement found through the descriptive and inclusive *"either... or... or..."*[108] We could say, therefore, that the freedom within memory is the freedom of movement found within the location of culture and the potentialities within its multiplicity. To put it another way, this mode of thinking presents a challenge to constitutive subjectivity (impotence) in that it would have us move from an objectifying (Cartesian) *"either/or"* view of the world, through the inclusive *"either... or...or..."*, and so to a more all-encompassing *"and/of"* view, a transition through perception and action to a deeper world understanding, with *"and"* referring to a sense of communion, and *"of'"* used in the non-isolated empathetic sense, which would be a shift toward a lived experience for both individual subject and community.

The screen as intervention: Compossibility and event

Deleuze will argue that the screen contains only compossibles, namely those contradictory elements that can exist together, such that, "chaos would be the sum of all possibles, that is, all individual essences insofar as each tends to existence on its own account; but the screen allows only compossibles – and only the best combination of compossibles – to be sifted through."[109] As an example, Deleuze offers that the screen is like Nature, in that Nature is like an infinitely refined machine, making compossibles out of an infinite number of possibilities.[110] If we return to Leibniz when he was seeking a theory of life that could be reduced to a series of straightforward propositions, he found that an individual "thing-in-itself" is characterized by all its properties, and these determine its relations with other individuals, yet the existence of one individual may contradict the existence of another, meaning it is possible to have a world made up of atomistic individuals that can exist together: hence, compossible. There may be other possible worlds (virtual), which exist as possibilities in the mind of God, but only one world among them is realized as this world (actual), and this world, by its very existence, must be the most perfect one. By definition, therefore, compossibles allow for the possibility of coexistence between the contradictory and conflicting beliefs of individual subjects to exist within the actual and the virtual, and limitations are essential in seeking the freedom of movement found through the individual and communal *"and/of."*

As a form of intervention, therefore, the screen is an encounter with action and perception, which is an event (*Ereignis*). In his interpretation of an event, Deleuze, inspired by Alfred North Whitehead, presents three components or conditions: extension, intensities, and prehensions.[111] In doing so, Deleuze returns to the Leibnizian harmonics to describe extension as a vibration or wave extending through space and time, and intensities are the measure or degrees of this vibration or series of vibrations, and prehension is the "datum" or other elements that are received, defined by an act of grasping or seizing, which suggests the "outside" of the event, such that "the event is inseparably the objectification of one prehension and the subjectification of another; it is at once public and private, potential and real, participating in the becoming of another event and the subject of its own becoming."[112] All of this is expressed through the action and perception of the individual subject who "feels in this prehension the *self-enjoyment* of its own becoming."[113]

Deleuze gathers Bergson, Leibniz and Whitehead in order to consider under what conditions the objective world allows for a subjective production of creativity, where the freedom to create something new (becoming), and not try to attain eternity (being) is the best of all worlds.[114] "Events are fluvia,"[115] Deleuze writes, and everything flows "in a perpetual flux,"[116] such that the screen is a kind of intervention that brings the compossibles into view. However, it follows that there are also incompossibles, beyond the borders of compossibility, that cannot be included in expressive units, even if their prehensive influence is attended by the event, as found in dissonance and divergent series, of folding and unfolding, whereby the process of creativity must remain one of openness, a synthesis that at once affirms incompossibilities and passes through them, allowing for "a world of captures instead of closures."[117] In doing so, Deleuze allows for an emancipation of dissonance and of unresolved accords, where mutually contradictory worlds can exist and where the process of creativity is a "chaosmos," that is, the affirmation of chaos within order, a "polyphony of polyphonies."[118]

An opposing view is offered by Badiou, who does not support Deleuze's application of the Leibnizian principle of harmonics, indeed, he will rather bluntly say, "Well, this 'resonance' has no charm for us."[119] Despite the ideas of divergent series and incompossible worlds, Badiou charges Deleuze with maintaining that "the event is the immanent consequence of becomings or of Life," whereas Badiou himself will claim "the event is the immanent principle of exceptions to becoming, or Truths."[120] Indeed, we might say this is a case of Deleuze's rule as opposed to Badiou's exception. Badiou declares this dispute amounts to a differend, to use Lyotard's term, incapable of being resolved without committing a wrong against one of the two parties. For one thing, Badiou sees the event being misinterpreted as "sense-event," which moves the event onto the side of language, where, in terms that suggest an eternal truth or the intervention of fate (which also suggests constitutive subjectivity that becomes constitutive impotence), and now "contains in germ the aestheticization of all things."[121] Badiou regards this as the empty and dogmatic proclamation of an eternal truth and as "latent religiosity," even when the "sense-event" is disguised as harmonics.

Evoking Lacan, Badiou writes that "if you consign what happens to sense or meaning, you work towards the subjective consolidation of religion, for, as he wrote, 'the stability of religion stems from the fact that meaning is always religious'."[122] Nonetheless, Badiou will allow that the creation of a site of compossibility may contain heterogenous truths and differing truth procedures. This heterogeneity might suggest the chaosmos (as well as the debate between Benjamin and Adorno), but for Deleuze compossibility refers to the interdependence of all events in the unity of a universe, whereas for Badiou compossibility refers to the unity of truths in the eternity of the present. Deleuze's compossibility renders meaning from chaotic multiplicity. Badiou's compossibility is essentially a fractal concept because it suggests the interdependencies of each event and their coming-into-view through the praxis of self-similarities, which must be composed of compossibles due to the constitutive subject and the consequent multiplicities. That said, it is the incompossible, with their divergence and dissonance, those exceptions to becoming, which prove to be more than the truth of compossibility, namely the truth of those truths, or the truth of truth itself.

Posthuman: I am Nobody

To return to Hiebert, from whom we began with the technology of reflection, he posits that to be human is to be alienated, whereas to be posthuman is to be self-alienated, such that the posthuman can say, "I have always been other, indeed that is my condition of being. I am unchosen."[123] This recalls Foucault when he wrote, "all discourses, whatever their status, form, value, and whatever the treatment to which they will be subjected, would then develop in the anonymity of a murmur," where "the author function would disappear," and so asks, as did Beckett, "What difference does it make who is speaking?"[124]

In the age of the posthuman, Hiebert argues, "the posthuman is 'post' not because it is unfree but because there is no a priori way to identify a self-will that can be clearly distinguished from an other-will," and therefore the "rhetoric of resistance" is no more than "intellectual self-fashioning in an age of subjective uncertainty and uncertain subjectivity."[125] In other words, the state of indistinction is that of an inability to make the distinction between fact and law, between what is and what ought to be, because there is an absence of will, or, more precisely, an absence of certainty due to the indistinction caused by self-determination as found in contemporary subjectivity. Hiebert points out that Lacan's mirror-stage explains how the self itself is formed out of self-alienation, hence a self-conception through the process of self-reflection is a form of alienation.[126] Unlike Foucault's epistemic turn, the mechanism of this alienation, Hiebert argues, is now a technological process, where Paul Klee's "Now objects perceive me" has become Paul Virilio's "automation of perception,"[127] which is merely a closed-circuit of "rational illusions" where the creative process is no more than a self-alienating technological process of synthetic images that have confused actual content with variations on mirror-like self-reflections: "a blurring of perception that affects the real as much as the figurative, as though our society were sinking into the darkness of a voluntary blindness, its will to digital power finally contaminating the horizon of sight as well as knowledge."[128]

Paradoxically, this may be the true vanishing point of the technology of reflection, where constitutive subjectivity eventually alienates the viewing subject through a process of self-objectification, which would be supported by Foucault's self-administration and the subject's conforming to a regime of normality. However, rather than the aesthetic place that is both solitary and communal, we find instead what Kracauer will call "group individuality,"[129] where the potentiality of the complete individual subject dissolves or disappears within the group. This was one of Kracauer's concerns for the "distraction industries," such as the cinema, whereby the viewing subject would have their individual subjectivity "dissolved," so to speak, making them more susceptible to the influence of the group. As a consequence, "that subject certainly no longer displays the endless manifold of traits proper to it as a single individual," and thus, "incapable of extending itself into many dimensions, it actually moves in one single direction, from which it cannot stray either to the right or to the left without disintegrating. Indeed, the linearity of its evolution is one of the fundamental characteristics of the nature of group individuality."[130] In addition, group individuality is only possible because it has embraced a single, validating idea, an idea whose validation is the key to the group individual's existence.[131] As a result, and with suggestions of the Volk who are susceptible to the initiative of a Führer, the group individual is no longer acting as a fully distinct and complete individual, but rather as an undistinguished element in an indiscriminate multiplicity.

Not unlike Adorno's argument in "Education After Auschwitz," this one-dimensional character will lose "those defining individual aspects, such as their flexibility and tenderness, and instead will now be linked to a uniformity and primitiveness, as well as a certain rigidity and cruelty, because many of the domains of reality and experience available to the individual now remain inaccessible to it."[132] Indeed, the essential point that Adorno makes, as noted by Henry Giroux, is that education had exceeded the bounds of "any critical practice could provide the means for disconnecting commonsense learning from the narrowly ideological impact of mass media, the regressive tendencies associated with hyper-masculinity, the rituals of everyday violence, the inability to identify with others, as well as from the pervasive ideologies of state repression and its illusions of empire."[133] In making this a pedagogical issue, unlike Sontag who had only noted the political nature of "reading images,"[134] Adorno includes the media in its ability to "educate," thus Giroux extends Adorno's concern to an "Education After Abu Ghraib," one that may call for an "*unlearning*,"[135] such that we can "imagine a future in which learning is inextricably connected to social change, the obligations of civic justice, and a notion of democracy in which peace, equality, compassion, and freedom are not limited to the nation state but extended to the international community. Education after Abu Ghraib must take seriously what it might mean to strive for the autonomy and dignity of a global citizenry and peace as its fundamental precondition."[136]

Kracauer's call for a redemption of reality and a return to real experience will propose, instead of distraction, that boredom is "the only proper occupation, since it provides a kind of guarantee that one is, so to speak, still in control of one's own existence."[137] Indeed, legitimate boredom is the experience of "a kind of bliss that is almost unearthly,"[138] which, as discussed, we may also interpret as an aspect of the power of the merely existent. On the other hand, as Rancière describes it, we may have simply returned to the much maligned and cretinous prisoner staring helplessly at images, where "the obtuse power of the image as being-there-without-reason becomes the radiance of a face, conceived on the model of the icon, as the gaze of divine transcendence. The works of the artists – painters, sculptors, video-makers, installers – are isolated in their sheer haeccity."[139] Or, as Sloterdijk will have it, we have arrived at the modern state of disillusionment and demoralization, and the cynicism of enlightened false consciousness, that "unhappy consciousness, on which enlightenment has laboured both successfully and in vain."[140] Sloterdijk argues that we might initially think that the order of things is an objective order, when in fact it is only constitutive subjectivity supported by the notions of perception and reflection, a realization that attends the paradoxical associations of the modern world, such as enlightenment and worthlessness, acceptance and apology, resignation and reconciliation, unfulfilment and contentedness, all wrapped up in the unrealized and unfulfillable promise of happiness.[141] Indeed, the miscarriage of enlightenment is to act against the better knowledge of things, to know oneself to be without illusions, and yet to move ever forward in the flight into illusion.

Just as Aaron formed the golden calf to assuage the people while Moses was upon the mountain, so Sloterdijk contends, "the dance around the golden calf of identity is the last and greatest orgy of counterenlightenment."[142] Thus, self-reflection and the search for identity, no matter whether it is personal, occupational, national, political, female, male, class, party, and so on, it will be resisted by even those who regard themselves as enlighteners, because enlightenment as counter-enlightenment must now continue its most intimate project: the transformation of being through consciousness.[143] But Sloterdijk isn't done yet, because now "There is, to be concise, not only a crisis of enlightenment, not only a crisis of the enlighteners, but even a crisis in the praxis of enlightenment, in *commitment* to enlightenment."[144] On a similar note, and having considered this passage in Sloterdijk, Jay notes that even Habermas, a loyal defender of the enlightenment project, admits the present era is one of "the new unsurveyability" (*die neue Unübersichtlichkeit*).[145] Consequently, the result of the final enlightenment will be the Nobody, the absolute non-identity, where the illusion of privacy and egoism comes to an end.[146]

Odysseus, Sloterdijk argues, is the true founding father of modern and everlasting intelligence, not Hamlet. By way of illustration, Sloterdijk presents the story of Odysseus and the Cyclops.[147] Imprisoned in a cave by the one-eyed Cyclops, Odysseus, the master of self-preservation, gets him drunk and then blinds him with a burning stick. When the Cyclops asked who blinded him, Odysseus replies, "It was Nobody who blinded you!" This is in response to the Cyclops saying earlier, "Friends, nobody slays me with cunning." The Cyclops calls for help on his attacker from his neighbours; they ask, on whom? The Cyclops answers, "On Nobody." The friends laugh at him and ignore his predicament. However, Odysseus also draws the envy of the gods. Having returned to his ship, he calls back to shore and reveals his true identity, but Cyclops is the son of Poseidon and will call for revenge.[148] As Benjamin claimed, as noted earlier, reason and cunning have placed tricks within myths so that their forces cease to be invincible. In any case, the laughter, if we take in Bergson's view, illustrates how stupidity or social inadequacy serves a reciprocal purpose when contextualized through humour, and its social function reveals aspects of society, and ourselves within that society, which might have remained hidden or unacknowledged, and in so doing contributes to our social development.[149] According to Sloterdijk, the lesson to be learned in this story is that when in danger, and between the poles of Nobodiness and Somebodiness, those who are mentally and spiritually alert will recognize the safety in Being-as-Nobody.[150] If so, then it is the very impotence of constitutive subjectivity that now serves as a means of self-concealment, an interstice of invisibility within the ubiquitous technology of reflection.

In reference to Beckett's writing, "*Continuez!*" and "Try again. Fail again. Fail better," Critchley refers to a "syntax of weakness,"[151] a humorous syntax that is characterized by the realization that one cannot *not* continue, where the events of existence are not heroic but merely hopeless, or Sisyphean as we have called it, and yet because of that very fact, because that struggle for meaning is the precondition and task of existence, the struggle is heroic. Perhaps, Critchley speculates, "we have had enough of the virile, Promethean politics of the will, the empty longing for total revolution."[152] Or perhaps there is strength in my weakness, as written in Corinthians: "For when I am weak, then am I strong."[153] Thus, Critchley is discovering in Beckett "a radical de-creation of these salvific narratives, an approach to meaninglessness as the achievement of the ordinary, *a redemption from redemption*."[154] We would add that this redemption is the redemption from constitutive subjectivity, to free ourselves from the impotence of constituting ourselves. In which case, Benjamin's "*weak* messianic power" may be our own, where we must offer ourselves the potential for the reconciliation of humankind. For Levinas, as noted by Jay, this would require an encounter with the "face of the other," but not in "seeing" them but in hearing their call, whereby "The 'turning' of the constituted into a condition is accomplished as soon as I open my eyes; I but open my eyes and already enjoy the spectacle," and yet to care for the Other is to refuse to submit to this spectacle and turn them into "an object of visual knowledge or aesthetic contemplation."[155]

Similarly, in terms of "unbecoming subjects," which supports a fluidity of gender interpretation, as well as a certain struggle for visibility, Judith Butler will propose that there is a question of ethics, as interpreted by Anika Thiem, one that asks how to continue dialogue, how to offer and receive recognition, particularly when the very conditions of the possibility for recognition and communication seem to have been eroded or are acknowledged to have never been there in the first place.[156] Nonetheless, the question of ethics could not emerge were there not the demand for recognition in play, the struggle for visibility, such that we must ask just what visibility is, just what recognition is, and how and why it has not succeeded, and what the ethical significance is of these different kinds of failures. In reference to Butler's *Antigone's Claim*, Thiem notes that Butler is questioning how we organize communal life and how Antigone lays claim to her identity, but Thiem also asks what is at stake, concluding that we must understand Antigone's self-understanding and how that informs her actions, which is "not a demand for public recognition of a private claim; rather her claim challenges how communal and political life is organized, whose lives are valued, and whose lives are considered dispensable."[157]

Self-understanding and social reality are a Möbius strip of constitutive subjectivity and communal existence where we self-conceive ourselves as an autonomous process within our social reality, which it both is and isn't, because thinking and being are the same, a two-centered world of the virtual and the actual, the verso and recto of the Möbius strip, where their unification is inherently impossible. Calling on Parmenides' aphorism, that thought and being are the same, where the way to truth is both the empirical "what is" and the contemplative "what is not," Badiou writes: "The same, itself, is both thinking and being."[158]

Badiou's argument is that we have always considered the One or oneness as our ontological goal, when in fact it should be the multiple--ness, or not one-ness, because the One or oneness is an unprovable and unfulfillable concept that is merely wishful thinking and thus creates a whole ontological lie. For example, multiple-ness, or not one-ness, can be structured through mathematics (set theory) and in fact is the real measure of our ontological processing. If so, then Being is not one-ness but the multiple (Being and being), and the event (*Ereignis*) is the one-ness, because it is a singularity, although we treat it like a multiple. Thus proving, as noted earlier, that we should have a fidelity toward the event because it is singularity that leads toward a "oneness" of Being that is in fact a multiple, but through set theory can become a totality, or, in terms used earlier, a multiple of ones, a community.

The impossibility of compossibility: The surprise of the event

Badiou sought fidelity, perseverance, and love, but not as the justification for norms of actions (system) but as an ethics of truths (position), where truth is interpreted as an act of fidelity to the event. The fidelity to the event may be described as "to weigh the judgement," which necessitates that the individual subject is incorporated into the broader concept of the *sensus communis*, or the public sense, where our critical faculties are engaged in an act of common human understanding, a self-formulating act that serves as a validity claim, in Critchley's terms, of "subjective universality" that we may now understand through the event as a "situated universality," where things come into themselves by belonging together, or as Rancière claimed, "being together apart." Therefore, in terms of the aesthetic through the aesthetic, we would consider the event itself, the coming-to-be that demands our fidelity, yet where the exceptions to that becoming that are beyond the event as intervention or screen or compossibles, beyond action and perception, will reveal the truth beyond truth itself.

If every truth is artificial, as stated earlier, even when it has the benefit of being a necessary lie, so that artificial-artistic or actual-virtual creation - what we may now call the compossible - is not simply a coping mechanism that allows the necessity of forgetting the truth, it also must promote the awareness of forgetting whatever we have understood, which, paradoxically, appears as fidelity to the leap of faith. Thus, we find there still remains the need for a "true" leap of faith in order to arrive at the truth beyond truth itself, which, if we return to Lyotard and the differend, is that unstable state where that which must be put into language cannot yet be.[159] We might call this the impossibility of compossibility.

Therefore, in order to change the aspect, as Wittgenstein would say, we should consider the event not so much as *the* event but as the *to be* event, emphasizing the aspect of action of the coming-to-be and the coming-in-to-view. Thus, the action of the *to be* event aligned with the "true" leap of faith also suggests Heidegger's concept of "throwness" (*Gewortenheit*), where the event comes to be through its projecting being-in-the-world (*Dasein*) onto the possibilities that lie before it (ground), thus occurring as an act that can neither be avoided nor anticipated, and may thus be considered violent, which then requires interpreting and understanding in terms of its possibilities and potentialities, which may be revealed or concealed, such that being-in-the-world is more actively becoming-in-the-world. The meaning of such projecting is disclosed through the action of throwness itself, but that does not mean we "have" possibilities as such, a discrete set of conditions and outcomes, but rather that we have the possibility of possibilities. As stated earlier, evoking both Heidegger and Critchley, the freedom to seek such possibility is not an abstract philosophical concept, but is in fact the experience of the human being demonstrating its potential through acting in the world, and that to act in such a way is to be authentic. As such, just as Heidegger would say that to be born or to die is not in itself "being" but a "leap into being," so we might say that the "true" leap of faith is fidelity to the coming-to-be of the *to be* event.

However, we have still not addressed how the *to be* event is able to surmount the "truth" found in compossibility in order to reveal the truth beyond truth itself. Once again we must return to the *to be* event, where, in terms expressed by Jean-Luc Nancy, the event is not only that which happens but that which "surprises," such that "the surprise of the event" is a tautology, because the event must surprise or it is not an event.[160] Nancy contrasts the eventfulness of the event (*das Geschehen*),[161] with the entelechy of the event, that is, the fully realized essence of the event.[162] In doing so, Nancy evokes Aristotle as well as Leibniz in order to make actual what was merely potential, and thus attaining the condition of fully realizing the possibility of one's own essence, where, in Heideggerian terms, the event is also a propriation in that it is an effort to save the sense of "own-ness." However, as we've noted, the truth can become a compossibility and thus loses it essentialness, such that, as Nancy argues, the event loses its surprise and then is no longer an event (a "happening"). In other words, if the *to be* event cannot be articulated without concealing its eventfulness, demanding, and here Nancy returns to Plato and Aristotle with their *topos* of "astonishment," where we (re)discover "simultaneously rapture and avowal of innocence," then the *to be* event "would set off the process of its auto-appropriation, that is, of its auto-resorption."[163]

The *to be* event is therefore linked to the action of self-presencing (self-determination, self-understanding) and to an action of self-similarity, or self-recognition, as found in the fractal network of the technology of reflection (*sensus communis*, communion, community). However, Nancy also recognizes that Hegel anticipated modern thought when he wrote that philosophy is "not meant to be a narration of happenings but a cognition of what is true in them, and further, on the basis of this cognition, to *comprehend* that which, in the narrative, appears as a mere happening [*événement*]."[164] This allows Nancy to interpret that the task of thinking must be to think the surprise of the event and therefore "be *thought surprised*."[165] If we return to the *to be* event and the "leap into being," we find that "thinking the leap can only be done by a leap of thought – by thought as a leap, as this leap that thought knows and senses itself necessarily to be."[166] In other words, the surprise is the leap, and the leap surprises itself: "It *is* surprised; inasmuch as it is surprised, it is."[167] Thus, Nancy acknowledges there is a "becoming-surprise of thought," which suggests the Deleuzian extension and intensities (the tension and extension of the leap in time and space, that surprises as intensities) and prehension (the surprise grasps hold of someone, appears where it is not), such that this prehension becomes the *self-enjoyment* of its own becoming, whereby the event/surprise is not recoverable in the existent, it is not gotten over, and that, Nancy concludes, is what it is to exist.

If we now return to the artificial-artistic creation and its struggle to apprehend the truth beyond truth itself, despite the fact that, in terms we've used earlier, its bonds are self-imposed through both form and interpretation, demanding it "frees itself from itself," thus demanding an aesthetic beyond the aesthetic itself, in other words, an aesthetic that is not restricted to the artificial and artistic "truth" of its own creation, but an aesthetic that escapes its own bonds in order to reveal the truth beyond truth itself through its own surprise/event, its *own* true leap of faith. Hence, in terms of the interpretation of the surprise/event, which is the very intervention that the artificial-artistic actual-virtual creation strives for, we might consider the psychoanalyst Wilfred Bion when he contends that the thing-in-itself can only be known through its sensory perception, and yet, to use our terms, the surprise/event within individual experience can only be known through its after-effects.[168]

In other words, if you think you are experiencing an aesthetic moment, then you are not, at least not anymore, because it is gone once you recognize it for what it is. Thus, the compossibility would come after the surprise/event that reveals itself from incompossibility through the creation. However, the (re)discovery of wonder and the process of its auto--appropriation or auto-resorption is to allow the event itself to serve as a kind of intervention, the recognition and self-enjoyment of its own becoming, such that the screen, or the artificial-artistic actual-virtual creation, is an encounter with action and perception, a self-sustained and self-sustaining compossibility within the fractal network of modern culture, and thus a threshold where one passes through the surprise/event.

Badiou makes the fundamental distinction between realizing a new possibility and creating a new possibility, such that to realize a possibility is to think that the possibility is there and one only needs to conceive the possibility (compossibility), whereas to create a new possibility is to invent a possibility where it did not exist before (surprise/event). In the same vein, Badiou would also state that "truths are eternal because they have been created and not because they have been here forever."[169] Nancy extends this insight when he claims that the surprise of the event necessitates that the *ex nihilo* event is non-present and therefore in "empty time," such that empty time is not a thing-in-itself, and where the leap of faith, the becoming-surprise of thought, is not the compossibility found in the creation of the world as the thought of God, but rather the self-presencing leap out of and into nothing, such that when the "true" leap of faith is fidelity to the coming-to-be of the *to be* event, then the "true" leap of faith is to leap where there is no hope or guarantee of recompense to that faith, and where thought can be thought without "God" and without a "creator." This would support the incompossibility where that which lies beyond the borders of compossibility, or that which is not a thing-in-itself, cannot be included in expressive units, even if their prehensive nature is attended by the surprise/event, as found in dissonance and divergent series, of folding and unfolding, whereby the process of creativity must be one of openness, a synthesis that at once affirms incompossibilities and yet passes *through* them.[170]

The intricacy of the event, therefore, contains the potentiality to initiate a new epoch of coming-to-be, a being-self that is precisely and appropriately revealed through the self-presencing of the self, and a new social reality that seeks the truth in truth itself, one that is the result of the questioning stance of genuine thinking. This stance also suggests a kind of active waiting until such time that we may answer the call into presencing, which Gunjević would describe as praying and watching,[171] or until such time, in Heidegger's terms, that the event reveals the essence of "the monstrousness that reigns,"[172] a monstrousness which suggests both the crisis in constitutive subjectivity and the critical state of modern society. However, to extend Nancy's proposal that the surprise/event is not recoverable in the existent, it is not gotten over, but that is what it is to exist, and if we also consider Badiou's claim that truths are eternal because they have been created, thereby containing, in Critchley's term, an ethics of truths, then we may look to the artificial-artistic creation itself as possessing the potentiality to aspire to the surprise/event of self-presencing. This is an event that demands fidelity not because it is making the truth that is the necessary lie, but because it is capable of rendering visible that which our social reality does not acknowledge as existing, which still must be a truth that we ourselves have created for ourselves, and, in recognizing it as such, perhaps reveal the truth of truth itself and so move toward the creation of true meaning, of separating chaos and cosmos, until such time, if ever, never, we understand what it is to be human. In the meantime, we persevere in our understanding of what it is to exist, and perhaps, as Badiou advocates, evoking Aristotle's enigmatic prescription, we should live "as an Immortal."[173] Of course, to live as an immortal is impossible with our mortal body, but conceivable for the soul if we lived with eternal truths, and those eternal truths may be found in the merely existent, which is not sterile, indeed it is essential to living our life.

Notes

1 Naomi Klein, *This Changes Everything: Capitalism vs. The Climate* (Toronto ON: Alfred A. Knopf Canada, 2014), p.62.
2 Benjamin, "The Work of Art in the Age of Its Technological Reproducibility: Second Version," p.122.
3 Benjamin, "Critique of Violence," p.252.
4 Ibid., p.252.
5 Rancière, "The Ethical Turn of Aesthetics and Politics," p.118.
6 Benjamin, "Critique of Violence p.252.
7 Hent de Vries, *Religion and Violence: Philosophical Perspectives from Kant to Derrida* (Baltimore MD: Johns Hopkins University Press, 2002), p.253.
8 See Benjamin, "The Task of the Translator," pp.253-263.
9 Buck-Morss, *The Origin of Negative Dialectics*, p.83.
10 De Vries, *Religion and Violence*, pp.254, 255.
11 Ibid., p.256. The quote is from Michel de Certeau, *Heterologies: Discourse on the Other*, translated by Brian Massumi (Minneapolis MI: University of Minnesota Press, 1986), p.88.
12 Ibid., p.257.
13 Ibid., p.259. The quote is from Ludwig Wittgenstein, *Tractatus Logico-Philosophicus* (New York: Cosimo, 2007), p.73.
14 Ibid., p.279.
15 Ibid., p.276.
16 Ibid., p.288.
17 Jacques Derrida, *Spectres of Marx: The State of the Debt, the Work of Mourning and the New International*, translated by Peggy Kamuf, with an Introduction by Bernd Magnus and Stephen Cullenberg (New York and London: Routledge, 2006), p.10.
18 Karl Marx, *The Eighteenth Brumaire of Louis Bonaparte*, translated by Daniel De Leon (Chicago IL: Charles H. Kerr & Company, 1914).
19 Jacques Derrida, "Spectres of Marx," *New Left Review*, No.205, May/June 1994, p.28. The title refers both to the ghosts that belong to Marx's legacy and to the ghosts with which he himself was haunted. The theme of spectrality appears in the opening sentence of the *Communist Manifesto* ("A specter is haunting Europe – the specter of communism"), and in the *Eighteenth Brumaire of Louis Bonaparte*, where Marx writes, "The tradition of all dead generations weighs like a nightmare on the brain of the living." Marx also characterizes commodity fetishism as a kind of "phantomalization" of things. Jacques Derrida, *Spectres of Marx: The State of the Debt, the Work of Mourning and the New International*, translated by Peggy Kamuf, with an Introduction by Bernd Magnus and Stephen Cullenberg (New York and London: Routledge, 2006), pp.4, 108, 159. See also Karl Marx, *The Eighteenth Brumaire of Louis Bonaparte*, translated by Daniel De Leon (Chicago IL: Charles H. Kerr & Company, 1914).
20 De Vries, *Religion and Violence*, pp.291, 292.
21 Ibid., p.299. See also Jacques Derrida, *Of Hospitality: Anne Dufourmantelle invites Jacques Derrida to respond*, translated by Rachel Bowlby (Stanford CA: Stanford University Press, 2000), p.71.
22 Ibid., p.299.
23 Ibid., p.377.
24 Ibid., p.366.
25 Jay, *Downcast Eyes*, p.593.
26 Ibid., p.398.
27 Critchley, "Violent Thoughts," p.3. An example of mythic violence is the story of Niobe. Niobe boasted of her superiority to Leto because she had fourteen children, seven male and seven female, while Leto had only two, Apollo and Artemis. Apollo would kill all of Niobe's sons, and Artemis all the daughters. A devastated Niobe turned into stone as she wept. See the painting of *Artemis and Apollo Piercing Niobe's Children with their Arrows* (Jacques-Louis David 1772).

28 Ibid., p.4. See also Critchley. *The Faith of the Faithless*, p.243.
29 Critchley, *The Faith of the Faithless*, p.243.
30 Critchley, "Violent Thoughts," p.5.
31 Agamben, *State of Exception*, p.88.
32 Critchley, "Violent Thoughts," p.3. The term is also used by Judith Butler in "Critique, Coercion, and Sacred Life in Benjamin's 'Critique of Violence,'" Political Theologies: Public Relations in a Post-Secular World, edited by Hent de Vries and Lawrence Sullivan (New York: Fordham University Press, 2006), pp.201-219.
33 Critchley, *Infinitely Demanding*, p.113.
34 Ibid., pp.113, 114.
35 Ibid., p.130. See also Alain Badiou, *Metapolitics* (London and New York: Verso, 2005).
36 Adorno, "Negative Dialectics and the Possibility of Philosophy," p.77.
37 Ibid., p.71.
38 Ibid., p.72.
39 Critchley, *Infinitely Demanding*, p.122.
40 Judith Butler, "From Performativity to Precarity," Lecture given at *Universidad Complutense de Madrid*, June 8, 2009, p.ii. [On-line]. Butler writes, "Precarity" designates that politically induced condition in which certain populations suffer from failing social and economic networks of support and become differentially exposed to injury, violence, and death. Such populations are at heightened risk of disease, poverty, starvation, displacement, and of exposure to violence without protection. Precarity also characterizes that politically induced condition of maximized vulnerability and exposure for populations exposed to arbitrary state violence and to other forms of aggression that are not enacted by states and against which states do not offer adequate protection. So by precarity we may be talking about populations that starve or who near starvation, but we might also be talking about sex workers who have to defend themselves against both street violence and police harassment." Judith Butler, "From Performativity to Precarity," Lecture given at *Universidad Complutense de Madrid*, June 8, 2009, p.ii.
41 Judith Butler, "Bodies in Alliance and the Politics of the Street," Lecture notes, Peter Wall Institute for Advanced Studies, Vogue Theatre, Vancouver BC, May 24, 2012, p.3. [On-line].
42 Ibid., p.8.
43 Ibid., p.9.
44 Kearney, *Poetics of Imagining*, p.97.
45 Ibid., p.101. The quote is from M. Préclaire, *Une Poétique de l'homme* (Montréal QC: Bellarmin, 1971). See also Gaston Bachelard, *The Poetics of Space*, (*La Poétique de l'espace*, 1958), translated by M. Jolas (Boston MA: Beacon Press, 1969).
46 Jay, *Downcast Eyes*, p.551.
47 Gaston Bachelard, *Water and Dreams: An Essay on the Imagination of Water*, translated from the French by Edith R. Farrell (Dallas TX: The Dallas Institute of Humanities and Culture, 1982), p.17.
48 Ibid., p.16.
49 Jacques Derrida, *Of Hospitality: Anne Dufourmantelle invites Jacques Derrida to respond*, translated by Rachel Bowlby (Stanford CA: Stanford University Press, 2000), p.135.
50 Steiner, *Heidegger*, p.71. Heidegger escaped to Die Hütte, a cottage in the Black Forest countryside near Todtnauberg, Germany.
51 Rancière, *The Future of the Image*, p.53.
52 Ibid., p.49.
53 Adorno, "Negative Dialectics and the Possibility of Philosophy," p.62. Adorno refers to "autarky," in the sense of self-sufficiency, as "Philosophical reflection makes sure of the nonconceptual in the concept. It would be empty otherwise, according to Kant's dictum; in the end, having ceased to be a concept of anything at all, it would be nothing. A philosophy that lets us know this, that extinguishes the autarky of the concept, strips the blindfold from our eyes." Ibid., p.62.
54 Rancière, *The Emancipated Spectator*, p.63.

55 Ibid., pp.70, 72.
56 Ibid., pp.66, 73.
57 Ibid., p.76.
58 Ibid., p.88.
59 Ibid., p.66.
60 Rancière refers to Jean-Luc Godard when he sought the restoration of cinema to its original potentiality by way of using another art, in effect "two cinemas," whereby, "the corpus of cinematographic works and the body of a fictional cinema that oversteps the corpus of works produced by that medium and can only be displayed by the means of another medium and another art." Because cinema has sacrificed the fraternity of metaphors to the business of stories, Godard does what cinema itself has not done, detaching metaphors from story in order to fashion a different "history'" and a cinema that has not existed. Rancière, *The Emancipated Spectator*, pp.68, 130.
61 Ibid., pp.60-61.
62 Benjamin, "The Work of Art in the Age of Its Technological Reproducibility: Second Version," p.122.
63 Rancière, *The Emancipated Spectator*, p.74.
64 Ibid., p.73.
65 Deleuze and Guattari, *A Thousand Plateaus*, p.23.
66 Badiou, "Art and Philosophy," p.7.
67 Ibid., p.3.
68 Freud, *Civilization and Its Discontents*, p.17. According to Freud, there are three sources of our suffering: the superior power of nature, the frailty of our bodies, and the inadequacy of the institutions that regulate people's relations with one another in the family, the state and society. And there are three kinds of distractions from reality: powerful distractions, substitutive satisfactions, and intoxicants. Freud, *Civilization and Its Discontents*, p.24.
69 Adorno, "Negative Dialectics and the Possibility of Philosophy," pp.54-55, 57.
70 Cutrofello, *Continental Philosophy*, p.118. The quote is from Kant, "Metaphysics of Morals," p.597. Stoicism was one of the new philosophical movements of the Hellenistic period. The name derives from the porch (*stoa poikilê*) in the Agora at Athens decorated with mural paintings, where the members of the school congregated, and their lectures were held. Unlike the term "epicurean," which is misleading in that it advocates luxury and the more exalted pleasures in life but perhaps not the simple life as advocated by Epicurus. The Stoics held that emotions like fear or envy (or impassioned sexual attachments, or passionate love of anything whatsoever) either were, or arose from, false judgements and that the sage - a person who had attained moral and intellectual perfection - would not undergo them. See Marion Durand, Simon Shogry, and Dirk Baltzly, "Stoicism," *The Stanford Encyclopedia of Philosophy*, Edward N. Zalta and Uri Nodelman (eds.) (Spring 2023 edition). [Online]
71 Jacques Rancière, "The Distribution of the Sensible." *The Politics of Aesthetics: The Distribution of the Sensible*, translated and with an Introduction by Gabriel Rockhill (New York: Continuum, 2004), p.22.
72 Jacques Rancière, "On Art and Work," *The Politics of Aesthetics: The Distribution of the Sensible*, translated and with an Introduction by Gabriel Rockhill (New York: Continuum, 2004), p.44. Rancière mentions, "the Flaubertian aesthete is a pebble breaker" and "the redistribution of the sensible" during the Russian Revolution. Rancière, "On Art and Work," p.45. In opposition to Romanticism would be Realism, where work would be respected, such as the paintings of Gustave Courbet (1819-1877), in particular *The Stone Breakers* (1850), that promote an ideology of objective reality and a revolt against the exaggerated emotionalism of the Romantic movement. In cinema, this objective realism may be found in the films of the Italian Neorealists (1946-1958), the work of Satyajit Ray, in particular the Apu trilogy (1950s), *Tokyo Story* (Yasujirô Ozu 1953), and the films of Ousmane Sembène, such as *Black Girl* (1966).
73 Ibid., p.45.

74 Rancière, "The Distribution of the Sensible," pp.20-23.
75 Ibid., p.26.
76 Deleuze, *Cinema 1: The Movement-Image*, p.xi.
77 Cutrofello, *Continental Philosophy*, p.37.
78 Buck-Morss, *Thinking Past Terror*, p.73.
79 Bergson, *Matter and Memory*, p.182.
80 Ibid., p.7.
81 Cutrofello, *Continental Philosophy*, p.301. See also Paul Ricoeur, *The Conflict of Interpretations: Essays in Hermeneutics*, edited by Don Ihde (Evanston IL: Northwestern University Press, 1974), p.176.
82 Michel Foucault, *The Archaeology of Knowledge*, translated by A.M. Sheridan Smith (New York: Routledge Classics, 2002), p.7.
83 Foucault, *Madness and Civilization*, p.xi.
84 Cutrofello, *Continental Philosophy*, p.302. See also Ricoeur, *The Conflict of Interpretations*, p.423.
85 Ibid., p.300.
86 Rancière, *The Emancipated Spectator*, p.110.
87 Ibid., pp.123-124, 126. Rancière offers the example of the Iranian filmmaker Abbas Kiarostami, whose work is poised between cinema, photography and poetry. Kiarostami said, "when we reveal a film's world to members of an audience, they each learn to create their own world through the wealth of their own experience. As a filmmaker, I rely on this creative intervention for, otherwise, the film and the audience will die together." Abbas Kiarostami, *An Unfinished Cinema*, written for the Centenary of Cinema, Paris, 1995. See also Jean-Luc Nancy, *Abbas Kiarostami: The Evidence of Film*, translated by Christine Irizzary and Verena Andermat Conley (Brussells: Yves Gevaert Publisher, 2001).
88 Ibid., pp.122-123, 127.
89 Ibid., pp.123-124.
90 Lyotard, *The Differend*, p.13.
91 Deleuze, *Cinema 1: The Movement-Image*, pp.3-8, 111-122
92 Paul Leduc, "Dinosaurs and Lizards," *New Latin American Cinema: Theory, Practices, and Transcontinental Articulations- Volume 1*, edited by Michael T. Martin (Detroit MI: Wayne State University Press, 1997), p.59. The "cinema of salamanders" also suggests "liberation theology," which emerged from Latin America in the 1980s. Liberation theology seeks a redefinition of "truth" in terms of a genealogy of oppression and liberation, particularly among the colonized nations, and thus offers a more revolutionary aspect to theological debate in that it is "an interpretation of scriptural traditions (and thus of human being, of history, and of political structures) by those who have not yet named the world – the marginal, the silenced, the defeated." Sharon Welch, "Dangerous Memory and Alternate Knowledges," *On Violence: A Reader*, Bruce B. Lawrence and Aisha Karim (Editors) (Durham NC and London: Duke University Press, 2007), p.365.
93 Deleuze, *The Fold*, p.104.
94 Cutrofello, *Continental Philosophy*, p.10.
95 Ibid., p.38. The quote is from Nietzsche, *The Birth of Tragedy*, p.5.
96 Ibid., p.38.
97 Deleuze, *The Fold*, p.107.
98 Binary Code was first introduced by Gottfried Wilhelm Leibniz (1646-1716), who was trying to find a system that converts logic's verbal statements into a pure mathematical one (although binary numbers were first described in *Chandashutram* written in 100 BCE by Pingala, who had a similar goal). After his ideas were ignored, Leibniz came across the classic Chinese text *I Ching* or *Book of Changes* (300 BCE), which used a type of binary code. A set of oracular statements represented by 64 sets of six lines each called *hexagrams*. Each hexagram is a figure composed of six stacked horizontal lines; each line is either *Yang* (an unbroken, or solid line), or *Yin* (broken, an open line with a gap in the center). With six such lines stacked from bottom to top, there are 26 or 64 possible combina-

tions, and thus 64 hexagrams represented. Although simple in form, they allowed for enormous complexity in terms of their comprehension. In his *Explication de l'Arithmétique Binaire* (1703), Leibniz used the hexagrams as a base for claiming the universality of the binary numeral system. He takes the layout of the combinatorial exercise found in the hexagrams to represent binary sequences, so that ¦¦¦¦¦¦ would correspond to the binary sequence 000000 and ¦¦¦¦¦| would be 000001, and so forth, thus creating a system consisting of rows of zeroes and ones, the precursor of computer language. See Brandon C. Look, "Gottfried Wilhelm Leibniz", *The Stanford Encyclopedia of Philosophy* (Spring 2020 Edition), Edward N. Zalta (ed.). [Online] See also (and hear) *Music of Changes* (John Cage 1951), based on the *I Ching*, and very difficult to perform, but proving, Cage has said, that "the impossible is not impossible." John Cage, "Lecture on Nothing" (1951), *Silence: Lectures and Writings* (Middletown CT: Wesleyan University Press, 1961).

99 Ibid., p.129.

100 A quote from Albert Einstein: "The most incomprehensible thing about the universe is that it is comprehensible." Robert Osserman, *Poetry of the Universe – A Mathematical Exploration of the Cosmos* (New York: Anchor Books, 1995), p.142. We might ask if it is not the other way around, that which is most comprehensible about the universe is that it is incomprehensible.

101 Mirzoeff, *An Introduction to Visual Culture*, p.25. The term "fractals" was coined by Benoit Mandelbrot (1924-2010) in *The Fractal Geometry of Nature* (1977), derived from the Latin *fractus* meaning "broken" or "fractured." See Osserman, *Poetry of the Universe*, p.159.

102 Ibid., p.25.

103 Richard Mankiewicz, *The Story of Mathematics* (London: Cassell & Co., 2000), p.182.

104 Ian Stewart, *Nature's Numbers – The Unreal Reality of Mathematics* (New York: Harper Collins, 1995), p.48.

105 Ibid., p.3. See also Susan Hayward, *Cinema Studies: The Key Concepts* (New York: Routledge, 2013).

106 The classic version of the "framing story" is found in *One Thousand and One Nights* (or *Arabian Nights*) where Scheherazade narrates a set of tales (most often fairy tales) to the Sultan Shahriyar over many nights - an early example of the "story within a story within a story" device. In most of Scheherazade's narrations there are also stories narrated, and even in some of these, there are some other stories. For example, "Sinbad the Sailor" is narrated by Scheherazade, yet within the story itself, the protagonist Sinbad the Sailor narrates the stories of his seven voyages to Sinbad the Porter. In film, the "framing story" is found in *Das Kabinett des Dr. Caligari* (Robert Wiene 1920), as well as the French New Wave (1950s) technique of showing film equipment within the frame, or the breaking of the "fourth-wall," where the actor addresses the audience directly, such as *Annie Hall* (Woody Allen 1977) and *Funny Games* (Michael Haneke 1997), and the "dream-within-a-dream" or "reality-within-another reality" can be found in *The Matrix* (Andy Wachowski and Lana Wachowski 1999) and *Inception* (Christopher Nolan 2010).

107 Elsaesser and Hagner, *Film Theory*, p.56.

108 Deleuze and Guattari, *Anti-Oedipus*, p.76.

109 Ibid., p.77.

110 Ibid., p.77.

111 Alfred North Whitehead (1861-1947) held metaphysical views that were called "process philosophy," which appeals to process (becoming) over substance (being). Similarly, "process theology" does not deny that God is in some respects eternal, immutable, and impassible, but it also contradicts the classical view by insisting that God is in some respects temporal, mutable, and passible. See Alfred North Whitehead, *The Concept of Nature* (Cambridge UK: Cambridge University Press, 1920).

112 Deleuze, *The Fold*, p.78.

113 Ibid., p.78.

114 Ibid., p.79.

115 Ibid., p.79.

116 Ibid., p.80.
117 Ibid., p.81.
118 Ibid., p.82. For example, the concept of Chaosmos is explored in the experimental writing style used by James Joyce in *Finnegans Wake* (1939) where he develops the polarity between disorder and order, liberty and rules, Chaos and Cosmos. See Umberto Eco and Ellen Esroc, *The Aesthetics of Chaosmos: The Middle Ages of James Joyce* (Cambridge MA: Harvard University Press, 1989).
119 Badiou, *Logics of Worlds: Being and Event, 2*, p.385.
120 Ibid., p.385.
121 Badiou, *Logics of Worlds: Being and Event, 2*, p.386.
122 Ibid., p.387.
123 Hiebert, "The Lacanian Conspiracy," p.5.
124 Michel Foucault, "What Is an Author?" The Foucault Reader, edited by Paul Rabinow (London: Penguin Books, 1984), p.119.
125 Hiebert, "The Lacanian Conspiracy,"p.2. The definition is from N. Katherine Hayles, *How We Became Posthuman: Virtual Bodies in Cybernetics, Literature, and Informatics* (Chicago IL: University of Chicago Press, 1999), p.4.
126 Ibid., p.4.
127 Ibid., p.4. See also Paul Virilio, *The Vision Machine*, translated by Julie Rose (Bloomington IN: Indiana University Press, 1994), p.59
128 Virilio, *The Vision Machine*, pp.75-76.
129 Kracauer, *The Mass Ornament*, p.152.
130 Ibid., p.152.
131 Ibid., p.154. Kracauer refers to the Golem, which "is annihilated if one removes from his mouth the sheet on which the life-giving formula is written, so too the group will expire if one separates it from the idea to which it owes its existence." Kracauer, *The Mass Ornament*, p.154. The Golem refers to the Jewish legend or folktale where a huge manmade effigy of lime or clay came to life by means of a sacred word. The story was recorded by the Brothers Grimm in 1808. Ibid., p.263*n*2. This suggests the interest in "soulessness" that would inspire other Borks such as Frankenstein and Dracula, as well as stories by E.T.A. Hoffman, Oscar Wilde and Edgar Allen Poe. In cinema, *The Student from Prague* (*Der Student von Prague*, Stellan Rye 1913) dealt with a similar idea, the dopplelgänger, where a student sells his soul to a sorcerer. While working on the film, German actor and director Paul Wegener (1874-1948) learned about the legend of the Golem. With writer Henrik Galeen, he made three film versions of the story, *The Golem* (1915, now lost), followed by a parody called *Der Golem und die Tänzerin*, and then a reworking of the original in *The Golem: How He Came into the World* (1920) which stands as one of the classics of early German cinema.
132 Ibid., pp.152-153.
133 Henry A. Giroux, "What Might Education Mean After Abu Ghraib: Revisiting Adorno's Politics of Education," *Comparative Studies of South Asia, Africa and the Middle East*, Vol. 24:1 (2004), p.13.
134 Ibid., p.11.
135 Ibid., p.14.
136 Ibid., p.21. The Abu Ghraib prison ("Place of Ravens"), also known as the Baghdad Central Prison, was built near Baghdad, Iraq by British contractors in the 1950s. In 2001, it was estimated to hold about 15,000 inmates. In 2002, Saddam Hussein added six new cellblocks. In October 2002, he gave amnesty to most prisoners in Iraq, and the now empty prison was vandalized and looted. After the US-led Iraq Invasion of 2003, the prison was used by both US forces and the Iraqui government. From late 2003 to early 2004, during the Iraq War, military police personnel of the US Army and the CIA committed human rights violations against prisoners, including physical and sexual abuse, torture, rape, sodomy, and death.
137 Kracauer, *The Mass Ornament*, p.334.
138 Ibid., p.334.
139 Rancière, *The Future of the Image*, p.23.

140 Sloterdijk, *Critque of Cynical Reason*, p.5.
141 Ibid., pp.59-60.
142 Ibid., p.60.
143 Ibid., p.82.
144 Ibid., p.88.
145 Jay, *Downcast Eyes*, p.592.
146 Sloterdijk, *Critque of Cynical Reason*, p.74.
147 The ancient Greek theatre recognized three distinct genres: Tragedy, Comedy, and Satyr. An example of tragedy would be *Antigonê* (Sophocles 442 BCE), of comedy, *Lysistrata* (Aristophanes 411 BCE), and of satyr, *Cyclops* (Euripides c. 430 BCE), a kind of tragi-comic burlesque, which is the only complete surviving satyr play that has survived.
148 In the afterword to Lyotard and Thebaud's *Just Gaming*, Sam Weber writes that Miltiades, the Greek general won the battle of Marathon (490 BC) despite being heavily outnumbered by the Persians (also, the commander who sent the day-runner to bring news of victory to Athens, hence a 'marathon runner'). But Miltiades became the "envy of the gods" and so the gods set out to destroy him, leading to his downfall, because he had been seduced and called attention to himself through a deed of *hybris* (excessiveness). Sam Weber, "Afterword: Literature – Just Making It," translated by Brian Massumi, in *Just Gaming*, Jean-François Lyotard and Jean-Loup Thebaud, translated by Wlad Godzich (Minneapolis MI: University of Minnesota Press, 2008), p.107.
149 See Henri Bergson, *Laughter*, translated by Drew Burk (New York: Atropos Press, 2009).
150 Sloterdijk, *Critque of Cynical Reason*, p.74.
151 Critchley, "On the Ethics of Alain Badiou," pp.232-233.
152 Ibid., p.234.
153 Critchley, *The Faith of the Faithless*, p.160. The quote is from Second Corinthians 12:10. Also note, "And he said unto me, My grace is sufficient for thee: for my strength is made perfect in weakness. Most gladly therefore will I rather glory in my infirmities, that the power of Christ may rest upon me." Second Corinthians 12:9 (King James Version).
154 Critchley, *Very Little... Almost Nothing*, p.27.
155 Jay, *Downcast Eyes*, p.556. The quote is from Levinas, *Totality and Infinity*, p.130.
156 Anika Thiem, *Unbecoming Subjects: Judith Butler, Moral Philosophy, and Critical Responsibility* (New York: Fordham University Press, 2008), p.248.
157 Ibid., p.249.
158 Badiou, *Logics of Worlds: Being and Event, 2*, p.38. In the 5th century BCE, in *On Nature*, Parmenides wrote, "For never shall this prevail, that things that are not are." See John Palmer, "Parmenides", *The Stanford Encyclopedia of Philosophy* (Winter 2020 Edition), Edward N. Zalta (ed.). [Online]
159 Lyotard, *The Differend*, p.13.
160 Jean-Luc Nancy, "The Surprise of the Event," translated by Lynn Festa and Stuart Barnett, *Hegel After Derrida*, edited by Stuart Barnett (London and New York: Routledge, 1998), p.97.
161 "The semantic origins and usage of the word *Geschehen* refer us less to process and what is produced than to the movment and the leap, to precipitation and suddenness. (Incidentally, and in contrast with the French '*événement*,' *Geschehen* does not have the sense of 'remarkable event,' for which there are other terms in German, such as the similar *Geschehnis*. The small difference between the two reveals all the more the verbal, active, mobile character of *Geschehen*.)" Jean-Luc Nancy, "The Surprise of the Event," p.94.
162 Entelechy, from the Greek *entelécheia*, is a term coined by Aristotle and then transliterated in Latin as *entelechia*. Aristotle invented the word by combining *entelēs* (complete, full-grown) with *echein* (also, *hexis*, to be a certain way by the continuing effort of holding on in that condition), while at the same time punning on *endelecheia* (persistence) by inserting *telos* (completion). According to Joe Sachs,

this is "a three-ring circus of a word," at the heart of everything in Aristotle's thinking, including the definition of motion. Sachs therefore proposed a complex neologism of his own, "being-at-work-staying-the-same." Joe Sachs, "Aristotle: Motion and its Place in Nature," *Internet Encyclopedia of Philosophy*, 2005. Leibniz, like Aristotle, understood entelechies as a metaphysical law, important not only for physics, but also for understanding life and the soul, where the soul, or spirit, can be understood as a type of entelechy (or living monad) which has distinct perceptions and memory. Leibniz writes, "the entelechy of Aristotle which has made so much noise, is nothing else but force or activity; that is, a state from which action naturally flows if nothing hinders it." Gottfried Wilhelm Leibniz, "On the Doctrine of Malebranche. A Letter to M. Remond de Montmort, containing Remarks on the Book of Father Tertre against Father Malebranche" (1715), *The Philosophical Works of Leibnitz* (New Haven CT: Tuttle, Morehouse, and Taylor, 1820), p.234. In terms of our earlier references to flux and flow, it is interesting to note Johann Hari in his book, *Stolen Focus: Why You Can't Pay Attention – and How to Think Deeply Again*, refers to flow and fragmentation. Fragmentation in thinking is due to "technological distraction" and the increase in speed, switching and filtering in a screen-obsessed world. For example, the average American college student switches tasks every 65 seconds. The average time on any given subject is 19 seconds. Flow, on the other hand, such as the making of art, takes time, reflection and mono-tasking. Flow is accomplished by doing something meaningful to you.

163 Nancy, "The Surprise of the Event," p.96. Auto-resorption is the sense of rebuilding oneself, or dissolving of one's self in order to build it again.

164 Ibid., p.91.

165 Ibid., p.96.

166 Ibid., p.101.

167 Ibid., p.102.

168 Mary Jacobus, *The Poetics of Psychoanalysis* (Oxford UK: Oxford University Press, 2005), pp.247,251-252. See also Nicky Glover, *Psychoanalytic Aesthetics: An Introduction to the British School* (London: Karnac Books, 2009). Wilfred Bion (1897-1979) studied with Melanie Klein (1882-1960), both of whom did work in "object relations theory" and "projective identification." During the 1950s and 1960s, Bion transformed Klein's theories of infantile phantasy by developing an epistemological "theory of thinking" of his own. For Bion, the foundation for both mental development and truth is emotional experience. See Donald Meltzer, *Studies in Extended Metapsychology: Clinical Applications of Bion's Ideas* (Perthshire UK: Clunie Press, 1986).

169 Badiou, *Logics of Worlds: Being and Event, 2*, p.512,

170 Nancy, "The Surprise of the Event," pp.103-104.

171 Boris Gunjević, "Pray and Watch – The Messianic Subversion," *God in Pain: Inversions of Apocalypse* (New York: Seven Stories Press, 2012), p.241.

172 Heidegger, "The Question Concerning Technology," p.16.

173 Badiou, *Logics of Worlds: Being and Event, 2*, p.507.

References

A

Adorno, Theodor W. Aesthetic Theory. Gretel Adorno and Rolf Tiedemann, editors. Newly translated, edited and with a translator's introduction by Robert Hullot-Kentor. Minneapolis MN: University of Minnesota Press, 1997.

---. In Search of Wagner. Translated by Rodney Livingstone. London: Verso Books, 1985.

---. Prisms. Translated by Samuel and Sherry Weber. London: Neville Spearman, 1967.

---. Minima Moralia: Reflections from Damaged Life. Translated from the German by E.F.N. Jephcott. London: Verso, 2005. (Originally published in 1951).

---. Negative Dialectics. Translated by E.B. Ashton. New York: Routledge, 1973.

---. "Education After Auschwitz." (1966). Critical Models: Interventions and Catchwords. New York: Columbia University Press, 1998.

---. "On The Fetish-Character in Music and the Regression of Listening." Popular Music: Cultural Concepts in Media and Cultural Studies. Edited by Simon Frith. London: Routledge, 2004.

---. Philosophy of Music. (First published in the U.K. in 1973.) London: Sheed & Ward, 1987.

---. The Adorno Reader. Edited by Brian O'Connor. Malden MA: Blackwell Publishing, 2000.

---. "Commitment." Aesthetics and Politics. With presentations by Rodney Livingstone, Perry Anderson and Francis Mulhern. Afterword by Fredric Jameson. London: Verso, 1980. Pgs. 177-195.

---. "Reconciliation under Duress." Aesthetics and Politics. With presentations by Rodney Livingstone, Perry Anderson and Francis Mulhern. Afterword by Fredric Jameson. London: Verso, 1980. Pgs. 151-176.

---. Notes to Literature Volume One. Edited by Rolf Tiedemann. Translated by Shierry Weber Nicholsen. New York: Columbia University Press, 1991.

---. *Notes to Literature Volume Two.* Edited by Rolf Tiedemann. Translated by Shierry Weber Nicholsen. New York: Columbia University Press, 1992.

---. "The Essay as Form." Translated by Robert Hullot-Kentor and Frederic Will. *New German Critique*, No. 32. (Spring - Summer, 1984), pp.151-171.

---. "Letters to Walter Benjamin." *Aesthetics and Politics*. With presentations by Rodney Livingstone, Perry Anderson and Francis Mulhern. Afterword by Fredric Jameson. Translation editor: Ronald Taylor. London: Verso Books, 1980. Pgs. 110-133.

---. *Quasi una fantasia: Essays on Modern Music*. Translated by Rodney Livingstone. (First published by Suhrkamp Verlag 1963). London and New York: Verso, 1992.

---. *Prisms*. Translated by Samuel and Sheirry Weber (Cambridge MA: The MIT Press, 1981.

Adorno, Theodor W. and Walter Benjamin. *The Complete Correspondence 1928-1940*. Edited by Henri Lonitz. Translated by Nicholas Walker. Cambridge MA: Polity Press, 1999.

Agamben, Giorgio. *Homo Sacer: Sovereign Power and Bare Life*. Translated by Daniel Heller-Roazen. Edited by Werner Hamacher and David E. Wellbery. Stanford CA: Stanford University Press, 1998.

---. *Nudities*. Translated by David Kishik and Stefan Pedatella. Edited by Werner Hamacher. Stanford CA: Stanford University Press, 2011.

---. *State of Exception*. Translated by Kevin Attell. Chicago IL: The University of Chicago Press, 2005.

---. *What is an Apparatus?* Stanford CA: Stanford University Press, 2009.

---. *The Highest Poverty: Monastic Rules and Form-of-Life*. Translated by Adam Kotsko. Palo Alto CA: Stanford University Press, 2013.

---. *The Coming Community* (Theory Out of Bounds, Volume 1). Translated by Michael Hardt. Minneapolis MI: University of Minnesota Press, 1993.

---. *The Time That Remains*. Translated by Patricia Dailey. Stanford CA: Stanford University Press, 2005.

---. *Remnants of Auschwitz: The Witness and the Archive*. New York: Zone Books, 2002.

Aitken, Ian. *European Film Theory and Criticism: A Critical Introduction*. Bloomington IN: Indiana University Press, 2001.

Alberti, Leon Battista. *On Painting* (*De pictura*, 1435) Translated with Introduction and Notes by John R. Spencer. New Haven CT: Yale University Press, 1966.

Althusser, Louis. "Ideology and Ideological State Apparatuses (Notes Towards An Investigation." *Media and Cultural Studies: Keyworks*. Edited by Meenakshi Gigi Durham and Douglas M. Kellner. Malden MA: Blackwell Publishing, 2006. Pgs. 79-87.

---. *Lenin and Philosophy and Other Essays*. Translated by Ben Brewster. New York: Monthly Review Press, 1971.

Anagnostopoulos, Georgios (Editor). *A Companion to Aristotle*. Malden MA: Wiley--Blackwell, 2009.

Anderson, Joseph and Barbara. "The Myth of Persistence of Vision Revisited." *Journal of Film and Video*. Vol. 45, No. 1 (Spring 1993). Pgs. 3-12.

Andrew, J. Dudley. *The Major Film Theories: An Introduction*. London and New York: Oxford University Press, 1976.

Arendt, Hannah. *On Revolution*. New York: Penguin Books, 1965.

---. "Introduction." *Illuminations*. Walter Benjamin. Edited and with an Introduction by Hannah Arendt. Translated by Harry Zohn. New York: Harcourt, Brace & World, 1968.

---. *Eichmann in Jerusalem: A Report on the Banality of Evil*. New York: Penguin Books, 1994.

---. *The Human Condition*. Chicago IL: The University of Chicago Press, 1998.

---. *On Violence*. New York: Harcourt, Brace, Jovanovich, 1970.

Aristotle. *The Complete Works of Aristotle: The Revised Oxford Translation – Volumes I and II*. Edited by Jonathan Barnes. Princeton NJ: Princeton University Press, 1984.

---. *A Companion to Aristotle*. Edited by Georgios Anagnostopoulos. Malden MA: Blackwell Publishing, 2009.

---. *Poetics*. General editor Stanley Applebaum. Editor of this edition Richard Koss. New York: Dover Publications, 1997.

Armstrong, Karen. *A History of God: The 4000-Year Quest of Judaism, Christianity and Islam*. New York: Ballantine Books, 1993.

---. *The Lost Art of Scripture: Rescuing the Sacred Texts.* New York and Toronto: Alfred A. Knopf, 2019.

Arnheim, Rudolf. *Film As Art.* Berkeley CA: University of California Press, 1957.

Aronson, Ronald. *Camus and Sartre: The Story of a Friendship and the Quarrel that Ended It.* Chicago IL: The University of Chicago Press, 2004.

Ashton, Dore. *The New York School: A Cultural Reckoning.* New York: Penguin, 1972.

Artaud, Antonin. *The Theatre and its Double.* Translated by Mary Richards. New York: Grove Press, 1994.

Atwood, Margaret. *Survival: A Thematic Guide to Canadian Literature.* Toronto ON: Anansi Books, 1972.

---. *The Handmaid's Tale.* Toronto ON: McClelland & Stewart, 1985.

Auerbach, Erich. *Mimesis – The Representation of Reality in Western Literature.* Translated from the German by Willard R. Trask. With a new introduction by Edward W. Said (2003). Princeton NJ: Princeton University Press, 2003.

---. "Realism in Madame Bovary" in *Madame Bovary* by Gustave Flaubert. Edited and with an Introduction by Leo Bersani. New York: Bantam Books, October 1976. Pgs. 372-382.

Augé, Marc. *Non-Places: Introduction to an Anthropology of Supermodernity.* London and New York: Verso, 1995.

B

Bachelard, Gaston. *The Poetics of Space.* (*La Poétique de l'espace,* 1958) Translated by Maria Jolas. With a new Foreward by John R. Stilgoe. Boston MA: Beacon Press, 1994.

---. *The Poetics of Reverie: Childhood, Language, and the Cosmos* [1960]. Translated from the French by Daniel Russell. Boston MA: Beacon Press, 1971.

---. *Water and Dreams: An Essay on the Imagination of Water.* Translated from the French by Edith R. Farrell. Dallas TX: The Dallas Institute of Humanities and Culture, 1982.

Badiou, Alain. *Manifesto of Philosophy: Followed by Two Essays "The (Re) Turn of Philosophy Itself" and "Definition of Philosophy."* Translated, Edited and with an Introduction by Norman Madarasz. Albany NY: State University of New York Press, 1999.

---. *Being and Event.* Translated by Oliver Feltham. London: Continuum, 2005.

---. *Logics of Worlds: Being and Event, 2.* Translated by Alberto Toscano. London: Continuum, 2009.

---. *Saint Paul: The Foundation of Universalism.* Translated by Ray Brassier. Palo Alto CA: Stanford University Press, 2003.

---. "Fifteen Theses on Contemporary Art." (2003)

---. *Handbook of Inaesthetics.* Translated by Albert Toscano. Stanford CA: Stanford University Press, 2005.

---. *Cinema.* Texts selected and introduced by Antoine de Baecque. Translated by Susan Spitzer. Cambridge UK: Polity Press, 2013.

Bagdikian, Ben H. *The New Media Monopoly.* Boston MA: Beacon Press, 2004.

Bakhtin, Mikhail. "Discourse in the Novel." *The Dialogic Imagination – Four Essays by M.M. Bakhtin.* Edited by Michael Holquist. Translated by Caryl Emerson and Michael Holquist. Austin TX: University of Texas Press, 1981.

Balázs, Béla. *Theory of the Film: Character and Growth of a New Art.* Translated by Edith Bone. London: Dobson, 1952.

Barnett, Stuart. "Eating My God." *Hegel After Derrida.* Edited by Stuart Barnett. London and New York: Routledge, 1998. Pgs. 131-144.

Barthes, Roland. "(i) Operation Margarine; (ii) Myth Today." *Media and Cultural Studies: Keyworks.* Edited by Meenakshi Gigi Durham and Douglas M. Kellner. Malden MA: Blackwell Publishing, 2006. Pgs. 99-106.

---. *Mythologies.* Selected and translated from the French by Annette Lavers. New York: Hill and Wang, 1987.

---. *Camera Lucida – Reflections on Photography.* Translated from the French by Richard Howard. New York: Hill and Wang, 2010.

---. "The Death of the Author." *Continental Aesthetics: Romanticism to Postmodernism: An Anthology.* Edited by Richard Kearney and David Rasmussen. Malden MA: Blackwell Publishers, 2001.

---. *Image-Music-Text.* Translated by Stephen Heath. New York: Hill & Wang, 1977.

Bataille, Georges. *Visions of Excess: Selected Writings, 1927-1939.* Edited by Allan Stoekl. Translated by Allan Stoekl with Carl R. Lovitt and Donald M. Leslie Jr. Minneapolis MI: University of Minnesota Press, 1985.

Bateson, Gregory. *Steps to an Ecology of the Mind: A Revolutionary Approach to Man's Understanding of Himself.* Chicago IL: University of Chicago Press, 1972.

Baudelaire, Charles. "The Painter of Modern Life." *My Heart Laid Bare and Other Prose Writings.* London: Soho Book Company, 1986.

Baudrillard, Jean. *America.* Translated by Chris Turner. London: Verso, 1988.

---. "Hystericizing the Millennium." Translated by Charles Dudas. (*L'Illusion de la fin: ou La greve des evenements, Paris: Galilee, 1992 CTheory*). Posted 5/10/1994.

---. "Disneyworld Company." Translated by Francois Debrix. (*Liberation, March 4, 1996 CTheory*). Posted 3/27/1996.

---. "The Precession of Simulacra." *Media and Cultural Studies: Keyworks.* Edited by Meenakshi Gigi Durham and Douglas M. Kellner. Malden MA: Blackwell Publishing, 2006. Pgs. 453-481.

---. *The Consumer Society: Myths and Structures.* London: Sage Publications, 2008.

---. *The Spirit of Terrorism and Other Essays.* Translated by Chris Turner. London: Verso, 2002.

---. "Simulations." *Continental Aesthetics: Romanticism to Postmodernism: An Anthology.* Edited by Richard Kearney and David Rasmussen. Malden MA: Blackwell Publishers, 2001. Pgs. 411-430.

Baudry, Jean-Louis. "Ideological Effects of the Basic Cinematographic Apparatus." Translated by Alan Williams. *Narrative, Apparatus, Ideology: A Film Theory Reader.* Edited by Philip Rosen. New York: Columbia University Press, 1986. Pgs. 286-298.

Bazin, André. *What Is Cinema? Volume 1.* Essays selected and translated by Hugh Gray. Foreward by Jean Renoir. New foreward by Dudley Andrews. Berkeley CA: University of California Press, 2005.

---. "Bicycle Thieves." *What is Cinema? Volume II.* Edited and translated by Hugh Gray. Berkeley CA: University of California Press, 2005.

---. "The Ontology of the Photographic Image." Translated by Hugh Gray. *Film Quarterly.* Volume 13. No. 4. (Summer 1960). Pgs. 4-9.

---. "The Myth of Total Cinema." *What is Cinema? Volume II.* Translated and Edited by Hugh Gray. Berkeley CA: University of California Press, 2005. Pgs. 23-27.

Belton, Ellen. "Reimagining Jane Austen: the 1940 and 1995 films versions of *Pride and Prejudice*." *Jane Austen in Hollywood.* Edited by Linda Troost and Sayre Greenfield. Lexington KY: The University of Kentucky Press, 1998.

Benedict, Ruth. *Patterns of Culture. With an Introduction by Franz Boaz and a New Preface by Margaret Mead.* New York: Mentor Books, 1960 (eighteenth printing). (Copyright 1934 by Ruth Benedict; First printed in 1946).

Benjamin, Walter. "Critique of Violence." *Walter Benjamin: Selected Writings Volume 1: 1913-1926.* Edited by Marcus Bullock and Michael W. Jennings. Cambridge MA: The Belknap Press of Harvard University Press, 1996.

---. "The Task of the Translator." *Walter Benjamin: Selected Writings Volume 1: 1913-1926.* Edited by Marcus Bullock and Michael W. Jennings. Cambridge MA: The Belknap Press of Harvard University Press, 1996.

---. "Exchange with Theodor W. Adorno on the Essay 'Paris, the Capital of the Nineteenth Century'." *Walter Benjamin: Selected Writings. Volume 3, 1935-1938.* Translated by Edmund Jephcott, Howard Eiland, and Others. Edited by Howard Eiland and Michael W. Jennings. Cambridge MA: The Belknap Press of Harvard University Press, 2002.

---. "Hashish in Marseilles." *Walter Benjamin: Selected Writings. Volume 2, Part 2. 1931-1934.* Translated by Rodney Livingstone and Others. Edited by Michael W. Jennings, Howard Eiland, and Gary Smith. Cambridge MA: The Belknap Press of Harvard University Press, 1999.

---. "Hitler's Diminished Masculinity." *Walter Benjamin: Selected Writings. Volume 2, Part 2. 1931-1934.* Translated by Rodney Livingstone and Others. Edited by Michael W. Jennings, Howard Eiland, and Gary Smith. Cambridge MA: The Belknap Press of Harvard University Press, 1999.

---. "Little History of Photography." *Walter Benjamin: Selected Writings. Volume 2, Part 2. 1931-1934.* Translated by Rodney Livingstone and Others. Edited by Michael W. Jennings, Howard Eiland, and Gary Smith. Cambridge MA: The Belknap Press of Harvard University Press, 1999.

---. "On Some Motifs in Baudelaire." *Illuminations.* Edited and with an Introduction by Hannah Arendt. Translated by Harry Zohn. A Helen and Kurt Wolff Book. New York: Harcourt, Brace & World, 1968.

---. "Paris, Capital of the Nineteenth Century – Exposé of 1939." *The Arcades Project.* Translated by Howard Eiland and Kevin McLaughlin. Prepared on the basis of the German volume by Rolf Tiedemann. Cambridge MA: The Belknap Press of Harvard University Press, 1999.

---. "Paris, the Capital of the Nineteenth Century." *Walter Benjamin: Selected Writings. Volume 3, 1935-1938.* Translated by Edmund Jephcott, Howard Eiland, and Others. Edited by Howard Eiland and Michael W. Jennings. Cambridge MA: The Belknap Press of Harvard University Press, 2002.

---. "Surrealism: the Last Snapshot of the European Intelligentsia." London: *New Left Review.* No. 108. March/April 1978.

---. "The Author as Producer." *Walter Benjamin: Selected Writings. Volume 2, Part 2. 1931-1934.* Translated by Rodney Livingstone and Others. Edited by Michael W. Jennings, Howard Eiland, and Gary Smith. Cambridge MA: The Belknap Press of Harvard University Press, 1999.

---. "Franz Kafka." *Walter Benjamin: Selected Writings. Volume 2, Part 2. 1931-1934.* Translated by Rodney Livingstone and Others. Edited by Michael W. Jennings, Howard Eiland, and Gary Smith. Cambridge MA: The Belknap

Press of Harvard University Press, 1999.

---. "The Formula in Which the Dialectical Structure of Film Finds Expression." *Walter Benjamin: Selected Writings. Volume 3, 1935-1938*. Translated by Edmund Jephcott, Howard Eiland, and Others. Edited by Howard Eiland and Michael W. Jennings. Cambridge MA: The Belknap Press of Harvard University Press, 2002.

---. "The Storyteller." *Illuminations*. Edited and with an Introduction by Hannah Arendt. Translated by Harry Zohn. A Helen and Kurt Wolff Book. New York: Harcourt, Brace & World, 1968.

---. "The Storyteller: Observations on the Works of Nikolai Leskov." *Walter Benjamin: Selected Writings. Volume 3, 1935-1938*. Translated by Edmund Jephcott, Howard Eiland, and Others. Edited by Howard Eiland and Michael W. Jennings. Cambridge MA: The Belknap Press of Harvard University Press, 2002.

---. "The Theory of Distraction." *Walter Benjamin: Selected Writings. Volume 3, 1935-1938*. Translated by Edmund Jephcott, Howard Eiland, and Others. Edited by Howard Eiland and Michael W. Jennings. Cambridge MA: The Belknap Press of Harvard University Press, 2002.

---. "The Work of Art in the Age of Mechanical Reproduction." (1935) *Media and Cultural Studies: Keyworks*. Edited by Meenakshi Gigi Durham and Douglas M. Kellner. Malden MA: Blackwell Publishing, 2006.

---. "The Work of Art in the Age of Its Technological Reproducibility: Second Version." (1937) *Walter Benjamin: Selected Writings. Volume 3, 1935-1938*. Translated by Edmund Jephcott, Howard Eiland, and Others. Edited by Howard Eiland and Michael W. Jennings. Cambridge MA: The Belknap Press of Harvard University Press, 2002.

---. "Theses on the Philosophy of History." *Illuminations*. Edited and with an Introduction by Hannah Arendt. Translated by Harry Zohn. New York: Harcourt, Brace & World, 1968.

---. *The Arcades Project*. [*Passagen-Werk*] Translated by Howard Eiland and Kevin McLaughlin. Prepared on the basis of the German volume by Rolf Tiedemann. Cambridge MA: The Belknap Press of Harvard University Press, 1999.

---. *The Origin of German Tragic Drama*. Translated by John Osborne. New York: Verso, 1998.

---. *Illuminations*. Edited and with an Introduction by Hannah Arendt. Translated by Harry Zohn. New York: Harcourt, Brace & World, 1968.

---. "Two Poems by Friedrich Hölderlin: 'The Poet's Courage' and 'Timidity.'" *Walter Benjamin: Selected Writings. Volume 1, 1913-1926*. Translated by Edmund Jephcott, Howard Eiland, and Others. Edited by Howard Eiland and Michael W. Jennings. Cambridge MA: The Belknap Press of Harvard University Press, 2002.

---. *The Writer of Modern Life: Essays on Charles Baudelaire*. Edited by Michael W. Jennings. Translated by Howard Eiland, Edmund Jephcott, Rodney Livingston, and Harry Zohn. Cambridge MA: Harvard University Press, 2006.

Berger, John. *Ways of Seeing*. New York: The Viking Press, 1972.

---. *On Looking*. New York: Pantheon Books, 1980.

Berger, Merrill and Stephen Segaller. *The Wisdom of the Dream: The World of C.G. Jung*. New York: TV Books, 2000.

Bergson, Henri. *Laughter*. [First published in 1900, under the title "Laughter, An Essay on the Meaning of the Comic" (*Le Rire, Essai sur la signification du* comique).] Translated by Drew Burk. New York: Atropos Press, 2009.

---. *Matter and Memory.* Translation by Nancy Margaret Paul and W. Scott Palmer. New York: Zone Books, 1988.

---. *Creative Evolution.* Translated by Arthur Mitchell. New York: Dover Publications, 1998.

Berlin, Isaiah. *The Proper Study of Mankind: An Anthology of Essays.* Edited by Henry Hardy and Roger Hausheer. With a Foreword by Noel Annan and an Introduction by Roger Hausheer. London: Pimlico, 1998.

Berman, Marshall. *All That Is Solid Melts Into Air – The Experience of Modernity.* New York: Penguin Books, 1988.

Bhabha, Homi K. *The Location of Culture.* London and New York: Routledge, 1994.

Bhaskar, Ira. "'Historical Poetics', Narrative, and Interpretation." *A Companion to Film Theory.* Edited by Toby Miller and Robert Stam. Malden MA: Blackwell Publishing, 2004. Pgs. 387-412.

Birri, Fernando. "For a Nationalist, Realist, Critical and Popular Cinema." *New Latin American Cinema: Theory, Practices, and Transcontinental Articulations. Volume 1.* Detroit, MI: Wayne State University Press, 1997. Pgs. 95-98.

Blake, William. *Songs of Innocence.* New York: Dover Publications, 1971.

Blanchot, Maurice. *The Infinite Conversation.* Minneapolis MN: University of Minnesota Press, 1992.

Borcherdt, Gesine. "Byung-Chul Han: "I Practice Philosophy as Art." *Art Review.* December 2021.

Bordwell, David, Janet Steiger and Kristin Thompson. "The Central Producer System: Centralized Management after 1914." *The Classical Hollywood Cinema: Film Style and Mode of Production to 1960.* Editors David Bordwell, Janet Steiger, and Kristin Thompson. New York: Columbia University Press, 1985.

Bordwell, David. *French Impressionist Cinema.* New York: Arno Press, 1980.

---. *Ozu and the Poetics of Cinema.* London: BFI Publishing, 1988.

---. *Making Meaning: Inference and Rhetoric in the Interpretation of Cinema.* New Haven CT: Harvard University Press, 1991.

Borges, Jorge Luis. "On Exactitude in Science." *Collected Fictions.* Translated by Andrew Hurley. London: Penguin, 1999.

Bourdieu, Pierre. "(i) Introduction; (ii) The Aristocracy of Culture." *Media and Cultural Studies: Keyworks.* Edited by Meenakshi Gigi Durham and Douglas M. Kellner. Malden MA: Blackwell Publishing, 2006. Pgs. 322-327.

Bowman, Paul. "The Tao of Žižek." *The Truth of Žižek.* Edited by Paul Bowman and Richard Stamp. New York: Continuum, 2007. Pgs. 27-44.

Brakhage, Marilyn. "Foreward," *By Brakhage: An Anthology, Volumes One and Two.* New York: Criterion Collection, 2002. Pgs.6-9.

Brakhage, Stan. *A Moving Picture Giving and Talking Book.* West Newbury MA: Frontier Press, 1971.

---. *Film At Wit's End: Eight Avant-Garde Filmmakers.* New York: Mc Pherson & Co., 1989.

Brecht, Bertolt. "The Essays of Georg Lukács." *Aesthetics and Politics.* With presentations by Rodney Livingstone, Perry Anderson and Francis Mulhern. Afterword by Fredric Jameson. London: Verso Books, 1980. Pgs. 68-69.

Breton, André. *Manifestoes of Surrealism.* Ann Arbor MI: University of Michigan Press, 1969.

Brown, Richard Maxwell. "Violence." *The Oxford History of the American West*. Edited by Clyde A. Milner II, Carol A. O'Connor, Martha A. Sandweiss. New York: Oxford University Press, 1994. pp. 393-426.

Brunette, Peter. "Post-structuralism and deconstruction." *The Oxford Guide to Film Studies*. Edited by John Hill and Pamela Church Gibson. Consultant Editors Richard Dyer, E. Ann Kaplan, Paul Willemen. London and New York: Oxford University Press, 1998. Pgs. 91-95.

Buchanan, Ian and MacCormack, Patricia (Editors). *Deleuze and the Schizoanalysis of Cinema*. London: Bloomsbury Academic, 2008.

Buchenau, Stephanie. *The Founding of Aesthetics in the German Enlightenment: The Art of Invention and the Invention of Art*. Cambridge MA: Cambridge University Press, 2013.

Buck-Morss, Susan. *Dreamworld and Catastrophe: The Passing of Mass Utopia in East and West*. Cambridge MA: The MIT Press, 2002.

---. *The Dialectics of Seeing: Walter Benjamin and the Arcades Project*. Cambridge MA: The MIT Press, 1991.

---. *The Origin of Negative Dialectics: Theodor W. Adorno, Walter Benjamin, and the Frankfurt Institute*. New York: The Free Press, 1977.

---. *Thinking Past Terror: Islamism and Critical Theory on the Left*. London: Verso, 2003.

Bürger, Peter. *Theory of the Avant-Garde*. Translation from the German by Michael Shaw. Foreward by Jochen Schulte-Sasse. *Theory and History of Literature, Volume 4*. Minneapolis MA: University of Minnesota Press, 1984. (Twelfth printing 2007).

Burke, Edmund. *A Philosophical Enquiry into the Origin of Our Ideas of the Sublime and Beautiful* (1757). London and New York: Oxford University Press, 1998.

Burton-Carvajal, Julianne. *Multiculturalism, Postcoloniality, and Transnational Media*. Edited and with an Introduction by Ella Shohat and Robert Stam. Piscataway NJ: Rutgers University Press, 2003.

---. "South American cinema." *The Oxford Guide to Film Studies*. Edited by John Hill and Pamela Church Gibson. London and New York: Oxford University Press, 1998. Pgs. 578-594.

---. "Film Artists and Film Industries in Latin America, 1956-1980: Theoretical and Critical Implications of Variations in Modes of Filmic Production and Consumption." *New Latin American Cinema: Theory, Practices, and Transcontinental Articulations. Volume 1*. Detroit, MI: Wayne State University Press, 1997. Pgs. 157-184.

Butler, Judith. *Precarious Life: The Powers of Mourning and Violence*. London: Verso, 2004.

---. *Antigone's Claim: Kinship Between Life and Death*. New York: Columbia University Press, 2000.

---. "Critique Dissent Disciplinarity." *Critical Inquiry*. Volume 35. No. 4. Summer 2009. pp. 773-795.

---. "From Performativity to Precarity." Lecture given at Universidad Complutense de Madrid. June 8, 2009.

---. "Bodies in Alliance and the Politics of the Street." Lecture. Peter Wall Institute for Advanced Studies, Vogue Theatre, Vancouver BC, May 24, 2012.

---. *Undoing Gender*. New York and London: Routledge, 2004.

C

Cage, John. "Lecture on Nothing" (1951). *Silence: Lectures and Writings*. Middletown CT: Wesleyan University Press, 1961.

Camus, Albert. *The Myth of Sisyphus and Other Essays*. Translated from the French by Justin O'Brien. New York: Vintage International, March 1991.

Caputi, Jane. "Small Ceremonies: Ritual in Forrest Gump, Natural Born Killers, Seven, and Follow Me Home." *Mythologies of Violence in Postmodern Media*. Edited by Christopher Sharrett. Detroit MI: Wayne State University Press, 1999. Pgs. 147-174.

Caputo, John. "Love among the Deconstructibles: A Response to Gregg Lambert." *Journal for Cultural and Religious Theory*, 5 (2), April 2004.

Cartier-Bresson, Henri. *The Decisive Moment*. New York: Simon and Schuster, 1952.

Cartwright, David E. *Schopenhauer: A Biography*. Cambridge UK, Cambridge University Press, 2014.

Caston, Victor. "Phantasia and Thought." *A Companion to Aristotle*. Edited by Georgios Anagnostopoulos. Malden MA: Wiley-Blackwell, 2009. Pgs. 322-344.

Celan, Paul. *The Meridian*. Edited by Bernhard Böschenstein and Heino Schmull. Translated by Pierre Joris. Palo Alto CA: Stanford University Press, 2011.

Certeau, Michel de. *Heterologies: Discourse on the Other*. Translated by Brian Massumi. Minneapolis MI: University of Minnesota Press, 1986.

Chatwin, Bruce. *The Songlines*. London: Jonathan Cape, 1987.

Chion, Michel. *Audiovision: Sound on Screen*. New York: Columbia University, 1994.

Christie, Ian. "Formalism and neo-formalism." *The Oxford Guide to Film Studies*. Edited by John Hill and Pamela Church Gibson. Consultant Editors Richard Dyer, E. Ann Kaplan, Paul Willemen. New York: Oxford University Press, 1998. pp. 58-64.

---. "The Avant-gardes and European Cinema before 1930." *The Oxford Guide to Film Studies*. Edited by John Hill and Pamela Church Gibson. Consultant Editors Richard Dyer, E. Ann Kaplan, Paul Willemen. Oxford UK: Oxford University Press, 1998. Pgs. 449-454.

Cixous, Hélène. "The Laugh of the Medusa." *Continental Aesthetics: Romanticism to Postmodernism: An Anthology*. Edited by Richard Kearney and David Rasmussen. Malden MA: Blackwell Publishers, 2001. Pgs. 388-399.

Clark, T.J. *Farewell to an Idea: Episodes from a History of Modernism*. New Haven CT and London: Yale University Press, 1999.

Clover, Carol J. *Men, Women and Chains Saws: Gender in the Modern Horror Film*. Princeton NJ: Princeton University Press, 1992.

Cocteau, Jean. *Diary of an Unknown*. Translation by Jesse Browner. New York: Paragon House, 1988.

Cole, K.C. *The Universe and the Teacup: The Mathematics of Truth and Beauty*. New York: Houghton Mifflin Harcourt, 1999.

Comolli, Jean-Louis. "Machines of the Visible." (1971) *Electronic Culture: Technology and Visual Representation*. Edited by Timothy Druckrey. Reading PA: Aperture Press, 1996.

Cook, David A. *A History of Narrative Film*. New York: W.W. Norton & Company, 2004.

Cornford, Francis MacDonald. *Plato's Theory of Knowledge: The Theaetetus and the Sophist*. London: Routledge, 2013.

Coupland, Douglas. *Bit Rot*. Toronto: Random House Canada, 2016.

---. "Douglas Coupland: I miss my pre-internet brain," *The Daily Telegraph*, September 14 2014. Excerpt reprinted from *Kitten Clone: Inside Alcatel-Lucent* (London: Visual Editions, 2014).

Cousins, Mark. *The Story of Film*. New York: Thunder's Mouth Press, 2004.

Crary, Jonathan. *Techniques of the Observer: On Vision and Modernity in the Nineteenth Century*. Cambridge MA: MIT Press, 1990.

Critchley, Simon. *Infinitely Demanding: Ethics of Commitment, Politics of Resistance.* London: Verso, 2007.

---. *Very Little... Almost Nothing: Death, Literature, Philosophy*. London: Routledge, 1997.

---. "Simon Critchley: What is Normal?" *Adbusters*. 14 December 2011.

---. "A Commentary upon Derrida's Reading of Hegel in *Glas*." *Hegel After Derrida*. Edited by Stuart Barnett. London and New York: Routledge, 1998. Pgs. 197-226.

---. *Continental Philosophy*. Oxford UK: Oxford University Press, 2001.

---. *On Humour*. New York: Routledge, 2002.

---. *The Book of Dead Philosophers*. London: Granta Books, 2008.

---. "Violent Thoughts about Slavoj Žižek." *Naked Punch*. First Posted: 10/21/09: Updated 09/19/10.

---. "Being and Time: part 3: Being-in-the-world. Posted 22-06-2009.

---. "Being and Time, part 4: Thrown Into This World." *The Guardian*. Posted 29/06/2009.

---. "Being and Time, part 9: Death." *The Guardian*. Posted 13/07/2009.

---. *The Faith of the Faithless: Experiments in Political Theology*. London: Verso, 2012.

---. "The Freedom of Faith: A Christmas Sermon." *The Stone*. Posted 23/12/2012.

---. *Impossible Objects: Interviews*. Edited by Carl Cederström and Todd Kesselman. Cambridge UK and Malden MA: Polity Press, 2012.

---. "On the Ethics of Alain Badiou." *Alain Badiou: Philosophy and its Conditions*. Gabriel Riera (Editor). Albany NY: State University of New York Press, 2005.

Croce, Benedetto. "Taste and the Reproduction of Art." *Continental Aesthetics: Romanticism to Postmodernism: An Anthology*. Edited by Richard Kearney and David Rasmussen. Blackwell Publishers. Malden, MA. 2001. Edited and translated by James Harkness. Berkeley CA: University of California Press, 1983.

Cutrofello, Andrew. *Continental Philosophy: A Contemporary Introduction*. New York: Routledge, 2005.

D

Dante. *Inferno*. Translated by Charles S. Singleton. Princeton NJ: Princeton University Press, 1970.

Darrigol, Olivier. *A History of Optics from Greek Antiquity to the Nineteenth Century*. London and New York: Oxford University Press, 2012.

De Beauvoir, Simone. *The Ethics of Ambiguity*. Translated from the French by Bernard Frechtman. Don Mills, ON: Syracuse Press, 1948.

Debord, Guy. "The Commodity as Spectacle." *Media and Cultural Studies: Keyworks*. Edited by Meenakshi Gig Durham and Douglas M. Kellner. Malden MA: Blackwell Publishing, 2006. Pgs. 117-121.

---. *Society of the Spectacle.* Detroit MI: Black & Red, 2000.

---. *Introduction to a Critique of Urban Geography.* Translated by Ken Knabb. *Les Lèvres Nues* #6, September 1955.

De Certeau, Michel. *The Practice of Everyday Life.* Translated by Steven Rendall. Berkeley CA: University of California Press, 1984

Deedes-Vincke, Patrick. *Paris: the city and its photographs.* London: Bulfinch Press (Little, Brown and Company), 1992.

Deleuze, Gilles. *Cinema 1: The Movement-Image.* (1983) Translated by Hugh Tomlinson and Barbara Habberjam. Minneapolis MN: University of Minnesota Press, 1986.

---. *Cinema 2: The Time-Image.* (1985) Translated by Hugh Tomlinson and Robert Galeta. Minneapolis MN: University of Minnesota Press, 2010. (Ninth printing)

---. *The Logic of Sense.* Translated by Mark Lester with Charles Stivale. Edited by Constantin V. Boundas. New York: Columbia University Press, 1969.

---. *The Fold: Liebniz and the Baroque.* Foreward and translation by Tom Conley. Minneapolis MN: University of Minnesota Press, 1993.

---. *Plato and the Simulacrum.* Rosalind Krauss (Translator). *The MIT Press.* Vol.27, Winter 1983.

---. *Difference and Repetition.* Translated by Paul Patton. New York: Columbia University Press, 1994.

---. *Foucault.* Translated and edited by Seán Hand. London and New York: Continuum. 2006.

Deleuze, Gilles and Félix Guattari. *A Thousand Plateaus: Capitalism and Schizophrenia.* (1987) Translation and Foreward by Brian Massumi. Minneapolis MN: University of Minnesota Press, 2007.

---. *Anti-Oedipus: Capitalism and Schizophrenia.* Translated by Robert Hurley, Mark Seem, and Helen R. Lane. Minneapolis MN: University of Minnesota Press, 1983.

Deren, Maya and Gregory Bateson. "An Exchange of Letters between Maya Deren and Gregory Bateson." *October,* Vol. 14 (Autumn 1980). Pgs. 18-20.

Derrida, Jacques. *Spectres of Marx: The State of the Debt, the Work of Mourning and the New International.* Translated by Peggy Kamuf. With an Introduction by Bernd Magnus and Stephen Cullenberg. New York and London: Routledge, 2006.

---. *Dissemination.* London: Althone Press, 1981.

---. *On Cosmopolitanism and Forgiveness.* Translated by Mark Dooley and Michael Hughes. With a preface by Simon Critchley and Richard Kearney. London: Routledge, 2001.

---. *Of Grammatology.* Translated by Gayatri Chakravorty Spivak. Baltimore MD: The Johns Hopkins University Press, 1977.

---. *Of Hospitality : Anne Dufourmantelle invites Jacques Derrida to respond.* Translated by Rachel Bowlby. Stanford CA: Stanford University Press, 2000.

---. "Structure, Sign, and Play, in the Discourse of the Human Sciences." *Writing and Difference.* Translated by Alan Bass. London: Routledge, 1978. Pgs. 278-289.

Descartes, René. *Discourse on Method and the Meditations.* Translated with an Introduction by F.E. Sutcliffe. Toronto ON: Penguin Books, 1968.

Dijksterhuis, E.J. *The Mechanization of the World Picture.* Translated by C. Dikshoorn. Oxford UK: Oxford University Press, 1961.

Doidge, Norman. *The Brain that Changes Itself: Stories of Personal Triumph from the Frontiers of Brain Science.* New York: Penguin, 2007.

Dostoevsky, Fyodor. *The Brothers Karamazov.* Translated by Richard Pevear and Larissa Volokhonsky. New York: Farrar, Straus & Giroux, 2002.

---. *The Idiot.* Ware UK: Wordsworth Classics, 1996.

Durand, Marion, Simon Shogry, and Dirk Baltzly. "Stoicism." *Stanford Encyclopedia of Philosophy.* Edward N. Zalta and Uri Nodelman (eds.), Spring 2023 edition. [Online]

Dyer, Richard. "Introduction to Film Studies." *The Oxford Guide to Film Studies.* Edited by John Hill and Pamela Church Gibson. London and New York: Oxford University Press, 1998. Pgs. 3-10.

---. "Entertainment and Utopia." *The Cultural Studies Reader.* Edited by Simon During. New York: Routledge, 1999. Pgs.371-381.

E

Eco, Umberto and Ellen Esrock. *The Aesthetics of Chaosmos: The Middle Ages of James Joyce.* Cambridge MA: Harvard University Press, 1989.

Edgar, Andrew. *Habermas: The Key Concepts.* New York: Routledge, 2006.

Eilenberger, Wolfram. *Time of the Magicians: Wittgenstein, Benjamin, Cassirer, Heidegger and the Decade That Reinvented Philosophy.* Translated by Shaun Whiteside. New York: Penguin Press 2020.

Eisenstein, Sergei. *The Film Sense* (1947). Translated by Jay Leyda. New York: Harcourt, Brace, Jovanovich, 1969.

Eisner, Lotte. *The Haunted Screen: Expressionism in the German Cinema and the Influence of Max Reinhardt.* Berkeley CA: University of California Press, 2008.

Elder, R. Bruce. *Body of Vision: Representations of the Body in Recent Film and Poetry.* Waterloo ON: Wilfrid Laurier University Press, 1997.

---. *Dada, Surrealism, and the Cinematic Effect.* Waterloo ON: Wilfred Laurier University Press, 2013.

Ekstrom, Arne D. and Hugo J. Spiers, Veronique D. Bohbot, R. Shayna Rosenbaum. *Human Spatial Navigation.* Princeton N.J. and Oxford: Princeton University Press, 2018.

Elkin, Lauren. *Flâneuse: Women walk the City in Paris, New York, Tokyo, Venice and London.* New York: Farrar, Straus and Giroux, 2017.

Elsaesser, Thomas. *New German Cinema: A History.* London: British Film Institute, 1989.

---. "Between Erlebnis and Erfahrung: Cinema Experience with Benjamin." *Paragraph.* Volume 32, Issue 3, 2009. Pgs. 292-312.

Elsaesser, Thomas and Malte Hagener. *Film Theory: An Introduction Through the Senses.* New York: Routledge, 2010.

Epperly, Bruce. *Process Theology: A Guide for the Perplexed.* London and New York: Bloomsbury T&T Clark, 2011.

Epstein, Jean. "On Certain Characteristics of *Photogénie.*" (1935) *French Film Theory and Criticism: Volume 1 - 1907-1939.* Richard Abel (Editor). Princeton NJ: Princeton University Press, 1988. Pgs. 314-318.

Espinosa, Julio García. "For An Imperfect Cinema." Translated by Julianne Burton. *Jump Cut: A Review of Contemporary Media.* No. 20, 1979. Pgs. 24-26.

Ettinger, Bracha. *The Matrixial Gaze*. Leeds, UK: Feminist Arts and Histories Network, 1995.

Euripides. *The Bacchae and Other Plays*. Translated by Philip Vellacott. London: Penguin Classics, 1978.

Evernden, Neil. *The Natural Alien*. Toronto ON: University of Toronto Press, 1993.

F

Faas, Ekbert. *The Genealogy of Aesthetics*. Cambridge MA: Cambridge University Press, 2002.

Farmer, Robert. "Jean Epstein." *Senses of Cinema*. Issue 69, December 2010.

Feenberg, Andrew. *Heidegger and Marcuse: The Catastrophe and Redemption of History*. New York: Routledge (Taylor & Francis Group), 2005.

Feuerbach, Ludwig. "Preface to the Second Edition" [1843]. *The Essence of Christianity* [1841]. Introduction translated by Zawar Hanfi, 1972, remainder translated by George Eliot, 1854.

Fichte, Johann Gottlieb. *Attempt at a Critique of All Revelation* (*Versuch einer Kritik aller Offenbarung* , 1792). Translated by Garrett Green. Edited by Allen Wood. Cambridge MA: Cambridge University Press, 2010.

Finger, Anke and Danielle Follett (Editors). *The Aesthetics of the Total Artwork: On Borders and Fragments*. Baltimore MD: The Johns Hopkins University Press, 2010.

Fink, Bruce. *The Lacanian Subject: Between Language and Jouissance*. Princeton NJ: Princeton University Press, 1997.

Finlayson, James Gordon. *Habermas: A Very Short Introduction*. Oxford and New York: Oxford University Press, 2005.

Fittko, Lisa. "The Story of Old Benjamin" in Walter Benjamin, *The Arcades Project*. Translated by Howard Eiland and Kevin McLaughlin. Prepared on the basis of the German volume by Rolf Tiedemann. Cambridge MA: The Belknap Press of Harvard University Press, 1999. Pgs. 946-954.

Foucault, Michel. "Dream, Imagination, and Existence: an Introduction to Ludwig Binswanger's 'Dream and Existence'." Translated by Forrest Williams. *Review of Existential Psychology and Psychiatry*. Volume XIX:1, 1985. Pgs. 31-78.

---. "This is not a pipe." Edited and translated by James Harkness. Berkeley CA: University of California Press, 1983. Reprinted in *Continental Aesthetics: Romanticism to Postmodernism: An Anthology*. Edited by Richard Kearney and David Rasmussen. Malden MA: Blackwell Publishers, 2001. pp.374-387.

---. "What Is an Author?" *The Foucault Reader*. Edited by Paul Rabinow. London: Penguin Books, 1984. pp. 101-120.

---. *Madness and Civilization: A History of Insanity in the Age of Reason*. Translated from the French by Richard Howard. New York: Vintage, 1988.

---. *Discipline and Punish: the Birth of the Prison*. Translated by Alan Sheridan. New York: Vintage Press, 1979.

---. *The Archaeology of Knowledge*. Translated by A.M. Sheridan Smith. New York: Routledge Classics, 2002.

---. *Speech and Phenomena and Other Essays on Husserls' Theory of Signs*. Translated by David B. Allison. Evanston IN: Northwestern University Press, 1979.

---. *The Hermeneutics of the Subject – Lectures at the Collège de France: 1981-82.* Edited by Frédéric Gros. General Editors: François Ewald and Alessandro Fontana. English Series Editor: Arnold I. Davidson. Translated by Graham Burchell. New York: Picador, 2001.

---. *The History of Sexuality - Volume I: An Introduction*. Translated by Robert Hurley. New York: Vintage Books, 1988.

---. *The Order of Things: An Archaeology of the Human Sciences* (Unattributed translation). New York: Routledge Classics, 2002.

---. "Technologies of the Self." *Lectures at Vermont University in October 1982.* Martin, L.H. et al (editors). Boston MA: University of Massachusetts Press, 1988. Pgs. 16-49.

---. *Aesthetics, Method and Epistemology: Volume 2.* Edited by James B. Faubion. Translated by Robert Hurley and others. New York: The New Press, 1998.

---. "What is Enlightenment?" *The Foucault Reader.* Edited by Paul Rabinow. New York: Pantheon Books, 1984. Pgs. 32-50.

Freud, Sigmund. "Selections from Three Essays on Sexuality." *The Freud Reader.* Peter Gay (Editor). New York: W.W. Norton and Company, 1995.

---. *Civilization and Its Discontents.* Translated by David McLintock with an Introduction by Leo Bersani. London: Penguin Books, 2002.

---. *Beyond the Pleasure Principle.* Translated and newly edited by James Strachey. Introduction by Gregory Zilboorg. New York: Norton, 1975.

---. "A Note upon the 'Mystic Writing Pad.'" ("*Notiz fiber den `Wunderblock,* 1925"') Translation by James Strachey. Reprinted from *International Journal of Psycho-Analysis*, 21 (1940), p.469.

---. *The Uncanny* (1919). Translated by David McLintock. Introduction by Hugh Houghton. New York: Penguin Books, 2003.

Frey-Rohn, Liliane. *From Freud to Jung – A Comparative Study of the Psychology of the Unconscious.* Translated by Fred E. Engreen and Evelyn K. Engreen. Forward by Robert Hinshaw. Boston MA: Shambhala Publications, 1974.

Friedberg, Anne. *Window Shopping: Cinema and the Postmodern.* Berkeley CA: University of California Press, 1993.

Friedman, Thomas L. *The World is Flat: A Brief History of the Twenty-First Century* (New York: Farrar, Strauss & Giroux, 2005).

Frye, Northrop. *The Modern Century – The Whidden Lectures 1967.* Toronto ON: Oxford University Press, 1967.

Fuller, R. Buckminster. *The Critical Path.* New York: St. Martin's Press. 1981.

Furedi, Frank. *How Fear Works: Culture of Fear in the Twenty-First Century.* London: Bloomsbury Continuum, 2018.

Gadamer, Hans-Georg. *The Beginning of Philosophy.* Translated by Rod Coltman. New York: Continuum, 2001.

---. *The Relevance of the Beautiful and Other Essays.* Edited by Robert Bernasconi. Translated by Nicholas Walker. New York: Cambridge University Press, 1986.

---. "The Ontology of the Work of Art and its Hermeneutical Significance." *Truth and Method* (Second Edition). Translated by Joel Weinsheimer and Donald G. Marshall. New York: Continuum, 1989.

---. "The Ontology of the Work of Art and its Hermeneutical Significance." *Continental Aesthetics: Romanticism to Postmodernism: An Anthology.* Edited by Richard Kearney and David Rasmussen. Malden MA: Blackwell Publishers, 2001. Pgs. 321-338.

G

Gardiner, Patrick L. (Editor and with an introduction.) *Nineteenth Century Philosophy*. General Editors: Paul Edwards and Richard H. Popkin. New York: The Free Press, 1969.

Gay, Hannah. "Clock Synchrony, Time Distribution and Electrical Timekeeping in Britain 1880-1925." *Past & Present: A Journal of Historical Studies*. Volume 181, Issue 1. Oxford UK: November 2003.

Gee, Dana. "Back to Books: Coupland looks at how we're spending our free time," *The Vancouver Sun*, October 1, 2016, p.D1.

Girard, René. *Mimesis and Theory: Essays on Literature and Criticism, 1935-2005*. Edited and with an Introduction by Robert Doran. Stanford CA: Stanford University Press, 2008.

Giroux, Henry A. "What Might Education Mean After Abu Ghraib: Revisiting Adorno's Politics of Education." *Comparative Studies of South Asia, Africa and the Middle East*, Vol. 24:1 (2004).

---. *The Mouse That Roared: Disney and the End of Innocence*. New York: Rowman & Littlefield, 2001.

Glover, Jonathan. *Humanity – A Moral History of the Twentieth Century*. New Haven CT: Yale University Press, 2000.

Glover, Nicky. *Psychoanalytic Aesthetics: An Introduction to the British School*. London: Karnac Books, 2009.

Gould, S.J. and R.C. Lewontin, "The spandrels of San Marco and the Panglossian paradigm: a critique of the adaptationist programme," *Proceedings of the Royal Society of London. Series B, Biological Sciences*, Vol. 205, No. 1161, The Evolution of Adaptation by Natural Selection, Sept. 21, 1979.

Gramsci, Antonio. "(i) History of the Subaltern Classes; (ii) The Concept of 'Ideology': (iii) Cultural Themes: Ideological Material." *Media and Cultural Studies: Keyworks*. Edited by Meenakshi Gigi Durham and Douglas M. Kellner. Malden MA: Blackwell Publishing, 2006. Pgs. 13-17.

---. *Selections from the Prison Notebooks of Antonio Gramsci*. Translated by Geoffrey N. Smith and Quentin Hoare. New York: International Publishers, 1971.

Gray, John. *The Silence of Animals – On Progress and Other Modern Myths*. New York: Farrar, Straus and Giroux, 2013.

Guignon, Charles B. "Introduction." *The Cambridge Companion to Heidegger*. Edited by Charles B. Guignon. Cambridge UK: Cambridge University Press, 1993.

Gunjević, Boris. "The Thrilling Romance of Radical Orthodoxy – Spiritual Exercises." Žižek, Slavoj and Boris Gunjević. *God in Pain: Inversions of Apocalypse*. New York: Seven Stories Press, 2012. Pgs. 193-220.

---. "Every Book is Like a Fortress – Flesh Became Word." Žižek, Slavoj and Boris Gunjević. *God in Pain: Inversions of Apocalypse*. New York: Seven Stories Press, 2012. Pgs. 127-153.

---. "Babylonian Virtues – Minority Report." *God in Pain: Inversions of Apocalypse*. Slavoj Žižek and Boris Gunjević. New York: Seven Stories Press, 2012. Pgs. 73-102.

---. "The Mystagogy of Revolution." *God in Pain: Inversions of Apocalypse*. Slavoj Žižek and Boris Gunjević. New York: Seven Stories Press, 2012. Pgs. 7-26.

Gunning, Tom. "Moving Away from the Index: Cinema and the Impression of Reality." *A Journal of Feminist Cultural Studies*. Vol. 18, Number 1. Durham NC: Duke University Press, 2007. Pgs. 29-52.

---. "The Cinema of Attraction: Early Film, Its Spectator and the Avant-Garde." *Wide Angle*. Vol. 8, nos. 3 & 4, Fall, 1986.

Guthrie, W.K.C. *The Greeks & Their Gods*. London: Beacon, 1954.

Gutting, Gary. "Bridging the Analytic-Continental Divide," *The Stone*. The New York Times; February 19, 2012.

Guy, Richard K. "John Horton Conway." *Mathematical People*. Donald J. Albers and G.L. Alexanderson (Editors). Introduction by Phillip J. Davis. Chicago IL: Contemporary Books, 1985. Pgs. 41-50.

Habermas, Jürgen. *The Structural Transformation of the Public Sphere – An Inquiry into a Category of Bourgeois Society*. Translated by Thomas Burger with the assistance of Frederick Lawrence. Cambridge MA: The MIT Press, 1991.

---. "On Leveling the Genre Distinction between Philosophy and Literature." *Continental Aesthetics: Romanticism to Postmodernism: An Anthology*. Edited by Richard Kearney and David Rasmussen. Malden MA: Blackwell Publishers, 2001.

---. *The Theory of Communicative Action Volume One: Reason and the Rationalization of Society*. Translated by Thomas McCarthy. Boston MA: Beacon Press, 1984.

---. "The Public Sphere: An Encylopedia Article." *Media and Cultural Studies: Keyworks*. Revised edition. Edited by Meenakshi Gigi Durham and Douglas M. Kellner. Malden MA: Blackwell Publishing, 2006. Pgs. 73-78.

H

Hall, Stuart. "Encoding/Decoding." Media and Cultural Studies: Keyworks. Revised edition. Edited by Meenakshi Gigi *Media and Cultural Studies: Keyworks*, edited by Meenakshi Gigi Durham and Douglas M. Kellner. Malden, MA: Blackwell Publishing, 2006. Pgs. 163-173.

Hamacher, Werner. "(The End of Art with the Mask)" *Hegel After Derrida*. Edited by Stuart Barnett. London and New York: Routledge, 1998. Pgs. 105-130.

Han, Byung-Chul. *The Burnout Society*. Translated by Erik Butler. Palo Alto CA: Stanford Briefs, 2015.

---. *Psychopolitics: Neoliberalism and New Technologies of Power*. Translated by Erik Butler. Brooklyn: Verso 2017.

--- *Non-Things: Upheaval in the Lifeworld*. Translated by Daniel Steuer. Cambridge UK: Polity Press 2022.

Hardt, Michael and Antonio Negri. *Empire*. Cambridge MA: Harvard University Press. Seventh Printing. 2001.

Hari, Johann. *Stolen Focus: Why You Can't Pay Attention and How to Think Deeply Again* (New York: Crown, 2023)

Harris, Michael. *The End of Absence: Reclaiming What We've Lost in a World of Constant Connection*. Toronto ON: HarperCollins 2014.

Hawking, Stephen. *A Brief History of Time*. New York: Bantam Books, 1988.

Hayward, Susan. *Cinema Studies: The Key Concepts*. New York: Routledge, 2013.

Heaney, Seamus. *The Poetry of Seamus Heaney*. New York: Columbia University Press, 2008.

Hearn, Lafcadio. *Kwaidan: Stories and Studies of Strange Things* (1903). Project Gutenberg, posted February 18 2010.

Hebdige, Dick. "(i) From Culture to Hegemony; (ii) Subculture: The Unnatural Break." *Media and Cultural Studies: Keyworks*. Edited by Meenakshi Gigi Durham and Douglas M. Kellner. Malden MA: Blackwell Publishing, 2006. Pgs. 144-162.

Hedges, Chris. *Empire of Illusion: The End of Literacy and the Triumph of Spectacle*. Toronto: Vintage Canada, 2010.

Hegel, Georg Wilhelm Friedrich. *Faith and Knowledge*. Translated by Waler Cerf and H.S. Harris. Albany NY: State University of New York Press, 1977.

---. "Lectures on Aesthetics." *Continental Aesthetics: Romanticism to Postmodernism: An Anthology*. Richard Kearney and David Rasmussen (Editors). Malden MA: Blackwell Publishers, 2001. Pgs. 99-126.

---. *Lectures on the Philosophy of World History* (1892). Translated by H.B. Nisbett. With an Introduction by Duncan Forbes. Oxford UK: Cambridge University Press, 1981.

---. *Hegel Selections: The Great Philosopher Series*. M.J. Inwood (Editor). London and New York: Macmillan, 1988.

---. *Elements of the Philosophy of Right or Natural Law and Political Science in Outline*. Edited by Allan W. Wood. Translated by H.B. Nisbet. Cambridge UK and New York: Cambridge University Press, 1991.

---. "The Oldest Systematic Program of German Idealism" (1797) Translated by Diana I. Behler. *Philosophy of German Idealism: Fichte, Jacobi, and Schelling*. Edited by Ernst Behler. New York: Continuum, 2003. [Note: Authorship is unknown, except it is assumed to be one of the Tübingen Three: Hegel, Schelling, Hölderlin].

Heidegger, Martin. "The Origin of the Work of Art." *Basic Writings – From Being and Time (1927) to The Task of Thinking (1964)*. Revised and Expanded Edition Edited, With General Introduction, and Introductions to Each Selection David Farrell Krell. Foreward by Taylor Carman. New York: HarperCollins, 2008. Pgs. 139-212.

---. "The Question Concerning Technology." *Basic Writings – From Being and Time (1927) to The Task of Thinking (1964)*. Revised and Expanded Edition Edited, With General Introduction, and Introductions to Each Selection David Farrell Krell. Foreward by Taylor Carman. New York: HarperCollins, 2008. Pgs. 307-342.

---. "Building Dwelling Thinking." *Basic Writings – From Being and Time (1927) to The Task of Thinking (1964)*. Revised and Expanded Edition Edited, With General Introduction, and Introductions to Each Selection David Farrell Krell. Foreward by Taylor Carman. New York: HarperCollins, 2008. Pgs. 343-364.

---. "What is Metaphysics?" [*Was ist Metaphysik?* 1929]. *Basic Writings – From Being and Time (1927) to The Task of Thinking (1964)*. Revised and Expanded Edition Edited, With General Introduction, and Introductions to Each Selection David Farrell Krell. Foreward by Taylor Carman. New York: HarperCollins, 2008. Pgs.89-110.

---. "What Calls for Thinking?" *Basic Writings – From Being and Time (1927) to The Task of Thinking (1964)*. Revised and Expanded Edition Edited, With General Introduction, and Introductions to Each Selection David Farrell Krell. Foreward by Taylor Carman. New York: HarperCollins, 2008. Pgs. 365-392.

---. "The Way to Language." *Basic Writings – From Being and Time (1927) to The Task of Thinking (1964)*. Revised and Expanded Edition Edited, With General Introduction, and Introductions to Each Selection David Farrell Krell. Foreward by Taylor Carman. New York: HarperCollins, 2008. Pgs. 393-426.

---. *Kant and the Problem of Metaphysics* (1929). Translated by James S. Churchill. Bloomington IN: Indiana University Press, 1962.

---. *On Time and Being* (*Zeit und Sein* 1962). Translated by Joan Stambaugh. New York: Harper & Row, 1972.

---. *Discourse on Thinking*. A Translation of *Gelassenheit* by John M. Anderson and E. Hans Freund. With an Introduction by John M. Anderson. New York: Harper Torchbooks, 1966.

---. "The Age of the World Picture." *Off the Beaten Track*. Edited and translated by Julian Young and Kenneth Haynes. Cambridge MA: Cambridge University Press, 2002. Pgs. 57-85.

---. "Only a God Can Save Us" [*Nur noch ein Gott kann uns retten - Der Spiegel 1966*] *Heidegger: The Man and the Thinker.* Translated by William J. Richardson. Edited by Thomas Sheehan. New Brunswick NJ: Transaction Publishers, 2010. Pgs. 45-67.

---. "What are Poets For?" (1946). *Poetry, Language, Thought*. Translated by Alfred Hofstadter. New York: Harper and Row, 1971.

---. *An Introduction to Metaphysics* (1953). New Haven CT: Yale University Press, 2000.

---. *Elucidations of Hölderlin's Poetry*. Translated by Keith Hoeller. New York: Humanity Books, 2000.

---. *Hölderlin's Hymn "The Ister"*. Translated by William McNeill and Julia Davis. Bloomington IN: Indiana University Press, 1996.

Herman, Edward and Chomsky, Noam. "A Propaganda Model." *Media and Cultural Studies: Keyworks*. Edited by Meenakshi Gigi Durham and Douglas M. Kellner. Malden MA: Blackwell Publishing, 2006. Pgs. 257-294.

---. *Manufacturing Consent: The Political Economy of the Mass Media*. New York: Pantheon Books, 2002.

Hesmondhalgh, David. *The Cultural Industries*. London: Sage Publications, 2007.

Hiebert, Ted. *In Praise of Nonsense: Aesthetics, Uncertainty, and Postmodern*. Montreal QC: McGill-Queen's University Press, 2012.

Higgins, Michael W. and Douglas R. Letson. *The Jesuit Mystique*. Toronto ON: Macmillan Canada, 1995.

Himmelfarb, Gertrude. *On Looking Into the Abyss: Untimely Thoughts on Culture and Society*. New York, Vintage Books, 1994.

Hockney, David and Paul Joyce. *Hockney on Art – Conversations with Paul Joyce*. London: Little, Brown and Co., 1999.

Hoffman, E.T.A. *The Collected Writings of E.T.A. Hoffman*. Edited and translated by Leonard J. Kent and Elizabeth C. Knight. Chicago IL: University of Chicago Press, 1969.

Hölderlin, Friedrich. *Friedrich Hölderlin - Poems and Fragments*. Translated by Michael Hamburger. Ann Arbor MI: The University of Michigan Press, 1966.

hooks, bell. "The Oppositional Gaze: Black Female Spectatorship"(1992). Edited by Amelia Jones. *The Feminism and Visual Cultural Reader*. New York: Routledge, 2003.

Horkheimer, Max and Adorno, Theodor W. "On the Theory of Ghosts." *Dialectic of Enlightenment*. Translated by John Cumming. (Original edition: *Dialektick der Aufklärung*. Social Studies Association. 1944.) New York: Continuum, 2000.

---. "The Culture Industry: Enlightenment as Mass Deception." *Dialectic of Enlightenment: Philosophical Fragments*. Translated by John Cumming. (Original edition: *Dialektick der Aufklärung*. Social Studies Association. 1944.) New York: Continuum, 2000. Pgs. 120-167.

Hornung, Erik. *Idea into Image: Essays on Ancient Egyptian Thought*, translated by Elizabeth Bredeck (New York: Timken Publishers, 1992). Pgs. 35-36.

Houlgate, Stephen, "Hegel's Aesthetics", *The Stanford Encyclopedia of Philosophy* (Winter 2021 Edition), Edward N. Zalta (ed.). [Online]

Hsu, Hua. "Affect Theory and the New Age of Anxiety: How Lauren Berlant's cultural criticism predicted the Trumping of politics." *The New Yorker*, March 19, 2019. Pgs.61-65.

Hughes, Robert. *The Shock of the New*. New York: Alfred A. Knopf, 1980.

Husserl, Edmund. *Ideas Pertaining to a Pure Phenomenology and to a Phenomenological Philosophy, First Book: General Introduction to a Pure Phenomenology*. Translated by F. Kersten. Dordrecht, Germany: Kluwer Academic Publishers, 1983.

Hutcheon, Linda. *A Theory of Adaptation*. New York: Routledge (Taylor and Francis Group), 2006.

Hyslop, Lois Boe. *Baudelaire, Man of His Time*. New Haven CT: Yale University Press, 1980.

I

Irigaray, Luce. "The Laugh of the Medusa" (1975). Translated by Keith Cohen and Paula Cohen, *Signs*, Vol. 1, No. 4 (Summer, 1976).

J

Jacobs, Jane. *Dark Age Ahead*. Toronto ON: Vintage Classic (Random House Canada), 2004.

Jacobus, Mary. *The Poetics of Psychoanalysis*. Oxford UK: Oxford University Press, 2005.

Jacoby, Russell. *Social Amnesia: A Critique of Contemporary Psychology from Adler to Laing*. Boston MA: Beacon Press, 1975.

James, David. "Is There Class in this Text? - The Repression of Class in Film and Cultural Studies." *A Companion to Film Theory*. Edited by Toby Miller and Robert Stam. Malden MA: Blackwell Publishing, 2004. Pgs. 182-201.

Jameson, Fredric. "Postmodernism, or the Cultural Logic of Late Capitalism." *Media and Cultural Studies: Keyworks*. Edited by Meenakshi Gigi Durham and Douglas M. Kellner. Malden MA: Blackwell Publishing, 2006. Pgs. 482-519.

---. "Reflections in Conclusion." *Aesthetics and Politics*. With presentations by Rodney Livingstone, Perry Anderson and Francis Mulhern. Afterword by Fredric Jameson. London: Verso Books, 1980. Pgs. 196-213.

---. *Postmodernism and its Discontents*. Edited by Ann Kaplan. London and New York: Verso, 1988.

---. *The Geopolitical Aesthetic: Cinema and Space in the World System*. Bloomington IN: Indiana University Press, 1995.

Jay, Martin. *Downcast Eyes: The Denigration of Vision in Twentieth-Century French Thought*. Berkeley and Los Angeles, CA: University of California Press, 1994.

---. *The Dialectical Imagination: A History of the Frankfurt School and the Institute of Social Research, 1923-1950*. Berkeley and Los Angeles CA: University of California Press, 1973.

---. "Scopic Regimes of Modernity." *Vision and Visuality*. Edited by Hal Foster. Seattle WA: Bay Press, 1988.

Jentsch, Ernst. *On the Psychology of the Uncanny* (1906).

Johnson, Paul. *The Birth of the Modern: World Society 1815-1830*. London: George Weidenfeld & Nicholson Ltd, 1991.

---. *Modern Times: The World from the Twenties to the Eighties*. New York: Harper & Row, Publishers, Inc., 1983. (Also published as *A History of the Modern World: From 1917 to the 1990s*. London: George Weidenfeld & Nicholson Ltd, 1991.)

Jung, Carl. *Synchronicity: An Acausal Connecting Principle*. (From Vol. 8. of the *Collected Works of C. G. Jung*) Princeton NJ: Princeton University Press, 2010.

---. *Two Essays on Analytical Psychology*. Translated by R.F.C. Hull. London: Routledge, 1999.

Jung, Carl and M.L. von Franz, Joseph L. Henderson, Jolande Jacobi, and Aniela Jaffé. *Man and his Symbols*. Coordinating Editor: John Freeman. London: Aldus Books, 1964.

K

Kadarkay, Arpad. *Georg Lukács: Life, Thought, and Politics*. Cambridge MA: Blackwell Publishers, 1991.

Kandel, Eric R. *The Age of Insight: The Quest to Understand the Unconscious in Art, Mind, and Brain, from Vienna 1900 to the Present*. New York: Random House, 2012.

Kant, Immanuel. *Religion and Rational Theology*. Edited and Translated by Allen W. Wood and George Di Giovanni. New York: Cambridge University Press, 1996.

---. *Perpetual Peace and Other Essays on Politics, History and Moral Practice*. Edited and translated by Ted Humphrey. Indianapolis IN: Hackett Publishing, 1988.

---. "Observations on the Feeling of the Beautiful and the Sublime." Translated by John T. Goldthwait. Berkeley CA: University of California Press, 1960.

---. "The Critique of Judgement." (1790) *Continental Aesthetics: Romanticism to Postmodernism: An Anthology*. Richard Kearney and David Rasmussen (Editors). Malden MA: Blackwell Publishers, 2001. Pgs. 5-42.

---. "Dreams of a Spirit-Seer Elucidated by Dreams of Metaphysics." *Theoretical Philosophy 1755-1770*. Edited and translated by David Walford in collaboration with Ralf Meerbote. New York: Cambridge University Press, 1992). Pgs. 301-359.

---. *Practical Philosophy*. Translated and Edited by Mary J. Gregor. General Introduction by Allen W. Wood. New York: Cambridge University Press, 1996.

---. *Critique of Pure Reason*. Translated and edited by Paul Guyer and Allen W. Wood. New York: Cambridge University Press, 1998.

Kaufmann, Walter. *Nietzsche: Philosopher, Psychologist, Antichrist*. Princeton NJ: Princeton University Press, 1974.

Kearney, Richard and David Rasmussen (Editors). *Continental Aesthetics: Romanticism to Postmodernism: An Anthology*. Malden MA: Blackwell Publishers, 2001.

Kearney, Richard. *Jacques Derrida - Dialogues with Contemporary Continental Thinkers: The Phenomenological Heritage*. Manchester UK: Manchester University Press, 1984. Pgs. 105-127.

---. *Poetics of Imagining: From Husserl to Lyotard (Problems of Modern European Thought)*. London: HarperCollinsAcademic, 1991.

Keats, John. *Selected Poems*. Edited with an introduction and notes by John Barnard. London: Penguin, 1988.

Kellner, Douglas M. "Culture Industries." *A Companion to Film Theory*. Edited by Toby Miller and Robert Stam. Malden MA: Blackwell Publishing, 2004. Pgs. 202-220.

Kellner, Douglas M. and Durham, Meenakshi Gigi. "Adventures in Media and Cultural Studies: Introducing the Keyworks." *Media and Cultural Studies: Keyworks*. Revised Edition. Edited by Meenakshi Gigi Durham and Douglas M. Kellner. Malden MA: Blackwell Publishing, 2006.

Kiarostami, Abbas. "An Unfinished Cinema." Text written for the Centenary of Cinema, Paris, 1995.

Kidd, John. "The Bridgewater Treatises on the Power Wisdom and Goodness of God as Manifested in the Creation: Treatise II." *On the Adaptation of External Nature to the Physical Condition of Man*. London, William Pickering, 1833.

Kierkegaard, Søren. "The Concept of Irony." *Søren Kierkegaard's Journals and Papers, Volume 2, F-K*. Edited and translated by Howard V. Hong and Edna H. Hong. Assisted by Gregor Malantschuk. Bloomington IN and London: Indiana University Press, 1970.

Kittler, Friedrich A. *Gramophone, Film, Typewriter*. Translated, with an Introduction, by Geoffrey Winthrop-Young and Michael Wutz. Palo Alto CA: Stanford University Press, 1999.

---. *Discourse Networks 1800/1900*. Translated by Michael Metteer, with Chris Cullens. Foreward by David E. Wellbery. Palo Alto CA: Stanford University Press, 1990.

---. "There is No Software." *CTheory*. Article: a032. Posted 10/18/1995.

Klages, Mary. *Literary Theory: A Guide for the Perplexed*. London: Continuum Publishing Group, 2006.

Klein, Naomi. *This Changes Everything: Capitalism vs. The Climate*. Toronto ON: Alfred A. Knopf Canada, 2014.

Kleinhans, Chuck. "Marxism and film." *The Oxford Guide to Film Studies*. Edited by John Hill and Pamela Church Gibson. London and New York: Oxford University Press, 1998. Pgs. 106-113.

Kleist, Heinrich von. "On the gradual production of thoughts whilst speaking." *Selected Writings*. David Constantine (editor). Cambridge MA: Hackett Publishing Company, 2004. Pgs. 405-409.

Koch, Gertrude. *Siegfried Kracauer: An Introduction*. Translated by Jeremy Gaines. Princeton NJ: Princeton University Press, 2000.

Koestler, Arthur. *The Act of Creation*. Ann Arbor MI: University of Michigan, 1978.

Kracauer, Siegfried. *The Mass Ornament* (1963). Translated, Edited and with an Introduction by Thomas Y. Levin. Cambridge MA: Harvard University Press, 1995.

---. *Theory of Film: The Redemption of Physical Reality* (1960). With an Introduction by Miriam Bratu Hansen. Princeton NJ: Princeton University Press, 1997.

---. *From Caligari to Hitler: A Psychological History of the German Film* [1947]. Princeton NJ: Princeton University Press, 1966.

Krell, David Farrell. "General Introduction: The Question of Being." *Basic Writings – From Being and Time (1927) to The Task of Thinking (1964).* Martin Heidegger. Revised and Expanded Edition Edited, With General Introduction, and Introductions to Each Selection David Farrell Krell. Foreward by Taylor Carman. New York: HarperCollins, 2008. Pgs. 1-36.

Kristeva, Julia. *Desire in Language: A Semiotic Approach to Literature and Art.* Edited by Leon S. Roudiez and translated by Thomas Gora, Alice Jardine, and Leon S. Roudiez. New York: Columbia University Press, 1980.

---. "Holbein's Dead Christ," *Black Sun: Depression and Melancholia*, Translated by Leon S. Roudiez (New York: Columbia University Press, 1989), pp.105-138..

---. "The Subject in Process," Translated by Patrick ffrench. The Tel Quel Project (London and New York: Routlege, 1998).

---. *Powers of Horror – An Essay of Abjection.* Translated by Leon S. Roudiez. New York: Columbia University Press, 1982.

Kundera, Milan. *The Unbearable Lightness of Being.* New York: Harper Perennial Modern Classics, 2009.

L

Lacan, Jacques. *Écrits: A Selection.* Translated by Alan Sheridan. New York: W.W. Norton & Co., 1978.

---. "The Mirror Stage as Formative of the Function of the I as Revealed in Psychoanalytic Experience," *Écrits: A Selection*, translated by Alan Sheridan. New York: W.W. Norton & Co., 1978.

---. "The Ethics of Psychoanalysis 1959-1960." *The Seminars of Jacques Lacan – Book VII.* Edited by Jacques-Alain Miller. Translated with Notes by Dennis Porter. New York: W.W. Norton & Co, 1992.

---. "The Mirror Stage as Formative of the *I* Function, as revealed in Psychoanalytic Experience." *Écrits: A Selection.* Translated by Bruce Fink. In Collaboration with Héloïse Fink and Russell Grigg. New York: W.W. Norton & Co, 1996. Pgs. 3-10.

---. "The Instance of the Letter in the Unconscious, or Reason Since Freud." *Écrits: A Selection.* Translated by Bruce Fink. In Collaboration with Héloïse Fink and Russell Grigg. (New York: W. W. Norton, 2002). Pgs. 138-168.

---. "The Subversion of the Subject and the Dialectic of Desire in the Freudian Unconscious." *Écrits: A Selection.* Translated by Bruce Fink. In Collaboration with Héloïse Fink and Russell Grigg. New York: W.W. Norton & Co, 1996. Pgs. 181-312.

---. *The Four Fundamental Concepts of Psycho-Analysis.* Translated by Alan Sheridan. London: Penguin, 1994.

Lampert, Laurence. *Nietzsche's Task: An Interpretation of Beyond Good and Evil.* New Haven CT and London: Yale University Press, 2001.

Langford, Michelle. "Alexander Kluge." *Senses of Cinema.* Issue 69. July 2003.

Latour, Bruno. *War of the Worlds: What About Peace?* Translated from the French by Charlotte Bigg. Edited by John Tresch. Chicago IL: Prickly Paradigm Press, 2002.

---. "War and Peace in an Age of Ecological Conflict," (lecture) *The Wall Exchange: Peter Wall Institute for Advanced Studies.* Vancouver, BC. September, 23, 2013.

Lawrence, Bruce B. and Aisha Karim (Editors). *On Violence: A Reader.* Durham NC and London: Duke University Press, 2007.

Lecercle, Jean-Jacques and Denise Riley. "A Voice Without A Mouth." *The Force of Language, Part 1.* London and Basingstoke: Palgrave Macmillan, 2004.

Léger, Fernand."A Critical Essay on the Plastic Qualities of Abel Gance's Film The Wheel," Functions of Painting, edited and with an introduction by Edward Fry, translated by Alexandra Anderson (New York: Viking Press, 1973), p.21.

Leibniz, Gottfried Wilhelm. *The Philosophical Works of Leibnitz, comprising The Monadology, New System of Nature, Principles of Nature and of Grace, Letters to Clarke, Refutation of Spinoza, and his other important philosophical opuscules, together with the Abridgment of the Theodicy and extracts from the New Essays on Human Understanding.* Translated from the original Latin and French, with Notes by George Trumbull Ladd, Instructor in Mental and Moral Philosophy, Yale University. (First published New Haven CT: Tuttle, Morehouse, and Taylor, 1820). New York: Andesite Press, 2015.

Leiss, William. *Under Technology's Thumb.* Toronto ON: McGill-Queen's University Press, 1990.

Letson, Douglas Richard and Michael W. Higgins. *The Jesuit Mystique.* New York: HarperCollins, 1995.

Lévi-Strauss, Claude. *The Elementary Structures of Kinship.* Revised Edition. Translated by James Harle Bell, John Richard von Sturmer, and Rodney Needham. Boston MA: Beacon Press, 1969.

Levinas, Emmanuel. *Totality and Infinity: an Essay on Exteriority.* Translated by Alphonso Lingis. Pittsburgh PA: Duquesne University Press, 1969.

---. *Otherwise Than Being, or, Beyond Essence.* Translated by Alphonso Lingis. Pittsburgh PA: Duquesne University Press, 2001.

Lewis-Kraus, Gideon. "Do Better: The gospel of effective altruism." *The New Yorker.* August 15, 2022. pp.48-59

Livingstone, Rodney and Anderson, Perry and Mulhern, Francis. "Presentation II." *Aesthetics and Politics.* With presentations by Rodney Livingstone, Perry Anderson and Francis Mulhern. Afterword by Fredric Jameson. London: Verso Books, 1980. Pgs. 60-67.

Locke, John. "An Essay Concerning Human Understanding" (1689). Revised edition. London: Penguin Classics, 1998.

Look, Brandon C., "Gottfried Wilhelm Leibniz", *The Stanford Encyclopedia of Philosophy* (Spring 2020 Edition), Edward N. Zalta (ed.). [Online]

Löwy, Michael. *Fire Alarm – Reading Walter Benjamin's 'On the Concept of History'.* Translated by Chris Turner. London: Verso, 2005.

Lucretius. *On the Nature of the Universe.* Translated by R.E. Latham. Revised and with an Introduction and Notes by John Godwin. London and New York: Penguin Books, 1994.

Luhmann, Niklas. *Art as a Social System.* Translated by Eva M. Knodt. Stanford CA: Stanford University Press, 2000.

---. *Essays on Self-Reference.* New York: Columbia University Press, 1990.

Lukács, Georg. "Realism in the Balance." *Aesthetics and Politics.* With presentations by Rodney Livingstone, Perry Anderson and Francis Mulhern. Afterword by Fredric Jameson. London: Verso Books, 1980. Pgs. 28-59.

---. *History and Class Consciousness.* Translated by Rodney Livingstone. Cambridge MA: The MIT Press, 1971.

---. "Reification and the Consciousness of the Proletariat." *History and Class Cons-*

ciousness. Translated by Rodney Livingstone. Cambridge MA: The MIT Press, 1971. Pgs. 83-222.

---. *The Meaning of Contemporary Realism*. Translated from the German by John and Necke Mander. London: Merlin Press, 1963.

---. *The Theory of the Novel: A Historico-philosophical Essay on the Forms of Great Epic Literature*. [First printed by P. Cassirer, Berlin, 1920. Hermann Luchterland Verlag GmbH, 1963.] Translated from the German by Anna Bostock. London: Merlin Press, 1971.

---. "Thoughts Toward an Aesthetic of the Cinema." Translated by Janelle Blankenship. *Polygraph*. No. 13, 2001. Pgs. 13-18.

Lyotard, Jean-François. *Libidinal Economy*. Translated by Iain Hamilton Grant. Bloomington IN: Indiana University Press, 1988.

---. *The Differend: Phrases in Dispute*. Translated by Georges Van Den Abbeele. Minneapolis MI: University of Minnesota Press, 1988.

---. *The Postmodern Condition: A Report on Knowledge*. Translated by Geoff Bennington and Brian Massumi. Minneapolis MI: University of Minnesota Press, 1984.

---. "Note on the Meaning of the Word "Post" and Answering the Question "What is Postmodernism?" *Continental Aesthetics: Romanticism to Postmodernism: An Anthology*. Edited by Richard Kearney and David Rasmussen. Malden MA: Blackwell Publishers, 2001. Pgs..363-373.

---. *Peregrinations: Law, Form, Event*. New York: Columbia University Press, 1990.

---. *Critical Evaluations in Cultural Theory*. Edited by Victor E. Taylor and Gregg Lambert. New York: Routledge, 2006.

---. *Why Philosophize?* Translated by Andrew Brown. Cambridge: Polity Press, 2013.

Lyotard, Jean-François and Jean-Loup Thebaud. *Just Gaming*. Translated by Wlad Godzich. Afterword by Samuel Weber. Translated by Brian Massumi. Minneapolis MI: University of Minnesota Press, 2008.

M

MacCormack, Patrick. "Julia Kristeva." *Film, Theory and Philosophy: The Key Thinkers*. Edited by Felicity Colman. Montreal and Kingston: McGill-Queen's University Press, 2010.

Magee, Glenn Alexander. *The Hegel Dictionary*. London: Continuum, 2011.

Magrini, James M. "'Surrealism' and the Omnipotence of the Cinema." *Senses of Cinema*. Issue 44. August 2007.

Mankiewicz, Richard. *The Story of Mathematics*. London: Cassell & Co., 2000.

Manovich, Lev. "Synthetic Realism and its Discontents." *The Language of Media - Film Theory and Criticism: Introductory Readings*. Edited by Leo Braudy and Marshall Cohen. (Seventh Edition) London and New York: Oxford University Press, 2009. Pgs. 785-801.

---. *The Language of New Media*. Cambridge MA: The MIT Press, 2001.

---. "An Archaeology of a Computer Screen." Kunstforum International, Germany, 1995. [Online]

Marcuse, Herbert. *The Essential Marcuse – Selected Writings of Philosopher and Social Critic Herbert Marcuse*. Edited by Andrew Feenberg and William Leiss. Boston MA: Beacon Press, 2007.

---. *An Essay on Liberation*. Boston MA: Beacon Press, 1969.

Martin, Michael T. (Editor). *New Latin American Cinema: Theory, Practices, and Transcontinental Articulations. Volume 1*. Detroit, MI: Wayne State University Press, 1997.

Marx, Karl. *The Eighteenth Brumaire of Louis Bonaparte*. Translated by Daniel De Leon. Third Edition. Chicago IL: Charles H. Kerr & Company, 1914.

---. *Theses on Feuerbach*. As an appendix to Ludwig Feuerbach and the End of Classical German Philosophy in 1888; *Marx/Engels Selected Works, Volume One*, pgs. 13-15, translated from the German by W. Lough. Progress Publishers, Moscow, USSR, 1969.

---. *Marx: Selected Readings*. Edited by Lawrence H. Simon. Cambridge MA: Hackett Publishing Company, 1994.

Marx, Karl and Friedrich Engels. "The Ruling Class and the Ruling Ideas." *Media and Cultural Studies: Keyworks*. Edited by Meenakshi Gigi Durham and Douglas M. Kellner. Malden MA: Blackwell Publishing, 2006.

---. *Capital: A Critique of Political Economy*. Introduction by Ernest Mandel (1976). Translation by Ben Fowkes (1976). Appendix translation by Rodney Livingstone (1976). New York: Vintage Books, 1977.

Mauss, Marcel. *The Gift: Forms and Function of Exchange in Archaic Societies*. Translated by Ian Cunnison. Foreward by E.E. Evans-Pritchard. Eastford CT: Martino Fine Books, 2011.

McLuhan, Marshall. *Understanding Me: Lectures and Interviews*. Edited by Stephanie McLuhan and David Staines. With a Foreword by Tom Wolfe. Toronto, ON: McClelland & Stewart, 2003.

---. *Understanding Media: The Extensions of Man*. Toronto, ON: Signet, 1964.

Melnyk, George. *One Hundred Years of Canadian Cinema*. Toronto, ON: University of Toronto Press, 2004.

Merleau-Ponty, Maurice. *The Phenomenology of Perception* (*Phénoménologie de la perception*, 1945). Translated by Colin Smith. New York: Routledge & Kegan Paul, 1962.

---. *The Primacy of Perception and Other Essays on Phenomenological Psychology - The Philosophy of Art, History, and Politics*. Edited and with an Introduction by James M. Edie. Evanston, IL: Northwestern University Press, 1964.

---. "Eye and Mind." *Continental Aesthetics: Romanticism to Postmodernism: An Anthology*. Edited by Richard Kearney and David Rasmussen. Malden, MA: Blackwell Publishers, 2001. Edited and translated by James Harkness. Berkeley, CA: University of California Press, 1983.

Metz, Christian. *The Imaginary Signifier*. Translated by Celia Britton, Annwyl Williams, Ben Brewster, and Alfred Guzzetti. Bloomington, IN: Indiana University Press, 1977.

---. "Problems of Denotation in the Fiction Film." *Film Language*. Translated by Michael Taylor. New York: Oxford University Press, 1974.

Thomas Metzinger. *Being No One: The Self-Model Theory of Subjectivity*. Cambridge, Massachusetts: MIT Press. 2003.

Mill, John Stuart. *Autobiography of John Stuart Mill*. Preface by John Jacob Coss. New York: Columbian University Press, 1924.

Miller, Toby. "Hollywood and the World." *The Oxford Guide to Film Studies*. Edited by John Hill and Pamela Church Gibson. London and New York: Oxford University Press, 1998. Pgs. 371-381.

Milloy, John S. *A National Crime: The Canadian Government and the Residential School System 1879–1986*. Winnipeg, MA: University of Manitoba Press, 1999.

Mirzoeff, Nicholas. *An Introduction to Visual Culture*. London: Routledge, 1999.

Mitchell, W.J.T. *What Do Pictures Want?: The Lives and Loves of Images*. Chicago, IL: University of Chicago Press, 2004.

Modrak, Deborah Karen Ward. "Sensation and Desire." *A Companion to Aristotle*. Edited by Georgios Anagnostopoulos. Malden MA: Blackwell Publishing, 2009. Pgs. 310-321

Monk, Ray. *Ludwig Wittgenstein: The Duty of Genius*. New York: The Free Press, 1990.

Montaigne, Michel de. *The Complete Essays of Montaigne*. Translated and edited by Donald Murdoch Frame. Palo Alto, CA: Stanford University Press, 1958.

Mulvey, Laura. "Visual Pleasure and Narrative Cinema." *Media and Cultural Studies: Keyworks*. Edited by Meenakshi Gigi Durham and Douglas M. Kellner. Malden MA: Blackwell Publishing, 2006. Pgs. 342-352.

Münsterberg, Hugo. *The Film: A Psychological Study*. New York: Dover, 1970.

Murray, Michael J. and Sean Greenberg, "Leibniz on the Problem of Evil," *The Stanford Encyclopedia of Philosophy* (Winter 2016 Edition), Edward N. Zalta (ed.). [Online]

N

Nancy, Jean-Luc. "The Surprise of the Event." Translated by Lynn Festa and Stuart Barnett. *Hegel After Derrida*. Edited by Stuart Barnett. London and New York: Routledge, 1998. Pgs. 64-90.

---. *The Evidence of Film: Abbas Kiarostami*. Translated by Christine Irizzary and Verena Andermat Conley. Brussels, Belgium: Yves Gevaert Publisher, 2001.

Nicholson, Shierry Weber. "'Now It Looks at Me': Aesthetic Experience and the Work of Psychoanalysis." (March 2013) Essay and lecture presented at the conference "On Psychoanalysis and Aesthetics." Institute of the Humanities, Simon Fraser University, Vancouver BC, April 27, 2013.

Nietzsche, Friedrich. *The Birth of Tragedy Out of the Spirit of Music*. (1872) Translated by Shaun Whiteside. Edited by Michael Tanner. London: Penguin Books, 1993.

---. *Human, All Too Human, Parts I and II*. Translated with an Afterword by Gary Handwerk. Palo Alto CA: Stanford University Press, 1995.

---. *The Gay Science: With a Prelude in Songs and an Appendix in Rhymes*. Translated by Thomas Common. Mineola NY: Dover Books, 1996.

---. *Beyond Good and Evil – Prelude to a Philosophy of the Future*. Translated, with Commentary, by Walter Kaufman. New York: Vintage Books, 1966.

---. *Thus Spoke Zarathustra – A Book for Everyone and No One*. Translated with an Introduction by R.J. Hollingdale. Middlesex UK: Penguin Books, 1961.

---. *Ecce Homo – How One Becomes What One Is*. Translated with Notes by R.J. Hollingdale. Introduction by Michael Tanner. London: Penguin Books, 1979.

---. *The Birth of Tragedy* and *The Genealogy of Morals*. Translated by Francis Golffing. New York: Anchor Books, 1956.

---. *The Antichrist* (1895). Translated by H.L. Mencken. The Project Gutenberg EBook. Release date Sept. 18, 2006. [Ebook #19322].

---. *The Will to Power* (1901). A new translation by Walter Kaufmann and R.J. Hollingdale. New York: Vintage 1968.

Ngai, Sianne. *Ugly Feelings*. Cambridge MA and London: Harvard University Press, 2005.

--- *Theory of the Gimmick: Aesthetic Judgement and Capitalist Form*. Cambridge MA: The Belknap Press of Harvard University Press, 2020.

Novalis, Friedrich von Hardenberg. "Monologue." (1907) Translation by Ferit Güven. *The Philosophical and Theoretical Works*. pp. 438-439.

---. "Monologue." (c. 1798) Translated by Robert Calasso. *Literature and the Gods*. London: Vintage, 2001. Pgs. 178-180.

---. *Novalis: Philosophical Writings*. Translated and edited by Margaret Mahony Stoljar. Albany NY: State University of New York Press, 1997.

Nowell-Smith, Geoffrey. "Introduction." *The Oxford History of World Cinema*. Edited by Geoffrey Nowell-Smith. Oxford UK: Oxford University Press, 1996. Pgs. 3-5.

Nussbaum, Martha. "Narrative Emotions: Beckett's Genealogy of Love." *Ethics*. Vol. 98, No.2. (January 1988). Pgs. 225-254.

O

Ondaatje, Michael and Walter Murch. *The Conversations: Walter Murch and the Art of Editing Film*. New York: Knopf, 2002.

Ong, Walter J. *Orality and Literacy – The Technologizing of the Word*. (First published in 1982 by Methuen and Co.) London and New York; Routledge, 2002.

Osserman, Robert. *Poetry of the Universe – A Mathematical Exploration of the Cosmos*. New York: Anchor Books, 1995.

P

Paley, William. *Natural Theology: or, Evidences of the Existence and Attributes of The Deity, collected from the Appearances of Nature*. London: R. Faulder, 1802. Independently published, 2019.

Panofsky, Erwin. "Style and Medium in the Motion Pictures." *Film Theory and Criticism: Introductory Readings*. Gerald Mast and Marshall Cohen (Editors). London and New York: Oxford University Press, 1974. Pgs. 151-169.

---. "What is Baroque?", *Three Essays on Style*. Cambridge MA: The MIT Press, 1995.

Pascal, Roy. *The Dual Voice: Free Indirect Speech and its Functioning in the Nineteenth Century Novel*. Manchester UK: Manchester University Press, 1977.

Pater, Walter. *Studies in the History of the Renaissance*. Edited by Matthew Beaumont. London and New York: Oxford University Press, 2010.

Pensky, Max. "Beyond the Message in a Bottle: The Other Critical Theory." *Constellations*. Vol. 10, No. 1. Oxford UK: Blackwell Publishing, 2003.

Plato. *The Republic*. Translated by Desmond Lee. Introduction by Melissa Lane. New York: Penguin Classics, 2007.

---. *The Symposium*. Edited, translated and with an Introduction by Christopher Gill. London and New York: Penguin Classics, 2003.

---. *Timaeus and Critias*. Translated with an introduction and an appendix on Atlantis by Desmond Lee. London: Penguin, reprinted with revisions 1977. Pgs. 7-26.

R

Rancière, Jacques. *The Emancipated Spectator.* Translated by Gregory Elliot. New York: Verso, 2009.

---. *The Politics of Aesthetics: The Distribution of the Sensible.* Translated and with an Introduction by Gabriel Rockhill. New York: Continuum, 2004.

---. *The Future of the Image.* New York: Verso, 2007.

---. *Aesthetics and Its Discontents.* Translated by Steven Corcoran. Cambridge UK and Malden MA: Polity Press, 2009.

Rapp, Christof. "The Nature and Goals of Rhetoric." *A Companion to Aristotle.* Georgios Anagnostopoulos (Editor). Malden MA: Wiley-Blackwell, 2009. Pgs. 579-596.

Ray, Robert B., "Impressionism, Surrealism, and Film Theory: Path dependence, or how a tradition in film theory gets lost." *The Oxford Guide to Film Studies.* Edited by John Hill and Pamela Church Gibson. Consultant Editors Richard Dyer, E. Ann Kaplan, Paul Willemen. New York: Oxford University Press, 1998. Pgs. 67-76.

Reiss, H.S. (Editor and with an Introduction and Notes.). *Kant: Political Writings.* Edited and with an Introduction and Notes by H.S. Reiss. Translated by H.B. Nisbet. (Second Edition) Cambridge MA: Cambridge University Press, 2011.

Ricoeur, Paul. "Metaphor and the Problem of Hermeneutics." *Continental Aesthetics: Romanticism to Postmodernism: An Anthology.* Edited by Richard Kearney and David Rasmussen. Malden MA: Blackwell Publishers, 2001.

---. *The Conflict of Interpretations: Essays in Hermeneutics.* Edited by Don Ihde. Evanston IL: Northwestern University Press, 1974.

Riera, Gabriel (Editor). *Alain Badiou: Philosophy and its Conditions.* Albany NY: State University of New York Press, 2005.

Rilke, Rainer Maria. *Selected Poems.* A Translation from the German and Commentary by Robert Bly. New York: Harper & Row, 1981.

---. *Requiem and Other Poems.* Translated from the German and with an Introduction and Notes by J.B. Leishman. London: The Hogarth Press, 1957.

---. *Duino Elegies.* The German Text, with an English translation, Introduction, and Commentary by J.B. Leishman and Stephen Spender. New York: W.W. Norton & Co., 1939.

Rombes, Nicholas. *Cinema in the Digital Age.* London: Wallflower Press, 2009.

Ronell, Avital. *The Über-Reader: Selected Works of Avital Ronell.* Edited by Diane Davis. Urbana and Chicago IL: University of Illinois Press, 2007.

---. *The Test Drive.* Urbana and Chicago IL: University of Illinois Press, 2005.

---. *Stupidity.* Chicago IL: University of Illinois Press, 2002.

---. "On the Misery of Theory without Poetry: Heidegger's Reading of Hölderlin's 'Andenken'" PMLA (Modern

Language Association), Vol. 120, No.1, Special Topics: On Poetry (Jan. 2005), pp. 16-32.

Rorty, Richard. *Philosophy and the Mirror of Nature.* Princeton NJ: Princeton University Press, 1979.

---. *Consequences of Pragmatism: Essays, 1972-1980.* Minneapolis MI: University of Minnesota Press, 1982.

Rosenfield, Kathrin H. "Getting inside Sophocles' Mind through Hölderlin's 'Antigone'." *New Literary History: Poetry & Poetics*. Vol. 30, No. 1 (Winter, 1999). Pgs. 107-126.

Rushdie, Salman. "Out of Kansas." *Step Across This Line – Collected Nonfiction 1992-2002*. Toronto ON: Alfred A. Knopf Canada, 2002.

S

Sallis, John. *Chorology: On Beginning in Plato's Timaeus*. Bloomington IN: Indiana University Press, 2020.

Sartre, Jean-Paul. *Being and Nothingness: A Phenomenological Essay on Ontology*. Translated by Hazel E. Barnes. New York: Washington Square Press, 1992.

---. *The Imaginary: A Phenomenological Psychology of the Imagination (L'Imaginaire: Psychologie Phénoménologique de l'Imagination*, 1940). Revisions and historical introduction by Arlene Elkaïm-Sartre. Translated by Jonathan Webber. New York: Routledge, 2004.

---. "What is Literature?" *Continental Aesthetics: Romanticism to Postmodernism: An Anthology*. Richard Kearney and David Rasmussen (Editors). Malden MA: Blackwell Publishers, 2001. pp. 276-287.

Saul, John Ralston. *The Unconscious Civilization*. Concord ON: House of Anansi Press, 1995.

Scarry, Elaine. *On Beauty and Being Just*. Princeton NJ: Princeton University Press, 1999.

Schelling, Friedrich Wilhelm Joseph von. *Philosophy of Art – Theory and History of Literature, Volume 58*. Edited and translated by Douglas W. Stott. Minneapolis MI: University of Minnesota Press, 1989.

Schiller, Friedrich. "Letter of an Aesthetic Education of Man." *Continental Aesthetics: Romanticism to Postmodernism: An Anthology*. Richard Kearney and David Rasmussen (Editors). Malden MA: Blackwell Publishers, 2001. Pgs. 43-45.

Schirmacher, Wolfgang. "Cloning Humans with Media: Impermanence and Imperceptible Perfection." *Poiesis: A Journal of the Arts and Communication*. Toronto ON: EGS Press, 2000.

---. "Mask, Role, and Identity: The Search for the Inner Person." *Philosophy and Technology Studies Center*. Paper presented at the International Symposium of Phenomenology. Cambridge MA: 1986. New York: Polytechnic University, 1986.

---. "Art(ificial) Perception: Nietzsche and Culture After Nihilism." *Poiesis: A Journal of the Arts and Communication*. Toronto ON: EGS Press, 1999. Pgs. 17-23.

---. "Indirect Communication and Aesthetic Ethics: An Ironic Reading of Kierkegaard." Translated from the German by Virginia Cutrufelli. *Poiesis: A Journal of the Arts and Communication*. Volume 9. Toronto ON: 2007.

---. *Just Living: Philosophy of Artificial Life*. New York: Atropos Press, 2007.

---. "Homo Generator in Artificial Life: From a Conversation with Jean-François Lyotard." *Poiesis: A Journal of the Arts and Communication*. Volume 7. Toronto ON: EGS Press, 2005.

Schjeldahl, Peter. "Paintings for Now – Neo Rauch at the Met." *The New Yorker*. 4 June 2007.

Schmitt, Carl. *Nomos of the Earth in the International Law of the Jus Publicum Europaeum* (1950). Translated by G.L. Ulmen. Candor NY: Telos Press, 2003.

Schulte, Joachim. *Wittgenstein – An Introduction*. Translated by William H. Brenner and John F. Holley. Albany NY: State University of New York Press, 1992.

Schwegler, Albert. *Handbook of the History of Philosophy*. Translated and Annotated by James Hutchinson Stirling. Edinburgh: Edmonston & Co., 1879.

Sedgwick, Eve Kosofsky. "Jane Austen and the Masturbating Girl." *Critical Inquiry*. Vol. 17. Summer 1991. Pgs. 818-847.

Serres, Michel, with Bruno Latour. *Conversations on Science, Culture, and Time*. Translated by Roxanne Lapidus. Ann Arbor MI: University of Michigan Press, 1995.

---. *The Natural Contract*. Translated by Elizabeth MacArthur and William Paulson. (Originally published in French as Le Contrat Naturel by Editions Francois Bourin 1990). Ann Arbor MI: University of Michigan Press, 1995.

Shelley, Percy Blythe. "Adonais." *The Oxford Book of Mystical Verse*. Chosen by D. H. S. Nicholson and A. H. E. Lee. Oxford: Clarendon Press, 1917.

Silverman, Kaja. "Lost Objects and Mistaken Subjects." *Feminist Film Theory: A Classical Reader*. Edited by Sue Thornton. New York: NYU Press, 1999. Pgs. 97-106.

Singer, Peter. *Practical Ethics*. "The Drowning Child and the Expanding Circle." *New Internationalist*. Oxford UK: New Internationalist Publications, April 1997.

---. "Hegel and Marx: Dialogue with Peter Singer." *Unsanctifying Human Life*. Oxford UK: Blackwell Publishers, 2002. pp.341-357.

---. "Is meat cooked?" *The Globe and Mail*. Opinion. Saturday August 25 2018. Pgs. 01,06,07.

Sloterdijk, Peter. *Critique of Cynical Reason*. Translation by Michael Eldred. Foreword by Andreas Huyssen. Minneapolis MN: University of Minnesota Press, 1987.

---. *The Aesthetic Imperative – Writings on Art*. Cambridge UK: Polity Press 2017.

Snider, Steven and Howard Curle (Editors). *Vittorio de Sica: Contemporary Perspectives*. Toronto ON: University of Toronto Press, 2000.

Sobchack, Vivian. *Carnal Thoughts: Embodiment and Moving Image Culture*. Berkeley CA: University of California Press, 2004.

Solanas, Fernando and Octavio Getino. *Towards a Third Cinema* (1969). *Film and Theory: An Anthology*. Edited by Robert Stam and Toby Miller. Oxford UK: Blackwell Publishing, 2000.

Sontag, Susan. "The Image-World" (1977). *A Susan Sontag Reader*. Introduction by Elizabeth Hardwick. New York: Farrar, Strauss and Giroux, 1982. Pgs. 349-367.

---. "The Literary Criticism of Georg Lukács" (1965). *Against Interpretation and Other Essays*. New York: Delta Publishing, 1990.

---. "A note on novels and films" (1961) *Against Interpretation and Other Essays*. New York: Delta Publishing, 1961. Pgs. 242-245.

---. *On Photography*. New York: Anchor Books, 1990.

---. *Regarding the Pain of Others*. New York: Farrar, Straus & Giroux, 2003.

Sophocles. *Antigone*. Mineola NY: Dover Publications, 1993.

Sreberny, Annabelle. "The Global and the Local in International Communications." *Media and Cultural Studies: Keyworks*. Edited by Meenakshi Gigi Durham and Douglas M. Kellner. Revised Edition. Malden MA: Blackwell Publishing, 2012. Pgs. 524-539.

Stam, Robert, Robert Burgoyne and Sally Flitterman-Lewis. *New Vocabularies in Film Semiotics: Structuralism, Post-Structuralism and Beyond*. London and New York: Routledge, 1992.

Steiner, George. *Heidegger.* (Second Edition) London: Fontana Press, 1992.

---. *George Steiner: A Reader* (Oxford UK: Oxford University Press, 1984).

Stewart, Ian. *Nature's Numbers – The Unreal Reality of Mathematics.* Science Masters Series. New York: Harper Collins, 1995.

Stoljar, Margaret Mahony (Editor and translator). *Novalis: Philosophical Writings.* Albany NY: State University of New York Press, 1997.

Szondi, Peter. *An Essay on the Tragic.* (*Versuch über das Tragische*, 1961) Translated by Paul Fleming. Stanford CA: Stanford University Press, 2002.

T

Talbot, Michael. *Mysticism and the New Physics.* London and New York: Penguin, 1993.

Tarkovsky, Andrei. *Sculpting In Time – Reflections on the Cinema*. Translated from the Russian by Kitty Hunter-Blair. Austin TX: University of Texas Press, 2005.

Taylor, Charles. *The Malaise of Modernity.* Toronto ON: House of Anansi Press, 1991.

Thiem, Anika. *Unbecoming Subjects: Judith Butler, Moral Philosophy, and Critical Responsibility.* New York: Fordham University Press, 2008.

Thomas, Nigel J.T., "Mental Imagery, Philosophical Issues About." *Encyclopedia of Cognitive Science* (Volume 2, pp. 1147–1153). L.Nadel (Editor). London: Nature Publishing/Macmillan, 2003.

Thomas, R.S. *Laboratories of the Spirit.* Boston MA: David R. Godine, 1976.

Thompson, Kristin and David Bordwell, Jeff Smith. *Film History: An Introduction.* Fifth Edition. New York: McGraw-Hill, 2022.

Tolstoy, Leo. *What is Art?* (1896) Translated by Aylmer Maude. Introduction by Vincent Tomas. Indianapolis IN and Cambridge MA : Hackett Publishing Co., 1996.

Tomkins, Sylvan. *Affect Imagery Consciousness.* Volumes I and II (1962). New York: Springer Publishing, 2008.

Townsend, Dabney. *Aesthetics: Classic Readings from the Western Tradition.* Belmont CA: Thomson Learning, 2001.

Turnbull, Herbert Westren. "The Great Mathematicians." *The World of Mathematics. Volume One.* Presented with commentaries and notes by James R. Newman. New York: Simon and Schuster, 1956.

Turner, Roger. *Capability Brown and the Eighteenth-Century English Landscape.* New York: Rizzoli, 1985.

V

Virilio, Paul. *The Vision Machine.* Translated by Julie Rose. Bloomington IN: Indiana University Press, 1994.

---. *Open Sky.* New York: Verso, 1997.

Vries, Hent de. *Religion and Violence: Philosophical Perspectives from Kant to Derrida.* Baltimore MD: Johns Hopkins University Press, 2002.

W

Warhol, Andy. *The Philosophy of Andy Warhol: From A to B and back again.* New York: Harcourt Brace Jovanovich, 1975.

Weber, Sam. "Afterword: Literature – Just Making It." Translated by Brian Massumi. *Just Gaming.* Jean-François Lyotard and Jean-Loup Thébaud. Translated by Wlad Godzich. (Sixth edition) Minneapolis MI: University of Minnesota Press, 2008. Pgs. 101-120.

Welch, Sharon. "Dangerous Memory and Alternate Knowledges." *On Violence: A Reader.* Bruce B. Lawrence and Aisha Karim (Editors). Durham NC and London: Duke University Press, 2007. Pgs. 363-376.

Welsch, Wolfgang. *Undoing Aesthetics.* Translated by Andrew Inkpin. London: Sage Publications, 1997.

Willett, John. *Art and Politics in the Weimar Period: The New Sobriety, 1917-1933.* New York: Pantheon Books, 1978.

Williams, Bernard. *Shame and Necessity* (1993). Foreward by A.A. Long. Berkeley CA: University of California Press, 2008.

Williams, Raymond. "Base and Superstructure in Marxist Cultural Theory." *Media and Cultural Studies: Keyworks.* Edited by Meenakshi Gigi Durham and Douglas M. Kellner. Malden MA: Blackwell Publishing, 2006. Pgs. 130-143.

Wittgenstein, Ludwig. "Lectures on Aesthetics." *Continental Aesthetics: Romanticism to Postmodernism: An Anthology.* Edited by Richard Kearney and David Rasmussen. Malden MA: Blackwell Publishers, 2001. Pgs. 212-215.

---. *Philosophical Investigations.* Translated by Gertrude Elizabeth Margaret Anscombe. Malden MA: Blackwell Publishers, 1968.

---. *Tractatus Logico-Philosophicus.* New York: Cosimo, 2007.

---. *L. Wittgenstein – Lectures and Conversations on Aesthetics, Psychology and Religious Belief.* Compiled from Notes taken by Yorick Smythies, Rush Rhees and James Taylor. Edited by Cyril Barrett. Berkeley and Los Angeles CA: University of California Press, 1972.

Wolfe, Tom. "Foreward" in Marshall McLuhan, *Understanding Me – Lectures and Interviews/Marshall McLuhan.* Edited by Stephanie McLuhan and David Staines. With a Foreword by Tom Wolfe. McClelland & Stewart. Toronto. 2003. Pgs. ix-xxiii.

Wollstonecraft, Mary. *A Vindication of the Rights of Woman* (1792). Edited with an Introduction and Notes by Miriam Brody. Revised edition. London: Penguin Books, 2004.

Woodruff, Paul. "Aristotle's Poetics: The Aim of Tragedy." *The Companion to Aristotle.* Georgios Anagnostopoulos (Editor). Malden MA: Wiley-Blackwell, 2009. Pgs. 612-627.

Woolf, Virginia. "Street Haunting: A London Adventure" (1927). *Virginia Woolf: Selected Essays.* Edited and with an Introduction and Notes by David Bradshaw (Oxford UK: Oxford University Press 2008), pp.177-187.

Y

Young, Nora. *The Virtual Self: How Our Digital Lives Are Altering the World Around Us.* Toronto ON: McClelland & Stewart, 2012.

Z

Zavattini, Cesare. "Some Ideas on the Cinema." *Vittorio De Sica: Contemporary Perspectives.* Edited by Howard Curle and Stephen Snyder, translated by Pier Luigi Lanza. Toronto ON: University of Toronto Press, 2000. Pgs. 21-37.

Žižek, Slavoj. *The Fragile Absolute.* New York: Verso, 2000.

---. *The Sublime Object of Ideology.* London: Verso, 1989.

---. *Did Someone Say Totalitarianism?* London: Verso, 2001.

---. "The Undergrowth of Enjoyment: How Popular Culture Can Serve as an Introduction to Lacan." *The Žižek Reader.* Edited by Elizabeth Wright and Edmond Wright. Malden MA: Blackwell Publishing, 1999. Pgs. 11-36.

---. "The Obscene Object of Postmodernity." *The Žižek Reader.* Edited by Elizabeth Wright and Edmond Wright. Malden MA: Blackwell Publishing, 1999. Pgs. 37-52.

---. *The Plague of Fantasies.* London: Verso, 1997.

---. "The Strange Case of the Missing Lacanians." *The Fright of Real Tears: Krzysztof Kieślowski Between Theory and Post-Theory.* London: British Film Institute, 2001.

---. *The Parallax View.* Cambridge MA: The MIT Press, 2009.

---. *Incontinence of the Void: Economico-Philosophical Spandrels.* Cambridge MA: The MIT Press, 2019.

Žižek, Slavoj and Boris Gunjević. *God in Pain: Inversions of Apocalypse.* New York: Seven Stories Press, 2012.

---. "Christianity Against the Sacred." *God in Pain: Inversions of Apocalypse.* Slavoj Žižek and Boris Gunjević. New York: Seven Stories Press, 2012. Pgs. 43-71.